W9-AAF-684

EXPOSITION OF THE REVELATION OF JESUS CHRIST

Exposition of the Revelation of Jesus Christ

WALTER SCOTT

FLEMING H. REVELL COMPANY
WESTWOOD, NEW JERSEY

This edition is issued by
special arrangement with
PICKERING & INGLIS LTD.
the British publishers

TENTH IMPRESSION OF
THE FOURTH EDITION

SBN 7208 0005 6

INTRODUCTION.

THE principle on which our "Exposition" proceeds is that the main contents of the Apocalypse are yet future, and that an exhaustive fulfilment of prophecy must be sought for in the near crisis of several years, culminating in the Return of the Lord in power. We cannot have the accomplishment of prophecy so long as the Church is the platform of God's activity in grace. But when it is taken up to Heaven, then God's suspended dealings with Israel and the nations are resumed. The Church—Christ's body and bride—is an election out of both, and is not itself a subject of prophecy, but of New Testament Revelation (Matt. 16. 16, 17; Eph. 3). Events, political and religious, are transpiring before our eyes which are the growth and result of centuries. But in the prophetic week of seven years (Dan. 9. 27) changes of the most startling character are witnessed. The whole political government of Europe is then rearranged under Satan's prime minister, *the* Beast of the Apocalypse—a gigantic confederation of ten powers. The old Roman empire will reappear under new conditions, guided and controlled by its active blaspheming and persecuting head, the little horn of Daniel 7. His partner in crime and sharer in everlasting ruin is the Antichrist who guides *religiously* in Christendom, as the Beast does *politically*. The whore, or the mystical Babylon, is the concentration of everything religiously vile. Her political dethronement in the revived empire is effected instrumentally by the ten kings (chap. 17. 16), who at first upheld her; her ruin is mourned over by kings, merchants, and peoples outside the Roman earth (chap. 18. 9-19), and she is subsequently destroyed by God Himself (vv. 2, 21-24) a short time before the destruction of the Beast. This latter is effected by the Lord in Person, and at His Coming in power (chap. 19). The destruction of Babylon and the Beast are separate events. The former precedes the latter.

There can be no public development of these and other events of a like character so long as the Church is on earth. Evil at present is a mystery, though actively at work, but it is restrained or kept in check by two powers: *what* restraineth (2 Thess. 2. 6) is the Church on earth, and *He* Who restraineth (v. 7) is the Holy Ghost. Hence there cannot be the public abandonment of the Faith till the Church and Spirit leave the earth. But the principles are at work which are surely and rapidly undermining the moral foundations of the professing Church and of society in general. The "Higher Critics" are the advance guard in the unholy crusade. The full-blown development may be expected ere long.

We have freely used the labours of many scholarly men in our translation of the text. *The New Translation* (Morrish, London) has been largely drawn upon.

Note to the Third Edition.

We are profoundly thankful to God for the *many* testimonies which have reached us of help and blessing, as also for the rapid sale of the second issue of our "Exposition." We bespeak a warm welcome for the third edition now in the hands of our readers.

The futurist application is, we are convinced, the only consistent and Scriptural one. "History is an old almanac," is ever repeating itself. There is nothing new under the sun. The principles and motives which govern men in thought and action are ever the same, while, of course, the facts are new; but even these are framed on old types and models; hence a *general* resemblance to the past may be traced in the prophecies. But the complete and exhaustive fulfilment of prophecy is undoubtedly future. "*The Revelation*" is regarded by many as a mystery, as a sealed book. It is not so. It is open for the simple to understand. Explanation of its every symbol may be found by diligent search in some part or other of the Sacred Volume, whose verbal inspiration is the faith of the writer.

Note to the Fourth Edition.

We adore our ever gracious God for His mercy in permitting us to issue a *fourth* edition of our "Exposition."

Before the study of the "Exposition" itself is entered upon we would advise, in the first instance, a careful reading of the three special papers indicated at head of Contents on next page.

WALTER SCOTT

GENERAL CONTENTS.

For Detailed Index see page 451.

EXPOSITION OF THE REVELATION.

GENERAL CONTENTS.

AUTHORS QUOTED

AUTHORS QUOTED OR REFERRED TO.

ALFORD, DEAN.—*New Testament for English Readers, etc.*
ANDREAS.—*The Apocalypse, with Notes and Reflections.*
AUBERLEN, C. A.—*Daniel and the Revelation.*

BAINES, T. B.—*The Lord's Coming, Israel, and the Church.*
B. (BELLETT), J. G.
BENGEL, J. A.—*Exposition of the Apocalypse.*
BLEEK, F.—*Lectures on the Apocalypse.*
BOUSSET, W.—*The Antichrist Legend.*
BRODIE, T.—*Notes on the Revelation.*
BULLINGER, E. W.—*Number in Scripture.*
BURDER.—*Notes on the Apocalypse.*

CAMPBELL, COLIN.—*Critical Studies in St. Luke's Gospel.*
CARPENTER, W. B.—*Commentary on the Apocalypse.*
CORFE, R. P. C.—*The Antichristian Crusade.*
CULBERTSON, ROBERT.—*Lectures on Prophecies of John.*

DANTE, A.—*Divina Commedia.*
DARBY, J. N.—*Synopsis of the Books of the Bible, etc.*
DELITZSCH, FRANZ.

ECUMENIUS.
ELLICOTT, BISHOP.—*A New Testament Commentary.*
ERASMUS (of Greek Testament Fame).

FARRAR, DEAN.—*The Early Days of Christianity.*

GIBBON, EDWARD.—*The Decline and Fall of the Roman Empire.*
GLOAG, P. J.—*Introduction to the Johannine Writings.*
GRANT, F. W.—*Facts and Theories as to a Future State, etc.*
GRANT, P. W.—*The Revelation of John.*

HENGSTENBERG, E. W.—*The Revelation of St. John.*
H. (HARTRIDGE), W. R.—*Revelation of Jesus Christ.*
HERODOTUS (the Father of History).
HERVEY.—*Meditations.*
HILGENFIELD.
HISLOP, ALEXANDER.—*The Two Babylons.*
HOOPER, F. W.—*The Revelation of Jesus Christ by John.*
HUSSEY, ROBERT.—*The Rise of the Papal Power.*

JOSEPHUS (the Jewish Historian).

KELLY, WILLIAM.—*Lectures on the Book of Revelation, etc.*

LEE, ARCHDEACON.—*The Speaker's Commentary.*
LUTHER (the Great Reformer).

MACLEOD, ALEXANDER.—*The Cherubim and the Apocalypse.*
MANNING, CARDINAL.—*The Temporal Power of the Vicar of Jesus Christ.*
MILLS, JOHN.—*Sacred Symbology.*
MOSHEIM, DR.—*Ecclesiastical History.*
MULLER, MAX.—*Science of Languages.*

AUTHORS QUOTED.

PHILO (the Celebrated Philosopher).
PLUMPTRE, E. H.
POOL, J. J.—*Studies in Mohammedanism.*
PORPHRY.—*Treatise against Christians.*

RAMSAY, WILLIAM.—*Lectures on the Revelation.*

SCOTT, WALTER.—*Doctrinal Summaries, etc.*
SEISS, DR.—*Lectures on the Apocalypse.*
SHEPHERD, H.—*The Tree of Life.*
STUART, C. E.—*Truth for the Last Days, etc.*
STUART, MOSES.—*A Commentary on the Apocalypse.*

TISCHENDORF, L. F.
TREGELLES, S. P.
TYNDALE, WILLIAM (the Reformor).

URSINIUS.—*Heidelberg Catechism.*

WARBURTON, WILLIAM.—*Lectures on Prophecy.*
WHITE.—*The Eighteen Christian Centuries.*
WILKINSON, W. F.—*Personal Names in the Bible.*
WORDSWORTH, CHRISTOPHER.—*Lectures on the Apocalypse.*
WYCLIFFE (the Morning Star of the Reformation).
WYLLIE, J. A.—*The History of Protestantism.*

HOW TO USE.

THERE are three ways in which this volume may be helpfully used.

1. By **reading straight through** as an ordinary book, making a pencil note in the margin of portions suitable for meditation and careful study.

2. Taking **chapter by chapter**, first reading the chapter in the Bible itself, then carefully noting the valuable and suggestive thoughts herein set forth in the fear of the Lord.

3. As a **book of reference**. The *Index* will readily indicate where any incident or event mentioned in the book may be found.

The Bible *chapters* are indicated at the head of each page, the *verses* at the beginning of each paragraph. **The black type clearly** indicates portions of the book quoted.

DISTRIBUTION OF THE CONTENTS OF THE BOOK OF REVELATION

"Revelation"—*the Veil rolled aside*.

The book was written and the visions seen by the beloved John in the island of Patmos about A.D. 96.

Two Parts.

The book is in two distinct and equal parts.

1. From chapter 1 to chapter 11. 18, in which the general condition of things and events is prophetically sketched from the close of the first christian century till the introduction of the eternal state. Compare "the time of the *dead* that they should be judged" (chap. 11. 18) with "I saw the *dead*, small and great, stand before the throne" (chap. 20. 12).

2. From chapter 11. 19 to chapter 22. 21, in which details are furnished connected with Israel and Christendom in the future awful crisis of their history.

Three Divisions.

The threefold division of the prophecy is noted in chapter 1. 19. This verse is the key to the interpretation and understanding of the book. It contains a past, a present, and a future.

1. "Write the things which thou *hast* seen." This constitutes a vision by itself, comprised within verses 10-18, in which Christ in the midst of the seven golden lamp-stands is the central object. PAST.

2. "Write the things . . . which *are*." These are embraced in chapters 2 and 3, in which the professing Church is traced through contemporary and successive stages of her history, from her decline (chap. 2. 4) till her rejection (chap. 3. 16). PRESENT.

3. "Write the things . . . which shall be *hereafter*," or *after these things*. This division commences with chapter 4, and runs on to chapter 22. 5. This is essentially the prophetic part of the book. FUTURE. The Seals, Trumpets, and Vials; Babylon, the Marriage, the Reign, etc., are each and all FUTURE.

Twelve Sections.

There are twelve sections into which the whole contents of the Apocalypse is distributed, and which if carefully noted and mastered will greatly facilitate the study of the book.

1. A general introduction, chapter 1. 1-9.

2. Christ in judicial glory in the midst of the seven Asiatic Churches, chapter 1. 10-18.

3. The Church in profession as God's witness on earth. Her growing departure from love and truth, chapters 2, 3.

4. The heavenly saints enthroned and glorified, including all embraced in 1 Thessalonians 4. 15-17; chapters 4, 5.

5. The seven Seals successively opened by the Lamb, chapters 6-8. 1. The seventh chapter is a parenthetical one of deep interest.

6. The seven Trumpets successively sounded by the angels, chapters 8. 2-11. 18. Here the revived Roman empire is in the forefront in these judgment prophecies.

7. Three Sources (chap. 12), two Actors (chap. 13), and seven Results (chap. 14), chapters 12-14.

8. The seven Vials of God's wrath successively poured out, chapters 15, 16. The closing dealings of God upon the empire, Israel, and the earth.

9. Babylon, the mystical, in her political and ecclesiastical associations, and utter destruction, chapters 17, 18.

10. Chronological sequence from the fall of Babylon till the eternal state, opening with rejoicing in Heaven, and closing with a picture of eternal misery in the Lake of Fire, chapters 19-21. 8.

11. The Bride of the Lamb in governmental and Millennial splendour. A thing of love, of life, and of beauty for ever, chapters 21. 9-22. 5.

12. Warnings, threatenings, and encouragements, chapter 22. 6-21.

Chronological Order

Chapters 2 and 3 unfold the moral history of the Church in successive periods of her history, from the close of the first christian century to its final rejection. Then chapters 4 and 5 are chronological in so far that Heaven and not earth is the scene of action, the heavenly saints having been removed to their home above. The fact of the

Rapture is not mentioned in the Apocalypse, but assumed as having taken place in the time between chapters 3 and 4. Paul unfolds the Rapture, John follows on assuming it has occurred. We place, therefore, the Rapture of the saints *after* the Church ruin shown in chapter 3, and *before* the glory witnessed in chapter 4.

The history on earth is then resumed from the close of chapter 3, but it is the history of the apostate world—Israel, the revived Roman empire, and Christendom generally. This will be found in chapters 6, 8, 9, 11. 14-18; 15. 5; 16. 21; 19. 11-21. 8.

Parenthetic Portions.

There are six distinctly marked parentheses in the book, which are as follows:

1. Chapter 7, between the sixth and seventh SEALS.
2. Chapters 10, 11. 1-13, between the sixth and seventh TRUMPETS.
3. Chapters 11. 19-15. 1-4, between the sounding of the seventh trumpet and the pouring out of the bowls of wrath.
4. Chapter 16. 13-16, between the sixth and seventh VIALS.
5. Chapters 17-19. 1-10, between the pouring out of the seventh Vial and the personal advent of the Lord in power and glory.
6. Chapters 21. 9-22. 1-5, between the description of the eternal state and the concluding section of the book.

The longest parenthesis is the third in which the hidden sources of good and evil are disclosed (chap. 12), the agents and chief instruments of evil named (chap. 13), and the results in grace and judgment fully stated (chap. 14).

General Notes.

The strictly prophetic part of the book commences with chapter 6 and concludes with verse 5 of chapter 22.

The chronological events under the Seals, Trumpets, and Vials transpire *after* the Rapture and *before* the Appearing in glory. It will be impossible to understand the Revelation if this is not clearly seen.

No date can be fixed for the opening of the Seals. The Roman empire *may* be forming while the Seals are being opened one by one. The empire is not recognised as existing under the Seals. It may be that under the throes of the sixth Seal (chap. 6. 12-17) the empire emerges out of the general chaos, but we cannot pronounce with certainty.

The first four Trumpets (chap. 8) specially concern the Roman world. The three "Woe" Trumpets announce judgment respectively upon apostate *Israel*, apostate

Christendom, and upon the guilty *world*. The Trumpets succeed the Seals, and the Vials succeed the Trumpets. The Seal judgments are comparatively light but widespread, with but one exception (chap. 6. 8). The trumpet-chastisements are heavier in character; the first four are more limited in extent, while the three last are "woe"—judgments.

The *martyred* company of Judah on the glassy sea harping and singing are noted in chapters 14. 2; 15. 2-4.

The *preserved* company of Judah on Mount Zion alone can learn the song of their brethren above, chapter 14. 1-5.

The *sealed* company of Israel (chap. 7) are not said to emerge out of the Tribulation, and are a distinct company from that of chapter 14. The hundred and forty-four thousand of chapter 7 are of all *Israel*, whereas the hundred and forty-four thousand of chapter 14 are of *Judah* only.

The *apostate* part of Israel is specially in view in chapter 9. 1-11. Thus all Israel is fully accounted for.

THE CELEBRATED PROPHECY OF SEVENTY WEEKS, OR 490 YEARS.

(Daniel 9. 24-27.)

The mass of Jews and Christians err alike in the understanding of this celebrated prophecy. The mistake lies in not perceiving that the last or 70th week is yet *future*, and that a long interval of time, one which has lasted for nigh 2000 years, occurs between the *close* of the 69th week and the *opening* of the 70th, and, further, that the prophecy concerns Jerusalem and the Jewish people. The apostle had no need to write of times and seasons to Gentile Christians (1 Thess. 5. 1). The prophecy itself clearly teaches a long gap or interval between the last two weeks.

We transcribe the words of the prophecy in full, adding a word here and there of explanation.

"Seventy weeks (490 *years*) are determined upon *thy* people (*the Jews*), and upon *thy* holy city (*Jerusalem*) to finish the transgression, and to make an end of sins, and to make reconciliation for iniquity, and to bring in everlasting righteousness, and to seal up the vision and prophecy, and to anoint the most holy (*six blessings*). Know therefore and understand, that from the going forth of the commandment to restore and to build Jerusalem (*Neh.* 2) unto the Messiah, the Prince (*Matt.* 21), shall be seven weeks (49 *years*), and threescore and two weeks (434 *years*); the street shall be built again, and the wall, even in troublous times. And after three score and two weeks (*in addition to the seven*) shall Messiah be cut off, but not for Himself; and the people (*the Romans*) of the Prince that shall come (*little horn of chap*. 7) shall destroy the city (*Jerusalem*) and the sanctuary (*the Temple*), and the end thereof shall be with a flood, and unto the end of the war desolations are determined. And he (*the Roman Prince*) shall confirm the ("*a*") covenant with many ("*the many*," *that is, the mass of the people*) for one week (*seven years*); and in the midst of the week he (*the Prince*) shall cause the sacrifice and the oblation to cease, and for the overspreading of abominations (*idolatry*) he shall make it desolate, even until the consummation, and that determined shall be poured upon the desolate (*i.e., the desolator*)."

To whom then does the prophecy refer—to Christians or Jews? To the latter undoubtedly. Daniel's people (the *Jews*) and city (*Jerusalem*)—the Jews and Jerusalem—are the subjects of the prophecy (v. 24). In a letter received a few years ago from one of the most distinguished students of the prophetic Word, he urged the writer to study carefully the celebrated prophecy of the seventy years, as he regarded them as "the *key* to all prophecy." The 70th week is yet future. The latter half of it is variously spoken of as 42 months, 1260 days—time, times, and half a time. It is that solemn period referred to in the central part of the Apocalypse, one profoundly interesting, and absolutely needful to understand if the prophecies are to be scripturally apprehended. Within these 70 weeks or 490 years the prophetic programme is mapped out.

Are the weeks periods of days or years? All competent Hebraists hold that the "week" simply denotes "seven," whether of days, years, or other denomination of time, must be learned from the context; the word itself does not determine. It is simply "seventy sevens." Says the learned Tregelles: "I retain the word 'week' for convenience sake, and not as implying seven days to be the import of the Hebrew word." That they are weeks of years is evident on the surface of the prophecy.

In chapter 10. 2 we have weeks of *days*; in that before us weeks of *years*. But another important inquiry meets us. *When* did the 70 weeks or 490 years commence? We are informed that it was "from the going forth of the commandment to restore and to build *Jerusalem*." Now, in the books of Ezra and Nehemiah we meet with several decrees, but only *one* in reference to the building of Jerusalem, the others refer to the *Temple*. This special commandment or decree is *that* to which the prophecy refers, and will be found fully recorded in the last historical book of the Old Testament—Nehemiah, chapter 2. This decree was promulgated in the 20th year of Artaxerxes, the king. Thus, then, we have the exact commencement of the 70 weeks—455 B.C.*

---

* "Dates and Chronology of Scripture," p. 44.

The prophecy is thus divided:

1. Seven weeks, or 49 years, occupied in the reconstruction of the city (see Neh. 2), which had been destroyed by the universal autocrat, Nebuchadnezzar—the head of gold (chap. 2. 38), and the lion amongst beasts (chap. 7. 4). The books of Nehemiah and Ezra give the history of this period, or "troublous times."

2. Three score and two weeks, or 434 years, which commenced from the city rebuilt, and the restoration of its social and ecclesiastical polity, which occupied 49 years, till Messiah the Prince. Thus, from the decree of Artaxerxes in the 20th year of his reign (Neh. 2) commanding the rebuilding of Jerusalem till the triumphal entry of Christ as Messiah into Jerusalem (Matt. 21) we have the two former periods multiplied; in all 483 years.

3. One week, or seven years, yet future. This interesting time, which introduces the closing sorrows of Judah, commences *after* the removal of the Church, and *after* the restoration of Judah to Palestine (Isa. 18). All prophecy, more or less, is concentrated in its final character in this interesting crisis. It is a week in which the gravest events which the world has ever known, political and otherwise, have their place.

4. 'Midst of the week of seven years, or three years and a half. This last week is divided into two equal parts. The attention of the reader in the books of Daniel and the Revelation is fixed on the history of the *second* half of the week. The *first* half will be one of general peace, one, too, of preparation for the awful outburst of satanic blasphemy, power, and cruelty, which characterises the closing half of the week. The history of the first three years and a half is not written, either by the Hebrew prophet or by the apocalyptic Seer.

TIMES, DAYS, MONTHS.

A time is a year (for the force of the term, *time*, see Dan. 4. 16-37); times, two years; dividing of time, or half a time, signifies half a year; months are of 30 days; days are literal days of 24 hours. Now these periods refer to the *same* time, namely, the last half of the 70th week. They cover the period of the tribulation. It will be observed that in Revelation 11. 3 and 12. 6, *days*, and not months or times, are spoken of, the reason being that God's suffering saints are in view; hence the days of their testimony and trial are carefully numbered. Days of interest to Him, Who has numbered the hairs of our heads. But when the power and blasphemy of the great political enemy of God and of the Lamb, as also the persecutor of the godly-fearing part of Judah, the king of the west is in question, and we may add, of the oppressing Gentiles as well, then the period is curtly spoken of as 42 *months* (chaps. 13. 5; 11. 2). The *days* are twice named in reference to God's saints. The *months* are twice named in relation to the enemy of God's people. "Times and laws," not the saints, are given into the hands of the little horn, or head of the revived Roman empire, "until a time, and times, and the dividing of time" (Dan. 7. 25). He rages and ravages in the wide scene of christian profession, but especially in Palestine is his iron hand felt, not against the nation as such, but against the God-fearing part of the people who boldly witness for God in these awful times. The Antichrist will support the pretensions of the arrogant, blaspheming king, energised by Satan cast down from Heaven, whose expulsion therefrom is noted in Revelation 12. Daniel 7. 25 and Revelation 13. 5 refer to the *same* personage and to the *same* period. The continuance of the last and satanic phase of the empire (chap. 17. 8) is limited to 42 literal months. Thus the 1260 days of suffering, 42 months of 30 days each of Gentile domination, and time, times, and half a time of Judah's abject misery synchronise.

Five Months.

Five months of torment (Rev. 9. 5-10). The locust judgment under the sounding of the *fifth* angel is a terrible one, and spite of the assertion of Hengstenberg to the contrary, we believe that the "five months" of torment is in allusion to the ravages of the natural locust which usually lasts five months. A limited and brief period is referred to, and one which may not exceed five months.

Hour, Day, Month, Year.

An hour, a day, a month, and a year (Rev. 9. 15). The angels of judgment bound at the Euphrates were to be loosed, not *during* the time specified, but at that particular moment. These evil agencies were to be let loose at an exactly defined moment. The very hour of the day of the month and year is noted. It is an exact note of time.

Three Days and a Half.

Three days and a half (Rev. 11. 9-11). The dead bodies of the witnesses lying unburied in the streets of Jerusalem, and exposed to the cruel and public gaze of the Gentiles, is a scene of three and a half literal days. Be it observed that the testimony of the witnesses extends during the last half of the unfulfilled week. Then they are killed, and after the public exposure of their bodies for three days and a half a public resurrection is granted them. The prophetic days in Daniel and in other parts of the Apocalypse are literal; why then should this particular passage form an exception? This is a special scene, confined in its peculiar features to events in Jerusalem. It is the Beast who murders the Jerusalem witnesses.

Two Thousand and Three Hundred Days.

2300 days (Dan. 8. 14) is an historical statement referring to the desecration of the Temple and the cruel treading down of the Jewish people by the Syrian monarch of infamous memory, Antiochus Epiphanes. That there is a typical bearing on the last days of Gentile supremacy and misrule over the restored Jewish commonwealth seems evident from verses 17 and 19. Antiochus figures the future Jewish antagonist, the king of the north.

Twelve Hundred and Ninety Days.

1290 days (Dan. 12. 11). These days exceed by a month the tribulation and the forced interruption of Jewish worship. They commence with the well-known and divinely-appointed sign (Matt. 24. 15), idolatry, which will mark the commencement of the closing sorrows of the coming crisis. The extra month is needed to complete the destruction of Israel's enemies. The prophet does not speak of blessing in connection with this period, because not only must judgment clear the scene of evil and evil men, but the people themselves must be morally prepared for the full tide of millennial blessing. The days are literal, of course.

Thirteen Hundred and Thirty-Five Days.

1335 days (Dan. 12. 12). Here 45 days are added to the former number. "Blessed is he that waiteth and cometh to the thousand, three hundred, and five and thirty days." Thus we have 75 literal days added to the 1260 before the full blessing of Israel is secured. What a busy two months and a half! The tale of judgment will be finished, "the filth of the daughters of Zion" washed away, temple worship restored under new conditions (Ezek. 40), and the people morally cleansed from all defilement in heart and life; then "blessed is he" who waits and reaches that moment of wondrous blessing for Israel and the earth.

Postponement of the Seventieth Week of Seven Years.

The present interval of grace and of Jewish degradation are co-existent, and are terminated by the translation of the heavenly saints, consisting of the changed living and raised dead. *Then* the last week, needed to complete the full tale of 490 years, opens with the apostate Roman prince and the apostate nation returned to Palestine, making a mutual agreement. The prince perfidiously breaks the treaty in the midst of the week. The great Tribulation with its horrors immediately ensue. It is enough. The throne is satisfied (Isa. 40. 2). The seven years close, and the ancient people, chastened, saved, and blest, enter into blessing. Her sun will never again set, and Jerusalem becomes the throne of the Lord (Jer. 3. 17).

Now unless this Dispensation is seen as having its place between the 69th and the 70th week of prophecy, there must be muddling and confusion. The interval between these weeks explains much.

THE SIX CHIEF ACTORS IN THE COMING CRISIS.

1. **The Great Dragon, the Old Serpent, the Devil, and Satan**—names and titles of ominous import—is the unseen leader of the moral darkness and wickedness of the closing days prior to the Lord's Return in power. The concentration of satanic wickedness on earth is consequent on the issue of the war in Heaven (Rev. 12. 7-9, 13-17), Satan, expelled therefrom, directs his untiring energies, and employs his almost unlimited resources in ruining the earth, filling it with anguish and misery. In his diabolic mission he is ably supported by his distinguished ministers, the Beast and the False Prophet, probably the two guiltiest men then on the face of the earth, satanically inspired.

2. **The Beast of the Apocalyptic Prophecies** (chaps. 11. 7; 12; 13. 1-8; 14. 9; 16. 17; 19. 19, 20; 20. 10). The little horn (Dan. 7. 7, 8, 11, 20, 21, 23-26). This little horn or king is the personal head of the revived empire. The little horn of Daniel 8 is a different personage. "The prince that shall come" (Dan. 9. 26).

3. **The Antichrist** of John's Epistles.* The false messiah (John 5. 43). Man of sin, son of perdition, and the wicked or lawless one (2 Thess. 2). The false prophet (Rev. 16. 13; 19. 20; 20. 10). Another beast (Rev. 13. 11-17). The king (Dan. 11. 36-39; Isa. 30. 33). The man of the earth (Psa. 10. 18). The bloody and deceitful man (Psa. 5. 6).

---

* For a fuller account see chapters 9 and 13

4. **King of the North** (Dan. 11). The overflowing scourge (Isa. 28). The Assyrian (Isa. 10; 14. 25; 31. 8). King of fierce countenance (Dan. 8. 23-25).

5. **King of the South,** *i.e.*, of Egypt (Dan. 11).

6. **Gog, the last Czar of Russia**, and head of the great northern confederacy against Israel and her land. In chapters 38 and 39 of the prophecy of Ezekiel we read: Gog, his allies and armies, ingloriously fall on the mountains of Israel. Of the hosts enticed by greed to plunder and spoil Israel, then the centre and storehouse of the world's wealth, but a sixth part are spared, and these are sent through the various lands of the east to proclaim the vengeance of the Lord on the enemies of His people, and to make known Jehovah's presence in the midst of His own, saved Israel. Jehovah is the defence of happy Israel.

The foregoing characters, save Satan their chief, are of different nationalities. Gog and the king of the north act together in the political oppression of Israel, the former the more distinguished of the two. The Beast and the False Prophet are confederates, the former wielding the royal and civil power, the latter the spiritual authority of Satan. The king of the south plays a comparatively unimportant part compared to that of his brother monarch in the north. The five persons referred to are actual men, not systems, although they may head them up, nor do they represent a succession of eminent persons. These five distinguished men have their various parts assigned them in the coming conflict betwixt good and evil, light and darkness. Their respective spheres of action, whether in the west against *Christ* (Rev. 19), or in the north-east against the *Jews* (Psa. 83; Zech. 14), are subjects with which all prophetic students should be thoroughly acquainted. To locate these future apostates, to apportion their work and doings as mapped out in the prophetic programme, is a necessity for all desirous of intelligently understanding the prophecies.

EXPOSITION OF
THE REVELATION:
AND PROPHETIC OUTLINES.

CHAPTER 1.

INTRODUCTION, VERSES 1-8; AND GLORIOUS VISION OF CHRIST, VERSES 9-20.

CHARACTER OF THE BOOK.

In this intensely interesting and only prophetic book of the New Testament the veil is rolled aside, and the future disclosed in a series of panoramic visions beheld by the apocalyptic Seer. Light and darkness, good and evil, are the moral forces in opposition. God, Christ, and Satan; men, saved and unsaved; and angels, holy and unholy, are the actors in this marvellous book of plan and purpose. The scenes shift and change, now time, then eternity. Heaven, earth, and abyss, and lake of fire form the platform and theatre of display. The song of the victor and the wail of the vanquished both gladden and sadden. In result, God triumphs, and the millennial and eternal glories of Christ shine forth in undimmed and undying splendour. *Then* shall be brought to pass the saying of the Hebrew prophet, "He shall see of the travail of his soul, and shall be satisfied."

The new-made Heaven and earth (chap. 22. 1) become the respective and eternal abodes of all that is holy and good, while the lake of fire (chap. 21. 8) shall have gathered into it all that is unholy and contrary to God.

Grace is the key-note of the previous epistolary communications. The public *government* of God in dealing with evil and in the exaltation of good is the characteristic burden of this profoundly interesting book.

THE TITLE.

The sacred writers did not title their respective books, and all the titles of the sacred books in our Bibles, save one or two, are destitute of divine authority. The title given to the Apocalypse in the Authorised Version and retained in the Revision of 1881 is faulty and misleading.

It is not "The Revelation of St. John,"* but as in the text, "THE REVELATION OF JESUS CHRIST." Whether the epithet, "the Divine," was added as an expression of the writer's supposed superlative sanctity, and to distinguish him from John the Apostle, are matters of unimportant controversy. We are at perfect liberty to reject the title as a whole. The Church tradition that John the Apostle was the writer dates from A.D. 170, or a little earlier. The John of the fourth Gospel, and of the three epistles to which his name is prefixed, is, we doubt not, the inspired writer of this book; *there*, however, he is described, *here* he is expressly named.

PREFACE (vv. 1-3).

The introduction contains a preface (vv. 1-3), a salutation (vv. 4-6), a prophetic testimony (v. 7), and a divine announcement (v. 8).

1.—"**The Revelation of Jesus Christ.**" Here Jesus Christ is viewed as Man, not in essential Deity as in John 1. 1, 2. The divine and human natures of our Lord, both absolutely perfect, are distinguished in office and action, but must not be separated. There is but one Saviour and one Mediator, Who is very God and very Man, and on this fundamental truth reposes the whole system of Christianity. Faith believes and grasps it firmly, while not pretending to solve the mystery of the Godhead. Our own complex being is a mystery, much more so the Being of our adorable Lord.

The Revelation is embodied in the visions beheld by the Seer of Patmos. The word "Revelation" gives unity to the many and diversified communications, whether in word or vision, contained in the book. Revelations there were, but these form one compact whole, and this belongs to Jesus Christ. Not only, however, is the Revelation Jesus Christ's as given Him by God, but He is the central object in these as in all prophecy. The rays of the prophetic lamp are directed onward to the millennial glory of Christ, no matter whether the lamp be held in the hands of Isaiah the Grand or John the Beloved.

1.—"**Which God gave unto Him.**" The kingdom is Christ's by right in virtue of what He is, yet as Man He *receives* it from God (Luke 19. 15), and shall *deliver* it up to God (1 Cor. 15. 24). So the Revelation, which mainly concerns the kingdom, is here given by God to Christ as Man.

---

* The book is sometimes spoken of as "*The Revelations*." But the revelations contained in the book are essentially one, and were communicated in vision in one day, viz., the Lord's day (chap. 1. 10). The unity of the whole is expressed in the title "*The Revelation*."

1.—**"To show unto His servants** (*bondmen*) **things which must shortly come to pass."** The term "bondmen" is applied in a narrow and restricted sense in both Testaments. The prophets of old were so designated (Amos 3. 7; Dan. 9. 6; 2 Kings 17. 13), as also the apostles and others of reputation in the Church (Phil. 1. 1; Col. 1. 7, see Greek). On the other hand, the word is employed in the New Testament to embrace *all* believers (Rom. 6. 19-22). It is, we judge, this wide and general application of the term which is to be understood here (compare with chaps. 2. 20; 7. 3; 22. 3).

The object, then, of the Revelation is to show Christ's servants or bondmen the near future. Servant is a more distant character of relation than that of son (*position*), or child (*relationship*), or friend (*intimacy*), and best suits the general character of the book which addresses itself to every individual Christian, and not by any means exclusively to an official class.

To ignore this book, therefore, to regard it as a profitless study, to consider its visions as day-dreams, and its symbols as inexplicable is to incur serious loss, dishonour God by Whom the book is inspired, and rob the soul of special promised blessing (v. 3). This warning applies to *every* servant of Jesus Christ, *i.e.*, every Christian.

1.—**"Shortly"** arrests our attention. The imminence of the fulfilment of the events herein foretold, as also the near Return of the Lord, the culminating point in the prophecies, are stated in precise terms both in the beginning and end of the book (chaps. 1. 1; 22. 7, 12, 20), thus forming an insuperable difficulty to its interpretation on the historical basis. A general application of the prophecies to certain past and present events is frankly admitted, for history is ever repeating itself. The facts may be new, but the underlying principles, as pride, love of money, love of power, are the same in all ages, and have ever produced a harvest which has gone to make up history. Thus while fully admitting a partial fulfilment of the strictly prophetic part of the book, *i.e.*, chapters 6-22. 5, yet we are forced to the conclusion that a yet *future* and *brief* crisis must be looked for under the Seals, the Trumpets, and the Vials, *after* the Translation of Old and New Testament saints to Heaven (1 Thess. 4. 17). We look for a successive series of judgments during the time that the saints of past and present ages are at home in the heavens. *Before* these begin (chap. 4), *during* their continuance (chap. 12), and *after* they have run their course (chap. 19), God's heavenly people are seen in their home above.

The futurist application therefore is the basis of our interpretation. If prophetic Scripture as a whole and in detail is to be interpreted soberly and fully, then we must discard the prevalent and pernicious error that history is its interpreter. We hold that the teacher of *all* Scripture is the Holy Ghost: "He will guide you into all truth" (John 16. 13). The full and precise fulfilment of the prophetic portion of the Apocalypse is yet future; and cannot possibly be shown as fulfilled. Take one central fact, the Beast or empire of Rome. Prophecy shows the Latin power in the last phase of its history, previous to its destruction, and in a condition in which it has never yet appeared. It is represented as a great blaspheming, persecuting power, distributed into ten kingdoms under ten vassal kings, subservient to one energetic chief or head, all reigning in willing subordination to their supreme lord (chaps. 13, 17), and in league with apostate Judah in Palestine. Neither under the imperial sway, nor since, has Rome appeared in this new form—one essential to the prophetic future; moreover, Rome destroyed the Jewish commonwealth instead of seeking to preserve it. Nor was Judah apostate when Rome was in the ascendant.

1.—It will be observed that the medium of communication between Christ and John is an unnamed angel, no doubt a spiritual being of prominence in the hierarchy of Heaven—"**His angel**." How unlike in character and mode the unfolding of the Lord's mind during His sojourn on earth. *Then* John was taught the Lord's will as he reposed *in* the Master's bosom (John 13. 23, R.V.). *Now* all is distant and in a way mysterious, but in exact keeping with the character of these communications. God is not here regarded as "*our* Father," but five times Christ's relation to *His* Father is affirmed (chaps. 1. 6; 2. 27; 3. 5, 21; 14. 1). We have only one recorded instance of our Lord, when on earth, directly addressing His Father as "My God" (Matt. 27. 46), but in this book we hear Him say both "My Father" and "My God," the former as Son, the latter as Man. The unfolding of certain governmental glories and titles in no wise enfeebles the blessed truth of Christ's more intimate relations as Son and Man.

The order of the Revelation, therefore, is from God to Christ, then by Christ's angel, whoever that may be, to John, and then on to us, *i.e.*, all Christ's servants or bondmen.

1.—"**Unto His servant John**." The beloved apostle always writes in the third person in the four inspired records bearing his name. Here he writes in the first person, naming himself three times in the introductory part (chap. 1. 1, 4, 9), and twice in the closing portion of the book (chaps. 21. 2; 22. 8).

2.—"**The Word of God and the testimony of Jesus Christ**" formed the sum of the visions beheld by the Seer. Omit the second "and" in the verse, and thus, "**all things that he saw**" constitute in brief the Word of God and the testimony of Jesus Christ. The third member of the text is really a summary of the preceding two. "The Word of God" is limited to the communications contained in this book, while "the testimony of Jesus Christ" is here of a prophetic character (see chap. 19. 10). "The Word of God" in the Gospels is one of grace, whilst "the testimony of Jesus Christ" has as its burden the revelation of the name and character of the Father. But as the Apocalypse treats mainly of the public government of God, both the "word" and "testimony" refer especially to the display of divine authority and rule over the earth. We regard the *Word* of God as that which He directly or mediately expresses, and the *testimony* of Jesus Christ that which He Himself, or by His angel, announces.

3.—In this verse, which completes the preface, the divine benediction, "**Blessed**," is pronounced on the reader, the hearers, and on those who keep these verbally inspired communications. The fact that the blessing is repeated at the close (chap. 22. 7), and judgment threatened on all who tamper with the whole or part of this book of prophecy (vv. 18, 19), imparts an unusually solemn character to this hitherto much neglected portion of Scripture. None can read it or hear it read without blessing, and none dare despise it with impunity. God is ever faithful to His Word, whether in the bestowal of blessing or in the execution of judgment.

The divine beatitude, "Blessed," occurs seven times (chaps. 1. 3; 14. 13; 16. 15; 19. 9; 20. 6; 22. 7, 14).

3.—"**He that readeth**" probably refers to the public reading of the Scriptures in the assemblies, and no doubt Paul's admonition to Timothy, "Give attendance to reading" (1 Tim. 4. 13), speaks of the same good old practice, and one which, we fear, is sadly neglected. Every reader of the Revelation, whether in public or private, may rest assured of the Lord's blessing. The synagogues, authorised by Jewish law wherever ten persons could be brought together to form a congregation, had as an integral part of their service the public reading of the Word of God and exhortation (Luke 4. 16-20; Acts 13. 14, 27; 15. 21). "They that hear" would signify the company present on these and other occasions when the prophecy was read. For the force of "keep those things," see John 14. 21-24.

3.—"**The time is at hand.**" Prophecy annihilates time, and all intervening and even opposing circumstances, and sets one down on the threshold of accomplishment. The activity of the divine will needs not, nor knows rest. But to our naturally impatient minds, weary and fretful of evil, it might seem at times as if God had let slip the reins of government and ceased to intervene in human affairs. But it is not so. Time, ways, men and their actions are in His hands and under His sole control. He is sovereign Lord and Master. "The time is at hand," and "the effect of every vision." God's lengthened delay of nigh 2000 years has proved a rich season of grace to the world. In the meantime faith rests assured that the hand of God, although unseen, is working out a scheme of good (Rom. 8. 28), which will result to His eternal glory, the true end of all.

A DIVINE SALUTATION (vv. 4-6).

We have had a brief but weighty prologue. Now we have a divine greeting. The former instructs, the latter cheers.

4.—"**John to the seven churches which are in Asia.**" What is here denominated Asia is not the old and dreamy continent as a whole, nor even Asia Minor, but that part of the latter on the western side or sea-coast of which Ephesus was the renowned capital, proconsular Asia. In this limited geographical area the professing Church was to be tested, and the salient features of her history depicted in the blaze of day, as represented by those seven Asiatic churches specially chosen for the purpose. Other and important churches in the same district are omitted, whilst those seven, and those only, are named, and that, too, in the order in which a traveller would naturally visit them. The seven selected assemblies form a symbol of the Church in its universality in successive periods of its history, as also at any given moment till its final rejection as an unfaithful witness to Christ (chap. 3. 16).

Why *seven* churches? That numeral is of more frequent occurrence than any other. There are *seven* feasts of Jehovah (Lev. 23); *seven* kingdom parables (Matt. 13); *seven* churches, *seven* Seals, *seven* Trumpets, *seven* Vials noted in the Apocalypse. In each of the foregoing there is a marked division into three and four. What is *divine* is expressed in the former, the *human element* enters into the latter. Combined they express what is COMPLETE. Thus the professing Church, as God's light-bearer on earth, is here regarded in its completeness at any given moment from its declension (chap. 2. 4) to its final and public repudiation by Christ (chap. 3. 16). In its public and responsible position it is solemnly warned. The threatened judgment, *i.e.*, absolute rejection, applies to the corporate body *only*. Believers are repeatedly assured of safety and blessing. An overcoming company of true saints is recognised in each of the first six churches. The mystic "seven" of the Apocalypse is pregnant with meaning.

John here announces himself simply by name. There is no assertion of his apostleship. No flourish of trumpets in calling attention to these sublime prophecies. There is a quiet dignity befitting the introduction and disclosure of subjects which have bowed in heartfelt adoration tens of thousands.

Then the Godhead, each in His own Person, unites in a message of grace and peace, and that, moreover, before the mutterings of the coming storm are heard. Not a Seal can be broken, not a Trumpet blown, nor a Vial poured out till the saints are divinely assured that the strength and blessing of God are for them. God for us in blessing, and in the maintenance of His own glory at all times and under all circumstances, is our mighty stronghold.

The hurricane of divine judgment could not roll over the plains of Sodom till Lot was delivered (Gen. 19); nor could the utter destruction of Jericho by fire take place till Rahab was saved (Joshua 6). But in this divine greeting, and in the place it occupies, we have far more than a guarantee of preservation from divine judgment. The salutation does not come in between threatened judgment and its execution, but before ever it is announced, and the true character of things in the Church, the world, and Israel disclosed, God's saints are assured of the deep interest He takes in them.

4.—The common and needed blessing of the redeemed is one of "**grace and peace**." Neither things nor persons can rob them of it, because given and maintained by God Himself. Grace is the source of all blessing, and peace the rightful and happy state before God. In the apostolic salutations grace always precedes peace; whilst in the individual epistles as those to Timothy, Titus, etc., "mercy" is generally added, as this latter takes account of personal need and circumstances.

The salutation, while eminently fitted to beget and strengthen confidence in God in view of impending judgment, is yet governmental in character. It is not the Father and the children, nor God and sons, but Jehovah and saints; hence, in the naming of the Persons of the Godhead, the order differs from that contained in Matthew 28. 19—*there* it is Father, Son, and Holy Ghost; *here* it is Jehovah; the Spirit, and Jesus Christ. Paul only once at the close of an epistolary communication (2 Cor. 13. 14) greets the saints in the Name of the three divine Persons; here John does so at the *commencement* of the book.

4.—The dread and sacred Name Jehovah signifies *underived existence, the Self-Existing One*. To Israel the Name was explained as "I AM THAT I AM" (Exod. 3. 14); to Gentiles as "**Him which is, and which was, and which is to come**" (Rev. 1. 4; 4. 8).* It is a Name of ineffable grandeur, and one which Israel was made fully acquainted with from the commencement of her history (Exod. 6. 3). It is God's memorial Name, even to generations yet unborn. "Which *is*" implies independent, unchangeable existence. "Which *was*" intimates Jehovah's relation to the past. "Which is to *come*" shows His connection with the future. God's relation to the universe in its vastness and greatness, as also in its minuteness, is a grand and invigorating truth.

In chapter 4. 8 the order of the sentences is reversed; "which *was*" precedes "which *is*." Chapter 4 contemplates the government of the whole earth, and not that of Israel only, hence the living creatures first say "which was." It is a question of time; whereas in chapter 1 the eternity of Jehovah's Being is first presented in the words "which is." Thus, too, it is intimated in the change of the sentence "which *was*" that Jehovah's past deeds of power are an earnest and pledge that eternal existence and omnipotent might are not quiescent attributes in the divine Being, but are exercised through all ages and under all circumstances.

4.—Next, the **Holy Spirit** is named, but not here regarded in the unity of His Being as "one Spirit" (Eph. 4. 4). The plenitude of His power and diversified activity are expressed in the term "seven Spirits," the fulness of spiritual activity (compare with Isa. 11. 2; Rev. 3. 1; 4. 5; 5. 6). "Before His throne," because the primal thought in the Apocalypse is the public government of the earth. In the history of Christianity for the first thirty years, the apostolic era, the Spirit is witnessed acting in energy and grace with individuals, as the book of Acts

* The heathen borrowed from the Jews. The truths of the Old Testament really lie at the root of anything good in the ancient faiths and mythology of the heathen. Thus, "Jupiter was, Jupiter is, Jupiter will be," is evidently taken from the Biblical explanation of the national Name of the God of Israel, Jehovah.

fully relates; whilst in the epistles, the Spirit's presence and action in the Church is the main truth disclosed. But here, as has been already remarked, the Spirit acts governmentally from Heaven on earth.

The governmental character of the book accounts for the mention of the Spirit before Christ. Had it been simply a question of grace, pure and simple, then necessarily the mention of Christ would have preceded that of the Spirit, *after* the Father as sent by Him (1 John 4. 14), and *before* the Spirit because sent by the Son (John 15. 26).

5.—"**Jesus Christ**" is next mentioned, uniting with Jehovah and the Spirit in saluting the saints. In the combination of Name and title is intimated the union of manhood and glory (Acts 2. 36). "Jesus" is composed of two syllables, signifying *Jehovah-saving* (Matt. 1. 21). It was a Name given Him before His birth, and one which exactly describes His Person and work. The greatest of all Names, the Name *par excellence*, is that of Jesus (Phil. 2. 9-11). It occurs upwards of 600 times in the New Testament, and is never prefixed by an adjective;* nor was the Lord ever, save by demons, directly addressed as Jesus. The Name "Jesus" occurs in the Apocalypse nine times, and in combination with Christ three times. Christ (Greek) and Messiah (Hebrew) both mean the anointed as in Psalm 2, etc.

Thus we have God in the greatness of His Being, the Spirit in the plenitude of His power, and Jesus Christ in holy humanity now glorified, united in blessing the saints who are about to have unfolded to them the prophetic counsels of God respecting the earth.

Then certain distinct attributes inseparable from the Name Jesus are introduced; glories which as Man He has earned, and to which He has right. There are three titles used of Him: the first referring to a certain relation to God; the second pointing to a special connection with all the dead, saved and lost; whilst the third directs attention to His supremacy over earth's governing authorities.

(1) "**The Faithful Witness.**" The whole life of our Lord from the manger to the Cross is embraced in this comprehensive title. The epithet "the faithful" is in marked contrast to all preceding witnesses for God. The path of human testimony is strewn with wreck and ruin. Christ alone passed through earth in His solitary

* We strongly deprecate the irreverent use (unwittingly, we are assured) of the most precious Name to a believer's ear and heart. "Dear Jesus," and such-like terms, are an offence against Him Who is our Lord and Master. His title of dignity, "Lord," should be employed in a thousand and one instances instead of "Jesus." This latter, when used in combination with other divine names and titles, is, of course another thing (see John 13. 13, 14).

and rugged path of unswerving devotedness to God, without break or flaw and in all holy separateness to God. "To this end was I born, and for this cause came I into the world, that I should bear witness* unto the truth" (John 18. 37).

(2) "**The First-born of the Dead.**" Christ is both "first-fruit" and "first-born" of the dead. The former title intimates that He is first in *time* of the coming harvest of those who sleep (1 Cor. 15. 20-23). The latter title signifies that He is first in *rank* of all who will rise from the dead. "First-born" is the expression of supremacy, of pre-eminent dignity, and not one of time or of chronological sequence (Psa. 89. 27). No matter when, where, or how Christ entered the world, He would necessarily take the first place in virtue of what He is. We may here remark that the change which the bodies of living believers will undergo at the Coming of Christ is equivalent to the raising of the sleeping dead. Both are to be like Christ morally (1 John 3. 2) and corporeally (Phil. 3. 21).

(3) "**The Prince of the Kings of the Earth.**" The proud monarch of the west, the haughty despot of the east, have each their Master. Christ is "higher than the kings of the earth." The kingdoms of the world are His by right and title, and before Him all must bow. He is "Lord of lords and King of kings." Lord of all who exercise authority, and King of all who reign. He has not yet put forth His power. His sovereign rights are yet in abeyance. But they will be asserted when the Father's time has come, and public universal government will pass into His hands. He shivers every imperial sceptre, and breaks the crown of all opposing authority. Then the pride of man is brought low, and his pomp withers in the dust.

In these titles, therefore, we have a tower of strength to the Christian and Church. We can see One, now in the heavens, Who has trod the path of faith and obedience without halting (Heb. 12. 1, 2); One Who has grappled with death, and him that had the power of it; Who overcame and is now great in His victory; One, too, Who is Lord and Master of all earth's governing authorities. But now the salutation abruptly passes on to a doxology.

6.—The preceding benediction, coupled with the Spirit's relation of *what* Christ is as man, at once rouses the heart of the redeemed. The affections are stirred, and the recital

* "The word *witness*, in its noun or verb form, is found not less than seventy-two times in the writings ascribed to John. It is pre-eminently his characteristic word."

of Christ's dignities is answered by the exulting song: **"Unto Him that loveth us, and loosed us from our sins by His blood"** (R.V.). He has won our hearts by His changeless love, and cleared our consciences by His precious blood. In this book, which reveals the crumbling to atoms of the consolidated power of evil established in high places, how positively refreshing to know, ere the coming judgments are announced, or the precursors of divine vengeance are seen and heard (chaps. 4. 5; 8. 5), that the whole redeemed company on earth can triumphantly sing of Christ's present and changeless love, and of His precious blood which has for ever freed them from their sins.

But the themes of the song are not exhausted. Our high dignity is next celebrated, and ascribed to Him Whose love and blood are our confidence and rest. "He made us a kingdom, priests unto His God and Father." It might be inferred from the expression, "made us a kingdom," that we are to be governed as subjects, but such is not the thought. Sovereignty is conferred upon the heavenly saints, and in a lesser degree upon Jewish millennial saints on earth. The character in which we shall rule is next intimated as "priests." What is meant is the union of kingly dignity and priestly grace. Zechariah 6. 13 states the position exactly: "He shall be a Priest upon His throne." But we shall reign with Christ; hence the character of His reign in part determines the nature of ours. There will be secured for the world in the coming age a thousand years' righteous and gracious government. Let us never forget, nor in practice sink below, our exalted rank. The constant remembrance of it will impart dignity of character and preserve from the money-loving spirit of the age (1 Cor. 6. 2, 3).

6.—**"To Him be the glory and the dominion for ever and ever. Amen."** The form of the ascription is nearly the same as in 1 Peter 5. 11, save that the Jewish apostle asserts that the glory and the dominion *are* Christ's; whereas John intimates the desire of the redeemed that the visible glory and far-reaching dominion foretold by prophet, seen by seer, and sung of by bards should be His Who alone is worthy; and not only during the millennial era, but through the ages or definite measures of time on to eternity. Neither is the "Amen" in the two passages used as prayer that it may be so, but is added as a solemn asseveration of the truth stated.

In the course of the successive disclosures contained in the book, and as their character deepens, the doxology increases in fulness. Here it is twofold; threefold in chapter 4. 11; fourfold in chapter 5. 13; and sevenfold in chapter 7. 12.

OUR PROPHETIC TESTIMONY (v. 7).

7.—"**Behold He cometh with the clouds.**" The Second Advent of our Lord is a vital part of christian testimony, and never more needed to be insisted upon than now, especially in light of the solemn reflection that both the Church and the world are *about* to enter on their final phases of accumulated guilt before being dealt with in sharp judgment. But it is essential to distinguish the two distinctive parts into which the Coming divides. There is a class of passages, confined to the New Testament, which directly refer to the Coming of the Lord *for* His saints, as John 14. 3; Philippians 3. 20; 1 Thessalonians 4. 15-17; and 1 Corinthians 15. 23. But there is another set of texts, common to both Testaments, which as distinctly teach the Coming *with* the saints, as Jude 14; Zechariah 14. 5; Colossians 3. 4; and Revelation 19. 11-14. Now, while both these aspects of the *one* Coming of our Lord should be increasingly pressed on the earnest attention of Christians as a part, and by no means the least important of the faith of God's elect, yet the *second* part or stage of the Coming is the one referred to here. The former, *i.e.*, the Translation of all saints at the epoch of the Lord's descent into the air (1 Thess. 4. 17) necessarily precedes the latter, *i.e.*, His Coming with His saints (Jude 14) and angels (Matt. 25. 31).

The apocalyptic testimony, "Behold He cometh with the clouds," coalesces with that of the Hebrew prophet, "I saw in the night visions, and behold one like the Son of Man came *with* the clouds of Heaven" (Dan. 7. 13); and also with the prophetic utterance of our Lord on Olivet, "They shall see the Son of Man coming *on* the clouds of Heaven with power and great glory" (Matt. 24. 30). All refer to the same time and event. The epiphany of the Son of Man in such majesty as has never been seen by mortal eye will strike terror to the hearts of all on earth save those of His own people.

The prophets of old, each in his own way, and according to his personal characteristics, but all under the direct guidance of the Spirit, descant on the two great prophetic themes: JUDGMENT and GLORY.

Immediately before the dawn of blessing the Gentiles, no less than the Jews, will be enveloped in gross moral darkness (Isa. 60. 2); whilst, instead of according a loyal welcome to the Coming One, the nations will be found gathered in open and armed rebellion, either in the west against the Lamb (Rev. 19. 19), or in the east against Jerusalem (Zech. 14. 2). Hence the earth must be cleared of evil and evil men ere the consecrating footsteps of its Lord and ours cause it to throb with a joy beyond that experienced in the brief and sinless moment of Genesis 2. It is the judgment aspect of the Coming to which the Seer of Patmos refers in verse 7.

Christ is nowhere said to come with the clouds to gather His own. On the contrary, *they* go up in the clouds (1 Thess. 4. 17). These are the royal carriages provided to convey us from earth to meet the Lord. The cloud of old was the well-known symbol of Jehovah's presence with His people (Exod. 13. 21; 40. 34-38; Luke 9. 35). But observe, Christ is not only said to come *in* the clouds (Mark 13. 26), but *with* them (Rev. 1. 7), and *on* them (Matt. 24. 30). The clouds which attend His Coming are symbols of His majesty (Psa. 18. 9-12). He sits on them as on His throne (Matt. 24. 30). We are caught up *in* the clouds (1 Thess. 4. 17). He ascended *in* a cloud (Acts 1. 9), and shall come *in* a cloud (Luke 21. 27). Such minute distinctions are interesting.

Here, then, we are directed to the culminating point of all prophecy—the pivot of blessing for Israel, the Church, and the world. The *first* and *last* testimonies in the book are to the Coming of the Lord (chaps. 1. 7; 22. 20), and we may further remark that the word "quickly" applied to the Coming is alone found in this sublime prophecy.

The Coming of the Lord to break the manifested power of evil on earth, to scatter the combined forces marshalled under the leadership of Satan, to grind to atoms every hostile power, will be an event of so public and overwhelming a character that it is added, "Every eye shall see Him." What a sight in the heavens! The descending Lord with many diadems on His head, clad in the insignia of royalty, saints and angels swelling His triumph, clouds around and beneath, will then appear in a manner befitting His majesty.

7.—But while the statement, **"Every eye shall see Him,"** must be accepted in its literality—need one add, not at the same moment—yet one class is singled out from the mass of mankind then in open revolt against God and His Anointed (Psa. 2), namely, "they which pierced Him." The Gentile spear which pierced the Saviour's side is a fact alone recorded by "the disciple whom Jesus loved" (John 19. 33-37). The weak and vacillating representative of Rome in her imperial greatness, sullied her vaunted reputation for inflexible justice by basely ordering his august Prisoner whom he thrice declared innocent to be scourged and crucified. But the Jews behaved even worse by clamouring aloud for His death, the death of their Messiah, and provoking the unhappy governor to pronounce the fatal sentence. Their children, who have inherited their guilt, and who refuse the shed blood of Christ as God's answer to their sin, shall see Him Whom they pierced, while Zechariah 12. 10 shows how grace will use it. The special class referred to as those "who pierced Him" are the Jews.

7.—"**All the tribes of the earth shall wail because of Him,**" more especially in the land and amongst the people where His grace has been so conspicuously displayed. The wailing, however, is not confined to the two tribes then in the land, Judah and Benjamin; nor to the ten tribes on the confines of Palestine ere entering it (Ezek. 20), but embrace the Gentiles also. "*All* the tribes of the earth." The substitution of "land" for "earth" is simply a question of interpretation, and not of translation. "Kindreds" or "tribes" in chapter 7. 9 undoubtedly designates Gentiles. Compare with Matthew 24. 30, which fixes the moment of the general wail of anguish, viz., the Coming of the Son of Man.

7.—The double affirmation, "**Even so, Amen,**" is the Spirit's seal to this striking prophetic testimony. The "Even so" is Greek, the "Amen" is Hebrew. To both Gentiles and Jews His Word is unchangeable.

A DIVINE ANNOUNCEMENT (v. 8).

8.—"**I am the Alpha and the Omega, saith the Lord God, which is, and which was, and which is to come, the Almighty.**" The announcement of these divine titles forms a fitting conclusion to the introduction. The dignity of the speaker and the character of His utterances demand profound attention. We listen here not to the voice of Christ as man, but God Himself is the speaker. He announces His own titles and glories. "I am the Alpha and the Omega"—first and last letters of the Greek alphabet—would intimate His relationship to creation. God is the source, the beginning of all truth revealed, of all promise given, and of all testimony committed to men. In this respect He is "the Alpha." But He is also the end. His glory is the goal. Everything finds its answer in Him. Our course, our testing lie between these points, God the Alpha and God the Omega. To Him as the end all gravitate. On *our* hands the threads are broken; in *His* hands they have never been rent. In the midst of failed and failing circumstances, and the Church ecclesiastically a ruin amidst the wrecked testimony of the ages, God's voice is heard above the din and strife. The beginning of all testimony is in God, and the end, too, centres in Him. In Him as the Omega is finished what as the Alpha He began.

Next we are introduced to the divine greatness of the speaker, who is none other than the Lord God of the Old Testament (Gen. 2, etc.).

Who is the Lord God? Jehovah Elohim, the God of men and of Israel, Who has been pleased to put Himself into moral relationship with both, speaks once again from Heaven. What a calm to the soul amidst the rush of life! Here the voice of the Eternal, and at once the murmur within and the din without are stilled. In the explanatory words which follow, "Which is, and which was, and which is to come," the essential and ever-abiding nature of His Being as Jehovah is stated. The three clauses form the interpretation of the Name Jehovah. The third member of the text, "which is to come," would at first sight seem to indicate an actual coming, but it is not so. The force of the whole is to present an eternal *Is*, yet not simply eternal existence, but a positive relation to the past and future.

How fitting that this truly weighty introduction should close with the title of God as the "Almighty," a title which has been a rock of strength to His afflicted people in all ages. "The Almighty" is not simply the witness of omnipotent power, but signifies Almighty in "sustaining resources," and it will be found in the course of this book that the circumstances of God's people make many a demand on this strong Name; hence its frequency in the Apocalypse, found only once elsewhere in the New Testament (2 Cor. 6. 18), and then as a quotation from Isaiah. "Almighty" used singly, or in conjunction with other names, occurs about sixty times, half of these instances in the ancient book of Job. *Almighty* God is a title full of strength and consolation. He is Almighty in sustaining His people, yet equally Almighty in judgment on His enemies.

It is to be noted that the Authorised Version of verse eight both interpolates and omits. The words, "the beginning and the ending," are right in the text of chapters 21. 6 and 22. 13, but wrong here. "God" after "Lord" is also an important omission. These and other blemishes are corrected in the Revised Version of 1881. It must be remembered that the excellent and, in general, godly men, who translated the Scriptures in 1611 had not the advantages of their successors in 1881. Neither the Vatican, Sinaitic (both most ancient of Biblical MSS.), nor the Alexandrian

Codex were available to the translators of our noble Authorised Version.

THE GLORIOUS VISION OF CHRIST (vv. 9-20).

9.—"**I John, your brother and partaker with you in the tribulation, and kingdom, and patience in Jesus.**" Daniel, more than any other of the Hebrew prophets, deals with subjects which come within the range of the visions beheld by John. There are numerous points of similarity between the two. Thus both the Prophet and the Seer unfold the character of the last holder of the civil imperial power of Rome; both disclose the last phase of the revived empire, as also its awful end (compare chap. 7 of Daniel with chap. 17 of the Revelation).

"I John" reminds us of "I Daniel" (chap. 7. 15, etc.). The former is not a borrowed style of announcement from the latter, but is an independent statement of quiet yet conscious dignity, befitting the character of the visions about to be disclosed.

John next intimates a common fellowship in life and suffering with God's sorely afflicted people. The Neronian and Domitian periods of martyrdom were, perhaps, the most bitter of any of the pagan persecutions, which, with an occasional lull, lasted about 250 years. According to some, John was a sufferer under Nero; others would rank him in the noble army of martyrs under Domitian. It is unimportant which tradition is true.* It should be noted that neither as an apostle nor as an elder does John here speak, but as a "brother and partaker" (or companion) with the saints in "the tribulation, and kingdom, and patience in Jesus."

"*The* tribulation" points to a definite character of trial, and not merely to the ordinary difficulties of christian life. There are three great periods of determinate suffering: (1) Under pagan Rome; (2) under papal Rome during the Dark or Middle Ages; (3) under the joint persecution of the *future* civil and ecclesiastical powers (Rev. 6. and 13).

The "kingdom" is next introduced as that in which John had a common participation with those to whom he writes. There are four distinct phases in which the kingdom is presented in the Scriptures: (1) In *responsibility* as presented to the Jews, the king being rejected (Matt. 1-12); (2) In *mystery* among the Gentiles as developed in Matthew

* The date generally assigned to "The Revelation" is as in our English Bible, A.D. 96, during the reign of Domitian. Some, however, assign a much earlier date. It has been put in the time of Claudius, A.D. 41-54, and by others in the reign of Nero, A.D. 54-68. The earlier date is extremely improbable.

13; (3) in tribulation as detailed in the central part of the Apocalypse; and (4) in *power* at the Coming of the Lord in glory (Matt. 25. 31), the great and grand subject of the prophets of old.

"Patience," or endurance, follows, for evil yet reigns unchecked in the world and in the Church. The petition, "Thy kingdom come," daily arising from the hearts and lips of thousands, is yet unanswered. Tribulation is the appointed path to the kingdom. The life of some is one of almost uninterrupted suffering, of others one of active service, while for the greater number it is one of weary routine of daily duty. Thus the need of patience by all in the hourly doing of God's will. The dreariness and solitude of Patmos called for "*much* patience," an essential characteristic of every true minister of God (2 Cor. 6. 4). Press on, wearied saint, till morning breaks, when God shall openly and publicly appear on the behalf of all who, in the meantime, in weakness cling by faith to His blessed Name.

But not only have we fellowship with the aged and honoured apostle in those three things, namely, "the tribulation," the "kingdom," and "patience,"* but the Lord has His part in them, and a distinguished one too. These things are "in Jesus." The introduction of the Name of sweetest import to the ear and heart of believers is brimful of comfort and solace to suffering saints.

THE ISLE CALLED PATMOS.

9.—**"Was in the island that is called Patmos, for the Word of God, and for the testimony of Jesus."** The place of John's banishment was almost unknown even by name; hence we are informed that it was an "island," and called "Patmos." This exceedingly dreary and inhospitable isle in the Aegean sea, lying off the south coast of Asia Minor, is about fifteen miles in circumference. In the Middle Ages it was known as Palmoso, now known as *Patino*. Its present population is about 4000, all Greek Christians. The ignorant and lazy monks possess a valuable library which they are unable to use. Says Tischendorf, that indefatigable Bible scholar: "Silent lay the little island before me in the morning twilight. Here and there an olive breaks the monotony of the rocky waste. The sea was still as the grave. Patmos reposed in it like a dead saint. John—that is the thought of the island. The island belongs to him; it

* "The three words, 'tribulation,' and 'kingdom,' and 'patience,' are intimately connected, being brought together under one head by one article in the Greek."—*J. N. D.*

is his sanctuary. The stones speak of him, and in every heart he lives." How fitting the geographical position! John in Patmos was, as it were, in the very centre of the prophetic situation. Jerusalem lay south, Rome lay behind the Seer to the west, Babylon to the east, and the land of Magog (Russia) to the north, while on the coast in front of him lay the seven Asiatic assemblies, whose history he was about to relate.

Moral superiority in his circumstances is expressed in the simple statement: "I was in the isle called Patmos." Not a word of reproach nor of complaint. The arrest, trial, and proceedings before the savage emperor Domitian are passed over in absolute silence as deemed unworthy of notice.

Tradition, not a safe instructor, has supplied us with interesting accounts of a legendary character, more numerous and truth-like than those related of the distinguished apostles, Peter and Paul.*

God made the wrath of the haughty emperor to praise Him. The circumstances were just what was needed to introduce John into the visions of God, one of which pictured the downfall of Rome's imperial greatness, its future revival, and final doom (chaps. 17. 8; 19. 20), while she was still in the zenith of her glory the unchallenged mistress of the world.

The same power which gave its legal sanction to the crucifixion of our Lord branded "the disciple whom Jesus loved" as a criminal. Here, however, the real cause of offence is stated in precise terms to be "the Word of God and the testimony of Jesus." These will ever incur the world's hostility.

John, although destitute of human learning (Acts 4. 13), and speaking in the rude vernacular of Galilee, fearlessly and faithfully preached and taught in public and private the Word of God. The apostles had not learned the art—a highly finished one in these days,—of trimming the truth to suit the varied tastes of people. In proportion as the Word of God is made known in its fulness and integrity, and the claims of God are pressed upon the conscience, the enmity of the world is roused into action.

9.—"**The testimony of Jesus**" is here especially regarded in its prophetic aspect. The birth of the King of the Jews awakened the cruel jealousy of Herod, and stirred Jerusalem to its centre (Matt. 2). The testimony to the royal rights of Jesus was a crime which neither the

* "Gloag, in his 'Introduction to the Johannine Writings' (Nisbet & Co.), discusses these legendary accounts in a calm and reverent spirit. There may be a basis of truth in some of them, but *certainty* there is not."

laws of Rome nor imperial greatness could brook, so Rome crucified Peter, beheaded Paul, and banished John.

10.—"**I became in** (the) **Spirit on the Lord's day.**" All Christians are "in Christ," in contrast with their former state "in Adam," and are "in the Spirit" in contrast with their previous condition "in the flesh." No Christian can ever be found again in either "Adam" or "flesh," both describing a *past* condition. In the former is signified that you are of that race of which "Adam" is head; in the latter is intimated the morally fallen condition in which the race is found. But being in the Spirit (Rom. 8), as every Christian undoubtedly is, does not convey the force of "*I became* in (the) Spirit." The meaning is, that John was held, controlled, and characterised by an absolute subservience to the Spirit. Taken out from the consciousness of everyday life and circumstances, he found himself in another state of being. From the absence of the article before "Spirit," it must not be inferred that the Holy Spirit is not meant. It is not the Holy Spirit as a Person, nor our own spirit that is referred to, but the omission of the article marks the phrase as indicating a characteristic state, a state characterised by the Holy Ghost, and one in which the human spirit and the whole inner being were for the time absorbed (compare Ezek. 11. 24 with 2 Cor. 12. 2, 3). Paul in his ecstatic state was not allowed then, nor afterwards, to record what he saw and heard. John, on the contrary, was commanded to do both.

The same form of words is found in the introduction to the subsequent visions recorded in chapters 4, 5, etc. The scene of the spiritual state of ecstasy of chapter 1 is on *earth*, whereas that of chapter 4 is in *Heaven*.

The whole contents of the book of Revelation were communicated in vision on the most interesting day of the week, "the Lord's day." The eight visions detailed in Zechariah were seen in one night (chaps. 1. 8-6.). The visions of Daniel were also beheld in the night (chap. 7).

THE LORD'S DAY.

10.—"**The Lord's day**" occurs but once in the Holy Scriptures, afterwards it became the common appellation of the Christian's special day of rest and worship. That the first day of the week is meant seems evident from the following considerations: First, the difference of the expression used in the original from that employed to set forth the prophetic "day of the Lord," for which see 1 Corinthians 5. 5; 2 Corinthians 1. 14; 1 Thessalonians 5. 2. Second, the character of the first vision (vv. 12-20), which is of *present* application. Christ glorified in the midst of the churches could have neither place nor meaning in the period of coming judgment, spoken of in both Testaments as the "day of the Lord," and which is dependent upon the setting aside of the Church as a public witness for God on earth. These, and other considerations, forbid the application of the disputed term to the "day of the Lord," yet future.

Two great facts stamp their character on the first day of the week, the resurrection of the Lord from the dead (John 20) and the founding of the Church at Pentecost (Lev. 23. 16, with Acts 2). Thus, "the Lord's *day*" is no ordinary day, nor is "the Lord's *supper*" an ordinary meal. Both the "day" and the "supper" are distinctively His. The sacred character of the "day" and of the "supper" should be maintained in their fullest integrity. The rude hand of the spoiler would rob us of these precious heirlooms which significantly speak to the Church of His resurrection and of His death.

10.—**"I heard behind me a great voice as of a trumpet."** The position of the Seer is significant. His back is to the Church and his face toward the kingdom. Ecclesiastical ruin foretold by Paul (Acts 20. 28-32; Rom. 11; 2 Tim. 3) had already set in. The polemical element in the writings of John was chiefly directed against Cerinthus (contemporary with the apostle) and others, who had commenced a vigorous and satanic crusade against Christianity. Certain Gnostic heresies, the principles of which were denounced by Paul in his Corinthian and Colossian epistles, were more fully developed in John's day, and in the second century had their distinctive schools, all in open and flagrant opposition to the Person of our Lord Jesus Christ. Added to these Church dangers was the persecuting power of the world. Little wonder, therefore, that the gaze of the aged and honoured prisoner was directed onward to the glory and strength of the kingdom, when right would be vindicated and wrong punished. But the Lord was not done with the Church, if John in spirit had turned his back upon it. He was to hear and see, and so must turn round and get occupied with that which was present to the Lord.

The "great voice as of a trumpet" would intimate that a matter of public importance had to be communicated, one in which the whole Church was interested. Moreover, the vision which John was called to witness behind him is introductory to the whole series subsequently revealed, thus fixing the commencement of these revelations. How fitting that the first vision presented to the rapt gaze of the Seer should be Christ in manhood, yet in power and majesty in the midst of the churches.

THE SEVEN CHURCHES.

11.—The divine titles, "**I am Alpha and Omega, the first and the last,**" should be rejected as forming no part of what John wrote. The first title was probably inserted from verse 8, and the second from verse 17;* besides which, the speaker is not revealed, nor His titles declared till John turns round. "I turned to see the voice that spake with me."

11.—"**What thou seest write in a book, and send to the seven assemblies**—to Ephesus, and to Smyrna, and to Pergamos, and to Thyatira, and to Sardis, and to Philadelphia, and to Laodicea." There were other assemblies of importance in proconsular Asia besides the seven specified. But the Spirit of God had a moral end in view in the choice of those particular churches, hence the definite article, "*the* seven assemblies." The order, too, in which they are named is worthy of notice. Hengstenberg in his commentary remarks, "Ephesus, Smyrna, and Pergamos must stand together, and be separated from the rest. For these three cities, and these alone, contended for the primacy in Asia." In the separate addresses to the churches (chaps. 2 and 3) there is a marked division into three and four. Thus the call, "He that hath an ear," seven times repeated, occurs in the addresses to the first three churches *before* the word to the overcomer (chap. 2. 7, 11, 17); whereas in the last four the call to "hear" comes *after* the promise to the overcomer (chaps. 2. 29; 3. 6, 13, 22). The assemblies are separately named. The independence of each is thus fully assured, and the responsibility of each to Christ is as distinctly taught. The vital unity of the Church as "one body," and the mutual dependence of its members, are truths exclusively taught by Paul. In the first three chapters of the Apocalypse the Church is, on the other hand, viewed in her public position on earth as God's light-bearer and witness. "*The* seven assemblies," without doubt, exhibited certain distinctly marked characteristics which separately stamp their

---

* Archdeacon Lee remarks: "The English version of the Apocalypse represents a Greek text which does not rest upon the same authority as that of the other books of the New Testament" ("Speaker's Commentary"). All competent Bible critics concur in this testimony. It is based on the Greek text (fifth edition) published by Erasmus, the most distinguished scholar of the 16th century. But Erasmus had only one Greek MS., found by Delitzsch in a German library in 1861 before him, and that so defective and mutilated that he actually supplied the last six verses wanting in his copy from the Vulgate. Besides which, it was too hurriedly done. There are fewer uncial MSS., that is, the oldest Greek copies, than of any other of the books of the New Testament. But the text has in recent years been recovered to almost the state of purity in which it was originally written, so that God's mind in the Apocalypse is a matter of ***absolute certainty***

character on the Church universal in successive stages of her history, while these same features collectively distinguish the Church throughout the earth at any given time, then and now.

Two of them, Smyrna and Philadelphia, are commended without a word of reproof. Suffering characterised the former, weakness the latter. Mingled praise and blame are meted out to Ephesus, Pergamos, Thyatira, and Sardis. Laodicea is the worst of "the seven." Her state is hopeless, *all* is blame without one word of commendation. In Thyatira a remnant is for the first time recognised.

(1) Ephesus,

the renowned capital of the Asia of the Apocalypse, the "Light of Asia," was the main seat and centre of heathen idolatry. It was the stronghold of Satan's power, and from it idolatry spread all over the known world (Acts 19). The small silver shrines representing the goddess Diana were eagerly bought by strangers, and set up as household deities in their distant homes; while the huge temple of the goddess, adorned and beautified by the wealth of Asia, was counted one of the seven wonders of the world. Ephesus became the scene of a fierce conflict between the powers of light and darkness. The devoted Aquila and Priscilla laboured for some time in this idolatrous city; previously twelve of John's disciples had helped in a small degree to break in upon the darkness, but their efforts must have been feeble owing to their own imperfect state (Acts 19); then the eloquent Apollos gave a further impetus to the work. Paul it was, however, who seems to have broken the power of darkness and roused to fury the devotees of idolatry and superstition, as they saw the whole system, like Dagon of old, trembling before the soul-emancipating truths of Christianity; lastly, the beloved John, after leaving his Jerusalem home, took up his residence in Ephesus, and for fully thirty years made it the centre of his work for Christ. The glory of Ephesus has departed, and the once proud heathen city is now but a miserable village known as *Ayasalook*.

(2) Smyrna

lay about 40 miles north of Ephesus, and is now one of the most important cities of the Turkish empire; its estimated population is about 200,000. It was anciently, in some respects, the rival of Ephesus. Its natural and commercial situation, its wealth and commerce, and the splendour of its buildings caused it to be termed "the beautiful." It was not much, if at all, behind Ephesus in idolatry. Smyrna is not named in the Acts, nor in the Pauline epistles, and we have no means of ascertaining conclusively *how* or *when* the Gospel was introduced there. The stringent imperial laws against Christianity were rigorously enforced in Smyrna, chiefly through the Jews and heathen combined, who pressed the unwilling hands of the local authorities to carry into execution the persecuting edicts. Polycarp, the friend of John, was, it is said, slain here in his ninetieth year, A.D. 168, the last disciple who had personally conversed with the apostle. The fierce persecution which raged in Asia Minor had its centre in Smyrna, and is no doubt referred to in the extended address to that assembly (Rev. 2. 8-11).

(3) Pergamos

lay still further north. This city had little or no commerce, but was remarkable for its learning, refinement, and science, especially medicine. A long succession of kings made Pergamos, or Pergamum, as the Greeks termed it, their royal residence. Its celebrated library, only second to that in Alexandria, with which it was ultimately incorporated, consisted of 200,000 books. It was here that the art of preparing skins of animals for writing upon was perfected, and from which our word *parchment* is derived. Thus the name of this scripturally ill-omened city (Rev. 2. 12-17) has been handed down through the christian ages, and no doubt many a literary *pergamena* MS. of value had been prepared in Pergamos. The worship of Artemis characterises Ephesus. Dionysos was the distinguishing deity of Smyrna. These two cities were evil, but Pergamos was pre-eminently so in its idolatry. The epithets, "Satan's throne" and "where Satan dwelleth" (Rev. 2. 13), must have had, in the first instance, a local application to Pergamos. The most conspicuous object in the celebrated temple of Æsculapius was the wreathed serpent, behind which was "Satan, that old serpent." The noble science of medicine was thus early identified with the worship of Satan, who usurped the place, functions, and titles of Christ. The names of "Preserver" and "Saviour" were applied to Æsculapius, and the cures wrought were ascribed to this chosen deity. It was, in short, substituting Satan for Christ.

(4) Thyatira

lay south-east from Pergamos. "The road from Thyatira to Pergamos . . . is one of the most beautiful in the world." The three cities previously named were much more noted than Thyatira, which, however, has an interest of its own. Indirectly, it connects itself with Paul's missionary labours in Europe. His first convert was a woman of Thyatira, engaged in selling the celebrated purple for which her city was famous (Acts 16. 14). Inscriptions, yet extant, show that the guild of dyers formed the most important trade of the city, and to this day the brilliant scarlet cloth dyed here is largely used throughout Asia and Europe, a weekly supply being sent to Smyrna. Thyatira is at present a flourishing town with a population of nearly 20,000.

(5) Sardis

lay about 27 miles due south from Thyatira. Sardis was anciently a proud and wealthy city, and the capital of the kingdom of Lydia. This once royal city, spite of the valour of its inhabitants, fell before the conquering hero, Cyrus. With the fall of the city the Lydian monarchy came to an end. The present name of the former capital is *Sart*. What a commentary on human greatness is furnished in the now degraded city of the wealthy, wise, and able Croesus. "Two or three shepherds inhabited a hut, and a Turk with two servants, at the time of Mr. Arundel's visit in 1826. In 1850 no human being was found dwelling in the once mighty and populous Sardis."*

(6) Philadelphia

is derived from its founder, Attalus *Philadelphus*, king of Pergamos, and it is situated about 25 miles south of Sardis. Its modern name, *Allah Shehr*, "city of God," is significant, although the Turks do not regard the city with any degree of veneration. The present town is large, and contains about 15,000 inhabitants, of whom a fair proportion are Greek Christians. The remains of early christian times are more numerous here than in any of the other Asiatic cities named by John; the ruins of no less than twenty-five churches are pointed out, while several marble pillars, almost entire, remind us of the apocalyptic reference (chap. 3. 12), probably to these very pillars. Its freedom from blame in the message to its angel (chap. 3. 7-13) is worthy of note in connection with the fact that it had the longest duration of any of the seven cities named. Says the sceptic Gibbon: "Among the Greek colonies and churches of Asia, Philadelphia is still erect; a column in a scene of ruins, a pleasing example that the paths of honour and safety may sometimes be the same."

(7) Laodicea

was situated about 40 miles east of Ephesus, and derived its name from Laodice, wife of Antiochus II., the Syrian

* "Imperial Bible Dictionary," article, "Sardis."

monarch. It was an exceedingly wealthy city, so much so, that although overthrown by an earthquake in the reign of Nero, A.D. 62, it quickly recovered from the blow, and from its own resources soon assumed its pristine glory, and at the date of the Apocalypse was a magnificent city. The assembly was infected with the "gold fever," being "rich and increased with goods" (chap. 3. 17). Pride, luxuriousness, and self-satisfaction characterised the general life of the population, and evidently stamped their character on the Church as well. The pride of Laodicea has been humbled, its wealth scattered amongst strangers, and its splendour laid in the dust. The site of the once opulent city is a scene of utter ruin and desolation.*

THE APPLICATION.

A special, but by no means exclusive, application of the first three chapters to the Asiatic assemblies named must be admitted. Thus, John greets "the seven assemblies which are in Asia" (v. 4); he has them equally in view in verse 11; while to each of "the seven" a special epistle is addressed (chaps. 2 and 3). But while a primary application to the seven Asiatic assemblies is undoubted, it is equally clear that they were representatives of the whole Church, not only at any given moment, but also in the successive moral stages of her history. After the third chapter we meet with no allusion to these Asiatic assemblies. "He that hath an ear let him hear what the Spirit saith unto the churches," seven times repeated, intimates a direct application of these addresses to the individual hearer, also to every company of professed believers on the earth at any given time. The *present* day application is of immense value and profit.

Questions have been raised as to John's ability, as a prisoner, to write and communicate with the assemblies. We hold that the Apocalypse as a whole was written in Patmos, and, further, that the seven assemblies had each their respective epistles sent to them from thence. We see no reason for the supposition put forth by some that the

---

* Paul's references to the Church in Laodicea (Col. 2. 1; 4. 13-16) afford a fine example of christian love and interest to saints personally unknown. "Likewise read the epistle from Laodicea" (v. 16) probably refers to the epistle to the Ephesians, then going the round of the assemblies. From the fact that there are no salutations to individuals, and from the character of the epistle generally, we consider it extremely probable that the epistle to the Ephesians was a circular letter, then at Laodicea. It is certain that the epistle to the Colossians was intended by the apostle to be read in the Laodicean assembly. What more fitting than the truths contained in these epistles to rescue the saints in Laodicea from the grave perils which beset them! The cross in the Roman and Galatian epistles was the emancipating truth of the sixteenth century. The heavenly glory of Christ in the Ephesian and Colossian epistles is the grand and delivering truth of the twentieth century.

visions were seen in Patmos, and afterwards written in Ephesus on the Seer's release from banishment under Nerva. The supernatural characterises a large portion of the book, and hence difficulties disappear like melting flakes of snow.

SEVEN GOLDEN LAMPS

12.—"**I turned back to see the voice which spake with me; and having turned, I saw seven golden lamps.**" The Seer on turning round to see the voice of the speaker necessarily turned round to the east, the scene of immediate interest. The first object he beheld was "seven golden lamps." What these signified we are informed in verse 20: "The seven lamps are seven assemblies." The numerical value of the number *seven* points to what is morally complete. Gold, the most precious of metals, signifies divine righteousness. The founding and constitution of the Church, whether viewed in relation to Christ as His body, or to God as His house, is the display of divine righteousness of the character of God. It could not be otherwise. In the symbol of "seven golden lamps" we have the Church in its completeness and perfection on earth, as in the thoughts of God, in its public position as His witness. It is not what the Church has become, but viewed in its origin and character as set up by Him. While the whole Church is in view it is here regarded as separate assemblies.

The seven golden lamps evidently allude to the seven-branched golden lamp-stand which stood at the *south* side of the outer compartment of the sanctuary of old. Here the lamps stand in the *east*. *There*, the seven lamps had one stem and one stand, while each lamp threw its clear light on the beautifully ornamented shaft or stem, discovering its beauties during the dark hours of night (Exod. 25. 31-40; Num. 8. 2-4), so only in the divine presence are fully expressed the moral glories of Jesus, God's beloved Son. *Here* each lamp rests on its own base. They represent separate and independent assemblies, each one in its place responsible to cast its beams of light athwart the gloom. It is the serious and urgent responsibility of every professed company of saints to be in its own locality a witness for God, and what, of course, is true of local assemblies is equally so of the Church universal. The seven Asiatic lamps have long since been removed according to the divine threat (chap. 2. 5), and a similar judgment, although expressed under a different symbol, is about to overtake the professing Church as a whole (Rom. 11. 22). Where are the golden lamps to-day? This is a solemn and searching question for us all.

THE VISION OF CHRIST (vv. 13-16).

The thing which first arrests the attention of the Seer is the seven golden lamps, not simply lamp-*stands*.* But what is the Church apart from Christ? The distinguishing glory of this introductory vision is not the churches in their divine standing on earth, but the grandeur and majesty of the One Who has deigned to be in their midst. Who is He? "One like unto (the) Son of Man." The omission of the definite article in the original, as also in Daniel 7. 13, is to be noted. Both the Prophet and the Seer beheld the Son of Man without doubt, but what morally characterised Him as bearing that Name or title is the thought presented in the omission of the article, not so much the person known as the Son of Man; but one is seen in Heaven by the Hebrew Prophet, and on earth by the christian Seer, in the moral characteristics belonging to Him who bore that title. It is characteristic, not personal.

13.—"**The Son of Man**" is a title used of Ezekiel about one hundred times, and once of Daniel (chap. 8. 17), the only Hebrew Prophet so spoken of. The Lord alone in the Gospels uses the title of Himself, about seventy times. John 12. 34 is only an apparent exception. The title is one which expresses a wider range of dominion and glory than that of king of Israel (compare Psa. 2 and 8). As Son of God He quickens the dead, spiritually (John 5. 25) and physically (v. 28). As Son of Man He judges (v. 22), and also executes His judgment (v. 27). It is a title of peculiar delight to the Lord.

13.—"**Clothed with a garment down to the foot,**" *i.e.*, to the feet of the glorious One, but not so low as to cover them (v. 15). Neither the material nor colour of the robe is specified. There is an evident allusion to the ephod, the pre-eminent garment of the high priest.† But the long flowing garment is neither girded about the loins (Luke 12. 35) nor laid aside (John 13. 4) as the activity of service would require, "rather dignified priestly judgment" is expressed thereby.

13.—"**Girt about at the breasts with a golden girdle.**" The materials in the girdle of the high

* The "candle" is distinguished from the "candle-stick," or, as in the Revised Version, the "lamp" from its "stand." It is the "lamp" which gives the light (Luke 8. 16; 11. 35, 36; Matt. 5. 15). There is prominence given to the "stand" in the ancient sanctuary, as in its chaste ornamentation, under the sevenfold light of the Spirit, were set forth the beauties of Jesus to the worshippers *within*.

† Exodus 28. 31 in the LXX. has the *same* word for "ephod" as in Revelation 1. 13 for "garment." Hence we infer the sacerdotal application of the word here.

priest were "gold" and "linen," in which latter the colours "blue, purple, and scarlet" were displayed (Exod. 28. 8), thus intimating the union of divine and human righteousness in Jesus our great High Priest, while the colours set forth His heavenly character (blue), sufferings (purple), and glory (scarlet). But the girdle here is one wholly of gold, divine righteousness. Girt about at the breasts instead of the loins (Dan. 10. 5) would intimate calm repose. The girdle in itself sets forth *righteousness* and *faithfulness*, attributes which ever characterised the Lord in all His ways (Isa. 11. 5). The angels of judgment (Rev. 15. 6), like our Lord, are girded with golden girdles at their breasts. The usual order, girt about the loins, is departed from in their case, as the place of the girdle at the breasts denotes that judgment to be executed is according to what God is in His nature.

14.—"**His head and His hair were white as white wool, as snow.**" "The Ancient of Days" (Dan. 7. 9) is similarly described. There are certain characteristics common to both Son of Man and Ancient of Days. They are distinct persons, yet so identified in action and character that it is not always possible to distinguish them. The identification of Jesus with Jehovah; of the wearied Man (John 4. 6) with the unwearied Creator (Isa. 40. 28) is a subject of profound interest. Divine wisdom in absolute purity seems, in the main, the thought intended by the dazzling whiteness of the head and hair. In the passage in Daniel the whiteness of the head is not mentioned. Here the head is uncovered. Personal attributes are in question, and not official or relative glories, which latter are found in verse 16.

14.—"**His eyes as a flame of fire,**" keen, penetrating judgment, which searches out, and exposes in all its nakedness, evil, however covered up. Who or what can escape the scrutiny of those eyes as of fire?

15.—"**His feet like fine brass, as burning in a furnace.**" An emblem of the most awful unyielding strength in judicial judgment (compare with chap. 10. 1).

15.—"**His voice as the voice of many waters**" (compare with Ezek. 43. 2). The grandeur, the majesty of His voice is beyond the ceaseless roar of many cataracts. "The LORD on high is mightier than the noise of many waters, yea, than the mighty waves of the sea" (Psa. 93. 4). The sign of His supreme sovereignty and majesty over all the waves of human passion, over the circumstances of a wrecked world and a ruined Church, is declared to be "*His voice* as the voice of many waters." It was His voice —"God said"—ten times repeated, which brought order out of chaos, light out of darkness, and life out of death (Gen. 1). It was His voice which stilled the angry Galilean sea, and hushed its boisterous winds and waves into the calm of a sleeping child (Matt. 8. 23-27).

16.—"**Having in His right hand seven stars.**" The stars are declared to be the angels or representatives of the churches (v. 20). The "stars" as a symbol are the expression, first, of countless multitudes (Gen. 15. 5); second, eminent persons in authority, civil and ecclesiastical (Dan. 8. 10; Rev. 6. 13; 12. 4); third, lesser or subordinate powers in general (Gen. 37. 9; Rev. 12. 1). All Church authority, all ministry, and all spiritual rule in every assembly are vested in Christ. His competency to give or withhold, to preserve and sustain every true minister of God is the fundamental idea in the stars being held in His right hand. When the eternal security of believers is in question they are said to be in His hand, and in the Father's hand, from whence no power can pluck them (John 10. 28, 29). But they are not said to be in His "*right* hand," as here. Spiritual rulers—we do not say official ones, for all such have not been set in the Church of God—are held and maintained in the right hand of the Son of Man. "The right hand" betokens supreme authority and honour (Psa. 110. 1; Eph. 1. 20; Rev. 5. 1, 7). What a responsible, yet withal honourable position every ruler in the Church occupies! Daniel 12. 3 points to a future class of Jewish ministers or rulers. Jude 13 refers to a class of christian apostates.

The responsibility of a star is to shine. During the night of the Lord's absence the assemblies are God's light bearers through the darkness, and are collectively the light of the world. But each christian ruler or guide is also to shine in his appointed sphere. The darker the night the greater need to shine, and to reflect the light of Heaven upon the increasing darkness around.

16.—"**Out of His mouth proceeded a sharp two-edged sword.**" The execution of divine judgment by the simple force of His Word—judgment, too, which cannot be warded off—for the sword as two-edged is the force of the figure. We never read of our Lord personally putting His hand on His enemies. He speaks, and it is done. His *personal* word is the point here, as the *written* Word in Hebrews 4. 12. The ungodly in the Church are the first to be threatened with judgment, which it is hopeless to escape unless they repent (Rev. 2. 16). At the commencement of the millennial reign we witness one of the saddest sights on earth, the congregated nations of the west, etc., under their leaders in open defiance of the Lamb of God

(Rev. 19. 19-21). The sword of the Almighty Victor, the resistless energy of His Word, finds out His enemies, and the universal slaughter of the multitudinous hosts of Gentiles glorifies His righteousness "in taking vengeance" on those who refuse to own His sceptre.

16.—"**His countenance was as the sun shineth in his strength**." Once the vile spittle of men rested on His patient face (Matt. 26. 67), now divine glory, more brilliant far, more resplendent than the midday tropical sun, is here seen in the face of the Lord. "The sun in his strength," on which no mortal eye can gaze, images forth the supreme glory of Jesus, Son of Man. We may remark that Christ is spoken of as the Light of the *World* (John 8. 12), as the Sun of Righteousness to *Israel* (Mal. 4. 2), and as the Bright and Morning Star to the *Church* (Rev. 22. 16). Hengstenberg draws a contrast between the glory of the sun and that of the stars (1 Cor. 15. 41), applying the lesson to the transcendent glory of Christ (the sun), to that of His ministers (the stars). The stars are mere reflectors. They have no independent light of their own. In the matchless yet simple story of creation (Gen. 1) the distinguishing orbs for day and night are appointed their place in relation to this earth, and then it is added as a matter of small import, "the stars also" (v. 16). Would that every servant would lay it to heart. Is there not in this a lesson to every minister? We are but of trifling importance save as held in the right hand of Christ. It is the servant's connection with the Lord which alone imparts dignity.

What a glorious vision of Christ we have had, so totally unlike the Christ of the Gospels. *There*, His attributes are those of tenderness, holiness, and love; *here*, He is seen clothed in majesty and power. *There*, the Man of Sorrows; *here*, in combined deity as the Ancient of Days, and humanity as Son of Man. He was, of course, ever Divine, always God, but on earth He veiled His eternal glory, or as Paul expresses it, "emptied Himself" (Phil. 2. 7, R.V.). Here His glory shines in the midst of the churches, a strength and consolation to every true heart, a terror to all morally opposed to it.

HUMAN WEAKNESS AND DIVINE CONSOLATION (vv. 17, 18).

17.—"**When I saw Him, I fell at His feet as dead;** and He laid His right hand upon me, saying, Fear not, I am the first and the last, and the living One; and I became dead; and behold, I am living to the ages of ages, and have the keys of death and of hades."

The effect of the glorious vision of Christ was overpowering. The same John who had pillowed his head on his Master's bosom (John 13. 23), outran Peter in the race to the sepulchre (chap. 20. 4), worshipped Him risen from the dead (Matt. 28. 17), witnessed with rapt gaze His ascending Lord (Acts 1. 9, 10), now fell at His feet as dead. Christ transfigured on the holy mount was an object of fear to the favoured three of the apostolic band (Matt. 17. 6, 7). Isaiah, who above all the Hebrew prophets revelled in the glorious future, was broken down in the presence of the glory of Christ; while seraphim covered face and feet, the glory too bright to look upon, and the place too holy to tread upon (Isa. 6 with John 12. 41). Ezekiel fell on his face before that same glory (chap. 1. 28), and Daniel more than once did the same (chaps. 8. 17, 18; 10. 7-10). But Christ is here beheld, not in the native region of glory, His palace-home in the heavens, but in the midst of the churches in the full display of attributes betokening power and majesty. Here we behold the incarnate Son of Man glorified. Hence, as answering to this representation of Christ, the effect is more marked than that hitherto produced. John fell at His feet as dead. Probably the most loving and loved of the disciples was John, but what avails even the strength of human affection in light of the overwhelming glory of Jesus, Son of Man! But human weakness is answered by divine consolation. The glorified Saviour and High Priest is "touched with the feeling of our infirmities." His grace and tenderness are equal to His majesty and greatness.

17.—"**He laid His right hand upon me,**" relates the Seer. The hand of power. On the mount the touch of the hand and the voice of Jesus instantly dispelled the fear of the disciples (Matt. 17. 6, 7). Here, too, the hand and voice of the glorious One restores the disciple from his death-like swoon. It was more than a touch, "He *laid* His right hand upon me." How the pressure of that hand in its life-giving energy and strength would thrill "the disciple whom Jesus loved," the very *same* Jesus in time and eternity, in earth and in Heaven.

17.—"**Fear not**" was the glorified Saviour's reassuring word as an accompaniment to His right hand. Both were needed. The "fear not," so often repeated on earth amidst its dreads and circumstances, again breaks on the ear of the apostle, for Jesus is *unchanged*. His circumstances are totally altered, but the heart that beat in Galilee is the same that *now* throbs in tenderest love toward His own.

17.—"**I am the first and the last.**" This is essentially a divine title. Jehovah claims it three times exclusively for Himself in the prophecy of Isaiah (chaps. 41. 4; 44. 6;

48. 12), and Christ correspondingly three times in this book (chaps. 1. 17; 2. 8; 22. 13). The application of this Jehovah title to the Son of Man is an absolute proof of His Deity. Eternal Self-Existence, with its necessary correlative, Absolute Supremacy, is thus intimated. As the "FIRST," He is before all, and above all, and from whom all proceed. As the "LAST," He is after all, and in Him all things centre. He is the source and sum of universal creation. What cause for fear then? In the calm contemplation of this magnificent title, claimed and borne by Jesus of Nazareth glorified in the heavens, fear disappears like mist before the rising sun. Here is a rock of strength for wearied feet and for life's heaviest burdens.

18.—"**The Living One**" is the next divine title. He was, is, and ever shall be the source of life. He is the Living One independently of the creature. The incarnation of the Lord did not originate life, but manifested what previously existed (1 John 1. 2). "*The Living One* in particular was the designation used by the Hebrews to distinguish the true God from all false ones." The eternal life of believers, the eternal existence of unbelievers, and the immortality of angels have each their source in Christ, "the Living One." What is predicated of God in the Old and New Testament Scriptures (Jer. 10. 10; 1 Tim. 3. 15) is equally true of Christ.

18.—"**I became dead.**" Even as man, death, the wages of sin, had no claim upon Him. But in grace to us He voluntarily "became dead," not merely died, but became truly and really dead. He laid down His life. Matthew writes, He "yielded up His spirit" (chap. 27. 50, R.V.); Mark, "He gave up the ghost" (chap. 15. 37); Luke, He committed His spirit to His Father and "gave up the ghost" (chap. 23. 46); John, He bowed His head and "gave up His spirit" (chap. 19. 30, R.V.). The moral grandeur of the statement, "I became dead," is enhanced as we reflect on the divine glory of the speaker. He, "the First and the Last," stooped from the glory of eternal existence to become a man, whose brief life here was measured by little over thirty years; and "the Living One," the life and originator of all intelligence, stoops down into death, that thereby He might annul him that had the might of death, the devil, and deliver his captives (Heb. 2. 14, 15). This victory over death is complete. Death's bands are broken. "He tore the bars away." The angels, though not seen at the cross, were witnesses, both outside and inside the tomb, of Christ's victory over death (Matt. 28. 2-7; John 20. 11-13). Our translation to the heavens will be announced by the shout of triumph,

"O death, where is thy victory? O death, where is thy sting?" (1 Cor. 15. 55, R.V.).

18.—"**Behold, I am living to the ages of ages.**" The Victor over death calls attention to the fact that He ever lives, He will die no more. He has emerged from the domain of death, and announces to His saints and Church for their everlasting strength and consolation that He lives, no more to die. The "Amen" in the Authorised Version is unanimously reject d by the critics.

18.—Then follows the fitting conclusion to this grand declaration of combined divine and human glory: "**And have the keys of death and of hades.**" In our English Bibles the order is reversed, hades preceding death. But clearly this is a mistake, and contrary to the general order in which the words are found in other parts of the book (chaps. 6. 8; 20. 13, 14). Death demands the body; hades claims the soul. The Lord became subject to the one, and entered the other. Our English word "hell" should be discarded, and "hades," signifying *the unseen*, substituted. Efforts have been made to fix the locality of hades. It is impossible to do so. It is rather a *state* than a place, and refers to that condition in which all, good and bad, are found after death and previous to the resurrection. For believers, hades is to be with Christ; for unbelievers, hades is to be in torment. Thus both the Lord and the rich man went to hades (Acts 2. 27; Luke 16. 23). Christ has come out of it; the rich man will do so when raised for eternal judgment. Hades as a state exists between death and resurrection. The word does not in itself signify either blessing or misery. The state is one of conscious blessedness for believers, and one of conscious misery for unbelievers.*

The "keys" denote Christ's complete mastery over the bodies and souls of all. The right to "open" and "shut" intimates His absolute authority over death and hades, the respective jailers of the dead, and is exercised at His sovereign pleasure. Satan has not now the power of death (Heb. 2. 14). For the force of "key" as a symbol of undisputed authority, see Isaiah 22. 22; Matthew 16. 19.

A THREEFOLD DIVISION OF THE BOOK. COMMAND TO WRITE REPEATED.

19.—"**Write therefore what thou hast seen, and the things that are, and the things that are about to be after these things.**"

---

* The reader desirous of studying this and kindred subjects would do well to procure "Facts and Theories as to a Future State," by F. W. Grant. The work contains a masterly *exposé* of current and widespread errors on questions affecting the eternal destiny of the race.

It will be observed that between the first command to write (v. 11) and the second (v. 19), we have the glorious appearance of Christ beheld by the Seer in vision (vv. 12-16), and this he is to record. The word "therefore" (omitted in the Authorised Version) is important here, as connecting the command to write with the dignity of the speaker. Divine greatness, combined with human tenderness in the Lord, have done their mighty moral work in the soul of John; hence the introduction of the word "therefore" as linking the command with the divine consolation, conveyed in two of the most precious verses (vv. 17, 18) in the Apocalypse.

THE THREE GREAT DIVISIONS.

The great divisions of the book are here written for the instruction of the Church of God. "What thou hast seen" refers to the vision of Christ just beheld (vv. 12-16). "The things that are" refer to the several successive, broadly-defined features of the professing Church, and of Christ's relation thereto, till its final rejection, not yet accomplished (chaps. 2 and 3). "The things that are about to be after these things." In this third division the world and the Jews, and, we may add, the corrupt and apostate Church, *i.e.*, that which is to be "spued out," are embraced in this strictly prophetic part of the Apocalypse (chaps. 4-22. 5).

Nothing has more contributed to throw discredit on prophetic studies than the erroneous principle on which it has been sought to understand this book. Here is the key for its interpretation hanging at the door. Take it down, use it, and enter in. There is simplicity and consistency in apportioning the main contents of the book to a *past*, a *present*, and a *future*. You cannot consistently lift events out of the future, or third division, and place them in the second. Each division has its own group of events, and to transpose them is to wrest Scripture. The breaking of the Seals, the blowing of the Trumpets, and the pouring out of the Vials are, with numerous other prophetic events, embraced in the third division, *i.e.*, are comprised within the time contemplated in chapters 4-22. 5, and that supposes the close of the Church's sojourn on earth.

The divisions do not overlap. The first is a complete vision by itself. The second is as distinct as either the first or third. The successive phases of Church history, traced from the close of the first century, are a full and comprehensive account by themselves. The third division is so plainly a prophetic outline that neither its details nor principles can be made to fit into the present. "The things that are" are running their course. The Church is yet publicly recognised and owned of God, and it is its history which is chronicled by the Spirit of inspiration in chapters 2 and 3, and not that of Jews and Gentiles to which the Seals, Trumpets, and Vials apply. Introduce these now and you make the Church the present subject of judicial judgment, which, in point of fact, it is not. It is the loathsome rejection of the professing Church (Rev. 3. 16) which terminates its history as God's public witness on earth, and introduces us into the prophetic scenes of the last days. The Church fills up the gap between the break with Israel and the resumption of divine dealing with the ancient people. Ecclesiastical history forms, in brief, "the things that are," whereas a prophetic crisis of but a few years is the period covered by the "things that are about to be after these things." History characterises the second division. Prophecy is the distinguishing feature of the third division. Ecclesiastical history for nearly nineteen centuries is graphically and energetically sketched in chapters 2 and 3.

The great political consummation is unfolded in chapters 6-19. The apostate civil power, guilty and rebellious Judah, and the whore—the corruptness of the earth—are the special subjects of God's providential dealings in judgment. It has been sought to distinguish between "fulfilled" and "unfulfilled" prophecy. All prophecy is concentrated in the close of the seventieth week of Daniel (chap. 9. 25-27), although it may have commenced centuries before. The desolation of Jerusalem by the Gentiles, foretold by the Lord thirty-seven years before its capture by Titus (Luke 21), culminates at that great gathering point of all prophecy, the Coming of the Son of Man (v. 27). Hence no prophecy has had an exhaustive fulfilment. The broken threads of prophecy are resumed with Israel at the close of the Church period. The principles of the coming apostasy are actively at work; the circumstances are forming, and it may be some of the main actors of the prophetic crisis are presently alive and ready for action when the devil begins to play his terrible *role*. But so long as the Church is recognised of God the full development of evil is hindered. The Holy Ghost in the Church is the main check to the awful outburst of evil, *i.e.*, the denial of all divine authority (2 Thess. 2. 7, 8). The "things that are" must necessarily terminate before any of the prophetic events embraced within the "things which shall be after these" can have their place. The character of the *present* forbids any application of the *future* save in present moral power.

MYSTERY OF THE STARS AND LAMPS.

20.—"**The mystery of the seven stars which thou hast seen on My right hand, and the seven golden lamps. The seven stars are angels of the seven assemblies; and the seven lamps are the seven assemblies.**" The word "mystery" alone used in the New Testament signifies what is *secret* and *hidden* till revealed, then, of course, it ceases to be a mystery. But certain truths after their revelation are yet spoken of as mysteries, as none but those taught of God can understand them or know them. Thus the mysteries of the Kingdom of Heaven (Matt. 13) are wrapped up in parables clear as sunlight to disciples, but dark as midnight to unbelievers (vv. 11, 13). Take another instance. The mass of Christendom dream of an improved and improving world, and actually pervert the word "leaven," which ever denotes *evil* (1 Cor. 5. 8; Gal. 5. 9; Matt. 16. 6), to signify its exact opposite to *good*. The numerous scientific, educational, and religious agencies are spoken of as "leaven," which will in time effect the moral regeneration of the world. Yet on this the Scriptures speak with no uncertain sound: "The mystery of iniquity doth already work," not "the mystery of good," but "of iniquity." The secret working of evil till it fully ripens and the "man of sin" appear—its public development and living expression—are to believers well-known and established truths, while the mass, who only bear the christian name, ridicule them. "Mystery" then signifies what has been kept *secret* or *hidden*, and which those only who have the mind of Christ understand.

The seven stars are said to be *in* His right hand in verse 16, and *on* His right hand in verse 20. The thought seems to be that in the former is denoted their security and blessing, while in the latter their public relation to Christ is expressed; He upholds them.

But why are the stars termed angels? In commenting on verse 16 we saw that the stars set forth spiritual rulers in the churches, eminent persons responsible to witness for God in the present dark night of the Church's history. But additional thoughts are suggested by the stars being termed angels. The word "angel" in itself does not denote *nature*, but *office*; it signifies a *messenger*. The context and the special use of the word can alone determine its application to persons or to spiritual beings. In Luke 7. 24; 9. 52; 2 Corinthians 12. 7; James 2. 25 the term "angel," or its plural, is used of those sent on messages of various kinds. Service is the great characteristic of the race of spiritual beings spoken of as "angels" (Psa. 103. 20, 21; Heb. 1. 13, 14).

But there is another sense in which the word angel is employed, namely, as a *representative*. Thus in Matthew 18. 10, "See that ye despise not one of these little ones; for I say unto you, that in Heaven their angels do always behold the face of My Father which is in Heaven" (R.V.). The word "angels" in this case cannot mean "messengers," but signifies those who in Heaven *represent* the little ones who belong to God. *Representation* is the thought. "It is his angel" (Acts 12. 15).

20.—"**The stars are the angels**." That is, not only do they witness for God in the Church as the stars do in the terrestrial heavens, but they are also angels, or messengers from God to the churches and from the churches to God, and, further, they morally represent the separate churches in their state, trials, failures, and general condition before God. The angel of the Church is "the symbolical representative of the assembly seen in those responsible in it, which indeed all really are." Thus in the full position occupied by the stars we have combined a threefold thought: spiritual rule, channel of divine and human communication, and moral representation before God.

The seven *golden* lamps signify that the Church is spiritually complete before God, that its original constitution and standing is according to God's very nature, and that its mission is to shine for Him.

20.—"**The seven lamps are seven assemblies**." There can be no doubt in the mind of the careful reader of the first three chapters of the Apocalypse that while the seven churches of Asia as a whole are representative of the Church universal, at the same time the separate assemblies are viewed as each resting on its own base, and all sufficiently apart for the Lord to walk in the midst. He is amongst them for reproof, for correction, for encouragement. Every ecclesiastical act of a high-handed character is witnessed by Him Who never slumbers nor sleeps. The arrogancy of many of the "clergy" on the one hand, and the democracy of the "laity" on the other, are rapidly destroying the Church in its outward character, so that scarce a trait of the true Church is presented to the world. Thank God that that which Christ builds is impregnable (Matt. 16. 18) and loved (Eph. 5. 25).

CHAPTER II

History of the Church from its Decline till its Rejection

REMARKS ON THE ADDRESSES TO THE CHURCHES.

All the visions contained in the Apocalypse refer to the future, save the first or introductory one, which is of present application. In this Christ is witnessed in the characteristic glory of Son of Man in the midst of the seven assemblies (chap. 1. 12-16). But did these assemblies as to their actual condition answer to the Spirit's designation of them as "golden lamps," and in keeping with the holy character of the glorious One in their midst? Alas, no! The features which distinguished the Church in the morning of her birth in holiness, truth, devotedness, unworldliness, power, and unity, are now in the evening of her days conspicuously absent. For a brief season the golden lamps shone brightly, now scarcely a glimpse is seen. Open infidelity, which once *hid* itself in the lecture room, the hall of science, and in the professor's chair is now securely and *openly* lodged in the Church, in the pulpit, and in the hall of divinity.*

In these addresses, called for by the state of the assemblies, there is disclosed the point of decline, heart departure from Christ (chap. 2. 4). As a consequence of cooled affections, longing for His personal Return from Heaven wanes (Matt. 24. 48), and thus the door is open for the enemy to enter. The external history of the Church as here depicted has been amply verified by contemporary records. *Once* the Church door was barred and bolted against the entrance of evil and Satan; *now* Satan's throne and dwelling is in the Church itself (Rev. 2. 13, 20, 24). Moral darkness is rapidly settling down on these christianised lands, and we are not far from its last development, the public disavowal of Christianity. It is when Christ gives up the Church as His vessel of light and testimony that it becomes a special subject of divine judgment.

In the brief epitome of ecclesiastical history as presented in these chapters not many details are specified, but rather the development of general forms of evil. One leading idea is kept steadily in view, namely, Christ's relation to the state of things, presenting Himself to each

---

* See the terrible indictment proved to the hilt, and the charges concisely put, in "The Anti-Christian Crusade, or Official Attacks on Christianity," by Robert P. C. Corte (Simpkin, Marshall & Co.).

assembly in a character suited to its condition. Christ is the one resource for spiritual decline and weakness.

The historian of "the times of the Gentiles" is Daniel. The historian of the Church is John. The former was for the special instruction of Daniel's people, the Jews. The latter is for the profit of the Church of God. The application of these addresses extends to the whole Church, and to every one who has ears to hear. The moral profit to be derived from an earnest and devout study of these addresses to the assemblies named is immense, and has ever proved helpful to prayerful readers.

In these addresses a principle is introduced by which the actual condition of the Church at any time may be determined. The history and testing of the Church come in between the revelation of its original standing in the full blessing of God, and its ultimate destiny in association with Christ in glory. Now its past and future condition is the principle by which it is presently judged. What a contrast exists between what the Church *was* and *is*! How unlike the resplendent glory awaiting it! In the addresses to the first three assemblies they are called to repent in view of "from *whence* thou art fallen," whereas in the addresses to the last four assemblies a return to pristine state is deemed impossible, the goal of hope being the Coming of the Lord, which is not directly referred to in the previous Church addresses.

Ecclesiastical pretension and departure from first love characterised the close of the apostolic period—*Ephesus* (chap. 2. 1-7). Next succeeded the martyr period, which brings us down to the close of the tenth and last persecution, under Diocletian—*Smyrna* (chap. 2. 8-11). Decreasing spirituality and increasing worldliness went hand in hand from the accession of Constantine and his public patronage of Christianity on to the seventh century —*Pergamos* (chap. 2. 12-17), The Papal Church, which is Satan's masterpiece on earth, is witnessed in the assumption of universal authority and cruel persecution of the saints of God. Its evil reign covers "the Middle Ages," the moral characteristics of which have been well termed "dark." Popery blights everything it touches—*Thyatira* (chap. 2. 18-29). The Reformation was God's intervention in grace and power to cripple papal authority, and introduce into Europe the light which for 300 years has been burning with more or less brilliancy. Protestantism, with its divisions and deadness, shows clearly enough how far short it comes of God's ideal of the Church and Christianity—*Sardis* (chap. 3. 1-6). Another Reformation, equally the work of God, characterised the beginning of last century—*Philadelphia* (chap. 3. 7-13). The present general state of the professing Church which is one of lukewarmness is the most hateful and nauseous of any yet described. We may well term this last phase of Church history on the eve of judgment the Christless period—*Laodicea* (chap. 3. 14-22).

Note, that the history of the first three churches is consecutive, whereas the history of the remaining four overlaps, and then practically runs on concurrently to the end, the Coming of the Lord. One other consideration of interest, and we bring these remarks to a close. The *divine* element, signified by the numeral three, is the predominant thought in the first group of churches, whereas the *human* enters more largely into the second group signified by the number four.

THE SPIRIT'S ADDRESS TO EPHESUS (CHAP. 2. 1-7).

1.—"To the angel of the Church in Ephesus write." The same form of words is repeated in the introduction to each of the seven churches. The Authorised Version, in chapter 2. 1, reads "of Ephesus," and in chapter 3. 14 "of the Laodiceans," but in the Revised Version the respective readings are correctly given as "in Ephesus" and "in Laodicea." The churches in these cities were composed of professing Christians, not of the pagan inhabitants, as the Authorised Version would imply. Each of the epistles is addressed to the "angel" of the Church. We have in these addresses the voice of the Spirit to the churches (v. 7, etc.), and of the Lord Himself, but they are not *directly* spoken to. Paul wrote to the *saints* in Ephesus (Eph. 1. 1). John to the *angel* of the Church. Why this? Intimacy characterises the former. Distance distinguishes the latter. The reason for the more distant style of address employed by John is found in the fact that the Church had sunk so low morally that the Lord could only address it through its representatives or angels, not spiritual beings, but men.

Some writers, as Dean Alford, argue for the guardianship of literal angels over the churches, and consider that these guardian angels are here addressed. But such a theory seems to us far-fetched and untenable. The Spirit on earth and the Lord on high make the Church their special subject of care. The spiritual powers in heavenly places learn through it God's manifold wisdom (Eph. 3. 10); lessons, too, of godly order are taught these heavenly beings (1 Cor. 11. 10). But the care of the Church is committed to higher and better hands than that of angels. Besides, it would be absurd to think of angels failing in their duty. They "do His commandments, hearkening unto the voice of His Word'' (Psa. 103. 20); whereas the angels of the churches are justly blameable, being held responsible for the moral state disclosed. Thus the words to the angel, ''I have against thee,'' ''Remember therefore from whence thou art fallen, and repent,'' etc., seem quite inapplicable to God's angels who are spoken of as ''elect'' and ''holy,'' and hence preserved from falling. It has, however, been more commonly understood that the ''angel'' represents a bishop, or presiding presbyter. But Scripture affords not the slightest countenance for the modern bishop of a diocese, or the more ancient bishop of a Church. Elders or bishops refer to the same persons (Acts 20. 17, 28). The term ''elder'' directs attention to the age and experience of the man, whilst that of ''bishop'' or ''overseer'' to spiritual oversight. The man and his work are thus respectively signified in the terms ''elder'' and ''bishop.'' Elders were made bishops, and there were several such in various assemblies, as in Ephesus (Acts 20. 17) and in Philippi (Phil. 1. 1). Timothy, Onesimus, and John have had the questionable honour thrust upon them by speculative divines of being after Paul's time the respective angels of the Church in Ephesus.

To insist upon a necessary application of the term ''angel'' to bishop or presbyter seems forced; besides, the other symbol used of the same persons, namely, ''stars'' (chap. 1. 20), would forbid such exclusive application. The ''stars'' are appointed to shine, to reflect the light of Heaven in the dark night of the Church's history. A person occupying the highest official position in the Church might not be a ''star.'' We regard the angel of the Church as symbolically representative of the assembly in its actual moral state. *Representation* is the thought. Hence in this book, the waters (chap. 16. 5), the winds (chap. 7. 1), the abyss (chap. 9. 11), and fire (chap. 14. 18) have each their representative angel. According to this view the angel of the Church may signify more persons than one. We would emphasise the remark that not official but *moral representation* is the idea conveyed in the word ''angel'' as used in connection with the seven churches. While, therefore, the Spirit has in view each local Church, and the assembly as a whole, yet each Church is addressed in its representative, and it will generally be found that in most companies of saints there are those who morally lead, apart altogether from official status.

THE SEVEN STARS AND SEVEN GOLDEN LAMPS.

1.—**''These things saith He that holdeth the seven stars in His right hand, that walketh in the midst of**

the seven golden lamps." The descriptive titles of Christ towards each of the churches are almost wholly taken from the detailed account of His Person as presented at the close of chapter one. In chapter 1. 20 the stars are seen *on* His right hand; in chapter 3. 1 He *has* the stars; but here a more intense action is intimated, He *holds* them. The stars are the Church's light bearers. They derive their light from Him, they are subject to His power, and sustained by Him. He guides, controls, and holds them fast. What a strength to the tried servant! How fitting, too, that the absolute authority of Christ over all responsible to shine for Him during the dark night of His absence should be shown at the commencement of this epitome of Church history in these two chapters.

The ecclesiastical place of our Lord (chap. 1. 13) is in the "midst" of the seven golden lamps; but here He walks in their midst, taking note of every corporate and individual difficulty. He observes if the lamps shine. He is present to sustain the vessels of testimony. His help is instantly available in every circumstance of need. The Church will never find itself in a position in which it is deprived of the active service of Christ, Who walks in and out amongst the churches, observing their ways, and according praise and blame. He trims each lamp, or, when it is proved utterly unfaithful, may remove it from its place of responsibility *on earth*. But this character of truth in no wise enfeebles the everlasting security of the Church, against which the gates of hades shall not prevail (Matt. 16. 18), nor against any individual member thereof (Rom. 8. 38, 39).

COMMENDED

2, 3.—**"I know thy works, and thy labour, and thine endurance, and that thou canst not bear evil (men); and hast tried them who themselves say (are) apostles, and are not, and hast found them liars: and endurest and hast borne for My Name's sake, and hast not wearied."** The Lord commends before He reproves. He loves to count up what grace—His own grace—has wrought in the souls and ways of His people. In these epistles the Church is witnessed in its downward course, going from bad to worse. But the Lord is unchanged. He loves to commend His saints when and where He can, and if things are drifting to their final consummation that does not hinder the fullest acknowledgment of the Spirit's work everywhere and in every saint. The fruit of the Spirit should more readily catch the eye than the works of the flesh. Be ever ready to heartily own and unqualifiedly express appreciation of all that is good and excellent, especially where evil may exist.

"I know," seven times repeated, intimates the Lord's absolute knowledge of the condition and circumstances of His people. Then He says, "I know thy works." These, no doubt, were many and varied. But all work is not accompanied by, nor is it the fruit of, toil or "endurance," as that spoken of here. The first christian lesson is patience (endurance) (Rom. 5. 3), and "much" of it the first trait of a true minister of God (2 Cor. 6. 4). Endurance is followed by intolerance of evil persons. Patience towards the weak, exercised in the midst of trial and opposition, did not make the Church indifferent to evil; the moral nature was roused. Moreover, they had tested the claim of some to be co-ordinate with the apostles, and this they did so thoroughly that all false pretension was exposed in light of those signs which characterised the Lord's apostles (1 Cor. 9; 2 Cor. 11; 12). The word "tried" signifies *tested*, or put to the proof (2 Cor. 13. 5; 1 John 4. 1). "Hast found them liars." The baseless assumption of these pretenders to apostolic office and authority was completely overthrown, and the men themselves branded as "liars," or, as Paul puts it, "false apostles" (2 Cor. 11. 13).

How unstinted is the praise! Yet, rich and copious as the foregoing declarations are, there is still more to follow. Not only had there been endurance, but it continued, "and endurest," and was in exercise even when the apostle, "the secretary of the Lord," wrote. Further, "and hast borne for My Name's sake." They had suffered much, had been sorely tried, but all had been cheerfully borne for the sake of the Name of Jesus Christ. On account of that same Name their sins had been forgiven (1 John 2. 12).

Lastly, they had not "wearied." There was no thought of giving up or giving over the conflict with evil; they had not wearied of the contest, nor had they wearied in it. What a beautiful picture of devotedness to the interests of Christ! But what about the springs of these holy activities? They are not mentioned; not because they were wholly wanting, else there could have been no commendation. What are these moral springs of christian life and activity? They are stated in the first of the Pauline epistles: "Remembering without ceasing your work of *faith*, and labour of *love*, and enduring constancy of *hope*" (1 Thess. 1. 3). There was work, and labour, and endurance witnessed in the Ephesian assembly, but the "work" would appear to have been to some extent separated from "faith," its moral source; "labour," too, appears not to have fully drawn its strength from "love," which is the activity of the divine nature, the very atmosphere in which the Church and Christians should live and act; and "endurance," for which Ephesus is twice commended (chap. 2. 2, 3), is not mentioned in connection with "hope," its spring and living energy.

BLAMED.

4.—"**But I have against thee that thou hast left thy first love.**" Here is disclosed the root of Church and individual failure: heart departure from Christ. The fine gold had become dim. The flower was fading. The first-named fruit of the Spirit is love (Gal. 5. 22), and that was but faintly seen, yet in Paul's day the Church in Ephesus was noted for its "love unto all the saints," a love begotten by love. When love, the very kernel of Christianity (1 Cor. 13), its crown too, and distinguishing glory is wanting, the moral power of Church and individual life is gone. Things may appear *outwardly* fair and promising, and none but an Omniscient eye may see the lack *inwardly*, coldness of heart to Christ. "Thou hast left thy first love" was the first step in the Church's downward career (compare with Matt. 24. 48). The loss of virgin love is a serious matter, and not to be regarded as a mere "somewhat," as in the Authorised Version. "But I have against thee"—first love given up. "But I have a few things against thee" (v. 14)—persons allowed in the midst holding the doctrine of Balaam, and others holding the doctrine of the Nicolaitanes. "But I have against thee" (v. 20)—Jezebel permitted to corrupt with her loathsome doctrines. Observe that in each instance the "But I have against thee" is in marked contrast with approval ungrudgingly bestowed.

THREATENED WITH JUDGMENT.

5.—"**Remember therefore whence thou art fallen, and repent, and do the first works; but if not I am coming to thee, and I will remove thy lamp out of its place, except thou shalt repent.**" The Lord has a positive, definite cause of complaint against the angel. "I have against thee that thou hast left thy first love." It is the only thing for which Ephesus is censured, but, oh, how serious! The coming shipwreck of the professing Church, its public and nauseous rejection by Christ is here traced to its *root*, first love given up. The Lord never forgets His joy in the first love of His people. "Thus saith the Lord; I remember thee, the kindness of thy youth, the love of thine espousals, when thou wentest after Me in the wilderness, in a land that was not sown'' (Jer. 2. 2). Judah's first love is never forgotten by Jehovah; the Church's first love, too, is equally remembered by the Lord, and *desired* by Him, which, in fact, "Ephesus'' really means. Now if the threatened judgment is to be averted there must be a recovery to ''first love'' and ''first works,'' hence the two admonitions needful to this end are ''Remember'' and ''Repent.'' Remember the moral elevation you once occupied, remember the heights of love, ''the mountain of myrrh'' and ''the hill of frankincense'' once trod in fellowship with the everlasting Lover of your soul! To what depths you have fallen! Repent. Judge the state of heart which has led to the first step in the downward course. Thus memory and repentance are presented as the two factors in recovery from a backsliding state. ''Quickly'' should be deleted. Ample time is given for restoration. The removal of the lamp as a light bearer in no wise weakens the question of eternal security of all who build on Christ—the Rock of Ages. Speaking in general terms, we may say, the lamps which once shone so brightly, and especially in the renowned capital of Ephesus, have been taken out of their place, and the gross darkness of Mohammedanism now wraps its deadly folds around these seven cities of proconsular Asia. A like removal awaits the western profession of Christianity. Unfaithfulness, whether corporate or individual, must be judged, and the present miserable condition of Ephesus, now known as *Agiosalouk*, is an object lesson to all. Has Christendom continued in the goodness of God? It has not, and ''gross darkness'' shall yet cover these lands, once brilliant with the light of the Gospel (Isa. 60. 2). According to the interpretation adopted in this Exposition we regard Ephesus as representing the Church in a special phase of its condition, a condition characteristically present at the close of the first century. We are pleased to know that love and faith were in a measure rekindled, and the lamp trimmed in the Ephesian assembly, so that in the third Ecumenical Council (A.D. 431) it gave forth no uncertain sound on the great underlying truth of Christianity, the incarnation of our Lord. But the hour of doom nevertheless came. In like manner various partial recoveries have been granted to the Church at large, but its doom, too, is fixed.

THE NICOLAITANES.

6.—**''But this thou hast, that thou hatest the works of the Nicolaitanes, which I also hate.''** The doctrinal faithfulness of the Ephesian assembly and its unswerving condemnation of evil have been already matters of warmest commendation (vv. 2, 3), followed by censure couched in terms of severe simplicity (v. 4), and judgment has been finally threatened, a judgment which repentance alone could avert (v. 5). Now one special character of evil is specified, hated alike by the Lord and by the angel. The absence of love has been deplored, but hatred, love's antithesis, was rightly present. The Nicolaitanes were not hated, for they shared in the general love of God (John 3. 16), but their works were, and for this the angel is commended. They must have been works of a decidedly evil character which called forth such a stern word of reprobation. Who, then, were the Nicolaitanes, and what their tenets and deeds? A satisfactory answer to these questions is wellnigh impossible. The Nicolaitanes as an immoral and exceedingly impure sect undoubtedly existed, but whether Nicolas of Antioch, the last of the "seven" (Acts 6. 5), was the originator of the sect bearing his name cannot be determined with any degree of certainty. Irenaeus is the first Church father or writer who affirms it. Others, however, consider that Nicolas is wronged when charged with the impure teachings and deeds of that sect; all the more evil that it existed under the cover of Christianity. If, indeed, the deacon was the founder of the sect, then he must have seriously lapsed from the faith. But on this we cannot pronounce with certainty. It has been conjectured that the Nicolaitanes are identical with the followers of Balaam.* But this is difficult to understand in the light of verses 14 and 15, where the evils are separately named. "So thou *also* hast those who hold the doctrine of the Nicolaitanes in like manner." The latter, it would seem, was the grosser evil of the two. All early writers, however, are agreed on the main features of this sect as being of an impure and licentious character.† Nicolaitanism therefore would appear to have combined the profession of Christianity with the impurities of Paganism. Fleshly indulgence is a practical denial of the holy nature of Christianity, and cannot be tolerated by the Lord, nor by any who are faithful to the Name of Him Who is "the holy, the true" (chap. 3. 7).

As to this evil, Ephesus and Pergamos, the first and

---

* "Nicolas ('Conqueror of the people') is identified with Balaam, according to one etymology of the latter word, as the 'lord' according to another, as the 'devourer' of the people. Both derivations are, however, uncertain, and the best Hebraists (Gesenius and Furst, the latter admitting the possibility of 'devourer') explain the name as meaning 'not of the people,' *i.e.*, an alien and foreigner."—*E. H. Plumptre D.D.*

† Ecumenius says they were "most impious in doctrine, and in their lives most impure." W. Kelly tersely sums up, saying: "The essence of Nicolaitanism seems to have been the abuse of grace to the disregard of plain morality."—"Lectures on the Book of Revelation," page 48.

third churches present a marked and striking contrast. The first turned in holy loathing from these impurities; the third sheltered the propagators of these filthy teachings. What was *hated* by Ephesus was *accepted* by Pergamos; the one "deeds," the other "doctrine;" but doctrine, good or bad, ever bears its own fruit. The point is, Ephesus would have none of it. Pergamos permitted it to corrupt and poison the sources of purity and morality.

THE CALL TO HEAR.

7.—**"He that hath an ear, let him hear what the Spirit saith to the churches."** This exhortation occurs seven times. In the addresses to the first three churches it immediately precedes the promise to the overcomer; whereas in the last four the exhortation forms the closing words of the address in each case. The Church as a whole is in view in the first group, and is called to repent.* But in the second group the hopeless condition of the Church is but too apparent, and hence a remnant company is marked off from the mass, whose one and only hope is centred on the personal Return of the Lord from Heaven. Now from the fact of the call to hear being placed *after* the words of cheer to the overcomers in the last four churches, we gather that none save overcomers or conquerors hear the voice of the Spirit.

Individual and direct responsibility to God is a cardinal truth in Christianity. In popery individual conscience is ignored. "Hear the Church" is the very essence of the papal system. But in truth the voice of the Church is never heard in Roman Catholicism. The higher orders of the clergy usurp the place of the Church; it is *their* voice which is declared to be the voice of the Church, a voice which the inferior orders of clergy and the mass *must* hear and obey under threat of Anathema, while the people are deceived with a semblance of truth. The favourite and oft-repeated formula from Matthew 18. 17, "Hear the Church," is employed to cover and defend the most cruel, superstitious, and soul-enslaving system which ever disgraced the earth; it is, indeed, Satan's masterpiece. How can the Church, itself threatened with judgment (chaps. 2. 5; 3. 16), become a source and ground of authority to any? Hence in these addresses to the churches the individual hearer is called upon to listen to the voice of the Spirit. It is He Who speaks, His voice alone to be heard. Thus we have linked together in this exhortation corporate and individual responsibility. Both exist. If the Church has become so

* The word *repent* occurs twelve times in the Apocalypse, but not in any other of St. John's writings.

utterly corrupt that the voice of God in Holy Scripture awakens no response there is the greater need for each one to open the ear of the soul to "Thus saith the Lord." The Lord when on earth repeatedly called attention to His teaching in the familiar words, "Who hath ears to hear, let him hear" (Matt. 13. 9, 43; 11. 15, etc.). Here the same Lord utters His voice, bespeaking earnest and devout attention to the new testimony and in almost the same verbal formula.*

THE OVERCOMER.

7.—**"To him that overcomes I will give to him to eat of the tree of life which is in the Paradise of God."** We have already referred to certain distinguishing features of the two broadly marked divisions of these seven churches —the first three and the last four. Each of these groups forms a separate unity of its own; while, of course, there are characteristics common to both. The *divine* element predominates in the first set of three churches, as that numeral signifies; while the *human* element enters largely into the composition of the second group of four churches, its numerical value.

But another distinction of interest meets us in the consideration of these promises and rewards to the overcomer. Those in the first group are not so full, nor of such a public character, as those in the second group. These latter are exceedingly grand in combining personal intimacies with Christ and scenes of public glory. We account for the difference in the fulness and character of these rewards, as respectively shown in the first and second group of epistles, by the fact that in the latter, overcoming is a matter of greater difficulty. The storm rages more fiercely, the adverse elements are more numerous, so the promises are proportionate to the severer character of the conflict. From Thyatira to Laodicea the Church is regarded as hopelessly corrupt. To swim against the tide, therefore, requires an energy of faith not called for to the same extent as when the Church was publicly owned—Ephesus to Pergamos. Not only are all these rewards and promises given to cheer the pilgrim band, and nerve each for the ever-deepening and narrowing conflict, but Christ Himself personally pledges His Word for their certain accomplishment, "I will give." His own hand crowns the victor. His own voice acclaims the overcomer, as he exultantly steps over the threshold of the heavenly portals.

In all cases the witnessing is individual, and of course the overcomer is one who in the energy of faith surmounts

* "Ears" in the Gospel; "ear" in the Apocalypse.

those *special* difficulties in which he finds himself. The overcomer in Laodicea has a more serious task before him than the overcomer in Ephesus. The position, circumstances, and character of the conflict are different in each Church.

This, the first promise to the overcomer, contains an evident allusion to the garden of Eden, with the tree of life in its midst (Gen. 2). Adam had not to overcome in the garden, he had simply to obey and keep his innocence, and the test of an innocent creature's obedience was the prohibition against eating of the symbolical tree of knowledge of good and evil. We have no ground to suppose that Adam ate of the tree of life although not forbidden to do so. But the scene presented to the gaze of the christian overcomer is one of a far more glorious character than that of Genesis 2. Here we have the Paradise of God with its tree of life, of which one may freely eat, and no tree of good and evil, the symbol of creature responsibility. The life of innocence (Gen. 2) was dependent on obedience. But here the tree of life, eternal life in its full character of blessedness, is enjoyed without alloy, without fear of failure. Eternal life becomes the everlasting feast of the conqueror in the Paradise of God. The word *Paradise* occurs three times in the New Testament (Luke 23. 43; 2 Cor. 12. 4; and Rev. 2. 7). It is of Oriental derivation, meaning a *pleasure garden*. It is three times used in this sense in the Old Testament.* To an Oriental mind "Paradise" is the expression and sum of blessedness. The Paradise of God is the expression of Heaven's blessedness. It is an actual place, of which the earthly garden (Gen. 2) was but a shadow. Here the blessedness is fixed and eternal. Paradise is the sum of all enjoyment, the aggregate of all pleasure, promised to the converted dying robber, and "into" it Paul was caught. It is the special and unique promise held out to the overcomer in the Ephesian state of the Church.

THE SPIRIT'S ADDRESS TO SMYRNA (CHAP. 2. 8-11).

SMYRNA AND LAODICEA CONTRASTED.

The briefest of these Church addresses is that to Smyrna, the longest that to Thyatira. Smyrna is wholly commended, and not one word of reproach or censure is addressed to it; Laodicea is in every respect blamed, and not one word of commendation or praise is bestowed. Again, the poverty

* The word *Paradise* is not used of the garden of Eden. There are six occurrences of the word in the Holy Scriptures: Nehemiah 2. 8, translated *forest*; Ecclesiastes 2. 5; Song of Sol. 4. 13, *orchard*; Luke 23. 43; Revelation 2. 7; 2 Corinthians 12. 4 Paradise is an actual place existing now and in the risen state. Moses never employ the word. Solomon is the first to do so.

and tribulation of Smyrna stand out in marked contrast with the rich and self-satisfied condition of Laodicea. There is but one other Church not censured, namely, Philadelphia. It must not, however, be supposed that there was nothing wrong in these unblamed assemblies, only the characteristic Church states represented by them were suffering (Smyrna) and weakness (Philadelphia). A child in affliction or in bodily weakness is spared words of censure, and surely our God is not less gracious than an earthly parent.

CONSOLATION IN TRIBULATION.

8.—"**And to the angel of the Church in Smyrna write: These things says the First and the Last, Who became dead and lived.**" Declension from first love had set in. The angel of the Church in Ephesus had fallen (v. 5), not, however, from Christ's right hand, but from love, whilst preserving doctrinal faithfulness and walking blameless in outward consistency. But the moral springs of action were relaxed, and Ephesian Church life thereby robbed of its fragrance. This consideration brings us to the second distinguishing Church period, one of Tribulation. The angel, the Church's representative, is addressed in words of rich and gracious consolation. The full blast of imperial pagan persecution was being endured. For about 250 years, with occasional lulls when the ruthless hand of the persecutor was stayed, the Church was passing through a "baptism of blood," and this in order to rekindle the smouldering flame of love wellnigh extinguished. What the suffering Church was to the Lord is imaged in the meaning of Smyrna, *myrrh*—a well-known fragrant perfume, a sacred one moreover (Exod. 30. 23), also one of the love perfumes of the spouse in the Canticles. The consolation that suited the Seer (Rev. 1. 17, 18) became the consolation of the Church. We have here the same combination of divine and human predicates which characterised Christ in the glorious vision of His Person as beheld by John. "The First and the Last" is one of the grandest of divine titles, a Rock against which the utmost power of the enemy is futile. As "the First" He is before all in time, and above all as supreme. As "the Last" He is after all, closing all up, for to Him all tend. He is eternal in His Being. But He stooped to die. Death had no claim on Him. He, "the first and the last"—Jehovah's special title (Isa. chaps. 41-48)—became dead. He breasted the waves of death. He rose out of it, and "lives" to die no more. This, then, was *their* "strong consolation." The One Who died and lives is none other than

Jehovah in the truth of His Being, the self-existing One. We have had the glory of the Speaker—what He was as God, and what He became as Man—now we are to listen to His consoling and animating message.

A MESSAGE.

9.—**"I know thy tribulation and thy poverty; but thou art rich; and the railing of those who say that they themselves are Jews, and are not, but a synagogue of Satan."** In the Authorised Version we read, "I know thy *works*." The word "works" should be deleted according to the critics, besides, it is to suffering and not to works that prominence is given in the message. "I know." What a tower of strength to an afflicted saint and Church! The One in Whose Person are combined at once the greatness of the Godhead and the sympathy of One Who has been in the utmost depths of suffering and death says, "I know thy tribulation and thy poverty." The measure, character, and duration of every phase of trial are known to Him. There is not a tear too many, not a blow too severe. The hardness, the unbrokenness of spirit, the self-confidence have to be broken down. We flourish best in suffering. Jacob was a better man morally after the night of wrestling than before it (Gen. 32. 24-32). Paul was kept humble and lowly by that continual reminder, whatever it was, "a thorn in the flesh" (2 Cor. 12. 7). But He also knows our "poverty." Not many grandees are numbered amongst the Lord's people. The Hebrew believers took joyfully the spoiling of their goods (Heb. 10. 34). Confiscation of goods and property, either to the imperial treasury or to those base enough to inform against the Christians, generally followed apprehension. But, says the Lord, "Thou art rich." Our treasure is in Heaven. Our inheritance is there. An inventory of christian wealth is furnished in 1 Corinthians 3. 21-23. Our *origin* is of God (1 Cor. 1. 30); our *position*, sons of God (Rom. 8. 14); our *dignity*, kingly authority (Rev. 1. 6); our *destiny*, conformity to God's Son (Rom. 8. 29); our *wealth*, limited only by Christ's millennial and eternal portion (Eph. 1. 10, 11). Truly the Church is rich, whatever its poverty on earth may be. Endowed with the love and riches of Christ, which are enduring and placed beyond the possibility of loss or corruption, we may well triumph in Him Who knows not only our tribulation and poverty, but knowing all pronounces us "rich."

Not only was the Church suffering from the pagan world *without*, but also from an enemy of a religious character *within*. There was a company, it would seem (not really

Jews), which took up the place and pretension of the Jews to be alone God's people on earth. We saw a company of higher clergy in Ephesus (v. 2), whose proud and lofty pretensions were exposed, and the pretenders styled liars. That movement for the time was crushed. But now a movement of a similar character, although on a lower scale, is again in evidence. Arrogant claims to be the Church, to be alone God's people, have been repeated again and again since the Smyrnean era, sometimes on a large scale, at other times on a smaller one. This body of religious pretenders railed against the suffering Church. False accusations, contempt, and contumely were the cruel work of these religious people. What were they in His sight? "A synagogue of Satan."* The two names, "Satan" and "Devil," are employed in the Revelation as everywhere else in Scripture with propriety and precision. The former means *adversary*, the latter *slanderer*. To the Church he is both. Satan "the adversary" set up a heretical party in direct antagonism to the lowly and suffering position of the Church. The devil, "the calumniator," forged lies and all manner of false accusations against God's saints, and succeeded, too, in getting the heathen powers to believe them, and thus *he* became the real author and source of the "ten persecutions"—ten legal outbursts of rage and fury against the Church which were only stopped on the accession of Constantine to the throne of the Caesars. Abounding suffering, however, was answered by abounding consolation, and both, no doubt, were the portion in full of the suffering Church. Christian and heathen contemporary records abundantly verify the truth of this.

TRIALS AND ENCOURAGEMENT.

10.—"**Fear nothing (of) what thou art about to suffer. Behold, the devil is about to cast you into prison, that ye may be tried; and ye shall have tribulation ten days. Be thou faithful unto death, and I will give to thee the crown of life.**" "Fear not," or "nothing," is a word of preparation for yet further trials, and is evidently taken from chapter 1. 17. *There* it fell on the ear of the fainting Seer, carrying absolute and unqualified assurance to his soul; *here* it is to reassure the Church in view of the gathering storm about to burst upon

* We again meet with this strong expression in the address to Philadelphia (chap. 3. 9). *Here* it opposed itself to the Church in *suffering*; *there* in antagonism to the Church in *weakness*. The Synagogue (Jewish assembly) and the Church (christian assembly) are distinguished by the apostle James: for the former see chapter 2. 2, R.V.; for the latter see chapter 5. 14.

it. Tribulation and poverty were bad enough, and hard to be borne. But worse still was in store. The closing imperial persecutions exceeded in savage cruelty the former ones. The dark clouds were gathering; the wild, hoarse roar of the coming storm was heard. Here the Church is forewarned and encouraged. These coming trials are traced from false accusers, and from the instruments and agents of cruelty to the devil. Persecution was *his* work. But faith rests on this mighty and grand sustaining truth that "Power belongeth unto God" (Psa. 62. 11). The power of the devil is limited and controlled, and he cannot put forth his hand and touch even the feeblest lamb of the flock without express permission (Job 1 and 2). "There is no power but of God" (Rom. 13. 1), whether satanic or human. The use and employment of the power is another question, involving responsibility of the gravest character. God's purpose was that His Church might be tried, and that to the utmost, and to this end the devil was His servant. Thus God's saints were purified. Love, faith, courage, and faithfulness were strengthened. The Church had a definite and appointed period of tribulation—"ten days." There may be here an allusion to the well-known "ten persecutions," and also to the tenth under Diocletian, which lasted just ten years. The expression "ten days" signifies a *limited period*, a brief time inconsistent with the lengthened period of pagan persecution covering 250 years. The following references to "ten days" will confirm the meaning of the term as implying a brief and limited time: Genesis 24. 55; Nehemiah 5. 18; Daniel 1. 12; Acts 25. 6; Jeremiah 42. 7, etc.

Some, not many, of the early witnesses for the truth, appalled by the dread of torture and death, denied their Lord. Here faithfulness every step of the way, even unto death, is urged. If the martyr's crown is to be won, then constancy and steadfastness to the end must be maintained. There are various crowns spoken of in the Word. There is the crown of *gold* on the head of every redeemed one in Heaven (Rev. 4. 4). The crown of *righteousness*, the reward of a holy and righteous walk on earth (2 Tim. 4. 8). Next, there is the crown of *glory* bestowed on all who shepherd the beloved flock of God (1 Peter 5. 4). Lastly, we have the martyr's crown, the crown of *life* (Rev. 2. 10). This crown, like other rewards and encouragements, is given personally by Christ, "I will give."

Then follows the usual call to hear. "He that hath an ear, let him hear what the Spirit says to the churches." Individual responsibility is ever and firmly maintained. In these addresses is contained the mind of the Spirit and of the Lord which is *one*, and is meant for all christian assemblies at all times throughout the earth.

PROMISE TO THE OVERCOMER.

11.—"**He that overcomes shall in no wise be injured of the second death.**" To be an overcomer in the Smyrnean condition of things requires endurance suited to the death struggle. The synagogue of Satan is raging on the one hand, and heathendom on the other, alike determined to crush Christianity, whilst between the two stand the lowly confessors of the Nazarene, patience and meekness their only defence. What was the human prospect? Loss of character, of goods, and of life itself. To overcome under such appalling circumstances required strong faith and clear spiritual vision as seeing Him Who is invisible, yet Who is never more near than when apparently His saints are forsaken, and never more true and tender in sympathy than when seemingly He has forgotten them. The overcomer may die under tortures prolonged and gloated over by the almost fiendish malice of men who delight in blood, but he is assured that he shall not be hurt of the "second death." He shall in "no wise," on no account—an exceedingly strong negative—be hurt of the "second death"* *which is* the lake of fire, *i.e.*, the everlasting abode and place of punishment for the devil and the wicked (chap. 20. 14; 21. 8).

The Spirit's Address to Pergamos (Chap. 2. 12-17).

PERGAMOS OR PERGAMUM.

12.—"**To the angel of the Church in Pergamos write.**" The most northern of the churches is next addressed. The ancient capital of Mysia still exists under the name of Bergamo, but shorn of its greatness and glory. Pergamos, or Pergamum more generally read, has been described as a "sort of union of a pagan cathedral city, a university town, and a royal residence." Attalus III. bequeathed his city to the great republic; then, and subsequently under the empire, it was considered one of the

* "The second death" stands in purposed contrast to the first. Death among men is the cessation of human life and activity on earth. It brings about a temporary separation of soul and body, but resurrection unites them and introduces the wicked to the "second death," the lake of fire. Extinction of being is not effected when one dies, nor does consciousness cease at death. *After* death and *before* resurrection we have a man in hades, the state between these two, namely, death and resurrection, with memory, consciousness, speech, reason, etc. This terrible picture, no doubt, is an everyday awful reality, and is *not* termed a parable (Luke 16. 19-31). "The second death" *is* the lake of fire. The raised body will be made capable of enduring the fierce wrath of Almighty God, whether by literal fire or not. The death of the body is a type of the "*second* death," but inasmuch as antitype exceeds its type, so does the "second death" in all respects exceed the first.

finest cities in Asia. Distinguished as it was for its idolatry, its learning, and medical science, nevertheless it was, from a christian standpoint, one of the worst of the seven cities named. Christianity reverses the judgment of the world, inasmuch as it reveals things, principles, and persons in their true relation to God.

THE SHARP SWORD OF JUDGMENT.

12.—"**These things says He that has the sharp two-edged sword.**" The glorious description of Christ, which constitutes the first vision beheld by the Seer (chap. 1. 12-16), is applied in its various parts in the addresses to the churches, or more correctly to their respective angels. The character of Christ to Pergamos is taken from verse 16 of the great introductory vision. *There*, however, the sword proceeds out of His mouth as denoting the character of judgment, the authority of His Word. *Here*, it is not said to be out of His mouth, but He has it. In neither passage is the sword seen sheathed, but drawn and ready for instant and thorough work, "sharp and two-edged." The sword is used as a symbol of judgment. It is employed to denote the Lord's vengeance on the guilty world (Rev. 19. 15), as also of thorough and unsparing judgment of evil, not *on* His people, but of evil *in* them (Heb. 4. 12). Christ ever holds the sword, and uses it on friends and foes alike. He fights against evil, and by the simple authority of His Word it is exposed and judged. To those, whether in the Church or in the world, who refuse to bow before Him and own His absolute authority, the sword *must* do its mighty and sure work in the execution of judgment; for, be it solemnly remembered, judgment and the execution of it also, are committed to the Son of Man (John 5. 22, 27).

The sword is not to wound or kill the angel of the Church, but to be used against those for whose presence in the assembly the angel was responsible (v. 16).

SATAN'S THRONE AND DWELLING.

13.—"**I know where thou dwellest, where Satan's throne is.**" In the Authorised Version the words "*thy works and*" coming after "I know" are an unwarranted interpolation, believed to be the work of a careless copyist. "Satan's *throne*" (not "seat"), as in the Authorised Version and other modern versions, alone suits the demands of the context and of the general truth of the passage. The decay of first love was the first characteristic feature of the Church in its downward career. The second, or Smyrnean condition, was one of open persecution from the heathen imperial power. Probably the most severe but the most useful and sanctifying periods of persecution were those under Decius, A.D. 249, and Diocletian, A.D. 284.* The effect of both was to separate the false from the true, and to purify the faith of the suffering Church. The cruelty of Satan from *without* was let loose against it, the heathen authorities being his instruments; but utterly baffled in his efforts to destroy Christianity his next move was to destroy the Church in its true character and testimony, and effect its ruin from *within*, using religious men and teachers to accomplish his deadly work. It has been said that "Paul feared the clergy, while Ignatius feared the people." Paul's prophetic forecast (Acts 20. 29, 30) was amply verified, as the Pergamos and Thyatiran states of the Church fully demonstrate.

Pergamos at the time of the Apocalypse was the capital of the Roman government in Asia. Heathenism reigned supreme. From it as a centre idolatry and persecution spread all over western Asia, the Asia of the Apocalypse; hence the local force of the expressions "Satan's throne" and where "Satan dwelleth." Satan had his throne and dwelling in Pergamos, and from thence he sought to strangle Christianity in that part of the earth.† Surely, however, a larger and more comprehensive use of these expressions must be sought for!

We must keep steadily in view that each of these three first churches describes a special condition of the whole professing Church at successive periods of its history. Thus the Pergamos period brings us up to the era of Constantine, the beginning of the fourth century. The repeated assaults of Satan as a "roaring lion" (1 Peter 5. 8) in open persecution for 250 years left the Church spiritually richer if poorer in the eyes of the world. Where Diocletian, the last of the persecuting emperors, failed, Constantine the first christian emperor succeeded. The seductions of Satan effected the moral ruin of the Church.

After the death of Licinius, the colleague of Constantine the Great, the latter became sole emperor. On his accession to the throne the persecuting edicts of his predecessor were

---

White, in his excellent and condensed history, "The Eighteen Christian Centuries," gives the ten pagan persecutions as follows: The *first* under Nero, A.D. 54; the *second* under Domitian, A.D. 81; the *third* under Trajan, A.D. 98; the *fourth* under Adrian, A.D. 117; the *fifth* under Septimius Severus, A.D. 193; the *sixth* under Maximin, A.D. 235; the *seventh* under Decius, A.D. 249; the *eighth* under Valerian, A.D. 254; the *ninth* under Aurelian, A.D. 270; the *tenth* under Diocletian, A.D. 284. It is impossible in all cases to determine the exact year when persecution commenced. The legal enactments against Christianity were suspended or enforced according to the will of the then reigning emperor. The persecuting laws of Domitian were repealed by the gentle Nerva, and those of Diocletian by the first christian (?) emperor, Constantine.

† Divine honours were paid to the Roman emperors, and in this impiety Pergamos took the lead in Asia. Says a Roman historian: "The city of Pergamos made a merit of having already built a temple in honour of Augustus," and petitioned Tiberius for the honour of erecting another. It is significant that the last phase of public idolatrous evil is to be the worship of the Beast, or revived power of Rome, in an intense and malignant form.

repealed, and liberty granted to the Christians to worship according to their conscience, A.D. 313. But the christian religion was then simply regarded as one of the many religions of the empire. All were equally tolerated. But as time wore on Constantine got better acquainted with Christianity, and was sagacious enough to discern in it principles of an enduring character, and such as would tend to consolidate his power; his christian subjects, too, could be relied upon to uphold the imperial dignity, whereas his pagan ones were continually raising insurrections in various parts of the empire.

Accordingly Constantine, A.D. 324, and frequently afterwards, issued edicts against paganism, and sought with might and main to force Christianity on the empire as its one and only religion. Pagans were banished from the court, and Christians advanced to posts of honour. Constantine offered his gold and patronage to the Church, and it eagerly swallowed the bait, sacrificed its conscience and allegiance to its Lord, and the Church and the world, which had hitherto walked apart (John 17; 2 Cor 6. 14-16), were soon locked in each other's arms. Fatal union! From this period we date the unhappy alliance of Church and State, and the rise of Church establishments endowed by the State. Christianity was in many instances forced upon unwilling subjects at the point of the sword. It was either the sword or baptism, although the august ruler himself put off observance of the christian rite till a few days before his death at Nicomedia. The gorgeous heathen temples and vestments of the priests were consecrated for christian service. Instead therefore of the plain and unpretending meeting rooms and halls, in which the early Church assembled, grand buildings and ostentatious display became the order of the day. Christianity walked in golden slippers. In order to reconcile the priests and people of the ancient superstitions to the new order of things many of the pagan rites and ceremonies were adopted by the Church. Thus it falsified its character as a witness for holiness and truth. The effects of that unholy alliance remain to this day, and although God has governmentally used it in checking the tide of infidelity, yet it has wrought incalculable mischief to the Church viewed as the body of Christ, and has done much harm in lowering the holy and unworldly character which the Church ought to show in this Christ-rejecting age. The true union of Church and State awaits the revelation of another day (Rev. 21. 9; 22. 5). The Church thus at her ease in the presence of the "throne" and "dwelling" of Satan, who is the god of this world, enables us to see the force of the unusually strong expressions in verse 13. Satan has both a "throne" and "dwelling" on earth, and for the Church to sit down thereon or therein is truly awful. There are enumerated twenty-eight items in chapter 18 of the Apocalypse as characteristic of the false Church; the *first* is "gold," and the *last* "souls."

This epoch of Church history is one of such importance that we have devoted to its consideration these lengthy remarks.

DWELLERS ON THE EARTH.

13.—The Lord was not indifferent. **I know "where thou dwellest"** has a deeply moral and ominous signification (compare with Phil. 3. 19 and Rev. 3. 10; 6. 10; 11. 10; 13. 14; 14. 6; 17. 8). These passages point to a class of persons who are not simply on the earth, but whose sole interests are in it and bounded by it. They refer to a class of persons morally characterised as "dwellers on the earth."*

COMMENDED.

13.—"**Thou holdest fast My Name, and hast not denied My faith.**" All that is vital in Christianity had been firmly maintained—the Name and faith of Christ. They had been tested and proved under the most appalling circumstances—confiscation of goods, torture, and death. "Swear by the genius of Caesar" they would not. They held fast the Name of Him Who is holy and true. Deny the faith of Christ as Son of God in divine relationship, as Son of Man in holy humanity towards men, and as Son of David in Judaic rights and glory they would not. They endured as "seeing Him Who is invisible." They shrank not from the fiery trial, and the Lord delights to recount it and commend them for it, even when He has to strongly censure them for dwelling in the high places of the earth where Satan had established his throne and dwelling. It was Satan really who had his throne first at Rome, afterwards at Constantinople, and who employed the Caesars as his instruments and agents; from thence he governed. He dwelt there while also having access to Heaven. His overthrow is determined and the moment fixed (Rev. 12. 7-13).

ANTIPAS, THE FAITHFUL.

The orthodoxy of the angel as to vital truth was unquestionable. Pergamos, in the main, had not surrendered one article of fundamental truth, and this especially,

* "The dwellers upon earth are a moral class, the worst in it, seemingly, apostates who have had the offer of the heavenly calling, but have deliberately chosen earth as their portion instead."—*C. E. S.*

"even in the days in which Antipas, My faithful witness (was), who was slain among you." The name of this noble witness for Christ who sealed his testimony with his blood has been handed down to all ages.* But although nothing certain is known of Antipas save the name, there is much wrapped up in that sentence, "My faithful witness, My faithful one" (R.V.). *What* Christ was to God (chap. 1. 5), *that* Antipas was to Christ.

BALAAMISM AND NICOLAITANISM.

14, 15.—"**But I have a few things against thee: that thou hast there those who hold the doctrine of Balaam, who taught Balak to cast a snare before the sons of Israel, to eat (of) idol sacrifices and commit fornication. So thou also hast those who hold the doctrines of Nicolaitanes in like manner.**" "But I have against thee," words of definite complaint to the angel of Ephesus (chap. 2. 4), and to that of Thyatira (v. 20); in the former, departure from first love; in the latter, corruption of doctrine. Here, however, the plural "things" point to more than one just cause of complaint. Those who held the teaching of Balaam were one class, and those who held the teaching of the Nicolaitanes were another. Both were tolerated in the Pergamos assembly. But what was hated in Ephesus was accepted in Pergamos (vv. 6, 15), Nicolaitanism being sternly rejected by the former, while permitted by the latter.†

Balaam's heart was not in the magnificent prophecies he was compelled by the Spirit of God to utter (Num. 23, 24). The honours and gifts of the king of Moab filled his soul's vision. For money he would curse the people of God. "He loved the wages of unrighteousness" (2 Peter 2. 15). Baffled in his attempts to curse those whom God had blessed, the wicked Mesopotamian prophet taught the wicked Moabite king to cast a stumbling-block in the path of Israel. We have no record of this transaction in the Old Testament. The prophet and the king went their respective ways (Num. 24. 25). But the stratagem succeeded. Under the direction of their guilty monarch the women of Moab caused Israel to sin (Num. 25-31). Thus Balaam, even more guilty than the king, was the real instigator under Satan of the fall of Israel, which led to

* "Andreas speaks of the account of the martyrdom of Antipas existing in his time and his bold expostulations against his accusers. It is said that in the reign of Domitian he was cast into the brazen bull."—"The Apocalypse, with Notes and Reflections," p. 30.

† There are certain parallel resemblances between the seven parables of Matthew 13 and the seven churches of Revelation 2 and 3, notably between the first and third parable with the first and third Church. The "*kingdom*" is the subject in Matthew 13; the "*Church*" the subject in the Apocalypse 2 and 3.

the signal judgment inflicted upon 24,000 of the people (Num. 25. 9).* Peter, Jude, and John are the only writers of the New Testament who specifically refer to Balaam. The two sins into which Israel was thus led were idolatry and fornication. These very evils were energetically denounced by Paul in a later day (1 Cor. 10. 19-28; and 1 Cor. 6. 15-18). Here the teachers and adherents of these impure practices were sheltered in the very bosom of the Church itself. These sins were the result of Balaam-teaching. For the Christian any object short of God Himself is idolatry (1 John 5. 21), and illicit intercourse with the world is fornication (2 Cor. 6. 14-16).†

15.—"**The doctrines of the Nicolaitanes**" were not quite the same as those of Balaam, although the result was the same in both cases, namely, the moral ruin of all contaminated by these unholy teachings and practices. Balaam, the false prophet, has his modern representatives in the Church to-day. Men occupy responsible positions in it, who, Balaam-like, cling tenaciously to their emoluments and preferments, while they labour with a zeal worthy of a better cause to overthrow the faith they are paid to defend and uphold. The honesty of these men is on a par with their soul-destroying work. The teachings of Balaam act *upon* the souls of men; whereas the doctrines of Nicolaitanism are sown *in* the souls of the people. Between the two the corporate body is wellnigh ruined. From the fourth century till to-day rapid strides have been made in the wrong direction, so that now there is scarcely a feature of early apostolic Church character left. The angel is not charged with holding these doctrines, but they had not been resisted. Indifference to evil is an insult to God. The moral relaxation of the angel of Pergamos stands out in marked contrast to that of Ephesus. ***The sin of the Church is toleration of evil and evil men.***

REPENTANCE OR JUDGMENT.

16.—"**Repent therefore: but if not, I come to thee quickly, and I will make war with them with the sword of My mouth.**" In the warning to Ephesus "remember" precedes the call to repent. Not one of the assemblies had been so richly blessed, had enjoyed so much of the goodness and grace of God, as the assembly in the

* In 1 Corinthians 10. 8 the number who perished is given at 23,000, but the words "fell in *one* day" sufficiently account for the apparent discrepancy in the numbers who perished. The full number destroyed would not necessarily be accomplished in one day. Moses states the larger number without reference to the time covered by the execution of the judgment.

† Israel is charged with *adultery* in having fellowship with the Gentiles (Jer. 3. 8), because viewed as married to Jehovah. The Church is charged with *fornication* in its illicit intercourse with the world (Rev. 2. 21), because not yet married to the Lamb.

capital of western Asia. Paul had laboured in Ephesus for three years. His service and tears had borne abundant fruit, and in his epistle to the saints of that city he had unfolded truths of the most exalted character without one accompanying word of rebuke or censure. Faith in Christ and love to all saints were characteristics of their Church life. How fitting therefore the words of divine admonition, "Remember therefore whence thou art fallen, and repent." But the assembly in Pergamos never had been in the enjoyment of such exalted grace and privilege; hence the omission of the word "remember."

"Repent *therefore*," omitted in the Authorised Version, is in view of the faithful exposure of grave evils in their midst. Personally the angel of the Church had neither imbibed the teachings nor practised the deeds reprobated, but, on the other hand, he had not denounced them, nor had he opposed their entrance into the Church which the angel of the Church in Ephesus had energetically done. If no self-judgment followed the call to repent, the Lord threatens speedy judgment: "I come to thee quickly." The imminence of the judgment is expressed in the use of the present tense, as also in the introduction of the word "quickly," wrongly inserted in verse 5, rightly here in verse 16 (see R.V. for both texts). The coming here referred to does not signify the personal return of the Lord, or what is spoken of as the second Advent, but points to an immediate dealing with the assembly by the Lord Who would visit it in judgment. To the angel He says, "I come to *thee*," but to the still more guilty, "I will make war with *them*." Thus the Lord distinguishes. There are degrees of sin and, proportionately, of punishment. We, too, should distinguish between leaders and led. In the various forms and phases of discipline enjoined in the New Testament in order to preserve the holiness of God's House this distinction should be carefully acted upon. "Of some," says the apostle, "have compassion, making a difference; but others save with fear, snatching (them) out of the fire; hating even the garment spotted by the flesh" (Jude 22, 23). "The sword of My mouth" refers to the judging power of His Word; it pierces.

A CALL TO HEAR.

17.—"**He that hath an ear, let him hear what the Spirit says to the churches**." In these addresses we listen to the voice of the Holy Spirit. In them He speaks to the churches of Christendom. Had Christendom listened to the voice of the divine Speaker the public ruin of the Church would have been averted. But whilst the

Spirit speaks to the churches, it is individuals who are called to hear. The Church throughout is regarded as a body insensible either to the pleadings or warnings of the Spirit; hence the churches are not called upon to hear, but individuals are: "*He* that has an ear to hear, let *him* hear." Corporate recovery is hopeless, hence individual responsibility, always of prime importance, is the more earnestly and continuously pressed. This is a cardinal truth in Christianity, on the denial of which the papacy flourishes. The very kernel of the papal system is the stern disallowance of individual thought and of one's direct relation to God.

SPECIAL AND PERSONAL REWARDS.

17.—"**To him that overcomes, to him will I give of the hidden manna; and I will give to him a white stone, and on the stone a new name written, which not one knows but he that receives** (it)." The overcoming here, as elsewhere, is an individual matter. If a company of overcomers is to be formed it can only be in the exercise of faith and spiritual energy by each one. The overcoming company, or "cloud of witnesses" of Hebrews 11, is separately presented. Each witness for God had to fight the foe alone, yet not alone, for the living God was for him and with him.

In our English Bibles the words "*to eat*" are not found in the *Sinaitic* and *Alexandrine* MSS., and are also deleted in the Revised Version, and rejected by Tregelles, Kelly, Darby, and others.

There is peculiar sweetness in these promises, as also in the way of their bestowal. "I give of the hidden manna." The twice repeated "I give" enhances the value of the promised blessings. The manna is termed "angels' food" (Psa. 78. 25) and "the bread of God" (John 6. 33). Manna, meaning "*What is this*?" is the standing expression of Israel's bewilderment at the manner and abundance of Jehovah's provision for them in the desert (Exod. 16. 15), but certainly it was not "hidden," since it lay on the face of the ground round their camp. For 12,500 mornings Jehovah rained down bread from Heaven for His people on earth. Isreal's God is our God, and He is even more to us than He was to them, owing to our present and living association with Christ in glory. As a memorial of God's grace to His people a pot full of manna was laid up before the Lord (Exod. 16. 33), a "golden pot" we are informed by Paul (Heb. 9. 4). For about 500 years this "hidden manna" told its tale of Christ in humiliation, but to God alone. Hid in the ark, the most sacred of vessels, it was screened from the gaze of the people; probably during the long period of five centuries no human eye beheld it.

Now, says Christ, "I give," not mediately, but personally, "of the hidden manna." It is, of course, a reward in the future when the struggle is over. What a blessing! To learn then from Christ Himself in glory the secrets of His life here, the depths of His humiliation, the moral beauties and perfections of His life hid from the eyes of men. It will then be seen that the path of the overcomer is but a reflex of the life of Jesus here. What communings in the glory between the Victor and His victorious people. Life's story understood and rehearsed above, but whose life's history?—ours or His? The unwritten records of His life, if penned, would require a larger world than this to contain them (John 21. 25). The manna of old was rained *from* Heaven for the blessing and satisfaction of the people on earth. The hidden manna is to be given to the overcomers in Heaven. The public place of the Church in closest fellowship with the world, in which Satan established his throne and dwelling, had been refused by the overcomers in Pergamos; hence they had to abide in the shade, and suffer as they trod a solitary path in fellowship with Jesus, Who Himself had trod that separate path—to Him more rugged and lonely surely than to any before or since.

But not only will He give the hidden manna, but also "I will give to him a white stone, and on the stone a new name written, which no one knows but he that receives (it)." What is to be understood by the white stone and secret name written thereon? A "white stone" was largely employed in the social life and judicial customs of the ancients. Days of festivity were noted by a *white* stone; days of calamity by a *black* stone. A host's appreciation of a special guest was indicated by a white stone with a name or message written on it. A *white* stone meant acquittal; a *black* stone condemnation in the courts of justice. Here the overcomer is promised a white stone and a *new* name written thereon, which none knows save the happy recipient. It is the expression of the Lord's personal delight in each one of the conquering band. It is by no means a public reward. There are common and special blessings now; there will be public and individual joys then. The Lord's approbation of, and special delight in, each one of the triumphant company will be answer enough to the rejection and scorn heaped upon the faithful witness now. The *new* name on the stone, alone known to the overcomer, signifies Christ, then known in a special and peculiar way to each one, and that surely is reward beyond all price and beyond all telling. It is a secret communication of love and intelligence between Christ and the overcomer, a joy which none can share, a reserved token of appreciative love. In the glory the hidden manna is the expression of *our* appreciation of Christ in His humiliation; while the white stone equally sets forth *His* appreciation in us as overcomers. His and our individual path here are the points respectively set forth in the glory by the symbols of the "manna" and the "stone."

The Spirit's Address to Thyatira (Chap. 2. 18-29).

DISTINCTIVE FEATURES.

18.—"**To the angel of the Church in Thyatira write: These things says the Son of God, He that hath His eyes as a flame of fire, and His feet are like fine brass.**" This is the only Church of the seven in which a woman's name is mentioned. Jezebel, the wicked consort of the apostate king of Israel, who was but a tool in her hands, the upholder and patroness of the worst forms of idolatry, a murderess, yet withal a clever and determined woman, is the prominent person named in the address to the angel. We cannot regard it as a mere coincidence that the earlier mention of Thyatira is in connection with a woman (Acts 16), but a very different character to the one named here. There are striking points both of contrast and resemblance between Lydia, the active, generous, decided Christian, and her relation to Paul (Acts 16), and Jezebel, the zealous and equally large-hearted pagan, and her relation to Elijah (1 Kings 18, 19).

This fourth epistle is the longest of the seven, and marks the commencement of the second group in which the history of each Church runs on till the second Coming of the Lord. The first direct reference in these epistles to the second Advent is found here (vv. 25-28).

The hopeless, helpless, corrupt condition of the Church —a condition out of which it cannot emerge, and one incapable of improvement, is another noted feature, distinguishing it thus from the three previous churches. Here, then, is an active propagation of evil and corrupting teaching from within. Pergamos tolerated certain grave evils; but Thyatira suffers them to be taught, and herself becomes the mother of similar evil systems, "her children." What a truly remarkable feature of this Church!

Another noticeable characteristic is that a remnant is now formally recognised and separately addressed (v. 24), thus clearly distinguishing the Church or mass from the remnant or faithful company.

Further, the call to hear which in Ephesus, Smyrna, and Pergamos *precedes* the promises to the overcomer, in Thyatira and succeeding churches is found *after* the promises, closing up in each case the respective address. In the first three epistles the Church stands related to the call to hear, whereas in the last four the overcomers are in relation to the words, "He that hath an ear, let him hear."

Another striking feature in the address to this Church is that for the first and only time, in the course of these epistles, the name of the divine Speaker is introduced—the Son of God; this title of personal and divine relationship is not used in any other part of the Apocalypse.

THE DIVINE SPEAKER.

18.—"**These things says the Son of God.**" The humanity of the Lord and His relation to the race are conveyed in the title "Son of Man." The Deity of the Lord and His relation to God are intimated in the title "Son of God." His glory and relation to the churches as beheld by John was as "Son of Man" (chap. 1. 13). Why, then, is this divine title "Son of God" introduced, and only here? The answer is at hand. Thyatira historically covers the Dark or Middle Ages, and pictures in brief terms and symbols the popish system, the worst bearing the christian name that has ever disgraced the earth. In popery every true thought of the Church is lost. True, she boasts loudly of unity, but it is a unity enforced when and where she can by the potent arguments of the faggot, the fire, and the dungeon—as unlike divine unity effected by the Holy Ghost (1 Cor. 12. 13) as light is to darkness. Popery shuts out Christ completely as Head of His Body, the Church, and as Administrator of the House of God. Hence the introduction of this title in the opening words of the address. Not Peter, but Christ, the Son of the living God, is the Church's foundation (Matt. 16. 16-18). Peter, too, is made the administrator of the Church instead of Christ. But the Lord never gives up His rights, and just *when* and *where* it were most needful to insist on His divine prerogative as Son of God it is done. If the Church has been drifting from bad to worse, so much the more need to insist on the divine glory and relationship of our Lord. If that goes, then truly all is lost. The title "Son of God" is in no wise a dispensational one; a title, moreover, which was given to Him on

His entrance into this world as Man (Psa. 2; Acts 13. 33, omit the word "again").

HIS EYES AND FEET.

18.—"**He that hath His eyes as a flame of fire and His feet like fine brass.**" This is part of the detailed description of the glorified Son of Man previously beheld (chap. 1. 14, 15). Here, however, these two attributes of stern sovereignty are exercised by the Son of God. It is well to remember that He to Whom all judgment is committed, and Who will infallibly execute His own judgment, is not only Man (John 5. 22, 27), but He is God as well. He who wields the sceptre is divine as well as human. His eyes as "a flame of fire" refer to His moral intolerance of evil. He will search out sin and discover it however hidden. *Who* or *what* can escape those eyes as a flame of fire? "His feet as fine brass." What His eyes discover, that His feet shall tread upon. Unbending judicial action, inflexible justice, is symbolised by the "feet like fine brass." Every systematised form of evil bearing the christian name (v. 23) must be destroyed. The mountains of Edom in the last days afford an awful example of divine vengeance and of the application of the striking symbol here employed (Isa. 63. 1-6). When the Lord comes in Person to make good His sovereign right over the whole scene under Heaven His feet are likened to "pillars of fire" (Rev. 10. 1, 2), a slight change in the wording of the imagery, implying the immovable, steadfast purpose and act of the Lord in the stern assertion of His universal rights. "Fire" is the expressive symbol of judgment, whether upon Christ, the sacrifice (Lev. 1), or upon the wicked (Mark 9. 43; Luke 16. 24; 2 Thess. 1. 8).

A WARM COMMENDATION.

19.—"**I know thy works, and love, and faith, and service, and thine endurance, and thy last works (to be) more than the first.**" Words of strong and stern rebuke are preceded by the warmest commendation accorded to any of the assemblies. "I know thy works" occurs in each address in our English Bibles. But in the Revised and critical editions of the Holy Scriptures the words are omitted in the epistles to Smyrna and Pergamos. The state of these assemblies precluded the idea of "works," the former being characterised by suffering, the latter by fidelity. The generic term "works" occurs twice in course of this commendation. The angel at Ephesus had declined in love, whereas the angel at Thyatira had increased in works. The darker the night the more devoted and zealous were the godly company; their "last works more than the first"—more numerous, more pure, and more elevated in character as the fruit of faith. But this Church is also commended for its love,* faith, service, and endurance, four practical features of christian life. Love, the first (Gal. 5. 22) and greatest of the christian graces (1 Cor. 13. 13), heads the list. Thyatira, too, alone amongst the seven is commended for its "love" and "service." This latter would, we judge, embrace ministry in its widest sense both of a spiritual and temporal character.

A GRAVE INDICTMENT.

20.—"**But I have against thee that thou permittest the woman Jezebel, she who calls herself prophetess, and she teaches and leads astray My servants to commit fornication and eat of idol sacrifices.**" The Authorised Version reads, "I have a *few things* against thee," but in the Revised Version and others we read, "I have against thee." The Lord had a grave indictment against the angel. The Church in its representatives was permitting an evil in its midst of a more serious character than any that had yet appeared. In other words the papacy is in the forefront of this address. The supremacy of the Roman See is simply the development in full of the dispute amongst the disciples "who was the greatest" (Mark 9. 33, 34, R.V.).† That the general state of the Church in the Middle Ages is represented by Thyatira seems self-evident.

HISTORICAL ORDER OF THE CHURCHES.

In the successional order of the churches attention is drawn to certain broadly marked features and distinctive epochs which lie open to every student of ecclesiastical history. The historian may furnish details, sometimes interesting, more often dreary, but the principles and broad characteristics of Church history, of which details are but the outcome and development, are plainly written

* Our translators here, and notably in 1 Corinthians 13, have followed Wycliffe, A.D. 1380, in rendering the Greek word *agapa* by "charity," instead of *love*, its only equivalent. In this he followed the Vulgate or Latin version of the Scriptures. The illustrious English Reformer, "The Morning Star of the Reformation," was not acquainted with the original tongues in which the Scriptures were written, but was an accomplished Latin scholar. Tyndale, who had carefully studied the Greek Testament of the learned Erasmus, published in A.D. 1516, gave to the English-speaking people the first printed New Testament in their own tongue. This was in A.D. 1526, nearly 150 years after Wycliffe's edition of the Scriptures. Tyndale rejected "charity" and rightly translated *love*. Cranmer followed suit. In Wycliffe's time and for long afterwards, the words *charity* and *alms* exactly represented our modern English words *love* and *charity*. The word *alms* is falling into disuse, *charity* being regarded as its equivalent.

† The historical development of the papacy from the fourth century, when the claim of supremacy was first advanced, to the eighth, when universal sovereignty, spiritual and temporal, was demanded, is ably traced in "The Rise of the Papal Power," by Hussey.

down in chapters two and three of the Apocalypse. Decay of first love closed up the first century, of which Ephesus was the representative. Then persecution raged with greater or less intensity at intermittent periods for more than two centuries, of which Smyrna was the sorrowful witness. Next, and in historical order, we are brought to the era of Constantine, when the emperor ruined the Church with his gold and honours. This sad event is of fourth-century notoriety, and was exhibited in Pergamos. Succeeding history shows the development of the papal system from the first claim of authority and supremacy in the council of Sardica, A.D. 347, till the seventh century, when its arrogant, pretentious claims clashed with the titles, honours, and worship due exclusively to our Lord and Saviour Jesus Christ. Then from the eighth century till the dawn of the Reformation the universal claim of the papacy over the kingdoms of the earth, and the souls and bodies of men, yea, as possessing even the keys of Paradise itself, was carried out as far as possible by force and fraud. The claim of universal sovereignty has never been withdrawn, and awaits another day for its enforcement. This, then, is the awful picture presented in Thyatira. The Reformation of the sixteenth century broke the yoke of the papacy and secured a measure of freedom for Europe. Luther with an open Bible was more than a match for the Pope, aided and abetted by the most potent monarch of his time. The blow then dealt at the papacy was not a deadly one, it is slowly but surely recovering from it. The Reformation and Protestantism are before us as prominent features in the epistle to Sardis. But another Reformation was needed, one of vital and practical Christianity. This was effected in the energy of the Spirit of God at the commencement of last century. Finally, the state neither hot nor cold; Christless, yet boasting of its wealth and supremacy; self-satisfied, too, is *the* main characteristic of the Church to-day. The cross outside and inside her buildings, with Christ outside at the door knocking for *individuals* to open is Laodicea. The *Church* refuses to hear His voice or own His authority.

JEZEBEL, OR THE PAPACY.

Jezebel was a woman, a queen, an idolater, a persecutor, and the virtual ruler and director of the government of Israel. Ahab was but a puppet in her hands (1 Kings 18-21). All this and more is the Jezebel of the Apocalypse. Combining in herself these and other features of the popish system (Rev. 17 and 18), she arrogantly assumes the title "prophetess." She professes to teach with authority.

Combined with teaching she can employ all the arts and seductions of minds specially trained to effect her fell purpose.* "Hear Mother Church" is the cry of every Romanist. "The Church cannot err in faith and morals," and it must be understood that by "the Church" is meant the papacy pure and simple. Her teachings and seductions, however contrary to Scripture and repellent to human understanding, must be accepted as authoritative and infallible. This is a dogma with Rome. She cannot err, therefore she cannot progress. It is thus that Rome and ignorance, Rome and superstition, Rome and no mind must necessarily, as history abundantly testifies, go together. Rome dreads the light and fears the Bible. "The Church teaches," says the Romanist. "The Church's mission is to evangelise," says the Protestant. Both are wrong. Teaching and preaching are not gifts conferred upon the Church, nor is it responsible to do either. The Church is taught, but does not teach. Both teaching and preaching are the exercise of gift by individual servants of the Lord (Eph. 4. 8-12).

She leads "astray My servants." This the Jezebel of modern days has done. She has turned the great mass of professing Christians (here designated "My servants," as bearing that name and character) from Christ to Mary; from Christ the one Mediator and Intercessor (1 Tim. 2. 5; Rom. 8. 34) to the dead; from Christ to the Pope; from the one offering of eternal value to the sacrifice of the mass; from the Word of God and its certainty to the traditions of men which all are uncertain; and, in general, from Christianity to christianised paganism. Is not the indictment a grave and true one?

Where does this wide departure from truth lead to? What is the natural result to those led astray? The *end* of popish error, of intrigue, of blasphemous teachings, of wicked practices, and undying hatred to all outside her communion is to get her adherents and dupes "to commit fornication and eat of idol sacrifices"—FORNICATION and IDOLATRY. These were the two great Pergamos errors, only here seen in a more settled and intensified form. It will also be noticed that in Pergamos the evils are stated in inverse order—*idolatry* and fornication (v. 14). These two satanic evils were taught and practised in the Church itself. There may have been in the Thyatiran assembly an actual counterpart to the impious Jezebel of old, who led in these very evils unchecked by the angel. But these

* The Jesuit is the real power behind the Pope. The ruling principle of the Jesuit lies in this, that the end justifies the means. Morality, honour, principle are sacrificed in order to effect this end. "The Jesuits spend the night in hatching plots, and the day in running about to execute them."—*Wyllie.*

heinous sins must be understood in a broad and comprehensive sense, and in keeping with the thought repeatedly pressed in this Exposition, viz., descriptive of the general condition of the Church as a whole at a given time. Those terrible evils were the characteristics of the mediaeval Church.

Fornication, employed as a symbol here and elsewhere, signifies for those professing the Name of the Lord, *illicit intercourse* with the world. What was commenced by Constantine was consummated in the papacy.* The assumption of combined temporal and spiritual power, both universal in their range, was the masterpiece of the papacy. Kingdoms were bestowed, crowns given, and principalities conferred according to the will of one styling himself "The vicar of Jesus Christ, the successor of Peter, the anointed of the Lord, the God of Pharaoh, short of God, beyond man, less than God, greater than man, who judges all men, and is judged by no man."† The unholy union of the Church with the world was as a system *perfected* in the papacy. It is spiritual fornication.

Participation in idol worship next follows, and is necessarily coupled with the former evil. Idolatry in the Church seems paradoxical, nevertheless it is true. We deliberately assert that the Romish Church and the Greek Church are systems of baptised paganism, and to some extent the Anglican Church is involved in the charge. Most of their doctrines, holy days, rites, ceremonies, vestments, titles, are heathen in their origin. The pagans refused to adopt christian worship and doctrine, and so the Church—more evil—adopted pagan customs, giving them christian names.‡ If the simple Church polity of the New Testament is compared with the unspiritual, mechanical worship and order in the Roman, Eastern, and Anglican churches, the reader may be surprised to learn that there is scarcely *one* point of agreement. But are the orthodox churches free from the taint of idolatry? Have they not more or less borrowed from Rome? Protestantism is not necessarily Christianity. The severance from the papacy by the churches of the Reformation was not as complete as it ought to have been. Numerous Romish practices and doctrines of pagan origin are yet retained in the Reformed churches. All mere forms of worship and doctrinal creeds

* The term "Popery" and "Papacy" are not equivalent terms. The former is the embodiment of doctrine and religious rite and ceremony; the latter signifies the whole system—sacred and secular—from its root to its utmost branch.

† Innocent III., who ascended the pontifical chair in the early part of the twelfth century. A cruel and relentless persecutor.

‡ All this is fully inquired into and proved beyond doubt in that remarkable book, "The Two Babylons," by Hyslop. See also "The Mystic Cities of Scripture," "Zion and Babylon," and "Mosheim's Ecclesiastical History," Vols. 1 and 2, English edition of 1845.

not of direct Scripture authority draw the heart and eye from Christ; other objects are substituted, and *that* is idolatry.

TIME FOR REPENTANCE.

21.—"**And I gave her time that she should repent, and she will not repent of her fornication**." Rome yet exists. In principle she is unchanged. She is slowly but surely recovering her strength and somewhat of her ancient prestige. Jezebel, *i.e.*, the papacy, reigned as queen for more than a thousand years, but repented not. Yet another period of grace from the Reformation till now—300 years—and the papacy is unchanged—wicked as ever, persecuting as ever, filthy as ever, idolatrous as ever. The Lord "gave her time to repent," but there has been no repentance. The Jezebel of the last 1300 years and more is the Apocalyptic Babylon of prophecy. Read her character and doings in chapters 17 and 18, and you will see that instead of repentance her character is blacker and her deeds are darker than in the past. How good the Lord is to grant such abundant mercy, such lengthened delay to induce repentance, though they be unavailing! The divine verdict is recorded, "She *will* not repent of her fornication." It is not she cannot repent, but she will not. Popery is utterly corrupt. Her character is fixed, so too is her doom.

JEZEBEL, HER ADHERENTS AND CHILDREN.

22.—"**Behold, I cast her into a bed, and those that commit adultery with her into great tribulation, unless they repent of her works, and her children will I kill with death**." Here are three parties threatened with judgment: (1) Jezebel; (2) those having intercourse with her; (3) her children. We have been already told that Jezebel will not repent, so her judgment is certain; those, too, who traffic with her are threatened unless they repent of "*her* works." Her children—persons and systems—who are born of Rome, who have imbibed her principles and teachings, are unconditionally threatened with death.

"Behold, I cast her into a bed." The word "bed" is evidently used in sharp contrast to the bed of the harlot with its illicit pleasure. It will be a bed of affliction. "Those that commit adultery with her." This is the first and only instance of the word "adultery" in the Apocalypse. Those who have tampered with the evil, who have defiled themselves by association with Jezebel, are the class here referred to—an increasing company in our times, a company born of the false spirit of toleration and of indifference to evil. Her children killed "with *death*" is a singular expression, and seems to denote the intensity of the Lord's judgment. This finds its answer in chapters 17 and 18 of the Apocalypse. Such is the character and doom of the papacy, and of all directly and remotely connected with it. There are varying degrees of guilt, but the main point to seize upon is that God judges evil according to the measure of each one's responsible connection with it.

A LESSON AND A PROMISE.

23.—"**And all the churches shall know that I am He that searches (the) reins and (the) hearts: and I will give to you each according to your works.**" The practical effect of the Lord's exposure of evil in Christendom and of its judgment is that the churches shall know that Christ searches the reins and hearts. Hidden evil is brought to light, and Christ is owned as the divine Searcher of the secret thoughts and hidden deeds of men. This was the sole prerogative of Jehovah in Old Testament times (Jer. 17. 10), and the churches are to learn the lesson, or rather know that Christ, with whom they have to do, exercises this solemn function. Omniscience belongs to Him.

But while systems, professedly good or bad, shall be judged, there is also an individual judgment of *each* one's works. Neither the believer's person nor his sins shall come into judgment (John 5. 24; Heb. 10. 17), but the works of each one shall be examined in light of that day, and blame or praise awarded by the Lord accordingly. The Lord shall pass righteous judgment on the works of each one bearing His Name. How needful to know this in view of the general toleration of evil and laxity of morals now so prevalent.

THE REST OR UNDEFILED.

24.—"**But to you I say, the rest (who) are in Thyatira, as many as have not this doctrine, who have not known the depths of Satan, as they say, I do not cast upon you any other burden: but what ye have hold fast till I come.**" The mediaeval Church was not wholly corrupt. The Albigenses and Waldenses in the thirteenth century stood aloof from the "mother of harlots." They with others constituted a noble band of witnesses against the corruptions of Rome. They were sound in the faith. Theirs, too, was no mere negative testimony. They boldly denounced the errors and heresies of the papal system. They were, as a rule, simple, unlettered peasants and hardy mountaineers, ignorant of the depths of evil, here termed in common parlance "the depths of Satan." The Lord would not add to their burdens; no fresh development of truth is taught them. What they had they were not to surrender, but "hold fast." There was no expectation held out of a reform, nor even an amelioration of the existing state of things. There could be no restoration of the Church; hence the eyes and hearts of the "rest," or remnant, are directed not backward but onward, "till I come." The Coming of the Lord is the goal of hope. A return to the pristine condition of the Church is deemed impossible. What then is the resource of the faithful? How long is their suffering, witnessing character to be maintained? "Till I come." That is the promised moment of deliverance.

FAITHFULNESS REWARDED.

26, 27.—"**And he that overcomes, and he that keeps unto the end My works, to him will I give authority over the nations, and he shall shepherd them with an iron rod; as vessels of pottery are they broken in pieces, as I also have received from My Father.**" It is not enough to deny Jezebel, her doctrines and works, but "he that keeps unto the end My works" is crowned. The chaplet of victory is placed on the brow of the one who perseveres in the path of faithfulness to the end. Death or the Coming of the Lord is that end. "My works" are evidently in contrast to the works of Jezebel (v. 23). "*Her* works" were unholy. "*His* works" are holy.

The large, grand, and public character of the promise exceeds anything we have yet had, namely, "authority over the nations." This very thing has ever been the goal of papal ambition. Metaphorically and literally the Pope has placed his foot on the neck of kings, and in the coming brief day of satanic rule (Rev. 12-19) the woman will ride the beast and command for a season the forces and authority of the revived western power with a completeness and breadth of authority never before witnessed. But the authority is usurped, the reign brief, and the instruments of her tyranny become the agents of her destruction (chap. 17. 16, 17).

The authority of the saints over the nations is co-extensive with that exercised by Christ, and for the lengthened period of 1000 years. The overcomer shall rule, or shepherd, the angry and rebellious nations with an iron rod. Their will shall be broken, their pride humbled, their glory laid in the dust like the crumbling to pieces of brittle vessels.

27.—"**As I also have received from My Father.**"

It is deeply interesting to notice that the grant of authority over the nations is made over to Christ alone (Psa. 2), but the same unlimited authority and dominion is assured to the conqueror who presses on till the end. The public place and portion of the Son are to be shared with the overcomers. The *very words* in which the Father gives the nations, the heathen, and the earth to its utmost limits to His Son are used by the Lord to endow His overcoming people with their public portion (compare v. 27 with Psa. 2. 9).

28.—"**And I will give to him the morning star.**" We have had association with Christ in His kingdom and glory, but now another and even richer promise is addressed to the overcomer: "I will give to him the morning star," a personal interest in Christ Himself. In His character as "Sun of Righteousness" to Israel He heals His people and brings in blessing, but in His character as the "Bright and Morning Star" He appears before the sun rises to His own alone. The former in connection with the *Church* (Rev. 22. 16); the latter in connection with *Israel* (Mal. 4. 2). The Lord then is coming to bring in a day of gladness for Israel and the world. The Sun will scatter the clouds and earth will rejoice, but the first faint streak of light which shall pierce through the gloom and darkness which have wrapped themselves round this dreary scene will be seen and rejoiced in by each overcomer, and then in company with Him we make our triumphal entry into the wide domain of His and our inheritance (compare v. 28; 22. 16, with Mal. 4. 2).

THE CALL TO HEAR.

29.—"**He that has an ear, let him hear what the Spirit says to the churches.**" In this epistle the Spirit has been speaking in solemn tones. The character and doom of the papacy have been sketched by a divine pen. The Spirit has been speaking to the churches. The call to hear in the preceding epistle is placed *before* the address to the overcomer. Here, and subsequently, the call to hear is placed *after* the address to the conqueror. Why so? In the first three churches the public body was ostensibly owned of God as His, and might "hear." In the last four churches the professing body is treated as incapable of repentance, and hence those alone who hear and respond to the Spirit's call constitute the overcoming company.

CHAPTER III.

THE SPIRIT'S ADDRESS TO SARDIS (CHAP. 3. 1-6).

THE EPISTLES TO SARDIS AND THYATIRA.

In this epistle to the angel we have the general state of the Church *after* the Reformation, as in the previous epistle we had a sketch in word and symbol of the Church *before* the Reformation. In Sardis Protestantism is before us; in Thyatira the papacy. The one overlaps the other, while both run on concurrently till the end, the Coming of the Lord. In the first three epistles are described consecutive states of the Church as a whole. The Reformation was a turning point in the history of western Christianity. The enforcement of the lofty and impious pretensions of the papacy in the seventh century was Satan's scourge of the west, while the rapid development of Mohammedanism at the same period equally blighted the east. The Reformation was a partial recovery in the west; for the east there has been none; it is apostate from God and the truth.

THE SEVEN SPIRITS AND THE SEVEN STARS.

1.—"**He that has the seven Spirits of God and the seven stars.**" "The seven Spirits of God" is a perplexing expression to some. In the epistles of Paul the unity of the Spirit, "*one* Spirit," is a cardinal truth. But in the apocalyptic phrase "seven Spirits" are taught the fulness, completeness, and diversified attributes and actions of the one Holy Spirit. The Spirit in diversified governmental action as distinct, yet in conjunction with Jehovah and Jesus Christ, seems the thought intended in chapter 1. 4; while in chapter 5. 6 the perfection of power and fulness of spiritual intelligence, exercised governmentally by the Lamb, is the force of the expression there used. The fulness of the Spirit is in Christ. He exercises the power of the Spirit whether towards the Church (chap. 3. 1) or towards the world (chap. 5. 6). Whatever, then, the state of the Church may be—fallen, ruined, corrupt, dead—there is in Him Who is in the midst of the golden lamps adequate spiritual power.

1.—"**He that has . . . the seven stars.**" The stars are the light bearers of the churches, responsible to shine for Christ and reflect the light of Heaven on the surrounding darkness. Christ has both the "seven Spirits" and the "seven stars," only the latter are not said to be in His right hand, as in chapter 1. 16. It is simply said He has them.

The ecclesiastical order of the Church was maintained in Ephesus, whereas in Sardis the ministry in general and the organisation of the Church were by no means according to the due order of the Spirit. A scripturally constituted ministry where all was in place, and every endowment of the Spirit was exercised under the Lordship of Christ might well be spoken of as "in His right hand." But after the Reformation churches were rapidly formed according to the will, caprice, or intelligence of certain leaders. Certain truths, not THE TRUTH, became a rallying point or centre round which congenial minds gathered, forming for themselves a Church polity, and establishing a ministry, paid for and duly ordered according to ability, talent, and the power to increase and consolidate their numbers. Hence it is here simply said "He has the stars." After all, ministry of every character proceeds from Christ. "He *has* the stars." The entire ministry of the Church is with Christ, but be it remembered that "the Spirits" and "the stars" must not be separated; distinguished they may be, but severed they cannot be without serious loss. A cold, carnal, intellectual, humanly-ordained ministry is a ministry divorced from the Spirit. The stars shine by the light of the Spirit. The union of the two is the point here. The Church's competency for inward and spiritual power and for an outward organisation of authority and ministry are ever with Christ. Herein consists the strength and weakness of Protestant profession of Christianity. Dependence upon and guidance by the Holy Spirit is true power; ministry and order which ignore the Spirit, practically or theoretically, are effete, and moral death is the sure result.

LIFELESS PROFESSION.

1.—**"I know thy works, that thou hast a name that thou livest, and art dead."** The Lord's omniscience is again asserted in the words, "I know thy works." Thus He Who walks in the midst of the churches searches Sardis, and pronounces this judgment, "Thou hast a name that thou livest, and art dead." Such was, and is, Protestantism. The Reformation was the result of the energy of the Spirit of God. Historically we trace that mighty intervention of God to its human instruments, Luther, Melanchthon, etc., and to the various causes which contributed to the grand result, as the invention of printing, etc., but behind all these the great operating cause was the Holy Ghost. We regard the papacy as the greatest curse and the Reformation as the greatest blessing since the introduction of Christianity. We distinguish between the Reformation and Protestantism; the former was a divine work, the latter a human system.

When the energy of the Reformers succeeded in breaking the chains and shackles of the worst tyranny which history records the crucial question arose: Will the energy and zeal be maintained? Will victory succeed victory? Alas, the Reformation, like every movement begun in the Spirit, soon lapsed into a cold, formal, lifeless, orthodox thing. The Reformers, and notably those who succeeded them, commenced the system of making churches instead of searching Scripture, from which they could alone learn what the Church of God is. Spiritual power was wellnigh gone; it might be found in individuals here and there, but, as a general and characteristic condition of the Church soon after the Reformation, the personal presence of the Holy Ghost in the Church (1 Cor. 3. 17) and in the individual believer (1 Cor. 6. 19) was either unknown, or, where a glimmering of the truth had penetrated, ignored. Yet things seemed fair enough, but within the power, the life, was not there. We refer to the general state. In Protestantism we have not the horrors nor gross corruption of the Middle Ages, but rather the sleep of death. There is a name to live, but only a *name*. The change from the papacy to Protestantism, from Thyatira to Sardis, may be described as a step out of the "chamber of horrors" into the "cell of death." There is the appearance of life, but He Whose eyes search all things and pierce through the outward covering says "art dead."

WORKS INCOMPLETE.

2.—"**Be watchful, and strengthen the things that remain, which are about to die, for I have not found thy works complete before My God.**" The general condition being one of death, the Church's spiritual representatives are to rouse up. Not only is watchfulness in view of the state then enjoined, but they were to become abidingly watchful. *Watching* and praying are coupled (Mark 13. 33) in the light of the Lord's return. *Praying* and watching are connected in the maintenance of the christian conflict (Eph. 6. 18). If moral death characterised the Protestant profession of Christianity inwardly, spite of deceptive appearances to the contrary, how needful the admonition to continue in a state of wakefulness and not slumber with the mass.

But while a continuous state of watchfulness was enjoined in order to arrest further paralysis (for death, not life, was fast becoming master of the situation), the energy of love was also needed.

2.—"**Strengthen the things that remain, which are about to die.**" The fruit of the Spirit (Gal. 5. 22, 23) yet existed, although in measure small and in expression feeble; whatever of life and grace remained was to be built up, cherished, strengthened. Whatever is of God hold fast, and the more so as practical religion is dying out of these christian lands. The exhortation was never more needed than now. The sword and the trowel are ever in demand, but the wise and diligent use of the latter is the crying need of the Church.

2.—"**I have not found thy works complete before My God.**" This charge forms the ground of the admonition addressed to the angel. The works of faith and of obedience were not complete, *i.e.*, in the sense of being *filled up*. The soul's practical relations with God were almost neglected in the public conflict with Rome. Individual godliness and Church life were at the lowest ebb. Protestantism as designating those who have seceded from Rome* is a poor designation of what a Christian ought to be. The exalted truths contained in the epistles to the Ephesians and Colossians were utterly unknown to the mass of the Reformers. Their efforts were mainly concentrated on the great struggle to recover for themselves, their children, and succeeding generations the Pauline truth of justification by faith, and even that is not presented in their writings in its scriptural fulness.† Exceedingly defective were they in their thoughts as to the personality and dwelling on earth of the Holy Ghost, of the Church as the Body of Christ, and of our individual and corporate relationships to Christ in Heaven.

Thus their works were not complete or filled up before "My God." This, then, was, and is, the great defect of Protestantism, and in this respect it compares unfavourably with the devotedness in works for which Thyatira was commended (chap. 2. 19). We must, however, in all this distinguish between the Reformation and the state subsequently known as Protestantism. The former was undoubtedly a divine movement, the latter is a public position taken up in opposition to the papacy in which, of course, there are many pious persons, while the system itself is one of moral death.

* At the famous diet of Spires, in 1529, on April 19th certain of the princes of Germany and many others *protested* against the usurpation of the papacy under *Clement VII.*; and again on Saturday, the 24th, the last day of the diet, they firmly renewed their *protest*. Hence from that day the Reformers and all who stood out in opposition to the papacy were termed *Protestants*, eight years after Luther had so nobly borne himself *alone* at the diet of Worms.

† Luther spoke in the most contemptuous terms of the epistle of James, because he foolishly thought that the Jewish apostle clashed with Paul in the presentation of the doctrine of justification.

THREATENED.

3.—**"Remember therefore how thou hast received and heard, and keep (it) and repent. If therefore thou shalt not watch, I will come (upon thee) as a thief, and thou shalt not know at what hour I shall come unto thee."** The "remember" to Ephesus (chap. 2. 5) was in view of the exceedingly rich endowment of truth revealed and grace bestowed, and from which the Church was declining; whereas the call to "remember" here is in the light of what God had recovered for them at the Reformation, *i.e.*, the Gospel, the Word of God, and liberty of conscience. Judgment is ever according to the measure of responsibility, and that exists in a greater or less degree as flowing from what God has given and where He has set one. They had both "received" and "heard." Protestantism was living on the renown acquired by her successful conflict with the papacy; was living on her *name*. The truths recovered and the Gospel heard to the joy of thousands were fading from memory and conscience; hence the command to "keep" and "repent"—to keep what they had, and to repent of the poor use they had made of their blessings.

They had been counselled to watch (v. 2), now unless they do so they are threatened with judgment. The character in which Christ would come to them is as a "thief in the night" (1 Thess. 5). He shall come as a Judge, unexpectedly, at an unknown and unlooked-for hour. Protestantism and the world are on the easiest terms possible. The mass of dissenters in pulpit, press, and Church courts are active politicians. State endowed churches must be to a considerable extent political in principle and practice. If, therefore, Protestantism identifies itself with the world, sharing its fortunes, it must also share its doom. Christ comes to the Church as the Morning Star, to Israel as the Sun of Righteousness, and to the world and religious profession in sudden surprise as a "thief in the night." The papacy (Thyatira) and Protestantism (Sardis) are running on together, but in opposition lines. Immense efforts are being made to heal the breach with popery. The differences between the two are lessening. The hour is approaching when the 1300 sects of Christendom will coalesce, headed by the personal Antichrist, but the end of every unity not formed by the Holy Ghost can only result in judgment.

PROMISE TO THE UNDEFILED.

4.—**"But thou hast a few names in Sardis, which have not defiled their garments, and they shall walk**

with Me in white, because they are worthy." In Thyatira the "rest," or remnant, and in Sardis the "few names" undefiled, formed a company in whom the Lord could delight. In principle and practice they were separate from the evil which they deplored; they walked apart from it. The weight of influence and numbers was with the popular side. The "few names in Sardis" had not defiled their garments. The mass had a *name* in the world, the "few" were unknown, and had no official standing, but each one of the company was personally known to Him Who "calleth His own sheep by name." How ample the gracious consolation: "They shall walk with Me in white." They had preserved their integrity *here*, they would walk with Him *there* in robes made white in the blood of the Lamb. We shall enjoy many a delightful walk and talk with our glorified Saviour and Lord (compare with Luke 9. 30-32). In that coming day of ample reward, and of holy companionship with our ever blessed Lord, no thought of personal unworthiness as now shall ever cast a shadow across the soul, for, adds the Lord in His wonderful grace, "They are worthy." Truly it is the reckoning of grace, for each one of the distinguished and honoured number is in himself as to worth but a "brand plucked out of the fire," one rescued from imminent judgment justly deserved.

REWARDS TO THE OVERCOMER.

5.—"**He that overcomes, he shall be clothed in white garments, and I will not blot his name out of the book of life, and will confess his name before My Father and before His angels.**" Here are three promises. (1) The overcomer who walked here in purity, in personal uprightness before God, shall be amply justified in the glorious scene outside this world. He shall be clothed in garments of white on which no speck or stain shall rest. (2) He who persevered in the path of life to the end would not have his name blotted out of the register of christian profession. Many standing high in the Church, whose names are as "household words," may be erased in the day when life's records shall be scanned by the all-searching eye of the Lord of the churches. (3) He who shrank not from the confession of the Name of Christ—always unpopular in merely religious society, and, of course, ever so in the world—shall be singled out in the august presence of the Father and His angels and have his name confessed before that grand assembly.

5.—"**The book of life**" here is not the same as that of chapter 13. 8. In chapter 3. 5 it is profession which may or may not be real. The end would show. Some names would stand, others be erased. But in that of chapter 13. 8 every name recorded was that of a true believer, because the names were written *from* the foundation of the world,* and hence before the course of human responsibility commenced. God knows the end from the beginning, and so in indelible letters wrote each name. In chapter 3. 5 "the book of life" is the record of christian *profession*; in chapter 13. 8 "the book of life" is the record of *reality*. In the former the true and false are found; in the latter the true only.

THE SPIRIT'S ADDRESS TO PHILADELPHIA (CHAP. 3. 7-13).

PHILADELPHIA: ITS MEANING AND PRACTICAL SIGNIFICANCE.

Philadelphia was the last christian city which submitted to the Turk, and of the seven cities named in these addresses it had the longest duration; moreover, it is the only one of the seven whose name is preserved in these modern times—in the name of the well-known American city founded by William Penn.

Philadelphia signifies "brotherly love," and evidently points to the characteristic feature of the work of God in our days. We are satisfied that the Philadelphian state has its rise, unique character, and development equally with the other Church states which have come before us. Why should Philadelphia with a character as equally pronounced as any of the others have no historical origin? We believe it has. At the close of the eighteenth century Christendom had settled down in the stupor of death. Protestantism was living on its name. *That* century was by no means the most wicked of the christian centuries, but it was the worst in the sight of God as to its moral state. We judge that the Philadelphian epoch of the Church and the sounding of the midnight cry (Matt. 25. 6) are associated events; if, indeed, the latter is not part and parcel of the Philadelphian movement. This was a true revival, a spiritual reformation. A work not of so public a character as the Reformation, but one of equal moment with it. The revival of long-forgotten truths, and their application to the souls and lives of God's saints, was the Philadelphian work of eighty years ago. Many New Testament doctrines and truths of vital importance to the standing and state of saints were forgotten soon after the

* The alternative reading in the margin of the Revised Version of chapter 13. 8 reads thus: "Shall worship . . . whose names hath not been written *from the foundation of the world* in the book of life of the slain Lamb." So also Tregelles, Darby, Kelly, etc.

death of the apostles. Thank God for their revival in our day. Multitudes who apparently stepped into the blessed grace won for them and us through the energy of the Spirit of God are now giving it up. What next? What follows? Laodicea, pure and simple. In Philadelphia true saints are caught up into the air to meet Christ. In Laodicea mere professors are spued out of His mouth; in the former the Church is preserved, in the latter the mass is rejected.

"Brotherly love"* intimates an exclusive company. Divine love in all its aspects is a holy love, one intolerant of evil, for *God* is love. "Brotherly love," therefore, must partake of the character of its source, which is God Himself. In this respect Philadelphia stands out in marked contrast to Sardis; this latter represents the mass of professing Christians, whilst distinguishing a remnant; the former brings into prominence a true-hearted company, the members of which may be scattered world-wide, but one characterised by love, a love holy and true in its character and one not narrower than the divine circle, "the household of God" (Eph. 2. 19).

PERSONAL ATTRIBUTES and ADMINISTRATIVE AUTHORITY.

7.—"**To the angel of the Church in Philadelphia write: These things saith the holy, the true: He that has the key of David, He who opens and no one shall shut, and shuts and no one shall open.**" It is a circumstance to be carefully noted that the character in which Christ presents Himself here forms no part of His glory as beheld in chapter one. He assumes a *moral* attitude towards the Church in Philadelphia, one which exactly fits its state of manifest weakness. Here, then, we have Christ in personal character, what He is essentially. He is the holy, He is the true. Others, however, might be that in a qualified degree, so that scarcely gives the force of

---

* There is a good deal of Biblical instruction wrapped up in the meaning of personal and common names practically unknown to most readers of the Holy Scriptures through inattention to this branch of study. On the other hand, there is danger, especially to persons of a mystic character of mind, in allowing imagination to take flights of fancy and play fast and loose in the domain of revealed truth. The Reformer, Ursinius, author of the Heidelberg Catechism, ingeniously constructed a statement of the Fall and Redemption from the alleged signification of the names of the first ten antediluvian patriarchs; others have followed in the same fanciful direction. To seek to establish a truth or doctrine on the real or supposed value of a numeral, or significance of a name *merely*, is to introduce a dangerous principle in Biblical interpretation. The value of numerals, and the signification of names throw many a sidelight on the teachings of Scripture. The origin of many words is lost, but if the origin and early history of names of objects and persons could in all cases be given with certainty it would be found that they express characteristic features or qualities in relation to special circumstances or events. The naming of the animals by Adam would no doubt be in relation to their several characteristics or habits. Professor Max Muller in his "Science of Languages" says: "Analyse any word you like and you will find that it expresses a general idea peculiar to the individual to which it belongs. What is the meaning of moon? The *measurer*. What is the meaning of sun? The *begetter*. What is the meaning of earth? The *ploughed*."

the words, "*the* holy, *the* true." He is both in His own Person. He ever is the embodiment of holiness and truth. Both personally and intrinsically He is "*the* holy" and "*the* true." Viewed essentially these are divine attributes (Hosea 11. 9; Jer. 10. 10; Rev. 4. 8; 1 Thess. 1. 9; Isa. 6. 3; 1 John 5. 20). Persons and things are spoken of as holy and true, but no created being has the essential moral glory of being The Holy One and The True One. As employed in our text they are really divine titles.

7.—"**He that has the key of David.**" In these words and in those that follow the reference is to Isaiah 22. 22. Shebna is deposed and degraded. The treasurer of the royal house of David used his high office to immortalise himself (v. 16). Then the prophet announced the investiture of Eliakim to the administration of the royal authority. The terms of the prophecy in depth and fulness are characteristically Messianic, going far beyond the historical circumstances in the days of Hezekiah. The prophetic announcement of Isaiah (chap. 22. 22) and the words of the Seer (v. 7 in our chapter), almost verbally the same, imply administrative authority; the former in connection with royalty in Judah, the latter in connection with grace to the Church. The "key" as a symbol denotes undisputed right to enter and exercise all needful authority.

Some, strangely enough, connect "the key of the house of David" with "the keys of death and of hades." They are not identical. The former intimates Christ's sovereignty in time, the latter His sway in the unseen world in all that concerns the bodies and souls of men. "The keys of the kingdom of Heaven" (Matt. 16. 19) were alone committed to Peter to signify delegated authority, which necessarily ceased when his work was done. Peter by his preaching opened the door of the kingdom for Jews in Acts 2, and for the admission of Gentiles in Acts 10. The keys having been used, and the doors opened, a successional and vested right in "St. Peter's keys" is absurd. Peter *left* the door open; hence they are of no further use.

7.—"**He who opens and no one shall shut, and shuts and no one shall open,**" does so in virtue of having "the key of David," *i.e.*, complete sovereignty. But the reference here is not to admission and rejection connected with either Church or kingdom. It is a "door" of service and testimony that is opened or closed according to Christ's sovereign pleasure (compare with Acts 14. 27; 1 Cor. 16. 9; 2 Cor. 2. 12; also with the words following, "Behold I have set before thee an open door"). The treasures of grace and blessing are under the absolute control of Christ. "He *has* the key," and will not pass it on to another. Hence when He opens or closes a door, who can shut or open? His right to direct His servants is unquestionable, His authority irresistible.

WHAT ALONE CAN MEET THE MIND OF CHRIST.

The zeal of many is unbounded, the orthodoxy of others is unquestionable, a scriptural ecclesiastical standing has been assumed by numerous assemblies of saints, and yet with it all there may be no real answer to Him, the holy, the true. We hold it to be impossible to point to any company of saints on earth and say, "There is the Philadelphian company" of Revelation 3. 7-13. What alone can suit the mind of the Lord (and no true-hearted saint would desire to come short of it) is a moral state, the reflex of what He is in essential moral character. God would stamp holiness and truth on His people, and in these morally associate them with His beloved Son. But the work must begin and be continued *within*, in the soul, and this will result in an *outward* display to the eyes of the Lord in which He can delight. Sardis is a sight for the *world*; Philadelphia for the *Lord*. Yet in painfully realising the poverty of our answer to Him Who is the holy, the true, we must brace ourselves up in the strengthening thought that the full administrative authority of the kingdom is with Him. He can make good every yearning after holiness and moral conformity to Himself. We abhor with Him every shade and shadow of falsehood. He rouses the integrity of the new man within us to desire only the true. He has, and ever retains, the key of David, and unlocks the treasures of strength and blessing for His beloved people. But sure we are that pretension, boasting, and the declaration of what we are morally or ecclesiastically are in every way opposed to the moral condition suitable to Him. Christ-like people are not occupied with their state or progress. The transforming process (2 Cor. 3. 4) ceases when self, *i.e.*, what we *are* and what we have *done*, is before the soul.

ENCOURAGED AND COMMENDED.

8.—**"I know thy works: behold, I have set before thee an open door, which no one can shut, because thou hast a little power, and hast kept My Word, and hast not denied My Name."** The Church in Sardis walked hand in hand with the world, and so must share its doom (Rev. 3. 3 with 1 Thess. 5. 2). Not so with the assembly in Philadelphia. It walked apart from the world, and so its end is bright (v. 12). The public position of the former, with its abundant religious machinery and works on a large scale and duly chronicled, is in marked contrast with the latter, which has no worldly status, no ecclesiastical organisation, and no works which the world can either admire or publicly note. The works of Philadelphia do not attract the world's admiration nor draw down the world's éclat. This is enough for the faithful: "I *know* thy works." A Philadelphian, one who answers to that character, flourishes spiritually in the shade. It is there, and not under the patronage or smile of the world that his deepest moments of communion are spent with the Lord. "I know thy works," poor and feeble as they are at the best, is enough for cheer and strength till the day of recompense arrives.

But the weakness of Philadelphia need not hinder service and testimony, nor prevent them being of the truest character. To Jesus on earth, Whose only care was to do His Father's will at whatever cost, the porter opened and none could shut. So here Christ has the unchallenged right to use the key, all authority in Heaven and in earth being committed to Him (Matt. 28. 18). He had set before the angel "an opened door." Service for Him and testimony to Him were to be the happy life work of the Church. They need not fear, for no created being can shut that opened door. "No *man* can shut it," reads the Authorised Version; "no one," or "none can shut," reads the Revised. What strength! In individuals or associations created might is powerless to hinder the service or crush the testimony of those called into personal association with Christ. Our only defence is our weakness. Do we realise it? We have a *shut* door in Acts 16. 6, 7, and an *open* door in 1 Corinthians 16. 9.

Then after this gracious and abundant encouragement the Lord proceeds in one unbroken strain of commendation. Not a word of censure. The Church in Smyrna was in *suffering*, and the assembly in Philadelphia in *weakness*, and so neither is blamed; the only two of the seven exempted from reproof.

8.—"**Thou hast a little power.**" Not exactly "strength," as in the Authorised Version. The Spirit wrought in resistless energy in the testimony and preaching in the commencement of Christianity, and had the Church continued its life of obedience and dependence the power of the Spirit would have remained in all its fulness.

The Lord has been pleased to make the plenitude of spiritual power dependent to a large extent on our individual and corporate faithfulness, but not so the *presence* of the Spirit in the Church; this latter is an ever-abiding fact pledged by the Word of the Lord Himself (John 14. 16). There was not much to show, nor marked spiritual energy, but there was a *little* power. The Church in profession is a wreck, and it would be a virtual denial of the corruption and ruin to expect a Pauline or Petrine energy of the Spirit. God cannot work in mighty power in a condition of things which is to the denial of the Name of His Son, the holy, the true. The amount of power was small, but it was actively employed, not held as a mere passive possession. Activity in service and faithfulness to the Word and Name of Christ characterised the angel.

8.—The testimony of Christ was both of a positive and negative character. Thou **"hast kept My Word"***—*positive*, and **"hast not denied My Name"**—*negative*. The former involves thorough subjection of soul and conscience to the written Word. In order to "keep" the Word obedience to it must be prompt and unqualified. A slipshod reading of Scripture as a matter of duty, or even its study for intelligence and to equip one more thoroughly for ministerial service does not constitute one a doer of the Word. To keep Christ's Word at all costs may involve the forfeiture of social and civil distinction and the abandonment of position in the professing Church and in the world. To a true Philadelphian saint Christ's Word is that which separates him from *all* to Christ alone at whatever personal cost.

Surely, too, in a scene where almost every religious abomination is attached to the holy Name of the Lord it is a matter of no small moment to stand aloof, to reject every association, even if good and learned men uphold it, if it is to the dishonour of Christ. Elijah in his day, Paul in his, and Luther at a later era were distinguished witnesses for God. During those and other critical periods God had always a company of negative witnesses. It is morally invigorating to trace the steps, reckon up the opposing forces, and mark the brilliant career of men who bravely battled for God and truth; but let us not overlook, as did Elijah, the 7,000 who had not bowed the knee to Baal (1 Kings 19. 18). *His* testimony was the grander of the two without doubt, but *theirs* was also valued by Jehovah.

A name represents a person, and necessarily supposes his absence. The value of what a person is has its force in the name. In the Name of Christ prayer is all-prevailing (John 14. 13, 14); to it alone God would gather

* "Word," meaning the mind of the Lord as a whole; "words" details; and "commandments," expression of His authority (see John 14. "Words," in verse 23 should read "word;" "sayings" in verse 24, "words").

His saints (Matt. 18. 20); in virtue of it our sins have been forgiven (1 John 2. 12); and because of it God leads His pilgrim people in paths of righteousness (Psa. 23. 3). It is no light matter therefore to be preserved from the denial of Christ in days of abounding iniquity. If we cannot have a bold, distinct, uncompromising testimony of an Elijah character, let us have at least a silent one, yet one that will not deny the Name of the blessed Lord.

CONDEMNATION OF MODERN JUDAISM.

9.—"**Behold, I will make them of the synagogue of Satan who say they are Jews, and are not, but lie; behold, I will cause that they shall come and shall do homage before thy feet, and shall know that I have loved thee.**" We meet with the same party here as in the address to Smyrna. The character of the opposition may not be the same in both Church periods, for the tactics of Satan are varied, but in both the opposition is termed a "synagogue of Satan." The company seems more formed and consolidated at the Philadelphian epoch of the Church; thus "*the* synagogue of Satan." Those here referred to are necessarily of Jewish nationality, but just as the Jews claimed to be God's people on earth, and that to the exclusion of all others, so here a traditional, successional Church order and position are assumed. Its true character is exposed by the Lord of the churches. It is a gathering under Satan, and all the more wicked that it has tacked on to it the Name of the holy and true. The pretension to be *the* Church, to be *the* people of God, is a false one, a "lie." Our souls and consciences have got somewhat blunted to the solemn state of things around us in which so many true saints are mixed up. The Church-state associations of the day are simply developed Judaism, with certain christian rites and doctrines added thereto. The saved and unsaved are together addressed as "brethren." The charge could be readily and abundantly proved. We have only to read the New Testament and contrast its teachings with Protestantism as a whole, and then ask: Have we not in our midst and around us a huge system of Judaism in its principles, traditions, practices, and character? Modern Judaism here meets the Lord's withering condemnation. Popularity, numbers, wealth, and influence are on their side. Philadelphian saints are few, feeble, and of no account. Confronted on every hand with a spurious character of Christianity, which adapts itself to every variety of taste and temperament, the special danger is lest the separate position be surrendered, that an easier path be sought at the expense of a deviation from truth and holiness. A large and increasing party in the professing Church is here termed "the synagogue of Satan." What is it if not that? There never was a moment when *human* charity was so in the ascendant, and surely never a moment when *divine* love is so needed. The former says "Union is *strength*," the latter says "Union in *obedience* is strength." But the relative positions of those composing "the synagogue of Satan" and the Philadelphian Church are soon to be reversed. The former are to be humbled; the latter exalted. What a reversal of the present order of things! But, more, these Church pretenders shall know that those whom they had despised are special objects of divine love. They "shall know that I have loved *thee*."

EXEMPTION FROM THE COMING HOUR OF TRIAL.

10, 11.—"**Because thou hast kept the Word of My patience, I also will keep thee out of the hour of trial which is about to come upon the whole habitable world, to try them that dwell upon the earth. I come quickly: hold fast what thou hast, that no one take thy crown.**" The patience or endurance of Christ was tested to its utmost, but the trial brought out, not impatience and fretfulness, as so often with us, but perfection of such sort as ascended to God as a sweet savour. "The Word of My patience," however, does not recall His *past*—fragrant as it is with moral beauty—but refers to the *present* attitude of our Lord. He sits at Jehovah's right hand patiently waiting till God makes His enemies a footstool (Psa. 110 with Heb. 10. 12, 13), or, in other words, He waits for the establishment of the millennial kingdom in power and glory. For that kingdom Christ patiently waits in Heaven. When God's time arrives the heirs are gathered up, changed and glorified (1 Thess. 4. 17; 1 Cor. 15. 51-55); then God brings into the world His First-Begotten, accompanied by all His heavenly saints (Jude 14) and holy angels (Matt. 25. 31). "And there was given Him dominion, and glory, and a kingdom, that all people, nations, and languages should serve Him: His dominion is an everlasting dominion, which shall not pass away, and His kingdom that which shall not be destroyed" (Dan. 7. 14). What a glorious prospect is thus opened up! A prospect grand to us, but infinitely more so to Him Who waits in patience in the throne of His Father. The Philadelphian saints had revived this testimony and kept it; here termed "the *Word* of My patience;" kept it midst the contempt and scorn of the proud, worldly, and pretentious party in the professing Church, whose arrogant claims to tradition and succession of ministry, priesthood, and sole right to dispense sacraments wore out the saints and demanded more than ordinary endurance. "*Because* thou hast kept the Word of My patience, I also will keep thee out of the hour of trial." How ample the recompense for the measure of faithfulness maintained by the Philadelphian assembly! The struggle was no light one. The conflict of Smyrna had been with the *pagan* world. The struggle of Philadelphia with the *religious* power. The Church had endured as seeing Him Who is invisible, and waited in patience as did the Lord for the intervention of God.

The wording of the promise is as precise as it is gracious, and effectually disposes of the theory advanced by some, and that to the fear and dread of believers, that the Church or a part thereof shall have to pass through the coming Tribulation to purge itself from its unfaithfulness. No, the guarantee is, "I also will keep thee *out* of the hour of trial," not brought *through* it, or kept *in* it, but entire exemption *from* it. No portion of the Church shall be in the Tribulation. Jews especially will be the most awful sufferers, for it is pre-eminently the day of Jacob's trouble (Jer. 30. 7). Gentiles, too, are embraced in it (Rev. 7. 9-17). Lot and Noah were preserved *through* the respective tribulations of their days; on the other hand, Abraham and Enoch were divinely kept *from* these same seasons of trial. It is these latter which figure the Church. The hour of trial is "about to come." It is nearing daily, and cannot in the nature of things be much longer deferred.

"**The whole habitable world,**" or civilised portion of the earth. The word here is the same as in Luke 2. 1, denoting the Roman empire. All apart from and outside the limits of the empire were regarded as without the pale of civilisation. The geographical sphere of the four Gentile universal monarchies (Dan. 2), the scene of special light and privilege, is to be subjected to a brief but awful period of trial. This crisis in the world's history has its place within the last week of Daniel's celebrated prophecy of seven years (Dan. 9. 27). Christendom has yet to answer to God for its abuse of the light vouchsafed and for privilege bestowed. Christianity will judge Christendom. Conscience and the testimony of creation will judge the heathen. But there is one class singled out, and one of ominous signification, "*them* that dwell upon the earth." This singular expression of moral import has its root in Philippians 3. 18, 19. These enemies of the cross have settled down in the earth, making it their home, the things and interests of earth bounding their horizon. As a class thus morally distinguished they are frequently referred to in the Apocalypse (chaps. 6. 10; 11. 10; 14. 6, etc.). Having deliberately chosen earth instead of Heaven they are tried in that coming hour when the rights of Christ over the earth which is, the prophetic testimony of this book, is to be made good by judgment, in Palestine particularly.

''**I come quickly**'' is the announcement of the Lord's speedy return from Heaven. It is three times repeated in the last chapter of the book (vv. 7, 12, 20). How can ''*quickly*'' be reconciled with a lengthened delay of nigh two thousand years? Ah! we have to adjust our modes of reckoning, and measure time as the Lord does. ''Beloved, be not ignorant of this one thing, that one day is with the Lord as a thousand years, and a thousand years as one day'' (2 Peter 3. 8). About two days thus measures the period between the two Advents, His first and second.

''**Hold fast what thou hast.**'' The characteristic possessions of Philadelphia were Christ's WORD, Christ's NAME, Christ's PATIENCE, and Christ's COMING. These were to be maintained. Death, desertion, and compromise may thin the company and reduce it to an insignificant, feeble few. But all the more need to ''hold fast,'' and on no account surrender one iota of the truth. The character of the times demands unflinching loyalty to the faith and unswerving devotedness to Christ and to all He has committed to our care. ''Know ye not that they which run in a race run all, but one receiveth the prize? *So run* that ye may obtain'' (1 Cor. 9. 24). It is not the *start*, but the *end* which determines the fitness to wear the crown. A true Philadelphian is one who continues to struggle on to the end. How needful, therefore, the admonitory words to one and all, to leaders and followers alike: ''Hold fast what thou hast, that no one take thy crown.'' Let go the truth and you lose the crown. What an irreparable loss!

PHILADELPHIAN REWARDS.

12.—**''He that overcomes, him will I make a pillar in the temple of My God, and he shall go no more at all out; and I will write upon him the Name of My God, and the name of the city of My God, the new Jerusalem which comes down out of Heaven from My God, and My new Name.''** An overcomer* in Philadelphia is one who, though in weakness, yet holds on his way. His progress is not marked by distinguished

* *Witnesses* in Hebrews 11. *Overcomers* in Revelation 2, 3. The former refer to Old Testament worthies the latter to New Testament saints.

achievements, but he struggles on. The deepening conflict strengthens faith, and leads to increasing faithfulness. He holds fast with a tight and tightening grip Christ's Word, Name, Patience, and Coming. Life itself may be surrendered, but not the things which constitute the crown of his testimony. The weakness of earth is to be exchanged for the stability of Heaven. "Him will I make a *pillar* in the temple of My God." There will be no material temple in Heaven (Rev. 21. 22); there will be one on earth in the time of the apocalyptic judgments (chap. 11. 1, 2). "The temple of My God" refers to the sanctuary above. Solomon set up two immense brazen pillars in the porch of the temple remarkable for strength and solidity (1 Kings 7. 21). The names of these pillars were Jachin, *establish*, and Boaz, *strength*. The allusion in our text is to these pillars. The weak and tried Philadelphian believer, cast out it may be of the orthodox and popular assembly on earth, shall be *established* and made *strong* in the eternal blessedness of Heaven. This high position is a fixed and eternal one: "He shall go no more at all out."

12.—"**I will write upon him the Name of My God.**" The blessedness of knowing God, too, shall be the conqueror's happy portion. But the tale of grace is not yet finished. The *city* of My God, the new Jerusalem which has her proper home in Heaven (chap. 21. 9, 10), pours out her wealth of blessedness to crown the overcomer. Then last, but not least, Christ's new Name will be graven for ever on each one of the conquering band. His new Name indicates His special relationship with the whole scene and sum of heavenly blessedness. While in all things He exceedeth, yet surely we may read these peculiarly rich and full promises as intimating association with Christ in the future scene of glory. How Christ loves to connect us with Himself in the enumeration of these rewards! *My* God, *My* Name, etc., occurring five times.

The address to the angel of the Church in Philadelphia closes with the usual call to hear. May the hearing ear be granted to each reader!

The Spirit's Address to Laodicea (Chap. 3. 14-22).

GENERAL CHARACTERISTICS.

In the first four churches Christ presents Himself in some part of the character in which He is beheld by the Seer in chapter 1. 12-16, but in each of the last three He gives fresh revelations of Himself. The circumstances in these latter are wholly different from those in the earlier churches, and hence the presentation of Christ is in exact keeping with the several closing Church states herein depicted.

Whatever the general condition of the Church may be at any period, Christ never deserts it. When it ceases to be a vessel of testimony for God, a light bearer in darkness, then the sentence of excision (chap. 3. 16) is finally executed, but that day, though nearing, has not yet arrived. The Church in its outward testimony for God is owned and recognised, and can be addressed in its Church standing. God has not yet rejected the professing Church, nor should we. We deplore its evils, and reject complicity with iniquity practised under its shadow, but it is still God's witness on earth, the pillar and ground of the truth (1 Tim. 3. 15) and the olive tree of testimony (Rom. 11). The unconditional threat and its execution are very different things. The former has been announced; the latter is yet future. Laodicea, representing as it does the last phase of the professing Church, has not yet been publicly disowned (v. 16). Its Church standing is a fact as positive as that of any of the previous churches. Laodicea may have departed in life and practice more than any of the others, but its position before God is unquestionable, and on that ground it is addressed.

The Church in these two chapters is spoken to in its public, professing character as the House of God in which the highest privileges are enjoyed; hence it is the scene of weightiest responsibility and the first subject of divine judgment (1 Peter 4. 17). The Church, when viewed as the mystical Body of Christ, being the aggregate of all true believers on earth, is necessarily exempt from judgment. Human administration enters largely into the former; whereas the latter is the fruit alone of God's Holy Spirit. The true and the false may enter the "House." The true only can enter the "Body." No real believer need fear being involved in the peremptorily expressed threat of judgment conveyed in verse 16. "Caught up" and "spued out" intimate the respective destiny of the true and the false, of believers and mere professors. This latter being so loathsome to Christ that thorough rejection by Him is the only way in which His holiness can be publicly vindicated.

In the address to Philadelphia there is no reproof. Here there is no praise.

TITLES OF THE DIVINE SPEAKER.

14.—"**To the angel of the Church in Laodicea write: These things saith the Amen, the faithful and**

true Witness, the Beginning of the creation of God." The marginal reading in our English Bibles, "in Laodicea," is correct, and not that in the text, "the Church of the Laodiceans." The titles are singularly appropriate to the Church of the last days; they just suit the present Laodicean condition of things. The angel as usual is addressed. The Church standing is thereby recognised. The spiritual condition of this assembly even in Paul's day, thirty years previously, caused the apostle great mental conflict (Col. 2. 1). Various causes contributed to this Church's ruin, the chief of which were pride, material wealth, and self-satisfaction. In these it gloried. How fitting therefore these titles!

(1) "**These things saith the Amen**." This is a Hebrew word signifying what is fixed, true, unchangeable. The force of the word may be found in Isaiah 7. 9 and 65. 16, where the words "believe" and "truth" are literally *Amen*. Its equivalent in Greek is in our well-known "verily," duplicated in the Gospel of John, and only there, occurring about twenty-five times. It implies divine certainty. Here, however, it is not employed as in other parts of the sacred volume as an adverb, but its use with the definite article "*the* Amen" points to another glory, another descriptive title of our blessed Lord. The Church has utterly failed in making good the promises and truth of God. In Christ both are secured. In His Person we have the guarantee that every promise and every truth will be Amened (see also 2 Cor. 1. 20).

(2) "**The faithful and true Witness**." The highway of the ages is strewn with wreck. Every witness for God, individual and corporate, has failed save *One*. The Church, so richly endowed with truth and privilege, is the worst offender of any of the witnessing company from Adam downwards. Has it been a faithful custodian of the treasures of divine grace? Is it a true witness to the character of God? Is it the living expression on earth of Jesus Christ, of what He *was* and *is*? Alas, no! The Church has shut Him out. Hear its jubilant strain, "I am rich and increased with goods, and have need of *nothing*," not even of Christ, the Church's life and glory. He, thus driven out, yet lingers about the door, taking His stand outside. "Behold!" this wonder of wonders, "*I* stand at the door and knock," and such is His attitude to-day. The Church is the most responsible witness which has ever appeared, and it is now a huge wreck. It is being morally ruined, not by open enemies, but by professed friends. Boastful, proud, loaded with wealth, and content while Christ is outside! Such was Laodicea, such is the Church

to-day. She has been neither a faithful nor true witness. But Christ is, and thus once again the heart is relieved as it turns from the wreck and ruin around to Him. What a rest to the spirit! Herein is a firm ground for faith amidst the ecclesiastical upheavings everywhere. Christ is God's Witness.

(3) "**The Beginning of the creation of God.**" The creation set up under the headship of Adam has, whether ecclesiastical, social, or governmental, gone from bad to worse. "The corruption of the best thing," *i.e.*, the Church, "is the worst of all corruptions." The world seems ready to enter on its last plunge into the vortex of iniquity. Ritualism is working towards popery, and Rationalism towards infidelity. The former system will be headed up, not in the Pope, but in the Antichrist; the latter will be fully represented in a man unnamed in the divine Word, but termed "the beast," characterised by brute force, a blasphemous, persecuting, murderous personage, inspired by Satan. These two men may be alive now for aught we know, and as Jew and Gentile were united in the crucifixion of our Lord, is it not fitting that the respective forces of Ritualism and Rationalism which are ruining the Church should, when the restraining influences are removed and things are fully developed, be headed up in a Jew and a Gentile? Laodicea is compounded of two Greek words signifying *people* and *righteous*, and really intimates the struggle now fiercely raging in every land by the peoples to obtain their rights, real or supposed. The forces of anarchy and order are confronting each other, and soon Europe, if not in a more extended area, will present the grim spectacle of the subversion of all constituted authority, with anarchy and the peoples for a brief season triumphant, turning earth into a pandemonium (Rev. 6. 12-17), when out of the moral, social, and political chaos a stern hand grasps the helm—one tyranny exchanged for another—and finally creation is again set up under Christ, the beginning of the creation of God (Psa. 8; Eph. 1. 10-22, etc.). This very title, therefore, intimates the ruin of the now 6000 years old creation, of which the Church is the last witness. The extensive and magnificent system of things, celestial and terrestrial, animate and inanimate, of which Christ as Man is here termed "the Beginning," is the creation spoken of in our text. The millennial kingdom is referred to. If, therefore, in the previous titles of the divine Speaker we are turned from the Church to Christ, from its ruined testimony to Him as the Securer of Truth and Promise, and the faithful and true Witness, here our hearts adoringly

rest on a scene of ineffable blessedness, on another creation of which Christ is "the Beginning."*

NAUSEOUS STATE OF THE CHURCH.

15, 16.—"**I know thy works, that thou art neither cold nor hot; I would thou wert cold or hot. Thus because thou art lukewarm, and neither cold nor hot, I am about to spue thee out of My mouth.**" "I know thy works" is seven times repeated in these addresses according to our English Version, but in the Revised and other critical editions of the Scriptures the formula is omitted in the address to Smyrna and in that to Pergamos. To the angel in Ephesus and Thyatira other items are added to the works of which the Lord says, "I know;" while in the case of Sardis, Philadelphia, and Laodicea, "I know thy works" refer to the general state and condition of these churches. The pregnant sentence, however, "I know" occurs seven times, being addressed to the angel of each assembly. Omniscience, a divine attribute, is thus seven times affirmed of our Lord. To Philadelphian weakness this assertion of the Lord's absolute knowledge of that which is unknown to man, yet known to Him, is a truth full of strength. To Laodicea in its lukewarmness, with its show, and boast, and wealth, the all-seeing eye of the Lord searching the recesses of the heart must be an intolerable thought. What the Lord here specially notes is the *lukewarm* condition of the angel. This last phase of the Church is the worst. Men would find a deeper evil in Thyatira. The Lord declares the most nauseous state to be that into which Laodicea was sunk, a state moreover in which the angel positively gloried. The terms used are "cold" and "hot," not "dead" and "alive." Had these latter been employed the truth of being saved or lost might have been in question, but "neither cold nor hot" is predicated in relation to their state to Him. Total indifference to Christ, not hatred, is implied in the term "lukewarm."†

We do not hold with some that the lukewarm condition of Laodicea springs out of the Philadelphian state of the Church. Such an interpretation is beset with insuperable difficulty, but, undoubtedly, the coldness and death of Sardis, with the weakness yet warmth of Philadelphia,

---

* There are at least four headships ascribed to Christ: (1) **Headship of the Body** (Col. 2. 19). (2) **Headship of the Race** (1 Cor. 15. 22, 45-49; *i.e.*, those in Christ, Gal. 3. 28; 2 Cor. 5. 17). (3) **Headship of Creation** (Col. 1. 15-17; 2. 10). (4) **Headship of everv Man** (1 Cor. 11. 3). United *to* Him gives the thought of the first; "*in* Him" is involved in the second; dignity is conveyed in the third; and lordship in the fourth. "The beginning of the creation of God" is a title involving His headship.

† "The Lord speaks here only of the condition of those who stand in relation to Himself."—*Hengstenberg*. It is not at all the question as to whether the angel was spiritually alive or dead, converted or unconverted, but of the moral state of one standing in a certain accredited relation to the Lord

had left but a *feeble* impression on the general condition of Laodicea. We take it that the legalism of Thyatira, the moral insensibility of Sardis, and the rejection of the truth and position of Philadelphia, with, of course, other causes, contribute to produce the Laodicean condition of that Church, *i.e., absolute indifference to Christ*. What can the Lord do with it? Had it been cold—an active position taken up—or hot—as manifesting a measure of spiritual activity—then something might have been done. But an undecided, neutral position towards Christ and the truth is one so hateful that it must be got rid of without delay. The last phase of the Church is its worst. Philadelphia is cheered with the promise, "I come quickly." Laodicea is threatened with judgment, "I am about to spue thee out of My mouth." Both promise and threat are presented as at hand. It has been remarked more than once that the last four phases of the Church run on concurrently to the end. The mass in Thyatira and Sardis are involved in the doom pronounced on Laodicea, whilst the remnants in these churches equally share in one distinctive blessing of Philadelphia—"caught up." The Lord's Coming is not referred to in the address to Laodicea. Its public repudiation as God's witness will be effected by the translation of the heavenly saints. In other words, the removal of Philadelphia and the rejection of Laodicea are coincident events, the latter being dependent on the former. Christendom, which commenced its history under the brightest auspices, will close under the darkest cloud which has ever rested on the course of human responsibility.

THE PROUD BOAST AND THE LORD'S CONDEMNATION.

17.—"**Because thou sayest, I am rich, and am grown rich, and have need of nothing, and knowest not that thou art the* wretched and the* miserable, and poor, and blind, and naked.**" Philadelphia has not a word to say for itself. Laodicea has. In fact, in almost every respect these two churches stand out in sharp contrast. "Thou sayest." There was not only a self-satisfied condition in the Church, but the proud boast of it is here recorded: "Thou sayest, I am rich." The *city* could boast of its material wealth, the *Church* would equally boast of its riches. It has added, moreover, to its wealth: "Am grown rich." Without doubt the Church in Laodicea had influence, numbers, gifts, showy

* The definite article is inserted by Darby, Kelly, Plumtre, and others.

attainments, intellectual acquirements, and other attractive qualities, and in the possession of these it prided itself. Alas! these things at the expense of spirituality, of a true and fervent love to Christ, can only be regarded as a curse, and must sooner or later, if not repented of, end in judgment. In their own estimation "they had need of nothing." They had neither heart for Christ nor desire for His presence. They could boast while immediate judgment was announced (v. 16), and Christ the Church's life and glory was standing outside (v. 20). The Laodicean condition is the special danger in these days.

What is the Lord's estimate of its state? What is the sum and character of Laodicean wealth in His eyes? "Thou art the wretched (one) and the miserable (one)," besides being "poor, and blind, and naked." The definite article (omitted in the Authorised Version) adds considerably to the point and force of the Lord's judgment of Laodicea. "*The* wretched" and "*the* miserable," or "pitiable," the concentration of extreme misery, and the subject beyond all others of pity. They were poor, as destitute of true riches; blind to their state and to the Lord's glory; and naked, as destitute of divine righteousness. There is one other feature to complete the awful picture presented of this Christless Church: "AND KNOWEST NOT." Its actual condition before the Lord was absolutely unknown to it. Had there been the slightest recognition of its need there would have been hope. All was utter insensibility. Nothing, therefore, remained but loathsome rejection.

LAODICEA'S THREEFOLD CONDITION AND THE LORD'S THREEFOLD GRACE.

18.—**"I counsel thee to buy of Me gold purified by fire, that thou mayest be rich; and white garments, that thou mayest be clothed, and that the shame of thy nakedness may not be made manifest; and eye salve to anoint thine eyes, that thou mayest see."** The three main characteristic features of Laodicea were their poverty, their nakedness, and their blindness; and these are what the Lord, ever gracious, here offers to meet. He might have commanded, but no, He counsels, "buy of Me gold purified by fire." "Buy" need present no difficulty. Christ has the treasures of grace, the wealth of Heaven at His disposal. He fixes the terms on which He sells: "Ho, every one that thirsteth, come ye to the waters, and he that hath *no money*; come ye, buy, and eat; yea, come, buy wine and milk *without money*, and *without price*" (Isa. 55. 1). Your title to come, to buy, is your need and poverty. "Gold" purified or refined by fire points to divine righteousness, tested and tried; without it, oh, how poor! with it, how rich! "White garments" are declared to be the righteousness of saints, *i.e.*, their righteous deeds (Rev. 19. 8), which would cover their moral nakedness and the shame of it as well. "Eye salve" is for spiritual discernment.

THE LORD'S LAST APPEAL.

19.—"**I rebuke and discipline as many as I love; be zealous therefore and repent.**" The Lord does not, as some suppose, speak in the first member of our text of saints in Laodicea. He states a truth common to both Testaments (Prov. 3. 11, 12, and Heb. 12. 5, 6). The passage does not assert its application to any special class of saints. The Lord had just been speaking in tones of unusual severity. The circumstances called for it. The stern rebukes administered to the angel were to be followed by an act of irremediable judgment—"spued out." But for Christians, then and now, they were to know that the Lord's rebukes, and His still severer chastening, were the fruit of love, not of an arbitrary dealing as perchance by an earthly parent. "Be zealous therefore and repent." The Lord would rouse them out of the torpor and insensibility in which they were sunk. He would rekindle their interest. Has this exhortation to be "zealous and repent" reached the conscience of the Laodicean Church? It is the first step towards recovery. Has it been taken? By the mass, *no*. Thank God, individuals have given heed, and do hear the call to repent. But the general mass is drifting on, and Laodicea is now being fully developed as *the* characteristic Church state of to-day. The judgment of the professing christian body, as announced in verse 16, is inevitable and at hand.

CHRIST STANDS, KNOCKS, AND SPEAKS.

20.—"**Behold, I stand at the door, and am knocking; if any one hear My voice, and open the door, I will come in unto him, and sup with him, and he with Me.**" This touching and tender call has for centuries been the foundation of christian song and sermon. The last appeal addressed to the collective body is contained in verse 19; *this* is spoken to individuals only. Between the threat of rejection (v. 16) and its execution the Lord takes an outside place: "Behold, I stand at the door," thus *morally* disowning the professing christian body. The Lord both knocks and speaks. What a rich display of grace in the worst of circumstances! The Lord neither commands to buy (v. 18) nor forces an entrance. He counsels in the one case, and knocks in the other. "I stand, . . . and am knocking." It is a present and continuous action. The continuity of both actions is affirmed: He stands, He knocks. The Lord will not force His presence where and when it is not desired. To the disconsolate travellers to Emmaus "He made as though He would have gone further" (Luke 24. 28). They constrained Him to enter, saying, "Abide with us: for it is toward evening, and the day is far spent. And He went in to tarry with them." In the presence of Jesus risen all is changed. *He* becomes the host and *they* His guests (v. 30). "If any hear My voice, and open the door, I will come in unto him, and sup with him, and he with Me." It is the last season of communion ere the night of judgment dawns. It is essentially individual. If denied Church fellowship, how exceedingly sweet the promise! The voice here is not that of Christ in quickening power, nor is it the knocking of salvation at a sinner's heart. The word to sinners is, "I am the Door: by Me if any man enter in he shall be saved" (John 10. 9). They have not to knock, for it is an ever open door, and they have simply to enter in. To believers the word is, "Knock, and it shall be opened unto you" (Luke 11. 9). But in our text He continues standing and knocking. He wants *the* place in the hearts of His own. He will make a feast for us even now; together with Him we joy and rejoice, but He dispenses the joy.

PROMISE TO THE OVERCOMER.

21.—"**He that overcomes, to him will I give to sit with Me in My throne: as I also have overcome, and have sat down with My Father in His throne.**" The "throne" is the sign and symbol of royal authority and dominion. How did Jesus reach His Father's throne and sit down with Him in that exalted seat? Not by inherent right only! But by His life of patience and death for His Father's glory. The conqueror's path lies open to us. His example is our cheer. His footprints our guide-marks. The reward to the overcomer is undoubtedly a glorious one, but by no means exceeding those addressed to the Philadelphian conquerors. Association with Christ as Son of Man in His kingdom is here the promised blessing. The kingdom will be universal in extent (Psa. 72. 8; Zech. 14. 9; Psa. 8); righteous in administration (Psa. 72. 1-7; Psa. 45. 7; Isa. 32. 1); and everlasting in duration (Dan. 7. 27; 2 Peter 1. 11; Dan. 4. 34). Jerusalem on high will be the capital seat of the heavenly department of the kingdom (Rev. 21). Jerusalem on earth forms the metropolitan city of the kingdom here (Jer. 3. 17). The Laodicean conqueror is promised association with Christ in His kingdom and glory. Surely a rich and full reward for the brief if rough struggle in overcoming the Laodicean element environing us on every hand. But the contest must be maintained to the end.

Then follows the usual call to hear, which fitly brings these Church addresses to a close.

Introduction to the Third or Prophetic Division of the Apocalypse.

SEVEN CHURCH MESSAGES.

The letters to the churches constitute the second division of the Apocalypse: "The things that are." The Church on the earth existed in John's day, and continues till now. That is the simple explanation of what the Seer beheld in symbol (chap. 1. 20). Then the moral state of the Church, but in successive and partly concurrent stages of its history, is developed in seven messages (chaps. 2, 3). The epitome of Church history contained in these two chapters is invaluable. To have Heaven's light thrown on the state of things during the whole of this Church period of nigh two thousand years is a mercy almost second to none. What lessons are here gathered up! How needful the warnings in a day of moral relaxation! How strengthening the promises in seasons of weakness!

These Church messages were first of local application, but the narrow and restricted sphere to which they first applied would not suit their breadth of instruction. The truths and principles therein unfolded have their application to the utmost bounds of the professing Church. They are applicable both to individuals and to churches.

The constitution, order, and discipline of the Church formed a special feature of Paul's ministry. Luke in "The Acts" unfolds its history for fully thirty years, from Pentecost till the imprisonment of Paul in Rome. But it was reserved for the Seer of Patmos to further unfold that history from the close of the apostolic period till its loathsome rejection by the Lord.

THE FUTURIST AND HISTORICAL APPLICATION.

The prophetic part of the book commences with chapter 4 and closes with chapter 22. 5, and forms the third division: "The things that are about to be after these." Prophetic action, however, does not begin till chapter 6, the heavenly scenes recorded in chapters 4 and 5 being clearly introductory to the first series of judgments detailed in chapter 6. There has been all along a conflict between good and evil, between light and darkness, and these respective principles have been governed by equally opposing powers, the Spirit of God and Satan. Hence we can easily understand a partial fulfilment in present and past ages. But while frankly allowing this, as also a past and present resemblance to many events in the prophetic part of the Apocalypse, yet we insist on their full, exhaustive, and complete fulfilment in the coming crisis of at least seven years. The futurist application is undoubtedly the right one. The historical application is always more or less conjectural, and one in which scarcely two of its exponents are agreed. Its principle of interpretation is untenable. History is made the interpreter of prophecy. This or that event is supposed to be indicated under Seal, Trumpet, or Vial. We have two serious objections to the presentist view of the prophecies contained in this book: first, by far the larger number of God's people are poor and illiterate, and would be practically debarred from understanding them if a knowledge of history is essential thereto; second, prophecy according to this system is robbed of its present moral value, for how can that act on the soul which cannot be understood till after its fulfilment?

THE SAINTS CAUGHT UP BEFORE THE APOCALYPTIC JUDGMENTS.

Now between the *close* of chapter 3 and the *opening* of chapter 4, that is, between the second and third divisions of the book, the overcomers have been "caught up" and the mass "spued out," but the Seer does not record these events; he takes them for granted. Paul unfolds by revelation, and in considerable detail, the translation of the saints of Old and New Testament times (1 Thess. 4. 15-17). We state three incontrovertible proofs that the Lord's dead and living saints are caught up before the opening of the prophetic section of the Apocalypse (chap. 4).

(1) The Church is not on the earth during the period of the apocalyptic judgments, under which you find a body of Jews and Gentiles, but not the Church, which is composed of both. The word "Church" or its plural occurs about twenty times in the first three chapters, and it is neither named nor referred to in the rest of the book till chapter 22. 17, which, of course, resumes the present state of things,

and is in no sense part of the prophetic visions. What then is the unmistakable deduction from the fact that the Church is not on earth from chapter 4 till chapter 22. 5? Why, that it is in Heaven. Where else could it be?

(2) The three divisions of the Apocalypse do not overlap, nor are they concurrent. The wording of the 19th verse of the first chapter is simplicity itself. "Write therefore what thou hast seen," the vision of Christ just beheld by the Seer, "and the things that are," the seven churches then existing, "and the things that are about to be after these," when the Church is removed and the government of the world is in question. The Holy Ghost has Himself fixed the divisions of the book into a past, a present, and a future. "The things that are about to be *after these*" signifies that "the things that are" must have ceased. These divisions are successive. The third commences in chapter 4. 1, "I will show thee the things," prophetic visions, "which must take place after these things," *i.e.*, the Lord's dealing with the churches on earth. One set of things succeeds another.

(3) The whole situation is changed. It is not the Lord in the midst of the candlesticks or churches on earth, but the throne set in Heaven. One great fact of vital importance to the understanding of the book is that the saints of God are witnessed in Heaven in chapter 4 and right on till chapter 19, when they accompany the Lord out of Heaven for the judgment of the world (vv. 11-14). All through the apocalyptic judgments, and before they commence, the heavenly body of saints is seen in Heaven. How did they get there? It can only be satisfactorily explained on the assumption that the Rapture of 1 Thessalonians 4 had taken place. *That* event would necessarily close the Lord's dealings with the Church, bring to an end "the things that are," and pave the way for the new and prophetic state of which "the throne set in Heaven" is the fitting symbol. All this is simple and consistent, and seems to us graven on the surface of the book.

CHAPTER IV.

THE THRONE OF THE ETERNAL.

THE ENTIRE SITUATION CHANGED.

1.—"**After these things I saw, and behold a door opened in Heaven, and the first voice which I heard as of a trumpet speaking with me, saying, Come up here, and I will show thee the things which must take place after these things.**" We have here an entire change in the situation. The Seer is caught up from earth to Heaven. Chapters 2 and 3 trace the fortunes of the Church on earth. Chapters 4 and 5 describe scenes and events in Heaven of incomparable majesty. The history of the Church has been written, the overcomers have been translated to meet the Lord in the air, and the guilty mass of mere christian profession has been "spued out." Thus the removal of the Church makes room for the subjects of prophecy to occupy their allotted place.

1.—"**After these things**" marks a new commencement. The various Church states on earth are over. Prophetic scenes and visions are now to occupy the attention of the Seer. The words "after these things" intimate not only the sequence of the visions, but the events also which follow in natural order.

1.—"**A door opened in Heaven**" signifies that Heaven must be entered if prophecy is to be understood. It is there where the sources of everlasting good are found, where the coming scene of millennial and eternal blessedness is arranged and duly planned, and where, too, the preparatory judgments have their source. "A door opened in Heaven" enabled the Seer to pass in. "Heaven opened" is for the saints to pass out (Rev. 19. 11).

1.—"**The first voice**" does not refer to the first of a successive series, but is a plain reference to the voice of the Lord already heard (chap. 1. 10). *There* the voice was heard on earth; *here* it speaks from Heaven. The trumpet voice summons John from earth to Heaven. Scenes in Heaven are to be disclosed, and it is only there they can be seen. Prophecy has its source in Heaven, and hence the Seer must make Heaven his standpoint if the prophetic visions about to pass before his rapt gaze are to be divinely understood. It is in Heaven that the prophetic plan is mapped out, and it is there, far above the mists and clouds of earth, and the wrangles, jealousies, and pride of man, where alone we can discern the mind of God as to the future. The moral lesson for each servant of God is a needful one.

MORAL COMPETENCY OF THE SEER; THE THRONE AND THE SITTER THEREON

2, 3.—"**Immediately I became in (the) Spirit; and behold a throne stood in the Heaven, and upon the throne One sitting, and He (that was) sitting like in appearance to a stone (of) jasper and a sardius, and a rainbow round the throne like in appearance to an emerald.**" The divine summons "Come up here" brooks no delay. "*Immediately* I became in (the) Spirit." The vision of Christ as Son of Man in transcendent glory in the midst of the seven golden lamps was a sight too much for mortal gaze. The Seer for the time being was under the absolute control of the Spirit; he lived and moved in another mode of existence. "He became in (the) Spirit" (chap. 1. 10). But this cannot in the nature of things be prolonged. The state had lapsed. Now fresh visions, and of the future, are to be witnessed and written, so in full accord with their solemn character the Seer is again the vessel of the Spirit's power. "I became in (the) Spirit." The absence of the article before "Spirit" marks the state as a characteristic one. Visions of things in Heaven were witnessed by certain prophets on earth, but to the distinguished prophet of the New Testament alone were visions beheld in Heaven itself. To John only were these words addressed, "Come up here." The moral competency of the Seer to behold and grasp the coming prophetic situation was not in himself, but in a power outside the domain of nature. The Spirit once again laid hold of the human vessel, and entirely occupied it. John for the time lived in a new mode and sphere of existence in which human weakness and frailty had no place. The Spirit filled and controlled him.

2.—"**Behold a throne stood in the Heaven.**" This was the first sight beheld by the Seer in this new vision. The throne is the central subject in this heavenly scene. It is the sign and symbol of God's universal government. It "stood in the Heaven." The stability of that government is conveyed in the word "stood" or set; "the Heaven" fixes definitely and precisely the seat of royal authority. What a contrast to the tottering thrones of earth! Here, at the outset, is an intimation that Jehovah reigneth. The throne is our security and strength. It is, too, the great central fact in the universe. It is the pledge that the fiat of the Eternal shall compel obedience from every created being. It is the sign of order, of rule, of authority. The throne set in Heaven is in contrast to the mutability of all earthly governments.

The Sitter upon the throne is unnamed, but is described in general yet significant symbols. Two precious stones are named, the jasper and sardius, and by these the glory and majesty of God are reflected. His essential glory cannot, of course, be communicated even to the most exalted of creatures. God dwells in light unapproachable: "Whom no man hath seen, nor can see" (1 Tim. 6. 16). But what can be witnessed by creatures is displayed. The jasper and sardius are mentioned in the list of precious stones adorning the breastplate of the high priest of old (Exod. 28. 17-20,) the sardius being *first* named and the jasper last; they are also named amongst those to describe the glory of the typical king of Tyre (Ezek. 28. 13), the sardius again coming *first* and the jasper *sixth*. We again meet with those precious stones in the description of the holy Jerusalem in governmental authority and glory towards the millennial world (Rev. 21. 19, 20), the jasper *first* and the sardius *sixth*. Is there no significance in the fact that in these three lists of precious stones—the reflectors of God in grace, in creation, and in glory—the numerical order is changed? Is this a mere coincidence or the evidence of design in inspiration? Of the latter assuredly. The brilliancy of the jasper and the deep red hue of the sardius reflect the glory and surpassing splendour of God in so far as these could be displayed. The glory of God, too, as symbolised by the jasper is the *light* (Rev. 21. 11), the *security* (v. 18), and the *foundation* (v. 19) of the Church or bride in future governmental display.

The Seer next proceeds, "And a rainbow round the throne like in appearance to an emerald."

The throne in vastness and majesty is one befitting the Lord of hosts. Encircled with a rainbow it is a witness that in the exercise of absolute sovereignty, of all-ruling power, God will graciously remember in covenant mercy His creatures. It is a sign to all in Heaven that God delights in goodness.

The complete, unbroken circle round the throne proclaims the truth, "His mercy endureth for ever." The bow set in the cloud of old, with its prismatic colours and varied beauties, is the token of God's covenant with the earth (Gen. 9. 9-17). It is rarely seen as a complete circle, but generally as an arch, or half-circle, and is God's object lesson for the race, a public sign hung out in the heavens that all may see and learn that God is good, a lesson from God and of God to men. In the last notice of the rainbow it is seen over the head of the Lord when in power He asserts His claim to the earth. He will sweep the defiled scene with the besom of destruction, but even then the old appointed token of divine goodness reappears (Rev. 10. 1). Instead of the combination of colours to which we are accustomed in the rainbow the heavenly one over the throne is "like in appearance to an emerald." The beautiful green, the characteristic colour of the vegetable world, and the only one which never tires the eye, is the chosen colour of the rainbow beheld by the Seer. The glorified saints will have constantly before their never-tiring gaze the rainbow in its entirety; the remembrance of God's grace to the earth even when He is about to deal with the race in judgment.

THE ROYAL AUTHORITY OF THE REDEEMED.

4.—**"And round the throne twenty-four thrones, and on the thrones twenty-four elders sitting, clothed with white garments; and on their heads golden crowns."** The thrones and crowns point to a royal company of redeemed and glorified saints in Heaven, clearly not before, but after, the resurrection (1 Cor. 15. 23). *Spirits* sitting, clothed and crowned, is an incongruous thought, and one entirely foreign to Scripture. Grouped round the vast throne in Heaven are twenty-four thrones of which the authority and stability are derived from, and sustained by, the measureless throne of the Eternal. "Seats," as in the Authorised Version, is a feeble and inadequate thought. The word "throne" is connected with a royal personage; "seat" with a private person.

These twenty-four elders, or chiefs, represent the general body of the redeemed then in Heaven. They play an important part in the scenes recorded and visions beheld from chapter 4 to chapter 19, where in verse four the last notice of them is recorded.* The elders are a distinct company from the beasts or living creatures, and from the angels. In chapter 5 the action of the elders, as distinguished from that of angels, makes it impossible to regard them as one and the same; verse 11 distinguishes by title the three companies. The elders *sing* (v. 9), the angels *say* (v. 12). The angels are never numbered (Heb. 12. 22), the elders are. Six times the representative number "twenty-four" occurs. Angels are not said to be crowned, the elders are.

* "Elders" as a term occurs twelve times. The varied actions and services in which they take part show clearly enough that they are the representatives of the redeemed and risen saints. They are enthroned; fall down and worship; one of them comforts the weeping Seer and interprets the mind of Heaven; they have harps and vials of incense; they sing (never said of angels); are the nearest company to the throne and to the Lamb; intelligently explain as to the redeemed on earth; celebrate the millennial and eternal triumph of God; and add their "amen" and "hallelujah" to the judgment of the whore—the corruptress of the earth. The passages where the word is found are as follows: chapters 4. 4, 10; 5. 5, 6, 8, 11, 14; 7. 11, 13; 11. 16; 14. 3; 19. 4.

The choral praise of Heaven, in harp and song, seems the peculiar function of the elders. Heavenly intelligence, especially in themes and subjects connected with redemption, is ascribed to the elders and not to angels. By the elders we understand, therefore, the innumerable company of the redeemed saints, raised and changed, and caught up to meet Christ in the air (1 Thess. 4. 17). Their crowns and thrones betoken their royal dignity; the harp and song their joy in worship, while their robes and vials point to priestly character and action. But why "*twenty-four?*" The significance of the numeral must be sought for in the first book of Chronicles 24, 25. David divided the priesthood into twenty-four orders or courses, each course serving in turn (Luke 1. 5, 8, 9). The respective elders or chiefs of these courses would represent the whole of the Levitical priesthood. There would thus be twenty-four chief priests and one high priest.* Their varied service corresponded to that of the elders in Heaven, for the temple (no less than the tabernacle) in structure, vessels, and services was framed according to things in the heavens. God's people are termed "an *holy* priesthood" (1 Peter 2. 5) and "a *royal* priesthood" (v. 9), and in both characters they are here seen in action.

The white garments indicate the purity and priestly character of the elders. "On their heads golden crowns" bespeak their royal dignity. Every redeemed and risen saint will be crowned; this is in no wise a distinctive crown peculiar to some, but intimates royal dignity and authority common to all the heavenly saints.

THE THRONE THE CENTRE OF ACTION AND INTEREST.

5, 6.—"**And out of the throne go forth lightnings, and voices, and thunders; and seven lamps of fire burning before the throne, which are the seven Spirits of God; and before the throne as a glass sea like crystal. And in the midst of the throne and around the throne four living creatures full of eyes before and behind.**" Having had the relation of the saints to the throne as surrounding it, and their royal authority derived from and dependent upon it, we have next the action of the throne itself. "Out" of it, not "from" it, issue the precursors of coming judgment, "lightnings, and

* Josephus, the Jewish historian, informs us that his family was "of the first course of the four and twenty"—no mean order. Some understand the twenty-four to represent the governmental number "twelve," thus signifying the sum of Old Testament saints as one body, and the sum of New Testament saints as another body of believers—thus the two twelves. We deem it unwarrantable to break up the symbol in this manner. We are satisfied however that the reference in the "twenty-four" is to 1 Chronicles 24, 25.

voices, and thunders.'' It has been said that ''the book hardly ever alludes to anything not Biblical,'' and we may add that the author of the Apocalypse assumes that the reader is tolerably acquainted with the previous parts of the sacred volume, and, further, that every symbol with which the book abounds may be interpreted and understood from its use in some part or other of the sacred Scriptures. *On no account seek the interpretation of any part of the Apocalypse outside the covers of your Bible. The meaning of every symbol must be sought for in the Word itself.* The threefold intimation of immediate judgment is eminently fitted to strike terror into the hearts of the guilty on earth. The throne is about to assert itself in power. God is preparing to break out in judgment and deal with the high-handed iniquity in the coming crisis lying between the Translation of the heavenly saints and their subsequent Return from Heaven. These signs of judicial dealing are Jehovah's premonitory intimations of His power in judgment (Psa. 29. 3-5). The same signs, with some additions, are mentioned in connection with the promulgation of the law (Exod. 19). The effect on the people is also stated, ''All the people that were in the camp trembled'' (v. 16). How much more widespread and alarming will these tokens of wrath be felt in a scene of almost unmixed evil governed by Satan!

5.—''**Seven lamps of fire burning before the throne**'' denote the fulness of the Spirit in governmental action. The Spirit here is not viewed as saving men through the preaching of the Gospel, nor in any of His varied services in the Church, but is here witnessed in moral keeping with the throne itself. Everything inconsistent with the absolute purity of the throne must be judged; hence the Spirit is here viewed in connection with the righteous character of the throne. ''Those seven (spiritual *perfection*) lamps of fire will search out and expose all contrary to the holy nature of God'' (compare with chap. 1. 4; and Isa. 11. 2).

6.—''**And before the throne as a glass sea like crystal**.'' The typology of the Old Testament enters largely into the structure of the Apocalypse. Here there seems an evident allusion to the laver in the tabernacle (Exod. 30. 18-21), and perhaps more directly to the molten sea in the temple (1 Kings 7. 23-37), both for priestly purification. But the sea of *glass* points to a fixed state of holiness, of purity inward and outward, while ''before the throne'' would indicate that the purity is in keeping with the holy character of the throne itself. ''**Like** crystal."* The clearness and beauty of that scene of holiness spread out before the throne are signified by the crystal. The two symbols, glass and crystal, are nearly allied, but are not quite the same. The former is a manufactured article, the latter is a native production. Thus the "glass" of the sea points to a settled state of purity, while the "crystal" intimates that the state is one according to God in His holy nature. The *divine* idea is connected with the employment of this latter symbol (Ezek. 1. 22; Rev, 21. 11; 22. 1). The sea of glass is again referred to in chapter 15, but "mingled with fire," expressive of the fiery ordeal, out of which the martyrs emerge. *They* stand on the sea of glass; *here* it is unoccupied.

The Seer next describes another class of beings, beasts rather, *living ones*, distinct, too, from the elders and angels, and more closely connected with the throne than either.

6.—"**In the midst of the throne**" shows that they are an integral part of it, "and around the throne" that they are externally connected with it. That is, the living creatures (not beasts) may be viewed either as vitally connected with the judicial authority of God, or as apart from, yet in relation to it. Intuitive intelligence, fulness of spiritual discernment, seems to be the force of the words "full of eyes before and behind."

THE LIVING CREATURES AND THEIR WORSHIP.

7, 8.—"**The first living creature like a lion, and the second living creature like a calf, and the third living creature having the face as of a man, and the fourth living creature like a flying eagle. And the four living creatures, each one of them having respectively six wings; round and within they are full of eyes; and they cease not, day and night, saying, Holy, holy, holy, Lord God Almighty, Who was, Who is, and Who is to come.**" Why "**four**" living ones? Because "four" represents the attributes of God in judicial dealing with man and creation. It is the signature of the world and of the race, and is employed when universality is in question. The representatives, or heads of the animal creation, are named as the lion for majesty, the ox (calf) for patient endurance, the man for intelligence, and the eagle for rapidity of action. Now these symbols express certain features in the exercise of divine government, and are fittingly introduced here in view of the immediate exercise

* "A sea of glass expressive of smoothness and brightness; and this heavenly sea is of crystal, declaring that the calm of Heaven is not, like earthly seas, ruffled by winds but is crystallised into an eternity of peace."—*Wordsworth*.

of these divine attributes. The whole scene under Heaven is to be visited in judgment; hence the employment of the numeral "four."* Thus in the four living creatures grouped together we have a complete and perfect view of God's judicial government. The symbols are taken from the most prominent animals, not from those in the sea. The first attribute of God's throne symbolised by a lion is majesty, strength, omnipotence (Gen. 49. 9; Dan. 7. 4; Amos 3. 8). The second symbol is an ox or calf in patient labour, assiduously working for the good of others (1 Cor. 9. 9, 10; Prov. 14. 4). The third creature had the face as of a man, denoting intelligence or reason (Job 9. 24; Ezra 9. 6). The fourth symbol of a flying eagle intimates keen sight and rapid action (Deut. 28. 49; Job 9. 26; Hab. 1. 8; Job 39. 27-30). Now these characteristics combined express the character of God's throne in relation to the earth. They are attributes of a judicial nature exercised through human or angelic instruments according to the sovereign pleasure of God. The living creatures represent the judicial authority of the throne. From the first mentioned of the cherubim (Gen. 3. 24) till the last (Heb. 9. 5) the same leading thought characterises all the passages, namely, the attributes of God's government.†

The differences between the living creatures of Ezekiel chapter 1, the cherubim in chapters 9 and 10 of the same

* "The numerals 'three' and 'four' significantly express the *divine* and the *human*. There are *three* persons in the Godhead. *Three* times the seraphim announce the holiness of God, crying, 'Holy, holy, holy, is the Lord of hosts' (Isa. 6. 3). *Three* times the living creatures say 'Holy' (Rev. 4. 8). Jehovah's relationship to time and eternity is expressed in a *three* fold way, 'which was, and is, and is to come' (v. 8). There are *three* specified temptations of our Lord (Luke 4). *Three* times our Lord on earth was publicly owned by God (Matt. 3. 17; 17. 5; John 12. 28). On the *third* day the Lord was raised. The darkness which gathered round the cross and over the land lasted *three* hours. Faith, hope, and love are the *three* cardinal christian virtues. Christ announces Himself in *three* characters, as the Way, the Truth, and the Life. The divine blessing is *three* times expressed (Num. 6. 23, 24). 'Three' is the signature of God. 'Four' is the signature of the world. *Four* divisions of the race, 'nations, and kindreds, and peoples, and tongues' (Rev. 7. 9). *Four* elements. *Four* winds. *Four* seasons. *Four* presentations of Christ in the Gospels. *Four* living creatures. *Four* universal empires (Dan. 7). *Four* great offerings, as the burnt offering (Lev. 1), the meal or flour offering (Lev. 2), the peace or communion offering (Lev. 3), and the sin offering (Lev. 4). God's *four* sore judgments (Ezek. 14. 21). *Four* women in the Lord's human genealogy (Matt. 1). The brazen altar had *four* sides and *four* horns. The golden altar had *four* sides and *four* horns. 'Four' is the signature of man and generally of the material creation.

"The old Rabbinical writers assert that the four standards for the tribes of Israel, round which they were ordered to pitch their tents on each side of the tabernacle, as in Numbers 2. 2, were as follows: for the tribe of Judah—a lion; for the tribe of Ephraim—an ox; for the tribe of Reuben—a man; for the tribe of Dan—an eagle."—"Notes on the Revelation," by F. Brodie.

Hengstenberg quotes an old Jewish saying: "There are four which take the first place in this world: Man among the creatures, the eagle among birds, the ox among cattle, and the lion among wild beasts."

† It has been sought to identify the cherubim and the living creatures with the Church, but this far-fetched idea cannot for a moment be entertained, for two reasons: first, the cherubim were fashioned out of the *same* piece of gold which formed the mercy-seat—the gold signifies Christ as *divine*, as the wood of the shittah tree sets forth His holy and incorruptible *humanity*; now we are not, and could not be, united to Him as God. The cherubim were *not* united to the mercy-seat, although they formed a part of it. Second, the judicial character of the cherubim would forbid the application to the Church, which is here to display the grace of God, not His judicial ways.

prophet, and the living creatures of the Apocalypse are numerous and interesting. In the description furnished by the prophet of the captivity each of the four living ones had four faces and four wings (chap. 1. 6). The apocalyptic Seer depicts only the third living creature with a man's face, and each of the four with six wings (chap. 4. 7, 8). *There* they had wheels; *here* they have none. *There* the throne was above them; *here* they are in the midst of it and also around it. *There* they were full of eyes, the "whole body, and their backs, and their hands, and their wings, and the wheels were full of eyes round about" (Ezek. 10. 12); *here* they are "full of eyes before and behind" and also "within." Many of these differences may be accounted for by the fact that the judgment of Judah and Jerusalem is specially treated of in Ezekiel, and as that judgment was to come from the north (Babylon), the wheels would run on earth as presenting the course of earthly judgment, whereas the living ones here are not yet seen in action; they are the ministers of the throne. In judicial activity they act from Heaven; hence wings and not wheels. Besides, a much more extended sphere of judgment is presented by the Seer than Judah and its guilty capital, Jerusalem, for the whole earth is about to tremble under the action of the throne.

The care of the cherubim is for the public, governmental *glory* of God (Ezek. 10). The care of the seraphim is for the *holiness* of God; these latter are named but once in Scripture (Isa. 6). The living creatures of the Apocalypse are a combination of both cherubim and seraphim.

Each of the four living creatures had "six wings." The seraphim of Isaiah (chap. 6. 2) had "six wings" each, two to cover face and feet respectively, and two for rapidity of action. The living creatures beheld by the prophet of the captivity had each "four wings" (Ezek. 1. 5, 6). The numeral "four" is largely employed in that chapter because the earthly government of God is in question. The "six wings" in each of the living creatures in the Apocalypse denote an activity beyond the powers of nature—supernatural activity.

8.—"**Full of eyes within**" signify inward spiritual perception of the governmental purposes and acts of God. In the previous part of the description the eyes are also said to be "before and behind" (v. 6). The future and the past come equally within the range of the perceptive faculties of the living creatures.

Having given a description of the living creatures the Seer next describes their worship. In this blessed and happy exercise there is no relaxation: "They cease not day and night." There is no imperfection in their service; neither lassitude nor weakness characterise their worship. Unceasingly they worship, saying, "Holy, holy, holy, Lord God Almighty, Who was, Who is, and Who is to come." We may here remark that in two respects the living creatures resemble the seraphim; in the number of wings and in the threefold ascription of worship (compare with Isa. 6). The works of God praise Him, but deeper still His attributes declare His holy, holy, holy nature, *i.e.*, what He is in Himself. The titles of the Deity here grouped and the respective truths connected with each are ceaselessly celebrated. The very powers which execute the righteous behests of the throne (chap. 6) here glorify Him in His divine Being. The living creatures symbolically represent the several attributes named, and "*give* glory and honour and thanksgiving to Him that sits upon the throne."

The divine titles are LORD, or Jehovah, the self-existing One; God in relation to creation; the Almighty in grace, power, and in "sustaining resources." In addition to these the divine Being is also celebrated as the God of the ages, Who was, is, and is to come. For this latter, *i.e.*, what God is in His own proper Being and nature, see chapter 1. 4. Here "Who *was*" precedes the term of independent and eternal existence "Who *is*"—this latter is first stated in the earlier reference. Thus the four living creatures worship God.

THE WORSHIP OF THE LIVING CREATURES, AND THE FULLER WORSHIP OF THE ELDERS.

9-11.—"**And when the living creatures shall give glory and honour and thanks to Him that sits upon the throne, Who lives to the ages of ages, the twenty-four elders shall fall before Him that sits upon the throne, and shall worship Him that lives to the ages of ages; and shall cast their crowns before the throne, saying, Thou art worthy, O our Lord and (our) God, to receive glory, and honour, and power; for Thou hast created all things, and for Thy will they were, and they have been created.**" Each of the living creatures is a characteristic symbol in itself of one or more of the divine attributes, and now the four unite, before they are witnessed in governmental action, in yielding to Him the glory, honour, and thanks due to His Name. They have announced, as we have seen, His essential purity in the threefold repetition of the word "Holy," now their doxology (v. 9), as that of the elders (v. 11), is threefold. Another feature as distinguishing the more profound worship of the elders from that of the living creatures is that the former directly address God in the second person; whereas the living creatures speak of God in the third person. It is important to observe that whoever may be the instruments, angels or men, in exercising the judicial authority of the throne, of which the living creatures are here the symbolical representatives, all must turn to Him in increased power and fulness. The doxology of the living creatures furnishes proof of this.

The worship of the elders is of a different character to that of the living ones. Theirs is the worship of redeemed persons, who, as having the mind of Christ (1 Cor. 2. 16), enter intelligently into the thoughts of God, and who know Him personally in His holiness and love. It is the worship of persons whose hearts have been won by His exceeding great love, and whose consciences have been cleansed by faith in the divine testimony to the precious blood of Christ.

"The saints here fall down before the throne, bow themselves before His place in glory, and worship Him in His endless being, and lay down their given glory before His supreme and proper glory, ascribing all glory to Him as alone worthy of it; but here, according to the nature of the celebration of it, the Creator for Whom all things are. In all changes these remain true. It will be remarked here that the living creatures only celebrate and declare; the elders worship with understanding. All through the Revelation the elders give their reason for worshipping. There is spiritual intelligence in them."*

It will be observed that in the declaration of the living creatures we have glory, honour, and *thanks*; in that of the elders it is glory, honour, and *power*. Further, the elders fall down before HIM Whom they love and reverence, and cast their crowns before the THRONE in the recognition of that from which their royal dignity is derived and sustained.†

The creatorial glory of God is here the ground of worship by the elders. "For Thy will they were," that is, all things exist according to His will or sovereign pleasure, "and they have been created." He caused them to exist, He is the origin and source of all creation. The worship here is grounded on the knowledge of God, what He is in His own Being and as Creator and Sustainer of the universe.

---

* "Synopsis of the Books of the Bible," vol. 5, p. 595.

† "The impressive nature of the scene presented in chapter 4 cannot but strike the mind of every intelligent reader. The holy Seer was duly prepared by such an august vision for the disclosures which follow; and the mind of the reader can hardly fail to be prepared also to look for them with deep interest. It cannot escape even the most unobserving how greatly this whole scene resembles the inaugural theophanies in Isaiah 6 and Ezekiel 1."—"A Commentary on the Apocalypse," by Moses Stewart, p. 514.

The first and fundamental claim of God on His creatures is this necessary recognition of His power and glory, creating and upholding all—men and angels, things animate and inanimate, of all in the celestial and terrestrial realms. The first subject revealed in the Scriptures is that of creation, and the first, moreover, in which faith is demanded (Heb. 11. 3). The worship in the next chapter is founded on redemption by blood, and hence the Lamb necessarily becomes the central figure. The throne itself is the prominent subject in our chapter; the Lamb in connection with the throne that of chapter 5.

The chapter we have been considering is one replete with interest. The main subject presented in vision being the throne of the Eternal, the guarantee that He governs the universe according to the truth of His nature. The throne, too, "set" or established in "the Heaven" on the fixed basis of eternal righteousness is the pledge of permanence and security. While "upon the throne ONE sitting," only one, intimates that there shall be no change of kings, no transference of the sovereign power, no succession; "sitting," not "sat," no vacation and no interregnum. There is no song in the chapter, no vision of a slain Lamb, and no mention of the blood of sacrifice; these are characteristic features of the next chapter, and hence, because of their absence here, the chapter is not so frequently read as chapter 5. But the throne, with its symbolic glories, its accessories and surroundings, invests this chapter with profound interest, which deepens the more carefully it is read and studied.

CHAPTER V

The Throne and the Slain Lamb

CONNECTION BETWEEN CHAPTERS 4, 5, and 6

In the previous chapter is witnessed the vast and glorious throne of the Eternal, the symbol of the governing power of God throughout the universe. Round it all persons and things are grouped in their respective positions. The main thought of the chapter is God the sovereign Ruler of all creation governing according to His nature and on the basis of eternal righteousness. It is not a portion of the divine Word which calls forth the affections of the soul. It is a vision which absorbs rather our being as creatures. The vision remains, the scenery is not changed, nor is the glory in anywise dimmed as the additional truths contained in chapter 5 come before us.

There is an intimate connection between chapters 4, 5, and 6. The first series of judgments is noted in chapter 6. The great actor is the Lamb, while the throne as seen in chapter 4 is the source of the judgments. We have here a continuation of the vision already beheld by the Seer, with two prominent and additional features, namely, the seven-sealed book, and a Lamb as slain. We may remark that in this chapter, preparatory to the proper action of the book, namely, JUDGMENT, the majesty of the lion and the meekness of the Lamb are combined, and centre in Him Who alone is worthy to bear these double glories.

This grand chapter is divided into four parts, the first two being introduced by the words "I saw" (vv. 1, 2); the second two parts are each prefaced with "I beheld" (vv. 6, 11). In brief, the subjects are: first, *the book*; second, *the challenge*; third, *the song*; fourth, *the worship*.

THE SEVEN-SEALED BOOK

1.—"**And I saw on the right hand of Him that sat upon the throne a book, written within and on the back, sealed with seven seals.**" This book or roll is, of course, a symbol. The book of life (chaps. 3. 5; 13. 8) is a register of *names*; the books of works (chap. 20. 12) are the divine records of human *actions*. But the book beheld by the Seer contains in full THE REVELATION OF GOD'S PURPOSE AND COUNSEL CONCERNING THE WORLD. It contains the history of the future, and gives us the successive steps needful for the inauguration of the world-kingdom of Christ. God is about to bring again His First-Begotten into the world amidst the acclaim of angels (Heb. 1. 6), and the seven-sealed roll unfolds *how* this will be brought about. The contents of the book cover the period from the breaking of the first seal (chap. 6) till the close of the kingdom reign and commencement of the eternal state (chap. 11. 18).

The book lay *on* the right hand of the Eternal. The position of the roll was in fitting accord with the proclamation of the angel (v. 2); in itself a challenge to the universe to produce one of sufficient worth to approach the place of distinguished honour (Psa. 110. 1; Eph. 1. 20) and take the book.

The book or roll was "written within and on the back,"* thus signifying that the *whole* counsel of God respecting this world was herein unfolded; no further revelation of God's purposes was to be vouchsafed. This book was fully written (compare with Ezek. 2. 10).

1.—"**Sealed with seven seals.**" Each seal closes a certain portion of the book; hence the contents are successively revealed as the seals are opened in order. But the whole is absolutely hidden from men and angels till opened by the Lamb. The "seven seals" express the perfection with which the hidden counsels of God are securely wrapped up in the divine mind till their open disclosure by the Lamb. The prophet Daniel (chap. 12. 4) was instructed to "shut up the words and seal the book even to the time of the end;" whereas the Seer of Patmos (Rev. 22. 10) is told the exact opposite, "Seal not the sayings of the prophecy of this book, for the time is at hand." The former was to seal; the latter was not to seal. Even Daniel, distinguished above all his contemporaries for the many and far-reaching revelations and visions granted him, says: "I heard, but I *understood not*" (chap. 12. 8, 9). Now, however, that we have reached "the *time* of the end," not exactly "the end," all is open. The book of prophecy is completely and openly revealed. For us the seven-sealed book, with its full and minute disclosure of the future, is no longer a hidden mystery. Prophecy, once a secret, is so no longer.

THE CHALLENGE OF THE ANGEL.

2, 3.—"**And I saw a strong angel proclaiming with a loud voice, Who (is) worthy to open the book, and to break its seals? And no one was able in the Heaven, or upon the earth, or underneath the earth, to open**

* Some would punctuate the clause thus: "written within, and on the backside sealed with seven seals," but where else could it be sealed save on the back? Why state that? It was customary to fill up a scroll and continue the writing on the back. The roll beheld by Ezekiel (chap. 2. 10) was, we are expressly informed, "written within and without." The fulness and completeness of the prophetic announcements about to be unfolded seem the thought designed in the scroll being written on both sides.

the book, or to regard it." The attention of the moral and intelligent universe is to be directed to the book resting on the open palm of the Throned One. The angels "excel in strength" (Psa. 103. 20), but their might is exercised only in the path of instant obedience to the will of the Creator. Each one of the countless myriads of the angelic hosts is held in dependence upon Him Whose will is their happy service. All angels are strong, but there are measures, and ranks, and orders amongst them. There are prominent angels amongst their fellows, as Gabriel, Michael, etc.* The loud voice of one of those angels of power penetrates to the utmost bounds of the universe, searching "the Heaven," the dwelling place of God; "the earth," the dwelling place of men; and "underneath the earth," the abode of other intelligent beings. Those three terms indicate the extent of the universe. Everywhere and to every being the angel's voice reaches.

2.—"**Who is worthy to open the book, and to break its seals**?" Moral competency to answer to the angelic proclamation there was not. The universe in all its parts—"The three kingdoms of creation" (Phil. 2. 10)—does not possess *one* being competent to disclose and execute the counsels of God; "no man," reads the Authorised Version; "no one," a term of much wider import, rightly reads the Revised. To "*open* the book and to *break* its seals" are regarded as separate actions. The natural order would have been to first break the seals in order that the book might be opened. The import of the angel's proclamation, however, is to open the book so as to unfold its contents; and the breaking of the seals, their execution as in chapter 6. The moral force of the acts is the point in question. The challenge is unanswered. The undertaking required moral worth and a proved capacity not found in any created being.

THE WORTHINESS OF THE LAMB.

4, 5.—"**And I wept much because no one had been found worthy to open the book nor to regard it. And one of the elders says to me, Do not weep. Behold, the Lion which (is) of the tribe of Judah, the Root of David, has overcome (so as) to open the book and its seven seals.**" The grief of the Seer is emphasised by the use of the pronoun "I," which is emphatic in the Greek. "*I* wept much." John is here regarded as the representative of the prophetic feeling at "the time of the end," or

* "Michael the Archangel" (Jude 9). Scripture never speaks of "Archangels." Jewish writers divide the angelic hosts into orders and classes as "Thrones, Dominations, Virtues, Princedoms, Powers," to which division Ephesians 1. 21 evidently alludes. In the region of the supernatural the unseen ministers of the divine will guide, control, and in every way influence human affairs. They are God's ministers.

"the last days." His soul is stirred within him as his eye rests on the sealed scroll lying on the open hand of the Sitter on the throne, with no one in the vast creation of God competent to disclose its contents and carry them into execution. The tears of John have been termed "the weakness of the creature," but if "wept much" is sometimes the expression of weakness, it is equally the expression of a right and godly feeling. It has been remarked, "Without tears the Revelation was not written, neither without tears can it be understood." But the book was to be opened. And since worship of the highest order and an intimate knowledge of the mind of God are characteristics of the crowned and glorified elders or representatives of the redeemed, it is one of these elders who consoles the weeping Seer by directing his attention to One in every respect qualified to unfold the divine counsels and carry them to a triumphant issue. Who is He? The Lion of the tribe of Judah, the Root of David. What has He done? He has overcome every spiritual power by His death on the cross. Thus He has an unchallenged right in Himself, and because, too, of what He has done, to advance to the right hand of the Eternal, take the book, and effectuate the counsels of God.

5.—"**The Lion of the tribe of Judah**" (Gen. 49. 9). The dying patriarch, however keen his spiritual vision, could not have dreamed that his glorious prediction (vv. 8-10) pointed to the advent of the Messiah nearly 4000 years afterwards, Who in irresistible might, majesty, and sovereignty would secure the blessing of Israel and of the whole earth. In His lion-like character He crushes every opposing force, and establishes His universal kingdom on the ruin of all opposition. Here worth and might are combined.

5.—But another title is here used of our Lord: "**The Root of David**." Why David? Why not Moses, or Abraham? David is the representative of *Royalty*. Moses the expression of *Law*. Abraham the depositary of *Promise*. Now these two chapters (4 and 5) have as their main subject the kingdom rights and glories of Christ. Thrones and crowns are frequently referred to, and in fact characterise this sublime portion of the Apocalypse. Hence, the introduction of the kingdom being *the* question, David is fittingly named. Christ is both the *Root* and *Offspring* of David (chap. 22. 16). He is the former as *Divine*, and the latter as *Man*. He is both Root and Branch (Isa. 11).

In verse 4 the words in the Authorised Version "and to read" are rightly omitted in the Revised.

VISION OF THE SLAIN LAMB.

6, 7.—**"And I saw in the midst of the throne and of the four living creatures, and in the midst of the elders a Lamb standing as slain, having seven horns and seven eyes, which are the seven Spirits of God (which are) sent into all the earth: and He came and took (it) out of the right hand of Him that sat upon the throne."** The Seer "wept much." The elders, heads of the heavenly priesthood, knew and could divinely interpret the mind of God. What was dark to John was light to them; what was cause of sorrow to him was gladness to them. One of the elders directed the attention of the weeping Seer to One Who, in majesty and resistless might, had besides personal and acquired rights which would entitle Him to disclose and effectuate the counsels of God. But when John looked he beheld a "lamb"* instead of a "lion." Seeming weakness instead of majesty.

In the midst of the heavenly scene stood a Lamb as slain. The wound prints in Him as risen beheld by the disciples (John 20. 20, 25, 27) are now seen by John in Him glorified. The memories of Calvary are treasured in Heaven.† John the *baptist* first pointed out Jesus on earth as the "Lamb of God" (John 1. 29-36); John the *apostle* now beholds Him in that same character on high. But how different the position! *There*, wounded and slain (Isa. 53); *here*, the centre of Heaven's strength and glory, yet bearing in His Person the marks and scars of the cross.

The "Lamb *standing*" between the throne and the elders is the first step to the assumption of the inheritance. He is about to take to Himself His great power and reign. At present He sits with His Father in His throne (Rev. 3. 21), and with Jehovah at His right hand (Psa. 110. 1). But the session of patience is seen by the Seer to be at an end. The Lamb vacates the "throne" and "right hand," and *stands* ready to act. *Standing* intimates readiness for action; *sitting* refers to a state of quiescence.

6.—**"Having seven horns and seven eyes, which are the seven Spirits of God sent into all the earth."** Here the mystic number "seven," denoting *perfection*, is thrice repeated. Strength and intelligence are denoted by the "horns" and "eyes," and the fulness of administration of the Holy Spirit in government in the "seven Spirits of God." All are perfect, and all connected with the government of the earth which is about to be asssumed by the Lamb in His redemption character "as slain."

* The term *lamb* occurs in the Apocalypse twenty-eight times; the word employed signifies a diminutive animal *Arnion*, not *Amnos*, as in the Gospel (chap. 1. 29, etc.). The word *lion* is only once applied to Christ in this book.

† We see no difficulty in supposing that in the glorified body of our blessed Lord the indelible marks and scars of the cross will be seen (John 20. 20-27).

The Lamb advanced and took the book "out of the right hand of Him that sat upon the throne." What a combination of glories and rights centre in God's beloved One! The majesty and might of the Lion, the meekness and sacrificial character of the Lamb, combined with all power and intelligence, are conspicuously displayed in the Person of the glorious One beheld by the Seer. Then how severely simple the words in which the majestic action is narrated. The opening of the seven-sealed roll on the hand of Jehovah intimates an undertaking of such a momentous character that the cross alone surpasses it, a work involving the glory of God and the blessing of creation, and one in which the whole universe is directly interested (vv. 11-14). "He came and took (it) out of the right hand of Him that sat upon the throne." Neither the pencil of the artist nor the pen of the historian is needed here. The artless simplicity of the account is God-like. "Simple and majestic, without any pomp of words, or any effort to decorate the scene," writes Moses Stuart. "How calm and sublime," says F. W. Grant. And with these testimonies we are in full accord.

THE LIVING ONES AND ELDERS; THE NEW SONG

8-10.—"**And when He took the book, the four living creatures and the twenty-four elders fell before the Lamb, having each a harp and golden bowls full of incenses, which are the prayers of the saints. And they sing a new song, saying, Thou art worthy to take the book, and to open its seals, because Thou hast been slain, and hast redeemed to God by Thy blood out of every tribe, and tongue, and people, and nation, and made them to our God kings and priests, and they shall reign over the earth.**" In the previous chapter Jehovah in the greatness and eternity of His Being, as also in His relation to all creation as its Lord, its Sustainer, and Creator, evokes the profound worship of the living ones and elders. No angels are mentioned as taking part in the worship. But here we have as the centre of Heaven's worship THE SLAIN LAMB, and accordingly all creation is stirred to its depths. There are additional features of *heart* interest, added grounds and reasons of worship, not found when Jevhoah, as such, is in view. The slain Lamb brings before us the holy Sufferer of earth given up to insult and wrong, rejected and crucified, uttering no word of reproach, nor exercising power on His own behalf save the passive might to suffer. Now all is blessedly changed. The Lamb once stood in the midst of the ribald band (Matt. 27. 27-31) silent, meek, unresisting, alone in holiness, in calm dignity, enduring to the utmost the mean and cruel contempt of the ferocious men around Him, who rained their blows on His defenceless head, bowed before Him the mocking knee, covered Him with their disgusting spittle, crowned and pierced Him with the prickly thorn, thrust a reed into His bound hands, stripped Him, and with blow and taunt indulged their vile and depraved nature. Silent and patient in His agony He stood in the midst. Now the self-same Lamb bearing in His Person the marks of His passion is here seen as the object of Heaven's worship. No voice is, nor can be, silent when the slain Lamb appears.

Here the living ones unite with the elders in profound prostration before the Lamb. Observe, too, the moment and occasion. How fitting! "When He took the book" they "fell before the Lamb." That supreme moment to which the ways of God all tend, for which creation groans, Israel yearns, and saints hope and pray, has come. Its first action is the transference of the reins of government to the slain Lamb. The kingdom is to be mediatorial in character. The sceptre will be wielded by Christ in association with His heavenly saints, here represented by the elders, and with other redeemed but martyred companies subsequently translated.

8.—**"Having each a harp and golden bowls"** applies to the elders, not to the living ones. These latter are of the executive government of God, and as that government is to be administered by Christ, the slain Lamb, they own His right and title to universal dominion. The living ones and elders worship *Jehovah* in chapter 4, they equally worship the *Lamb* in chapter 5. What does this prove but that the Son is equal with the Father, and that whatever added glories He acquired by incarnation and atonement, yet He, the Son, *is* God, and as such entitled to the worship of every created being.

8.—**"A harp."** In earth's millennial praise various musical instruments are named (Psa. 149, 150). But the choral praise of the heavenly hosts is represented by the harp only. The harp and song correspond as in that of the martyred company of Judah (chap. 15. 2). In the direct praise and worship of Jehovah of old the harp seems more frequently employed than any other musical instrument, owing to its rare combination of solemn, grand notes with soft and tender strains under the hand of a skilful player (Isa. 24. 8; Psa. 33. 2; 43. 4; 1 Chron. 25. 6). Song and harp are generally named together.

8.—"Golden bowls* full of incenses, which are the prayers of the saints." Priestly praise (the harp) and service (the bowls) are here united. In 2 Chronicles, chapters 3 and 4, the temple and its holy vessels prefigure the millennial scene in some of its highest aspects. What the gold basins were in the temple (chap. 4. 22), such with their own characteristic differences are the golden bowls in the hands of the heavenly saints. "*Golden* bowls" mark their value and attest the high and holy service for which they are used. "Full of incenses."† It is not one perfume, but many. The fragrance is full and diversified. The "incenses *are* the prayers of the saints." Prayer on earth is incense in Heaven. We sometimes deem our prayers as worthless. Ah! it is not so. God in His own inimitable way and rich grace values our cries and intercessions, and they ascend to Him as incense.

But who are the praying company of saints in whom the heavenly priesthood are so deeply interested? The central part of the book clearly enough points to the existence of a witnessing company on earth during the course of the apocalyptic judgments, a company saved from amongst Jews and Gentiles (chaps. 11. 3; 12. 17; 13. 7-10). These holy sufferers under the apostate civil power (the Beast), and under the religious apostate power (the Antichrist), will have the rage of Satan let loose upon them working through his chiefs on earth. All suffer in the awful week of seven years (Dan. 9. 27) preceding the millennial dawn. Many are martyred, and thus have a heavenly place and portion assigned them; others survive and form the nucleus of the millennial inhabitants who will joy in the public advent and righteous reign of Christ, Lamb of God, and Son of Man. The prayers of these saints are incense.‡ But carefully note that the elders neither act as mediators nor intercessors. They do not present these supplications to God, nor add by mediation to their value. The elders in Heaven are the brethren of those holy sufferers on earth. Strange, therefore, that they should not be interested in the struggles and conflicts here in which they formerly had their part. But theirs, while deeply sympathetic, is a passive attitude. The angel-priest who adds incense to the prayers

* "A broad open vessel or basin;" see useful footnote, p. 158, "Lectures on the Book of Revelation," by William Kelly.

† "I have ventured to make a plural to suit the original, which implies a variety of sweet odours."—*Hooper*. See also "New Translation."

‡ Many writers on the Apocalypse contend that the harp and bowls of incense signify the praise and prayers of the redeemed in Heaven. The former is true, but certainly not the latter. Prayer as the expression of need would be out of place in Heaven. It is idle to cite chapter 6. 9 to the contrary. "Under the altar" and awaiting the resurrection of the body is not the same as raised and glorified in Heaven and beyond need as the elders undoubtedly are.

of the saints is no created being (chap. 8. 3, 4); Christ, and He alone, is competent to do this. He alone is the Mediator (1 Tim. 2. 5) and Intercessor (Rom. 8. 34). *One* Mediator, Who is "the Man Christ Jesus." *Two* Intercessors, Christ in Heaven, and the Holy Spirit in us now.

9.—"**They (the elders) sing a new song.**" There is no song recorded in the book of Genesis. The patriarchs were men of deep thought and of serious, not joyous mind. The first song on earth of which we have any account is narrated in Exodus 15. The deliverance which had been wrought for Israel (chap. 14) formed the ground and material for both song (chap. 15. 1-19) and refrain (v. 21). The *old* song is God celebrated in creation glory (Job 38. 7). The song in our text is termed "new" because of its theme—redemption, not typically, but actually accomplished; "new" because sung in Heaven on the eve of the full burst of millennial joy. We may observe that there is no song in chapter 4, nor is it said in Scripture that angels sing. The song of Moses and the song of the Lamb (Rev. 15. 3) unite to celebrate God's past ways with Israel and His present grace in and through the Lamb. "The song over creation must give place, in compass and melody, to the song over the triumphs of Jesus" (J. G. B.), and this is the new song which has as its burden and theme the conquering Lamb of God; a song which embraces the past and the future, the cross and the kingdom. Grand as the song of Israel was when sung on the eastern bank of the Red Sea, *this* in its character and occasion is incomparably greater. The redeemed sing *of* Him and *to* Him.

9.—"**Thou art worthy to take the book, and to open its seals.**" It is remarkable how the introduction of the Lamb shuts out all else. In that character which presents Him as slain He absorbs the attention of Heaven. Where is the Lion of the tribe of Judah? The Lion gives place to the Lamb. Under the former title, which is one of might and power, He will defend the cause of His oppressed people of Israel, and in His career of victory He rests not till the triumph of that people is secured. But *that* title of assertive power is meantime in abeyance, and the Lamb is all the glory in Heaven and earth. Of course the power of the Lion and the grace of the Lamb centre in Jesus. Here the Lamb is personally addressed in song. His worthiness to disclose and to execute the counsels of God are celebrated. Next, the ground of the Lamb's worthiness to carry out the purposes of God into full and glorious result is stated.

9.—"**Because Thou hast been slain and hast re-**

deemed to God by Thy blood out of every tribe, and tongue, and people, and nation." As the Lion of the tribe of Judah He acts in power, but as the Lamb He was slain. Here the accomplishment of God's counsels of grace and glory is traced to the cross as the basis. "*Because* Thou hast been SLAIN." Without the cross, Christ would have entered into spheres of glory *alone*; without it there could have been no redemption for sinners. The cross is the grandest counsel of eternity and the grandest fact of time. It is the immovable basis on which rests the blessing of Israel and creation, as also the glory of the Church and of saints in the heavens.

The redemption of the race is a figment of the theological brain, and absolutely destitute of scriptural authority. Do Philippians 2. 10, 11; Colossians 1. 20; Acts 3. 21 lend the slightest support to the notion that all things, persons, and demons shall be redeemed, or restored to their pristine condition? We emphatically answer, "No!" Philippians 2. 10, 11 asserts the subjection of the universe to Christ, but subjection is not redemption. Colossians 1. 20 limits the reconciliation of all things (not persons) in Heaven and earth, the under world being exempted. Acts 3. 21 refers to the fulness of millennial blessing, the testimony of prophecy. But instead of proclaiming the redemption of all men, the prophets of old expressly refute it (Dan. 12. 2; Isa. 66. 24). What, too, of the solemn testimony of the Seer of Patmos? (Rev. 19. 19, 20; 20. 7-15). There is no redemption of the race, but of persons out of it, and this distinction is quite in accord with the ancient testimony of Moses in Psalm 90. 3. "Thou turnest man (the race) to destruction, and sayest, Return, ye children of men" (individuals). Purchase is universal, and intimates a change of ownership. Redemption is special, and refers to a change of state. "Redeemed to God," then we are His. Not only so, but, writes the apostle, "We also joy in God" (Rom. 5. 11), the highest moral state compatible with creaturehood. At what an infinite cost has our blessing been secured! "By blood." The past redemption of Israel was effected by *power* (Exod. 15. 13; Psa. 106. 10); the redemption of sinners out of the race is by *blood* (1 Peter 1. 18; Rom. 3. 24). The distribution of the human family is under its usual and well-known significant factor *four*, *i.e.*, tribes, tongues, peoples, and nations. Out of these God gathers and redeems a people for Himself.

10.—"**And made them to our God kings and priests, and they shall reign over the earth.**" The pronouns "them" and "they," instead of as in the Authorised

Version "us" and "we," mark an important distinction in the interpretation of this important passage. The elders do not sing of their own redemption, but that of a people on earth. Their priestly service was on behalf of others, so here their song is of the redeemed then on earth. They sing and celebrate the blessing of others, not their own. How unselfish! How unjealous! How intense the interest in God's work of grace in the earth during the interesting interval between the Translation (1 Thess. 4. 17) and the Advent of the Lord in power (Rev. 19. 11-14). The redeemed in Heaven delight to declare the blessing of the redeemed on earth. "Made them to our God kings and priests," royal dignity and priestly nearness. "They shall reign over the earth." Jerusalem will become the capital seat of government on earth during the blessed coming era (Jer. 3. 17), and the Jewish people, then all saved, take the headship of the nations (Ezek. 48. 15-35; Isa. 52. 1-10; Psa. 47). But the heavenly saints shall reign "*over*," not *on*, the earth. The kingdom of the Father and the kingdom of the Son (Matt. 13. 41, 43) intimate respective spheres of blessing. All saints who die, along with those changed at the Coming (1 Thess. 4. 15; 1 Cor. 15. 51, 52), reign over the earth in blessed association with Christ. They are not subjects of the kingdom; they *are* kings, and are in full number presented as about to assume royal functions in Revelation 20. 4. Our reign as to its character takes its pattern from His, the union of royal authority and priestly grace (see Zech. 6. 13, "He shall be a *priest* upon His *throne*").

THE WORTHINESS OF THE LAMB. THE INTELLIGENT UNIVERSE IN PRAISE TO GOD AND TO THE LAMB.

11-14.—**"And I saw, and I heard (the) voice of many angels around the throne, and the living creatures and the elders; and their number was ten thousands of ten thousands and thousands of thousands: saying with a loud voice, Worthy is the Lamb that has been slain to receive power, and riches, and wisdom, and strength, and honour, and glory, and blessing. And every creature which is in the Heaven, and upon the earth, and under the earth, and (those that are) upon the sea, and all things in them, heard I saying, To Him that sits upon the throne, and to the Lamb, blessing, and honour, and glory, and might to the ages of ages. And the four living creatures said, Amen: and the elders fell down and did homage."** "I saw" and "I heard" are expressions which denote the rapt attention of the Seer.* The introduction of angels into the heavenly scene and the place which they occupy is of profound interest. They announced the birth of Jesus and praised God in words of never-dying fame (Luke 2. 8-14); an angel ministered to Him in the gloomy garden as the dark shadow of the cross and agony rested on His spirit (Luke 22. 43); two angels witnessed to His resurrection (John 20. 12, 13); and two also testified of His ascension (Acts 1. 10, 11). When He re-entered His heavenly home, then was made good that article of the christian faith "seen of angels" (1 Tim. 3. 16). The whole system of Christianity is a matter of inquiry and interest to the heavenly hosts (1 Peter 1. 12). They delight to serve the heirs of salvation now (Heb. 1. 14), even as it will be their joy to serve them in glory (Rev. 21. 12). They accompany the Lord in innumerable hosts in His triumphal entry into this world (Matt. 25. 31; Heb. 1. 6). It is not predicated of angels that they love or are loved.

In the centre stands the slain Lamb, around the throne the living ones and the redeemed, while the outer circle is formed of angels whose numbers are beyond human computation (see Dan. 7. 10).† In the response of the angelic hosts to the song of the redeemed they *say*, whereas the elders *sing*. There is more than a verbal difference in this, for while angels know the Lamb they cannot say "He was slain for us." We know Him in a deeper, fuller, more personal way than do angels. He died for us, not for them; hence the difference, we *sing*, they *say*. Angels are never said to sing. Observe, too, that the elders in their song directly address the Lamb, whereas the angels, in keeping with their place and service, adopt a more distant form of address. The former sing *to* Him, the latter speak *of* Him. The full burst of praise from the angelic hosts is grand. The symphony is unmarred by one discordant note. They ascribe to Him the fullest number (seven) of attributes,‡ as

* The former, *i.e.*, "I saw," occurs forty-four times; the latter, *i.e.*, "I heard," twenty-seven times. They are found in conjunction in the closing section of the book. In the fifth and last mention of John as the writer of the Apocalypse he twice assures us that he "*saw* these things and *heard* them" (chap. 22. 8). The testimony of the apostle to the fact that these visions were actually seen and the various voices and sounds actually heard is personal and decisive.

† In the relation of the numbers by the Seer and Prophet the order observed is not the same. John first names the *larger* number. Daniel first mentions the *smaller* number. But substantially there is no difference.

‡ "Power" is first named because the circumstances call for its immediate exercise. "Power" in its widest and most comprehensive character is ascribed to Him. "Riches," the wealth of the universe, physical and moral, is His due. "Wisdom," as seen in all the ways and works of God next follows in the list. "Strength" is that quality which enables one to execute what the will determines to be done. "Honour" implies that every mark of public distinction is worthy to be conferred on the Lamb. "Glory" refers to public and moral display, of which the Lamb is deemed alone worthy. "Blessing," every form and character of blessedness or happiness is here ascribed to the Lamb.

they also do in chapter 7. 12; in the former, however, the slain Lamb is the burden of their testimony, whereas in the latter it is "our God," the God of angels and of men. The order in which the attributes are named in the two respective angelic strains differs. There are also other minor points worth noting in these ascriptions of praise. The seven terms denote the highest and most perfect expression which a creature can offer. They embody the full and perfect praise of the most exalted of God's creatures.

But the full tide of praise is not yet exhausted. It rolls on, gathering force and volume, till the whole universe is embraced. "Every creature which is in the Heaven, and upon the earth, and under the earth, and (those that are) upon the sea, and all things in them," the vast universe of God in all its parts. Jehovah on His throne and the Lamb are the objects of universal adoration. The fourfold ascription of praise—"blessing, and honour, and glory, and might"—marks the universality of this spontaneous burst of worship. The praise is never ceasing—"to the ages of ages."

The living creatures add their "Amen," whilst the elders again "fell down and did homage." In drawing our comments to a close on this peculiarly precious page of divine revelation we would observe that the song and its accompanying responses are anticipative. Millennial and eternal themes are celebrated and spoken of as accomplished. The past tense is generally employed. The slain Lamb is the object round which all are grouped. In the person of the Lamb we have the firm guarantee for the glorious display of all God's counsels. Hence, ere the work is performed, faith exultingly cries, "*It is done.*"

Important Emendations in Chapters 4 and 5.

	Authorised Version.	*Corrected Text.*
Chap. 4.	1, "After this."	"After these things."
,,	1, "Hereafter."	"After these things."
,,	4, "Four and twenty seats."	"Four and twenty thrones."
,,	6. etc., "Four beasts."	"Four living creatures."
,,	9, 10, "Ever and ever."	"Ages of ages."
,,	6, 8, 11, 14, "Four beasts."	"Four living creatures."
,,	8, "Golden vials full of odours."	"Golden bowls full of incenses."
,,	9, "Redeemed us to God."	"Redeemed to God."
,,	10, "Made us."	"Made them."
,,	10, "We shall reign."	"They shall reign."
,,	10, "On the earth."	"Over the earth."
,,	12, "Power."	"The Power."
,,	13, 14, "Ever and ever."	"Ages of ages."

Delete in verse 14 the words "that liveth for ever and ever" (see the "Revised" and other critical helps).

CHAPTER VI.

Opening of the First Six Seals.

INTRODUCTION TO THE SEALS.

The Church period closes with the Lord's repudiation of that which publicly bears the christian name (Rom. 11. 21, 22; Rev. 3. 16), and with the gathering of all saints, the raised dead and changed living, at the Coming of the Lord in Person (1 Thess. 4. 15-17; 2 Thess. 2. 1). The present position of the Lord walking in the midst of the churches, overseeing all and awarding mingled praise and blame, is the characteristic truth graven on chapters 2 and 3 of the Apocalypse. To us how great the profit! How full and valuable the lessons!

Now a consideration of the formula "after these things" will assist us here. It occurs twice in verse one of chapter 4; is also found in chapters 7. 9; 15. 5; 18. 1; 19. 1; see Revised Version; also Genesis 15. 1; and 22. 1. The formula seems to form a connecting link between a series of events already past and of others to follow. What then is the obvious inference from its double occurrence in chapter 4. 1? Is it not that the history of the Church on earth, chapters 2, 3, as beheld by the Seer in vision, is past, and that consequently a new series of events is to be unfolded?

The twenty-four elders who take an important part in the heavenly actions and scenes described by the Seer are first mentioned in chapter 4. Their representative number and title evidently point them out as signifying the whole company of the redeemed of the past and present age. Now it is frankly conceded that no express apocalyptic statement affirms the translation of the saints to Heaven. Chapter 11. 12 refers to a small and special company. Paul is the only one of the New Testament writers who affirms it. John, on the contrary, dwells on the manifestation of the saints with Christ at His appearing. The former shows our gathering together *to* Him, and our subsequent return *with* Him. John writes of the latter only. The twenty-four elders signify the redeemed *in* Heaven (so that their translation had already taken place); the Seer also shows them in vision coming *out* of Heaven (chaps. 19. 11-14; 21. 10). In what part of the book can you put their translation? *After* chapter 3, which closes the Church period, and *before* chapter 4, which introduces a new series of events, and in which the elders or redeemed in Heaven are prominent. We look, therefore, for the fulfilment of John 14. 3, and 1 Thessalonians 4. 15-17, between these two chapters of the Apocalypse. The twenty-four elders are seen on high, but the fact of their Rapture is assumed, not stated, and unless this is admitted an intelligent understanding of the book is impossible. It follows, therefore, that the Church is not on earth during the apocalyptic judgments. As we have seen from the first mention of the elders (chap. 4. 4) till the last (chap. 19. 4) Heaven is their home.

We are about to enter on an examination of the strictly prophetic part of the book, and we do so with this fact before us, that the three different series of judgments—Seals, Trumpets, and Vials—have their place in the interval between our gathering to the Lord Himself, and His and our manifestation to the world at the close of Daniel's last prophetic week.* The translated saints are in Heaven during the 70th week of Daniel, a period of seven years, during the latter half of which "The Great Tribulation" rages fiercely on earth, involving in its unparalleled sorrow a godly Jewish and a godly Gentile company, called out to witness for God after the "partakers of the heavenly calling" have been translated. The Church is expressly promised exemption *from* the Tribulation (chap. 3. 10). Prophecy relates to the earth, but the Church as Christ's body and the Lamb's bride, that which is nearest and dearest to Him, is necessarily associated with Him in the heavens, and consequently outside the sphere of prophetic dealing. Still, while insisting upon the full and precise fulfilment of the prophetic section of the Apocalypse in the brief crisis covered by Daniel's last week of years, we are far from denying a historical application to the past and present; but analogy is one thing and literal fulfilment another. This latter can only be sought for at the end.†

THE FIRST SEAL.

PECULIARITIES.

1, 2.—"**And I saw when the Lamb opened one of the seven seals, and I heard one of the four living creatures saying, as in a voice of thunder, Come. And I saw, and behold a white horse, and he that sat upon it having a bow; and a crown was given to him, and he went forth conquering, and that he might conquer.**" The judgments under the Seals and Trumpets are not contemporaneous, but successive. The former cover a larger area than the Trumpets,

* See chapter on "The Celebrated Prophecy of the Seventy Weeks."

† "The visions of the book may have preliminary applications, because the principles on which they are constructed are eternal ones."—"New Testament Commentary."

but these latter, on the other hand, are more severe and searching in character.

Observe, too, that the Lamb is connected with the Seals, the angels with the Trumpets, and God with the Vials or Bowls of wrath.

In this preliminary announcement of coming judgment there is a fulness and precision of statement not found in the opening of the remaining six Seals, or even in the first Trumpet and first Vial. Here the cardinal *one* is alone used, and not the ordinal *first*, etc., as in all the others.

"And I saw" is uttered twice. John was an intensely observant eye-witness. He "saw" the act of the Lamb in opening the Seal (v. 1). He also "saw" the minister of judgment (v. 2).

The various coloured horses in the first four Seals represent in symbol the human agencies employed in the execution of these judgments on earth, which are providential in character. But as Christians having the mind of Christ, *i.e.*, the discerning faculty, we look behind the mere historical course of events and trace all to the unseen source, God Himself. So the living creatures, the executive of the throne, successively call on the human instruments of vengeance to execute their divinely-appointed task. They cannot move in judgment till summoned by the throne to do so. What a strength to the heart in days of evil! The first four Seals are characterised by the living creatures and horses. In the remaining three there is no mention made of either.

In the first Seal only a living creature speaks, "as in a voice of thunder," and at once the first prophetic event foretold in the Apocalypse comes into view. Prophecy opens.

The words in verses 1, 3, 5, 7, "*and see,*" should be omitted, as in the Revised Version. With this Tregelles, Kelly, and others agree.* The retention of the words would make it a call to John to "come and see," but why the incongruity of speaking to him in a voice of thunder? Their deletion makes the "Come"

* Some consider the deletion of the words, especially in verse 1, a doubtful matter, but the question is, we judge, satisfactorily answered by the writer of the exposition of The Revelation in Bishop Ellicott's "New Testament Commentary": "The words 'and see' are doubtful. They are found in some MSS. and omitted in others; the authority for their omission and for their retention is about equally divided. Under these circumstances we may fairly be guided by the context. To whom is the summons addressed? Who is bidden to come? If it was taken to be addressed to the Seer we can understand why some copyist should add the words 'and see.' But are they addressed to the Seer? It seems difficult to see the purpose of such a command. He was near already. He had seen the Lamb opening the Seal. There was no object in his drawing near. Are the words then addressed, as Alford supposes, to Christ? It is difficult to believe that the living creature would thus cry to the Lamb who was opening the scroll. The simplest way of answering the question is to ask another: Who did come in obedience to the voice? There is but one answer: The horseman. The living beings cry, 'Come,' and their cry is responded to by the appearance of the several riders."

a summons to the human instrument employed in these earthly chastisements.

THE LOUD SUMMONS AND ITS IMMEDIATE ANSWER.

The response to the loud and imperative command of the living creature was instantly obeyed. "And behold a white horse, and him that sat upon it." A war-horse is evidently referred to. Now the horseman cannot, as the mass of expositors allege, signify Christ on a career of conquest. Psalm 45, and especially Revelation 19. 11, have been confidently alleged in proof of the application of the first Seal to Christ. But both the Psalmist and the Seer direct us to Christ in that grand moment of His Coming to assume the sovereignty of the world, whereas the first Seal epoch refers to a time some years before the introduction of the kingdom in power. In chapter 19 the rider is named; here he is not named. From what part of the earth the Seal horseman emerges we are not informed. We have here a symbol of conquering power. A white horse denotes victorious power. It points to the advent on the prophetic scene of a power bent on conquest. A career of unchecked, brilliant, yet almost bloodless victory lies before this coming royal warrior of world-wide fame. A Cyrus, an Alexander, or a Napoleon in triumphs and conquests, but without bloodshed and slaughter, is the horse and rider of the first Seal.

"Having a bow."* The returned Jews from Babylon in the rebuilding of Jerusalem were armed with "swords, their spears, and their bows" (Neh. 4. 13). Hand-to-hand conflict demands the use of the sword; a little distance off the spear would be required; while more distant warfare is expressed by the bow. This latter weapon would not do much execution; hence its employment as a symbol of war afar off, and that not of a very deadly character.

"A crown was given to him." This must be more than the chaplet of victory bestowed on the conqueror at the *close* of a successful campaign, for here the crown is given ere victory is spoken of. Imperial or royal dignity is conferred on this distinguished personage before he enters on his wonderful career of conquest.

"He went forth conquering, and that he might conquer." Victory after victory, conquest after conquest, without reverse or cessation, marked the royal progress of the hero

---

* When active warfare with the bow and arrow is in question, then the latter is specifically mentioned (Num. 24. 8; Psa. 45. 5; Zech. 9. 14, etc.). But here nothing is said as to the bow being strung or ready for action (Lam. 2. 4), but simply the white horse rider has it. Bloodless victory is the main idea.

of the coming day and hour. The symbols under this and the succeeding Seals are simple enough and full of meaning.*

THE SECOND SEAL.

CHARACTERISTICS OF THE SECOND SEAL.

3, 4.—**"And when He opened the second Seal, I heard the second living creature saying, Come. And another, a red horse, went forth; and to him that sat upon it, to him it was given to take peace from the earth, and that they should slay one another; and there was given to him a great sword."** In all the Seal judgments, save the second, the Seer informs us that he was an eye-witness: "I saw." Then under the other Seals the word "behold" precedes the description of the horse, whereas it is here omitted. Instead of "behold" the word "another" is added, not found in the other Seals. These may be termed trivial differences, but as we are firm believers in the verbal inspiration of the Holy Scriptures we are satisfied that there is a divine meaning in these seemingly unimportant details. The occurrence of the words "I saw" and "behold" in the first Seal, and their omission in the second, may be accounted for by the fact that the word "another" in the latter connects the two Seals. Thus "I saw," and "behold . . . another, a red horse."

In answer to the summons, "Come," of the second living creature, a "red horse went forth." Why "red,"† and what is its special significance? The *white* horse denotes a series of peaceful victories. The *red* horse, on the other hand, intimates a period of slaughter and bloodshed (Isa. 63. 2; Rev. 12. 3). The rider is unnamed. It is the day of the Lord's vengeance on the guilty scene; hence the repetition of the pronoun "him," emphasising the fact that the direct agent of judgment is a man appointed by God for that purpose, "to him it was given." Whatever motives or political aspirations may actuate this coming man of blood, yet he is God's scourge for the time

---

* In the four horses under the first four Seals there is an evident allusion to the horses of Zechariah 1 and 6. In this latter vision the coloured horses, red, bay, and white, represent the character and energy of the three imperial powers of Persia, Greece, and Rome. The man riding on the red horse sets forth Cyrus, the renowned Persian, the destroyer of Babylon and deliverer of the Jews, prefiguring Christ, Israel's Saviour in a coming day, and the Judge of the mystic Babylon. In the latter vision (Zech. 6) the character and geographical course of the four Gentile empires are set forth, empires which effected unknowingly the governmental will of God. The black horses (the Persians) go forth into the north country (Babylon) and destroy it while they in turn are destroyed by the white horses (the Grecians); the grisled horses (the Romans) establish themselves in the south (v. 6). God grants universal dominion to Rome (v. 7), and rests in the destruction of Babylon (v. 8). The two Babylons, the literal (Jer. 51) and the mystical (Rev. 18), are doomed to utter destruction. Both have held captive the people of God.

† "A forfeiture of life is figuratively represented by the several colours of red, scarlet, crimson."—"Sacred Symbology," by Mills, p. 160.

being. A brief time of peace immediately succeeds the translation of the saints to Heaven, and even, as we have seen under the first Seal, the rise and progress of a mighty conqueror will not be marked by much bloodshed. His career of unchecked triumph will scarcely break the general peace. But under the second Seal we track the footsteps of one who strides through the earth on a mission of blood. He has a divine mandate "to take peace from the earth," and "that they should slay one another." In his progress he everywhere stirs up the angry passions of men. Ah! little do the governments of Europe dream that in the arming and training of their respective populations those murderous weapons perfected by the applied science of the day shall be used not merely in aggressive or defensive wars, but in civil broils and party conflicts. It is not here "nation against nation," but that "they should slay one another." The wild passions of men are let loose. A time of mutual slaughter ensues. The authority of the civil power is unavailing to check the riot and bloodshed in cities, towns, and villages, if indeed it does not lend itself to the awful work of destruction. "A great sword" given to the rider intimates that the broils and commotions which he brings about will be marked by great carnage and bloodshed. War, whether aggressive or defensive, is surely at all times deplorable enough, but a state of open, armed, civil rebellion of man against man, of fellow against fellow, glutting their vengeance and spilling blood like water is infinitely worse than any state of war conceivable, and such is the awful scene portrayed under this Seal.

THE THIRD SEAL.

A FAMINE.

5, 6.—"**And when He opened the third Seal, I heard the third living creature saying, Come. And I saw, and behold a black horse, and he that sat upon it having a balance in his hand. And I heard as a voice in the midst of the four living creatures saying, A choenix of wheat for a denarius, and three choenixes of barley for a denarius; and do not injure the oil and the wine.**" The *white* horse is the symbol of power in victory. The *red* horse denotes power in bloodshed. The *black* horse intimates power in bringing about a time of lamentation and mourning. Here, as in Zechariah 6. 2, the black horse follows the red. "Our skin was black," says the weeping prophet, "like an oven because of the terrible famine" (see Lam. 5. 10; Jer. 4. 28; Jude 13, etc., for the symbolic force of this colour).

Various things are predicated of each of the other three horsemen under their respective Seals, but here one thing only. The rider holds "a balance in his hand." The two main cereals which constitute the staff of life are to be doled out by weight and sold at famine prices. Wheat and barley are named. The latter grain was generally eaten by slaves and the poor of the people, being much cheaper than the former, and of a coarser nature. The English penny in the Authorised Version, retained in the Revised Version, is misleading. The Roman denarius was equal to about eightpence of our money; was the daily pay of a soldier, and the daily wage of a labouring man (Matt. 20. 2). Usually eight measures or choenixes of wheat could be bought for a denarius, but here only one, just barely sufficient, and no more, to sustain life.* But what about the numbers of aged people, women and children unable to work? If the denarius can only procure the necessary food for one, what about multitudes who through infirmity or other incapacity are unable to work! Must starvation be their bitter experience, and death anticipated as a happy release from the agonies of hunger?

But the living creatures are not themselves the source of this providential chastisement. They are vitally connected with the throne (chap. 4. 6), but God is the Sitter thereon, and ever will be. The Seer hears a voice from the very centre and throne of the Eternal, the announcement of a famine. God Himself is the source of these preliminary and providential judgments upon men on earth. They are inflicted by Him whoever He may employ as agents in accomplishing His purpose.

THE RICH SPARED.

The prohibition, "Do not injure the oil and the wine," is by some supposed to signify a mitigation of the famine as intimated in the preceding declarations. But that can hardly be. People could not subsist on oil and wine. Wheat and barley are essentials. Oil and wine were regarded as luxuries found alone on the tables of the rich (Prov. 21. 17; Jer. 31. 12; Psa. 104. 15). Hence the chastisement under this Seal falls especially on the working classes. The rich, the wealthy, and the governing classes are markedly exempted. But *they* shall not escape. For under the sixth Seal (vv. 12-17) judgment is impartially meted out to all alike, from the monarch down to the slave.

---

* Bread doled out by weight is a marked sign of scarcity (Lev. 26. 26; Ezek. 4. 10-17). Under this Seal, however, both weight and measure are recognised, but of such a limited character that large numbers of the populations affected thereby must suffer the misery of an actual want of food.

SOCIALISM.

Is there not righteous retribution in the fact that the masses of the people of these and other lands are first visited in judgment, and made to suffer in the very circumstances in which they now seem to triumph? An ominous sign of the times is the spread of Socialism, of the gospel of equality amongst the nations of Europe. The time-honoured distinctions of master and servant, of rulers and ruled, are scorned; wealth and social position, with their respective claims, are treated with contempt; and labour and capital are regarded as opposing forces. The working classes are rapidly getting power into their hands, and are not slow in seizing their opportunities, while demanding further rights and privileges. The spirit of insubordination and contempt of authority is abroad. The seed is being sown, the harvest is sure to follow. The masses are here seen suffering from scarcity of the staff of life, while the rich in their affluence and luxuries remain untouched, although doomed to suffer at a later period.

THE FOURTH SEAL.

DEATH AND HADES.

7, 8.—"**And when He opened the fourth Seal, I heard the voice of the fourth living creature saying, Come. And I saw, and behold a pale horse, and he that sat upon it his name (was) Death, and Hades followed with him; and authority was given to him over the fourth of the earth to slay with sword, and with hunger, and with death, and by the beasts of the earth.**" Another power is now summoned. These initial judgments are increasing in severity. The *pale* horse implying a cadaverous hue is the new harbinger of approaching judgment.

In the three preceding Seals the riders are unnamed. Here the name of the horseman is Death. "The four Seals turn upon living men; and so death, by which they are carried off, is most prominently represented; but Hell (Hades) only in so far as he receives those who have been cut off by death, acting as death's hearse, on which account no separate horse is assigned him."* Hades follows not after, but *with* death. These two are the respective custodians of the bodies and souls of men. At the close of the thousand years' reign they give up their prisoners, and are themselves destroyed, are personified, and cast into the lake of fire (chap. 20. 14). Hades refers to that condition

* Bengel as quoted by Hengstenberg.

immediately following on death, and one which resurrrection necessarily closes, the state between death and resurrection. Death and Hades are here used in relation to the ungodly only. The latter word simply means *"the unseen,"* and therefore the English term "Hell" is no just equivalent for "Hades." In this vivid description the king of terrors himself appears. The corpse-like colour of the horse is in keeping with the name and character of the rider. Death and Hades are inseparable companions. Together they act in judgment and divide the spoil.

GOD'S FOUR SORE JUDGMENTS.

We are again reminded of the interesting fact that these judgments in their sequence, character, duration, and severity have their source in the throne of God. "Authority," we read, "was given to him," not to "them." The reading "him" or "them" is disputed, but internal evidence would decide. Death acts upon living men. Hades claims the souls of the dead. Death necessarily precedes Hades. Death deals with the living, Hades with the dead.

Under the previous Seals one instrument of judgment under each is noted, but here there are four, the four by which Jehovah threatened guilty Jerusalem of old. "For thus saith the Lord God, How much more when I send my *four sore judgments* upon Jerusalem, the sword, and the famine, and the noisome beast, and the pestilence, to cut off from it man and beast?" (Ezek. 14. 21). The only difference between them is that in the apocalyptic judgments the "beasts" are last named; "death," too, the third in the list, should be understood as "pestilence," as in the margin of the Revised Version. The sword under the second Seal, and hunger under the third, are here reproduced under the fourth Seal coupled with two others. The unsheathed sword in the hands of the remorseless rider will not be withdrawn till its divinely-appointed task is finished. Hunger also will do its deadly work, a more protracted and painful death than by the sword. Then death or pestilence will ply its sickle with fatal effect and reap a full harvest. Lastly, "the beasts of the earth" will complete the destruction.

Under the previous Seals agricultural pursuits, without which no civilised people can exist, must have been abandoned. The masses under the second Seal were using the sword instead of the ploughshare. The ground would lie untilled, and in the absence of crops starvation would follow as a consequence, and the beasts, leaving their usual haunts, would add to the general misery by preying on men. These "four sore judgments," the sword, hunger, pestilence, and beasts are to be in active operation at the same time. They are contemporaneous judgments. To spiritualise them, as many do, to make them speak a language foreign to their simple and natural meaning, is to twist Scripture and not interpret. Thank God that the sphere in which these judgments operate is limited to a "fourth of the earth." The then Roman world is spoken of as a "third" (Rev. 12. 4). The extent of the sphere of judgment is a circumscribed one. What an awful future lies before the christless populations of these lands!

THE FIFTH SEAL.

DIVISION OF THE SEALS.

9-11.—"**And when He opened the fifth Seal, I saw underneath the altar the souls of them that had been slain for the Word of God, and for the testimony which they held; and they cried with a loud voice, saying, How long, O Sovereign Ruler, holy and true, dost Thou not judge and avenge our blood on them that dwell upon the earth? And there was given to them, to each one, a white robe; and it was said to them that they should rest yet a little while until both their fellow-bondmen and their brethren, who were about to be killed as they, should be fulfilled.**" The first four Seals are broadly marked off from the remaining three, as in most of the septenary divisions. Each of the four is characterised by a living creature* and a horse, both of which disappear in the Seals to follow. The living creatures are connected with the providential government of the world; they are the unseen powers behind the human actors and instruments. But in the Seals to follow the scene darkens, and the public intervention of God in the affairs of men is more marked. A similar break in the septenary series of Trumpet and Vial judgments occurs (for the former see chap. 8. 13; for the latter see chap. 16. 10). The last three Vials give the full expression of God's wrath on guilty Christendom.

THE FIRST CONTINGENT OF THE MARTYRED BAND.

9.—"**I saw under the altar the souls of them that had been slain.**" How changed the scene! Believers now "are the salt of the *earth*" (Matt. 5. 13). Their

*No doubt there is a moral correspondence between the characteristics of the living ones (chap. 4. 7, 8) and the respective Seals with which they are severally connected. The first living creature and the first Seal, the lion and the imperial conqueror, is a correspondence easily seen. So between the fourth living one and the fourth Seal the eagle (see **Matt. 24. 28.** ***judgment***) **and the march of Death, is a striking resemblance.**

presence in it preserves these lands meanwhile from apostasy, corruption, and consequent judgment. But they are also "the light of the *world*" (v. 14). Their testimony to the grace of God, however defective in fulness and character, is yet the world's best and highest blessing. But when the term of God's patience is run out, and the "salt" and "light" removed, then *corruption* and moral *darkness* shall characterise the scene given up in retributive righteousness to judgment (Isa. 60. 2). The opening page of judgment is before us in the first four Seals.

When the home of the Spirit on earth, the Church (1 Cor. 3. 16), is broken up (for it has to be presented by Christ to Himself in glory, Eph. 5. 27), the Spirit will work from Heaven on earth, quickening souls by His divine power. Those first converted and saved, by no known human agency,* will incur the active and cruel hostility of the christless populations of the earth. It is possible, as under the early pagan persecutions, that the future witnessing company of believers will be regarded as the cause of the national calamities, and hence the fierce blast of bitter and cruel persecution. Here, however, the true and real reason of their martyrdom is named, "Slain for the Word of God, and for the testimony which they held." The Word of God when faithfully declared in its incisive claims on man's conscience ever stirs into action the hostility of the world, and its most faithful exponents in life and public testimony must seal that witness with their blood. The Lord at present, by the power of the Holy Spirit on earth, bridles the passions of men, but let the presence and power of the Spirit be withdrawn, and the world's enmity to Christ and to those who are His shall burst out in fierce and bitter persecution even unto death. "The testimony which they held" is not to the grace of God as now, but to the righteous claims of God in establishing His kingdom on earth. The answer to these claims is the sword of power in the hands of the then apostate, persecuting power. Judgment is let loose on these holy sufferers. The kingdom rights of Christ (Matt. 24. 14), then the subject of testimony, will be trampled under foot and the witnesses cruelly slain. The sacrificial word "slain" is used in keeping with the special character of these, probably Jewish, witnesses. The later company under the Beast (chap. 13. 7) are said to be "killed" (v. 11), a more general word than the former. The altar of burnt offering which

* This first company of witnesses on earth after the translation will go through the Roman world preaching the Gospel of the kingdom. The result of their labours is stated in Matthew 25. 31-46. We gather that these first preachers will be chiefly converted Jews. "These my brethren," are the Lord's Jewish brethren according to the flesh (v. 40).

stood both in the court of the tabernacle and of the temple is here referred to. This altar of brass typifying the endurance of divine judgment is also noticed in chapters 11. 1; 14. 18; 16. 7. The golden altar of intercession twice comes into view in these apocalyptic scenes (chaps. 8, latter part of verse 3; and 9. 13). "The altar" in verses 3 and 5 of chapter 8 refers to the brazen altar.

Under the altar, on which they had been sacrificed by the ruthless hand of the persecutor, their souls cry aloud for vengeance on their enemies. The imagery is cast in Jewish mould, but is none the less easily read. The cry does not breathe the accents of divine grace, but of righteous judgment. The appeal of the future Jewish remnant to the God of judgment is as much in accord with the divine mind as the touching words of the Lord on the cross: "Father, forgive them; for they know not what they do" (Luke 23. 34), or the prayer of the first christian martyr: "Lord, lay not this sin to their charge" (Acts 7. 60). The change of the dispensation alters the character of God's dealings with the world. *Law* was the principle on which God dealt in Old Testament times. *Grace* is the platform of His present acts and ways. *Judgment*, in dealing with evil and evil workers, characterises the future brief crisis before glory dawns upon the earth. The cry, therefore, of the slain under the altar is quite in keeping with Psalm 94: "O Lord God, to whom vengeance belongeth; O God, to whom vengeance belongeth, show Thyself. Lift up Thyself, Thou Judge of the earth; render a reward to the proud. Lord, how long shall the wicked, how long shall the wicked triumph?" (vv. 1-3). The judgment of sin on the cross is the foundation on which securely reposes our glory in Heaven. The judgment of sin on the wicked on earth is needful to clear it from evil and fit it as a dwelling place for God's earthly people.

Their souls are seen in vision "**underneath the altar.**" *On* the altar would express the holocaust being offered, but "*underneath*" it, where the blood of the sin offering was poured out (Lev. 4. 7), signifies the completion of the sacrifice. The martyrdom of the saints was not taking place. The scene was over. There are no details furnished. The cruelty of the oppressor and the sigh of the steadfast witness for Jesus and His royal rights are alike unrecorded. The martyrs are not here seen in life, nor as risen, but in the separate state, "the *souls* of them that had been slain."

With a loud voice they cry "**How long?**" the well-known cry of the suffering Jew in the coming hour of unparalleled sorrow. Anguish and faith are expressed in the cry (Psa. 74. 9, 10; 79. 5; 89. 46; 94. 3, 4). The appeal is to God as "Sovereign Ruler." This is a title implying supreme authority, and is found nowhere else in the Apocalypse. The epithets "holy" and "true" are added. The cry is to One Who has right and power to avenge the blood so wantonly shed; Who is holy in His nature and true to His Word and promise. The circumstances contemplated under this Seal are similar to those noted in Psalm 79, only the Psalmist witnesses to a later moment and to a more circumscribed area. Vengeance is invoked "on them that dwell upon the earth." A moral class is here indicated, for in chapter 11. 9 the inhabitants of earth are referred to under the well-known enumeration, "people, and kindreds, and tongues, and nations;" then in the next verse a moral class, the guiltiest of all, are spoken of as those "that dwell upon the earth." The significance of this term is found in Philippians 3. 19. The cry for vengeance is heard, but the answer is deferred. In the meantime the Lord gives a token of special approval. Each one of the martyred band is singled out for honour and vindication. "**There was given to them, to each one, a white robe.**"*

If this verse stood alone it would itself render untenable the historical school of interpretation. Christians are in connection with the Father, not the Sovereign Ruler; they pray for those who despitefully use them; they do not invoke vengeance upon them. To a Christian such an invocation is impossible. To one who had been a martyred Jew this legal call for vengeance was absolutely consistent with the law under which he had lived, and his own Scriptures, and the Lord by giving each one a white robe stamps His approval on their utterance.

How good and gracious of our Lord thus to express with His ready approval the righteous attitude assumed by His martyred saints. But the sword of the Lord was not yet to be drawn. The iniquity of man awaited a fuller development of evil ere the righteous and holy wrath of the Lord bursts forth in its fury on the ungodly. The time of vengeance was measured by a "little while." Another company here termed "fellow-bondmen" and "brethren" were to swell the ranks of the noble army of martyrs. Two separate companies of martyred saints are evidently referred to in these verses, the earlier company slain under the fifth Seal;† the later killed at a subsequent period, here called "a little while." There can be no full answer to the cry "underneath the altar" till this second contingent of the martyred band is complete.

* Not "Robes," as in the Authorised Version. See Revised.

† See Matthew 24. 9, which synchronises with the time and events here referred to.

It must be distinctly borne in mind that neither the Old Testament martyrs from Abel, nor the christian martyrs from Stephen, are referred to here. The two companies are those who seal their testimony with their blood *after* the translation of the saints of past and present ages to Heaven. The coming brief crisis will witness in its earlier and later stage fierce outbursts of cruel persecution against those then witnessing for God.

THE SIXTH SEAL.

COMPLETE SUBVERSION OF ALL GOVERNMENTAL AND CIVIL AUTHORITY.

12-17.—"**And I saw when He opened the sixth Seal, and there was a great earthquake; and the sun became black as hair sackcloth, and the whole moon became as blood, and the stars of Heaven fell upon the earth as a fig tree, shaken by a great wind, casts its unseasonable figs. And the Heaven was removed as a book rolled up, and all mountains and islands were removed out of their places. And the kings of the earth, and the great, and the chiliarches, and the rich, and the strong, and every bondman and freeman hid themselves in the caves and in the rocks of the mountains; and they say to the mountains and to the rocks, Fall on us, and have us hidden from (the) face of Him that sits upon the throne, and from the wrath of the Lamb; because the great day of His wrath is come, and who is able to stand**?" Under the former Seal we witnessed a fierce struggle between light and darkness. The conflict between good and evil knows no cessation. But God shall triumph in the end. The full answer to the appeal of the martyred saints must await the completion of the martyred band. A second outburst of rage against God's witnesses, directed by the Beast and his satellite, the Antichrist, is there intimated. *Then* will come the hour of awful tribulation. *Then* will an angry God deal in judgment with the cruel persecutors of His people. "It is a righteous thing with God to recompense tribulation to them that trouble you" (2 Thess. 1. 6). But under this Seal God begins to deal judicially with the world, thus giving an earnest of the full answer yet to be vouchsafed to the cry underneath the altar.

The scene here described is an awful and sublime one. The symbols employed are the powers of nature. The whole fabric of civil and governmental power on earth breaks up. Disorder reigns supreme. It is not simply the collapse of this or that government, but the total subversion of *all* governing authority, both supreme and dependent. The general idea which the metaphors present is a universal overthrow of all existing authority; a revolutionary crisis of such magnitude that kings and slaves are in abject terror. The coming crash will involve in one general catastrophe everything on earth deemed secure and strong. A vast civil, social, and political chaos will be created. What an awful scene to contemplate! A world without a magistrate! Without even the semblance of rightful power! Without government! Without the authority of repression!

12.—"**A great earthquake**" denotes a violent disruption of the organised state of things, a complete subversion of all existing authority. Under the seventh Seal, and preparatory to the infliction of yet severer chastisements (chap. 8. 5), an earthquake, along with other signs, is mentioned as a public intimation of coming wrath. But here the earthquake is termed "great," as its effects upon men amply testify. Under the seventh Vial (chap. 16. 18) there will be another social and political revolution exceeding in its effect what we have in our text, a catastrophe of such an appalling character that history affords no parallel to it. It must be borne in mind that the Seals unfold a series of consecutive and preliminary sorrows. The "great earthquake" does not usher in the day of the Lord. There are two groups of signs mentioned by the Lord in His great prophetic discourse (Matt. 24, 25). The first group applies to the period *before* the great tribulation (chap. 24. 6-14), the second group has its application *after* the tribulation, and announces the immediate Return of the Lord in power (v. 29). Now the events under the Seals are prior to the tribulation, and really coalesce with the earlier state of things described in Matthew 24. 6-14. The "great earthquake" of our text does not, therefore, announce the final judgment, nor is it the immediate precursor of the Lord's return, whatever men may say in their fear and terror (Rev. 6. 17). The very fact that a yet more awful earthquake succeeds the one of our text should settle the question (chap. 16. 18). The state of things described under the sixth Seal is to be followed by more awful horrors.

12.—"**The sun became black as hair sackcloth**."* The sun symbolises the supreme governing authority (Gen. 37. 9; Rev. 12. 1). "Black as hair sackcloth" denotes the darkening power of Satan, and points to the supreme

* Hair sackcloth was originally made of camel's hair (Matt. 3. 4), and was the Prophet's usual garment (Zech. 13. 4). But it was pre-eminently the mourning garb (Rev. 11. 3; 2 Sam. 3. 31, etc.). It is in this latter sense in which it must be viewed here.

authority of earth (on which all were dependent) in a condition of utter collapse (Isa. 50. 3; Ezek. 7. 18). The darkening of the heavenly bodies is an awful calamity in the physical world, and hence the aptness of the figure here.

12.—"**The whole moon became as blood.**" All authority immediately derived from and dependent on the supreme power is here figured by the "whole* moon." The moon in the material realm is a secondary planet, and symbolises derivative authority in the moral realm. It is the chosen figure of Israel as dependent upon Christ the Sun of Righteousness (Cant. 6. 10; Psa. 81. 3). "Became as blood." The moral death and apostasy of every subordinate authority is intimated. "Blood" is a universal figure of death (Rev. 11. 6; 19. 2, 13).

13.—"**The stars of Heaven fell upon the earth** as a fig tree, shaken by a great wind, casts its unseasonable figs." All lesser authorities, as individual rulers, civil and ecclesiastical, morally fell from their exalted station. God and their relation to Him were morally given up. The unripe or unseasonable figs are those concealed under the leaves which never ripen, and which are cast off in winter by a strong wind. When the wintry winds of God's wrath sweep across the scene, then those who were never truly His, however exalted their position, shall openly apostatise and abandon all external relation to Him (Isa. 34. 4).

14.—"**The Heaven was removed as a book rolled up.**" The political, civil, and ecclesiastical systems, the constitution, bonds, and frame work of society, shall as completely disappear as a book or scroll is unreadable when rolled up. The physical removal of the heaven (Rev. 21. 1) and of the heavens (2 Peter 3. 10), not, of course, the dwelling place of God, of saints, and of angels, is one of the most stupendous events which the Word of God records. But the entire cessation of all governmental order, the moral Heaven, is one of those coming events most awful to contemplate. We have had the ruin of all greater and lesser authorities, but here the whole system in which they were placed itself collapses.

14.—"**All mountains and islands were removed out of their places.**" A system of settled power is represented by a mountain (Dan. 2. 35; Jer. 51. 25), a long established, stable, and powerful government. Islands were regarded by the Jews as sources of wealth, as centres of trade and commerce (Isa. 23. 2; Ezek. 27. 3-15). The

---

* "Whole," omitted in the Authorised, but inserted in the Revised, as also by Tregelles, Kelly, Darby; is found in the Sinaitic, Alexandrian, and Vatican Codices

removal of all, regarded as enduring and great, as also the sources of wealth and commerce, are here declared.

UNIVERSAL TERROR.

The effect of this mighty and universal revolution in civil and political life will be a scene of awful terror. In keeping with a marked characteristic of the Apocalypse, in which the numeral seven is largely employed, there are enumerated seven classes of men, and, as usual, these again are divided into two groups of three and four. The first consists of those who govern: "kings," the highest and most exalted; "great," or princes, see Revised Version; and "chiliarches," or military tribunes.* The second group includes the non-official class presented in pairs: "the rich" and "strong," "bondman and freeman."†

15.—All, high and low, rich and poor, "**hid themselves in the caves and in the rocks of the mountains.**" What a vivid emblem of terror! The fear of the Lord and the glory of His majesty in governmental power, as witnessed in the universal disruption of society, will strike men with such awful dread that the caves and rocks of the mountains ‡ shall be eagerly sought as hiding places from His wrath and to screen them from His face. It is an hour of mortal fear. In their terror they appeal not to God, but to the mountains and rocks to fall upon them and hide them from the face "of Him that sits upon the throne, and from the wrath of the Lamb." Their guilty fears add, "Because the great day of His wrath is come, and who is able to stand?" It is not so. Heavier judgments are looming, darker clouds are gathering ere the final hour of concentrated agony known as the "wrath of the Lamb" transpires. Under the sixth Seal the first droppings of the coming storm of divine wrath cause universal terror and fear. When the storm actually bursts at the personal return of the Lord, then, instead of dread of His wrath, bold, high-handed contempt of the Lamb will characterise the scene (Rev. 19. 17-19) which the warrior king will drench in blood.

We have to be exceedingly careful not to allow the consideration of details to weaken in our souls the general

---

* In Mark 6 21 we read of Herod making a supper to his nobles and the chiliarches or military officers, and the chief men of Galilee, but these latter would not necessarily be officials; they were probably eminent persons in a private station.

† In chapters 13. 16; 19. 18 the order is reversed as the *free* and bond.

‡ This second and further reference to the mountains would in itself show that the physical heaven, moon, stars, mountains, etc., are not actually contemplated, but are to be understood symbolically. How could every mountain be removed (v. 14) and yet be sought for subsequently as a hiding place (v. 15)? There will be physical changes in the heavens and earth at the commencement (Zech. 14) and close of the millennial reign (2 Peter 3), but the time under which this Seal has its place would forbid anything but a moral and symbolical signification.

effect of this thrilling description of coming events, and the consequent fears of men. Even a cursory reader must feel awed at the "almost unparalleled magnificence and sublimity" of the scene about to be enacted, which is revealed in terms so full and plain that their bearing cannot, save by the wilfully ignorant, be misunderstood. The consideration of the seventh Seal* must be reserved till we enter upon the study of chapter 8.

* We had thought of presenting a condensed summary of the historical application of the Seals, but on further reflection decided not to do so. We are amazed at the conflict of opinion by the historicalists. Scarcely two are agreed in their interpretations, while their assigned dates to this and that event are in hopeless confusion. Little wonder that the mass of Christians regard the study of the Apocalypse with an amount of suspicion difficult to get rid of. The principle of interpretation is clearly erroneous. If the Revelation is to be interpreted by the light which the facts of history record, it necessarily shuts out by far the greater number of God's people from the study of the book, for how can they study history? Besides, if those who have done so and seek to interpret the book on this principle differ so widely that scarcely two are agreed, how hopeless the task for others. We are satisfied that the principle on which this book is sought to be interpreted by the historical school is utterly false. God's Spirit alone is the power by which prophecy is to be understood, and not the facts of history. The Revelation from chapter 4 refers to the future.

CHAPTER VII.

Parenthetic Visions of Grace.

VISIONS OF TWO SEPARATE COMPANIES.

There are two separate visions contained in this chapter. The first concerns *Israel* (vv. 1-8); the second refers to the *Gentile* (vv. 9-17). There can be no question as to the parenthetic character of both. The contents of our chapter form no part of events under the Seals. There is no historical sequence. In the previous chapter we had the opening of the first six Seals in succession; then in chapter 8 the Lamb opens the seventh or last Seal. Thus between the sixth and seventh, yet forming no part of either, a deeply interesting episode of blessing to Israel and to the Gentiles is introduced. The course of judgment is suspended and the veil drawn aside that we may witness the heart of our God. It is not all judgment in those dark and evil days. It must not be supposed, however, that the salvation of these respective companies from amongst Israel and the Gentiles necessarily takes place between the sixth and seventh Seals, much less their public place and blessing. The chapter is without dates. The sealing of Israel is in view of their millennial position, but *when* the sealing took place we are not informed. The vision of the saved Gentile multitude after coming out of the great tribulation regards them in full millennial blessing on earth, for it is an earthly scene (vv. 16, 17). But *when* the testimony of God reached them and saved them we are not told. Immediately after the translation of the heavenly saints (1 Thess. 4. 15-17) God will work in grace amongst His ancient people and amongst the Gentiles at large outside the apostate part of the world. This testimony will be continued for several years, probably during the whole, and it may be longer, of the 70th week of Daniel, a period of seven years. Here we have in vision the results of that testimony. The revelation of these companies is a refreshing sight. Coming as it does *after* the power of the enemy has been let loose against the saints of God (chap. 6. 9-11) and *before* the infliction of yet severer judgments (chaps. 8, 16) it triumphantly proves that nothing can thwart the purposes of God nor hinder the working of His Spirit on the earth. How good of God to give us this interesting parenthetic chapter!

JUDGMENT RESTRAINED.

1.—"**And after this I saw four angels standing upon the four corners of the earth, holding fast the**

four winds of the earth, that no wind might blow upon the earth, nor upon any tree." The phrase *after this*, repeated in verse 9, marks a new commencement. It introduces the Israelitish section of our chapter, as also the vision of the Gentile palm-bearing multitude. The intentional employment of the phrase and its repetition should have preserved certain interpreters from confusing the two companies. They are separate and distinct both in nationality and in blessing. The one is from among Israel, the other from among the Gentiles. The millennial earth is the scene where both are displayed. But it is essential to the understanding of the chapter to bear in mind that the time of the vision and the time when the companies come into their appointed public blessing are very different.

1.—"**Four angels standing upon the four corners of the earth**, holding fast the four winds of the earth." The banished Seer here views the earth as a vast extended plain, bounded by the four main points of the compass, north, south, east, and west. At these respective corners an angel stands so as to have full control over the destructive forces of evil.

The threefold repetition of the numeral "four" marks the completeness and the universality of the action. We see no reason for limiting the term "earth" here to the Roman world. The winds are not to blow till an ideal number of Israel is sealed (vv. 3, 4). Now the two houses of Israel, Ephraim and Judah, are embraced in this work. Jehovah "shall assemble the outcasts of Israel, and gather together the dispersed of Judah from the four corners of the earth" (Isa. 11. 11, 12), Thus both the Prophet and the Seer refer to the full extent of the inhabited earth, and not to the territorial limits of the Roman world, whether past or future. Clearly, too, verse 9 refers to the result of a divine testimony amongst the Gentiles far exceeding the extent of the empire in any period of its history. The earth here must be understood in its largest sense.

The four restraining angels,* the unseen, yet real, spiritual powers, are here seen controlling the forces and instruments of evil, "the four winds of the earth."†

* Wordsworth, in his "Lectures on the Apocalypse," p. 120, attempts to show that the "four angels standing upon the four corners of the earth" are the same as those "bound at the great river Euphrates" (chap. 9. 14). But the world-wide position of the former compared with the circumscribed sphere of the latter would forbid such interpretation. Besides, the actions and time essentially differ. Wordsworth is one of the most fanciful and uncertain of interpreters.

† Political and other troubles are expressed in the term "winds of the earth" (Dan. 7. 2; Job 1. 19; Jer. 49. 36). "Winds of the *Heaven*" and "winds of the *earth*" are to be distinguished. The former expression points to the providential agencies employed by God to execute His purposes; whereas the latter denote attention to the guilty sphere of these judgments and calamities, *i.e.*, the earth. We may also observe that the first mention of the "earth" in the text is unrestricted in its application. The second mention of the word limits it to the civilised portion of the globe in contrast to the "sea" the uncivilised part (see also Rev. 10. 2).

1.—"**Holding fast**" with a firm grip, implying that the winds were struggling to get loose. How irresistible the grasp of Omnipotence on the powers and forces of evil. They are effectually bridled till the plans of God are ripe and ready for action.

The situation is one of intense interest. We are about to enter into yet deeper sorrows. The climax of judgment so far was under the sixth Seal when all government, political, social, supreme, and subordinate, utterly collapsed, and a scene of universal terror ensued. But deeper woes are looming. All were not slain in the martyrdom under the fifth Seal (chap. 6. 9-11), nor will coming and severer judgments hinder a universal testimony for God, as the consolatory visions of this chapter conclusively prove. Hence the universal calamities and troubles, indicated by the expression "winds of the earth," are for a season held in check till God takes measures for the preservation of a complete number of His people Israel and of an innumerable company of Gentiles.

1.—"**That no wind might blow upon the earth,**" the scene of settled government (Rev. 10. 2; Psa. 46. 2); "nor upon the *sea*," nations and peoples in anarchy and confusion (Dan. 7. 2, 3; Isa. 57. 20); "nor upon any *tree*," the might and pride of earth (Dan. 4. 10, 22; Ezek. 31. 3-9, 14-18). The reason of the cessation of judgment is stated in precise terms : "until we shall have sealed the bondmen of our God upon their foreheads" (v. 3).

THE SEALING ANGEL AND HIS CRY.

2, 3.—"**And I saw another angel ascending from (the*) sun-rising, having (the*) seal of (the*) living God; and he cried with a loud voice to the four angels, to whom it had been given to hurt the earth and the sea, saying, Hurt not the earth, nor the sea, nor the trees, until we shall have sealed the bondmen of our God upon their foreheads.**" Judgment attributed to the winds in verse one is here ascribed to the angels. By the former are symbolised the agencies of political and other evils; by the latter are to be understood the spiritual powers which direct and govern these agencies of evil, the instruments of judgment in verse one; the powers which wield them in verse two.

"Another angel," not one of the four, and certainly not Christ,† as some have strangely supposed. The sentence

* The absence of the article (bracketed by J.N.D. in his "New Testament," and inserted in italics by W.K. in his valuable "Lectures on the Book of Revelation") marks the respective actions before which it is omitted as characteristic.

† The angel-priest of chapter 8. 3-5, and the strong angel of chapter 10. 1-6, 8-10, seem undoubtedly to refer to Christ. The terms used and actions described in both Scriptures could not truthfully be applied to any created being, however exalted.

"until *we* shall have sealed" would be derogatory to the pre-eminent dignity of Christ; so also the concluding words of the angel's cry, "the bondmen of *our* God." The language and spirit of John 20. 17, "I ascend unto My Father and *your* Father; and to My God and *your* God," is maintained throughout the New Testament. We never meet with the terms "*our* God" and "*our* Father" as signifying Christ and believers.

The angel referred to in our text is evidently a distinguished spiritual being having an exalted mission on hand. He ascends from the east or sun-rising, "having (the) Seal of (the) living God."* The sealing angel ascending from the sun-rising for the preservation and blessing of Israel seems a herald of the Messiah, Who as the Sun of Righteousness shall arise with healing in His wings (Mal. 4. 2), and shine upon the land and people with undimmed splendour. The firstfruits of national blessing is predicated of the angel; the harvest awaits the revelation of Christ from Heaven.

"The seal of the *living* God" implies immunity from death, and the seal upon the forehead intimates public, open acknowledgment that those who are sealed belong to God. What the seal is we are not informed.

"The *bondmen* of our God." Such is the title applied to the sealed of Israel. They had maintained the testimony of God through trial and difficulty; their course had been marked by conflict and service; hence the appropriateness of the title "bondmen."

The sealing is not alone the work of the angel; others are associated in the happy service of preserving from judgment a complete number of Israel, "until *we* shall have sealed." There is a dignity of action here neither found in the sealing recorded by the prophet of the captivity (Ezek. 9. 4) nor in that of Judah on Mount Zion (Rev. 14. 1). The angel ascending from the sun-rising is in keeping with the exalted mission on hand. His is no ordinary service, and hence the surrounding circumstances bespeak the greatness of the work.

"He cried with a loud voice" to the angels of judgment, "Hurt not the earth, nor the sea, nor the trees." The imperative summons is obeyed, and saved Israel is sealed for millennial blessing.

THE NUMBER OF THE SEALED.

The Gentile company (v. 9) is not numbered. The Israelitish company, on the contrary, is carefully reckoned, and the result stated, not in round numbers, but in precise

* Sealing in the present dispensation is no outward mark as here. It is the Holy Ghost given by God to indwell the believer (2 Cor. 1. 21, 22; Eph. 1. 13). God (not Christ) seals; the Holy Ghost Himself, a *Person* is the Seal.

terms as a hundred and forty and four thousand. Twelve thousand out of each of the twelve tribes of Israel. The numbers, whether singly (12) or multiplied (144) denote a complete and definite number. *Twelve* is the signature of Israel, and is largely employed in Jewish connection. *Earthly administration, rule, government,* seem to be the moral value of this numeral.* The number of the sealed is of course symbolic, and simply denotes that God has appropriated a certain, complete, yet limited number of Israel for Himself.

PECULIARITIES

In the enumeration of the tribes throughout Scripture, of which there are about eighteen, the full representative number twelve is always given; but as Jacob had thirteen sons,† one or other is always omitted. Levi is more generally omitted than any other. In the apocalyptic enumeration Dan and Ephraim are omitted. Both these tribes were remarkable as being connected with idolatry in Israel, the probable reason for the blotting out of their names here (Deut. 29. 18-21). But in the end grace triumphs, and Dan is named first in the future distribution of the land amongst the tribes (Ezek. 48. 2), but, while first named, it is the farthest removed from the temple, being situated in the extreme north. In our English version there are three tribes named in each verse, but in reality the arrangement of the tribes, as of the apostles, (Matt. 10. 2-4) is in pairs. *First,* Judah and Reuben, the fourth and first sons of Leah, the former the royal tribe, the latter the representative of the nation (Gen. 49. 3). *Second,* Gad and Asher, the two sons of Zilpah, associated in the prophetic blessings of the last days (Gen. 49. 19, 20). *Third,* Naphtali and Manasseh, linked in the enumeration of Ezekiel 48. 4. *Fourth,* Simeon and Levi, the second and third sons of Leah, associated in the prophetic enumeration (Gen. 49. 5-7), also in the Lord's revelation of Himself to saved Israel (Zech. 12. 13). *Fifth,* Issachar and Zebulun, the fifth and sixth sons of Leah, both are associated in the prophetic (Gen. 49) and in the territorial (Ezek. 48) enumerations of the tribes. *Sixth,*‡ Joseph and Benjamin, the two sons of Rachel, the beloved wife of the patriarch.

* The *twelve* hours of the day, *twelve* hours of the night, direct us to the sun and moon as the ruling and governing powers of day and night. There were *twelve* tribes of Israel and *twelve* apostles in relation to the future government of Israel (Matt. 19. 28). *Twelve* gates in the holy Jerusalem (Rev. 21. 12). Israel was represented in the *twelve* precious stones on the breastplate of the high priest and in the *twelve* loaves of show bread on the holy table (Exod. 28; Lev. 24). *Rule* on the earth is the predominant factor in the use and value of this numeral.

† Counting the two sons of Joseph instead of the father as Jacob's.

‡ We have Joseph, not Ephraim; the father instead of the son. But Ephraim in blessing takes precedence of his elder brother Manasseh, and again grace shines (Gen. 48. 8-20).

It is to be noted that in the Revised Version and other critical helps the word "sealed" is omitted in naming each of the tribes save the first and last. Thus, "out of (the) tribe of Judah twelve thousand sealed" (v. 5), and "out of (the) tribe of Benjamin twelve thousand sealed" (v. 8). The tribes of Judah and Benjamin respectively open and close the enumeration. The characteristics of these tribes (Gen. 49. 8-12, 27) both centre in Christ.

THREE COMPANIES OF MILLENNIAL SAINTS.

The two companies of Israel and the Gentiles were beheld by the Seer in separate visions. The elect company from the twelve tribes (vv. 4-8) is not only distinct from their Gentile associates (vv. 9-17), but is equally distinct from the 144,000 from amongst Judah who emerge out of the horrors of the coming hour of trial standing on Mount Zion (chap. 14). There are two Jewish companies of equal number—the hundred and forty-four thousand of all *Israel* (chap. 7), and the hundred and forty-four thousand of *Judah* only (chap. 14). The palm-bearing Gentile multitude must not be confounded either with the Church or with Israel. The innumerable multitude here beheld in vision is the fruit of an extensive work of grace begun immediately or soon after the translation of the heavenly saints (1 Thess. 4), and continued during the future prophetic week of seven years (Matt. 24. 14). This world-wide testimony actively carried on between the Translation and the Appearing will be signally owned of God. Thus ample time under the good and controlling hand of God is afforded for the mighty work of grace, which in extensive results remind us of the palmy days of Pentecost.

We may also note another interesting distinction between the two companies of millennial saints in our chapter. The elect of Israel are beheld *before* they enter into "the time of Jacob's trouble," whereas the Gentile saved multitude are here witnessed *after* having come out of "the great tribulation."

THE SAVED GENTILE MULTITUDE AND THEIR CRY.

We have already remarked that the white-robed, palm-bearing multitude come out of the great tribulation, and while their blessing is strictly millennial in character and time, they must not be confounded with another class of Gentiles who will be saved at the commencement of the millennial era *after* the close of the tribulation; hence the special position and characteristic blessings of the "innumerable multitude" here referred to. Both the position and blessing are in beautiful keeping with the previous trial, out of which they have emerged, and in which many of their brethren, Jewish and Gentile, were slain. "Out of every nation, and tribes, and peoples, and tongues." We have already met with this fourfold distribution of the race (chap. 5. 9). It is a technical formula expressing *universality* (see also chap. 11. 9).

This vast multitude beyond all counting, and in this respect in marked contrast to the more limited and exactly defined number of Israel, is witnessed by the Seer "standing before the throne and before the Lamb, clothed with white robes, and palm branches in their hands." These saints are on earth. "*Standing* before the throne and before the Lamb" is, of course, a position of exalted dignity, but the thrones of the heavenly saints are "around" the throne of God (chap. 4. 4) and of the Lamb (chap. 5. 6). Moreover, they are seated on them (see also chap. 20. 4). It is not said that these earthly saints have thrones and crowns; the heavenly ones have both. In these and other respects the heavenly company of the redeemed occupy a higher and more exalted position of dignity than the "innumerable multitude" who on earth stand before the throne—a designation of moral force.

9.—"**Clothed with white robes.**" They had maintained the rights and claims of God against a rebellious and apostate world amidst circumstances, too, of unparalleled sorrow and affliction (Mark 13. 19). Now God remembers and rewards their faithfulness, they are "clothed with white robes," robes of *righteousness* (see chap. 19. 8). "Palm branches" express the *joy* of complete deliverance (Lev. 23. 40; John 12. 13). God had brought them safely through their awful period of appointed affliction termed "*the* great tribulation" (Rev. 7. 14, R.V.), and now they triumph in the triumph of their God. The palm is the only tree named in the construction of the millennial temple (Ezek. 40; 41); is also named chiefly in connection with the Feast of Tabernacles, the last and closing joyous feast of Israel (Lev. 23. 40). The white-robed multitude is the only company in the Revelation said to have palms; the word occurs but once in the Apocalypse.

10.—"**They cry with a loud voice**, saying, Salvation to our God Who sits upon the throne, and to the Lamb." Their struggles and trials are over. The throne before which they stand is now and for ever their strength and security. The countless multitudes of these redeemed ones break out in one loud and united cry.

What is the burden of this intense and thrilling cry? Salvation in its most comprehensive sense is ascribed to God and to the Lamb. Not a member of that redeemed host is silent. "*They* cry with a loud voice." Sovereign grace has done its mighty work. It has gathered out of all lands and tongues a Gentile host beyond all human computation—each and all once "dead in sins"—and placed them saved and blest before God's throne. How fitting then that the triumph of divine grace should be grandly celebrated and traced to the source—God in divine sovereignty, and to the Lamb, the expression of His love and grace.

THE ANSWER OF THE ANGELIC HOST.

11, 12.—"**And all the angels stood around the throne, and the elders and the four living creatures, and fell before the throne upon their faces and worshipped God, saying, Amen: Blessing, and glory, and wisdom, and thanksgiving, and honour, and power, and strength to our God, to the ages of ages. Amen.**" We have two distinct heavenly scenes in which the throne is the central figure here, and in chapter 5. 11, 12. In both scenes the angels form the outer circle around the throne. In these beatific visions we have the doxology of the angelic host in a sevenfold ascription of worship. In the former scene (chap. 5. 11, 12) the *Lamb* is the object of praise; in the latter vision (chap. 7. 11, 12) *God* is the object of adoration. The position of the angels in both scenes is around the throne, while the elders and living creatures form inner circles. The order in which these last, *i.e.*, the elders and living ones, are presented differs in the two scenes. In the earlier one the elders form the innermost circle; in the later the living creatures are nearest the throne. The difference is easily accounted for. In the former the Lamb is in immediate view and the redeemed in Heaven (the elders) naturally gather around Him; whereas in the latter vision, God sitting on His throne. the symbol of universal sovereignty, would account for the near place of the living creatures who represent the executive authority of the throne. The Gentile crowd on earth had ascribed salvation to "*our* God," but He is also the God of angels; hence they, too, in their place in the heavens say "*our* God." To the cry of the exultant redeemed the angels, which are as countless as the redeemed host on earth, in whom they are so deeply interested, fall down and worship, saying, Amen. How profound their worship may be gathered somewhat from their position, they fell down upon "their faces." The cry of the multitude is answered by the angels' "Amen." The terms in the angelic doxology differ in their order from that contained in chapter 5. There the *last* two terms, "glory and blessing," are the *first* named in our chapter. There "riches," here instead is "thanksgiving."*

The two redeemed companies on *earth* in our chapter are the elect of Israel and the white-robed multitude of Gentiles. The companies in Heaven are the angels, the elders, and the living creatures. Neither of the last two take part in the celebration of praise. This is confined to the Gentile crowd on earth, and to the angels in Heaven. The special object of the whole passage (vv. 9-17) is the relation of the palm-bearing multitude to God and to the Lamb. This really is the burden of their cry, which the angels fully own by adding their "Amen."† The relation of the elders and living ones to God is disclosed in chapters 4 and 5, and hence in those portions their worship is appropriately introduced, not here.

THE ELDER'S QUESTION AND ANSWER.

13-17.—"**And one of the elders answered, saying to me, These who are clothed with white robes, who are they, and whence came they? And I said to him, My Lord, thou knowest. And he said to me, These are they who come out of the great tribulation, and have washed their robes, and have made them white in the blood of the Lamb. Therefore are they before the throne of God, and serve Him day and night in His temple, and He that sits upon the throne shall spread His tabernacle over them. They shall not hunger any more, neither shall they thirst any more, nor shall the sun at all fall on them, nor any burning heat; because the Lamb which is in the midst of the throne shall shepherd them, and shall lead them to fountains of waters of life, and God shall wipe away every tear from their eyes.**" The Seer stood in silent wonder. He heard the exulting cry of the redeemed host and beheld their joy, but he did not personally participate in either. "One of the elders

* W. Kelly, F. B. Hooper, Bishop Ellicott, and others in their respective works on the Apocalypse read verse 12 with the definite article before each noun, thus: "*The* blessing, and *the* glory, and *the* wisdom, and *the* thanksgiving, and *the* honour, and *the* power, and *the* strength." Says an able writer: "The force of the article is to express each quality in its highest degree and excellence."

† The first "Amen" is the answer to the cry of the saved multitude. The second "Amen" is a confirmation of the truth of their own praise.

answered,'' not the spoken, but the unspoken inquiry of the heart of the Seer. The elders are characterised by the most elevated character of worship and intelligence in the mind and ways of God. They themselves were redeemed from earth, and hence it was fitting that one of them, and not a sinless celestial being, should be the interpreter to John, and through him to us, of the origin and history of this remarkable company for the first time beheld by the Seer. John was not unacquainted with the heavenly service of the elders. In a previous vision (chap. 5. 4, 5) one of them had comforted and instructed him. Hence the two questions put to John exactly expressed what he wanted to know: ''These who are clothed with white robes, *who* are they? and *whence* came they?''

It is not without significance that attention is called three times to their ''white robes'' (vv. 9, 13, 14). Their public acceptance by God, their recognition by Him in perfect purity of character and ways, are witnessed in those robes of purest white.*

THE GREAT TRIBULATION.

14.—''**These are they who come out of the great tribulation**.'' Our venerable Authorised Version is at fault here. It reads: ''These are they which came out of great tribulation.'' But the Revised Version and other versions give undoubtedly the Spirit's meaning, ''come,'' not ''came,'' and ''the tribulation,'' not ''tribulation'' simply. It is not the record of a past act, but they ''come out.'' It is regarded as a characteristically present action. ''*The* tribulation'' points to a definite prophetic period, and not simply to tribulation in general in which *all* saints share. ''*The* great tribulation''† cannot be the general troubles which afflict God's people in all ages. The insertion of the definite article marks its speciality. The Neronian‡ and other pagan and papal persecutions have been variously referred to as ''the great tribulation'' by the historical school of expositors. More frequently still the expression is thought to refer to the general troubles of life. But every interpretation of the Apocalypse which has history and not God's Word as its basis is necessarily confusing and uncertain. The force and import of the term must be sought for in Scripture and not in the records of

* An old Scotch divine remarks on this passage: ''The word translated robes properly signifies a marriage robe; and as both this word and the one translated *white* have the article prefixed it gives a peculiar force and beauty to the expression The allusion is to a marriage garment of the richest and most splendid appearance To take in the full idiom of the expression it would require to be rendered thus: 'Who are these clothed in the richest marriage robes, in robes of the purest white?' ''

† ''Out of the tribulation, the great one.''—*Alford*.

‡ ''The Early Days of Christianity,'' p. 448.—*Dean Farrar*.

human history. The interpretation of the Word, as also its application to the conscience, is the sole prerogative of the Holy Ghost Who inspired it.

"The great tribulation" is yet future. It pre-supposes the Jewish nation restored to Palestine in unbelief to serve Gentile political ends, and brought there by the active intervention of a great maritime power (Isa. 18). The duration of the coming hour of trial, which in its intensity will exceed all past and subsequent sorrows endured on earth (Mark 13. 19), is limited to the *second* half of Daniel's prophetic week of seven years (Dan. 9. 27 with Matt. 24. 15), or, speaking more correctly, to 1260 days, *i.e.*, 42 months of 30 days each* (Rev. 11. 3; 13. 5). Satan cast out of Heaven into the earth is the instigator of this unparalleled outburst of fury and hatred against God's witnesses, Jewish and Gentile (Rev. 12. 7-17). Satan's chief persecuting ministers will be "the beast," *i.e.*, the revived imperial power of Rome in the person of its head, the "little horn" (Dan. 7. 7, 21; Rev. 13. 1-8); the Antichrist, only so termed in John's epistles, the ally and confederate of the beast (Rev. 13. 11-17); and the king of the north, or the Assyrian (Dan. 8, 11; Isa. 10. 24-34).† The two former will be the active agents in persecuting the saints; the latter will be politically hostile to the restored Jewish commonwealth, but Jewish saints will also have to suffer as part and parcel of the nation. "The great tribulation," then, embraces Gentiles as well as Jews. Apostate Christendom is the wide sphere which will come under the direct judgment of Christ in the coming day, nor will the sword be sheathed till the heathen, too, feel the stroke (1 Peter 4. 17). But while the tribulation will embrace Jews and Gentiles, the former will suffer most severely (Jer. 30. 7). The Gentile company of our text comes *out* of the great tribulation. They have been preserved

---

* "The tribulation ends before the coming of Christ to reign (Matt. 24. 29); and I believe it will virtually close by the pouring out of the vials (Rev. 16). Writhing under these inflictions, neither the beast nor his myrmidons will be in a condition to persecute any longer. So it seems to me.

"The 1260 days of persecution (Rev. 11. 3), or 42 months, counting 30 days to a month, will end before the three and a half years are concluded. They fall short of this last period by 17 days, or more exactly 17¼ days. Till the 42 months end the beast's power is unchallengeable (chap. 13. 5). The seventh trumpet sounds, and the *mystery* of God is then finished. He will henceforth deal *directly* with the apostates, as the vials describe. It will be mystery as to that no longer.

"The days will be shortened, as the duration of the beast's power will be curtailed by the above mentioned days that will remain of the three and a half years of the week (Dan. 9. 27). Shortening or lengthening of days, not a day, refers to a period of time, and not to a natural day of twenty-four hours.

"The clue to me of a deal of all this is the difference between 1260 days and three and a half years. The former can by no possibility be made to equal the latter. At the end of the latter the Lord comes to reign. At the end of the former the trumpet sounds; and the balance of days between the 1260 days and the three and a half years leaves room for the outpouring of the vials."—"Truth for the Last Days," No. 4, p. 163, C.E.S. See also article, "The Celebrated Prophecy of the Seventy Weeks."

† See article "The Chief Actors in the Coming Crisis."

while Christendom, and Judea especially, have been bathed in the blood of God's saints.*

Their mystical robes derive their whiteness solely from the blood of Christ.

Next we have the standing or position of the Gentile throng. "*Therefore* are they before the throne of God." It is the shed blood of Christ which alone entitles anyone to stand before the throne. "This grace wherein we stand" (Rom. 5. 2) is ground common to all saints. The demonstrative pronoun points *not* to grace in general, but to that special grace of God witnessed in the death and resurrection of the Lord.

14.—"**Have washed their robes and made them white in the blood of the Lamb. Therefore are they before the throne of God.**" Washing robes is one of those expressions peculiar to the Apocalypse. Whatever may have been the special testimony addressed to these Gentiles,† evidently the blood of the Lamb was its grand and distinguishing feature. Their mystic robes could alone be made white in the blood. The ground on which they stood before the throne of God is one common to all saints in time and eternity. The blood of the Lamb, shed in divine purpose from the foundation of the world, is the only but adequate basis of appearing before the throne of God. "Therefore," or on this account, "are they before the throne," *i.e.*, because of the blood. The blood constituted these sinners *saints*; the tribulation made them *sufferers*.

15.—"**Serve Him day and night in His temple.**" We have had the historical origin of this innumerable redeemed company (v. 9); victorious too, and ascribing salvation to God and to the Lamb (vv. 9, 10). Then attention is called to the fact that they emerge out of the great tribulation, while, not their sufferings, but the blood of the Lamb gives them divine fitness to appear before the throne of God. Next we have their unceasing service, they "serve Him day and night in His temple." Another proof is here furnished that these saints are on earth, not in Heaven, for, says the Seer in a subsequent vision, "I saw no temple therein." Jerusalem on earth will have its temple, one of vast proportions, in which

---

* The location of the saved Gentile company, when the testimony of God reached their consciences, must not be confined to the territorial limits of Christendom. The largeness of the scene in verse 9 intimates a breadth which probably covers the whole Gentile world. Rejecters of God's grace—grace now fully and freely preached—are in the time of the tribulation given up to judicial dealing (2 Thess. 2. 10-12), and are punished with everlasting destruction at the Appearing of Christ (2 Thess. 1. 6-9). Hence these apostates are precluded from any share in the work of grace—widely and rapidly carried out (length of time uncertain) between the Translation and the Appearing.

† We do not read of any testimony borne by them.

Jews and Gentiles will worship and serve in millennial days (Ezek. 40-44; Isa. 56. 5-7). They are here viewed as a vast worshipping company, priests to God.*

15.—"**He that sits upon the throne shall spread His tabernacle over them.**" The Authorised Version reads, "shall dwell among them;" a poor and utterly inadequate rendering of the divine thought here expressed. God spread His tabernacle over the tent of meeting of old, which thus became the centre and rest of the thousands of Israel. It covered them in the desert. Two millions and a half of people, the typically redeemed host of Jehovah, were sheltered from scorching suns and winter's blasts by the huge canopy which God spread over them. It was the nation's glory and defence. The marginal reference in the Authorised Version, rightly so, directs us to Isaiah 4. 5, 6: "Jehovah will create over every dwelling place of Mount Zion, and over her assemblies, a cloud and smoke by day, and the shining of a flame of fire by night; for over all the glory (shall be) a canopy. And there shall be a booth (or tabernacle) for a shadow in the day time from the heat, and for a refuge and for a covert from storm and from rain." In the eternal state the tabernacle of God is with men (Rev. 21. 3); in millennial times God's tabernacle will be *over* them (chap. 7. 15, R.V.). What a sense of security the white-robed multitude will enjoy as they bask under the glorious overspread canopy, each member of the countless throng equally sheltered, equally protected! God's tabernacle spread over them, and the throne in all its strength and majesty for them!

The special millennial blessings of the redeemed Gentiles are next presented, negatively and positively, and suited exactly to the new order of things under the personal sway of Christ. In the enumeration of these earthly blessings one cannot fail to see how transcendently superior are those enjoyed by the saints in Heaven. Glory *with* Christ in the heavens, and blessing *under* Christ on the millennial earth define the difference. "They shall not hunger any more, neither shall they thirst any more, nor shall the sun at all fall on them, nor any burning heat." The reference to millennial days is undoubted (see Isa. 49. 10). In these emphatic negatives† the saved Gentile multitude is assured that the privations of life, hunger and thirst, and persecution and tribulation, sun and burning heat, shall never

---

* "They are not only as Israel in the courts, or the nations in the world; they have a priest's place in the world's temple. The millennial multitudes are worshippers—these priests. As Anna, the daughter of Phanuel, even in the temple itself they have always access to the throne."—"Synopsis of the Books of the Bible," vol. 5, p. 603.

† " 'No more,' or 'never,' is a mode of negation so often repeated in the Apocalypse (cp. chap. 18. 22, 33) that it is somewhat peculiar to this book in respect to *frequency*."—"A Commentary on the Apocalypse," p. 561.—*Moses Stuart.*

again be their sad lot. There shall be no recurrence of past evils.

17.—"**Because the Lamb which is in the midst of the throne shall shepherd them, and shall lead them to fountains of waters of life; and God shall wipe away every tear from their eyes.**" The Lamb "in the midst of the throne,"* exercising its power and expressing in Himself its majesty, will graciously provide for every need. Not angelic and providential care as now (Heb. 1. 14), but the shepherd grace of the Lamb will then be in exercise—tending, caring, preserving, and guiding each and all of the redeemed Gentile multitude. He "shall lead them to fountains of waters of life," not to channels or springs merely, but to the sources of life. The fulness and joy of earthly blessing shall be theirs, the Lamb Himself being their guide to these fountains or sources of unalloyed delight (see Isa. 12. 3).

The closing words are unequalled in their combined depth and tenderness: "And God shall wipe away every tear from their eyes," not the Lamb, be it observed, but God, against Whom they and we have sinned, shall Himself remove the causes and occasions of sorrow. If He wipes away every tear they shall never weep again. "Everlasting consolation" is the happy and assured portion of all His people, heavenly and earthly. The words in our text are verbally repeated in chapter 21. 4. *There* the eternal state is in view; *here* the millennial condition is in question. Both passages apply to saved people on earth, not to those in Heaven.

---

* See remarks on chapter 5. 6.

CHAPTER VIII.

First Four Trumpets.

GENERAL VIEW OF THE SEVEN TRUMPETS.

The coming great events which overshadow all others are the Translation *to* Heaven (1 Thess. 4. 16, 17) and the Return *from* Heaven (Rev. 19. 11-14). Paul alone treats of the former; John more fully than any of the other New Testament writers unfolds the latter. Now, in the interval between these two, the septenary series of judgments under the Seals, the Trumpets, and the Vials run their course. These divine chastisements increase in severity as we pass from one series to another. The judgments are not contemporaneous but successive. The Trumpets succeed the Seals, and the Vials follow the Trumpets. Strict chronological sequence is observed. The general symbol of the previous prophecy was a *Seal*; in the second series of judgments it is a *Trumpet*; in the third it is a *Vial* or bowl. These respective symbols impress a certain character on the events grouped under them. The Seals were opened in order that the successive parts of God's revelation of the future might be disclosed, but to faith only the mass would regard the judgments as merely providential. Such things had happened before. But the Trumpets' loud blast by angels intimates a public dealing with men of an intensely judicial character. These mystic Trumpets sound an alarm throughout the length and breadth of apostate Christendom. The public intervention of God in the guilty and apostate scene is thus intimated. Then in the third general symbol, that of the Vials or bowls poured out, the concentrated wrath of God overwhelms the whole prophetic scene under Heaven. Chapter 16 reveals a series of judgments hitherto unsurpassed in range and severity. During the progress of the Seal judgments the Lamb and His suffering people on earth are prominently introduced, but under the Trumpet judgments the Lamb wholly disappears, and saints are only incidentally noticed, and then as praying.

The prophecy under the first four Trumpets refers to the general state of things, civil and ecclesiastical, of the western Roman empire then revived. Chapter 8. 2-13 covers this ground. The recurrence of the expression, *third part* (twelve times repeated in our chapter, see R.V.), points to the resuscitated power of Rome, the same power which gave its legal sanction to the crucifixion of the Lord and scattered the Jews throughout the earth (see chap. 12. 3, 4).

Then the fifth Trumpet, or first Woe judgment (chap.

8. 13), falls on apostate Judaism, and is the subject of the first eleven verses of chapter 9. The sixth Trumpet, or second Woe judgment, deals directly with the guilty and apostate inhabitants of the Roman earth, and is the burden of chapter 9. 12-21. The final blast of the Trumpet, or third Woe, is universal in its effects, and in result reaches on to the end of the kingdom reign of 1000 years, even to "the time of the dead that they should be judged" (Rev. 20. 11-15). The momentous issues under the seventh Trumpet are briefly detailed within the compass of four verses, chapter 11. 15-18.

It will be observed that a "third part," so prominent in chapter 8, is not mentioned under the fifth and seventh Trumpets, but occurs again under the sixth. The omission in the two former is accounted for on the ground that the Roman power does not there come into view, whereas in the latter, *i.e.*, the sixth Trumpet, it is the immediate subject of the Lord's vengeance. The Trumpets, therefore, begin with chapter 8. 2 and close with verse 18 of chapter 11. Between these, however, an interesting and needful parenthetic portion occurs. This occupies chapters 10, 11. 1-13.

We have before remarked that the Seals, the Trumpets, and the Vials are respectively marked off into groups of four and three. Men in their circumstances and persons are judicially dealt with under the Seals, Trumpets, and Vials as a whole, but in the groups of three the strong arm of God is more distinctly witnessed. The source of all these apocalyptic judgments is God Himself, as the numeral three (*divine*) intimates. The human causes and instruments of judgment are prominent in the groups of four, just what that numeral speaks of.

THE SEVENTH SEAL
(Chap. 8).

1.—**"And when He opened the seventh Seal there was silence in the Heaven about half an hour."** The seven-sealed book, or scroll, seen in the open hand of Jehovah (5. 1, 2) has its Seals successively opened by the Lamb. Six of the seals were broken in chapter 6, and now, in the first verse of our chapter, He opens the final one, with the result that the book of God's counsels respecting the earth lies open before us. The plans, the counsels of our God regarding the vast interests of earth, as also the means and manner by which these counsels will be effected, are no longer a secret. All are disclosed. But why is the seventh Seal separated from the preceding six? Naturally one would suppose that it would have concluded chapter 6.

But instead a whole chapter (chap. 7) comes in between the sixth and seventh Seals, a parenthetic interruption breaking the orderly sequence of events. The sixth Seal (chap. 6. 12-17) announced judgment of such an appalling character that in the universal terror which ensued the fears of men, from the king to the slave, supposed the general horror to be the great day of the wrath of the Lamb. But no, and so ere the seventh Seal is opened, which is *preparatory* to the infliction of yet further and severer judgments, the veil is drawn aside, and two great millennial companies from amongst Israel and the Gentiles are introduced into the scene, the result of an extensive work of grace carried on even while judgment is desolating the earth (chap. 7).

"Silence in Heaven"* does not mean that the songs and hallelujahs of the redeemed are silent. The silence must be interpreted in connection with the immediate subject on hand, which is *judgment*. But, inasmuch as the source of these judgments on earth is the throne set in Heaven, the silence is there. The course of judgment is arrested. There is a pause both as to the announcement and execution of further chastisements. The silence is of brief duration. "Half an hour" simply denotes an exceedingly brief period during which judicial action is suspended. The breaking of the seventh Seal is followed, not by judgment, but by an ominous silence. It is a calm before a storm, like a stillness in nature preceding a tempest. How long the awful suspense lasts we are not informed, but in the meantime we are called to witness an action of an entirely different character from anything which has yet passed before us, and one which fills up the interval of the *half an hour*, whatever may be the precise length of time thereby indicated.

THE SEVEN ANGELS.

2.—"**And I saw the seven angels who stand before God, and seven trumpets were given to them.**" That the angels here referred to are a distinguished and select number seems evident from the insertion of the definite article, "*The* seven angels," as also from the highly honoured place assigned them, "who stand before

* Hengstenberg and some other expositors argue for a silence on *earth*, and quote in proof Habakkuk 2. 20, Zephaniah 1. 7, Zechariah 2. 13; these passages speak of a silence on earth, whereas our text, which so far as we can judge has no parallel or proof text in the Old Testament, speaks of "silence in *Heaven*." We are satisfied that the force of the expression simply denotes a brief pause during which the course of judgment is suspended. This is confirmed by a consideration of two texts, in both of which premonitory intimations of coming judgments are stated in substantially the same words. Under the *first* text, chapter 4. 5, we have a course of divine inflictions down to the close of chapter 6. Then comes a pause intimating a brief cessation of judgment. Then in the *second* text, chapter 8. 5, a further and similar intimation of divine chastisements is announced, and these latter take effect under the Trumpets. The silence is in Heaven because the judgments proceed from it.

God." "The seven" are distinguished from the seven who pour out the Vials (chap. 15. 1). Only of the trumpet angels is a special position ("before God") predicated.

There are distinctions amongst the angelic hosts. They are distributed into various orders and ranks, but all, from the archangel down to the least, are servants. They have no relationship to God founded on redemption. They are servants, and never rise out of that position, nor do they desire it. The two great characteristics of angel life are unquestioning obedience and activity in service (Psa. 103. 20; Heb. 1. 7, 14). The "*presence angels*" is a familiar Jewish thought. They are supposed by some to be identical with the seven Spirits before the throne (Rev. 1.4), and by others the term is regarded as a borrowed expression from the apocryphal book of Tobit. Both are wrong. Why depart from obvious simplicity and force an interpretation for which there is really no adequate reason? What the angel Gabriel said of himself, "I am Gabriel, *who stand before God*" (Luke 1. 19), is here said of these seven *presence angels*. As to the number, seven, they represent the full power of God in judical judgment.

2.—"**And seven trumpets were given to them.**" The place of subjection is ever the place of even the most exalted of God's creatures; the trumpets were *given*. Sovereign action is the prerogative alone of the Creator. But why trumpets? No wind instrument was more generally used in the national life of Israel than the trumpet. It convened them in public assembly. Its loud blast summoned them for war, and directed them when to advance and when to retreat. On the promulgation of the law "the voice of the trumpet sounded long, and waxed louder and louder." In their solemn feasts the trumpet was largely employed. Its loud warning notes announced the near approach of danger or an enemy. By sound of trumpet the journeys in the wilderness were directed. The year of jubilee, and, in fact, on all important national occasions the trumpet was employed (see Lev. 25. 9; Exod. 19. 19; Num. 10. 2-10; Lev. 23. 24, etc.). The circumstances calling for the public interference of God in judgment, as detailed in our portion of the Apocalypse, are somewhat similar to the coming days of Joel 2. 1, 2, "A day of darkness and of gloominess, a day of clouds and of thick darkness." Both Joel and John refer to the blast of the trumpet, intimating that God is about to deal openly and before all in judicial chastisement with the iniquity before Him, a public and loud announcement that He is about to do so. "The *seven* trumpets" signify a complete and full announcement. The *mystic* trumpets of the

Apocalypse must not be confounded with the *literal* trumpets of Old Testament times.

THE ANGEL PRIEST.

3-5.—"**And another angel came and stood at the altar, having a golden censer; and much incense was given to him, that he might give (efficacy) to the prayers of all saints at the golden altar which (was) before the throne. And the smoke of the incense went up with the prayers of the saints, out of the hand of the angel before God. And the angel took the censer, and filled it from the fire of the altar, and cast (it) on the earth: and there were voices, and thunders and lightnings, and an earthquake.**" The scene before us is one of profound interest, and cast moreover in the mould of familiar Jewish imagery. "Another angel." Who is he? We are satisfied that the angel priest is Christ, our great High Priest. The service at the altars proves it, for both the brazen altar and the golden altar are referred to. No mere creature could add efficacy to the prayers of saints, for that could only be effected by One having in Himself independent right and competency. Further, the action recorded at the altars is of a mediatorial character, one between suffering and praying saints on earth and God; and as Christianity knows of but "one Mediator between God and men, the Man Christ Jesus" (1 Tim. 2. 5), the proof is undeniable that the angel priest is Christ and Christ alone, not a representative person or company, as some expositors understand it. There is a pretty general consensus of thought amongst the early expositors of the Apocalypse in rightly regarding the angel here as meaning Christ to the exclusion of all others. "Another angel" is three times used of Christ in the apocalyptic visions (chaps. 8. 3; 10. 1; 18. 1). This title is one which supposes *reserve* and *distance*. The appellation "Lamb" is characteristic of the Apocalypse as a whole, and of the Seals in particular, and seems to be the chosen title expressive of Christ's interest in His saints, as also of their *intimacy* and *nearness* to Him. Under the trumpet series of judgments Christ morally retires and invests Himself in angelic title and character. When the saints come distinctly and prominently on to the prophetic scene then the title Lamb appears (see chaps. 7. 17; 14. 1, etc.).

3.—"**And another angel came and stood at the altar, having a golden censer.**" The reference here is to the altar of burnt-offering which stood in the court of the tabernacle of old. The fire at first miraculously kindled (Lev. 9. 24) was to be afterwards fed by the daily, yearly, and other sacrifices. This altar is mentioned six times in the Apocalypse, and simply as "the altar" (chaps. 6. 9; 8. 3, 5; 11. 1; 14. 18; 16. 7). It is only from Hebrews 9. 4 we learn that the censer in use in the yearly day of atonement (Lev. 16) was of gold. The censer was employed to carry the fire from off the brazen altar.

3.—"**And much incense was given to him that he might give (efficacy) to the prayers of all saints at the golden altar which (was) before the throne.**" The incense employed in the tabernacle service was composed of four ingredients, specified in Exodus 30. 34-36. It was a special preparation compounded according to a divine formula. Any unhallowed make, or use of it, was punished with death (vv. 37, 38). No doubt the *four* precious ingredients, three of which are only named once, set forth the moral beauties and perfections of Christ as witnessed in the *four* Gospels, but it needed the fire of judgment to draw out the full fragrance of Christ, and this Calvary alone could accomplish. The golden altar, twice referred to in the Apocalypse (chaps. 8. 3; 9. 13), stood within the tabernacle in the holy place, right in front of the veil. Blood, the witness of death and judgment, was put upon its four horns yearly (Lev. 16. 18, 19), as also on other occasions for atonement (Lev. 4. 7, 18). Incense was also burned upon it each morning and evening (Exod. 30. 7-10), "a perpetual incense before the Lord." The deep, deep meaning of the incense is more than tongue can tell or pen delineate. The sweet savour of Christ, what He was, what He did, and what He suffered is set forth by the incense.

Now let us put the various parts of the scene together and seek to understand its true bearing. The whole action is called for by the fact that a large body of suffering saints are on earth during the time of the sounding of the Trumpets, and for them intercession is needed. In an early period, under the fifth Seal, a company of martyrs is beheld. Their souls are under the altar, and they cry and pray (chap. 6. 9). But no priestly intercession is made for them; they need it not. This grace is provided for the living, not for the dead. The prayers of these saints, at the solemn crisis of the world's history in which their lot is cast, are not recorded. No doubt their general burden will be appeals to God for deliverance from, and judgment on, their ungodly oppressors. Their prayers do not breathe the accents of grace, but rather the reverse.*

Prayer for judgment then will be right and godly in accordance with the character and spirit of the Dispensa-

* "The character of the answer determines the nature of the petition that had been offered."

tion, as it would be most unsuitable now and contrary to the spirit of this period of God's long-suffering mercy. Spiritual prayer at the very best is necessarily imperfect, and so Christ adds His own perfectness in life and death. Thus the smoke of the incense, *i.e.*, the savour of Christ and the prayers of the saints went up together, not out of the golden censer, but "out of the *hand* of the angel before God," more intimate, more near surely than "out of the *censer*." How prevailing then the prayers of even the weakest saint when accompanied *with* the sweet savour of God's beloved One. The Angel (Christ) having gone from the altar of burnt-offering to the altar of incense, and presented the prayers of "all saints" then on earth to God, adding to them the sweet savour of His life and sacrifice, returns to the altar of burnt-offering and fills His now empty censer with fire from off it. But not with incense, for that was on behalf of saints. Judgment, pure judgment, will be meted out to the apostate earth, and of this we have the stern intimation in the forcible act of the angel who "took the censer and filled it from the fire of the altar, and cast (it) on the earth." A striking intimation of judicial procedure. God is about to punish the earth, and as the altar was the expression of His holiness and righteousness in dealing with the sin of His people of old, so that same holiness and righteousness will search the earth and judge and punish accordingly. The angel's act is immediately followed by the symbolic signs of almighty power. "There were voices, and thunders and lightnings, and an earthquake," harbingers of the coming successive outbursts of divine wrath on the earth. "These terms compose a FORMULA OF CATASTROPHE; and the fourfold character here denotes the universality of *the catastrophe in respect of the thing affected*."* We have the same divine formula intimating immediate judgment substantially repeated four times (chaps. 4. 5; 8. 5; 11. 19; 16. 18). In the first of these references the concentration of coming wrath is limited to these three tokens: "lightnings, and voices, and thunders." In the second and third references an "earthquake" is added; while in the fourth (chap. 16. 21) we meet with a still further addition, "and great hail." But in the four texts we have, with slight variation in the order of the terms, "lightnings, and voices, and thunders."

PREPARING TO SOUND.

6.—"**And the seven angels who had the seven trumpets prepared themselves that they might sound with their trumpets.**" These seven angels do

* "The Revelation of Jesus Christ by John," p. 341.—*Hooper*.

not themselves execute the judgments which they announce. The four judgment angels (chap. 9. 14) are distinguished from the seven trumpet angels. The seven *presence angels* received their trumpets before the episode of the angel priest's intercession (v. 2). But the greatness and solemnity of the work on hand is intimated by the signs and tokens of almighty power. Now the angels prepare themselves. There is no hurry, but premonitory signs by Christ, and careful preparation by the angels, certainly indicate the serious nature of the situation, one calling for unsparing judgment.

FIRST TRUMPET.

7.—**"And the first sounded (his) trumpet: and there was hail and fire, mingled with blood, and they were cast upon the earth; and the third part of the earth was burnt up, and the third part of the trees was burnt up, and all green grass was burnt up."** "Hail and fire mingled with blood." These are not to be understood as literal destructive agencies. They are symbols. The seventh plague in Egypt was one of "hail and fire," a tempest unexampled in the history of that most ancient of kingdoms (Exod. 9. 18-25). The coming judgment here announced will be of a more appalling character, more ruinous and widespread, not one, moreover, effected by the destructive forces of nature, "hail and fire." The introduction of a third element, not as a separate devastating agency, but the two first named, "mingled with blood," stamps a peculiar and superhuman character on this judgment. It is one which in its singular combination of forces is entirely outside the domain of nature. The judgment is not of a providential kind, not a literal hail and fire storm. What then do these symbols teach? How are we to read and understand them? On this Scripture is by no means silent.

Hail signifies a sudden, sharp, and overwhelming judgment from above, God the executor of it (see Isa. 28. 2, 17; Rev. 11. 19; 16. 21). **Fire** is the expression of God's wrath. As a symbol it is more largely employed than any other in the Sacred Volume. Thorough, unsparing, agonising judgment is denoted by fire. It has, of course, other significations, but we are only concerned now with its judicial application (see Deut. 32. 22; Isa. 33. 14; Luke 16. 24; Rev. 20. 10, 14, 15). **Blood** signifies death, both physical and moral. In the latter it would assume the form or character of apostasy, *i.e.*, the utter abandonment of revealed truth, all religious profession given up;* for blood

* Jude 12, "twice dead;" first as dead in sins, second dead by apostasy.

as physical death, see Genesis 9. 5, 6; Ezekiel 14. 19; for blood as moral death, see Acts 2. 19, 20; Revelation 6. 12; 16. 3-6. Now while the two former symbols may be regarded separately, "hail *and* fire," we cannot so treat the third. The "blood" was mingled with those two elements of destruction. Combined they express a truly awful outburst of divine wrath, whoever or whatever the agencies may be to accomplish the divine purpose. The trumpet sounds, the judgment is a public one.

7.—"**And they were cast upon the earth,**" thus covering as a subject of judgment precisely the same sphere on which the angel scattered the fire from the altar (v. 5). In both cases (vv. 5 and 7) the term "cast" implies irresistible power behind. That the judgment of the hail and fire with blood is not traceable to natural causes is evident from the fact that they were cast down, not falling from the heavens in an ordinary way, but impelled by an unseen yet powerful arm. The area affected is said to be *the earth*. But as *earth* and *sea* are separately referred to in the symbolism of the Apocalypse we have to inquire what they respectively signify. In chapter 10 we have a vision of Christ characterised by the insignia of divine majesty. He descends from Heaven to claim the world as a whole. It is His. Significantly, therefore, in the assertion of His universal and sovereign right He plants His right foot on the *sea* and His left on the *earth*, thus taking possession of the whole scene under Heaven. Those two parts of the natural creation present a picture of (1) *restlessness* (sea), and (2) *stability* (earth). The same symbolic representations in other parts of the Apocalypse, as elsewhere, fix and determine a meaning as precise and full as if the words and not the symbols were used. A symbol brings before the mind a complete picture of what is intended to be conveyed, oftentimes much more forcibly than by the use of a lengthened statement; hence the universality of symbols in the expression of human thought. The *earth*, then, denotes that part of the world civilised and under constituted authority, fixed and settled government. The *sea*, on the contrary, represents that portion of the world in disorder, the scene of anarchy and of wild rebellion, without divine and civil government.* The

* It has been asserted that the symbolism of the Hebrews was borrowed from Egypt and Assyria, where in both kingdoms the system of representation had attained to a high degree of excellence. But are we to conceive of God borrowing from the pagan nations of antiquity? The thought betrays gross ignorance, and in its conception is thoroughly infidel. The truth is that symbolism is much more ancient than the kingdoms referred to, and is coeval with the existence of the race. Thus in the earliest period revealed (Gen. 2) the symbolic trees of life and of the knowledge of good and evil arrest our attention as being the first symbols presented to men. It is part of the universal language. A symbol presented to the mind conveys in a forcible manner the moral features or characteristics of the thing on hand. Thus a lion, "the lord of the forest," at once suggests the idea of *majesty*, of *royal*

public rejection of God will be quickly followed by the repudiation of civil and magisterial authority, and when lawlessness and impiety have reached their climax then God intervenes in judgment. Of this the prophetic part of the Apocalypse affords a striking witness, as we hope to see in the course of these studies.

"The third part of the earth was burnt up," also the third part of the trees, and all green grass. We now witness the dire results produced by this manifest judgment from Heaven. Those lands on which Christianity has shone so brightly are then given up to judgment. God in His relation to the nations as supreme has, in the time of the Trumpets, been forsaken, and Christianity abandoned. What then remains but the mighty arm of God to be bared in judgment? The destructive symbolic elements were cast upon the earth. The results are threefold.

(1) **"The third part of the earth was burnt up."** This is wholly omitted in the Authorised Version, but inserted in the Revised on unimpeachable authority. The western part of the prophetic earth is here designated as *the third part.** The revived empire with its personal,

power; hence these moral characteristics denoted by the symbol may be applied to Christ (Rev. 5. 5), or to the first of the great universal empires (Dan. 7. 4). It is not that the lion represents either Christ or the mighty Babylonian empire, but rather the characteristics of the lion in *greatness* and *majesty*, and of course these qualities may be applied to persons or objects as the case may be. The symbol represents a certain moral characteristic or idea. It must not be supposed that the frequent use of symbols is a mark of the poverty of language. In fact in every language and amongst all peoples, civilised and barbarian, a representative system of speech is in general use. The language of symbols quickly became incorporated in the religions of the ancient world. "It was the language of the shrine, the oracle, and the temple." With many invisible realities are more easily conceived of when represented by objects presented to the eye and mind. Our readers will find help in the perusal of "Sacred Symbology," by John Mills; but especially in an article entitled "Symbols" in vol. 1 of "Notes and Comments on Scripture," by the late J. N. Darby.

* The four universal empires, and there are but four, are represented as metals (Dan. 2) and beasts (chap. 7). These are Babylon, Persia, Greece, and Rome. The first three are expressly named in Scripture by the Hebrew prophet. The fourth, or Roman, is pointed out in Luke 2. 1, "There went out a decree from Caesar Augustus that all the world should be taxed." Rome was founded 753 B.C., shortly before the ten tribes were taken captive by Shalmaneser. Romulus, its first king, gave name to the city, which was destined to play such an important part in the world's history. Carthage, the African rival of Rome, was the only power which seemed to check its growing greatness. The African was the elder of the two, and of great wealth. But Ham had to succumb to Japheth. Rome increased in power and in territorial extent till the known world lay at her feet (Luke 2. 1). Says Gibbon: "The empire of the Romans filled the world." After the conquest of Greece the early virtues of the Roman character became impaired and degeneration set in. Integrity and justice, once so characteristic of early Rome, were now wantonly sacrificed and trampled under foot, while personal ambition, instead of care for the State and its interests, became the distinguishing features of its emperors and generals. After the empire had existed for more than five hundred years, undivided and universal, its dismemberment in the fourth and fifth centuries took place. It ceased to exist. The rise of the papacy and decline of the empire were coeval and connected events. The supremacy of the See of Rome dates from the fourth century. The present European situation, with its numerous and conflicting interests, is the result really of the complete break up of the once undivided empire of the Caesars. The pen of the historian has traced the history of Rome from its rise, 753 B.C., till its inglorious fall, A.D. 476, but there it stops. God lifts the veil and shows the future of the now defunct empire. The Hebrew prophet (Dan. 2; 7) and the christian apostle (Rev. 17; 19) clearly show that the empire will be revived and shown to be in existence at the Coming of the Lord in power. Its utter destruction by the Lord in Person will be immediately succeeded by the millennial and universal kingdom of our Lord Jesus Christ, which will surpass in greatness, character, and in territorial extent every power on earth since the world began (Dan. 7. 26, 27).

persecuting, and blasphemous head, the "little horn" (Dan. 7. 8), with its ancient and renowned capital, Rome (Rev. 17. 18), will again dominate the earth, but the empire, at least in its most guilty part, the west, will be given up to feel the Lord's vengeance. Whether the term "burnt up" refers to the desolating ravages of war or other heaven-sent agencies we know not, but that the empire will be wasted and desolated by several combined judgments seems evident.

(2) **"The third part of the trees was burnt up."** Here the stern hand of judgment reaches out to the great and distinguished; to men in the haughtiness of pride and position. Destruction overtakes all such, all, of course, within the sphere contemplated in the prophecy. A tree is an apt and familiar figure of human greatness; of pride and of high position amongst men (Ezek. 31; Dan. 4. 4-27; Judges 9. 8-15, etc.).

(3) **"All green grass was burnt up."** There is no limitation here, no "third part," or even "fourth part," as under the fourth Seal (chap. 6. 8). *Grass* refers to the people of Israel (Isa. 40. 7); the human race is also spoken of as grass (1 Peter 1. 24). "*Green* grass" would naturally signify a highly prosperous condition of things amongst the inhabitants of the empire generally. The association of trees and grass, as in chapter 9. 4 and here also, would intimate judgment upon all, high and low, involving the utter destruction of all their happy surroundings. The condition indicated by the "green grass burnt up" points to a general scene of desolation. What awful days are in store for these countries *now* so highly blest and favoured, but *then* in retributive justice given up to the stern judgment of God.

SECOND TRUMPET

8, 9.—**"And the second angel sounded (his) trumpet: and as a great mountain burning with fire was cast into the sea; and the third part of the sea became blood; and the third part of the creatures which were in the sea, which had life, died; and the third part of the ships were destroyed."** "A great mountain burning with fire." Scripture itself gives the force of the figure. The mighty Babylonian monarchy is thus spoken of by the prophet Jeremiah (chap. 51. 25), "Behold, I am against thee, O destroying mountain, saith the Lord, which destroyest all the earth; and I will stretch out Mine hand upon thee, and roll thee down from the rocks, and will make thee a *burnt mountain*." Jehovah here threatens the Chaldean kingdom—apparently so firmly established in its might and greatness as to defy an overthrow—with consuming judgment, a "burnt mountain." Again, the stone which no human hand or tool had touched falls with crushing effect upon the feet of the image, the figure of Gentile power, and *then* becomes "a *great mountain*, and filled the whole earth" (Dan. 2). The world-wide dominion of the Son of Man is thus set forth. A mountain as a symbol represents a kingdom (Isa. 2. 2; Zech. 4. 7; Jer. 51. 25) or a firmly established power (Psa. 46. 2; Rev. 6. 14; 16. 20). The abstract idea, important to lay hold of in these prophetic symbols, is that of a strong, consolidated, established power, and this power itself the subject of God's governmental vengeance, for the Seer saw it burning with fire, becoming in the divine hand the instrument of judgment upon the heathen. The weeping prophet, Jeremiah, exactly defines the force and value of the imagery in our text (chap. 51. 25).

8.—**"Was cast into the sea."** In the previous Trumpet (v. 7) the *earth* was the scene of judgment; here it is the *sea*. The earth is the Roman world in general, the third part being the western portion of the empire. The sea sets forth a state of rebellion against constituted authority; of peoples in a condition of unrest, and consequently outside the limits of the Roman world. Within this latter, in the past as in the future, authority and government are upheld. The ever-restless sea (Isa. 57. 20; Dan. 7. 2, 3; Rev. 13. 1; 18. 21) is here the chosen figure to denote the peoples of the earth in dire anarchy, owing to the want of a strong controlling power or firm hand. Civil and governmental authority are ordained of God (Rom. 13. 1). The state of things in the future amongst the nations outside the territorial limits of the revived Roman power may be compared to the condition of France during the reign of terror in the eighteenth century—a nation without God, without religion, and with but the semblance of government, controlled by the wild passions of the mob, the devil's playground in Europe. The prophetic sea, therefore, represents the general condition of the nations without civil and spiritual government. Into the seething masses of mankind, of heathenism, this burning power is cast. We now witness the dire results produced. These are threefold, as in the first trumpet.

(1) **"The third part of the sea became blood."** Does blood here symbolise a violent natural death, or does it refer to the spiritual death of apostasy? In our judgment these two forms of death are here combined. Those nations in political or in outward relation to the dominant power of the Roman empire are destroyed.

The destruction of life amongst the Gentiles, in association with the guiltiest of the four universal empires, is what the symbol sets forth. Spiritual and physical death is the sure result of any connection with the apostate, blaspheming, and persecuting power of Rome.

(2) "**The third part of the creatures which were in the sea, which had life, died.**" That part of the world not brought into orderly subjection to constituted authority, but in external relation to the empire, is next seen in vision, as visited in judgment. Persons, and not peoples or nations in general, as in the first judgment, are in question. The term "creatures" would imply as much. Even in heathenism varying measures of responsibility and commensurate degrees of guilt exist. "The third part," *i.e.*, the worst is before us in this series of divine chastisements. "The third part of the creatures which were in the sea, which had life, died." The interpretation of the Seals is a simple matter compared to that of the Trumpets. In the latter there is a purposed mysteriousness in the symbols employed which makes a minute examination somewhat difficult. Here, however, with chapters 2. 23 and 3. 1 before us we are on firm ground. Moral, spiritual death is the undoubted force of the judgment here executed. Death towards God, towards principles of truth and righteousness, and, in fact, death viewed morally in its widest aspect and character.

(3) "**The third part of the ships were destroyed.**" Now this destructive power, whether a nation or a system, violently thrown into the unformed masses of mankind not only works awful destruction, physical and moral, on peoples and persons, it wrecks also the commerce and means of communication with distant countries. "The third part of the ships were destroyed." But the tale of judgment is not yet told. The darkness thickens as the night wears on. Horror succeeds horror. O that Christendom would wake up to the stern reality that the Judge is at the door!

THIRD TRUMPET.

10, 11.—"**And the third angel sounded (his) trumpet: and there fell out of the Heaven a great star, burning as a torch, and it fell upon the third part of the rivers, and upon the fountains of waters. And the name of the star is called Wormwood; and the third part of the waters became wormwood; and many of the men died of the waters, because they were made bitter.**" At the blast of the trumpets the four restraining angels let loose the four winds of the earth, the providential agencies of judgment (chap. 7. 1). The dark cloud of vengeance upon a guilty scene is lifted for a brief space, during which God in sovereign grace works amongst Israel and the Gentiles (chap. 7). Then under the Trumpets the orderly course of judgment is resumed. The previous blasts announced judgments of the most appalling character on the *earth* and on the *sea*: the former the scene of governmental order, and where, too, God had been more or less professedly owned; the latter the sphere where the forces of anarchy and the will of man reigned supreme, which is ever to the denial of spiritual and civil authority. This Trumpet intimates a judgment equal in terrible severity, and in some respects even more awful than the preceding ones. "There fell out of the Heaven a great star." The Heaven is the source of authority; it is a definitely fixed position; hence the introduction of the article "*the* Heaven." All spiritual, civil, and political authority has its source *above*. "The heavens do rule" (Dan. 4. 26). Under the two preceding trumpets the instruments of judgment were "*cast*" upon the earth and sea respectively, but from whence we are not informed. Here this apostate dignitary "*fell*" out of the Heaven.* The word "cast" would imply the exercise of irresistible power on the part of the unseen actor, as also the violence of the judgment; whereas "fell," as also in chapter 9. 1, would rather point to a sudden, unexpected downfall. The "star" as a symbol is one of frequent occurrence in the Apocalypse, and denotes a ruler, or one occupying a place of influence and position in responsibility to God (chaps. 12. 1-4; 6. 13, etc.). Supremacy is denoted by the *sun*; derived and subordinate authority is figured by the *moon*; while *stars* point to lesser authorities. This "great star" evidently symbolises a distinguished ruler responsible as set in the moral firmament to give light in the then dark night of the world's history, but he is an apostate personage, one under the immediate judgment of God, "burning as a torch;" in this respect like the "great mountain burning with fire." The epithet "great" is attached to the mountain, and also to the star; only in the former a corporate power or system is referred to, whereas in the latter an exalted individual is meant. Who this degraded and apostate person is we are not informed. Some regard the great fallen star as denoting the personal Antichrist.†

* The "great star" of chapter 8. 10 must not be confounded with the falling star of chapter 9. 1. Both are spiritual rulers, viewed as morally fallen from their high position. They are, however, distinct personages.

† The symbolic name of the star (v. 11) gives no indication of the person referred to, but rather of the baneful influence exercised.

But that does not amount to more than conjecture. The Antichrist plays an important part in the coming crisis, as we shall see in subsequent studies.

10.—"**It fell upon the third part of the rivers, and upon the fountains of waters.**" *Waters* in general signify peoples (chap. 17. 15; Isa. 17. 12, 13); the *sea* points to a state of commotion, of unrest amongst those peoples (Isa. 57. 20; Dan. 7. 3); *floods*, fulness of earthly blessings (Isa. 44. 3), as also earthly calamities (Amos 8. 8); *rivers*, the ordinary life of a nation or people characterised by certain principles (Ezek. 29. 3; Isa. 18. 2); *fountains*, the sources of the principles and influences which act upon the life of a nation (Joel 3. 18; Jer. 6. 7).

11.—"**The name of the star is called Wormwood**; and the third part of the waters became wormwood; and many of the men died, because they were made bitter." The name "Wormwood" is significant of character. Many of the older expositors regard the personage here as Satan, but, as has already been remarked, we have no means to identify the person by name. The geographical area affected is the "third part." The fountains, the sources of national life, are poisoned. All under the withering influences of this fallen being partake of his character, "Wormwood." Evidently there is a reference to that interesting incident in Israel's history detailed in Exodus 15. 22-25. *There* the bitter waters were made sweet; *here* the sweet waters are made bitter. National life and character are corrupted. A judicial dealing of an intensely solemn character overtakes a third part of the nations; their springs of action, their motives, principles, and moral life are poisoned, with the result that "many" die. It is not physical but moral death that is in question, truly more awful than the former. "When you look at these bitter ingredients infused into the waters by the fall of this great star, the wonder is not that many died, but that any lived."*

FOURTH TRUMPET.

12.—"**And the fourth angel sounded (his) trumpet: and the third part of the sun was smitten, and the third part of the moon, and the third part of the stars; so that the third part of them should be darkened, and that the day should not appear (for) the third part of it, and the night the same.**" The sun, moon, and stars collectively symbolise the whole governing body, from the supreme head down to all lesser authorities —a complete system of government in all its parts. Under

* "Lectures on the Revelation," p. 181.—*Ramsay.*

the sixth Seal (chap. 6. 12, 13) the same symbols are presented to express an utter collapse of all governing authority on earth. The might of man is broken. Every power under Heaven is overthrown. Long established governments, and all dependent power and authority fall in the universal crash. *There*, however, the disruption of the whole social fabric, and the overthrow of every seat of power, is in no wise restricted. The only limitation under the Seals is a "fourth part," which occurs but once (chap. 6. 8). *Here* under the fourth Trumpet the judgment and its effects extend to the "third part" of the prophetic scene, the western part of the revived empire. In this connection the term "third part" occurs five times (v. 12). The effect of this judgment is that moral darkness, like a funeral pall, settles down upon the empire.

A LOUD AND UNIVERSAL ANNOUNCEMENT OF THE THREE WOE TRUMPETS.

13.—"**And I saw, and I heard an eagle flying in mid-heaven, saying with a loud voice, Woe, woe, woe, to them that dwell upon the earth, for the remaining voices of the trumpet of the three angels who are about to sound.**" "I saw and I heard," both eye and ear were engaged, thus intimating the rapt attention and interest of the Seer in the events which passed before him in the vision. The Authorised Version reads "*angel*," but we have substituted "*eagle*" on decisive and competent authority. There is a mission entrusted to a flying angel (chap. 14. 6), as also one, but of a different character, to a flying eagle (chap. 8. 13). Mid-heaven, or the firmament, is the sphere traversed by both, so that they could scan the earth from its centre to its remotest bounds. The former is a messenger of mercy, this latter is a herald of judgment. The triple cry of "woe" finds its fitting announcement by the eagle. In its rapid and lofty flight across the meridian sky it aloud proclaims the coming doom of the christianised portion of the earth, of those who proudly rejected the "heavenly calling," of whom Paul writes, "Whose end is destruction, whose god is their belly, who mind earthly things" (Phil. 3. 19). A special class is here singled out from earth's inhabitants, a moral class, spoken of as those "that dwell upon the earth," and twice previously referred to (chaps. 3. 10; 6. 10). On these apostates, the worst in these dark and evil times, direct and irremediable judgment is publicly and loudly announced. A more fitting symbol could not be employed than an eagle in its aerial flight across the heaven, scanning from afar its prey. The eagle is the harbinger of approaching judgment (see Deut. 28. 49; Jer. 48. 40; Matt. 24. 28). The four preceding judgments were of a general character, but in those to come the climax of horror is reached; hence this preliminary announcement.*

* "Woe, specially on those who had their settled place on earth, in contrast with the heavenly calling, and who were unawakened and unmoved by the judgments on the earth, but cling to it as their home in spite of all is then announced. Threefold woe! The term 'dwellers on,' or 'inhabiters of,' the earth has not yet been used, save in the promise to Philadelphia and the claims of the souls under the altar, for both of these were in contrast with such. After all these dealings of God, they are a distinct and manifested class, and spoken of in what passes on the earth as such. Against this perversely unbelieving class the earthly judgments of God are now directed; the first against the Jews, the second against the inhabitants of the Roman earth, the last universal."—"Synopsis of the Books of the Bible," vol. 5, p. 605

CHAPTER IX.

FIFTH AND SIXTH TRUMPETS.

THE FIRST WOE TRUMPET.

1-12.—**"And the fifth angel sounded (his) trumpet: and I saw a star out of the Heaven fallen to the earth; and there was given to it the key of the pit of the abyss. And it opened the pit of the abyss; and there went up smoke out of the pit as (the) smoke of a great furnace; and the sun and the air were darkened with the smoke of the pit. And out of the smoke came forth locusts on the earth, and power was given to them as the scorpions of the earth have power. And it was said to them that they should not injure the grass of the earth, nor any green thing, nor any tree, but the men who have not the seal of God on their foreheads. And it was given to them that they should not kill them, but that they should be tormented five months; and their torment (was) as (the) torment of a scorpion when it strikes a man. And in those days shall men seek death, and shall in no way find it; and shall desire to die, and death flees from them. And the likenesses of the locusts (were) like to horses prepared for war; and upon their heads as crowns like gold, and their faces as faces of men. And they had hair as women's hair, and their teeth were as of lions. And they had breastplates as breastplates of iron, and the sound of their wings (was) as the sound of chariots of many horses running to war. And they have tails like scorpions, and stings; and their power (was) in their tails to hurt men five months. They have a king over them, the angel of the abyss; his name in Hebrew Abaddon, and in Greek he has for name Apollyon. The first woe has past; behold, there come yet two woes after these things."** The details of this "woe" are wrapped up in mysterious language and symbol, but the general bearing seems evident. The Trumpets present more difficulties in minute exposition than either the Seals or Vials. But care, patience, and waiting upon God for light and intelligence are vital factors in the elucidation of Scripture. We "have an unction from the Holy One," said of even babes in Christ (1 John 2. 20, 27), and we "have the mind of Christ" (1 Cor. 2. 16), *i.e.*, the intelligent reasoning faculty, and are thus made divinely competent to understand the written Revelation of our God.

TWO FALLEN STARS.

1.—**"A star out of the Heaven fallen to the earth."** The Authorised Version reads, "I saw a star *fall* from Heaven," whereas what the Seer beheld was the star when *fallen*, not in the act of falling.

Under the third and fifth Trumpets (chaps. 8. 10; 9. 1) apostate personages of high position and of commanding influence figure in the prophetic scene. The "great star" of chapter 8. 10 and the "star" of chapter 9. 1 do not set forth systems of civil or ecclesiastical power singly or combined, nor a succession of eminent persons, but point to those once set in the moral Heaven, *i.e.*, recognised authorities of a religious character now fallen and degraded and acting under satanic influence. In the earlier reference (chap. 8. 10) the degraded ruler fills the western part of the Roman world (the guiltiest) with misery and death. In the later scene he is about to let loose the malignant and darkening power of Satan on the apostate part of Judah.* Apostate *Gentiles* are the subjects of judgment under the third Trumpet; apostate *Jews* are the sufferers under the fifth Trumpet. The state of things under the first Woe, or fifth Trumpet, surpasses anything we have hitherto witnessed. Direct satanic influence and power energise the agents and instruments of evil.

HISTORICAL RESEMBLANCE AND SEQUENCE.

Under the successive judgments and events revealed in the Apocalypse a certain historical correspondence and sequence may be traced. But by no means a partial, much less an exhaustive, fulfilment is to be sought for in the annals of the historian.

The Revelation, from chapter 4 to 22. 5, is not history, but prophecy. The shadows only of the future are thrown on the masterly pages of Gibbon and others. But inasmuch as the principles which govern men and nations are ever the same, for there is "nothing new under the sun," an historical resemblance to the prophecies under the Seals, Trumpets, and Vials is fully allowed. We are satisfied, however, that the historical application of the Apocalypse, especially the central part, as set forth in most of the literature on the subject to-day, is a serious mistake. The course of prophecy is resumed in connection with the last of Daniel's 70 weeks or 490 years (Dan. 9. 27), and *after* the translation of the heavenly saints (1 Thess. 4. 17).

*** Judah, in the coming crisis, in her closing hour of sorrow and unbelief, and previous to the public intervention of Christ on her behalf, seems to be completely under the power and influence of Satan. The last state of Israel is worse than the first. Idolatry rampant in the land (Matt. 12. 45), and her chiefs and guides in league with death and hell (Isa. 28. 15-18), make an awful picture of combined satanic and human wickedness.**

Paul witnesses to the translation. John in the Apocalypse views the translated in Heaven (chap. 4). The whole of this Church period, the history of Christianity itself, is a great and intensely interesting episode, and has its place between the *close* of the sixty-ninth and the *opening* of the seventieth week of Daniel, and yet forming no part of either. The Church is not the subject of prophecy but of Revelation. It was a mystery hidden from men and angels till revealed to and by Paul to us (Eph. 3). The Jew, and subordinately the Gentile, is the subject of prophecy. The supreme importance of the Jew is the key to unlock prophecy. The prophetic periods are all in relation to the Jews and Jerusalem (Dan. 9. 24*); those contained in the central part of the Apocalypse equally so. But, as we have said, history presents a resemblance (*not* fulfilment) to the prophetic portions of the Apocalypse; a resemblance not devoid of interest. According to the ablest of the historical school—and in this there is substantial agreement amongst his confrères—the first four Seals represent four successive periods of pagan Rome. Then on the downfall of paganism and the historical triumph of Christianity large numbers, both of Jews and Gentiles, were converted to God, and of this it is supposed chapter 7 speaks. Then the first four Trumpets are said to pertain still to pagan Rome, but in its decline, downfall, and extinction in the west. The northern irruptions of Gothic, Lombard, and Hungarian into the fertile fields and rich and prosperous towns of Italy soon culminated in the destruction of the empire of the Caesars. The rule of the uncivilised barbarian in Rome itself, once the proud and haughty mistress of the world, was a sorrowful but instructive spectacle. Rome fell A.D. 476.

Again, the fallen star of chapter 9 is generally supposed to point to the great Arabian impostor Mohammed, and certainly he may well be regarded as the prototype of the coming false prophet, the man of sin, and the Antichrist—titles referring to one and the same person. Mohammed†

* "Seventy weeks (490 years) are determined upon *thy* people (the *Jews*), and upon *thy* holy city (*Jerusalem*)."

† Mohammed (lit. "The Praised One") was born in Arabia, at the famous city of Mecca, A.D. 570. The Koran (lit. "The Reading") is the Bible of the Mohammedan world, and was cleverly compiled by Mohammed, partly from materials supplied by a renegade Jew and an apostate Christian, and added to by the impostor himself as occasion required. Whatever is really good in it is from Judaism and Christianity. But there is much that is disgusting and filthy in the book. Mohammedanism as a system is the greatest curse on the face of the earth, and has effected the spiritual ruin to-day of fully 150 millions of the earth's teeming population, and what of the countless millions in the past who lived and died in the faith of the hellish creed of the Arabian prophet? The professing Church has broken up into fragments, and by far the largest and worst of these fragments is Roman Catholicism. But bad as it is, with its mixture of paganism and Christianity, Mohammedanism is infinitely worse. Its founder was, without doubt, devil inspired. Mohammed, the fallen star, opened the pit and let loose the darkening power of Satan, and flooded the east, and partially the west, with doctrines which can justly be termed hellish in their nature and effects. For information on this system of deadly error, see "Studies in Mohammedanism," by J. J. Pool.

founded the most satanic system the world has ever known. The Antichrist yet to come will head up under Satan the most awful combination of soul-destroying and blasphemous doctrines conceivable. Pursuing the historical application, the locust army would be the Saracens, whose military achievements, equalled by their spiritual conquests, are a wonder to this day. The east was conquered. The Crescent displaced the Cross. The ruin of the east may be well likened to a locust devastation. Only the glorious victory of Charles the *Hammer* (so termed because of his military prowess) at Tours, in France, checked the career of the Saracenic host and preserved the west as a whole from Mohammedan apostasy, with its awful consequences for time and eternity. The five months of torment (chap. 9. 10) are supposed to refer to the 150 years of unchecked conquest by the Moslem hordes on the year-day theory. Then the sixth Trumpet, or second Woe, is applied to the revival of Mohammedanism under the Turks, and the extinction of the Greek-Roman empire in the ever memorable siege and capture of Constantinople. For nearly eight hundred years repeated efforts had been made to establish Islamism in the eastern half of the empire, but beautiful Constantinople, standing on the borders of Europe and Asia—the Bosphorus dividing the two continents—defied capture. Its hour, however, had come. The decree had gone forth. Mohammed the Second entered Constantinople on the morning of the 29th May, 1453. The great Greek Church was purified and then transformed into a mosque, and the Crescent floated over the walls of the city of the Caesars.

But the corrupt Turkish power is waning, and the predicted drying up of the Euphrates (chap. 16. 12), that famous river, is claimed by historicalists to point to that cruel Mohammedan power now and for many years past almost tottering to its fall. Its complete destruction is certain. Such, then, in brief, are a few of the leading points in which, in the interpretation of the prophetic parts of the Apocalypse, the historical school feel on firm ground. In our judgment the position is untenable. It is an impossibility to square these prophetic visions with the facts of history. There is at the most but a general resemblance, and fulfilment in the past of the visions and prophecies there is *not*. God will "Amen" them to the full in that brief and solemn crisis for Israel and Christendom, after the translation of the heavenly saints, in the coming reign of Antichrist and his political chief and confederate, the Beast or revived empire, with its great personal head, the little horn of the west (Dan. 7. 7, 8).

THE FALLEN STAR; OR, THE PERSONAL ANTICHRIST

The rise of a personal Antichrist in the last dark days of Gentile and Jewish apostasy was an undoubted article of belief in apostolic and succeeding christian times. There have been many Antichrists and antichristian systems of deadly error, but there is yet a blacker outlook. The Antichrist to come, an apostate of Jewish extraction, will be the incarnation of satanic wickedness and the greatest soul-destroyer who has ever trod the earth; moreover, he will sum up in himself every form and phase of sin, and head the most awful system of corrupt and damnable evil ever known—a combination of Jewish and christian profession, and "natural religion" too—in open daring rebellion against God. He assumes Christ's place, titles, and functions on earth. He works miracles. Supernatural signs accredit his mission, and by these he deceives guilty Christendom, and thus lures it on to hopeless destruction.

It is during the last phase of the revived power of Rome when distributed into ten kingdoms that the personal Antichrist arises.* This final character of Rome was therefore dreaded by the early Christians. In their minds the future revival of the civil power of Rome and the presence of the Antichrist were coeval and connected events. They were wont to pray for the continuance of the empire in its imperial form, and even for the rule of the cruellest of the Caesars, as the last bulwark against the coming sway of the Antichrist. The subject of the Antichrist was a common one to the fathers of the Church. Some held that he was the devil incarnate; others spoke of him as "the devil's son." The relation of Satan and the Antichrist in the traditional lore of the first four christian centuries may be resolved into two distinct thoughts: first, that the coming Antichrist (as delineated by John), or the man of sin (as described by Paul), is a real man of earthly Jewish parentage, controlled directly by Satan; second, that he is Satan incarnate, and thus in his conception simulating the miraculous birth of our blessed Lord. The former notion is undoubtedly the scriptural one, and it is an interesting fact that Jerome in the west, and Chrysostom in the east, distinctly taught that the Antichrist is a man energised by Satan, in direct

---

* The rise of the Antichrist—*after* the subversion of the one undivided empire of the Caesars, and *during* its prophetic revival when portioned into ten kingdoms with a great central and controlling chief—was taught and "expounded with confidence, definiteness, and unanimity by the whole body of patristic writers."—"The Antichrist Legend," Englished from the German W. Bousset. There may be much in this remarkable work to condemn, but it contains a vast amount of able research and valuable information as to what the early Christians taught and held on the doctrine of a personal Antichrist.

opposition to those who maintained that he was the devil in human form. "Henceforth the assumption that the Antichrist is the devil himself practically dies out of ecclesiastical tradition." The early Christians regarded Nero* and Claudius, especially the former, as precursors of the Antichrist. The almost superhuman wickedness of Nero marks him out in the page of history as the most apt and fitting historical type of the coming man of sin and blood.

The mass of Protestant expositors apply the term Antichrist to the papal system. But this we conceive is a blunder. The term Antichrist, whether employed in the singular or plural, denotes a person or persons, never a system. The Roman Catholic interpreters have written much and learnedly on this theme, and, we are compelled to add, more correctly than many of their Protestant opponents. The former look on to the end for the rise of a personal Antichrist,† and in this they are right. He is yet to come. Dr. Manning, one of the most distinguished of Roman Catholics, held that the Antichrist, or "the man of sin," is one individual, and neither a succession of persons nor a system. He says: "To deny the personality of Antichrist is therefore to deny the plain testimony of Holy Scripture."‡ The learned Cardinal adds: "He (the Antichrist) may indeed embody a spirit, and represent a system, but is not less therefore a person."§ Bellarmine, second to none as a Roman Catholic writer, tersely sums up papal belief on the subject of the Antichrist, saying, "All Catholics hold that Antichrist will be one individual person." One special person, a man, a Jew, an apostate, is the Antichrist of the prophetic Scriptures.

Some modern expositors regard the Antichrist as the civil head of the Roman empire, but this is not so. He is the false messiah, the minister of Satan amongst the Jews in Jerusalem, working signs and displaying wonders through direct satanic power. He sits in the temple of God then set up in Jerusalem, and claims divine worship. The Beast (Rome), the false prophet or the Antichrist, and the dragon (Satan) are deified and worshipped, counter-

---

* It was during the reign of Nero that Christianity and paganism first came into open conflict. The history of these thirteen years, in which for the first time persecution of the Christians was legalised by imperial edict, has never yet been fully written. The unchronicled events of that reign await full disclosure at the judgment seat of Christ.

† To the Protestant the Pope is an Antichrist. To the Papist Luther is an Antichrist. Both are wrong, for both miss the scriptural characteristics of Antichrist, and these, as described by John and Paul, do not apply to the Pope, much less to the illustrious reformer.

‡ "The Temporal Power of the Vicar of Jesus Christ."

§ Dr. Manning further shows that the rise of the papacy in the west and its hindrance in the east is accounted for in the fact that the throne of the Caesars removed from Rome paved the way for the establishment of Roman Catholicism in Italy; whereas the political imperial power in Constantinople hindered and checked the claims of the papacy in the east. This witness is true.

feiting the worship of Father, Son, and Holy Ghost. The apostate nation accepts the Antichrist as king. In no sense is he a great political power. True, he influences Christendom, but religiously, not politically. The government of the world, civil and political, is then in the hands of a great Gentile chief. It is he whose throne is in Rome who rules politically under Satan. The Antichrist has his seat in Jerusalem. The head of Gentile dominion in Rome. The two men are ministers of Satan, confederates in wickedness; the one a Jew, the other a Gentile. Both exist at the Coming of the Lord in judgment, and both are then consigned *alive* to the lake of fire—an eternal doom.

The term Antichrist is used only by the writer of the Apocalypse, and by him four times (1 John 2. 18, 22; 4. 3; 2 John 7), and once in the plural (1 John 2. 18). From these texts we gather several important points. The rise of Antichrists is a definite mark of "the last time;" they are apostates. The Antichrist sets himself in direct opposition to what is vital in Christianity—the revelation of the Father and of the Son—and also to the distinguishing truth of Judaism—Jesus the Christ (1 John 2. 22). The holy Person of the Lord is also the object of satanic attack by Antichrists (2 John 7). Evil of this character is found fully developed in the coming Antichrist, in whom every form of religious evil culminates.

Paul, in one of his earliest and briefest epistles (2 Thess.), sketches a personage characterised by impiety, lawlessness, and assumption towering far beyond all the world has ever seen, a character clearly identical with the Antichrist of John. They are one and the same person, and on this, in all ages, there has been an almost complete concensus of opinion.

It is evident that Paul had personally instructed the Thessalonian Christians on the solemn subjects of the coming apostasy or public abandonment of Christianity, and, consequent thereon, the revelation of the man of sin (2 Thess. 2. 5). He now adds to former verbal instruction. There are three descriptive epithets here used of the Antichrist: "The lawless one" (R.V.), "the man of sin," and "the son of perdition." The first intimates that he sets himself in direct opposition to all divine and human authority. The second, that he is the living and active embodiment of every form and character of evil—sin personified. The third, that he is the full-blown development of the power of Satan, and as such perdition is his proper doom and portion. This frightful character usurps God's place on earth, and sits in the temple then set up in Jerusalem, claiming divine worship and honour (v. 4). His religious influence, for he is not a political person of any account, dominates the mass of professing Christians and Jews. They are caught in Satan's snare. *They* had already given God up, had publicly renounced the christian faith and the essential truth of Judaism, and now in retributive justice *He* gives them up to the awful delusion of receiving the man of sin whilst believing him to be the true messiah (v. 11). What a lie! The Antichrist received and believed on instead of the Christ of God! If verse 9 is compared with Acts 2. 22 a remarkable correspondence is shown. The very same terms are found in both texts, namely, power, signs, and wonders. By these God would accredit the mission and service of Jesus of Nazareth (Acts 2. 22), and by the same credentials Satan presents the Antichrist to an apostate world (2 Thess. 2. 9). In the latter case, however, lying and deceit significantly characterise the more than human signs of that day (2 Thess. 2. 9, 10).

The Lord Himself refers to the Antichrist and to his acceptance by the Jews as their messiah and prophet (John 5. 43). In the book of Psalms he is prophetically written of in his character as "the man of the earth" (Psa. 10. 18), as also "the bloody and deceitful man" (Psa. 5. 6), whilst these descriptive epithets are in themselves characteristic of the wicked in general in the coming crisis, yet there is one person, and but one, to whom they can in the fullest sense refer. It is the character of the Antichrist, and not his person, that is before us in these and other Psalms.

Daniel in chapter 11 of his prophecy refers to three kings: The king of the north (Syria); the king of the south (Egypt); and the king in Palestine (the Antichrist). The wars, family alliances, and intrigue so minutely detailed in the first thirty-five verses of this interesting chapter have had an exact historical fulfilment in the history of the Syrian and Egyptian kingdoms formed after the break up of the mighty Grecian empire. It was this prophecy in its literal and detailed fulfilment which so roused the ire of that bitter pagan and opponent of divine truth, Porphyry, in the third century. His "Treatise against Christians" is the armoury which from the seventeenth century has supplied material for attacks upon Christianity. Think of christian (?) teachers eagerly availing themselves of the help of a pagan philosopher in their wicked campaign against the truth!

In verse 36 "*the* king" is abruptly introduced into the history. This king is the Antichrist whose reign in Palestine precedes that of the true Messiah, even as King Saul preceded King David, the former pointing to the antichristian king, and the latter to Christ, the true King of Israel. This portion of the chapter (vv. 36-45) is yet future, carrying us on to the time of the end (v. 40). The king exalts himself, and magnifies himself above man and every god. The pride of the devil is embodied in this terrible Jewish character. God's place alone will satisfy his ambition. What a contrast to the true Messiah, to Jesus Who humbled Himself as none other ever did. He Who was God humbled Himself, even to the death of the cross (Phil. 2. 5-8).

That the Antichrist is of Jewish descent seems evident from Daniel 11. 37, as also from the consideration that otherwise he could have no claim even with apostate Jews to the throne of Israel. The king, or the Antichrist, is attacked from the north and south, his land, Palestine, lying between the two. He is unable, even with the help of his ally, the powerful chief of the west, to ward off the repeated attacks of his northern and southern enemies. The former is the more bitter and determined of the two. Palestine is overrun by the conquering forces of the north; but its king, the Antichrist, escapes the vengeance of the great northern oppressor, of whom Antiochus Epiphanes of infamous memory is the prototype. The Antichrist is the subject of the Lord's judgment at His Return from Heaven (Rev. 19. 20).

In the Apocalypse, chapter 13, two Beasts are seen in vision. The first is the Roman power and its blasphemous head under the direct control of Satan (vv. 1-10). The second Beast is the personal Antichrist (vv. 11-17). The *first* is characterised by brute force. It is the political power of earth in those days, and the one to whom Satan "gave his power, and his throne, and great authority" (chap. 13. 2). The *second* Beast is clearly subordinate to the power of the first (v. 12). It is religious, not political, ends he has in view. Religious pretension is supported by the might and strength of apostate Rome; thus the two Beasts act together under their great chief, Satan. The three are jointly worshipped.

The second Beast, or Antichrist, is identical with "the false prophet," named three times (chaps. 16. 13; 19. 20; 20. 10). The respective heads of the rebellion against Christ in His royal and prophetic rights are two men directly controlled and energised by Satan—a trinity of evil. "The dragon has given his external power to the first Beast (Rev. 13. 8); to the second he gives his spirit, so that having this spirit it speaks as a dragon" (v. 11).*

Finally, Zechariah refers to the Antichrist as the "idol shepherd," utterly regardless of the flock (Israel) over whom he assumes royal, priestly, and prophetic power.

* "Daniel and the Revelation," p. 309.—*Auberlen.*

But his boasted authority (his arm) and vaunted intelligence (his right eye) by which his pretensions in the land are supported are utterly blasted, while personally he is cast alive into the eternal abode of misery, the lake of fire (Zech. 11. 15-17; Rev. 19. 20).

In our judgment, therefore, the fallen star under the first Woe unmistakably designates the Antichrist. To whom other of the apocalyptic personages could the description apply? The *spiritual* aims and religious pretensions of Satan are supported and enforced by the Antichrist, whilst his *temporal* sovereignty on earth is established in the kingdom and person of the Roman prince.*

Now the agony here depicted is that of soul and conscience; not bodily anguish. The Antichrist seems the devil's chosen instrument in the infliction of the former, whereas in the latter kind of torment the brute force of the Beast is let loose, indulging itself in scenes of cruelty and bloodshed, tormenting the bodies of men.

After this long but needful digression we return to our chapter.

THE FALLEN STAR.

1.—"**I saw a star out of the Heaven fallen to the earth; and there was given to it the key of the pit of the abyss.**" This symbolic fallen star, once set in the moral Heaven to reflect and uphold God's authority in government, is neither a religious nor a political system, but an actual person, a degraded ruler. The reference is not to the fall of Satan, as prophetically beheld and announced by the Lord to the Seventy (Luke 10. 18), but to the king of Babylon. "How art thou fallen from heaven, O Lucifer,† son of the morning! How art thou cut down to the ground which didst weaken the nations!" (Isa. 14. 12-15). The haughty, great, and proud king of Babylon is here alluded to in his awful fall from a height never before attained by any earthly potentate, down to the lowest depths of infamy. "Yet thou shalt be brought down to hell (*sheol*), to the uttermost parts of the pit." Some regard the "day star" of the prophet (Isa. 14. 12), and fallen star of the Apocalypse (chap. 9. 1), as both pointing to the fall of Satan from Heaven, but we are satisfied that the king of Babylon ‡ is signified by the former and the Antichrist by

* The blessed Lord peremptorily refused to accept from Satan universal lordship and glory (Matt. 4. 8, 9). But the coming prince will gladly receive both at the hands of Satan; the awful compact is ratified, the Beast worships the dragon, and Satan then endows his political minister with the world's sovereignty.

† Lucifer signifies *day star*, and is so rendered in the Revised Version of Isaiah 14. 12.

‡ The first and fourth of the universal imperial powers (Dan. 2; 7), to whom Judah was enslaved, were Babylon and Rome. The former is doomed to everlasting

the latter. The context of both Scriptures confirms the prophetic application to the secular and religious chiefs of the last days—the Beast and the False Prophet.

This fallen dignitary has committed to him "the key of the pit of the abyss." "The key" symbolises competent authority (see Matt. 16. 19; Rev. 1. 18; 3. 7; 20. 1). "*The pit* of the abyss" is a singular expression, only used in connection with the judgment recorded in verses one and two of our chapter. "The bottomless pit," or abyss, occurs seven times in the Apocalypse. The deep, or abyss, (Luke 8. 31) seems the prison house of demons, in which Satan is to be confined for one thousand years (Rev. 20. 3)—the duration of the kingdom reign. The lake of fire, *not* the abyss, is the eternal abode of the devil and of the lost. Says the Rev. W. B. Carpenter in his commentary on the Apocalypse: "The verse before us suggests the picture of a vast depth approached by a pit or shaft, whose top, or mouth, is covered. Dante's *Inferno*, with its narrowing circles winding down to the central shaft, is somewhat similar. The abyss is the lowest spring of evil, whence the worst dangers arise" (cp. chaps. 11. 7; 17. 8; 20. 1-3). Here, then, the abyss is regarded as locked up, but commission is given to unlock it. It has been contended that, as a result of this vast prison house being opened, swarms of evil spirits issue therefrom and overrun the earth. But smoke, not spirits, rose up out of the pit, and out of the smoke emerged a devastating swarm of symbolic locusts.

SATANIC DELUSION AND ITS DARKENING EFFECT.

2.—"**And there went up smoke out of the pit as (the) smoke of a great furnace; and the sun and the air were darkened with the smoke of the pit.**" A satanic delusion bred in the abyss, and characterised by its moral blinding and withering effect is here intimated. Probably the same delusion to which Christendom will be given over referred to by Paul (2 Thess. 2. 11, 12). The effect of the smoke or darkening influence and power of Satan will be to blight the supreme government (the sun), and darken and corrupt the whole social life and principles of men (the air). The air denoting *moral influence* occurs

---

desolation. "Thus shall Babylon sink and shall not rise from the evil that I will bring upon her" (Jer. 51. 64). It is a mistake to suppose that either Babylon as a city, or the ancient Chaldean empire will again flourish. The last holder of the imperial power on earth, "*the* Beast," takes up and completes the story of Babylon. The historical Nebuchadnezzar is a type of the great coming Gentile chief who will combine, with features peculiar to himself, the main characteristics of the three preceding empires. The king of Babylon (Isa. 14) is a type of the king in the last days of Gentile supremacy prior to the Lord's Return.

twice in the Apocalypse, under the fifth Trumpet (chap. 9. 2) and in the pouring out of the seventh Vial (chap. 16. 17).

THE LOCUST ARMY.

3-10.—Neither the smoke nor the locusts are literal. The smoke gives birth to the locusts. "**Out of the smoke came forth locusts on the earth.**" Satanic agencies are let loose upon the prophetic scene. The intense anguish caused by these hordes of satanic instruments and agents is likened to the torment caused by the poisonous sting of the scorpion, a creature which shuns the light, and is justly dreaded by the native races of Africa and the various Arab tribes of Asia. It is not often that the sting proves fatal, but the suffering is dreadful. "The scorpion is constantly shaking his tail to strike, and the torment caused by his sting is very grievous." In Luke 10. 19 the Lord connects serpents, scorpions, and the power of the enemy with the fall of Satan, as here scorpions with the fallen star. But these hellish instruments of vengeance let loose upon guilty Israel are powerless, save as authority is given them to act: "**And power was given to them as the scorpions of the earth have power**" (v. 3).

That the locust army is a symbolical representation of judgment of a superhuman kind is evident from the whole description, as also from the prohibition to injure the grass and trees (v. 4), their natural food. There is a further reason why the vegetable world was to be spared. A general condition of prosperity in the temporal circumstances and position of men is intimated by the grass, "any green thing," and trees. Now the locusts were commissioned to invade Palestine, the country above all others of grasses, and injure alone "the men who have not the seal of God on their foreheads" (v. 4). The Gentile multitude is not sealed; the 144,000 of Israel are (chap. 7. 3, 4). Here, then, the unsealed part of the nation is given up to drink the cup of the Lord's vengeance, yea, to the dregs thereof. Death would be a welcome release from the torment, the anguish of soul inflicted by these myrmidons of Satan, but that last refuge of despair is denied them, "death flees from them" (v. 6). The gnawing anguish and horrible torment of a guilty and sin-defiled conscience is beyond all telling; it can only be weighed and balanced by those enduring it.

The duration of the satanic scourge is limited to five months (v. 5), the time of natural locust life.* The time specified points to a brief and determinate period of woe, not necessarily one of five iteral months.

* From May to September.

Next follows a detailed description of the locust army, each item in the delineation being significant and full of meaning.

(1) They are seen fully prepared and eager in warlike energy to execute their commission, "like to horses prepared for war."*

(2) They lay claim to royal dignity. The crown of gold adorns the head of the Son of Man (Rev. 14. 14), and also those of the triumphant elders or redeemed (chap. 4. 4). But these satanic invaders from the smoke of the pit are not really crowned, nor is real gold in question. They lay claim to a dignity not divinely conferred. "Upon their heads *as* crowns *like* gold." Their pretension to royal authority is spurious.

(3) They profess to be guided in their movements by human intelligence, but in appearance only, "their faces *as* faces of men." Their assumed dignity and intelligence are as worthless as their claim to royal authority.

(4) Their effeminacy and subjection, not to God, but to Satan their leader, are next intimated: "They had hair as women's hair."

(5) They are savage, rapacious, cruel: "Their teeth were as of lions" (Joel 1. 6).

(6) They know no pity. Neither force nor entreaty is of any avail in turning them from their purpose. Their hearts are hardened, their consciences steeled, "they had breastplates as breastplates of iron."

(7) In resistless energy the satanic host swept on, causing fear and terror to their victims. Their approach is heralded thus: "The sound of their wings (was) as the sound of chariots of many horses running to war" (Joel 2. 5).

(8) In the next part of this extraordinary description the past tense is departed from and the present tense employed. Surely this is intentional, and marks off the worst and most characteristic feature from what has preceded, "they *have* tails like scorpions, and stings;" again, "and their power was in their tails to hurt men five months," referring back to verses three and five.

These scorpion locusts overrun the once Holy Land, and prey upon the unsealed and ungodly part of Israel. The venom of falsehood, born in the pit—doctrines, teachings, and principles conceived in the abyss are received by the apostate part of the nation, and create in their souls and consciences intolerable anguish. Without God, yea, given up judicially by Him to receive Satan's lies and delusions, little wonder that they, *his* dupes and disciples,

---

* In Italy and in some other countries locusts are termed "little horses," because of the resemblance of the head to that of the horse (see Joel 2. 4). Hostile armies, especially cavalry, are in the Sacred Writings symbolised by locust invasion (Joel 2; Jer. 51. 27). For the desolation caused by a locust plague see Exodus 10. 12-15.

share, as far as men on earth can, the full tale of misery. The scorpion-like tails of the locusts contain the moral poison which so awfully torments those who receive it. *There* lie the venomous stings, and there the power to torment (Isa. 9. 15).

IDENTICAL PERSONAGES.

11.—"**They have a king over them, the angel of the abyss: his name in Hebrew Abaddon, and in Greek he has (for) name Apollyon.**" The king of the symbolic locusts* and the angel of the abyss are identical, as the singular pronouns "his" and "he" show. Both terms directly refer to Satan. Now the judgment we have been considering is a judgment executed on earth. It is not eternal judgment. The human leader in this awful woe is the fallen star, or the Antichrist, while the unseen chief of all is the devil himself. But the Antichrist is the personification of Satan in malignant influence, representing him religiously amongst men, hence certain expressions are employed in this locust vision which seem to regard them as one. They are in a sense, for the devil gives his character to his human subordinate, but, on the other hand, they are distinct. Satan is a spirit, and the leader of the hosts of evil; while the Antichrist is a man, an apostate Jew, and has as his sphere of operation corrupt and semi-infidel Judaism and apostate Christendom.

We regard, therefore, the fallen star as signifying the Antichrist; and the king of the locust army and the angel of the abyss as designating Satan.

The two descriptive epithets, Abaddon and Apollyon, while practically meaning the same, and both applied to the same awful personage, yet present in their exactness of signification a difference worth noting. Abaddon is Hebrew, and literally means *destruction*. Apollyon is Greek, and signifies *the destroyer*. Why this seemingly unimportant distinction in these suggestive titles? And why does the Hebrew precede the Greek one? Inasmuch as the Jew is more guilty than the Gentile, the Hebrew title Abaddon, *destruction*, emphatically asserts judgment on apostate Judah, its certainty and finality. And as the *first* Woe has its direct application to the mass of Judah, Abaddon is first named. The *second* Woe directly concerns the inhabitants of the Roman empire, hence, fittingly, the order of the names: first, Abaddon; second, Apollyon. The order in grace as in judgment is the Jew first, then the Gentile. The Greek name Apollyon, *the destroyer*, intimates Satan's character in relation to Christendom, as his former

* "The locusts have no king," so said Solomon the monarch, that keen observer of nature (Prov. 30. 27).

title his connection with Judaism. Both systems in "the last days" will be fully represented in the person and doings of the Antichrist, who will head up the revolt against the priestly and prophetic rights of Christ, denying the essential truths of Judaism (Dan. 11. 36-39; 1 John 2. 22), and of Christianity (1 John 2. 18-22). The Beast out of the abyss will head the civil and political rebellion against Christ in His royal rights, His kingly authority. Hence the two names in Hebrew and Greek used of Satan have their counterpart on earth in the double connection of the Antichrist with the corrupt systems of Judaism and Christendom. The denial of *the* Christ, *i.e.*, the Messiah, is the characteristic feature of the former; the denial of the Father and of the Son is as truly the distinguishing character of the latter system.

If further proof were needed that the fallen star is a personage subordinate to the angel of the abyss it is to hand in the fact that the former exercises delegated authority. "To it," the star, or "him," the personage intended, "was *given*" the key of the pit of the abyss. The insertion of the definite article, "*the* angel of the abyss," marks him off as an independent personage in authority. Further, it will be noted that "*the pit* of the abyss" is spoken of in connection with the star, whereas the "abyss" simply is referred to as under the control of "the angel." This latter term by itself gives the full expression of satanic power. *Out* of it the Beast emerges (chap. 11. 7), and *into* it Satan himself is cast, and it becomes his prison for one thousand years. The fallen star (v. 1) is the Antichrist; the king and the angel (v. 11) both designate Satan.

SIXTH TRUMPET, OR SECOND WOE.

THE TWO ALTARS.

13-21.—**"And the sixth angel sounded (his) trumpet: and I heard a voice from the four horns of the golden altar which (is) before God, saying to the sixth angel that had the trumpet: Loose the four angels which are bound at the great river Euphrates. And the four angels were loosed, who are prepared for the hour, and day, and month, and year, that they might slay the third part of men. And the number of the hosts of horse (was) twice ten thousand times ten thousand; I heard their number. And thus I saw the horses in the vision, and those that sat upon them, having breastplates of fire, and jacinth, and brimstone; and the heads of the horses (were) as**

heads of lions, and out of their mouths goes out fire and smoke and brimstone. By these three plagues were the third part of men killed, by the fire, and the smoke, and the brimstone which goes out of their mouths. For the power of the horses is in their mouth and in their tails; for their tails (are) like serpents, having heads, and with them they injure. And the rest of men who were not killed with these plagues repented not of the works of their hands, that they should not worship demons, and the golden and silver, and brazen and stone, and wooden idols, which can neither see nor hear nor walk. And they repented not of their murders, nor of their witchcrafts, nor of their fornication, nor of their thefts.'' In the tabernacle of old there were two altars. One stood *without* in the court; the other *within* in the holy place. The golden altar is twice referred to in these apocalyptic visions, here and in chapter 8. 3. The brazen altar is mentioned six times simply as "the altar." It was this latter which stood in the court. The kernel of the Levitical system was the brazen altar—the altar of sacrifice. What "the altar" was to Judaism, namely, the moral foundation of the people's relations to Jehovah, *that* "the cross" is to Christianity—its centre and distinguishing glory. Now the golden altar derived its force and value from the brazen altar. Every morning and evening, save on the annual day of atonement, incense (the merits of Christ) was burned on the golden altar, while on *that* special day in the history of Israel, as on other occasions, the blood of the sacrificial animals was put on its four golden horns (Lev. 16. 18, 19; 4. 7, 18). The fragrance of the incense was brought out by fire taken from the brazen altar, while the blood on the golden horns was that shed on the north side of the altar in the court (Lev. 1. 11). Thus the efficacy of the worship and communion of the people with Jehovah, maintained and carried on at the golden altar, had as its basis the shedding of blood at the altar of sacrifice.

A VOICE FROM THE FOUR HORNS OF THE GOLDEN ALTAR.

13.—"**I heard a voice from the four horns of the golden altar.**" We have already noted the fact that the golden altar is twice mentioned in the Apocalypse. In the earlier reference the prayers of the saints on earth are heard (chap. 8. 3). The Beast out of the abyss comes upon the scene. Blasphemy and persecution characterise his closing career. During the time of which we have read in chapter 6. 11, a body of witnessing, and hence suffering, saints are recognised. Their prayers for God's intervention on their behalf are about to be answered (chap. 9. 13). Under the first four Trumpets the general condition of the empire is subjected to a course of judicial dealing. Its social, moral, commercial, and political state comes under the rod of God's anger, but the sixth Trumpet, or second Woe, is far more dreadful in its character and effects than any of the preceding chastisements. The peoples of the Roman earth are here the direct subjects of woe, not torment as in the preceding one, but a wide-spread and extensive slaughter of the inhabitants from hordes of external enemies, added to which satanic delusion and falsehood will play sad havoc in the souls and consciences of the people. Judicial plagues upon men's circumstances are one thing, but dealing with the men themselves, the open and declared enemies of God and of His saints, is a very different matter. Hence God's answer to the cries and prayers of His suffering saints is answered from the altar of intercession. *To* it their prayers ascended (chap. 8. 3). *From* it the answer goes forth (chap. 9. 13).

The "voice" which the Seer heard is either the voice of God or of one commissioned by Him to act.

The voice is heard "from the *four horns* of the golden altar." Why not from the altar itself, as in chapter 16. 7? And why are the horns and their number so specifically mentioned? "Four" expresses *universality*.* "Horn" denotes *power*.† The whole strength and power of the altar of intercession is put forth in the divine answer to the mingled prayers and incense which gathered around it. Both altars had each four sides and four horns. *All* sinners from every part of earth may use the brazen altar. *All* saints wherever found are heard at the golden altar. We refer, of course, to the truths respectively set forth by the altars.

Another minute distinction may here be pointed out. In chapter 8. 3 the connection is between the altar and the *throne*, whereas in chapter 9. 13 the connection is between the altar and *God*. This latter is the nearer and more intimate relation, and brings out God's personal interest in His saints.

AN AUTHORITATIVE COMMAND.

14, 15.—**"Loose the four angels which are bound at the great river Euphrates. And the four angels were loosed, who are prepared for the hour, and day, and month, and year, for to slay the third part of**

* Four metals (Dan. 2) and four beasts (chap. 7) representing the four universal empires. Four divisions of the human family (Rev. 7. 9).

† See Psalm 118. 27; 89. 17, 24; 92. 10; 132. 17; Revelation 5. 6, etc.

men." The voice from the place of intercession and power is evidently one of divine authority, and is addressed to the sixth angel. The repetition of the ordinal "*sixth*" (vv. 13, 14) and of the cardinal "*four*" (vv. 14, 15) intimates the precision with which this Woe will be executed. The exactness, too, of the appointed hour of vengeance (v. 15) and the number of the instruments employed (v. 16) all go to mark this divine infliction as one of an unusually solemn character. The four *restraining* angels (chap. 7. 1-3) must not be confounded with the four *bound* angels at the river Euphrates (chap. 9. 14, 15). The former are stationed at the extremities of the earth, the latter in the circumscribed region of the Euphrates. Besides, not only are the times and circumstances different, but the action in each case is exactly opposite. The four angels of chapter 7 *restrain* the forces of evil, whereas those of chapter 9 let *loose* the human and satanic instruments of vengeance.

The Euphrates is twice mentioned in the Apocalypse, here and in chapter 16. 12. The epithet "great" is used in both instances: "The great river Euphrates." Its entire length is about 1780 miles, and it is by far the longest and most important river of western Asia. It is famous in Bible history and prophecy. Israel's great progenitor, Abram, came from its other side into the land of Canaan. The rivers Nile and Euphrates are prophetically designated as the limits of the promised land (Gen. 15. 18). For a brief season David and Solomon extended the royal authority to the Euphrates (1 Chron. 18. 3; 2 Chron. 9. 26). This extensive dominion was greatly curtailed in the disruption of the kingdom under Rehoboam. The Euphrates was the natural boundary separating the nations of the east from Palestine. Its broad stream flowed between Israel and her powerful enemy Assyria. The Euphrates was also the limit of the Roman conquests in that part of the world. We understand, therefore, that the *literal* Euphrates is here signified, and not the Turkish power. So also in chapter 16. 12.

The mandate to the sixth angel is to loose the four angels bound at the great river. These angelic ministers of judgment are under divine control; they cannot act without express command. The very hour when the Lord in retributive justice would deal with the apostate peoples of the revived Latin empire is carefully noted, for that hour the angels were prepared.* What hindered an earlier

* One would gather from the Authorised Version that the time during which the four angels were to act in judgment would be "for an hour, and a day, and a month, and a year," whereas these exact denominations of time refer to the moment when the angels *begin* to act, not the duration of their action.

action by these angelic ministers of God's providence we are not informed. The hour of vengeance in the prophetic scheme had not arrived. The iniquity of the empire had not risen to the height foretold in Scripture; now it has, and judgment, sharp and overwhelming, can no longer be delayed.

15.—**"To slay the third part of men."** There is no "third part" in the previous Woe. There Palestine is the sphere of judicial action, and the unsealed of Israel only are the subjects of judgment. Gathered in rank unbelief to the land, the last state of Israel will exceed in idolatrous wickedness any former condition (Matt. 12. 45). But a recurrence to the "third part," so prominent in the earlier Trumpets, brings once again the Roman empire into the sphere of divine operation. A terrible slaughter of the inhabitants takes place. We are now to consider the human instruments which are to drench the empire in blood.

THE NUMBER OF THE AVENGING HOST.

16.—We have had the number of the invisible leaders, *four*; now both the reader and the Seer are informed as to the number of the invading and avenging host, stated to be **"twice ten thousand times ten thousand,"** or two hundred millions. This immense host is a number too vast for human conception. The mind gets bewildered in the effort to comprehend such an army, which for number surpasses anything ever seen on earth. The unseen chariots of God are similarly numbered (Psa. 68. 17). May the lesson be graven on our hearts that the seen and unseen powers of good and evil are all under the direct control of God. A literal army consisting of two hundred millions of cavalry need not be thought of. The main idea in the passage is a vast and overwhelming army, one beyond human computation, and exceeding by far any before witnessed.* "An army of prevailing, imperial, congregated power."† The Revised Version reads, "the *armies* of the horsemen." It is not one army, but "armies," not a host, but "hosts." The reason why the plural is employed and not the singular is that more than one invasion into the territory of the Beast from beyond the Euphrates will be attempted and succeed. The future antagonist of the revived empire is Gog (Russia), the great north-eastern power. Persia and, generally, the kingdoms and powers situated north and east of Palestine follow in the train of the great northern despot (Ezek 38; 39;

* The largest army ever brought into the field recorded in history was that under Xerxes in the invasion of Greece. On the testimony of Herodotus it exceeded two and a half millions of men.

† "Notes on the Book of Revelation," p. 45

Psa. 83). The repeated attacks upon the kingdom, or empire of the Beast, will be commenced by the king of the north, then established in the present Syrian possessions of Turkey. This king, the determined political enemy of restored Israel, is subordinate to his great chief, the autocrat of the vast Russian power. Hence "hosts" or "armies" is the fitting word employed.

DESCRIPTION OF THE HORSEMEN AND THEIR HORSES.

17.—The riders have "**breastplates of fire, and jacinth, and brimstone.**" These lands on which the light of the Gospel has shone so brilliantly will ere long be given over to satanic darkness and delusion. The devil will take possession of the doomed scene. His influence will permeate and poison the springs and sources of national and individual thought and action. He will command the spiritual and human forces of evil. Demon worship will prevail (v. 20). Judea and Christendom will be given over to the direct worship and homage of Satan and of his two main supporters on earth—the Beast and the False Prophet (Rev. 13; 2 Thess. 2). Satan, then, is divinely permitted to furnish his countless hosts with a defensive armour which makes them invulnerable. The combination of fire, jacinth,* and brimstone as a breastplate has been well termed "the defensive armour of hell." Fire and brimstone are destructive elements not of a providential kind, but judicially inflicted (Gen. 19. 24). They are also the symbols of everlasting torment.

Next follows a description of the horses "in the vision." In the previous Woe we had a combination of locust and scorpion, denoting destruction and agony; here horses are prominent—the aggressive and military agents of rapine and slaughter. Their heads "as heads of lions" invest the warlike host with a certain majesty, courage, and boldness, well-known characteristics of "the king of the forest."†

17.—"**Out of their mouths goes out fire and smoke and brimstone.**" These military expeditions are under the direction **of Satan**. He it is who out of the pit supplies his agents with a *defensive* armour against which all opposing weapons of war are powerless (v. 17). Here he arms the host with a trinity of *offensive* destructive forces.

---

* "The jacinth was of a deep blue colour, similar to the blue which we see in flame, or burning brimstone. The blue flame of the pit is indeed a widely different thought from the blue of Heaven."

† We have the *roar* of the lion causing terror (Rev. 10. 3). The *teeth* of the lion denoting ferocity (chap. 9. 8). The *head* signifying majesty (v. 17). The *mouth* pointing to its destructive character (chap. 13. 2).

The men of the empire under which Christ was crucified, Jerusalem destroyed, and the Jews dispersed, are to suffer on earth, so far as men can, the agonies and torments of the lake of fire. To fire and brimstone, the symbols of inconceivable anguish (chaps. 14. 10; 19. 20; 21. 8), are added "smoke," the moral darkness and delusion of the pit.

A HARVEST OF DEATH.

18.—The **fire, smoke,** and **brimstone** are separate plagues, but here they are associated in the work of slaughter. The death to which the mass are doomed is one inflicted by the judicial power of Satan, and hence more dreadful than sudden death by the sword. The scene described is not one simply of human slaughter by scientific methods of modern or ancient warfare; the destructive forces of the pit are let loose upon a "third part of men" who are killed, probably the worst in the empire, as there is a remnant spared (v. 20), who, however, repent not. *Twice* the three plagues are named, and *twice* as going out of the mouths of the horses. The repeated mention of these destructive forces would emphasise the fact that the judicial power of Satan is at work; and, further, that the agents are not mere mercenaries, but are energised by Satan, and delight to kill. "Out of their mouths" would show the heart's diabolic pleasure in the work. See chapter 16. 13 for what is evil; also Matthew 12. 34 for the general principle.

THE MOUTH AND TAILS OF THE HORSES.

19.—"The clause stating **the power to be in their mouth** serves only as a connecting link with what is still to be said of their tails. The injurious and dreadfully destructive tendency had not been sufficiently represented by what proceeds out of the mouth of the horses. It still farther embodies itself in the symbol of the serpent—tails."*

It may be noted that *mouth* is here in the singular, whereas it has just been used twice in the plural, and that *tails*, the plural, is employed. Mouth and tails, singular and plural, would express that all are animated by *one* spirit, but that the teachings and lies of Satan are multifarious. "The power of the horses is in their mouth and in their tails." There is not only the *open* power of Satan, but in addition his *secret* malignant and soul-destroying influence. Both are contemplated here. In the previous Woe the power to injure was in the tail (v. 10). Here the power to destroy is in the mouth and tails (v. 19). *There* he is the liar. *Here* he is both murderer and liar.

* Hengstenberg, vol. 1, p. 370.

19.—"**Tails like serpents**." The serpent was the chosen creature in which the devil hid himself in deceiving Eve (Gen. 3. 1), and is probably the only member of the animal creation doomed to perpetual degradation, even during the lengthened and universal blessing in millennial days (cp. Gen. 3. 14 with Isa. 65. 25). The serpent is synonymous with *craft, deceit, guile, subtility*. The "tail" of the serpent is the expression of *malignant influence, falsehood, mischief* (Isa. 9. 15; Rev. 12. 4).

Further, the tails have "heads," intimating that the mischievous influence is intelligently directed. The purpose to injure is pursued with relentless and intelligent activity.

NO REPENTANCE.

20, 21.—The two closing verses of the chapter reveal an astounding picture of human depravity. The loud blasts of the Trumpets successively sounded are God's public announcements to the world—heralds of woe. Increasing in severity, judgment succeeds judgment. The prophetic scene is turned into Satan's special sphere of action. He triumphs for a season. What a scene is depicted in these last of "the last days!" Western Europe, so boastful of its light and knowledge, given up to the grossest idolatry and most shameful wickedness. We here witness a distinct return to the paganism of early days. What! Shall these christianised populations retrogade to such an extent that the most disgusting forms of idolatry and the sins of the flesh in their vilest character be again practised? *Yes*. Romans 1. 21-32,* 2 Timothy 3. 1-5, and verses 20, 21 of our chapter remove the veil, and give us to witness a seething mass of iniquity and wickedness. "**The rest**," or spared apostates, repented not. The awful doom of their fellow-associates in idolatry and general wickedness had made but a passing impression. They "**repented not**" is repeated. Their obduracy of heart in turning from God to Satan and continuing there, spite of warning examples before their eyes, is stated in verse 20.

Their impenitence in turning from righteousness to wickedness, and persisting therein, is stated in verse 21.

20.—"**The works of their hands**," of which they did not repent, is a phrase peculiar to heathen idolatry (Isa. 2. 8; Jer. 1. 16; 25. 6, 7, 14; Deut. 4. 28; Psa. 115. 4-7; 135. 15).

20.—"**That they should not worship demons**,"

* The state of the world from the introduction of idolatry (Joshua 24. 2) till the introduction of Christianity is described in Romans 1. 21-32. Christianity abandoned, a return to the ancient pagan state is most sure. There are signs which unmistakably point in that direction—signs which the observant may see *to-day*.

not "devils" as in the Authorised Version. Demon worship is here distinguished from that of lifeless idols made of various materials. Demons are living spiritual beings who dread a judgment to come (Matt. 8. 28, 29). The abyss is their proper home (Luke 8. 31, R.V.). They are a class of wicked spirits (Rev. 16. 14). Satan is their leader, "the angel of the abyss" (chap. 9. 11). The demon host of the pit is worshipped. Gentile idolatry, so sternly denounced by Paul (1 Cor. 10. 20, 21), will yet be openly and universally practised within the bounds of the lands termed christian.

The whole scene is given over to idolatry. The rich have their gods of gold and silver, the middle class have theirs of brass and stone, while the poor are equally provided for in idols of wood. The character of the worship and the conduct of the worshippers must necessarily correspond. If God, Who is light and love, is given up for Satan, a murderer and a liar, the character of the latter is stamped upon his devotees and worshippers. Assimilation in nature and ways is the natural result. Hence there follows a short but comprehensive list, the crimes to which the demon worshippers were addicted. As verse 20 gives their religion, verse 21 shows their deeds. These latter are pre-eminently heathen vices. The crimes enumerated are four in number, a brief list, but sufficiently comprehensive.

(1) "**Murders**," and not as an exceptional occurrence, the result of passion, etc., but habitually practised.

(2) "**Witchcrafts**," or "sorceries," the claim of supernatural power, illicit intercourse with spirits, professed telling of the future. The witch of Endor (1 Sam. 28. 7) and Elymas the sorcerer (Acts 13. 8) are examples of those who practised "the black arts of witchcraft." This ancient Canaanitish iniquity was sternly denounced by God, and death was the decreed penalty for those who practised it (Deut. 18. 10-12; Lev. 20. 27; Exod. 22. 18). Sorcerers are classed with dogs, murderers, fornicators, and idolaters as shut out from the heavenly city (Rev. 22. 15). Spiritualism is making rapid strides, and soon Christendom will be given over almost wholly to its practice.

(3) "**Fornication**," which we understand in its actual and literal sense. The marriage tie is that which binds society together; its safeguard and bulwark against the grossest impurity. With no fear of God, with no magistracy to punish, with no check against the wildest indulgence of unbridled lust, *this*, the pre-eminent sin of the heathen at all times, will flourish in these very lands of christian morality. What a picture of moral debasement is here

depicted! The morals of Christendom are rapidly degenerating.

(4) "**Thefts.**" The bonds of society loosened, all mutual respect for each other's rights, even in the most sacred relationship, completely gone, what follows? Greed will lure on the mass of men "not killed" to enrich themselves at the expense of society. "Each one for himself" is the order and motto of these coming days. A certain respect for property, for others' rights, for others' goods may exist, but "thefts" will be part of the characteristic life and history of these awful times. A world without God, given up judicially by Him, and Satan received as its prince and ruler! What a caricature of Christianity verse 20 presents, and what a code of morals is unfolded in verse 21!

THE TWO WOES COMPARED.

The first Woe desolates Palestine. The second is wider in its range, and more disastrous in its effects, reaching to the limits of the Roman earth. The delusions of Satan are more marked in the first, the violence of Satan is characteristic of the second, although the former is also present in the second Woe. This latter is by far the worst. "The scene of this wave of trouble is wider than that of the preceding, for its waters were circumscribed by the bounds of the Hebrew and Greek tongues. Here the trouble springs up in the Euphrates, and has a fourfold energy, going whithersoever there is idolatry. There is a haste and a wildness in the mighty rush here presented, and an all-devouring character of action prominently displayed in their first appearance, very unlike the character of action in the last Trumpet. There is no presenting of any such idea of order, preparedness, dominion, intelligent lordship, or apparent gentleness, as in the fifth Trumpet; but the two hundred millions are presented at once, brilliant as the flames in action; and consumption, rather than victory, marking their progress; while behind them is felt the stinging wretchedness of subjection to them. The sorrow rolls on in judgment over heathenism, but leaves it, in moral result, just where it was."* The seventh Trumpet, or third Woe, is dealt with in the next chapter.

* "The Bible Treasury," vol. 13, p. 239.

CHAPTER X

Descent of the Strong Angel
The Little Opened Book

INTRODUCTORY.

Previous to the opening of the seventh Seal to the sounding of the seventh Trumpet, and to the pouring out of the seventh Vial, a break in the course of judgment in each case is witnessed. The briefest pause is the Vial one (chap. 16. 15). The Trumpet interlude is the longest (chaps. 10-11. 13).

The seventh Seal, under which no separate action or judgment is witnessed, introduced the Trumpet series of divine chastisements. Similarly the third Woe, or seventh Trumpet, prepares the way for the final outpour of God's wrath upon the apostate scene. These last septenary judgments, *i.e.*, the Vials, are of an open, manifested character. They are clearly seen by all to issue from Heaven. God is owned as the source of these horrors, not in true repentance, but in open blasphemy of God and of His Name. In the episode between the sixth and seventh Trumpets we read, "In the days of the voice of the seventh angel, when he shall *begin* to sound, the mystery of God should be finished, as He hath declared to His servants the prophets" (chap. 10. 7). The sounding of the seventh Trumpet brings the patience of God to a close. The apostate power on earth is to be openly dealt with, not providentially, as under the two previous series of judgments. Heaven and earth, angels and men, witness that these last strokes under the Vials are inflicted by the hand of God. Hence the sounding of the seventh Trumpet heralds the pouring out of the concentrated wrath of God on the guilty and apostate scene. The blows are short, sharp, and unsparing (chap. 16).

It has been held that as the *immediate* result of the seventh presence angel sounding his Trumpet the Lord takes to Himself His great power; at once commencing His millennial reign. But this we conceive is a mistake. The active hostility of the Beast against the saints ceased with the expiration of the 1260 days, the exact period of suffering measured by days and months (chaps. 11. 3; 13. 5-8). This leaves seventeen and a half days to make up the three and a half years needed to complete the seventieth week of Daniel, that eventful week of seven literal years (Dan. 9. 27). The Vials are poured out during these seventeen and a half days.*

* See article, "The Celebrated Prophecy of the Seventy Weeks."

The power of the Beast to further harass God's saints comes to an end when the angel begins to pour the Vials out. How can the Beast persecute when he is himself the direct subject of these last judgments? We gather that chapter 11. 15-18 does not present events which directly come under the seventh Trumpet, but rather groups millennial and eternal scenes, and celebrates in the near anticipation Christ's universal reign and God's triumph. The kingdom is anticipated, not yet come. After the sounding of the seventh angel the Vials are successively poured out. Thus the Trumpets succeed the Seals, and the Vials follow the Trumpets.

But before Rome becomes the direct subject of intense judicial dealing (chap. 16) the public intervention of God is witnessed in symbol and word (chap. 10), and another testimony is shown, one hitherto undisclosed in any previous vision (chap. 11). This testimony has a character peculiar to itself (v. 4), and is a much more restricted one than either that of chapter 6. 9, or the yet more extensive one shown in chapter 7. The city of Jerusalem, then trodden down under the iron heel of the Gentile oppressor, becomes the sphere of the operation of the very special testimony of chapter 11.

GLORIOUS DESCRIPTION OF THE MIGHTY DESCENDING ANGEL

1-3.—"**And I saw another strong angel coming down out of the Heaven, clothed with a cloud, and the rainbow upon his head, and his countenance as the sun, and his feet as pillars of fire, and having in his hand a little opened book. And he set his right foot on the sea, and the left upon the earth, and cried with a loud voice as a lion roars. And when he cried the seven thunders uttered their own voices.**" Things are drawing to a close. The half-week of sorrow (three years and a half) is nearly spent, but its last hours reveal the world in mad and open rebellion against God, and His saints on whom the Beast and the Antichrist wreak their fury. Before, however, the last dregs of the Lord's vengeance are drunk by the Gentile and Jewish apostates and their dupes this consolatory vision breaks through the dark clouds of judgment. It is a stern reminder to the world that, in spite of the raging of the wicked, the government of the earth is the just claim of the Creator and one about to be made good in power. But the vision is also one eminently fitted to strengthen and console believers, and especially suffering saints, for the same power which will crush the enemy exalts the sufferers to honour.

The vision is easily read. It is one of the most profound in the book, yet withal exceedingly simple in its main features. The mysteriousness of the Trumpet visions here disappears.

1.—"**Another strong angel**" carries us back in thought to chapter 5. 2, but the only thing common to both references is the epithet "strong." In the earlier text a *created* being endowed with might is referred to, whereas in the passage before us an *uncreated* Being of divine majesty and power is witnessed. It is the Lord Himself. We have had already a vision of the Lord in angelic, priestly intercession (chap. 8. 3); here He asserts in angelic power His undisputed claim to the dominion of the earth.

1.—"Coming down out of the Heaven," not simply "from" it as a point of departure, but "out" of it as being His native home (1 Cor. 15. 47, R.V.; John 3. 13, last clause); "*the* Heaven" fixes a definite locality. The insertion of the preposition *from* and the omission of the definite article *the* in the text of the Authorised Version may seem to some veriest trifles, but for those maintaining the verbal inspiration of the Sacred Scriptures, as we trust *all* our readers do, an unwarranted interpolation, or the omission of an inspired letter or part of one, jot and tittle (Matt. 5. 18), must be regarded as a distinct loss. God warns and threatens in unusually solemn terms against tampering with the inspired Word, either in *adding* to it (Rev. 22. 18) or in *taking* from it (v. 19).

In the descent of the strong angel to earth is intimated the close of providential dealing. The former scene of prophecy was viewed as having its source in Heaven; here the scene of operation is openly shown to be on earth. The whole prophetic scene under Heaven is openly and publicly occupied. The Lord in thus coming out of His place to establish His world-wide kingdom on earth changes the point of view, which in the vision is earth, not Heaven.

1.—"**Clothed with a cloud**." In the ancient oracles the cloud figures largely as representing the presence and majesty of Jehovah. There is great fu ness and boldness in the symbols employed to set forth the glorious majesty of the Lord, symbols, too, which in their interpretation leave little room for discussion. "Clothed with a cloud" is a public sign of His majesty.

1.—"**The rainbow upon his head**." The same rainbow* as previously witnessed by the Seer (chap. 4. 3). In the earlier reference a rainbow encircles the throne and its august Occupant, here *the* rainbow with its many and

*** In chapter 4 the appearance of the rainbow is "like in appearance to an emerald," the never-tiring green, so restful to the eye.**

variegated colours and glories rests on the head of the angel. The use of the definite article *the* in our text (R.V.) connects the scene of chapter 10 in some of its essential features with that of chapter 4. It is the same rainbow, "this crest of divinity" which surrounds the throne (chap. 4) and the head (chap. 10). Amidst the apocalyptic scenes of judgment God's remembrance of mercy is constant and unfailing. The bow in the cloud,* that ancient token of divine goodness (Gen. 9), here reappears, and just at the time and season when most needed.

1.—"**His countenance as the sun**, and his feet as pillars of fire." Substantially the description here is that of the glory of the Son of Man in chapter 1. 15, 16. There, however, the feet of the glorious One are mentioned before His countenance. Both descriptions apply to the *same* blessed Person in different connections. In the former (chap. 1) the expression of His character and glory as man are set forth. In the latter (chap. 10) the majesty of angelic strength and glory are witnessed. Supreme majesty and government are reflected in His face, while "His feet as pillars of fire" indicate stability and firmness, the unbending holiness of His judicial action.

2.—"**Having in his hand a little opened book.**" In chapter 5 Jehovah holds in His right hand a *closed* seven-sealed book or roll; here the angel holds in his hand an *open* book. Why closed in the one and open in the other? In the former hitherto unrevealed counsels of God are successively disclosed by the Lamb, whereas in the latter "the book is open as part of well-known prophecy, and now brought to a direct issue on known ground." Further, this is a "little" book, diminutive in contrast to the larger book of chapter 5, which was so full that it was written without and within. A book both in size and contents larger and fuller than the one in the hand of the angel.

2.—"**He set his right foot on the sea, and the left upon the earth.**" Three times in the course of this vision the angel is seen standing on the sea and the earth, and in each instance the mention of the sea precedes that of the earth (vv. 2, 5, 8), whereas in other parts of the Apocalypse the order is reversed (chaps. 7. 1-3; 14. 7; 5. 13; 12. 12,

* "The rainbow could not, consistently with the mythology of the heathen, constitute a part of the regalia of any particular deity. They had such exalted notions of it, they thought it was not properly a bow, but a goddess. The Greeks supposed Iris to be the daughter of Thoumas and Electra. The Romans considered her as a particular favourite of Juno. Among the Peruvians the highest acts of worship were paid to the rainbow; in the celebrated temple of the sun at Cusco, an apartment was dedicated entirely to the worship of the rainbow, and an order of priests set apart to perform the customary services."—"Lectures on Prophecies of John," by Robert Culbertson, vol. 1, p. 387. The bow of an archer round the head of some of the heathen deities is different from the rainbow. The heathen could neither open the clouds nor bind them up, and hence adds the above writer: "They were not therefore entitled to wear this badge of distinction." The rainbow is pre-eminently a symbol exclusively used of the divine Being or of His throne (see also Ezek. 1. 28).

etc.). This latter is certainly the natural order, *i.e.*, the earth and the sea. We have already remarked upon the force of these symbols; the *earth* denoting the civilised portion of the globe, the *sea* referring to the masses of mankind in an unformed, uncivilised condition. But in our passage the sea, the turbulent heathen, is first named. Is it random or divine precision that the *right* foot is set down on the rebellious nations and peoples, and the left on the professed scene of light and government? How firm the tread of the angel? How complete the action! How thorough the subjugation of all to Him! He *set* those pillars, or columns, of fire on all beneath the sun. Right and might, both in exercise, are characteristic of the significant **act** of the angel as He takes possession of the whole scene under Heaven.

3.—He **"cried with a loud voice as a lion roars."** Accompanying the *act* of the angel we have His *voice* of majesty and power causing intense terror throughout the whole earth (Hosea 11. 10; Joel 3. 16). It is the voice of Christ. "He doth send out His voice, and that a mighty voice" (Psa. 68. 33). We have here the roar of the lion of the tribe of Judah. He was named as such in conjunction with the Lamb in that heavenly and magnificent scene unfolded in chapter 5. But *there* we witness the action of the lamb; *here* that of the lion.

3.—**"When he cried, the seven thunders uttered their own voices."*** The cry of the angel was a cry to Jehovah which is immediately answered. The answer is one of power and judgment. Thunder is God's voice in judgment, the expression of His authority therein (1 Sam. 7. 10; Psa. 18. 13; Job 26. 14). "The seven thunders" intimate a full and perfect response to the angel's cry. "*The* seven" gives precision and definiteness to the answering voices of the thunders. It was not a crash like the thunder of nature, but these thunders intelligently expressed the mind of the God of judgment, they "uttered their own voices."

THE SEER FORBIDDEN TO WRITE.

4.—**"And when the seven thunders spoke, I was about to write,† and I heard a voice out of the Heaven saying, Seal what the seven thunders have spoken, and write them not."** The prophet was about to record the words of the thunders. He heard and understood.

* The *seven* thunders seem to answer to the *seven* times in which the voice of Jehovah is heard (Psa. 29. 3-9). The seven thunders point to "the perfection of God's intervention in judgment."

† "The intimation here plainly is that John was employed in writing during the intervals of his vision."—"Stuart on the Apocalypse," page 585. We question this statement.

This vision is full of voices. That of the angel of the thunders, and another "out of Heaven." This was a voice of authority, "Seal what the seven thunders have spoken, and write them not." Those to us unrevealed communications were to be sealed. It was not the time to make them known. The exact import of these revelations has not been disclosed; probably they are embodied in the after communications directly concerning the end. There are two commands addressed to the Seer: first, to seal up the sayings of the thunder; second, to write them not (compare with Dan. 8. 26; 12. 9). It may be, as in the case of the Hebrew prophet, that this part of the apocalyptic vision, containing the unwritten words of the angel and of the seven thunders, is "closed up and sealed *till the time of the end*." Sealing these prophetic revelations supposes that the end is a long way off. If the end is near, then the prophecies are not to be sealed. In one case the words are sealed, for the end is *far* off (Dan. 12. 9); in another the sayings are not sealed, for the end is *nigh* (Rev. 22. 10).

SOLEMN OATH OF THE ANGEL.

5-7.—"**And the angel whom I saw stand on the sea and on the earth lifted up his right hand to the Heaven. And sware by Him that lives to the ages of ages, Who created the Heaven and the things that are in it, and the earth and the things that are in it, and the sea and the things that are in it, that there should be no longer delay. But in the days of the voice of the seventh angel, when he is about to sound the Trumpet, the mystery of God also shall be completed, as He has made known the glad tidings to His own bondmen the prophets**." One of the most sublime of apocalyptic actions is here recorded. How strengthening and how consolatory! We turn from the din and angry strife amongst the nations to the eternal purpose of God respecting this earth. It belongs by native right and purchase to Christ. What a sight! Sea and earth under His feet, the book of closing prophecy in His left hand, while He lifts up His right to Heaven,* and swears by the ever-living God and Creator† that there should be *no longer delay*.

* In Daniel 12. 7 the man in linen swears holding up both hands.

† "The description of this angel has been admired by every classical scholar. Abstracted from its spiritual meaning, and considered merely as a literary production, it stands unrivalled by anything we meet with in all the pages of Grecian and Roman literature." Here is another eloquent tribute. "Be pleased to observe the *aspect* of this august personage. All the brightness of the sun shines in his countenance; and all the rage of the fire burns in his feet.—See his *apparel*. The clouds compose his robe, and the drapery of the sky floats upon his shoulders; the rainbow forms his diadem, and that which compasseth the Heaven with a glorious circle is the ornament of his head.—Behold his *attitude*. One foot stands on the ocean, the other rests on the land. The wide extended earth and the world of waters serve as pedestals for those mighty columns.—Consider the *action*. His hand is lifted up to the height of the stars, he speaks, and the regions of the firmament echo with the mighty accents,

It is not "no longer time" as in the Authorised Version and retained in the Revised Version. The translators have corrected their blunder by substituting for "time" *delay* in the margin. Either the text or margin is right, for both cannot be. After the accomplishment of the oath of the angel at least a thousand years run their course ere time ceases and eternity opens; hence it cannot mean that there shall be no longer "time." Tregelles, Stuart, Darby, Kelly, and a host of others competent to judge, read "no longer delay." The meaning is that "man's day," which commenced with the Ascension of the Lord and is closed up by His Advent in power, is drawing to an end. The age of secret, providential dealing with evil is about to close. For 2000 years God has not openly interfered in the government of the world. The Church is a ruin, and the world a wreck. It is the time when the will of man is everywhere rampant. It is, too, the time of God's patience with evil, the era of His long-suffering with men. There will be no longer delay in setting up the kingdom and taking the government of all creation into His own hands. Man's day is to be closed up in sharp and severe judgment, and the Lord's reign and kingdom set up. The oath of the angel not only assures us of this, but guarantees the immediate execution of it. There is to be no longer delay in bringing the present age with all its evil to an end.

7.—"**In the days of the voice of the seventh angel, when he is about to sound the Trumpet, the mystery of God also shall be completed.**" What is signified by the mystery of God?* Does it not seem strange that Satan has been allowed for 6000 years to wrap and twist his coils around the world, to work evil and spoil and mar the work of God? What havoc he has wrought! He is the god of this world and the prince of the power of the air. God's saints have ever been the objects of his fiercest malignity. Is it not a mystery why God, the God of righteousness and holiness, allows evil to go unpunished and His own people to be crushed and broken on every hand? Truly this *is* the mystery of God. Is it that He is indifferent to the wrong, indifferent to the sorrows of

---

as the midnight desert resounds with the lion's roar. The artillery of the skies is discharged at the signal; a peal of sevenfold thunder spreads the alarm, and prepares the universe to receive his orders.—To finish all, and give the highest grandeur, as well as the utmost solemnity to the representation, he swears by Him that liveth for ever and ever."—"Hervey's Meditations."

* The mystery of His will (Eph. 1. 9). The mystery of iniquity (2 Thess. 2. 7). The mystery of godliness (1 Tim. 3. 16). The mystery of Christ and the Church (Eph. 5. 32). The mystery of God (Col. 2. 2). The mystery of the seven stars (Rev. 1. 20). The mystery of the woman and the beast (Rev. 17. 7). The mystery of Israel (Rom. 11. 25). These and other mysteries are distinct from the mystery of God in the passage before us. Mystery signifies something previously unknown but now revealed; when made known it ceases to be a mystery of course; it is then "an open secret." All the mysteries are unfolded in the New Testament. The word "mystery" does not occur in the earlier oracles.

His people? Nay, that were impossible. God bears with evil till the hour of judgment arrives, when He will avenge the cry of His elect, and come out of His place to punish the wicked. The checks and restraints upon evil now are unseen as to their source, and are only of partial application. Everything in the world and in the Church is out of order save what God by His Spirit produces.

Now, however, this mystery of God is about to be finished, and God by His Son, the Heir of all things, will wrest the government of the world from the iron grasp of Satan, confine him as a prisoner in the abyss for 1000 years, finally casting him into the lake of fire for eternity, and then rule and reign in manifested power and glory. Evil now tolerated and allowed, spite of numerous checks to hinder its coming to a height, will then be openly punished. The mystery is at end. Christ is about to reign.

This is indeed glad tidings proclaimed to His prophets of old, not declared by them (although they did that as their books testify), but *to* them, "Surely the Lord God will do nothing, but He revealeth His secrets unto His servants, His prophets" (Amos 3. 7). The public intervention of God on behalf of His afflicted saints to crush the power of evil, to expel the usurper Satan from the earth which he has been, so far, permitted to destroy morally and physically, and to set up the world in more than primitive beauty and order: such is God's decree. This was the glad tidings which roused the energies, stimulated the faith, brightened the hope, and gladdened the hearts of the prophets of God in all ages. The *same* blessed hope with added glories is our strength to-day.

Not exactly ***when*** the seventh angel sounds, but in the *days of the voice* of the angel, the mystery of God shall be completed.

THE LITTLE BOOK OF DIVINE COUNSEL AND THE RECOMMENCEMENT OF JOHN'S PROPHETIC MINISTRY.

8-11.—"And the voice which I heard from the Heaven (was) again speaking with me, and saying, Go, take the little book which is opened in the hand of the angel who is standing on the sea and on the earth. And I went to the angel, saying to him to give me the little book. And he says to me, Take and eat it up; and it shall make thy belly bitter, but in thy mouth it shall be sweet as honey. And I took the little book out of the hand of the angel, and ate it up; and it was in my mouth as honey, sweet; and when I had eaten

it my belly was made bitter. And (he) says to me, Thou must prophesy again as to peoples, and nations, and tongues, and many kings.'' The prisoner of Patmos again hears the voice from ''the Heaven,'' the dwelling of God. The limbs of John may have been fettered, and the wild waves of the sea dash against his rocky prison, but the island was no lonely place for the man whose soul was wrapped up in the visions of God, whose ears heard the songs of the redeemed, and the spoken worship of angels, and who was personally addressed out of Heaven again and again. He is commanded to go to the angel and take out of his hand the little opened book. Instantly he complied. The Speaker was none other than God Himself, and hence obedience was prompt and unqualified. The majesty of the angel had no terrors for John. Undismayed by the divine dignity and grandeur of the all-glorious One Who held the book in His hand the Seer goes in the authority of the Creator and asks for the book. The soul who is obedient, who yields unquestioning submission to the expressed will of God, is for the time omnipotent. He walks and acts in the strength of the Creator, the Maker of Heaven and earth. Fear! He knows it not. The invisible God, seen by faith, makes him invincible in the path of obedience, ''immortal till his work is done.''

A further command is given by the angel. The first command was from Heaven to *take* the book, the second was from earth to *eat* it. Why *bitter* in the belly, and *sweet* in the mouth? Prophecy is both bitter and sweet. We are here dealing with symbols. There should be no more difficulty in understanding the prophet eating the book than in Jeremiah eating the words of Jehovah (Jer. 15. 16). To eat is to make the thing one's own, to incorporate it into one's being (John 6. 49-58). The christian prophet eating the roll, and finding it both sweet and bitter, reminds us of a similar symbolic action by the Jewish prophet (Ezek. 2. 8; 3. 1-3). The first effect of prophetic communication, the roll in the mouth, was sweetness, the sweetness of honey; but as the revelations are weighed, the judgments they announce considered, the next effect is to cause bitterness and sorrow. Prophecy both gladdens and saddens, as it contains announcements both of joy and grief.

Finally, the Seer was to recommence his prophetic ministry, not *to* ''peoples, and nations, and tongues, and many kings,'' but *concerning* them. He was to prophesy of them. This we find him doing in the following chapter; hence the last verse of chapter 10 naturally leads us into new scenes and circumstances, of which this later prophetic ministry treats. Its character we shall now, through grace, examine.

CHAPTER XI.

JEWISH TESTIMONY AND THE SEVENTH TRUMPET.

INTRODUCTORY.

We have pointed out the mysteriousness of the Trumpets. Whatever difficulty there may be in a minute exposition of certain figures and symbols this, at least, may be granted, that the devastation of Gentile christianised lands and peoples is unmistakably graven on the Trumpet series of judgments as a whole; their general bearing, even though couched under a wealth of figure, is plain. It is the judgment of Christendom, which is in the main the subject of the Trumpets.

But now in the vision before us the situation is changed; we pass on to the ground of well-known prophecy. The Prophets and the Psalms have made us acquainted with the state of things in Judea and Jerusalem at the epoch referred to in our chapter, hence the interpretation is comparatively simple. We are on Jewish ground. But why is the interest of prophetic dealing transferred from the Gentile to the Jew, and why is Jerusalem so prominent in the vision, the centre of the situation? The reasons are not far to seek. Providential dealing with the apostate part of the Gentile world is now closing up. The government of the earth is about to be assumed openly, and it only remains to pour out under the Vials the concentrated wrath of God upon the guilty scene. But Israel is the centre of Gentile blessing and of judgment too. The course of judgment is drawing to a close. We are in the second half of Daniel's celebrated seventieth week of seven years. At that time *man's* centre of earthly government will be Rome (Rev. 17. 18). *God's* centre and capital seat of earthly government is Jerusalem. There are many cities of note, but in importance Jerusalem dwarfs them all. "Thus saith the Lord God; This is Jerusalem: I have set it in the midst of the nations and countries that are round about her" (Ezek. 5. 5). Jerusalem is the capital of the millennial world, and the centre from whence the Lord governs the nations (Isa. 2. 1-4), "the city of the great King." When the Gentile world is brought into blessing it is not apart from but in direct connection with Israel. "Rejoice, ye Gentiles, *with* His people" (Rom. 15. 10). The settlement of the nations, the respective territory assigned to each, is in no wise dependent on conquest, or war, or purchase, but on the fiat of the Most High. When He "divided to the nations their inheritance, when He separated the sons of Adam, He set the bounds of the peoples according to the number of the children of Israel. For the Lord's portion is His people; Jacob is the lot of His inheritance" (Deut. 32. 8, 9). The purpose of God to make Israel and her land the centre round which He shall gather the nations is not frustrated, but postponed. Our chapter presents the initial stages in the development of this glorious earthly purpose.

The Jews and Jerusalem are in the forefront of the prophecy, and viewed as trodden down of the Gentiles. The circumstances in this most affecting period of their national history are touchingly described in Psalm 79. Here we have first the storm, then the calm; the agony of Israel's closing hours of unbelief are here depicted, but joy cometh in the morning, and on this latter the Hebrew prophets grandly descant.

In the beginning of the chapter we are introduced to the most familiar of Jewish imagery—the temple, altar, court, holy city, etc.

THE TEMPLE AND JERUSALEM.

1, 2.—"**And there was given unto me a reed like a staff, saying, Rise and measure the temple of God, and the altar, and them that worship in it. And the court which (is) without the temple cast out, and measure it not; because it has been given (up) to the nations, and the holy city shall they tread under foot forty-two months.**" "A reed like a staff." The reed was a measuring instrument,* and is frequently mentioned by the prophets of old. The temple, altar, and worshippers measured by the Seer intimate their appropriation, preservation, and acceptance by God. An angel with a golden reed measures the glorified Church (Rev. 21. 15). The Seer with a wooden reed does a like office for the temple. "Like a staff," or firm rod, signifies the strength, stability, and firmness of the emblematic action referred to.

"Rise and measure." The Seer had been a passive yet deeply interested spectator of the scenes witnessed under the previous Trumpets, but now that Israel, his own nation, is in question he is commanded to "rise." He is roused into activity by the divine mandate. It is more than a mere question of posture.

The temple, the altar, the worshippers, all are measured. Christian worship comes in between the suspension of

* In Ezekiel 40. 3 the measuring rod is applied to the temple; then the city itself is measured (Zech. 1. 16). These both, *i.e.*, temple and city, are for God's appropriation in millennial times. There seems two distinct thoughts connected with measuring. First, *set apart* for God, as in the foregoing passages; second, *devoted to destruction* by God, as Moab (2 Sam. 8. 2), Jerusalem (Lam. 2. 8), Israel (Amos 7. 8, 9, 17).

Jewish worship in the past and its resumption in the future. Christians have no *place* of worship on earth; they enter no earthly temple. The holiest in the sanctuary above is their one and only place of worship (John 4. 21, 23, 24; Heb. 10. 19-22); their sacrifices are praise to God and practical benevolence to men (Heb. 13. 15, 16). But this is very different from Jewish worship both in the past and in the future. A temple and altar are essential to Jewish worship. While for the force of the figure it is not essential to suppose the existence of a material temple then in Jerusalem, yet prophecy demands the erection of a stone temple, and the reconstruction of the Jewish polity, both secular and religious, during that deeply solemn period between the Translation (1 Thess. 4. 16, 17) and the Appearing (Jude 14, 15).

The Jews as a nation are restored in unbelief both on their part and on that of the friendly nation who espouse their cause (Isa. 18). They then proceed to build their temple,* and restore, so far as they can, the Mosaic ritual. God is not in this Gentile movement for Jewish restoration, which is undertaken for political ends and purposes. But amidst the rank unbelief of these times there shall be, as ever, a true, godly remnant, and it is this remnant which is here divinely recognised. Gentile oppression and Jewish national apostasy but bring into bold relief the faithful and consequently suffering witnesses of that day, the closing hours of the unbelieving nation's history. "The temple of God" is so termed, because He owns and accepts the true worshippers found therein. The altar refers to the brazen altar which stood in the court of old. It signifies the acceptance of those who in faith draw nigh to it, of course, as ever, on the righteous and holy ground of sacrifice. As to the moral value of the terms the "temple" would express the *worship*, and the "altar" the *acceptance* of the godly remnant of Israel. The unmeasured and rejected court given over to the Gentiles signifies the apostate part of the people, the mass in outward religious profession abandoned by God to the nations, who will wreak their vengeance on the guilty people, spite of the promised assistance of the Beast (Isa. 28. 17-22). The

* The following are the material temples referred to in the Word of God: *Solomon's* (1 Kings 7), destroyed by Nebuchadnezzar, 588 B.C. *Zerubbabel's* (Ezra 3; 6), pillaged and dedicated to the heathen god Jupiter by Antiochus Epiphanes, 168 and 170 B.C. *Herod's* (John 2. 20), reconstructed and almost rebuilt in a style of surpassing magnificence, commenced in the year 17 B.C. *Antichrist's* (2 Thess. 2. 4), to be built by restored Judah. *Christ's* millennial temple (Ezek. 40), entirely new, grand and capacious. In all, five temples. The Church (1 Cor. 3. 16) and the bodies of believers (1 Cor. 6. 19) are each spoken of as the temple of God. Jerusalem is the only city on earth where a temple of stone is divinely sanctioned. The force of the word "temple" in Revelation 7. 15 is that a vast crowd of worshipping Gentiles are recognised; probably these may pray and worship in the literal millennial temple then "a house of prayer for all peoples" (Isa. 56. 7).

"court" signifies *Judaism* in alliance with the Gentiles, and that in its most corrupt and apostate character.

JERUSALEM TRODDEN DOWN.

2.—"**The holy city shall they tread under foot forty-two months.**" Jerusalem is here as elsewhere spoken of in its sacred character as "the holy city" (see Neh. 11. 1, 18; Isa. 52. 1; Dan. 9. 24, etc.). She is to be trodden under foot for an exactly defined period, forty-two months. This denomination of time is elsewhere spoken of as 1260 days (v. 3; 12. 6), a time, times, and half a time (chap. 12. 14). It is also referred to in Daniel 9. 27 in the expression, "The midst of the week." Now these periods refer to the *last* half-week of seven years of Daniel's prophecy (chap. 9. 24-27).*

The forty-two months during which Jerusalem is trodden down, trampled upon by the Gentiles, are months of thirty days each, thus corresponding to the 1260 days of sackcloth testimony borne by the two witnesses or prophets. Jerusalem's coming hour of agony is limited to forty-two months. She will have to drink the cup of the Lord's fury, and drink it for 1260 days. The Gentiles will tread down the people as mire in the streets (Isa. 10. 6, etc.). Even those nations which at first politically befriended the Jew will turn round and glut their vengeance on the restored nation. "They," Judah restored by Gentile intervention, "shall be left together unto the fowls of the mountains, and to the beasts of the earth; and the fowls shall summer upon them, and all the beasts of the earth shall winter upon them" (Isa. 18. 6). Thus the Gentile enemies of Israel are let loose upon the people of Jehovah's choice, then in open idolatry and apostate from God and truth (Matt. 12. 43-45). "The *last* state of that man (Judah) is worse than the first. Even so shall it be also unto this wicked generation" (v. 45).

JEWISH WITNESSES.

3, 4.—"**And I will give (power) to My two witnesses, and they shall prophesy a thousand two hundred (and) sixty days, clothed in sackcloth. These are the two olive trees and the two lamps which stand before the Lord of the earth.**" The worshippers in the *temple* are a distinct company from the witnesses in the city. The worshippers and the prophets respectively set forth the truths of priesthood and royalty which unite in Christ in His millennial reign, "He shall be a priest upon His throne" (Zech. 6. 13); of this the witnesses testify.

* See separate article, "The Celebrated Prophecy of the Seventy Weeks."

On the question of the number of witnesses* conjectures innumerable have been advanced, such as the two Testaments, the law and the Gospel, Huss and Jerome, the Waldenses and the Albigenses, etc. Others with more show of reason, and with an apparent sanction of Scripture, suppose that Moses and Elijah are the two witnesses, quoting Malachi 4 in proof of their contention.† "*Remember* ye the law of Moses My servant" (v. 4) would not imply a personal presence of the great lawgiver in the scenes of the last days; whereas verse five does seem a very express declaration that the distinguished prophet has again to reappear in Palestine: "Behold, I will send you Elijah the prophet before the coming of the great and dreadful day of the Lord." *A full and adequate testimony* is the thought purposely intended in the number of the witnesses. It seems to us that a larger number than actually two is called for in the solemn crisis before us, also that verse eight supposes a company of slain witnesses. But the point is immaterial. Jewish law, and here we are in the midst of Jewish circumstances, called for two witnesses to give competent evidence (Deut. 17. 6; 19. 15). Two angels bore testimony to the resurrection of the Lord (John 20. 12), and two men to His ascension (Acts 1. 10).

3.—"**I will give.**" The Revised Version, Tregelles, and others omit the interpolated word "power." The sense of the passage requires a word for its completion, and hence the translators of the Authorised Version rightly enough inserted in italics in the text, "I will give *power* unto My two witnesses." *Power* or *efficacy* is imparted to the testimony of the witnesses. Such seems the obvious sense of the passage as demanded by the context.

The days of their testimony are carefully numbered. Theirs is not an intermittent testimony, but is continued daily till the allotted period is exhausted, not, however, a day longer. It will be observed that the 1260 days come short of three years and a half by seventeen and a half days. At the close of the period indicated the seventh Trumpet sounds, the Tribulation ends, the power of the Beast to further persecute God's saints abruptly terminates (chap. 13. 5).

---

* "I concur with Lowman, Newton, Woodhouse, Cunningham, and others in the opinion that we are to understand by the two witnesses a competent number of faithful servants of Christ."—"Notes on the Apocalypse."—*Burder*.

† It was an ancient idea that some of the old prophets would reappear before the Second Advent of the Messiah. "As to the persons of these witnesses for the faith, it may be assumed as certain, as all the ancients allow, that the prophet Elijah is one of them, since the opinion was widely prevalent that he, having been carried up to Heaven without dying, would return at the time of the Messiah, or as His forerunner according to Malachi 4. 5. The ancients generally suppose the second to be Enoch, especially because it was assumed of him, according to Genesis 5. 24, that he was received up to Heaven whilst still alive."—"Bleek's Lectures on the Apocalypse." page 252.

3.—"**Clothed in sackcloth**" would express the *afflicted* condition of the witnesses (Joel 1. 13; 1 Kings 20. 31; Jer. 4. 8).

"These are the two olive trees and the two lamps." Why are the two prophets so peculiarly designated? The undoubted reference is to Zechariah 4. The olive, vine, and fig trees have each its distinctive signification. The olive is *testimony* (Rom. 11). The vine *fruitfulness* (John 15). The fig *Israel* nationally (Luke 21. 29). The witnesses in Jerusalem are termed "olive trees," because in that day they represent the testimony of God, and maintain prophetically the royal and priestly rights of the Messiah. They are also termed "the two lamps," for the light of the Spirit is in them. Their testimony is of no uncertain character, for it is carried on in the clear light of God. God is with them spiritually and in power.

But, further, the witnesses are said to "stand before the Lord of the earth," not *God*, as in the Authorised Version. There is One and only One Who has right and title to all here below. Jehovah, the Saviour of Israel, has in Himself an indisputed right to the earth. It belongs to Him. The right is denied, of which the resistance and conflicts of apostate Jews and Gentiles detailed in the Apocalypse are the sorrowful witness. The prophets stand before the Lord of the earth; they know in whose presence they are, and they endure as seeing Him by faith, Who to mortal sight is invisible.

Thus, then, the witnesses, be they two or many, prophesy uninterruptedly for an exact 1260 days. Their office and the sorrowful circumstances under which their testimony is carried on are signified in their clothing of sackcloth. Their testimony is one of power, and also one of spiritual light in the midst of the gloom which settles down like a funeral pall over the guilty city of Jerusalem, the guiltiest city on earth.

MIRACULOUS POWER OF THE WITNESSES.

5, 6.—"**And if anyone wills to injure them, fire goes out of their mouth, and devours their enemies. And if anyone wills to injure them, thus must he be killed. These have power to shut the Heaven that no rain may fall during the days of their prophecy;* and they have power over the waters to turn them into blood,† and to smite the earth as often as they will with every plague.**" We have had the concentration of light and power in the witnesses; now they are empowered

* Elias-like (James 5. 17, 18).

† Moses-like (Exod. 7. 17).

to protect themselves and accredit their mission to the "rebellious" of Israel (Psa. 68. 18) by inflicting signal judgment on their enemies, and by exhibiting signs of a supernatural kind. None, be they high or low, are beyond the reach of judgment. Death is the certain portion of those who "wills to injure" the witnesses. No doubt the testimony will be received by some, perhaps by many (Dan. 12. 3); others, and by far the greater number, proudly and disdainfully reject the message; while another class will seek to injure (not hurt as in the Authorised Version) the witnesses by violence or calumny. On these last stern judgment is executed, not on the mass, but individually, as the opposition to the witnesses assumes a violent character. *Now* grace works in saving the souls of men, *then* judgment is active in clearing the earth of Christ-rejecting sinners. The difference of the dispensations must not be overlooked. The principle is illustrated in the two Psalms (22 and 69). In the first part of both Psalms we have the sufferings of Christ. But in the former the effect of His sorrows is *blessing* even to the ends of the earth and for all time to come (vv. 22-31); whereas in the latter *judgment* is invoked on those who contributed to the anguish of the suffering Saviour (vv. 22-28). Christ suffered for sin (Psa. 22) and also for righteousness (Psa. 69). When the day of grace has run its course the day of vengeance surely follows.

But while verse five asserts the possession by the witnesses of conferred authority (v. 3) to protect themselves and vindicate in stern judgment their mission—a power which, without doubt, will be exercised—verse six intimates a bolder and wider commission. The miracles of Moses when Israel was in *subjection* to the Gentiles (Exod. 7-12), and of Elijah (1 Kings 17; 18) when Israel was *apostate* from God, are again to be witnessed in like character. Jerusalem will be the centre of these miraculous signs of a public kind. What a testimony to the apostate nation of that day! The miracles of Moses repeated, at least in character, will remind them of their ancient slavery to Egypt, and a token of their subjection to Gentile rule once again; while the miracles of Elijah, re-enacted before the public gaze, will surely lead their thoughts back to their former state of apostasy from God to Baal. Jehovah, the Lord of the earth, has again to assert His claims before His apostate people. Thus the condition of Israel, at least of Judah and in Jerusalem, is similar to that in the days of Moses and Elijah—*slavery* and *apostasy*, necessitating on the part of Jehovah a ministry adapted to both states with their corresponding miraculous signs.

A Moses and an Elias character of ministry is predicated of the witnesses.

THE BEAST AND THE WITNESSES.

7.—**"And when they shall have completed their testimony, the Beast who comes up out of the abyss shall make war with them, and shall conquer them, and shall kill them."** The witnesses are invincible and immortal till their mission is completed. They have prophesied in Jerusalem, the centre of prophetic and political interest during the last half of the coming week, less a little over a fortnight, during which time the Vials are poured out. But now the Beast, *i.e.*, the revived empire of Rome, comes upon the scene. This is the first mention of the Beast in these apocalyptic visions. He is named as one well known. In Daniel 7. 2, 3 and Revelation 13. 1 the Beast, or Rome, rises from the sea, that is, out of the struggling masses of mankind, out of a scene of anarchy and confusion. The Antichrist rises after the historical formation of the empire, and out of a settled condition of civil and political government, spoken of as the land or earth (Rev. 13. 11). But in our text the Beast is said to come "up out of the abyss." That is to say that whilst its *historical* rise is human, its *revival* is satanic. The Beast has been ravaging in Christendom, aided by his political subordinate the Antichrist (chap. 13). Judea has especially felt the cruel and relentless hand of the persecutor (Matt. 24. 15-28; Rev. 12. 13-17). But now Jerusalem itself is visited. The witnesses in the city were safe, while their brethren in the faith and companions in sorrow were passing through the horrors of the Great Tribulation, a period of affliction unparalleled in the annals of history (Mark 13. 19). The wickedness of earth has risen to a height in the holy city. The man of sin is there. But God interposes and publicly vindicates His servants by miraculous signs and tokens of power and judgment. The testimony in Jerusalem (v. 3) is coeval with the existence of the Beast as a persecuting power (chap. 13. 5). The *continuance* of the Beast is for at least seven years, but his *power* to persecute is limited to 1260 days, or forty-two months of thirty days each. The Beast is then permitted, at the close of his active career, to enter Jerusalem and slay the witnesses; "his last political act," as one has said. The Beast has triumphed. He wars against the saints, conquers them, and kills them. Goodness and faith seem banished from the earth (Psa. 4. 6; Luke 18. 8). The question is asked whether they will then exist at all. But the story of the witnesses is not yet finished; God's vindication, if delayed, is most sure. The triumphing of the wicked is short, and of that we are now to read, after which God's approval of His faithful witnesses is publicly expressed. The Beast in cruelty and blasphemy exceeds every power which has ever appeared on the earth. His doom and that of his confederate is an awful one (chap. 19. 20).

SCORNFUL TREATMENT OF THE SLAIN WITNESSES, AND GENERAL REJOICING.

8-10.—"**And their body (shall be) on the street of the great city, which is called spiritually Sodom and Egypt, where also their Lord was crucified. And (men) of the peoples, and tribes, and tongues, and nations, see their body three days and a half, and they do not suffer their bodies to be put into a sepulchre. And they that dwell upon the earth rejoice over them, and are full of delight, and shall send gifts one to another, because these, the two prophets, tormented them that dwell upon the earth.**" In the passage before us we have both the *body* and the *bodies* of the witnesses spoken of. In the use of the singular is intimated *one* common contemptuous treatment. Jerusalem is here termed "the great city." Rome (civil) and Babylon (mystical), as also all human consolidated power within the limits of the empire, are similarly designated—chapter 17. 18 for the first, chapter 18. 10 for the second, and chapter 16. 19 for the third. The moral degradation of Jerusalem is expressed in the title "the great city." It is not named, but characterised as "spiritually Sodom and Egypt." The former because of its filthiness and wickedness (Gen. 18; 19; Jude 7; 2 Peter 2. 6-8), and the latter because it was the first enslaver and oppressor of God's people (Exod. 1. 14). "Where also their (not *our*) Lord was crucified." This clause positively forbids a mystical application to the Church.* The historical city of Jerusalem is here identified by that which was the crowning act of her guilt, the crucifixion of "*their* Lord," *i.e.*, the Lord of the slain witnesses.

It will be noted that there are three classes in this dark picture: (1) The Beast who murders the witnesses. (2) Those "of the peoples, and tribes, and tongues, and nations,"† who look upon the bodies of the prophets cast out upon the street or public places of the city, and thus

---

* "*Jerusalem* denotes the Church."—"Hengstenberg on the Revelation," vol. 1 page 403.

† This fourfold distribution of the human family expresses *universality* (see also Rev. 7. 9; 10. 11). In this latter reference "kings" are substituted for "tribes." as supreme authorities are in view—rulers as well as the ruled

exposed to the vulgar gaze; further, they express their hatred and scorn in forbidding the burial of the bodies, a shameful proceeding. (3) "They that dwell upon the earth,"* the worst amongst the apostate peoples of that day. All the classes here named literally reside on the earth, but the phrase referred to is one of moral signification and import. They are apostates from Christianity, having deliberately and determinedly rejected the heavenly calling and chosen the earth instead. *God* may have Heaven, *they* are determined to have the earth as their place and portion. Bad, therefore, as the Beast and his allies are these dwellers on the earth are infinitely worse. The former, *i.e.*, the Gentiles in alliance with the Beast, deny burial to the bodies of the martyred witnesses; the latter keep high and joyous holiday, and exchange gifts and congratulations on the slaughter of the prophets. It will be noted that the general rejoicing is in the present tense, whereas the sending of gifts is in the future. The sending of presents or gifts on occasions of public joy is an old and universal custom (Prov. 19. 6; Esther 2. 18; 9. 19-22). The voice of the witnesses is hushed in the silence of death, and this is the cause of the public rejoicing. So long as the rights of God to the earth were pressed by voice and sign (vv. 3-6) the christian apostates were "tormented" in their consciences and perhaps in their bodies as well. The Word of God wherever faithfully preached makes men unhappy. Sin with its awful consequences is a tormenting subject to even the most hardened and seared conscience.

GOD'S PUBLIC VINDICATION OF THE SLAIN WITNESSES.

11, 12.—"**And after the three days and a half (the) spirit of life from God came into them, and they stood upon their feet; and great fear fell upon those beholding them. And I heard a great voice out of the Heaven saying to them, Come up here; and they went up to the Heaven in the cloud, and their enemies beheld them.**" The energy of life, eternal life, from God is put forth, and the witnesses rise in its power and stand upon their feet. Their witness borne, their trials past, they stand in the strength and stability of a life which death cannot touch. The effect of this publicly witnessed act of resurrection, proved in the sight and to the consciences of the apostate Gentiles to be *of God*, is to cause terror and alarm. "Great fear fell upon those beholding them." The three and a half days twice mentioned (vv.

---

* See on chapter 3. 10.

9, 11) are literal days. It is impossible to regard them otherwise. We are here on the eve of the events concluding the last prophetic week. Probably not many days have to run, much less years, ere the Lord returns to take to Himself His power and kingdom. He comes at the end of the week, and we are here about its close. There is neither room nor need to interpret the time specified other than literally. The four denominations of time mentioned in the chapter are literal and exact periods, and have their place not in the historical past, but in the coming crisis.

12.—The Seer then heard "**a great voice out of the Heaven.**" This was the voice of Jehovah or of one empowered by Him. The voice was addressed to the witnesses raised in bodies immortal and incorruptible (1 Cor. 15. 54), and standing in the presence of their enemies, then overcome with fear. "Come up here." In Heaven they are to find their place and portion. What an answer to earth's scorn, reproach, and murder! What a sight for their enemies! *We* are to be caught up in the clouds (1 Thess. 4. 17); *they* went up in the cloud, not in a cloud. Why "*the* cloud?" Evidently a special and known cloud is referred to, probably that in which Christ descended (chap. 10. 1). The cloud is the symbol of the presence of Jehovah (Exod. 40. 34-38). Only here and in Luke 9. 34 do we read of persons entering into the glory cloud, the cloud of the divine presence.

12.—"**And their enemies beheld them.**" Both the resurrection of the witnesses and their triumphant departure out of the scene of testimony and suffering were publicly witnessed (for the former see v. 11, for the latter see v. 12). In these two respects they differ from that of Christ and of the heavenly saints. No human eye beheld Christ emerge from the sepulchre; His disciples alone witnessed His ascension. There is not a hint afforded that our coming resurrection and translation are witnessed by any on earth. While the order in which the resurrection of the just, the change of the living, and the subsequent translation of both classes of saints (1 Thess. 4; 1 Cor. 15) is traced out even in minute detail, yet all is so quickly done that it would be impossible for the world to witness the sight. All is accomplished "in a moment, in the twinkling of an eye" (1 Cor. 15. 52).

JUDGMENT.

13.—"**And in that hour there was a great earthquake, and the tenth of the city fell, and seven thousand names of men were slain in the earthquake. And the remnant were filled with fear, and gave glory**

to the God of the Heaven." "In that hour there was a great earthquake." Under the sixth Seal (chap. 6. 12), as here under the sixth Trumpet, there is a "great earthquake," *great* because of the appalling effect produced. Under the seventh Vial there is witnessed one even more terrible, one so disastrous as to overshadow all previous judgments of a like character (chap. 16. 18). It is without doubt a violent disruption of society, of all governmental and social order, that is referred to under the sixth Seal. But here in the narrow and circumscribed sphere before us we judge that a literal earthquake is meant, one which will destroy a part of the city and kill seven thousand—a complete number devoted to death. Jerusalem has been the scene of similar visitations in the past, as it will be in the future (Zech. 14; Matt. 28. 2). An upheaval of the forces of nature, carrying in its train destruction of life and property, would be eminently fitted to impress the rest of the guilty inhabitants with the solemn fact that Jehovah's intervention in judgment was a stern reality.

13.—"**The tenth* of the city fell.**" The hour of triumph for the witnesses was the hour of retributive justice on the city wherein they had testified, and in which their blood had been wantonly shed. We understand a "tenth" here as signifying a complete judgment. Thus the *ten* plagues upon Egypt were the sum of Jehovah's completed judgments upon that land (Exod. 9. 14). The *ten* commandments expressed the full measure of Jehovah's demands upon His people—the measure of their obedience (Exod. 20).

13.—"**Seven thousand names of men were slain in the earthquake.**" In the Authorised Version and Revised Version "names of men" is omitted in the text but inserted in the margin. We have inserted the deleted sentence in the text. The definiteness of the judgment seems purposely intended in the peculiar phraseology employed, "*names* of men." We have already remarked on the analogous circumstances of the Jews in Jerusalem as shown in our chapter to the apostate times in which Elijah stood for God. The same character of miracles are here wrought. Compare the first part of verse six with James 5. 17, 18. As to the number "seven thousand" here by God devoted to death, we are reminded of "the seven thousand in Israel" whom God had reserved for Himself (1 Kings 19. 18), another allusion by contrast to the times of Elijah. An exact company of just seven thousand need no more be thought of than literal numbers

---

*For an elucidation of this and other numerals, see "Number in Scripture: Its Supernatural Design and Spiritual Significance." by E. W. Bullinger, D.D.

mentioned in chapters 7. 4-8; 14. 3 of the Apocalypse. What is before us is simply a full and perfect number, be it large or small. A certain defined number is doomed to death.

13.—"**The remnant were filled with fear, and gave glory to the God of the Heaven.**" The remnant is in contrast with the seven thousand slain. Thus the mass of the guilty inhabitants of Jerusalem really form two classes, the slain and spared. This latter company tremble. The arm of God has been bared in judgment and the "remnant" fear. The effect of the appalling judgment on the city and people is not to lead the survivors to repentance and faith, but in their terror they give "glory to the God of the Heaven." Till the conscience is thoroughly searched and the soul brought into the light there can be no communion with God. They wish Him away from the scene of their interests. They are willing enough when their souls are overwhelmed with terror to "give glory to the God of the *Heaven*," because that keeps Him at a distance. But the special testimony of the Apocalypse is to God's right and title to the *earth*, and that is the very question in dispute with these apostates, whether Jewish or christian. Hence till God's right and claim to the earth is recognised, further and severer judgment is needed. God's claim is unqualified and peremptory, and He cannot forego nor abate one iota of His righteous demand. Glory given to the God of Heaven, in the manner of those affrighted apostates, cannot avert the stern course of judgment.

The first Woe, or fifth Trumpet, is announced as past in chapter 9. 12; here in verse 14 we have a similar intimation as to the second Woe, the prophet adding, "Behold the third Woe cometh quickly," the final consummation is at hand.

THE WORLD KINGDOM OF OUR LORD.

15-18.—"**And the seventh angel sounded (his) Trumpet: and there were great voices in the Heaven, saying, The kingdom of the world of our Lord and of His Christ is come, and He shall reign to the ages of ages. And the twenty-four elders, who sit on their thrones before God, fell upon their faces, and worshipped God, saying, We give Thee thanks, Lord God Almighty, (He) Who is, and Who was, that Thou hast taken Thy great power and hast reigned. And the nations have been full of wrath, and Thy wrath is come, and the time of the dead to be judged, and to give the recompense to Thy servants the prophets, and to the saints, and to those who fear Thy Name,**

small and great; and to destroy those that destroy the earth." The seventh Seal and the seventh Trumpet are alike in this respect, that no immediate judgment is announced, no events directly fall under them (see chaps. 8. 1; 11. 15-18). The consummation so grandly celebrated in the verses before us do not record events properly falling under the sounding of the seventh Trumpet. Nothing is recorded as immediately resulting from the Trumpet being blown. This will be evident from even a slight examination of the passage we are now considering. The kingdom and the power taken, the doxology of the elders, the anger of the nations, the wrath of God, the judgment of the dead, and the reward to servants and saints constitute the great and distinguishing truths of the millennium kingdom during its whole course and even on till eternity. Compare "the time of the dead to be judged" with chapter 20. 12. The last Trumpet sounds. Then the present mysterious ways of God with men are completed. God is about to act openly, and inflict a series of short, sharp, and decisive judgments on the vast consolidated and apostate power then dominating the earth, *i.e.*, the Beast (chap. 16). This concluding series of divine chastisements is seen to issue from God Himself. There is no mystery in them. But before these are inflicted, the world kingdom of our Lord and of His Christ is announced as come. Great voices in Heaven proclaim it. Not that the kingdom has actually come, but it is anticipated. The ruin of all opposing power and authority must necessarily precede the establishment of the kingdom, and to this chapters 16 and 19. 17; 20. 3 conclusively witness.

The *anticipation* of the kingdom, and not the actual *setting* up of it, is the cause of the rejoicing in Heaven. When the kingdom is established in power earth as well as Heaven will unite in thanksgiving and song. We repeat, that it is in Heaven only where the kingdom is celebrated as come. Whilst rejoicing characterises the inhabitants of Heaven—the angels and the redeemed—the earth is preparing to enter into its last throes of agony ere the light of the millennial morning dawn and dispel the gloom. It is only in Heaven that our Lord and His Christ take the kingdom; only there is it celebrated. The seventh Trumpet does not bring in the kingdom, but intimates its nearness. The strong angel in chapter 10. 6, 7 had solemnly sworn that at the sounding of the seventh Trumpet the mystery of God should be completed, and that without delay. He here makes his oath and word good. The Trumpet sounds, and open, public judgment seen by all to be from Heaven is the witness that *now* God has risen up to publicly intervene in the affairs of men. But before we are called to see these last judicial chastisements on the apostate scene, Heaven in its calmness looks forward and exults in the near establishment of the kingdom.

The Authorised Version reads, verse 15, **"The kingdoms of this world,"** the Revised Version rightly substitutes "The kingdom of the world." It may seem a trivial difference, but it is not really so. "The kingdoms of this world" at once suggest many kings, numerous conflicting interests, international jealousies, and the like, whereas "The kingdom of the world (or world kingdom) of our Lord and of His Christ is come" intimates one universal kingdom covering the globe; all parts of the earth brought into subjection to the *One* reigning monarch. The government of the earth will be exercised by One who will control all evil and establish righteousness. *His* beneficent sway will be in every respect in happy contrast to past and present kingly rule and government. One undivided and universal kingdom covering the whole earth and righteously and graciously governed is the thought intended.

Next, the duration of the reign is stated to be **"to the ages of ages,"** that is, throughout all time to come, so long as sun, moon, and earth endure (Psa. 72. 5, 7, 17). The reign extends to eternity. It shall never cease.

The many voices of the heavenly host are answered by an act of profoundest worship on the part of the elders or representatives of the redeemed. Their normal place is as enthroned and crowned before God. Twice in chapter 5 the elders fall down and worship (vv. 8, 14). Here only is it said "They fell upon their faces, and worshipped God." In no other instance do the elders so prostrate themselves. The occasion demands it. Then follows a doxology from the elders in which they not only rejoice, but give intelligent reasons for so doing* (see chaps. 5. 5, 8-10; 7. 13-17, etc.). There are seven doxologies mentioned in the course of these apocalyptic visions, of which this is one. These are introduced only on occasions of deep interest (chaps. 5. 12; 7. 12; 11. 15; 12. 10; 14. 2; 15. 2; 19. 1).

Thanks are given to Jehovah (Lord) God Almighty, a strong combination of divine titles. Jehovah the self-existing One; God (Elohim), Who as such is the Creator; Almighty too in power, in resources. Then the eternity

* "Voices in Heaven announce the fact of the reign of Jehovah and of His Christ according to Psalm 2, and that He (for, as ever, John unites both in one thought) should reign for ever and ever, and so it will be. But both the earthly and eternal kingdom are celebrated. Only in the eternal kingdom the distinction of the worldly kingdom and of Christ's subordination is omitted. In the thanksgiving of the elders Jehovah Elohim Shaddai is also celebrated; as the great king who takes to Him His power and reigns, for it is God's kingdom."—"Synopsis of the Books of the Bible," vol. 5, page 534.

of His Being is declared, "Who *is*" (*eternal existence*), and "Who *was*" in relation to the past. "And art to come" is in the text of the Authorised Version, but should be omitted, as in the Revised Version and other translations. "To come" would be out of place in the doxology before us, as the kingdom in its time and eternal features is regarded as present. The deleted sentence is correct in chapter 4. 8.

17.—"**Thou hast taken Thy great power and hast reigned.**" It is interesting to observe that while the kingdom is that of our Lord and of His Christ, or Anointed (Psa. 2), yet *He* takes it, not they. While Jehovah and Christ are here severally distinguished, yet they are united in taking the kingdom and in the subsequent reign, hence the use of the singular pronoun, where one might expect rather the employment of the plural.

Well may it be termed "Thy great power." The fulness of divine power, the might of the Eternal God, is put forth, and the kingdom in its widest sweep as embracing the heavens and earth, and as stretching on through time into eternity, has been wrested from the grasp of the enemy, and "*hast* reigned" is the term employed, so sure that it is spoken of as past.

Next, the elders in a passing sentence historically summarise the feeling of the nations toward God and His people—heavenly and earthly—"And the nations have been full of wrath," spoken of in the past tense. "And Thy wrath is come." Note the difference in the tenses. The wrath of the nations *has* been. The wrath of God *is* come.

18.—"**The time of the dead to be judged**" carries us on in thought to the close of the kingdom (chap. 20. 12). The judgment of the nations (Matt. 25. 32) is at the commencement of the kingdom reign; that of the world, or inhabited earth (Acts 17. 31), during its whole term or course; while the dead are judged after the earthly kingdom has passed away (Rev. 20. 11, 12).

18.—"**And to give the recompense.**" Both the judgment and recompense are characteristic actions of the kingdom. The distribution of reward is both common and special. The recompense of rest and glory is bestowed upon all God's saints alike. But there are special crowns and rewards. In the very conception of a kingdom varying degrees and stations of honour are necessarily thought of. "The recompense" is not only therefore God's answer to the state of His afflicted people here, but embraces also the several and distinctive positions which they will occupy in the kingdom. The reward in this latter is proportioned to the faithfulness, suffering, and service of each individual saint.

18.—"**Thy servants the prophets, and to the saints, and to those who fear Thy Name, small and great,**" are the persons specified to whom "the recompense" is given. There are three classes referred to: (1) "Thy servants the prophets" evidently point to those who have in all ages witnessed for God. The witnesses of our chapter are termed "prophets" (vv. 3, 10), hence the term "servants" must be understood in a narrower sense than that employed in chapters 1. 1; 2. 20; 22. 3. It is used in chapter 7. 3 to designate the sealed of Israel. "Servants" is here qualified by the additional noun "prophets." "Thy servants the prophets." To witness for God in a dark and evil day is a service which God never forgets. All such are peculiarly His servants. (2) "The saints." This term is the common one in the New Testament to designate the general body of believers, and is nowhere used in the New Testament Scriptures to express a select company. It is the common appellation of the redeemed in both Testaments. (3) "Those who fear Thy Name, small and great." This latter company embrace all so characterised who own the Name of the Lord. There are, no doubt, many hidden ones in all ages whose moral separation from the world is of such a feeble character that there may be grave difficulty in terming them saints.* But there *are* those who fear the Name of the Lord in all ranks and classes of society. The technical expression, "the small and great," designates the respective status of each in the world and before God (see chaps. 13. 16; 19. 5, 18; 20. 12). Thus those who fear His Name, wherever found, be they amongst the low or exalted, come in here for their special reward.

18.—"**And to destroy those that destroy the earth.**" That is, the time has also come when the destroyers of the earth, *i.e.*, the Beast, the Antichrist, and their followers, are themselves destroyed. This latter class is a contrasted company to the dead who are judged. The active workers of evil corrupting the earth are surprised in their terrible work, and are subjected at once to divine judgment. The earth is the Lord's, part of that inheritance purchased by Christ and about to be redeemed by power (Eph. 1. 14), hence it must be cleared of all who are destroying it,

* The term *saint*, as used in the New Testament, does not at all signify a practical and advanced state of holiness—its theological signification. A saint is a *separated* one, as the derivation of the word implies, but this separation from the world is effected by the call of God. Called saints, or saints by calling (see Rom. 1. 7; 1 Cor. 1. 2). "Called *to be* saints" is misleading. Delete the italicised words and the meaning is simple. When God's call reached their souls and consciences *that* made or constituted them saints.

whether physically by the Beast or morally by his coadjutor the Antichrist.

THE SITUATION REVIEWED.

The chapter opens with a temple and closes with one (vv. 1 and 19), only the latter introduces a new series of events, and resumes the general history. Verse 19 forms no part of the preceding vision. The subject-matter of the chapter closes with verse 18.

We pass from the interesting episode of the mighty angel and its attendant circumstances (chap. 10) on to Jewish ground (chap. 11). Our stand is Jerusalem, here termed "the great city."* God's acceptance of the true worshippers is signified in the measuring of the temple and altar, whilst His rejection of apostate Judaism is expressed in the court being cast out (vv. 1, 2). The mass of the people ally themselves with the Gentiles, then in open revolt from God and truth. It must be remembered that we have not the heathen before us, but Christendom, which is infinitely worse. But God does not leave Himself without a witness in the midst of the seething mass of corruption in Jerusalem, *then* the sport and plaything of Satan. A special testimony is raised up in the city, distinct from that elsewhere. The witnesses, or prophets (for they are termed both), are endowed with miraculous power. They work miracles, and protect themselves by signs of a divine character for 1260 days. Slavery to the Gentiles and apostasy from God characterise the general condition of Judah, especially those in the city of Jerusalem. Hence the miracles wrought resemble those in the days of Moses and of Elijah. Both the miracles and the character of the times are alike (vv. 3-6).

The Beast who has found his way from Rome—the capital seat of Gentile power, civil and ecclesiastical—to Jerusalem, ravages and murders at his pleasure, but both his power and the period of its exercise are under divine control. We have not here his historical rise "out of the *sea*" (chap. 13. 1), but his satanic revival "out of the bottomless *pit*," or abyss (chap. 11. 7). Jerusalem is morally described as filthy like Sodom, and idolatrous like Egypt, and the stigma is added, "where also their (not *our*) Lord was crucified." In the city thus characterised, the bodies of the slain are cast out on the places of public resort and cruelly denied burial. All classes and representatives of the apostate world gather in the city,

---

* The expression "great city" occurs nine times in the Apocalypse, but not once in a good or holy sense. Chapter 21. 10 is a seeming exception, but the epithet *great* should be deleted (see R.V.).

feasting their eyes on the murdered dead, the worst being those morally spoken of as "they that dwell on the earth" (vv. 8-10). But in the midst of the universal scene of rejoicing God intervenes and vindicates His witnesses by granting them, in full view of their enemies, a public resurrection and translation to Heaven (vv. 11, 12). Judgment on the city and its guilty inhabitants follow. No saving effect is produced in the remnant spared, only that in their great fear they "give glory to the God of the Heaven" (v. 13).

The second Woe, or sixth Trumpet, is announced as past, "the third Woe comes quickly" (v. 14). The seventh angel sounds, and at once "great voices" break out in Heaven, saying, "The kingdom of the world," of Jehovah and of His Christ, is come. Separate nationalities and political organisations may exist under the reign of Christ, but they all own His sway, all are under His authority, and exercise their kingly rule in subjection to Him Who is "King of kings and Lord of lords." The contest between God and Satan, as detailed in the Apocalypse, is not for any or all of the separate kingdoms of the world, but for the world as a whole; *it* becomes the kingdom of our Lord and of His Anointed. The sovereignty of the whole world is the question in dispute. His perpetual reign, *i.e.*, to the ages of ages, is celebrated, not as yet on earth, but in Heaven. The establishment of the world kingdom is anticipated, not actually come; when it does, then the earth as well as Heaven will join in celebrating its virtues and glories. "O clap your hands, all ye peoples," *i.e.*, Gentiles. If there is joy in Heaven as the kingdom is anticipated (v. 15), there is *sorrow* on earth.

The elders next take up the strain, and profoundly worship God in the greatness and eternity of His Being, thanking Him for taking His great power and reigning. The power of the kingdom is regarded as an accomplished fact, although not then actually come. Next, the elders proceed in a statement which, for boldness and fulness, leaves nothing to be desired. The great outstanding facts of the kingdom are mentioned. The nations angry, God's wrath come,* the judgment of the dead, the recompense to His people, and, finally, the destruction of those then corrupting the earth (vv. 16-18). These eighteen verses are replete with interest, and will well repay careful study. Much spiritual insight as to the condition of Jerusalem, and of the feelings and exercises of God-fearing Jews, both inside and outside the city, at the time of which this

* Satan's woe had been specially on Jews; man's woe, specially on the men of the Latin empire; this is God's woe when the nations are angry, and God's wrath is come, and full reckoning and final deliverance come."—*J. N. D.*

chapter treats may be gleaned from a careful study of the *prophetic* character of the Book of Psalms, a study which has been much neglected.

GOD'S REMEMBRANCE OF ISRAEL.

19.—"**And the temple of God in the Heaven was opened, and the ark of His covenant was seen in His temple: and there were lightnings, and voices, and thunders, and an earthquake, and great hail.**" The Apocalypse, as we have noticed, is divided into three divisions—a past, a present, and a future (chap. 1. 19). But besides this threefold division we have the contents of the book arranged under two great parts. The eighteenth verse of our chapter records the last historical action—the judgment of the dead. There is no history beyond it. This last and most solemn assize has its place *after* the millennial heavens have passed away and the earth burned up, and *before* the new eternal Heaven and new earth come into view. The judgment of the dead (chap. 20. 12) is, if we may so say, the link between time and eternity. In the first part of the Apocalypse (chaps. 1-11. 18) we have unfolded the general history of the Church, of Israel, and of the world from about the close of the first christian century down to the close of the kingdom. The second part commences with chapter 11. 19, and occupies the rest of the book. In this part many interesting details are found, Satan is more openly in the foreground, the closing issues both in relation to the Church and the world are more fully unfolded than in the first part of the book. Verse 19 therefore is in relation to events about to be disclosed, and is not to be regarded as part and parcel of what has just been unfolded. Chapter 12 really commences with verse 19 of the previous chapter. In that which follows we have an entirely new prophecy, beginning with verse 19 and closing with chapter 14. It is one mainly relating to Israel, as the opening visions show. In chapter 12 are witnessed in Heaven the sources of good and evil. In chapter 13 Satan's two chief ministers on earth are seen in active hostility against God and His saints. In chapter 14 a series of seven events is disclosed in which the activity of God in grace and judgment is shown.

19.—"**The temple of God in the Heaven was opened, and the ark of His covenant was seen in His temple.**" Neither of these, *i.e.*, the temple and the ark of the covenant, so rich and sacred in Jewish history, is actually located in Heaven. "I saw no temple therein," says the Seer in a subsequent vision (chap. 21. 22). What then do they signify? What are their moral value and lessons to us "upon whom the ends of the ages are come?" The temple is the sign that God is taking up the cause and the interests of Israel, and when seen in Heaven, that it is *there* He is occupied with His people then on the earth. The ark of His covenant is the token of Jehovah's presence with, and His unchanging faithfulness to, His earthly people. The rainbow round the throne (chap. 4. 3) and encircling the head of the angel of might (chap. 10. 1) is the sign to all who behold it of God's covenant with creation, one of goodness and mercy. Here the ark, enclosing the tables of the law, and surmounted with its pure gold lid or mercy-seat, tells a rich tale of grace to Israel. What the rainbow was to creation, that and more the ark* was, and is, to Israel.

19.—"**There were lightnings, and voices, and thunders, and an earthquake, and great hail.**" These terms point separately and in conjunction to a storm of divine wrath, having its source in Heaven. We have already drawn attention to the signification of these terms in former parts of our Exposition. Hail from Heaven, here specially singled out by the epithet "great," intimates the sharpness and suddenness of judgment on earth, as also its source as manifestly from God (Exod. 9. 18-25; Rev. 8. 7; 16. 21). The combination of destructive elements is not employed when the throne is set up. No need of it, as judgment will then proceed from the throne on earth, and not, as here, from Heaven.

---

* Whether the ark shared the fate of the temple, which was burned a month after the sack of Jerusalem by the Chaldeans (Jer. 52. 12, 13), or whether it was hidden by Jeremiah according to Jewish tradition (for the prophet was in the city during the whole of the siege), or included amongst the vessels carried by the conqueror to Babylon, we know not. Certain it is that the ark in the future is not to be brought to light, spite of speculation and guess-work to the contrary. On this Jeremiah speaks with no uncertain voice (chap. 3. 16). The ark, the sign of Jehovah's presence and faithfulness, will no longer be needed in the palmy days of the kingdom, for *that* which it signified will then be an accomplished fact. Jehovah will have made good His unchanging grace to His people, and His throne and presence in their midst will gloriously supersede the ark in the tabernacle and temple of old. To Israel the ark was the sign and token of grace (Joshua 3. 14-17), to the uncircumcised heathen it only brought judgment (1 Sam. 5). In the former case the people were redeemed, hence Jehovah's presence with them was a blessing; in the latter the people were not redeemed, and hence His presence was intolerable.

CHAPTER XII.

Events as God Views Them.

THE WOMAN AND THE MAN CHILD.

1, 2.—"**And a great sign was seen in the Heaven: a woman clothed with the sun, and the moon under her feet, and upon her head a crown of twelve stars; and being with child she cried (being) in travail, and in pain to bring forth.**" We have already remarked that chapters 12, 13, and 14 form one connected prophecy. We regard this section as one of pre-eminent interest to prophetic students. An intelligent understanding of it will enable anyone of devout mind to grasp in the main the prophetic situation. What a sweep! From the birth of Christ (v. 5) till He treads the winepress of God's wrath (chap. 14. 20)—a sweep of two thousand years more or less! From the weakness of the infant to the manifestation of His almighty power in judgment. And this marvellous history is comprised in symbol and word within the compass of fifty-five verses.

1.—"**A great sign was seen in the Heaven,**" not "*wonder,*" as in the Authorised Version. A "wonder" is a surprise. A "sign" has a meaning, and points to a definite subject or object (chap. 15. 1). The adjective *great* is used six times in the chapter, which is one of great subjects. The first of these in order, but not in greatness, is a woman. The Man-Child is the pre-eminent subject of the chapter. The woman is not in Heaven actually, but on earth. The sign only is there. Why in "the Heaven," for her greatness and sorrow are on earth? It is that *God's* thoughts and purposes about her in His dwelling-place, "the Heaven," might be known. It is history read and known in Heaven, in the light of God's presence.

1.—"**A woman clothed with the sun**, and the moon under her feet, and upon her head a crown of twelve stars." There are four representative women in the Apocalypse, each of whom is the expression of a corporate body of persons or a system. (1) Jezebel (chap. 2. 20), or the papal system. (2) The woman invested with the fulness of governmental authority (chap. 12. 1), or Israel. (3) The great harlot (chap. 17. 1), or the future, corrupt and apostate professing Church. (4) The Bride, the Lamb's wife (chap. 19. 7), the Church glorified in Heaven. The celestial luminaries sun, moon, and stars are seen in their assembled glory. A complete system of government is thus presented. All authority supreme as the sun, derived and subordinate as the moon, and lesser lights and rulers as the stars, centre in the woman. She has, too, royal dignity, as the crown on her head signifies. But why *twelve* stars? The undoubted reference is to Joseph's dream (Gen. 37. 9), in which the future glory of Israel, of the twelve tribes, is symbolised.* The woman is invested with the splendour and fulness of governmental authority on earth, for although the sign is in Heaven the reality is to be witnessed here.

2.—"**Being with child she cried (being) in travail, and in pain to bring forth.**" The woman has been before us as a queen, now we witness her as a mother. Her glory and majesty in the former relation, her suffering and pain under the latter designation (Jer. 4. 31). Who is the woman? and who is the child? The woman is ISRAEL. The child is CHRIST. The larger number of expositors apply the vision of the woman to the Church. Now both Israel and the Church stand closely related to Christ—Israel as the mother, the Church as the wife. If it is only seen that verse five applies to Christ, and in fact *must* and *only* refer to Him personally, all controversy is at an end. Israel, and not the Church, was the mother of the Messiah (Isa. 9. 6; Micah 5. 2; Rom. 9. 5; Matt. 1, etc.).

It may be difficult to reconcile the maternal anguish as applicable to Israel with the facts of the case when Christ was born. But however put together these things are in the wisdom of God, and seemingly contradictory (for when was the crying, the travail, and pain when the Messiah came into the world?), yet there is no *real* difficulty. The solution of the matter is contained in Isaiah 66: "*Before* she travailed she brought forth; *before* her pain came she was delivered of a man-child" (v. 7). The travailing and pain refer to Israel's coming hour of trial, the Great

* It is not a safe principle to apply the symbology of the ancients to the interpretation of prophetic imagery. Owing to their numerous and dissimilar religious systems, in all of which hieroglyphic and symbol were largely employed, frequently in the expression of exactly opposite ideas, there can be no certainty in applying their symbology in the interpretation of *that* in the Bible. Scripture interprets itself. Every symbol in the Apocalypse may be intelligently understood by reference to other portions of the divine Word. The Bible does not need the borrowed light of the pagan world. It *gives*, but never borrows. On the numerals of Scripture the late Mr. W. F. Grant, of America, has ably written; Dr. Bullinger of this country, and the late Mr. E. C. Pressland, and others have contributed a good deal that is truly valuable in this department of Biblical knowledge. But the subject is by no means a new one, nor one confined in its elucidation to modern times. In all ages the science of numbers has engaged earnest minds in its study. Apocalyptic numerals have largely employed the thought and pen of theologians in all ages. The sacred number *seven* is without question the ruling number of the Apocalypse, occurring about fifty-three times. Its signification points to what is *perfect* or *complete*. This number is frequently broken up into three and four, the former directing attention to what is *divine*, the latter with what is connected with *man* at large, or generally that of *universality*. The numeral twelve, as employed in our text, and frequently elsewhere, denotes *administrative rule* in the hands of men, thus a civil or ecclesiastical polity, or the two combined, as in the true union of Church and State exhibited in chapter 21. Twelve is of very frequent occurrence in the Apocalypse. Amongst heathen nations this number was largely employed in *administrative* action. The history of China, Egypt, Persia, Greece, Rome, etc., supplies abundant evidence in confirmation of our statement.

Tribulation. But *before* that great event the Messiah, the Man-Child, is born. The prophet Micah confirms this in a clear and unmistakable passage. After referring to the birth of the Messiah (chap. 5. 2), he adds, "Therefore will He give them up, until the time that she which travaileth hath brought forth; then the remnant shall return unto the children of Israel" (v. 3). The travail of the woman is at least two thousand years subsequent to the birth of the Messiah, and refers to her sorrow in the coming Tribulation. "Before she travailed she brought forth; before her pain came she was delivered of a Man-Child." It only remains to inquire: Why then is the travail of the woman put in juxtaposition to the birth of the Messiah? First, notice that the present lengthened period of Israel's rejection, coming in as it does between the birth and the travail, is passed over in silence in the chapter before us; it is a parenthesis, the history of which is not given in prophecy, but found elsewhere of course. Second, it shows the deep interest which the Messiah takes in His people. He thought of the Tribulation, and made certain conditional provisions so as to lighten it many centuries ago (Matt. 24. 15-28). Third, at the time in which our chapter has its place the nation is about to pass into its awful sorrow, and the object of going back in the history to the birth of Christ is to connect Him with them in it.

THE DRAGON AND THE WOMAN.

3-5.—**"And another sign was seen in the Heaven: and behold a great red dragon, having seven heads and ten horns, and on his heads seven diadems; and his tail draws the third part of the stars of the Heaven, and he cast them to the earth. And the dragon stood before the woman who was about to bring forth, in order that when she brought forth he might devour her child. And she brought forth a male son, who shall shepherd all the nations with an iron rod; and her child was caught up to God and to His throne."** The next remarkable sign is that of "a great red dragon." Satan is here before us in his worst character confronting the woman. See verse 9, also chapter 20. 2, in which the identity of the dragon with Satan is established without a doubt. Why is the dragon used as a symbol of Satan? Pharaoh, king of Egypt, in his cruelty to God's people, and in proud and haughty independence of God, is termed "the great dragon" (Ezek. 29. 3, 4). Nebuchadnezzar is similarly spoken of in respect to his violence and cruelty (Jer. 51. 34). Gathering up the numerous Scripture references in the Book of Psalms, and in the first three of the greater prophets, to the crocodile, the sovereign of the seas, who is identified with the dragon, *insatiable cruelty* seems the main feature. The Egyptians regarded the crocodile, or dragon, according to their hieroglyphics, as the source and author of all evil, worshipped under the name of Typho. The colour of the dragon, *red*, denotes his murderous, bloodthirsty character. This is the first time in Scripture that Satan is directly spoken of as a dragon. The heathen monarchs, Pharaoh and Nebuchadnezzar, enslaved and oppressed the people of God, and, thus far acting in satanic power, merited the appellation of dragon. But at the time treated of in our chapter Satan is the prince of the world, its virtual ruler. The Roman power is the instrument through which he acts. Hence the title "great red dragon" can now for the first time be used of him.

3.—"**Having seven heads and ten horns, and on his heads seven diadems**," not "crowns," as in the Authorised Version. What is said of the dragon here is also predicated of the Beast (chap. 13. 1), only here the heads are encircled with the golden fillet, or diadem, the emblem in the East of arbitrary, despotic power; whereas the ten horns of the Beast are crowned. The heads in the one case; the horns in the other. The seven heads on the dragon must not be interpreted as the seven-hilled city of Rome. The dragon and the Beast are distinct, however closely related. The former is a spiritual power, the latter the historical world power. The seven crowned heads of the dragon refer to the concentration of earthly power and wisdom in cruel and despotic exercise. His ten uncrowned horns point to the future limits of the empire as distributed into ten kingdoms, the government of which he administers. If his heads are crowned there is no need for the horns to be. When we come to the actual history the ten horns or kings are crowned (chap. 13. 1). The simple thought is that the heads of the dragon are crowned, while his ten horns signify that his power is exercised administratively through the empire in its ten-kingdom form. The dragon represents the unseen force behind the empire; hence the diadems are on his heads, not on his horns. His heads are encircled with the golden fillet, or badge of royalty, as expressing his complete power and wisdom on earth, centred, however, in the Beast, the royal power then dominant on earth. He is the virtual ruler of the world-wide Gentile monarchy. He administers its government through its personal head "the little horn" (Dan. 7), who is but an instrument in his hands. The despotism and cruelty of the empire are due to the fact that Satan is behind it, governing it in the fulness of his power, and imparting his own character to it, one of undying hatred to God and to those who are His.

4.—"**His tail draws the third part of the stars of the Heaven, and he casts them to the earth.**" We have had the deliberative power and wisdom of the dragon, "seven heads;" here we have in his tail the emblem of his soul-destroying influence; in other words, his lies (Isa. 9. 15). Satan is said to be a murderer and a liar. He murders the bodies, and ruins the souls of men. His power is in his head; his malignant influence in false and damnable teachings in his tail. The western part of the Roman earth, the scene above all others of Gospel light and privilege, seems intended in the expression, "the third part," so commonly met with in the Trumpets. "Stars of the Heaven" mean individual rulers set in outward relationship with God in positions and places of authority. These christian rulers and teachers are caught in Satan's snare, and believe the devil's lies. "He cast them to the earth."* Their moral ruin is complete. Note the use of the present tense, "his tail draws," not "drew," as in the Authorised Version. His work is viewed as present.

Then we have the impressive spectacle of the dragon confronting the woman to "devour her child." What a lurid light this throws on the history and circumstances connected with the birth of the Lord as detailed in Matthew 2. It was not the woman nor Israel that was the special object of Satan's hatred. It was not *her*, but her Seed which he wanted to destroy. In the early days of Genesis 3. 15 the undying hostility of Satan to the woman's Seed was first prophetically announced. In Matthew 2 that hatred is shown. But there only the human agents are seen. Now in the light of Revelation 12. 4 we learn that the real instigator of the attempt to destroy the woman's Seed was Satan, the seven-headed, ten-horned dragon. Herod, the vicegerent of the Caesar in Palestine, the representative of the Roman empire, was really Satan's minister in his subtle attempt to compass the death of the Lord. Here the curtain is rolled aside, and Satan, not Herod, stands fully disclosed as the real murderous enemy of Christ. Herod was a true child of his father the devil (John 8. 41, 44). When his plans were frustrated he turned his cruel rage against the innocent male children in the fond hope that the infant Jesus might be sacrificed amongst the number.

---

* The somewhat similar expression in Daniel 8. 10 refers to eminent Jewish persons, and is the work of the king of the north in Palestine. What is before us here is the malignant work of Satan in Europe amongst eminent christian persons.

5.—"**She brought forth a male son**." This somewhat singular expression does not mean mere distinction of sex. A worthier purpose is intended. The moment that Christ is born, unlike every other male child, universal dominion is conferred upon Him, He steps, so to speak, at once into the rights and glories of Messiah and the yet wider range of sovereignty as Son of Man (see Psa. 2 for the former; Psa. 8 for the latter).

5.—"**Who shall shepherd* all the nations with an iron rod**." There is more than an allusion in these words to Psalm 2. 9. The ancient prediction is here reasserted, and that, moreover, on the very threshold of its accomplishment. The "iron rod" in the hand of the Shepherd of the nations is first laid on the guilty kings and peoples of the west (Rev. 19), then on those of the north and east (Isa. 10; Zech. 12; 14). He breaks up the consolidated powers of earth, whether gathered against Himself or His people. He breaks the iron will of the nations. His hands grasp the reins of universal government, crushing to atoms every opposing power, shivering sceptres, and crashing crowns and kingdoms till kings and peoples bow before Him and own His sovereign sway. In that day of irresistible might and power, the overcomers, forming a body distinct by themselves, as it seems to us, shall be with Him (Rev. 2. 26, 27), associated with Him in His rule over the nations. What an exalted dignity! What an ennobling prospect! (see also 1 Cor. 6. 2, 3).

5.—Next follows the rapture of the Child: "**Caught up to God and to His throne**." This, of course, refers to the ascension, forty days after the resurrection. The fact is briefly stated by Mark (chap. 16. 19), but is more fully and circumstantially related by Luke, the beloved physician (chap. 24. 50, 51; Acts 1. 9-11). The nearest and highest place is His. It is sometimes said "The Church is included in the rapture of the Man-Child." We think not. The ascension of Christ and our translation are always treated of as distinct events. His ascension is a mark of *personal* glory, one in which we cannot share. In truth the word "ascension" is never used of saints. We cannot find Scripture to warrant the assumption that the Church is embraced in the rapture of the Man-Child.

There are three statements in verse 5: (1) The birth of the Man-Child; (2) His destiny; (3) His rapture. Now there is nothing said here about His life and death. His birth and rapture are put together as if no period of thirty-three

* The kings of Israel are termed shepherds (Ezek. 34). David, Christ, and the Antichrist are so spoken of.

years separated the two events. Why is this? The reason is that in this chapter we have not history. The historical course of events must be sought for outside this portion of Scripture, which deals with things from God's standpoint. The moral purpose and aim, as seen and interpreted in Heaven, is what we have in our chapter. The signs are in Heaven; the reality and history on earth. The object here is a twofold one. First, to connect the Messiah with Israel, at least with Judah about to enter her appointed hour of sorrow, Jacob's trouble (Jer. 30. 7); second, to connect the Child with His marvellous destiny, the rule of all nations. Now both these are dependent on His birth, not on His life here, which is omitted, only the necessary links being given, viz., His birth and ascension. To connect the Messiah with Israel and the nations His life is not needed, and thus it is passed over. It only remains to add that Christ is caught up to God and to His throne, where His claim as the Heir of all is allowed, if denied on earth. God and the throne shall make good that claim, and from thence Christ will pass on to the destined Inheritance in God's time and way.

FLIGHT OF THE WOMAN.

6.—**"And the woman fled into the wilderness, where she has there a place prepared of God, that they should nourish her there a thousand two hundred (and) sixty days."** What happened to the Man-Child, and what to the mother, might be supposed to be contiguous events. But it is not so, for just as we have a parenthesis of thirty-three years between the birth and rapture of the Child, so an interval of nigh two thousand years comes in between the rapture and the flight. In fact the whole history of Christianity bridges the time from the ascension of Christ till the woman flies into the wilderness. To make the present dispersion of Judah unto "the four corners of the earth" (Isa. 11. 12) to signify the flight of the woman into the wilderness is too absurd to need refutation. Some have, strangely enough, supposed a double flight, as verse 14, in which it is repeated comes after the war in Heaven. Now it is true that there is a break between the statement of the flight in verse 6 and its repetition in verse 14. But the object is to show *why* the woman had to fly. The dragon cast out of Heaven persecutes the woman, who is then providentially assisted in her flight from the face of her great enemy. The interrupted statement in verse 6 is resumed in verse 14. Between these verses we have the episode of the war in Heaven and the rejoicing consequent on its success. "The first six verses," as another has said, "give us the complete picture." Satan's expulsion from Heaven is antecedent to the flight, and indeed is the immediate cause of her rapid journey. So *that* had to be explained in order to account for the flight into the wilderness. The force of the term "wilderness," as also in chapter 17. 3, signifies a condition *destitute of natural resources, a place of isolation*. The afflicted and sorrowing circumstances of Judah in the Tribulation may well be termed "wilderness." It is the great day of Jacob's trouble (Jer. 30. 7), "when all faces are turned into paleness" (v. 6); the awful time sketched in detail by our Lord in His great prophetic discourse on the mount of Olives (Matt. 24. 15-28; Mark 13. 14-22; see also chapters 13, 17 of the Apocalypse).

6.—"**There a place prepared of God**." Nourished "*there* a thousand two hundred (and) sixty days." The repetition of the adverb is not a mere "Hebraistic pleonasm," as one has said, but is purposely intended to mark the definiteness of the place prepared for her, and where she is nourished or cared for. God provides for the woman both place and nourishment for 1260 days. The same period is expressed in briefer terms as months of thirty days each (chaps. 11. 2; 13. 5). But here the careful numbering of the days intimates the Lord's tender interest in His sorrowing saints. He counts them up one by one, so to speak. These periods *all* refer to the last half week of prophetic sorrow, the closing period of Daniél's years, 490 in all. The suffering Jews in Jerusalem (chap. 11), and those outside (Matt. 24. 16), form one body of Jewish witnesses. We gather, however, that those who witness in Jerusalem itself are probably all martyred, whereas those who escaped to the mountains from the various towns of Judah on the outburst of the persecution survive it. The *martyred* company of Judah are the harpers and singers on the sea of glass (chap. 15). The *preserved* company of Judah, the brethren and companions of the slain, are those on Mount Zion with the Lamb* (chap. 14. 1).

WAR IN HEAVEN.

7-9.—"**And there was war in the Heaven: Michael and his angels went to war with the dragon. And the dragon fought, and his angels; and he prevailed not, nor was their place found any more in the Heaven. And the great dragon was cast out, the ancient serpent, he who is called Devil and Satan, he who**

* The martyred company is not numbered; those preserved are spoken of as 144,000, verse 3 of chapter 14. The 144,000 of chapter 7 are a distinct company. The former is of Judah only, the latter of all Israel.

deceives the whole habitable world, he was cast out into the earth, and his angels were cast out with him.'' The scene described in these verses is not spoken of as a sign. The presence of Satan in Heaven is a *reality*. A war there between the hosts of good and evil under their respective leaders, Michael and the Dragon, is most sure. The statement that Satan has a place in "the Heaven," not in the immediate presence of God, is received with surprise by many and with incredulity by others; and it is deemed stranger still to speak of actual conflict in the place beyond all others of peace and rest, in the place of

> **" No midnight shade, no clouded sun,**
> **But sacred, high, eternal noon."**

But when the vastness of the heavens is considered we cease to wonder. No child in the Father's house, no saint there, need ever fear the conflict of contending hosts. But sin was conceived in the heart of Satan. Not content to occupy a creature's place, although probably the highest of spiritual intelligences (Ezek. 28. 12-17), he aspired to the throne itself. He sinned. He morally fell from his exalted position. But he was not then cast down from the heavens. Other spirits are associated with him in his moral degradation. The blessings of saints are in the heavenly places (Eph. 1. 3), there also they sit, but in Christ (chap. 2. 6). Others besides saints are in the heavenlies (chap. 3. 10); and there our christian conflict is carried on *now* (not after death or the Coming—no warfare then) against wicked spirits (chap. 6. 12). Now, however, the moment has come for his final expulsion from "the Heaven," and the hosts of evil with him. He has to be cast down to the earth, then into the abyss, and finally into the lake of fire, not to reign, but to suffer eternally, the most abject and degraded of beings. The first step in the execution of judgment upon Satan is his forced dislodgment from above. It is the time and occasion referred to by the prophet Isaiah. "And it shall come to pass in that day, that the Lord shall punish the host of the high ones on high, and the kings of the earth upon the earth" (chap. 24. 21). Jehovah will mete out punishment to the sinning angels in their place "on high," and to the mighty on earth as well. None, however exalted in rank and position, can escape.

MICHAEL.

But who is Michael (*who is like unto God*)? This distinguished angel is named five times in the Scriptures (Dan. 10. 13, 21; 12. 1; Jude 9; Rev. 12. 7). He seems to be the leader of the angelic hierarchy, as he is termed by

Jude "*the* archangel,"* and in Daniel 10. 13, where Michael is first named, he is spoken of as "first of the chief princes" (see margin). In each of the five passages where his name occurs, and in their several contexts, the Jewish people are in question. Evidently he is the angel to whose guardian care the interests of Israel are committed. "And at that time shall Michael stand up, the great prince which standeth for the children of *Thy people*," *i.e.*, the Jewish people (Dan. 12. 1). The period referred to by the prophet is the same time beheld in vision by the Seer of Patmos. The Great Tribulation is to be entered upon. But Michael makes it his business to see that Israel does not perish. "He (Jacob) shall be saved out of it" (Jer. 30. 7). Michael is a militant angel. The contests between Persia and Babylon were to all appearance decided by the generalship and force of arms of the renowned Persian, Cyrus, the prophetically designated overthrower of the Babylonian monarchy and the deliverer of the Jewish people from their lengthened exile of seventy years (Isa. 44. 28; 45. 1-4), but it was not really so. The movements of nations, their wars, politics, and social policy are shaped and directed by higher and spiritual powers. There are angels, good and bad, who are constantly influencing men and governments, and of this chapter 10 of Daniel is a conspicuous example. Wars and strife on earth are but the reflex of opposing spiritual powers in the lower heavens. The invisible struggles between the powers of light and the forces of darkness are real and earnest (1 Sam. 16. 13-15; 1 Kings 22. 19-23), and by the influence of these spiritual beings the world is providentially governed. Angelic agency toward the saints of God on earth (Heb. 1. 14; Acts 12) is a generally admitted truth, but their action in determining the issue of battles and shaping national policy, and human interests generally, is not recognised as it ought to be. Of course all is under the wise, strong, and controlling hand of God. He is the supreme Arbiter in human life and history. In the chapter referred to (Dan. 10) Michael goes to the help of an unnamed angel who had wrought at the court of Persia for twenty-one days (v. 13). With the assistance of the archangel the destinies of Persia were directed, resulting in the two associated facts: Babylon the oppressor overthrown, and Judah the oppressed delivered. Michael, too, figures in the contest about the body of Moses. Satan sought possession of the

* Scripture does not speak of *archangels*, only of one, and that in two passages in the New Testament (1 Thess. 4. 16; Jude 9). The Pauline reference is to Christ, the true, real head of angelic power; the other by Jude speaks of that angelic created being who presides over the destinies of Israel. The only two angels who are specifically named are Michael and Gabriel.

body no doubt to ensnare Israel to worship it, as they did the brazen serpent (2 Kings 18. 4). But no human hand dug the grave of Moses. Jehovah "buried him in a valley in the land of Moab, over against Beth-peor: but no man knoweth of his sepulchre unto this day" (Deut. 34. 6). Jude in a few energetic sentences informs us of the cause of dispute between Satan and Michael. Now the contest in our chapter in the Apocalypse is not one between two chiefs simply, as mentioned by Jude, but here the respective forces gather under their distinguished leaders. "Michael and his angels went to war with the dragon. And the dragon fought, and his angels."

THE HEAVENS CLEARED.

The issue of the war between the contending spiritual hosts is in no wise a doubtful one. Satan and his angels are overthrown.

8.—"**He prevailed not, nor was their place found any more in the Heaven.**" The dragon personally suffered an ignominious defeat, while the whole company of sinful angelic intelligences is for ever banished from "the Heaven." On the return of the seventy disciples from their mission they tell their Lord, and that with joy, how "even the devils (demons) are subject to us through Thy Name." That, however, was but the germ of full and final victory over the enemy and his power, and this the Lord prophetically announced when He immediately added, "I beheld Satan *as lightning fall from Heaven*" (Luke 10. 17, 18). Whatever the resistance offered to his expulsion from Heaven, his downfall will be effected completely and instantaneously like a flash of lightning. From the day that pride and lofty ambition entered his heart, for *then* he sinned, he has not only a place in Heaven, where he unceasingly accuses God's saints, but He traverses the earth as well on his mission of mischief. He is the leader of the demon host, and of every form and kind of sinful, spiritual agency. The devil is a *real* person, not an influence, but a living spiritual being. The vision before us has its actual fulfilment in the midst of the prophetic week—about the close of the first half. The treaty made between the Roman prince and the restored nation, or "the many," *i.e.*, the mass of the people, is respected, and its terms observed for the half of the stipulated period of seven years (Dan. 9. 27). But instigated by Satan, the Roman prince breaks the covenant in "the midst of the week." The scene before us is preparatory to it, and, in fact, accounts for the last uprising of evil, civil and religious, on the earth. Cast down from Heaven, Satan takes possession of the doomed scene, and exerts his untiring energy in the ruin and destruction of all then standing for God. The war in Heaven results in the victory of Michael and his associated angels. The dragon and his angels are cast down, never to regain a heavenly position. Then Satan turns his baffled rage against the woman, or what represents her before God in testimony, *i.e.*, the Jewish remnant on the earth. The Tribulation (which in its range covers the whole prophetic area, but in its worst and severest forms of suffering especially affects Palestine) lasts the exactly defined period of 1260 days. We consider it clear, therefore, that the expulsion of Satan from Heaven and his downfall to the earth is on the eve of the Tribulation, and is really the procuring cause of it.

JUDGMENT ON SATAN.

There are three distinct stages in the judgment on Satan. First, he is cast down from Heaven to earth with his associated angels (v. 9); second, he is confined as a prisoner in the abyss for one thousand years (chap. 20. 3); third, he is consigned to eternal torment in the lake of fire (v. 10). The first two acts of judgment are executed by the instrumentality of angels; the third and final one is an exhibition of divine power irrespective of the agency employed to execute it, which is not named. The lake of fire! *There* the wail of anguish is never hushed, and the tear is never dry. No ray of light nor gleam of hope ever enters those caverns of eternal despair. Mind cannot conceive nor pen trace the horror of such a doom. Satan's *reign* in the lake of fire is but the dream of the poet, and is without a shred of Scripture to support it. *There* he suffers—not reigns—the most degraded and abject of God's creatures. How patient is our God, but how sure His threatened judgments! Satan after seven thousand years of active hatred against God, and of hostility to those who are His, is at length crushed, shorn of power and ability to work further mischief, and shut up with his angels to his and their "prepared" doom, "everlasting fire" (Matt. 25. 41).

NAMES AND WORK OF SATAN.

The dragon is here viewed in relation to earth and the human race; hence these four names, as also in chapter 20. 2, in the same order.

(1) **"The great dragon,"** so termed because of his remorseless cruelty. Legend and hieroglyphic paint the dragon as a monster in form and appearance outside the pale of the animal kingdom, a combination of superhuman craft and cruelty.

(2) "**The ancient serpent**" reminds us of his first and successful attempt to effect the ruin of the happy and innocent pair in Eden (Gen. 3). Subtilty, craft, deep cunning are characteristic features of Satan from the beginning of his history in connection with the race. He has ever been a murderer and a liar (John 8. 44; 1 John 3. 8). "The *ancient*" serpent refers to his first historical connection with the race, and the title "serpent"* to his *subtilty* (2 Cor. 11. 3). Satan, needless to say, is a spirit and a real person.

"He who is called," referring now to personal names, (3) "**Devil**," and (4) "**Satan**." The two former titles are descriptive of character—cruelty and subtilty; the two latter names, Devil and Satan, refer to the dragon as a person. The devil is an actual historical being, and in the Greek of the New Testament is used only in the singular. "Devils" should be "demons" (R.V.). As the devil, he is the *accuser*, the *traducer*, and *tempter*. As Satan, he is the open and declared *adversary* of Christ, the public *enemy* of God and of His people (see Job 1; 2; Zech. 3; Matt. 4; Eph. 6. 11; 1 Peter 5. 8).

The special work of Satan is next stated, and one to which his untiring energy is directed. He "deceives the whole habitable world." The human instruments in effecting his purpose (chap. 13), and God's judicial judgment upon Christendom, *i.e.*, the habitable earth, are not here named. The prime mover in all is alone before us. By God's permission Satan deceives all embraced within the prophetic scene (2 Thess. 2. 7-12), whoever may be the persons employed, or whatever the means used, Satan himself is the leader in luring on the world to its moral ruin. Christianity having been abandoned, God gives up in retributive justice the guilty and apostate Church, and the mass of Judah as well, to believe the lie of Satan, in presenting the Antichrist as Israel's promised Messiah and king, backed up by signs of a miraculous character. The bait is eagerly swallowed. "The whole habitable world"

---

* We are satisfied that Genesis 3 is a true and historical account of what actually took place. That Satan spoke through a real serpent seems unquestionable. There is no need of supposing, with Josephus and his learned translator, Whiston, that serpents along with other reptiles of a similar species had the faculty of speech before the Fall, but lost it consequent on its wicked misuse under the dominion of Satan. There are three remarkable instances in the Old Testament of the miraculous use of the lower animals: (1) Speech given to the serpent (Gen. 3); (2) a certain intelligence and speech granted to the ass ridden by Balaam (Num. 22. 21-30); (3) The great fish which swallowed up Jonah, answering to the voice of Jehovah in throwing up the repentant prophet on dry land (Jonah 2. 10). We firmly believe in the exact historical accuracy of these narratives, which, moreover, are vouched for in the New Testament (see 2 Cor. 11. 3; 2 Peter 2. 15, 16; Matt. 12. 40). The stater or piece of money in the mouth of the *first* fish caught by the hook (Matt. 17. 27) is another instance of divine power and foreknowledge in support of the claim of the Creator over the works of His hands. The *creation* of the serpent species is stated in Genesis 1. 24, 25; 3. 1. The governmental *curse* pronounced on the reptile is noted in Genesis 3. 14. Its *degradation* even in millennial days is stated in Isaiah 65. 25.

is deceived thereby. *Then,* however, Satan keeps in the background; *here* in the light of Heaven he stands fully exposed. He was the unseen but spiritual and personal power behind Herod (compare v. 4 with Matt. 2. 16). He is equally so in the judicial blinding of Christendom by his great satellite, the Antichrist, or second Beast of Revelation 13.

9.—"**He was cast out into the earth, and his angels were cast out with him.**" The threefold repetition of the verb *cast out* is meant to emphasise the fact of the ignominious expulsion of Satan and his angels from Heaven. Who these angels are is a question shrouded in mystery. All we know is that they constitute Satan's militant host, and are cast out of Heaven with their distinguished chief. Satan can then no more enter God's presence and accuse the saints to Him, nor can his poisonous breath ever again infect the holy atmosphere of the heavenly places. The heavens have to be cleared of evil as well as the earth, and the ground on which both spheres are to be purified and reconciled (Col. 1. 20) is the sacrifice of Christ (Heb. 9. 23). How complete, therefore, and far-reaching in its results is the blood of Christ!

TRIUMPH—WOE.

10-12.—"**And I heard a great voice in the Heaven saying, Now is come the salvation, and the power, and the kingdom of our God, and the authority of His Christ; for the accuser of our brethren has been cast out, who accused them before our God day and night; and they have overcome him by reason of the blood of the Lamb, and by reason of the word of their testimony, and have not loved their life even unto death. Therefore be full of delight, ye heavens, and ye that dwell (or tabernacle) in them. Woe to the earth and to the sea, because the devil has come down to you, having great rage, knowing he has a short time.**" "A great voice in the Heaven" heard by the Seer is that of the already risen (1 Cor. 15; 1 Thess. 4) and glorified saints. In a subsequent vision an angel addressing John says "*thy* brethren" (chap. 19. 10); whereas it is here "*our* brethren," language unsuitable in the lips of an angelic being. In the doxology which follows "the salvation, and the power, and the kingdom" are announced as *come*. But that is as yet in anticipation. As a necessary and preliminary step to the accomplishment of the kingdom set up in displayed power Satan has been cast out of the heavenlies. "The prince of the power of the air" (Eph. 2. 2) is a title henceforth lost to him for ever. The power of the kingdom having been so gloriously vindicated in Heaven all is announced *there* as "come," although not actually so on earth.

The insertion of the definite article before each of the subjects named gives definiteness and force. "*The* salvation" is not that of the soul now, nor even of the body at the Coming, but is a wide and comprehensive thought embracing the overthrow of the enemy and the deliverance of creation from its present thraldom and agony (Rom. 8. 21). "*The* power" refers to the irresistible might which shall crush and grind to atoms all opposing authority—whether satanic in the Heavens or human on the earth. Now it is the kingdom in *patience*, then it will be the kingdom in *power*. "*The* kingdom" must be understood here in its largest extent, as embracing the heavens and the earth. The kingdom of the Father, and the kingdom of the Son (Matt. 13. 41-43), respectively set forth the two main departments, heavenly and earthly, of the vast and universal kingdom of our God and of His Christ (see Psalm 2).

The casting out of Satan is an event almost second to none in those coming days of stirring interest. The ceaseless activity of "the accuser of our brethren" in denouncing the saints to God, whose ways afford him abundant cause of complaint and ground of accusation, is a solemn feature of what goes on above unseen by mortal eye. Thank God, we have in Christ, the Righteous One, an Advocate with the Father (1 John 2. 1, 2), whose all-powerful intercession, founded on His sacrifice, maintains us ever before God, and renders the charges of the enemy nugatory and powerless. "The accuser of our brethren has been cast out." Satan is completely vanquished and overthrown in the scene and seat of his power. Never again shall his accusations, just or unjust, be listened to in the court of Heaven.

We take it, therefore, that, as a result of the war in Heaven, the celestial regions are for ever freed from the presence of Satan and wicked spirits against whom our conflict, as Christians, is carried on (Eph. 6. 12, R.V.).* "The prince of the power of the *air*" must not be confounded with the title "The prince of this *world*." As the former he heads the *spiritual* powers above, as the latter he

* "It may not be in every one's mind that the aerial regions, the air, the cloud-heavens, the spaces above the earth, are now the chief lurking places of evil spirits. But so the Bible teaches. Paul says we wrestle not with flesh and blood, but with principalities and powers, with *wicked spirits in high places*, literally, '*in the heavens*,' 'in the aerial regions' (Eph. 6. 12). Hence also Satan is called 'the prince of the power of the air,' more literally, 'the prince of *the aerial host*,' meaning wicked spiritual powers dwelling in the aerial heavens (Eph. 2. 2). Thus the satanic confederation has its seat in the upper air, in the atmospheric heaven, in the spaces above and around our world. There they are permitted to have place up to the time of this war."—"Lectures on the Apocalypse." Dr. Seiss, vol. 2, page 362.

neads the *temporal* powers on earth. The Lord having judged "the host of the high ones that are on high" it only remains to fulfil the second part of the prophetic utterance, "and the kings of the earth upon the earth" (Isa. 24. 21).

10.—"**Our brethren.**" Who are they? If the voice in Heaven is that of the heavenly saints, then the brethren referred to would be saints on earth whom Satan accuses, fellow-saints with those in Heaven. These saints were overcomers in their severe conflict with evil. The machinations of Antichrist, and the wiles and even open hostility of the devil were powerless against men whose consciences had been purged by the blood of the Lamb, the holy and righteous ground, moreover, of their standing before God, and in virtue of which the accusations of Satan could not be entertained nor even listened to. There are two grounds stated for their victory over Satan. First, the blood of the Lamb which gave them boldness before God; second, their testimony to men. In this case it would be, of course, of a prophetic character. A third and supplementary statement is added, which shows that the martyr spirit was mighty in them, "and have not loved their life even unto death." As "partakers of the heavenly calling" resurrection is assured them, for all saints who have died, or shall die, share in the blessedness of the first resurrection. The company here referred to are not yet seen raised, but wait for it. These martyrs are distinct from those who subsequently suffer under the Beast, *i.e.*, revived Rome.

12.—"**Therefore be full of delight, ye heavens,**" that is for this cause, that Satan and his angels have been for ever ejected from Heaven. Rejoice, let gladness reign throughout the whole of the heavenly spheres. This is the only instance in the Apocalypse of the word "heavens," otherwise it is invariably employed in the singular. But not the heavens alone are to share in the joy consequent on the victory of Michael, for it is added, "and ye that dwell (or tabernacle) in them." The whole company of the redeemed and angels as well (for the heavens are their native region) are embraced in the call to rejoice. The word *dwell* or *tabernacle* is the same as in chapters **7. 15; 13. 6; 21. 3.**

12.—"**Woe to the earth and to the sea.**" The Authorised Version wrongly inserts "the *inhabiters* of the earth." The interpolation is uncalled for. This is not a denunciation of wrath, but a prophetic announcement of coming judgment on the *earth*, *i.e.*, on all settled and stable governments and peoples; also on the *sea*, *i.e.*, the restless and revolutionary part of the world. We have already referred more than once to the symbolic representation of *earth* and *sea*.* The former denoting what is *fixed*, the latter what is *unstable*. These terms may be used of either things, persons, or governments.

The cause of the prophetic woe on the world at large is next stated, "the devil has come down to you." His expulsion from the heavens is a matter of jubilant praise above, his deportation to the earth will fill the whole scene under Heaven with sorrow, wickedness, and woe.

12.—The **"great rage,"** or wrath, of Satan exceeds that of the nations (chap. 11. 18), inasmuch as the former is the prime mover and invisible leader. His rage in being for ever exiled from his heavenly place is intensified by the knowledge that he has before him but a short career on earth. Whether the devil knows the *exact* period allotted him before he is banished to the abyss we know not. This, however, Christians know, or at least should know, that Satan, when cast down, is permitted to rage against and persecute God's saints on earth for 1260 *literal* days; after this a breathing space is granted, a lull in the storm which lasts for seventeen days and a half, the time during which the Beast, the apostate civil and imperial power, is itself the subject of special judgment under the Vials (chap. 16), and therefore cannot persecute. These two denominations of time added make up exactly three years and a half, at the close of which the Lord appears, and Satan is confined in the abyss for a thousand years. This is the second stage in the judgment of the devil. The first was his casting down from the heavens. It only remains to execute the third, which is accomplished at the close of the kingdom reign, cast into the lake of fire, his eternal doom. Since the sphere of his operation is restricted to the earth, and Satan knows that his brief career must soon end in utter disaster to himself and his followers, spiritual and human, he gives himself in untiring determination to wreak his vengeance on the woman (Judah), the mother of the Man-Child, and this he is permitted to do during the *last* half of Daniel's future prophetic week, less seventeen and a half days. This shortening of the days is what the Lord prophetically referred to in His Mount Olivet Discourse (Matt. 24. 22).

THE DRAGON AND THE WOMAN.

13-17.—**"And when the dragon saw that he had been cast out into the earth, he persecuted the woman which bore the male (child). And there were given to the woman the two wings of the great eagle, that**

* See pages 163, 164, 184.

she might fly into the wilderness, into her place, where she is nourished there a time, and times, and half a time, from (the) face of the serpent. And the serpent cast out of his mouth behind the woman water as a river, that he might make her be (as) one carried away by a river. And the earth helped the woman, and the earth opened its mouth and swallowed the river which the dragon cast out of his mouth. And the dragon was angry with the woman, and went to make war with the remnant of her seed, who keep the commandments of God, and have the testimony of Jesus.'' The deeply interesting episode of the war in Heaven (vv. 7-12) had to be introduced in order to account for the woman's flight into the wilderness. Satan, baffled in his attempt to destroy the Man-Child, turns his rage against the mother (Israel). So long as he had a place in Heaven his fitting title was "the accuser" of the brethren, and chief, too, of the mighty spiritual host against which we war (Eph. 6. 12). But the war in Heaven is decisive so far as Satan and wicked spirits in the heavenlies are concerned. They are cast down; the heavens are for ever cleared of their presence. But on the completion and victory of the heavenly war the earthly contest begins. The issue of the former is an everlasting expulsion from the heavens; the issue of the latter will be the confinement of Satan in the abyss for a millennium.

The broken thread of history is then resumed (v. 13); the parenthesis (vv. 7-12) accounting alone for the flight of the woman. The dragon is on earth. He seeks to wreak his vengeance on Judah then restored to the land, and representing the whole nation before God, for as yet Ephraim, or the long lost ten tribes, has not come into view. In verse 6 the flight of the woman is mentioned, being repeated in verse 14. Persecution caused her to fly (v. 13).

14.—"**There were given to the woman the two wings of the great eagle.**" The insertion of the definite article, omitted in the Authorised Version, marks the definiteness of the action. *Wings* convey a double thought, namely, *rapid motion* and *guaranteed protection*. Both these are granted to the woman. Evidently the allusion to the wings of the eagle refers to Jehovah's past care of His people and deliverance from then impending danger (Exod. 19. 4; Deut. 32. 11, 12). In the earlier reference the wings are attributed to Jehovah; here they are given to the woman. All in this part of our chapter is providential.

The symbolic force of the term *wilderness* into which the

woman fled has been already considered.* She has a place prepared of God, and can also count upon the exercise of divine care. In verse 6 the period of her isolation in the wilderness is counted by days, 1260, but here it is spoken of in more ambiguous terms as "a time (one year), and times (two years), and half a time"† (six months), in all three years and a half. This mode of reckoning is taken from Daniel 7. 25. We have months (chaps. 11. 2; 13. 5), days (chaps. 11. 3; 12. 6), and times (v. 14). All these variously expressed periods refer to the *same* time, the last half week of sorrow spoken of by the Hebrew prophet as the "midst of the week" (Dan. 9. 27). When the period is spoken of as days the suffering saints are specially in view.

14.—"**The face of the serpent.**" Nations and peoples in the time of Satan's activity on earth fall under his malignant influence; are directed and controlled morally and politically. The former is that special form of evil referred to here, from which the woman is preserved. The dragon *persecutes*, the serpent *ensnares*.

15.—"**The serpent cast out of his mouth behind the woman water as a river**"‡ that she might be carried away by it. The devil here uses a certain power, or powers, which are under his influence to accomplish the destruction of the Jewish nation. God providentially frustrates the effort of the serpent. "And the earth helped the woman, and the earth opened its mouth and swallowed the river which the dragon cast out of his mouth." The settled governments of that day befriend the Jew, and providentially (how we know not) frustrate the efforts of the serpent. The means employed by Satan are rendered abortive, not by war, but in neutralising and circumventing Satan's plans to destroy the people. This, we gather, is signified by the earth swallowing the river.

The failure rouses the ire of the dragon, and in his baffled rage he goes "to make war with the remnant of her seed," *i.e.*, individual Jews who had not escaped when the Tribulation burst forth (Matt. 24. 15-20). These individual and faithful witnesses are doubly characterised: "they keep the commandments of God"—the great and distinguishing mark of a godly life, and one common to all believers at all times—"and have the testimony of Jesus." This, of course, is special, and refers to His Coming

---

* See page 253.

† "Seven times" (Dan. 4. 16, 23, 25, 32); times are years. Seven years Nebuchadnezzar lived as a beast, *i.e.*, without heart or conscience to God, just what his and the succeeding empires became, beastly in character and action (chap. 7). See also separate article, "The Celebrated Prophecy of the Seventy Weeks."

‡ For the force of the symbol see page 188

in His kingdom. "The testimony of Jesus" in this book is prophetic in character.* In the Gospels it is of a different nature—one of grace and moral display.

REVIEW OF THE CHAPTER.

The last verse of the previous chapter intimates that Israel comes on the prophetic scene, but not as viewed on earth, although actually there. The *sign* is in Heaven, the first instance of the word in the Apocalypse (chap. 12. 1). The woman is not the Church, but Israel. The Church is the bride of the Lamb (Rev. 19. 7). Israel is the mother of the Lord according to the flesh (Rom. 9. 5). The Male Son—a singular expression—is Christ, so called as He alone is the sum of human excellence, and by birth steps into the rights and dignities of Psalm 2. Who but He could shepherd the nations with a rod of iron? Others through grace are associated with Him in the exercise of universal dominion (Rev. 2. 26, 27). But the Male Son† can only refer to One, the embodiment of all masculine virtue.

The woman is represented as the possessor of all supreme earthly authority—the sun. The pale and silvery moon, the queen of the night, is under her feet. She is royal in rank, too, for on her head reposes a crown in which is gathered up in grand display the fulness in earthly administration of all lesser powers—twelve stars. This is Israel as God sees her; not what she is now, nor even what she has been, but it is "a great sign" of what awaits her in millennial times.

Another sign is then seen in "the Heaven." A dragon, *great*, for he is the unseen yet mighty leader of the hosts of evil in the heavens and on earth; *red* because of his murderous character, delighting in bloodshed; with seven heads crowned with diadems signifying that the fulness of imperial, autocratic power is his; ten horns, the latter condition of the empire in its ten-kingdom form, but not yet in existence, so the horns are not crowned; then his tail in which his venom and deceit lie sweeps across the political horizon, and casts down to the ground, morally, of course, the sum of eminent persons in the western part of the empire.

The dragon is Satan—the former denoting his character, the latter the personal opponent of Christ and adversary of the saints—who is witnessed confronting with murderous purpose the woman in order to destroy her seed. He is baffled, for the Son is caught up to God. The life and

---

* See page 21.

† "The Man-Child is the Lord Jesus Christ, and none other."—*Alford.*

even death of the Lord, rich as these are in fundamental truth and teaching, are passed over in silence. The ascension follows the birth, all between being regarded as a parenthesis.

Then the woman flees into the wilderness, and we meet with another and yet more lengthened parenthesis. Between the ascension of the Man-Child and the woman's flight, *yet future*, the history of Christianity comes in. The great point to lay hold of is the connection between Christ and *Israel*, not Christ and the Church, hence the two omitted parenthetic periods: (1) between the birth and ascension; (2) between the ascension and the flight.

Then follows the interesting account of the war in Heaven, introduced here to show *why* the woman had to flee. Satan and his angels are for ever cast down from Heaven, which fact, along with the knowledge that his career on earth is of brief duration, rouses his anger against the *mother*; previously his rage was directed against the *Child*. The means he employs to accomplish her ruin are in the providential ordering of God rendered ineffectual. Both the Son and the woman escape his vengeance. But individual God-fearing Jews become the objects of his murderous hate.*

So closes this wonderful chapter, in which are grouped perhaps the greatest events related in this marvellous book. It is a chapter second to none in its range of subjects, and goes further back in its historical grasp than any other portion of the book. Who but God could have furnished such a connected grouping of events?

---

* "To make war" (v. 17) implies every form of attack upon the bodies of the saints, whether by persecution or war. Physical hurt and evil of every kind is referred to under this technical expression (see chaps. 11. 7; 16. 14; 17. 14; 19. 19).

CHAPTER XIII

The Two Beasts

THE DRAGON AND THE TWO BEASTS

The victory of Michael over the dragon resulted in the complete overthrow of Satan's power and influence in the heavens. The dragon and his host were cast down to earth, an event of unusual importance, and one of grave significance. The earth is now to become the scene of satanic operation, and God-fearing Jews and Gentiles the special objects of Satan's murderous hatred. He also blinds and darkens the peoples and countries in which once shone so brilliantly the light of Christianity. Although Satan is a spirit, and therefore unseen by mortal eyes, he is nevertheless actually in person on the earth during the last half prophetic week of Daniel, three years and a half. His two principal ministers are before us in this chapter, two *men*. These instrumentalities are also spoken of as beasts, wild, fierce beasts.* As men they are, of course, responsible to God, but they are here viewed as the tools and instruments of Satan, who gives them their power and wields it. Satan is the master mind which acts in and by those two apostates. The first Beast is a *Gentile*, characterised by brute force (vv. 1-10); the second Beast is a *Jew*, characterised by subtile influence (vv. 11-18). These, then, are the two chief ministers of Satan on earth, in and by whom he works to accomplish the destruction of Israel, and, failing that, "the remnant of her seed" (chap. 12. 17). At a later period he urges on his blind dupes to stand in battle array against Christ Himself and His heavenly army (chaps. 19. 11; 20. 3). How utter the rout! How complete the overthrow!

THE FIRST BEAST

(Verses 1-10)

HISTORICAL REVIVAL OF THE ROMAN EMPIRE

1.—**"And I stood upon the sand of the sea."** Some read "*he* stood." If the former reading be adopted, then the reference is to the Seer, but if the latter, then the dragon is meant. Hengstenberg remarks, "One cannot decide on *external* grounds between the two readings." Authorities are divided. But a careful study of the context

* Beasts are powers or kingdoms, but the expression is used ofttimes for the personal head of the kingdom, as the ruler gives his own character to it. Thus in this very chapter masculine and personal pronouns are applied to the Beast, denoting, of course, the actual personal ruler (see chap. 20. 10 in confirmation). Hence the term *Beast* may be used interchangeably for the empire or its personal and energetic head. The beasts of chapters 4-6 are *living creatures* (see Revised Version).

shows conclusively that it is the Seer and not the dragon that "stood upon the sand of the sea."* The apocalyptic prophet always takes his place or stand as a point of observation in keeping with the subject on hand. Thus Heaven (chap. 4. 1), the sand of the sea (chap. 13. 1), the wilderness (chap. 17. 3), and a high mountain (chap. 21. 10) are respective points of view from which he can contemplate the various panoramic visions as they pass before his gaze.

1.—"**The sand of the sea**" on which the Seer stood denotes *vast multitudes* of people (chap. 20. 8). The symbol is common enough as thus employed in all literature. The *sand* directs attention to the countless masses of mankind, while the *sea* as a symbol speaks of the wild and revolutionary forces and principles at work amongst them. In other words, the mass of the human race is here indicated as in a state of unrest and turmoil. In this state of things the Seer takes his stand, and "saw a beast rising out of the sea."

This Beast is without doubt the ancient Roman empire reappearing upon the prophetic scene. It arose in a similar way to the three preceding empires. "Four great beasts came up from the sea" (Dan. 7. 3); that is, out of the unsettled, restless masses of mankind. The four universal empires, Babylon, Persia, Greece, and Rome are represented both as metals (Dan. 2) and beasts (chap. 7), and not only in the rise and initial stages of their history but at the end they are there when the Lord comes.† The first three powers,‡ shorn of their strength, are at the end merely existing, but the fourth (the Roman) will be, as in the past, the dominant power on earth. Rome originally rose out of the throes of revolution and anarchy. The city was built shortly before the ten tribes were taken captive to Assyria. The many omens and legends connected with the birth of Rome all pointed to its future greatness. But while Daniel 7. 3, 7 refers to the historical rise of the empire, 753 B.C., the Seer in Revelation 13. 1 points to its future reappearance. For more than fourteen hundred years the western Roman empire has ceased to exist,§

* The Revised Version reads, the dragon "*went away* to make war." How inconsistent with the next notice of him, "*he stood* upon the sand of the sea!" Just as the Hebrew prophet by the river Ulai beheld the rise of the Persian and Grecian empires their conflicts and history (Dan. 8), so the christian Seer on the sand of the sea beheld the reappearance of the fourth Beast—Rome in imperial splendour emerging out of the wild and tumultuous forces of a revolutionary crisis.

† The prophet takes no account of the break up and non-existent Roman power for many centuries. John shows its revival.

‡ The first will not exist territorially, but will be found merged in her characteristics in the fourth. Babylon is doomed never to rise as a temporal power (Jer. 51. 63, 64).

§ Rome fell A.D. 476. The last who bore the imperial crown was named Romulus Augustus, a young and feeble ruler. The former name recalled to memory the founder of the empire, whilst the latter that of the first of the imperial line.

but its future revival is unquestionable, and it is to this that the first verse of our chapter refers. Whether the empire is in existence or only being formed during the time of the Seal-judgments we have no means of ascertaining. It may be that out of the general collapse of all governing authority under the sixth Seal (chap. 6. 12-17) the Beast emerges. The earlier martyrs (chap. 6. 9-11) are not slain under the persecution of the Beast, but are to wait until they were joined by those subsequently slain, showing that the Beast is not on the scene, at least not active, during the time covered by the Seals.

THE BEAST OUT OF THE SEA, AND OUT OF THE ABYSS.

The Beast then is here first viewed in its historical revival "out of the *sea*." But it is said also "to come up out of the *abyss*" (chap. 17. 8, R.V.). Both are future. The empire is to exist for seven years, but when it comes up at first it will do so out of a political and social chaos, while in its last and final stage its diabolic origin and character are intimated. The ***sea*** refers to its future historical rise, the ***abyss*** to its state under satanic power. This latter aspect of the empire dates from the casting down of Satan in "the midst of the week." Satanic character and action characterise it during the last period of its existence, three years and a half.

THE HORNS AND HEADS OF THE BEAST.

1.—Then the Beast is described as having "**ten horns and seven heads, and upon his horns ten diadems**." The mention of the horns precedes that of the heads (see R.V.). In the Authorised Version they are named in inverse order. But in chapters 12. 3; 17. 3 we find the heads first, then the horns. Probably the reason why the horns in our text are named before the heads is that the Beast's historical appearance when revived is in a ten-kingdom form. Attention is thus called to this new and hitherto unknown feature of the empire. The diadems are on the heads of the dragon (chap. 12. 3); here they are seen on the horns of the Beast. In the former seven diadems; in the latter ten. We should read diadems, not crowns. The former denotes despotic power, the latter constitutional monarchy. Now these ten crowned horns are ten kings (chap. 17. 12). There will be witnessed *soon* ten distinct kingdoms in western Europe. It would be the merest guess-work to enumerate them or allocate exactly their territorial limits, but their identification will be simple enough when God in His providential arrangements brings them into view. In the history of the empire it never had this character. When it ceased to exist, then numerous kingdoms and petty states were formed, fragments of the one vast colossal empire with its one despotic head. But when revived ten kingdoms will be formed within its territorial limits. These ten kings, tired, we suppose, of continued international jealousies and quarrels, "have one mind, and shall give their power and strength unto the Beast" (chap. 17. 13). There shall then be but *one* ruler over the empire, the "little horn" of Daniel 7, the Roman prince who makes a covenant with the apostate nation for seven years (Dan. 9. 27), breaks it in the midst of the period, and finally perishes at the Coming of the Lord in judgment (Rev. 19. 20).

NAMES OF BLASPHEMY.

1.—Another and more awful feature is added, "**upon his heads names of blasphemy**." To a careless observer the empire in its vast strength and territorial extent would be most striking, but to a reflecting mind its blasphemous character as displayed in its heads, its governing authority, is an awful sight to contemplate. The seven heads on the Beast represent, not successive forms of rule, as in chapter 17. 10, but the fulness and completeness of government with which the Beast is invested in its latter-day history. It is not simply the concentration of power signified by "seven *horns*" (chap. 5. 6), but "seven *heads*," the fulness of intelligent government (chap. 12. 3).

"Upon his heads names of blasphemy."* The profession of Christianity having been abandoned (2 Thess. 2. 3), public, open blasphemy of God is the sad result. The Beast will openly defy God, and set himself in determined opposition to all who are His (v. 6). This is an entirely new feature of the empire, and one characterising the last stage of its existence. Ancient Rome was heathen in character. We might reasonably have looked for those names (not *name* as in the A.V.) on the heads of the dragon, but no, they are on the Beast, for he it is who is to be the public witness of direct and flagrant opposition to God and His Anointed, and to all Heaven as well. Every form and character in which God could be dishonoured in the eyes of men are referred to in "*names* of blasphemy."

---

* On the historical application the "names of blasphemy" would be those impiously borne by the emperors, several of whom insisted that divine honours and worship should be paid them. Nero was saluted as "the eternal one." Caligula commanded that his image should be placed in the temple to be worshipped side by side with Jehovah. In fact the deification of the emperors was a standing law in Roman life. This awful feature was introduced on the accession of the Caesars to imperial dominion.

CHARACTERISTICS OF THE EMPIRE.

2.—But the Beast is further represented as "**like to a leopard, and his feet as of a bear, and his mouth as a lion's mouth.**" That is, the Beast, or imperial Rome, besides being marked by features peculiar to itself, combines and concentrates the main characteristics of the three preceding empires, "absorbs them" as another has said.* We turn to the Hebrew prophet for needful explanation as to these empires. The chapter is one connected prophecy given in vision to Daniel (chap. 7), stretching from the advent of the conqueror of Judah to the seat of universal sovereignty, and on through the ages till the star of Judah is again in the ascendant; in other words, from the reign of Nebuchadnezzar to that of Christ as Son of Man. Now the first three empires are briefly described (Dan. 7); the Babylonian in verse four, the Medo-Persian in verse five, and the Grecian in verse six. The rest of the chapter is devoted in the main to the consideration of the fourth Beast, characterised but not named (v. 7). It will be observed that the Seer mentions the wild animals in the inverse order to that of the prophet. In Daniel the historical succession of the empires necessitates the mention first of the lion, the chosen symbol of Babylonian greatness. In Revelation 13. 2 is first mentioned the leopard or third empire. Celerity of movement and sudden spring, so characteristic of the mighty Grecian, Alexander, are denoted by the leopard; the grasping, crushing tyranny of the Persians on their conquered provinces (on Judah perhaps excepted) is likened to the feet of a bear; while the terror inspired by the lion's roar, as also its ferocity in tearing to pieces its prey, are next spoken of. These characteristics of a bestial nature are here seen combined and embodied in the fourth Beast of Daniel 7, the revived Roman dominion.

THE DRAGON AND THE BEAST.

2.—"**And the dragon gave to him his power, and his throne and great authority.**" The Beast, in whom are combined the distinguishing features and characteristics of its predecessors, as well as their sovereignty, is thus a fitting instrument through which the dragon can

* "All the ferocious and powerful beasts which Daniel (chap. 7. 3, *seq.*) has *successively* brought upon the scene of action as the representatives of different empires John has here combined in one monster. There is much of significancy in this. The Roman empire combined in itself all the elements of the terrible and the oppressive which had existed in the aggregate in the other great empires that preceded it; its extension too was equal to them all united. Hence the propriety of the composite symbol which unites the symbols of other empires in that of Rome, and thus makes the complex unity of the latter a most significant index of power and cruelty and extent of imperial dominion."—Stuart on "The Apocalypse," page 638.

work. Thus not only is the Beast the inheritor of the world-wide dominion directly bestowed upon Nebuchadnezzar, but he also represents the dragon in cruelty and brute force in the world. The subtilty of the serpent is expressed in the second Beast (v. 11). Satanic power from the abyss, Satan's own throne* in the midst of a God-defying scene, and unlimited authority on the earth make up the awful picture here presented. Christ refused the sovereignty of the world from Satan (Luke 4. 5, 8); here is one who accepts it. It only remains to add that the period referred to when the dragon gives his throne and authority to the Beast is the time and occasion when the Beast ascends out of the abyss (chap. 17. 8), consequent upon Satan's expulsion from Heaven.

The satanic character and history of the empire covers the most interesting and solemn crisis in the world's future—the three years and a half preceding the Lord's Advent in glory. At the close of this period, the seventieth week of Daniel, the Beast and his coadjutor in evil go "into perdition," *i.e.*, the lake of fire. The two Beasts of our chapter are in the end seen to be two devil-inspired men. These chiefs of the apostasies in the closing days are consigned alive to their eternal doom (chap.. 19. 20).

THE DEATH AND RESURRECTION OF THE BEAST A UNIVERSAL WONDER.

3.—"**And one of his heads (was) as slain to death, and his wound of death had been healed; and the whole earth wondered after the beast.**" Here we have the political death and resurrection of the Beast. The wounded head and the Beast are evidently identified. It was the Beast in its imperial head that was slain. The empire ceased to exist A.D. 476. The world-wide dominion of the Caesars has lain in the iron grip of political death from that date till now. But God in His providence will call the empire again into being, out of a scene of revolutionary passion and conflict, like that out of which the empire of the first Napoleon arose—out of the sea (v. 1). "His wound of death had been healed." The Seer views it as an accomplished fact, referring, we take it, to the statement in verse 1. But his resurrection, as also his presentation to the world, is connected with his satanic revival in the midst of the week (Dan. 9. 27). The *historical* rise and continuance of the Beast precedes, or at least is coincident with, the seven years' treaty with Judah. The *satanic* revival (v. 2; chap. 17. 8) is in the last

* "*Seat*" read *throne*; also in chapter 4 read *thrones*, not "*seats*." Royal position is in view in both passages. *Seats* suppose a private station in life, *thrones* a royal one.

half of that prophetic week of seven years. "The whole earth wondered after the beast." The Beast will present a picture hitherto unknown and unseen, one unexampled in the history of the race. A human power endowed with satanic energy, openly defying God, and invested with the royal power and world-wide authority of Satan will engage the rapt gaze of the whole earth. It will marvel at the sight. We see no reason to limit the phrase "the whole earth." The revival of the empire must be a matter of interest to all embraced within its range and influence. The authority of the dragon and his far-reaching influence go beyond the geographical limits of the ten kingdoms. The Beast to whom Satan delegates his authority exercises a commanding influence all over the earth, reaching even to the limits of heathendom.

WORSHIP OF THE DRAGON AND THE BEAST.

4.—"**And they worshipped the dragon, because he gave the authority to the Beast; and they worshipped the Beast, saying, Who (is) like the Beast? and who can war with him?**" Here God is set aside, and the dragon usurps His place. Not the Creator, but Satan becomes the object of universal worship. Mere profession is worthless in that awful day. Reality alone can avail in a scene wholly given up to Satan. Only those whose names have been written in the Lamb's book, or, in other words, the elect (v. 8), can confront Satan in the hour of his apparent triumph. In the eyes of men the dragon has just done what it was supposed God alone could do, given supreme authority to the Beast; on that account divine honours are paid to him. But the Beast also is worshipped. The *wonder* which, with super-human features added, his reappearance in the scene of history arouses is succeeded by *worship*. Both the astonishment and the worship are universal, the latter in character and extent exceeding anything ever before witnessed in Rome. Spiritualism, which has been making gigantic strides of late years, is working for one definite object, the worship of the devil. In Europe and America devil-worship is largely practised. In 2 Thessalonians 2 we learn that the man of sin, who is identical with the second Beast of our chapter, is also worshipped. What horrible blasphemy! What a mockery and parody of Christianity! Not the Godhead: Father, Son, and Holy Ghost, but triune devil-worship: the dragon, the Beast, and the man of sin. And is this what christian (?) England is coming to? The higher critics are doing their best under the influence of Satan to hand over Christendom to the devil, and they are making rapid progress in that direction. "Who *is* like the Beast? and who can make war with him?"* intimate that his power and war-like prowess are the dazzling qualities which win the admiration of the world, and hence the homage due to his exalted position, but not worship is the special point here. We think, however, more is implied, and that divine honours shall be paid to the personal head of the restored empire; to effect which is the work of the second Beast (vv. 12-15).

THE BLASPHEMY, PERSECUTION, AND WORLD-WIDE AUTHORITY OF THE BEAST.

5-7.—"**And there was given him a mouth, speaking great things and blasphemies; and there was given him authority to pursue his career forty-two months. And he opened his mouth for blasphemies against God, to blaspheme His Name and His tabernacle, and those who have their tabernacle in the Heaven. And there was given to him to make war with the saints and to overcome them; and there was given to him authority over every tribe, and people, and tongue, and nation.**" Interwoven in the very texture of the dark account here furnished of satanic wickedness and human arrogance is a ray of consolation to God's beloved saints (now and then) in the frequency of the expression "given him." Behind the Beast there lies the hidden yet omnipotent power of Jehovah. Satan has no power in himself. All power is of God. Its individual and governmental exercise is another matter, and for that all are responsible, even the devil himself. The power which lashed the Sea of Galilee into fury and tempest in order to sink the vessel which contained the richest freight that ever sailed, Christ and His disciples, had its source in the divine Sleeper reposing in the hinder part of the ship. Satan for the moment was granted authority over the elements of nature to demonstrate to us that his power, as also its continuance, is controlled and checked by God at His will and pleasure (Matt. 8. 23-27). In the pride of his heart the Beast boasts and blasphemes. Who he *is* and what he has *done* constitute, no doubt, the sum of the "great things" spoken, and added to this are the significant words "and blasphemes." God, and all His in earth and Heaven, are openly railed upon, and spoken against in words not recorded, but bitter enough surely, as the expression of an apostate heart inspired by the devil.

* In this proud and defiant challenge the claim of omnipotence is advanced. Beyond all power which has ever appeared on earth the Beast stands forth as acting directly in the super-human power of the dragon—a power which spares not and knows no pity.

Once again we meet with the duration of incarnate satanic power on the earth. "There was given him authority to pursue his career forty-two months." Observe that it is not the *existence* of the Beast or empire simply as such that is affirmed in our text, but that great crisis in its history when Satan takes possession of it forty-two months, or three years and a half previous to its final destruction. It is during this time that the Beast pursues his career of blasphemy and violence under the direct influence of the dragon. The continuance of the empire from its rise (v. 1) till its final destruction by the Lord in Person at His Advent in glory (chap. 19. 19-21) covers at least the whole of the last week of prophecy (Dan. 9). Its revival out of the abyss is in the midst of the week, and from thence we date its satanic career of forty-two months.

Then God and His tabernacle and the dwellers in Heaven are the subjects of satanic blasphemy. Words, bold and bad, are uttered. What is said we know not, but we may be sure that the utmost of undying hatred to God which the malice of the dragon can suggest is publicly and loudly expressed. Probably, too, the blasphemy may take the additional character of contempt and mockery in image and representation of divine subjects. Then the saints on earth standing for the rights of God against the dragon and his satellites are given over to the power of the Beast. The saints in these times are not of the character of the seven thousand negative witnesses in the time of the prophet. They are all Elijahs, bold and uncompromising in their testimony. The Beast is allowed to wreak his vengeance on the saints "to overcome them." See also chapter 11. 7, 8, which, however, is confined to Jerusalem. Whatever may be the territorial extent of the empire in the future, the authority of the Beast seems unlimited in its range and extent, as it embraces "every tribe, and people, and tongue, and nation"—the four divisions of the human race. Thus we find a gathering to Jerusalem of people from all parts of the earth in association with the Beast in the murder of Jewish saints (chap. 11. 9). Countries and peoples outside the Roman empire will yet be found under its powerful influence and authority. The Beast and the woman (Babylon) are in closest connection, but, besides, there are other nations in external relation to the Beast over whom he exercises authority (chap. 17).

WORSHIPPERS OF THE BEAST.

8.—**"And all that dwell on the earth shall worship him (every one) whose name had not been written from (the) foundation of (the) world in the book of**

life of the slain Lamb." We have more than once remarked upon the moral significance of the expression "dwell on the earth"* as signifying a class of persons who had deliberately rejected the heavenly calling, who, in fact, were apostates from Christianity. They are distinct from nations, peoples, tongues, and tribes (chap. 11. 10). Here, however, "the dwellers on the earth" can have no special moral significance, as *all* save the elect are referred to. All then dwelling on the prophetic earth are contrasted with those whose names are in the Lamb's book of life, hence the spiritual meaning of the phrase *earth-dwellers* cannot apply in this case. In the passage before us all worship the Beast save the elect. The slain Lamb who had redeemed them by His Blood takes special account of these sufferers. The book of life in which their names are recorded belongs to Him. In its pages their names were written *from* the foundation of the world, hence there can be no erasure, as undoubtedly there shall be from the book or register of profession (chap. 3. 5). Names, true and false, are found in this latter book, as God takes account of all christian profession. But the Lamb's book of life can only contain the names of the redeemed, as these were written *from* the foundation of the world, *i.e.*, from time's commencement. It is the same book and the same class that are referred to in chapter 17. 8, only there the Name of the Lamb is omitted. The Beast conquers and kills, but eternal life is the portion of those martyrs. The Lamb by His death redeemed them, and thus made good in time, and revealed at the fitting moment the strengthening and consoling fact of their names having been written in *His* book of life. Our blessing as Christians dates further back than that of the elect here and those of Matthew 25. 34. We are foreknown, chosen, and predestinated from *before* the foundation of the world, before time began, hence in eternity (Eph. 1. 4, 5; Rom. 8. 29). We may remark that the elect of Matthew 24. 22 constitute a company of God-fearing Jews, whereas those of our chapter and the sheep of Matthew 25. 34 are chosen out of the world at large.

A CALL AND WARNING.

9, 10.—"**If any one has an ear, let him hear. If any one (leads) into captivity, he goes into captivity. If any one shall kill with (the) sword, he must with (the) sword be killed. Here is the endurance and the faith of the saints.**" The formula, "If any one has an ear, let him hear," is one frequently employed in the ministry

* See pages 74 and 234.

of our Lord (Matt. 11. 15; 13. 9, 43; Luke 8. 8, etc.). It is substantially the same, too, but shortened from that found in each of the addresses to the seven churches (Rev. 2; 3). The added clause, "what the Spirit saith unto the churches," could have no application here, as churches are no longer in existence during the course of the apocalyptic judgments. The call to hear supposes the exercise of spiritual understanding, as distinct from the natural hearing common to men.

Then a principle is stated applicable to the Beast as to God's saints in all ages—to enemies and friends alike. However much grace and the power of the Spirit may work in saints, and modify the application of the principle, it yet abides. But what is the truth here so strongly inculcated? It is the certainty of retributive justice, or in the words of Scripture, "with what measure ye mete, it shall be measured to you again" (Matt. 7. 2). Whoever leads into captivity must himself go into it. Whoever kills must himself be killed. What a word of warning, and how seasonable to saints then crushed under the iron rule of the Beast! They must not resist. Their weapons are not carnal, but spiritual. "Here is the patience (endurance) and the faith of the saints." In this way only can they triumph. Their victories are moral and spiritual, not physical. Helpless and hopeless, their resource is in God Himself. The Beast they would not worship, but on the other hand they must not resist, hence captivity and death would be their sad lot. Well, be it so; they had a life beyond the utmost power of the enemy. Their names were written in the Lamb's book of life, and no power in hell or earth could erase the writing or rob them of their eternal portion founded on the death of the Lamb of God.

We may remark that both in Revelation 13 and Daniel 7 the revived empire is the prominent subject. But in the former the general character of the world power is the prominent feature, whereas in the latter it is more especially the personal head of the empire that is in view. The blasphemy and persecution of the Beast (Rev. 13. 5-7) are in terms nearly identical with those employed in connection with the little horn (Dan. 7. 8, 25). Both the Hebrew prophet and the christian Seer vitally connect the empire with its personal head, the last emperor. The character of the empire is embodied in its last great chief. There are other features of the fourth Beast and its relation to the whore which are taken up in chapter 17 of the Apocalypse, the consideration of which must be reserved till we reach that chapter. "*The* beast," *i.e.*, the empire, is characteristically apocalyptic as being the great civil power in the last days.

THE SECOND BEAST (VERSES 11-18).

THE TWO BEASTS CONTRASTED.

The two beasts of our chapter present a series of strikingly marked contrasts. The first came out of an unsettled state of things—the *sea*; the second arises out of a settled and established condition of civil and political government—the *earth*. The former is a secular power; the latter a religious one. The first Beast had ten horns; the second has two. In subtle soul-destroying influence the second is the more dangerous of the two executive ministers of Satan, but the first is paramount in civil and military authority. The second Beast is clearly subordinate to the first, and, in fact, uses the military and other forces of the empire to accomplish his purpose—the deification of the first Beast. The second is the lieutenant of the first. The first is a Gentile; the second a Jew. Chronologically, too, the second Beast succeeds the rise of the first. There is considerable confusion in the minds of many as to the respective spheres of action of these two beasts. The first is a vast political and military system, and as such perishes at the Coming of the Lord. While the territorial extent of the empire is more limited than it was in its past imperial character, its authority and influence extend throughout the civilised and christianised parts of the earth, embracing numerous nations and peoples. To it Satan gives his throne and authority, *that* which Christ refused from Satan (Luke 4. 6, 7). He receives it from His Father (Psa. 2. 8). No power can withstand the Beast. It is the dominant power on earth.

The second Beast rules in Palestine, but his political power soon wanes, as the first Beast, in the person of its prince, meddles in Jewish political and religious matters, and is for the time the virtual master of Palestine. The Antichrist is viewed as a Beast at the beginning of his history, but at the end perishes as the false prophet, having lost his temporal sovereignty. Princely and kingly authority on earth are merged in the first Beast, who remains sovereign all along and perishes as such. The second becomes the minister of the first. But it is the second Beast who deceives the world, who labours to put Judaism and Christendom into the arms of Satan. The most abject slavery of all to the first Beast is another awful feature of these times. Liberty and freedom there shall be none. Both beasts share the same doom at the same time, in or near Jerusalem, at the Coming in power (chap. 19. 20).

A VILE IMITATION OF CHRIST.

11.—"**And I saw another Beast rising out of the earth; and he had two horns like to a lamb; and spake as a dragon.**" Who is the Beast here referred to as "another?" His lamb-like appearance points him out at once as the false Messiah. He has "two horns." The Lamb has "seven horns." The horn is an emblem of *power*, physical, moral, or kingly. We gather that the two horns on the Beast are a travesty of the seven horns on the Lamb (chap. 5. 6). Fulness of power is with the Lamb; limited power is with this Beast. The *two* horns of power signify the dual office of king and prophet assumed by the Antichrist. As king he reigns in Jerusalem, but in subordination to his great chief, "*the* Beast" (Dan. 11. 36). Under this apocalyptic title, "the false prophet" (chaps. 16. 13; 19. 20; 20. 10), he exercises great spiritual authority amongst the Jews and the peoples of Christendom generally.

He "spake as a dragon." In spite of a certain outward resemblance to the Lamb in the assumption of official power to which he has no right he is at once exposed when he speaks. His draconic voice and speech betray him, and mark him off as Satan's minister. He is the instrument by which Satan works in ruining Judaism and Christendom, spiritually and morally, as his great coadjutor, the first Beast, is instrumental in the prophetic spheres of political and civil government. Ruin, physical and moral, is the great aim of the dragon, and in seeking to accomplish his purpose he is ably supported by His two chief lieutenants, the beasts of our chapter.

We may remark that Rome and Jerusalem are the respective centres of influence from which Satan acts in Europe and Judea and all over the earth.

THE SECOND BEAST THE MINISTER OF THE FIRST.

12-15.—"**And he exerciseth all the authority of the first Beast before him, and causeth the earth and those that dwell therein to worship the first Beast, whose deadly wound was healed. And he doeth great signs, that he should cause even fire to come down from Heaven to the earth before men. And he deceiveth those that dwell on the earth because of the signs**

which it was given him to do before the Beast, saying to them that dwell on the earth that they should make an image to the Beast, who hath the wound of the sword, and lived. And it was given him to give breath to the image of the Beast, that the image of the Beast should also speak, and should cause that as many as would not worship the image of the Beast should be killed." These beasts are political organisations, whoever their respective chiefs may be. The second is a subordinate power, and its royal head the active minister of the first Beast. One might at first sight almost gather that the first Beast is a mere passive machine, and that the energy and force of character are alone found concentrated in the second Beast, as "he exerciseth all the authority of the first Beast before him," *i.e.*, in his presence. But that is not so. The first Beast is a powerful federation of ten kingdoms, harmoniously welded into one vast colossal power (chap. 17. 13) under an imperial leader, active, bold, persecuting, and blaspheming. Now the religious Beast has no royal authority outside Palestine, hence he employs the authority of the first Beast, its force and prestige, to accomplish his truly diabolical design to get Christendom to bow down in worship before the revived Roman empire. The second Beast has no great force or military power of its own; *that* has been given by the dragon to the first Beast. The second influences men religiously and spiritually, and is the worst of the two. Bad as the first undoubtedly is, the second Beast surpasses him. He arrogates to himself divine worship; sits in the literal temple built by the restored nation in unbelief; sets himself above all authority, divine and human; and, in fact, takes God's place so far as he can, but all this in the land of Palestine.* *There* he reigns, having set up his throne in Jerusalem, and *there*, too, he fully occupies the temple as God. This Beast is a combination of religious and secular power, the former predominating. Unlike Christ, Who came in His Father's Name (John 5. 43), this awful personage pushes his own claims as the Messiah to Israel, too, as king and prophet amongst the people then restored in unbelief. The nation (save the godly remnant), judicially blinded, own the pretension and claim of the Antichrist who will head up

* He is publicly worshipped, yet, strange to say, he himself worships a god of his own creation, one hitherto unknown in the history of Israel. This idol-god he loads with honours (Dan. 11. 38). "The king," whose abrupt introduction into the history of the contests between the Syrian and Egyptian monarchs (Dan. 11), and who is of Jewish descent (v. 37), is without doubt the false Messiah; the same, too, as the man of sin and lawless one (2 Thess. 2), the Antichrist of John, the false prophet of the Apocalypse, and the second Beast of our chapter. He claims exclusive worship in Palestine, and associates worship with his great confederate, and with the dragon in the world outside

in himself Jewish and christian apostasy (1 John 2. 22). *Within* the limits of the Holy Land he is impiously deified. *Outside* the bounds of Palestine, in the wider scene of Christendom, he forces upon the nations and peoples the worship of the first Beast, "whose deadly wound was healed," then satanically revived.

13.—"**He doeth great signs**" which are not specified, but one pre-eminent sign is expressly named, he causes "even fire to come down from Heaven," and that publicly "before men." It is the character of miracle by which Elijah accredited the claims of Jehovah over those of Baal (1 Kings 18. 38, 39). In this manner, then, the second Beast supports the claim of the first to be universally worshipped; similarly the second Beast is accredited by Satan (2 Thess. 2. 9). It is the time when God in retributive judgment gives up the guilty scene of Christendom, which had already given Him up. Their punishment *begins* here. Judicially God hands Christendom over to "a working of error, that they should believe a lie" (2 Thess. 2. 11, R.V.). The consequence is that Satan takes his seat in the professing house of God, and so absolutely sets God aside that devil-worship in a triune form is the terrible result. This, then, is the end of our boasted civilisation and material and moral progress. It must either be God and Christianity, or the devil and Christendom. Reality is alone connected with the former; mere profession, which is worthless, is preparing the way for the latter.

The public intimation to "make an *image* to the Beast who hath the wound of the sword, and lived," is an advance upon what we have hitherto had. It is remarkable that at the beginning of Gentile supremacy men were compelled under pain of death to worship an image representing the greatness and majesty of the first empire (Dan. 3). Now at the close of Gentile dominion it is repeated. How incorrigible is human nature! Likeness and image are distinguished in Scripture. Man has lost the likeness (moral) to God (Gen. 1. 26), but fallen as he is he is yet God's image or representative in power (Gen. 9. 6). An image is something that represents another, not necessarily *like* one. We are satisfied that the "image to the Beast" will be an actual, literal, vast representation set up in the centre of Christendom by means of which the Beast will be worshipped. It was an actual image that was set up in the plains of Dura, and by which Nebuchadnezzar was worshipped.

The death wound of the Beast is three times stated (vv. 3, 12, 14). In the third notice of it the wound is said to have been given by the sword, implying not a natural break-up of the empire, but a violent one. The hordes of barbarian savages from the north swept down upon the decaying empire and quickly brought it to a political end.

IMAGE OF THE BEAST WORSHIPPED UNDER PAIN OF DEATH.

15.—**"It was given to him to give breath** (not life) **to the image of the Beast."** The Antichrist has no power in himself. He could not of himself energise the image or give it a real or even spurious vitality. The power behind is Satan. It is he who acts through the beasts. It is *breath* that is given, not life, for this latter God ever keeps in His own hand. It is an image "*to* the Beast," that is, to his glorification; but it is also an image "*of* the Beast," that is, it represents him, calls the attention of the world to him, and keeps the thought of the Beast before the eyes and minds of men. Hengstenberg remarks, "It is not *images* that are spoken of, but an image. But in regard to the sense a multitude of images is meant." Whether the image here spoken of is to be multiplied and scattered throughout the length and breadth of Christendom is a point on which we cannot pronounce with certainty. The object, however, whether the image is one or many, is to bring the world down to the feet of the Beast in worship. The image is made to speak. What it says shall only be known to those who hear it. Death is the appointed portion of those who refuse divine honours to the Beast, or to its distinguished chief, "the prince (Roman) that shall come" (Dan. 9. 26). Thus by signs and wonders of a miraculous kind, wrought by the second Beast, he deceives the guilty and apostate christian mass, so that not only is all true conception of Christianity lost, but idolatry of the rankest character is openly and unblushingly practised. What a future lies before these lands!

UNIVERSAL SUBJECTION TO THE BEAST—COMMERCE AND TRADE CONTROLLED.

16, 17.—**"And he causes all, the small and the great, and the rich and the poor, and the free and the bondmen, that they should give them a mark* upon their right hand or upon their forehead; and that no one should be able to buy or sell save he that had the mark, the name of the Beast, or the number of**

* "'Literally, 'that they should give them,' *i.e.*, that a mark should be given them. Compare Revelation 10. 11, 'they say to me,' *i.e.*, it is said. (See Luke 6. 38; 12. 20; 16. 9, for a similar usage, the first and especially the last of which are often misunderstood)."—"Lectures on the Book of Revelation," by William Kelly, page 413, footnote.

his name." In those awful days individual thought and action are crushed out. The most abject submission to the vilest tyranny ever witnessed is demanded, and none dare refuse. The various classes named are a comprehensive designation of all within the range of the influence of the Beast, and are mentioned in pairs. None, however insignificant in station, none, however exalted, can escape. Neither riches nor poverty can buy nor find exemption from the iron rule of the Beast. The free and the bond are alike on one dead level—absolute submission to the Beast. All, from the least to the highest, are equally his slaves. To resist his will is to be deprived of the right to live (for he effectually controls all commerce), and to court certain death. A certain mystic mark is put either upon the right hand or upon the forehead* of all, save the martyrs who lay down their lives in stern and faithful protest against satanic assumption. The mark upon the "hand" would denote that the person so branded was an *active* slave of the Beast; stamped upon the "forehead" would serve as a *public* acknowledgment of slavery. In either case all must own the absolute supremacy of the Beast and worship him. It was usual to brand slaves with the name or special mark of their owner. Paul (Gal. 6. 17), Israel in her tribes (Rev. 7. 3), the preserved of Judah (chap. 14. 1), the glorified and heavenly saints (chap. 22. 4) are marked by God as belonging to Him, and that publicly (see also Ezek. 9. 4).

Let it be carefully noted that Satan gives unity and strength to this vast political and social organisation termed "the Beast," hence all must belong to it under the pains and penalties of a relentless ostracism. The necessaries of life, obtained by legitimate trading, will be denied those who, in faithfulness to God and fidelity to the truth, refuse allegiance to the Beast and to his powerful and wily supporter and satellite, the Antichrist. Social ostracism and death are the appointed portion of all faithful to God in this most awful crisis in human history. Combination is the order of the day. Religion demands it, the political world demands it, wealth and capital demand it, labour, skilled and unskilled, demands it. All are working for the one great end, Satan's fusion of all religious parties under the Antichrist, and of all political and social parties under the Beast. Out of the seething masses of democracy, out of the wild forces of revolution and of anarchy which know no law, out of the struggles and conflicts between capital and labour, out of

* The Brahmins of India bear a mark upon their foreheads in honour of the god they worship, by which every one can readily distinguish them.

the crashing of crowns and overturning of kingdoms, a strong and imperial power will emerge by direct satanic influence, and will crush all standing in its way or bars its progress, and to this power all without exception must submit or pay the penalty—*death*.

17.—"**The mark, the name of the Beast, or the number of his name.**"* We have not three specific items. The "mark," the "name," and the "number" are not independent things. The mark is general, and consists of either the *name* or *number* of the Beast. The two latter are embraced in the first, and are explanatory of the mark. The name of the Beast is withheld from us, as also that of the personal ruler of Russia in the last days destined to play such an important part in connection with Israel (Ezek. 38; 39). We do not hold that it is impossible to know *who* and *what* are meant by the name and number of the Beast; but no doubt God will give full light and intelligence on these points to saints then in the scene, to whom such knowledge will be most useful and even necessary in order that the true character of the Beast may be known. We leave it where God leaves it, till He makes it plain, as undoubtedly He will; if not to us, at least to those who will be in a position to profit by it. Those who receive the mark of the Beast in either its name or number are doomed to eternal misery. The words in which their awful fate is recorded are unequalled for horror. We know of nothing in the Word to exceed in dread solemnity the utter, irrevocable, and everlasting ruin of the adherents of the Beast. God alone could describe it, and He has done so in words and terms which express unspeakable anguish (chap. 14. 9-11). The door of hope is closed to the Beast, his fellow-associate in evil, and his numerous worshippers. The rejection of Christ by Christendom is most surely followed by the acceptance of the false Messiah, and *that* crowning act of guilt and human folly, when fully consummated, can have but one end, the lake of fire.

THE NUMBER OF THE BEAST.

18.—"**Here is wisdom. He that hath understanding let him count the number of the Beast; for it is a man's**

* "The Number of the Beast.—The various attempts made in recent years to solve this famous apocalyptic riddle seem to show that students are so far as ever from agreement. Weyland finds the number in the phrase, 'Caesar of the Romans,' written in Hebrew characters; Schmidt and Vischer recognise it in the name 'Nero,' so written; Pfleiderer in the phrase 'Nero Caesar;' and Voelter in 'Trajan Adrianus.' Erbes, Spitta, and Zahn, who follow Irenaeus in reading 616 instead of 666, identify the Beast with Caligula, that is, 'Gaius Caesar;' but this result is obtained by the use of Greek, not Hebrew, letters. After eighteen centuries it is still uncertain whether any one has yet arisen with sufficient understanding to count the number of the Beast."—"The Thinker," vol. 5 page 98.

number; and its number (is) six hundred (and) sixty-six.'' Expositors have brought skill, learning, and in some instances great research to the elucidation of the question: What is meant by the number 666?

There is divine wisdom wrapped up in this symbolic numeral—the only instance of its occurrence—and it requires spiritual understanding to unlock the mystery therein. No doubt its full, precise, and final solution will be apparent to the wise or godly in the near crisis when the Beast power under the craft of Satan will exhibit the highest human development in pride, impiety, and in combined religious and political opposition to God and to His Anointed, for such, in general, is the moral significance of 666. The meaning being obvious to the saints to whom it immediately concerns will call for prompt repudiation of the Beast and his claims, who will be the political minister of Satan in blasphemous opposition to God.

Six hundred and sixty-six (666) is man's number; the unit *six* being impressed upon him at his creation and on his subsequent history. Man was created on the sixth day. His appointed days of labour and toil are *six*. The Hebrew slave was to serve *six* years. For *six* years the land was to be sown. Under the *sixth* Seal an appalling and universal catastrophe upon mankind ensues. As the numeral seven denotes what is *perfect* or *complete*, six being short of that signifies *human imperfection and toil*. But in the growing development of man's history he goes from bad to worse, hence six combined with six increases in moral significance, till man is witnessed in open and direct opposition to God. Goliath and his brother giant were men of abnormal strength and height, and open enemies of God and of Israel. The numeral six is stamped upon both (1 Sam. 17. 4-7; 1 Chron. 20. 6).

In the yet further development of man in his progressive evil history the culmination is reached in the ominous signification of 666, the number of the Beast. There is an obvious connection between the first and the last of the world powers. In character they are identical, save that the last is the *worst*. The image of gold set up by Nebuchadnezzar for his own glorification was sixty cubits high and six cubits broad (Dan. 3). No doubt the image on the plain of Dura was meant to consolidate and unify the numerous and diversified religions of the mighty Babylonian empire. Under threats of an awful death the image of gold must be worshipped. Surely Daniel 3 points forward to the yet even deeper and truly satanic evil of Revelation 13. The one foreshadows the other. In both Scriptures the pride, self-will, and haughty independence of God by men placed above human law is the sad picture. It only remains to ask: What is the signification of this trinity of *six*? *It is the fullest, highest development of man under direct satanic control*. It is the combination of civil, religious, and political power satanically inspired. It is, so far as man can do it, the complete setting aside of God as the Supreme Ruler and *a* man taking His place, not in heathendom, but in Palestine itself, and in the wider range of Christendom. Beyond what is signified in this trinity of evil—666—man cannot go. We here reach the *height* of human folly, of human pride, of human arrogance, of human unbridled will. Such, we believe, is the meaning of this mystic numeral—666. It is not a conundrum to be solved by ingenious minds, but it contains a wisdom which the spiritual in that day, as now, may understand and profit by the knowledge thereof.

THE PROPHETIC SITUATION REVIEWED.

In chapter 11 the Jews and Jerusalem, but in captivity to the Gentiles, are in the forefront of the vision, at least down to verse 13. The rest of the chapter is general, and joyously anticipates the end. In chapter 12 we have the light of Heaven thrown upon the unseen sources of good and evil, which are respectively the Man-Child and the dragon; then Israel's relation to both, especially during the last half week of coming sorrow. Satan having been cast down from the heavens, and his angels with him, seeks to wreak his vengeance on Judah, persecutes God's saints—Jewish and Gentile—and blasphemes God, Heaven, and all therein. His activity is incessant, his energies are boundless, as he knows that his career is but a brief one. It is marvellous how events are crowded into so short a time as three years and a half. What in other circumstances would take hundreds of years to bring about by the force and application of ordinary causes are here rapidly brought to fruition under the skilful generalship of Satan. It must also be remembered that the many providential and governmental checks now in operation to hinder the last outburst of evil will then be removed. The Church will have been caught up to Heaven, and the Spirit, too, have left the earth. "He who hinders (or letteth) will let till He (the Holy Ghost) be taken out of the way, and *then* shall that wicked (one) be revealed" (2 Thess. 2. 7, 8). There is a double hindrance: "*what* withholdeth" and "*He* who now letteth"—a thing (the Church) and a person (the Holy Spirit).

Then in chapter 13 we have the two Beasts through whom Satan seeks to accomplish his purposes in Christendom and in corrupt Judaism. The first Beast is without doubt Rome, civil and political, the great world power to whom Satan gives his seat, throne, and authority. The second Beast acts in almost supreme power religiously in Palestine, but in the larger field outside the Holy Land his services are required by Satan, and there he acts in subordination to the imperial power. It is not enough that the latter end of Judah exceeds in idolatry anything ever witnessed in the past (Matt. 12. 45), beyond even that horrible picture so graphically drawn by the prophet of the captivity (Ezek. 8), but Christendom, too, must be reduced to a corrupt and loathsome mass of idolatry and wickedness. This the second Beast accomplishes in the presence of his superior in power.

Then as to the external enemies of Israel* at this time, not noted in the Apocalypse, the chief is the Assyrian, or king of the north, the political scourge of the restored nation. The king of the south, or Egypt, is the ally of the Beast, and is opposed to his great northern neighbour, the Assyrian, who is the bitter opponent both of the antichristian king in the land (the second Beast of chap. 13) and of the king of the south. Palestine lying between those two opposing powers is made, as in the past, their battleground. The past (Dan. 11. 1-35) and future (vv. 36-43) of these respective monarchies in their relation to the Jews form a study of exceeding interest. We may remark that chapter 11 of Daniel is an enlargement, with fuller detail, of chapter 8. The prophets Isaiah, Micah, and Daniel especially should be read to understand the great external enemies of Israel in the last days. Gog, or Russia, the master of the king of the north, falls ingloriously on the mountains of Israel after the destruction of the Assyrian, and *after* the Lord has come, thus completing the sum of judgments ere the Lord's reign in its Solomon or peaceful character, and establishes the earth in its long-expected and ardently-desired jubilee of one thousand years. Gog heads the north-eastern nations and peoples in opposition to the Beast—the power in the west. The former is politically hostile to the Jews, the latter is politically friendly to the restored nation. The Jews restored to the land previous to the Lord's Return in power is the occasion of quarrel and hostility between Gog and the Beast. The political aims of these latter are different, and this brings them into conflict. Events in Europe and Asia are fast ripening for the closing struggle. May our souls be kept in peace!

---

* See separate article, "The Chief Actors in the Coming Crisis."

CHAPTER XIV.

God's Sevenfold Intervention in Grace and Judgment.

The point at which we have arrived in these apocalyptic visions is a most sad one. Truth has fallen in the streets; the blood of God's saints shed as water; open defiance of God and proud boasting are witnessed and heard; good is almost banished from the earth (Psa. 4. 6), and faith in God almost gone (Luke 18. 8). "The man of the earth," or the Antichrist, ravages in Palestine amongst the saints, glorifies and deifies himself in Jerusalem and in the temple, deceives the world, and turns the whole prophetic scene into a playground for Satan. The Beast in pride, persecution, and blasphemy is equally busy as Satan's powerful vicegerent in the wider sphere allotted him. Now is heard the oft-repeated cry to Jehovah of the Jewish remnant, suffering more than all others under an accumulated load of distress, "How long?" The touching appeal strikes a responsive chord in our hearts, as in spirit we take our part in the circumstances: "Why standest Thou afar off, O Lord, why hidest Thou in times of trouble?" (Psa. 10. 1). Chapter 14 of the Revelation is the answer to the cry of the remnant. It records God's intervention in grace and judgment. We have had the marvellous activity of Satan and his seeming triumph—for are not Christendom and Judaism the spheres of his special operation?—so it might be supposed that God is indifferent, and had abandoned His people to the cruel mercy of the enemy. But it is not so, as the contents of this chapter conclusively show.

We have already remarked that chapters 12, 13, and 14 form one connected prophecy. The hidden source of evil is shown to be the dragon; the Man of God's purpose is the Child; Israel the mother of the Man-Child flees from the dragon's vengeance; these are the three main subjects of chapter 12, not, however, presented as history, but as seen in Heaven. Then, as the subjects of chapter 13, we have the character, history, and doings of the two Beasts through whom Satan works out his evil plans on earth. We are next to be shown in a series of events the hand of God (chap. 14). There are seven distinct subjects in the chapter: first, the spared remnant of Judah on Mount Zion (vv. 1-5); second, God's closing testimony, or the Everlasting Gospel (vv. 6, 7); third, the announcement of the fall of Babylon (v. 8); fourth, the awful doom of those who worship the Beast (vv. 9-11); fifth, the immediate blessedness of those who die in the Lord (v. 13); sixth, the harvest of the earth reaped, discriminating judgment (vv. 14-16); seventh, the vintage of wrath, unsparing vengeance (vv. 17-20). Thus, then, those three chapters form an episode of great interest. Their place between the Trumpets and the Vials explains much. It is shown *who* is the real author of earth's horrible iniquity, the human instruments by *whom* it is practised, and, lastly, the intervention of God in the scene. Moreover, as we have had the *wickedness* of the Beast, we are about to see its awful *judgment* under the Vials. Those chapters, too, serve as a necessary prelude to the yet severer chastisements inflicted in sharp and rapid succession, which sum up the providential judgments of God, and are followed by the vengeance of the Lamb in Person.

I.—THE SPARED JEWISH REMNANT (VERSES 1-5).

MOUNT ZION, THE LAMB, AND THE JEWISH REMNANT.

1.—**"And I saw, and behold, the Lamb standing upon Mount Zion, and with Him a hundred (and) forty-four thousand, having His Name and the Name of His Father written upon their foreheads."** The Revised Testament reads "a Lamb," and omits "having *his Name*." Both blunders are corrected in the Revised Version.

Zion is only named once in the Apocalypse. "Out of about 110 times that Zion is mentioned, ninety are in terms of the Lord's great love and affection for her, so that the place has great, very great significance, and Heaven knows it too."* The first mention of Zion when captured from the Jebusites by David (2 Sam. 5. 7) is pregnant with interest, for, adds the sacred historian, "the same is the city of David." Saul, the predecessor of David on the throne, was the man of the *people's* choice, and typified "the king" who reigns in Jerusalem before the Lord comes. David, the true king of Israel, was *Jehovah's* chosen, and Zion the seat of his government. He is thus the prototype of our Lord, Who will reign in Zion, "and before His ancients gloriously" (Isa. 24. 23). Zion is rich in sacred memories to the Jew. It is his goal of hope. It is, too, God's chosen city. "For the Lord hath chosen Zion: He hath desired it for His habitation. This is my rest for ever; here will I dwell; for I have desired it" (Psa. 132. 13, 14). "Beautiful for situation, the joy of the whole earth, is mount Zion, on the sides of the north, the city of

* "Revelation of Jesus Christ," by W. R. H., page 54.

the great King" (Psa. 48. 2). It is the seat of universal government for earth, and the centre of interest to the millennial world (Isa. 2). It is where Jehovah has in purpose set His King (Psa. 2. 6). There are three distinct thoughts connected with mount Zion: (1) It is the seat of royal power; (2) of God's intervention in grace; (3) of Jehovah's sovereignty, but all in respect to Israel.

The vision is a bright and gladdening one, a calm after a storm. Christ does not yet reign on Zion, but the time is near, and in the meantime He stands as the Lamb with His chosen ones. The vision is an anticipative one. Both the crowd of saved Gentiles (chap. 7. 9) and the millennial kingdom (chaps. 11. 15; 12. 10) are anticipative visions which have their actual fulfilment at the Advent in power. Here the Lamb stands on mount Zion, but the Vials have yet to be poured out. The 144,000 here witnessed are of *Judah*; a similarly numbered company of all *Israel* (chap. 7. 4) forms a separate vision. This company has the Name of the Lamb and His (not their) Father's Name written upon their foreheads. The mark of the Beast is on each one of *his* worshippers. The Name of the Lamb and His Father's Name as well on the forehead of each confessor of Christ. These witnesses are viewed as having come out of the fiery trial under the Beast. They are Jews who steadfastly maintained the rights of God and of the Lamb; now they are publicly owned of Him. Many of their brethren suffered even unto death, sealing their testimony with their blood. Those here were spared through the horrors of the Tribulation. We gather that the innumerable company of Gentiles (chap. 7. 9) are identical with the sheep who go into everlasting life (Matt. 25. 34, 46); further, the "third part," refined as silver and tried as gold (Zech. 13. 8, 9), the same as are here spoken of as 144,000 Jewish saints who occupy the leading place in the earthly millennial kingdom. They stand with the Lamb on the seat of royalty. What an exchange! From the tyranny of the Beast to fellowship with the Lamb! From the place of suffering to the seat of glorious power!

HARPERS AND SINGERS.

2, 3.—**"And I heard a voice out of the Heaven, as a voice of many waters, and as a voice of great thunder. And the voice which I heard (was) as of harp-singers harping with their harps; and they sing a new song before the throne, and before the four living creatures and the elders. And no one could learn that song save the hundred (and) forty-four thousand who were bought from the earth."** Heaven is stirred and breaks out into song. We have had the Babel sounds of earth, the mingled cry of the victor, and the wail of the vanquished. We have witnessed the Beast treading down the earth and breaking it in pieces (Dan. 7. 23)—an exhibition of insensate brute force—and his fellow in crime, the Antichrist, morally darkening and deceiving the world. But now other sights delight the eye, and other sounds and songs greet the ear. We meet with a new company in Heaven, distinct from either the living creatures or elders, for they harp and sing "before the throne, and before the four living creatures and the elders." *Harps* are mentioned three times in the Apocalypse, in each instance associated with song (5. 8; 14. 2; 15. 2). Thus is set forth the choral praise of the redeemed and heavenly host. The elders, representatives of the redeemed of past and present ages, each celebrates with song and harp God's intervention in mighty saving grace (chap. 5. 8-10). Then, again, the martyred company of Judah tell out their gladness and triumph similarly to those of the elders (chaps. 14. 2, 3; 15. 2, 3). We understand the harpists of our chapter and those on the sea of glass (chap. 15. 2) as being one and the same class. The song and harp are so blended that they are spoken of as "a voice" majestic as "many waters," and powerful as "great thunder." Then this company of harpists sing a "*new* song" in contrast with the *old* song. The former has as its theme redemption; the latter has as its subject creation (Job 38. 7). The *Lamb* and the new song are conjoined (chap. 5. 8; 14. 2). *God* and the old song are united. "The song of Moses" and "the song of the Lamb" (chap. 15. 3) link up in one God's past ways of power toward Israel with His present grace to them and to us. The crowd of saved Gentiles who form the nucleus of earth's millennial inhabitants is said to stand "before the throne" (chap. 7. 9). So here the company sing "before the throne." But as the former are on earth, while the latter are in Heaven, the position differs accordingly. The saved Gentiles have a standing *morally* before the throne, whereas the martyred Jewish company have an *actual* place in relation to the throne.

3.—"**No one could learn that song save the hundred (and) forty-four thousand.**" The choristers in Heaven and those with the Lamb on Zion are evidently in closest sympathy. The two together formed one company on earth. Nationally they were Jews, spiritually fellow-saints. They had been companions in labour, in testimony, and in suffering under the oppression of the Beast and the Antichrist. Many sealed their testimony with their blood, others passed through the Tribulation, keeping themselves free from the corruptions of the wicked scene. The former class are the harp-singing company in Heaven; the latter are the preserved of Judah on mount Zion; thus the intimate connection between the two companies. How fitting, therefore, that the saved and delivered Jews on Zion should be those who alone on earth enter into and learn the song of their brethren "before the throne" in Heaven. On earth they *learn*; in Heaven they *know* (1 Cor. 13. 12).

As showing the ground of blessing even though victors over the Beast and occupying the place of royalty on Zion, the words are added, "who were bought from the earth," not "redeemed" as in the Authorised Version, but "*bought*," or *purchased*, as here and in verse four. All saints in Heaven and in earth are both purchased and redeemed. The former term applies to all men and all things on earth, the latter to believers only, and to things on earth at the Coming.*

THE HUNDRED AND FORTY-FOUR THOUSAND ON MOUNT ZION.

4, 5.—"**These are they who have not been defiled with women, for they are virgins: these are they who follow the Lamb wheresoever He goes. These have been bought from men, firstfruits to God and to the Lamb: and in their mouths was no lie found; they are blameless.**" In this first vision we have three companies of redeemed people: (1) The elders, the saints of past and present ages; (2) the praising company of martyred Judah in Heaven; (3) the victorious part of Judah who had emerged out of "the great Tribulation." This latter company are associated with the Lamb in His triumph, standing on mount Zion, the seat of royalty and of sovereign grace. Amidst the grossest corruptions, open idolatry, proud boasting, daring blasphemy, and open wickedness, these saints had not defiled themselves. They had walked through a scene abandoned to Satan without defilement. They lived and walked in virgin purity† (2 Cor. 11. 2). They had "kept themselves unspotted from the world." But not only is there virgin purity of life, but there is also virgin love, undivided heart affection for the Lamb. We have had their *purity* attested, now we

* For a fuller elucidation of the truths of purchase and redemption, see page 140. The reader is also referred to our "Doctrinal Summaries; or, Expositions of Important Scriptural Truths." Fifth edition. Price 2d.

† "These are they who have not been defiled with women, for they are virgins." To refer this to *literal* impurity, as some do, manifests a lamentable want of spiritual discernment; moreover, the absurdity of such an interpretation would necessarily confine the company on mount Zion to men only.

witness their *obedience*, which is full and unqualified; they "follow the Lamb wheresoever He goes," their discipleship is unquestionable.

4.—"**Bought from men**" and "bought from the *earth*" (v. 3) respectively signify the *race* and the *place* out of which God in His grace had taken them. Their purchase is regarded as a special act of sovereign grace.

"**Firstfruits to God and to the Lamb.**" These are an earnest of earth's coming blessing. God and the Lamb are to reap a rich and bountiful harvest, and these are a sample. Priority in time and blessing of a like character are indicated in the term "firstfruits" (see Rom. 8. 23; 1 Cor. 15. 20-23; James 1. 18, etc.).

5.—"**In their mouths was no lie found.**" Truthfulness in word characterised them. Their confession of Christ as the real Messiah was a true one (1 John 2. 21-27), in contrast to the mass given over to believe a lie in the reception and acknowledgment of the false Messiah, the Antichrist (2 Thess. 2. 11; 1 John 2. 22).

5.—"**They are blameless.**" Thus ends the beautifully descriptive character of the 144,000 on mount Zion. The Authorised Version substitutes *guile* for "lie," and adds "without fault *before the throne of God*." This is a serious interpolation. The meaning and force of the simple statement, "they are blameless," is that they were so in practical ways and conduct generally. They refused to conform to the persecuting and blaspheming edicts of the Beast, they neither wondered after the Beast nor worshipped him. The seductions, too, of Antichrist, by which the mass were deceived, were avoided with holy loathing. In these respects "they were blameless." Were the absolute holiness of God, the claims of His throne and nature in question, none on earth could stand and say, "I am blameless in myself." This the passage does not assert, but is simply God's estimate of their practical conduct when under the Beast.

REVIEW.

The opening vision is that of the Lamb standing on mount Zion immediately preparatory to His assumption of royal power as King of Israel. With Him is associated a defined number of Jews who have emerged out of the great Tribulation. They publicly bear the Name of the Lamb and His Father's Name, and are thus, in light of the full blaze of millennial glory, openly owned of God. Then a voice is heard "out of," or proceeding from, Heaven, grandly majestic and loud and powerful. It is *one* voice in which the harp and song of many are expressed. These singers and harpers are in Heaven. Who are they? They are as a company distinct from the elders, the raised dead and changed living of 1 Thessalonians 4. 15-17. The harpist choir are the brethren of those on mount Zion. They had laid down their lives rather than succumb to the Beast and his minister who dominated the conscience of the mass. They are here seen as raised in vision only; actually the whole scene is an anticipative millennial one. Their brethren on earth, once their companions in confession and sorrow, alone can learn the song of Heaven. How near is Heaven to earth in those days! How interested and how real the fellowship of saints in Heaven with those on earth! It is the day of Hosea 2. 21, 22, and the day of John 1. 51.

Then we get the ground (twice stated) on which these saved ones stood in holy and royal fellowship with the Lamb. They had been purchased at what a cost, even the blood of the Lamb. Then we have their practical conduct (not the inward state), which is equally true in principle of every child of God. (1) *Separation*, thorough and unqualified, from the wickedness and idolatry of their surroundings. They maintained virgin purity from evil and virgin affection for Christ. (2) *Obedience* and *Discipleship* are marked features. They followed the Lamb wheresoever He went at a time and in a crisis when all save the elect wandered after the Beast. Following the Lamb is a characteristic truth. They followed Him in His rejection; they equally follow Him in His glory. The word translated "follow" is in the present tense. (3) *Truthfulness*, in word and confession, is another feature of the practical character of these saints. When Christendom as a whole had been given over to believe the devil's *lie* (2 Thess. 2. 11) these godly Jewish saints clung to the truth of Holy Scripture in its teachings as to the true Messiah and Prophet. (4) *Blamelessness* in outward conduct and ways before men, not "before the throne of God" (an interpolation), is a fitting and condensed epitome of their practical character and life. They were the first-fruits of the harvest gathered out of Israel, a joy to God and to the Lamb.

II.—PROCLAMATION OF THE EVERLASTING GOSPEL.

6, 7.—**"And I saw another angel flying in mid-heaven, having the everlasting Gospel to announce to those settled on the earth, and to every nation, and tribe, and tongue, and people, saying, with a loud voice, Fear God, and give Him glory, for the hour of**

His judgment has come; and worship Him that made the Heaven, and the earth, and the sea, and fountains of waters." The chapter from verse six to the end unfolds the order of events. The first vision anticipates the happy scene when, after the dark clouds of judgment have rolled aside, the bright dawn of the coming day fills the earth with gladness. The first and most joyous company in the scene delivered from the thraldom of Satan is the 144,000, the godly remnant of Judah standing in safety and in holy fellowship with the Lamb on mount Zion. The time and place of the vision itself (vv. 1-5), therefore, must be distinguished from its fulfilment. The sequence of events as the end is drawing to a close commences with verse six, the announcement to the world at large of the Everlasting Gospel.

6.—**"I saw another angel flying in the mid-heaven."** The word *another* angel does not connect itself with the seventh angel (chap. 11. 15), nor with the militant host under Michael in chapter 12, but with the eagle messenger flying in mid-heaven announcing woe (chap. 8. 13). It may be said that the connection does not hold good, inasmuch as one is an eagle and the other an angel, but the objection is more apparent than real. The term "angel" in itself does not denote *nature*, but *office*, and is used both of spiritual beings and of men. The context, and not the word merely, must determine its application to men or spirits. Angel literally signifies *messenger*. Both the eagle and the angel are messengers. Both are witnessed flying across the firmament so as to scan the earth, even to its remotest bounds, and aloud proclaim their message. The flying eagle is a herald of *judgment*, the flying angel is a messenger of *mercy*.

6.—Will there be a *literal* announcement of the "**Everlasting Gospel**" by an angel? Will a spiritual being *actually* proclaim the glad tidings from mid-heaven in his rapid course? Angels will be largely employed in the providential and governmental economy both prior to and during the millennial kingdom. But the preaching of the Gospel, whether it be that of the kingdom, of the grace, or of the glory of God, is a task committed to men and not to angels, while the latter will, without a doubt, providentially expedite the work of declaring the good news in the closing days of the last prophetic week. But we apprehend that the preachers of the Everlasting Gospel will be converted Jews chiefly, and that the result of their mission will be an ingathering of a vast and countless throng of saved Gentiles for millennial blessing (Matt. 25. 34; Rev. 7. 9). Isaiah 66. 19-21 is by some applied to the same mission as we have here, but that is a mistake. The Isaiah mission has its place *when* the Lord comes in Person to plead with all flesh, as the previous part of the chapter conclusively demonstrates; whereas the Everlasting Gospel is announced to the nations *before* the Lord comes. The angel flying on his mission indicates that a *widespread* and *rapid* testimony to grace and a warning note of judgment are proclaimed on the eve of "the day of vengeance of our God" (Isa. 61. 2). It is only in vision that the angel announces the Everlasting Gospel.

The Gospel preached now is that of God's rich and sovereign grace to guilty sinners (1 Cor. 15. 1-4; Rom. 1. 16); and of the Gospel of the glory of Christ (2 Cor. 4. 4). The Gospel of the kingdom was preached prior to the death and resurrection of Christ (Matt. 10. 7), and will be preached again after the removal of the Church (Matt. 24. 14). We gather that the Everlasting Gospel is in substance that of the kingdom, here termed *everlasting*, because it is an ever-abiding truth that the Creator and not the creature is the only object of worship. This, too, is the only instance of the word "everlasting" applied to the Gospel. The earliest mention of the good news is contained in Genesis 3. 15, and on through the dark and ever-changing ages of man's history this Gospel remains unchanged in character, for God is everlastingly merciful, and from the entrance of sin into the world till its judgment at the Coming God *alone* is the hope of His creatures.

Those to whom the Gospel is announced are stated under five terms: (1) "To those settled on the earth." We have had the same moral* class of persons brought before us on several occasions (chaps. 3. 10; 6. 10; 11. 10, etc.). They are christian apostates who had rejected God's call to Heaven (Heb. 3. 1), and deliberately chose the earth and its interests instead. They have been described as those that "*dwell* on the earth," but here a somewhat stronger expression is used, "*settled* on the earth." (2) "To every nation." (3) "And tribe," or a part, a division of a nation or people. (4) "And tongue," signifying the numerous languages and dialects spoken. (5) "And people," whether organised or not; the masses of mankind. These last four terms really embrace the race, and express as a formula *universality* (chaps. 7. 9; 11. 9). Those then are the persons to whom this Gospel is preached.

---

* See pages 74, 156, 235. We may add that we greatly question whether any of this class bow to the proclamation and receive the glad tidings; when the results of this mighty and extensive work of grace are before us, as in chapter 7. 9, there is no mention of those "that dwell on the earth." *Here* we have five classes to whom the Gospel is preached, *there* only four when the results are stated (see also 2 Thess. 2.10,12).

As to its reception by some and its rejection by others we are not here informed; that must be learned elsewhere.

7.—What is so publicly and widely announced is next declared. "**Fear God, and give Him glory, for the hour of His judgment has come.**" The first duty of the creature is to "fear God," which is indeed the "beginning of wisdom"—twice repeated (Psa. 111. 10; Prov. 9. 10). It is, too, a call to turn from the Beast to God; from the creature to the Creator. The mass were glorifying a *man* whom Satan had deified. Him they worshipped. God alone was, is, and ever shall be glorified both in His character and in His works and ways. The world is here recalled to this grand and fundamental truth, almost entirely forgotten, "Give Him glory." The solemn ground on which this call is based is next stated, "*For* the hour of His judgment has come." What an awful moment in human history! God is about to intervene in judgment, and no power can arrest the stroke. It is about to fall on the ungodly world and apostate peoples, christian and Jewish. "And worship Him that made the Heaven, and the earth, and the sea, and fountains of waters." The primary truth that God is the Creator of all, the visible and the invisible (Col. 1. 16), has been lost sight of. Man has usurped the place of God, and the claim of the Creator to the homage of the creature is wellnigh effaced from the minds of men. The truth of creation is the first and fundamental subject of divine revelation (Gen. 1). Here it is recalled and enforced in light of immediate judgment. The worship of the Creator is a necessary law for men and angels. As we have had the race under a fourfold designation—nation, tribe, tongue, and people—so here creation is stated in four terms equally *universal* with the other: Heaven, earth, sea, and fountains.

How good, how gracious in God, ere His righteous vengeance search out the guilty of earth, to send to the race at large this final message couched in terms forcible and solemn! The moment is opportune, for every true thought of the Creator has been almost banished from the earth. *All* worship the Beast save the elect, then in a weak and feeble minority.

III.—THE FALL OF BABYLON.

8.—"**And another, a second angel, followed, saying, Great Babylon has fallen, has fallen, which of the wine of the fury of her fornication has made all nations drink.**" It will be observed that there are three specific angelic announcements (vv. 6, 8, 9). The first and the third are proclaimed with a "loud voice." Not so the second. Babylon, civil and religious, figures largely in Bible history. Whether viewed as a city (Jer. 51), or as a religious system (Rev. 14. 8; 17; 18), it is a vast consolidated system and the enslaver of God's people. Babylon of old was the first and only Gentile power on which God directly conferred governmental authority (Dan. 2. 37). Its doom, and the deliverance of Judah from the seventy years' captivity were associated events. It will be so at the end. The Beast of the Apocalypse, which inherits the civil and political power of ancient Babylon, perishes at the Coming (Rev. 19), and God's people are delivered. But what is before us now is the mystic Babylon, that huge system of spiritual adultery and corruption which holds sway over the whole prophetic scene. It is scarcely possible to conceive of a huge system of wickedness eagerly embraced by the nations once called christian. It will nevertheless be so. Babylon here is the full development of the state of things under the Thyatiran condition of the Church (chap. 2. 18-23). Protestantism as a system is destroyed *at* the Coming (chap. 3. 3). Babylon falls *before* the Coming (chap. 17).

Babylon, the city of old, was the oppressor of the nations, and the centre and stronghold of the world's pride and idolatry. Satan stamped his own character upon it. But Israel and her renowned capital, Jerusalem, should have been the people and city from whence the knowledge of Jehovah and power over the nations emanated. But Israel, having falsified her position as set on earth to administer righteous government in headship over the nations, and also having proved unfaithful to her mission in making known the character of the true and only God, is set aside. Babylon is the contrast to what Israel should have been, and, in fact, to what she will be when under the new covenant (Jer. 31). The Church should have been a witness to God's character as light and love, instead of which she has shown herself an unfaithful steward of the truth, and has failed as a witness to God and to Christ. *Then*, consequent on the moral ruin of the Church, the ground is prepared for Satan to introduce the mystic Babylon, the corruptress of the earth, and the spiritual enslaver of the nations who are madly intoxicated with her adulteries and corruptions. Her meretricious charms are guilded chains; her cup is full. The nations have yielded to her seductions, and have eagerly drunk out of her golden cup. Here her downfall is intimated, and that with intensity of utterance. The repetition of the word "fallen" must not be regarded as a mere Hebraism.

The fall of the literal, as of the mystic, Babylon is similarly announced (Isa. 21. 9; Rev. 18. 2).

In the passage before us we have merely the fact announced that Babylon has fallen. It is regarded as an accomplished judgment. Particulars are reserved. The character, doom, and human instruments of her destruction are specified in chapters 17 and 18, while her utter and everlasting ruin is grandly celebrated in Heaven in the first three verses of chapter 19, and that as preliminary to the marriage of the Lamb. The *whore* is destroyed, and then the *bride* is displayed.

8.—"**The wine of the fury (or wrath) of her fornication**" drunk by all nations is a singular expression, and exceeds what is said of the Euphratean city (Jer. 51. 7). The Babylon of the Apocalypse has by her seductions, unholy allurements, and incitements to evil enthralled the nations. Their passions have been fearfully roused, and they are not only mad (morally, of course), but her illicit intercourse with them has wrought them up to frenzy. In the height of the ungodliness and folly of the unholy union between the corrupt Church and the equally corrupt nations, the welcome message falls upon our ears, "Babylon has fallen, has fallen." In every respect the Babylon of the Apocalypse may be termed "great" in contrast to the city of old.

Delete the word "city," erroneously inserted in the text of the Authorised Version (v. 8). It is almost unanimously rejected by the authorities.

IV.—THE AWFUL DOOM OF THE WORSHIPPERS OF THE BEAST, AND ENDURANCE OF THE SAINTS.

9-12.—"**And another, a third angel, followed them, saying with a loud voice, If any one worshippeth the Beast and his image, and receive a mark upon his forehead or upon his hand. He also shall drink of the wine of the fury of God prepared unmixed in the cup of His wrath, and he shall be tormented in fire and brimstone before the holy angels and before the Lamb. And the smoke of their torment goes up to the ages of ages, and they have no rest day and night that worship the Beast and his image, and if any one receive the mark of his name. Here is the endurance of the saints, who keep the commandments of God and the faith of Jesus.**" We have had the fall of Babylon proclaimed in the previous announcement. The empire, in its full and consolidated strength of will and power, is the human destroyer of Babylon (chap. 17.

16, 17). Read "The ten horns which thou sawest *and* the Beast." These, the horns and Beast, work together in united purpose to destroy the woman, or Babylon. This leaves the Beast unchecked in his career of wickedness and blasphemy. He had previously carried the woman, *i.e.*, supported her. But now, utter hatred and disgust take the place of a former admiration for her spiritual pretensions. He must reign without a rival, be the sole possessor of power. A system of brute force is established, and its decrees unrelentingly enforced. After the destruction of Babylon the Beast assumes its worst character. The full development of evil, in the absence of the harlot, is rapidly consummated, and a stern and inflexible policy is pursued with the determination that all—rich and poor, great and small—must bow down and worship the Beast. Absolute subjection to the Beast is the law in the coming crisis. It is under these appalling circumstances that the loud note of warning is sounded to the Beast worshippers. The awful doom here announced, unequalled in its severity, is proportioned to the guilt and horrible iniquity then openly practised.

The Beast and his image must both be worshipped, and his mark received either in the hand or forehead, and that under the dread penalty of death. There is no escape. The alternative to the worship of the Beast is *death*, probably in its severest forms, and all commerce, trade, and barter are sternly prohibited to those who refuse to recognise his claims (chap.13. 17).

The devotees of the Beast are here warned and threatened with punishments of so terrible a character that the very mention of them is enough to make one's flesh creep. But what of those who will have to endure them? The "third angel" says "with a loud voice"—so that all may hear, and thus be without excuse—"*he*," who has worshipped the Beast and received his mark, "also shall drink of the wine of the fury of God." The nations had drunk out of the harlot's cup (v. 8); now in retributive justice they shall drink out of God's cup (v. 10). In this cup there are no palliative ingredients (Psa. 75. 8). It is pure, *unmixed* wrath. "*He* shall be tormented in fire and brimstone." The awful torment is individual. Each one shall suffer eternal misery in his own person. "Fire and brimstone" (Isa. 30. 33; Rev. 20. 10) are symbols of unutterable anguish. Another awful feature of the agony inflicted upon each adherent of the Beast is that the torment has to be endured "before (or in the presence of) the holy angels and before the Lamb" The *holy* angels had been witnesses from their place on high of the horrible wickedness of the Beast and his abettors; now they will witness God's vengeance, and each tormented one will *know* that the angels are looking down upon the scene of indescribable anguish,* and also "before the Lamb,"† Whom they had openly defied, and Whose blood had been wantonly trampled upon. This will, of course, add greatly to the horror of the situation.

11.—"**The smoke of their torment goes up to the ages of ages.**" In the previous clauses of this deeply solemn passage we have had the individual before us, as indicated in the use of the personal pronouns. Now, however, that the company is made up, the aggregate is spoken of—"the smoke of *their* torment." What a lurid picture of complete and overwhelming judgment! (Gen. 19. 28; Isa. 34. 10). The harlot is similarly judged and punished (compare with chap. 19. 3).

The expression "for ever and ever" is translated "the ages of ages" in all its eleven occurrences in the Apocalpyse in the margin of the Revised Version. It is used to express:

The eternal‡ existence of God (chaps. 4. 9, 10; 5. 14; 10. 6; 15. 7).

The eternal glory of the Lamb (chap. 5. 13).

The eternal reign of believers (chap. 22. 5).

The eternal doom of the devil (chap. 20. 10).

The eternal torment of the lost (chap. 14. 11).

The torment of the lost and of the devil is eternal. "No *rest* day and night" is the solemn pronouncement in chapter 14. 11, and "*tormented* day and night" is the equally emphatic declaration of chapter 20. 10—no cessation, no alleviation; the agony is ceaseless. The endless horror of the Beast worshippers is beyond human conception. The eternal punishment of the lost is graven on the imperishable records of revelation. Sin and its punishment are measured by the greatness, the glory, and the eternity of God. He alone can reveal *who* and *what* He is. Sin against an infinite Being must necessarily entail infinite and eternal consequences.

"Here is the endurance of the saints who keep the commandments of God and the faith of Jesus." In this state of

* At the period referred to, especially at its commencement, angels will be largely employed in the execution of decreed judgment (Matt. 13. 49, 50; Rev. 20. 1-3). Then we read of that terrible expression, "The wrath of the Lamb." Both the Lamb and the angels take part in executing the vengeance of Almighty God on the Beast and his followers.

† "The specific torment here alluded to for those who receive the mark of the Beast is that of fire and brimstone, 'in the presence of the Lamb,' and this latter clause seems to contain the pungency of the curse, in the same way as is expressed in chapter 6. 16, which expresses the horror felt by the wicked at seeing 'the face of Him that sitteth on the throne.' "—"Notes on the Revelation," by Brodie, page 133.

‡ In eternity nothing is either past or to come but subsists.—*Philo.*

things, unequalled in the history of the race, the saints can only hold fast and hold on. They are forbidden to resist with the sword, even if they could (chap. 13. 10). But faith and patience at length, however sorely tried, win the day. Death is before them, but better to be killed *by* the Beast than to be tormented *with* the Beast. The afflicted saints cling to the clear commands of God and the faith of Jesus. In the apocalyptic record the martyrs are the martyrs of Jesus (chap. 17. 6). The name of sweetest sound is but rarely introduced in the book, but the connections in which it appears are full of interest (chaps. 14. 12; 17. 6; 22. 16).

V.—THE BLESSED DEAD WHO DIE IN THE LORD.

13.—"**And I heard a voice out of the Heaven saying, Write,* Blessed are the dead who die in** (the) **Lord from henceforth. Yea, saith the Spirit, that they may rest from their labours; for their works follow with them.**" The voice, but not the name, of the speaker falls upon the ear of the christian Seer. The Authorised Version interpolates *unto me*. The message was not addressed to John, although he heard it, but it is one for *all* saints, while it has its own special application to saints in that critical hour preceding the Coming of the Lord in judgment. It is ever true that those who die in the Lord are blessed, but why is the statement reserved for this awful juncture in human history? and why is it added, "from henceforth?" Why from that particular moment? The answer to these questions is a simple and satisfactory one. The word "henceforth" intimates the *near* end, and that the blessing is *just* about to be entered upon.

In chapter 20. 4 we have the complement of the heavenly saints who reign with Christ a thousand years. There are three classes of such: (1) A recognised and well-known company sitting upon thrones. These are the raised dead and changed living at the Coming into the air (1 Thess. 4. 16, 17; 1 Cor. 15. 51-54). When caught up they are spoken of as "elders" throughout the prophetic part of the Apocalypse. (2) "The souls of those beheaded on account of the testimony of Jesus, and on account of the Word of God." This company forms a class of martyrs by themselves, who were slain before the Beast was in existence as a persecuting power. They are witnesses under the fifth Seal (chap. 6. 9-11). (3) "Those who had not worshipped the Beast, neither his image, and had not received the mark on their forehead and hand." There is an interval

* "This command to write is repeated *twelve* times in the Revelation to indicate that all the things it refers to are matters of importance."

of some time, probably years, between the martyrdom of the two latter companies. If, therefore, the whole company of reigning saints is embraced in the three classes referred to (chap. 20. 4), in which of them are we to place those who "die in the Lord from henceforth?" Undoubtedly amongst those martyred under the Beast.

Another and helpful consideration follows. If the two martyred companies named comprehend *all* who die after the Rapture, then it is evident that no saint during the "crisis week" of seven years dies a natural death. Those who "die in the Lord" are slain; hence the inapplicability of our text engraved on stone and monument in memory of our precious dead. Those who "die in the Lord from *henceforth*" do so as martyrs. They are about to share in the blessedness of "the first resurrection" (chap. 20. 6). Their blessing in character and fulness greatly exceeds those who survive the Tribulation. The former take a distinguished place in heavenly glory, the latter are accorded the highest place on earth; the former reign with Christ, the latter are reigned over; the former are kings, the latter are subjects.

The Spirit responds to the voice from Heaven, "Yea," and adds a word of rich consolation, "that they may rest from their labours; for their works follow with them." Probably none amongst "the cloud of witnesses" had so walked in the vigour of faith as these; none so served and suffered under the most appalling circumstances. But now these witnesses of whom "the world was not worthy" are about to enter on their everlasting rest—toil and suffering for ever past. God is not unrighteous to forget their work and labour of love. When these saints are raised and taken up, their works accompany them, not come after them, but "with them." Their works will be appraised at their true value by the righteous Judge, Who will reward every man according to his work. Rest and reward are the *immediate* portion of those then dying in the Lord.

VI.—THE HARVEST OF THE EARTH REAPED.

14, 15.—**"And I saw, and behold, a white cloud, and on the cloud one sitting like (the) Son of Man, having upon His head a golden crown, and in His hand a sharp sickle. And another angel came out of the temple, crying with a loud voice to Him that sat on the cloud, Send Thy sickle and reap; for the hour of reaping is come, for the harvest of the earth is dried. And He that sat on the cloud put His sickle on the earth, and the earth was reaped."** Judicial judgment is about to sweep the guilty earth with the besom of destruction and clear it of evil. The harvest and the vintage are the familiar figures employed to express God's closing dealings. The former is discriminating judgment, the latter unsparing wrath. In the harvest the wheat is separated from the tares. In the vintage these latter, *i.e.*, the tares, are alone in the prophetic scene, and form the subjects of the Lord's righteous vengeance.

14.—"**I saw, and behold.**" This expression is only employed in the introduction of subjects of unusual interest. There are two matters of weighty import selected out of the seven series of events contained in our chapter, to which special attention is called by this word "behold" (see vv. 1, 14).

14.—"**A white cloud**" is peculiar to this action, so also is the *white* throne in the judgment of the dead (chap. 20. 11). The cloud symbolises the divine presence (chap. 10. 1; Matt. 17. 5; Ezek. 10. 4), "white" the purity and absolute righteousness characterising and governing the action.

14.—"**On the cloud one sitting like (the) Son of Man.**" Christ is said to come *in* a cloud (Luke 21. 27), but He is also said to come *on* the clouds (Matt. 24. 30, R.V.). In the former His Person is veiled; in the latter He is publicly displayed. He sits on the cloud. It is a calm, deliberative judgment; no hurry, no haste. "Like (the) Son of Man." It is under this title that Christ deals with the state of things on the earth, and judges the ungodly (Matt. 25. 31; John 5. 27). As Son of God He quickens now the spiritually dead (John 5. 25), as in the future the physically dead (v. 28). We have before called attention to the absence of the definite article in this title as used in the Apocalypse and in Daniel 7. 13.* As Son of Man He comes and claims universal dominion. His connection with the race and with the world in general is intimated in the title Son of Man, but in that very character He bears the attributes and moral glories of the Ancient of Days (compare Dan. 7. 13 with verse 14 of our chapter, also with Rev. 1. 13, 14). Without doubt the Seer beheld in vision the Son of Man, but in the absence of the article it is what morally characterises Him that is prominent. The article would make it definite and personal. The attributes of the Son of Man are called into exercise, and to these we are directed—to what is characteristic of such a One, rather than to the Person Himself.

14.—"**Upon His head a golden crown,**" the sign of royal dignity (chaps. 4. 4; 6. 2). The crowns upon the

* See on chapter 1. 13.

heads of the locusts were "*like* gold" (chap. 9. 7). Their assumption of royal authority was spurious. Here it is real, divinely conferred. But the crown of *gold* is also the expression of divine righteousness in victorious action.

14.—"**In His hand a sharp sickle.**" It is not the execution of judgment either moral (Heb. 4. 12) or physical (Rev. 19. 15), else a sword would have been named. But the sickle is needed to reap the harvest. It is "sharp" in order to do its work thoroughly, and in the "hand" of the Reaper, Who is about to begin the separating process —the wheat garnered and the tares gathered in bundles.

15.—"**Another angel came out of the temple.**" *Another*, as distinct from those previously numbered in the chapter (vv. 6, 8, 9). The *throne* and the *temple*, both in "the Heaven," are the respective sources of judgment on earth. The throne judgments are characteristic of the first great portion of the book, closing with chapter 11. 18. The temple chastisements are in question from chapter 11. 19, and on to the pouring out of the Vials (chap. 16). In the seventh Vial, which brings the wrath of God to a con clusion, the temple and throne are united in action (v. 17). For the throne see chapter 4. 5; for the temple see chapter 11. 19. The throne sets forth the exercise of divine government; the temple refers to the immediate presence of God. In the second main part of the Apocalypse, from chapter 11. 19, the judgments are of a severer character than the preceding ones, as the evil to be dealt with is of a more acute kind, more open, daring, blasphemous, and of a religious-secular character. Hence judgment comes out from the very presence of God, *i.e.*, the temple—the nature of God as light is roused to action.

15.—The angel from the temple cries "**with a loud voice.**" It is a call for immediate action on the part of the divine Reaper. "Send Thy sickle and reap; *for* the hour of reaping is come, *for* the harvest of the earth is dried up," or "overripe" (R.V.). There are two reasons assigned why the Son of Man should at once proceed to gather in the harvest. First, the appointed hour of final dealing has come; second, the harvest was fully ripe, yea, "dried up" (see chap. 16. 12). The hour of judgment (v. 7) and the hour of harvest (v. 15, R.V.) are both said to have come, and both refer substantially to the same character of action.

15.—"**Send Thy sickle and reap.**" The Son of Man does not Himself personally reap. He superintends. Instrumentally He reaps. The actual reapers are the angels (Matt. 13. 39).

15.—"**The harvest of the earth**" is both political

(Joel 3. 9-14) and religious in character (Matt. 13. 24-30). The former is directly connected with Israel, and has its sphere of operation in the valley of Jehoshaphat (Joel 3. 12); the latter is of much wider extent, embracing within its range the whole scene of Christendom (Matt. 13. 38).

16.—"**He that sat on the cloud put His sickle on the earth, and the earth was reaped.**" The result is instantaneous, but that is in vision only. We must not regard these actions as signifying a momentary exercise of divine power. Events are regarded in the various visions—which may extend over a considerable time and employ many agencies—as completed in a single act. In the visions the completed results are briefly and tersely summed up. But in other portions of Scripture the details, equally important to know, are unfolded. But how gracious in God to afford us the certainty that His purposes shall be fulfilled; *that* these apocalyptic visions affirm.

We have already observed that the harvest discriminates and separates the wheat from the tares. "Gather ye together first the tares, and bind them in bundles to burn them; but gather the wheat into My barn" (Matt. 13. 30). This, then, is harvest work. It is the same character of separating work in which the good fish are gathered into vessels and the bad cast away (v. 48). This severing process is at the end of the age. There is no *actual* execution of judgment in the harvest. *That* is accomplished in the vintage; nor is the harvest here the completion of the firstfruits of the company of virgins of verse 4. *That* harvest is one of blessing, and is reaped when the millennial kingdom is set up. The harvest here is one of discriminating judgment prior to the kingdom being established. Reaping is in view of judgment.

VII.—THE VINE OF THE EARTH AND ITS JUDGMENT

17-20.—"**And another angel came out of the temple which (is) in the Heaven, he also having a sharp sickle. And another angel came out of the altar, having power over fire, and called with a loud cry to him that had the sharp sickle, saying, Send thy sharp sickle, and gather the bunches of the vine of the earth; for her grapes are fully ripened. And the angel put his sickle to the earth, and gathered the vine of the earth, and cast (the bunches) into the great winepress of the fury of God; and the winepress was trodden without the city, and blood went out of the winepress to the bits of the horses for a thousand six hundred stadia.**"

17.—"**Another angel**." In these visions there is mention made of six angels (vv. 6, 8, 9, 15, 17, 18). The ordinal numbers, second and third (vv. 8, 9, R.V.), are evidently meant to form a group of three angels as distinct from those which follow and are not numbered. The numbered angels announce specific events which are closely related. The fourth and the fifth come out of the temple (vv. 15, 17), from whence all the Vials are poured out (chap. 16. 1). The sixth angel comes out of the altar (v. 18).

17.—"**Having a sharp sickle**." There is a certain minuteness in the previous description not observable in this one. *There* "in His hand a sharp sickle" (v. 14); *here* it is simply "having a sharp sickle." In the one "a loud *voice*" (v. 15); in the other a "loud *cry*" (v. 18). These and other minute distinctions are to be noticed if full profit is to be gained. There are, of course, certain things in common, as "harvest" and "vintage" would necessarily suggest.

Then "another angel" is seen coming "out of the altar, having power over fire." This is the brazen altar, the altar of judgment. The loud and urgent cry of the souls of the martyrs under the altar for righteous vengeance (chap. 6. 9-11) was but partially answered. Now the full measure of judgment is to be inflicted on their enemies. The brazen altar speaks of acceptance (Lev. 1), and, with the blood upon its horns, of forgiveness (chap. 4). But it is a holy altar, and hence it demands the judgment of sin; it is also the ground of divine forgiveness. Here the thought is one of pure, unmingled judgment—divine judgment on the vine of the earth (compare with Ezek. 9. 2).

The altar angel "called with a loud cry." It was a loud, peremptory, urgent call, and one which could brook no delay.

18.—"**Gather the bunches of the vine of the earth**; for her grapes are fully ripened." Israel of old was the vine brought out of Egypt (Psa. 80. 8)—Jehovah's fruit-bearing system on earth. After centuries of cultivation and care the vine only produced "wild grapes" (Isa. 5. 2-4). The noble vine planted by the Lord God of hosts had in the days of the weeping prophet "turned into a degenerate plant of a strange vine" (Jer. 2. 21). Israel therefore was set aside, to be morally replaced by Christ the *true* Vine, Who alone could and did bear fruit (John 15). The mark of a true disciple is not simply to be a branch in the vine (Judas was that), but to be a *fruit-bearing* branch. The expression "the vine of the earth" contemplates the whole religious system in the coming crisis, not Judaism only. The grapes are ripe for judgment. They are gathered in bunches and cast into the great winepress of the wrath of God. The great religious apostasy of earth is now to be unsparingly dealt with in judgment. "The winepress was trodden without the city." The tares are now cast into the fire (Matt. 13. 40-42)—"a furnace of fire." It is, too, the consuming of the fruitless branches (John 15. 6). There is no mercy, no separating judgment, but absolute vengeance. The winepress signifies this. It is the day of vengeance of our God. It is the time of Isaiah 63: "Wherefore art Thou red in Thine apparel, and Thy garments like Him that treadeth in the winefat?" asks the prophet. The Messiah answers, "I have trodden the winepress alone; and of the peoples there was none with Me; for I will tread them in Mine anger, and trample them in My fury; and their blood shall be sprinkled upon My garments, and I will stain all My raiment. For the day of vengeance is in Mine heart, and the year of my redeemed is come" (vv. 2-4). The vine of the earth is a far-reaching expression, embracing apostate Jews and apostate Gentiles (Psa. 85. 5; 83; Isa. 34; Jer. 25. 15, 16; Joel 3).

20.—"**The winepress was trodden without the city.**" Jerusalem is the city here referred to. The valley of Jehoshaphat was outside Jerusalem, and it is there that the fullest vengeance of God shall be poured out, "the press is full" (Joel 3. 13). In fact, both the harvest and the vintage are directly grounded on the prophecy of Joel (chap. 3), with, of course, a wider application. Outside the city, or "without," signifies Palestine as a whole.

20.—"**Blood went out of the winepress to the bits of the horses for a thousand six hundred stadia.**" Blood, not wine or the juice of the grape, but that which it signified, poured out of the winepress to the depth of the horses' bits; the length of the stream of blood nearly two hundred miles. There may be certain measurements of the Holy Land* to which these would apply, but nothing certain can be affirmed. What is signified is a vast destruction of human life over a circumscribed area. Certainly what is stated of the vast slaughter is beyond anything ever known. We gather that the scene of the vintage in its worst form is that referred to by Joel (chap. 3. 9-14), as also where the battle of Armageddon is to be fought (Rev. 16. 14-16); the scene, too, of Revelation 19. 19. All these have their centre in Palestine. It is there that the wickedness of earth will be concentrated. The Beast and the Antichrist both fall there, and their

* As from Dan to Beersheba.

followers as well. Gog, too, and his subordinate, the king of the north—the political oppressors of Israel—meet their doom in Palestine (Ezek. 38; 39, for Gog and his allies; Isa. 14. 25; Dan. 11. 45, for the Assyrian or king of the north). The final dealings of God at the end of the age as expressed in the harvest and vintage are centred in Palestine, but are not confined in their effects to Israel, then the most guilty of all peoples, but extend to the utmost bounds of Christendom. We do not, of course, hold that the actual valley of Jehoshaphat and Armageddon are literally meant, as both are utterly inadequate to serve as a gathering place or centre for the nations who will assemble in close proximity to Jerusalem, and thus Judea becomes the battlefield of the nations. May God graciously preserve His beloved people from the unholy principles and spirit so characteristic of the day in which our lot is cast!

CHAPTER XV.

The Seven Vials or Bowls of God's Wrath.

INTRODUCTORY.

The two closing scenes of the previous chapter are the harvest and the vintage. But in both it is assumed that the Lord has come. The white cloud on which the divine Reaper sits betokens His presence (chap. 14. 14). Then in Joel, where the harvest and the vintage are united (chap. 3. 13), the Lord sets up His judgment seat in the valley of Jehoshaphat (v. 12). In Matthew 13. 36-42 the actions are more carefully distinguished, but both assume the actual presence of the Lord. He has come to deal with evil on the earth. It is not Babylon, the organised religious system in direct opposition to God, that is judged under the figures of the harvest and the vintage, but the world at large and by the Lord Himself. The judgment of Babylon precedes the harvest and vintage; in fact, must do so. The doom of Babylon is under the seventh Vial (chap. 16. 19), and synchronises with the third of the eries of events noted in chapter 14. 8. Hence, the doom of the worshippers of the Beast (v. 9), the blessedness of the righteous dead (v. 13), the discriminating judgment of the harvest (v. 14), and the unsparing vengeance of the vintage (v. 17) are events which have their place *after* the Bowls of wrath have been poured out. The pouring out of the seventh Vial completes the wrath of *God*, to be followed by the wrath of the *Lamb*. The seventh Vial does not introduce the personal presence of the Lord into the scene. There is an interval, a brief one no doubt, between the close of the Vial judgments and the Coming of the Lord. In the Vials we have God's wrath upon the guilty scene—upon specific subjects of judgment. In these the Lord does not appear. But He comes *after* the Vials to reap the harvest of the earth and to tread in vengeance the winepress of wrath, not in Edom only (Isa. 63. 1-6)—the centre of bitter past hostility to Israel (Psa. 137. 7)—but the world at large (Rev. 19. 15; Zeph. 3. 8). The harvest and the vintage come after the fall of Babylon.

The two chapters should be read and studied together. These Bowls of wrath are really the filling up in detail of what is stated in general terms in the ten opening words of verse 18, chapter 11. There are no specific judgments under the seventh Trumpet, under the seventh Vial there is. The termination of the Vials completes God's wrath. The wrath of the Lamb next follows—*personally* executed judgment.

ANOTHER SIGN. Chap. 15.

1.—"And I saw another sign in the Heaven, great and wonderful: seven angels having seven plagues, the last; for in them the fury of God is completed."

We have had the "great sign" of the woman, Israel (12. 1), then "another sign," that of the dragon (v. 3), now we have "another sign" spoken of as "great and wonderful." Those three signs are each seen in the Heaven—the dwelling place of God and angels. What makes the third one of such solemn import, even more so than the two preceding, is, that corresponding to the third Woe, the fulness of God's wrath is poured out upon the Beast, the diabolic persecutor of the woman. The *first* sign directs attention to Israel, the *second* to the real instigator of the evil, the dragon, and the *third* to the apostate civil power, who under Satan blasphemes God and persecutes Israel.

"Seven angels." There are three numbered groups of angels: of four (chap. 7. 1), of seven (chaps. 8. 2; 16. 1), and of twelve (chap. 21. 12). In the ministry of judgment under the Trumpets and under the Vials there are two distinct groups of seven angels. Those connected with the Trumpets are evidently a highly honoured company, as they are spoken of as those "who stand before God,"* and are likewise introduced by the definite article "*the* seven angels" (chap. 8. 2). Not so the Vial angels.

"Having seven plagues, the last." The Seal judgments were succeeded by the Trumpet series, and now the seven Vial plagues are about to be poured out, in which the pent-up and concentrated wrath of God is fully expressed. These providential judgments are the *last*. Emphasis is laid upon this expression of finality; not that the Vials close up the story of divine wrath, but they bring to an end the providential judgments of God. Further strokes of the divine vengeance are most surely inflicted, but these are by the Lamb in Person at His Coming (chap. 19; Matt. 25. 31-46).

"*For* in them the fury (or wrath) of God is completed." The reason is here given why these seven plagues are the last. "For" therein the wrath of God is exhausted, that is, His providential dealings in judgment with a wicked and apostate scene.† On the conclusion of the Vials, the wrath of the *Lamb*, even more terrible than the wrath of *God*, is openly expressed on the subjects of vengeance. "Commission to act is given to Christ as soon as the ministration of the Vials ends." The secret, providential

* See page 178.

† "The wrath of God," as an expression occurs six times in the Apocalypse: chapters 14. 10, 19; 15. 1, 7; 16. 1; 19. 15. In chapter 19. 15, 16 God's wrath and the Lamb's wrath are united in action.

dealings of God are brought to an end with the Vials, or Bowls of wrath, after which the Lamb in Person publicly assumes the government of the world. But as the nations at His Coming are in armed rebellion—apostate and wicked beyond all human conception—the wrath of the Lamb burns in its fierceness. The wrath of God is finished in the Vials, to be succeeded by the wrath of the Lamb.

THE VICTORIOUS MARTYRED COMPANY OF JUDAH.

2-4.—"**And I saw as a glass sea, mingled with fire; and those that had gained the victory over the Beast, and over his image, and over the number of his name, standing upon the glass sea, having harps of God. And they sing the song of Moses bondman of God, and the song of the Lamb, saying, Great and wonderful (are) Thy works, Lord God Almighty; righteous and true (are) Thy ways, O King of nations. Who shall not fear (Thee), O Lord, and glorify Thy Name? for (Thou) only (art) holy; for all nations shall come and worship before Thee; for Thy righteousnesses have been made manifest.**" In the earlier vision (v. 1) we had a solemn intimation of what is coming on the organised political (chap. 16. 10) and religious (v. 19) systems then dominating the earth, as also on those connected with them. On these the wrath of God in resistless force spends itself, while the civil and ecclesiastical leaders are reserved for special punishment under the wrath of the Lamb inflicted at His Coming in power. The vision of judgment in verse 1 is resumed in verse 5. In the parenthesis between the visions of wrath we are introduced into an exceedingly grand scene of victory and song (vv. 2-4). The awfulness of the Vials (v. 1) is an occasion for God to bring into bold and striking relief His thoughts about His suffering people, and that before a blow is struck at the enemy. They are here witnessed in a parenthetic vision *after* the announcement of wrath, and *before* its execution. Historically the Beast triumphed (chap. 13. 7) over the saints in the great Tribulation. They were not preserved from his brutal power. Now, however, we see the position reversed. The saints who had been martyred are here the victors on high, and the Beast on earth a subject of the fullest vengeance of God.

A SEA OF GLASS.

2.—"**As a glass sea, mingled with fire,**" like it in appearance. In the first of these heavenly visions (chap. 4) the Seer beheld a sea of glass like crystal spread out before the throne of the Eternal, intimating a fixed state of purity in keeping with the holy character of the throne. The glassy sea like *crystal** signifies the solid calm of that scene of unsullied light. But in the vision before us the *crystal* is omitted. In beautiful accord with the divine character of the scene detailed in chapter 4 it would be morally out of place in our chapter. Here the sea is "mingled with fire," evidently referring to the fiery persecution under the Beast, a trial exceeding far in its combination of suffering anything hitherto experienced (Mark 13. 19). The pagan persecutions of early times, and the still more exquisite and refined torments under papal Rome, come short of the horrors of the great Tribulation.

The victory of the conquering band standing on the sea of glass is assured. The Beast concentrated his power and energies to overthrow the faith of the martyrs. Paradoxical as the statement may seem, yet it is true that in death they triumphed. In the victory of the Beast we behold the triumph of the saints. They "gained the victory over the Beast, and over his image, and over the number of his name." The victory was thorough and complete.

2.—"**Standing upon the glass sea**." They stand in keeping with their new position as conquerors and worshippers; the elders *sit*, save when engaged in praise or other service. The glass sea in the early vision is unoccupied; here we witness the happy, victorious, and praising company standing upon it.

HARPS.

2.—"**Having harps† of God.**" The Authorised Version wrongly inserts the article before harps. There are two heavenly companies spoken of as having harps, the only musical instrument mentioned in the Apocalypse. First, the glorified saints who had been translated at the Coming into the air (chap. 5. 8); second, the martyrs under the Beast, a victorious company on the sea of glass (chaps. 14. 2; 15. 2). We gather that the harp singers of chapters 14 and 15 are the same company. It will be noted likewise that harp and song are conjoined in each of the three references. The words "*of God*" signify that they are provided by Him for His direct praise and worship—God's harps; inasmuch as the instruments, the musicians, and the themes are His.

Each one of the rejoicing band is a skilful minstrel and

---

* For the force of the imagery see page 125.

† See page 137.

each a joyous singer. Harp and song correspond; no jar, no discord to mar the harmony of the strains of the heavenly and triumphant host. Neither voice not heart can be out of tune when the leader of their song is Jesus, the Saviour and Lord (Heb. 2. 12). There is a somewhat striking parallel between this triumphant company and Israel of old in the day of her deliverance and gladness. Egypt, the oppressor, smitten with plagues; Israel across the Red Sea, saved and emancipated, and singing on the eastern bank of the sea, the *first* song recorded in Scripture (Exod. 15); all this has its spiritual counterpart in the Beast, the enslaver of God's saints smitten in a series of plagues; the godly remnant beyond the malice of the Beast, saved and triumphant, and singing the song of Moses on the sea of glass, the *last* song recorded in Scripture (Rev. 15).

THE SONG.

3.—**"They sing the song of Moses, bondman of God, and the song of the Lamb."** The songs are united. The song of Moses celebrates Jehovah's mighty deliverance of His people, His acts of power, and His ways of grace with and for Israel from the beginning of their history till their final triumph. Grace and glory are celebrated in the magnificent song sung on the eastern bank of the Red Sea (Exod. 15)—pre-eminently the song of Moses.* But it was an earthly redemption, and won with power over the might of the enemy. The song of the Lamb intimates two main subjects: first, redemption from guilt and sin's consequences by the blood of God's Lamb; and, second, the exaltation of the Lamb to which this book bears ample testimony.

The song of the martyred victors, the harp singers of chapter 14. 2, 3, the brethren of the spared Jewish remnant on mount Zion (chap. 14. 1), is not so elevated nor characterised by such depth as that sung by the elders (chap. 5). The worship of the latter is more profound, yet both companies are partakers of the heavenly calling.†

* The prophetic song of Moses (Deut. 31. 30; 32), when a hundred and twenty years old, cannot be entitled to the appellation, "*The* Song of Moses." That the song of Exodus, and not the Deuteronomy one, is meant seems evident from the following considerations: The apocalyptic reference to the victors on the sea on which they stand; their conscious triumph over their enemy; the term "plague" common to the Mosaic and apocalyptic judgments on Egypt and on the Beast, as also the *character* of the plagues alike in both. These and other considerations which might be adduced prove conclusively that "The Song of Moses" is that of Exodus 15, and not the subsequent one on the eve of his death.

† "Their song is very peculiar. The song of Moses is triumph over the power of evil by God's judgments. The song of the Lamb is the exaltation of the rejected Messiah, of the suffering One, and like Whom they had suffered; for it is the slain remnant amidst unfaithful and apostate Israel whom we find here. The song celebrates God and the Lamb, but by victorious sufferers who belong to Heaven."—"Synopsis of the Books of the Bible," *in loco*.

THE SUBJECTS OF THE SONG.

3.—**"Great and wonderful (are) Thy works, Lord God Almighty; righteous and true (are) Thy ways, O King of nations."** The opening words of the song, "Great and wonderful," occur also in verse 1. The connection, of course, is different, but one cannot overlook the recurrence of the phrase in a scene admittedly closing up the manifested wrath of God upon public evil. The sign of closing judgment is "great and wonderful" (v. 1), so also are the works of God (v. 3). The time of the pouring out of the Bowls of wrath will be brief, but acts of stupendous and wonderful power will characterise it.

It will be observed that the *works* are ascribed to JEHOVAH, the Self-Existing, Sovereign, Independent One; ELOHIM, the Creator, the God of gods; and SHADDAI, Almighty in power, Almighty in resources, Almighty to sustain. As Jehovah He was known to Israel (Exod. 6. 2, 3). As God He stands related to creation (Gen. 1). As the Almighty He revealed Himself to the patriarchs (Gen. 17. 1). The order in which the divine names and titles are here employed differs from that of their revelation. God, Jehovah,* and the Almighty is the historical order. But the true, real Israel is before God in the victorious company on the sea of glass, and thus the representatives of the nation use the appropriate divine title first. How true God is to His own Word and Name! Jehovah from the early days of Exodus 6 still stands related to Israel. Jehovah and Israel! Ah, then the people can never perish; never cease to be remembered. What a tower of strength in the combination of these divine titles! How consoling in their application to believers in all ages! How awful to contemplate their exercise to the enemies of God and of His saints!

But the *ways* of God also form part of the song. His tenderness, His grace, His love, His wisdom, and every gracious, moral feature manifested in His dealings with His saints pass before the victors in review. The holiness and pity of God to His saints form a tale that never can be fully told. The conspicuous acts of Jehovah were displayed before the eyes of Israel. These acts of power did not call for an intimate knowledge of Jehovah's character; they were self-evident to all. But the ways of God—those dealings flowing from what He is—could alone be discerned by the spiritual, hence we read, "He made known His *ways* unto Moses, His *acts* unto the children of Israel"

---

* "By My Name JEHOVAH was I not known to them *i.e.*, Israel (Exod. 6. 3), means that it was not known as a title of ordinary relationship. To Israel, of course, the name was familiar, but not known formally in special relation to them as a people.

(Psa. 103. 7). His ways here, however, are ways of judgment, and *that* judgment, however variously expressed, is "righteous and true." The ways of God in His dealings with His people are ever just and true, but equally so in the chastisement of His enemies; this latter is specially in view in the passage before us.

3.—"**O King of nations.**" In the text of the Authorised Version we have *saints* instead of *nations*; the latter, however, is inserted in the margin. Without doubt, the correct reading, on competent authority, should be *nations*, not *saints*. Christ is King of kings, King of the earth, King of Israel, King of the nations, but is never spoken of as "Our King," and never as the King of saints. Believers in the present dispensation have kingly rule and authority conferred upon them (1 Cor. 4. 8; 6. 2, 3; Rev. 1. 6); its exercise is yet future. We shall reign *with* Christ (2 Tim. 2. 12). The nations comprising the Roman earth are about to come under judgment, hence the appropriateness of the title "King of nations" (see Jer. 10. 7). We gather that in this song of praise both God and Christ are worshipped, the former in the greatness of His Being, but in relation to Israel, and the latter in His ways of judgment with the Gentiles or nations.

4.—Then the victors in their song throw out a universal interrogation. "**Who shall not fear (Thee), O Lord, and glorify Thy Name?**" The threefold repetition of the conjunction *for* supplies three reasons, each grounded upon the character of God, why all should comply with the interrogative claim to fear the Lord and glorify His Name. (1) "*For* (Thou) only (art) holy." The word here rendered "holy" is not the word usually applied to God in speaking of His holy character. It is used here and in chapter 16. 5 of Him, otherwise it is applied to men as denoting the sum of moral qualities of a divine character. But in the two apocalyptic references it signifies that the sum of qualities in God alone entitles Him to the exclusive worship of the creature. The word "holy" as employed here denotes therefore *all* in God entitling Him alone to worship. In the Septuagint we have the same word in "the sure *mercies* of David" (Isa. 55. 3). How fitting the application of this word to the Lord at a time when the world wonders after and worships the Beast, a worship and homage to which God alone is entitled, as signified by this word "holy." (2) "*For* all nations shall come and worship before Thee." The prophecies of the book are generally cast in the present tense, but the one before us is an exception. The future is employed. As a result of these ways of judgment by the "King of nations" the iron will of the peoples is broken, and they turn from human props and confidences to God, and worship in His presence. It will be the time and fulfilment of such Scriptures as Psalm 100; 148; Isaiah 2. 2-4; 56. 6, 7; Zechariah 14. 16, 17, etc. (3) "*For* Thy righteousnesses* have been made manifest." The manifestation of God's *righteous acts of judgment* is indicated in the plural "righteousnesses." God declaring Himself in judgment is surely a powerful reason why His Name should be glorified.

THE MINISTERS OF GOD'S WRATH EQUIPPED FOR JUDGMENT.

5-8.—"**And after these things I saw, and the temple of the tabernacle of witness in the Heaven was opened. And the seven angels who had the seven plagues came out of the temple, clothed in pure bright linen, and girded about the breasts with golden girdles. And one of the four living creatures gave to the seven angels seven golden bowls, full of the fury of God, Who lives to the ages of ages. And the temple was filled with smoke from the glory of God and from His power; and no one could enter into the temple until the seven plagues of the seven angels were completed.**" The opening words of this vision constitute a technical expression signifying a complete break, introductory of an entirely new subject (see chap. 4. 1, R.V.). Thus the Vial plagues are altogether unique, and form a body of special judgments by themselves. There are two important respects in which they differ from the Seal and Trumpet chastisements: the *throne* in "the Heaven" is the source and authority of these latter, while the *temple* is the scene from whence the Vials of wrath are poured out. The fact that the temple takes the place of the throne changes the situation entirely, and introduces a severer course of dealing, one flowing from what God is in His righteous and holy character. Hence the second marked difference of the Vials from preceding judgments is that in them the wrath of God against the organised systems of evil is finished up or completed. "After these things" is a technical formula several times found in the Apocalypse.

5.—"**The temple of the tabernacle of witness in the Heaven was opened.**" We have already remarked

* The same word in chapter 19. 8. Only in our text it is applied to judgments on the wicked, whereas in the other Scripture it is employed to set forth the righteousness or righteous acts of the saints. In a footnote to Revelation 19. 8 in "The New Translation (Morrish, London) the learned translator says: "In Hebrew the plural of acts expressing a quality is used for the abstract quality itself. This may be the case by analogy here (also in chap. 15. 4). So Psalm 11. 7, where in Hebrew it is 'righteousness,' but it is actual, not imputed."

upon the interesting fact that in all this part of the Apocalypse, from chapter 11. 19 to chapter 19, the temple, not the throne, as in the earlier part of the book, is the source from whence action on earth proceeds. Both here and in chapter 11. 19* the temple is opened in "the Heaven," the residence of God and of angels. But in the earlier reference the ark of the covenant is seen, the token of God's presence with and interest in His people, as also the pledge and witness of His purpose and grace. Here it is the tabernacle of witness, or testimony. This was a testimony really to the rights of God then openly denied. The former, *i.e.*, "the covenant," was the sign of security to Israel. The latter, *i.e.*, "the witness," of judgment according to the nature of God on the enemies of God and of His people. The "*temple* (or house) of the tabernacle of witness" is a singular expression, and alone occurs here. We understand by the term *naos*, meaning the structure or building itself, to the exclusion of court, etc., God's dwelling place, where He is approached and worshipped. Now inside the golden furniture and tables of stone constituted the witness, or testimony, but as they were found within the temple, or house, this could be spoken of in a higher and fuller way than "the tent of the testimony" merely (Acts 7. 44). It was "the *temple* of the tabernacle of witness."

What a strange sight meets the gaze of the Seer! Not the priests ministering in the holy place, or the high priest in the holiest of all, but "the seven angels who had the seven plagues came out of the temple," not priests the ministers of grace, but angels the ministers of judgment. They are commissioned and equipped for their service by God Himself, and come out from His immediate presence fully empowered to maintain the rights and vindicate the character of the God of Israel in judgment. The temple of old was a witness of *grace*, here it is opened for *judgment*. The wickedness of man deserved it, and the holiness of God demands it.

The righteous character of their mission is signified by the pure and bright linen in which they are clothed (compare chap. 19. 8), while the golden girdles round their breasts set forth that divine righteousness and faithfulness characterise their action (see Isa. 11. 5; Rev. 1. 13). Why girded at the breasts, and not, as usual, at the loins? Because the wrath about to be poured out is measured by the holy nature of God.

7.—"And one of the four living creatures gave to

* In the early part of the chapter (11) the temple in Jerusalem is referred to (v. 1). "The temple of God in *the Heaven*" must not be understood as a literal one. The point is what it symbolically represents.

the seven angels seven golden* bowls† full of the fury of God, Who lives to the ages of ages.'' The living creatures are the executors of the judicial government of God. There are three distinct steps in this work of judgment. First, the angels are commissioned and equipped in the sanctuary (v. 6). Second, they then receive golden Bowls full of God's fury from one of the living creatures (v. 7). Third, not a step in the act of judgment can be taken till God authoritatively gives the command (chap. 16. 1). How calm and measured are the ways of God in judgment! The Ever-Living, Eternal God is the God of judgment. Who is He Who is about to plague the earth and visit it with His utmost fury? He **''Who lives to the ages of ages.''**

The temple was darkened with smoke from the glory of God—not incense but smoke filled the temple. Nothing could be seen and none could enter. God's glory was moved to intense action. Intercession was of no avail. Neither incense nor blood could arrest the coming storm of divine judgment. The temple was given over, not to worship or intercession, but to the fiercely burning wrath of God. The smoke here is not that of *incense*, but of *fire*, the symbol of divine consuming judgment (Isa. 6. 4; Exod. 19. 18). The house filled with smoke‡ intimated that none then need seek Him in grace. He could not be seen or found by any in the temple. Judicial action was then in question, and till the seven angels had completed their allotted work of judgment God was for the time being hidden in the thick darkness of His own glory and power in righteous vengeance on the corrupt mass on earth.

---

* Gold, brass, and linen, viewed as symbols, each sets forth the truth of *righteousness*. Gold is intrinsic, divine righteousness (chaps. 1. 12, 13; 3. 18; 21. 18-21). Brass is righteous judgment, or, as another has expressed it, ''Righteousness in dealing with man in his responsibility'' (chaps. 1. 15; 2. 18). Linen, righteous acts or deeds; human righteousness (chaps. 15. 6; 19. 8).

† ''The word means *bowls* or *cups*, and is taken from the vessels used for pouring out drink-offerings, etc., before the Lord.''—''Lectures on the Book of Revelation,'' by William Kelly.

‡ In the dedication of the tabernacle Moses could not enter into the tent of testimony (Exod. 40. 34, 35), and when the temple and its services were inaugurated (1 Kings 8. 10, 11) the priests could not enter. In both the glory of the Lord filled the house. Here, however, it is not the glory but the smoke of it, that is, the glory of God in judgment.

CHAPTER XVI.

THE SEVEN VIALS OR BOWLS OF GOD'S WRATH.

THE COMMAND FROM THE TEMPLE.

1.—"**And I heard a great voice out of the temple, saying to the seven angels, Go and pour out the seven bowls of the fury of God upon the earth.**" The terms, "voice," "voices," a "strong voice," a "loud voice," and a "great voice," have each their own special significance.

The word *voice* is variously used of Christ, of God, of angels, of the living creatures, of the altar, of the throne, etc. Wherever the word occurs, or to whom or to what it refers in the Apocalypse, there is implied an intelligent apprehension of the subject in question. Its metaphorical application as in chapter 9. 13 is no exception.

The plural, *voices*, occurs eight times, and with one exception (chap. 11. 15) is directly associated with judgment. It is one of the premonitory signs of coming wrath (chap. 4. 5; 8. 5, 13; 10. 3, 4; 11. 19; 16. 18), and implies that the judicial dealing is not simply the exercise of arbitrary power, but is intelligently governed and directed.

Then we read of a "*strong* voice" (chap. 18. 2), of a "*loud* voice" (chap. 5. 2), and of a "*great* voice," as in our text (see also chap. 21. 3). The adjectives respectively set forth the character of the voice, which, again, is in exact keeping with the nature of the announcement.

1.—The Seer hears "**a great voice out of the temple.**" The sanctuary itself, the holiest spot in the universe, is roused to action. The demand for judgment on the apostate scene proceeds not from the throne, but from the holy of holies. God's wrath burns fiercely, and its strength is derived from what His holy nature demands and necessitates (Isa. 6). The voice heard in the temple may well be termed "great," when the holiness of the place and the majesty of the Speaker are considered.

The completeness of the service in which these judgment angels are employed is signified by the number *seven*, the predominant and ruling numeral in the Apocalypse. These ministers of God's wrath, although divinely equipped and commissioned, cannot act till God commands. "Go and pour out the seven bowls of the fury of God." These broad-rimmed vessels had been filled in the sanctuary, not with incense, but with wrath—God's righteous wrath. The voice which orders the execution of these seven plagues (v. 1) announces their completion when all are poured out (v. 17).

1.—"**Pour out**," not sprinkle; the expression refers to the fulness of divine wrath, each vessel overflows, and is to be poured out without stint or measure in succession till all are emptied. A similar phrase is not uncommon in the Old Testament (Zeph. 3. 8; Psa. 69. 24; Jer. 10. 25). These *seven* apocalyptic plagues seem like an answer to the prayer of the suffering Jewish remnant in the coming crisis. "Render unto our neighbours *sevenfold* into their bosom their reproach, wherewith they have reproached Thee, O Lord" (Psa. 79. 12).

The scene of these plagues is "the earth," not geographically but prophetically viewed, hence the course of judgment takes a wider sweep than that under the Trumpets (chap. 8). Not the apostate Roman earth only, but the whole of the guilty scene within the range of prophetic vision is here given up to feel the vengeance of an angry God.

We are now about to witness these truly awful visitations of divine wrath successively inflicted out of the sanctuary, and from the Bowls, hallowed by temple use and service, now devoted to purposes of judgment.

FIRST BOWL OF WRATH.

2.—"**And the first went and poured out his bowl on the earth; and there came an evil and grievous sore upon the men that had the mark of the beast, and those who worshipped his image.**" In the enumeration of the respective Trumpets each of the seven angels is referred to as "second angel," "third angel," "fourth angel," and so on (chap. 8), but not so here. The introduction is more brief, the ordinals as first, second, etc., being simply employed, and the word angel omitted.*

The plague here referred to as "an evil and grievous sore" reminds us of the sixth Egyptian plague (Exod. 9. 10, 11). This was the first of the plagues which attacked the persons of the Egyptians, and one under which the magicians, or wise men, specially smarted. It was a disgusting and loathsome disease (see Deut. 28. 27, 35). There are two other New Testament references to this painful character of boil. Under the fifth Bowl it is mentioned in conjunction with other judgments (v. 11), and in Luke 16. 20, 21 we learn that Lazarus, dying amongst the dogs on the street, was covered with

---

* Bengel, remarking on the omission of the word angel in the Vials, tersely adds, "The Vials make short work."

these painful and generally incurable boils or sores, but the soul of the pauper was waited upon by the angels of God, and *carried* up and into the bosom of Abraham—the reserved place of Jewish blessing.

The literality of the apocalyptic plagues (chap. 16) is a moot question with some. It has been argued that because the Egyptian plagues were literal, so must these be, because of their general resemblance. Now, while strongly protesting against any limitation of divine power, or intruding on the region of sovereignty which God alone can and must necessarily occupy, yet we judge that the plagues of our chapter must be understood symbolically in keeping with the general character and design of the book. What is signified is a *moral* sore which will cause intense mental suffering. Physical suffering, no doubt, will also add to the anguish endured by men, but the chief and predominating feature will be judicial dealing with the soul and conscience—a suffering far exceeding any bodily infliction. It is called an "evil and grievous *sore*." The word literally means a bad ulcer, that which produces and draws to it unhealthy humours, discharging these in a highly offensive form. Persons bearing the mark of the Beast and his worshippers—the active supporters of the apostate civil power then under the direct authority of Satan—are the sufferers under the first Bowl. It is God's wrath on the adherents and devotees of the Beast throughout the prophetic earth. This truly awful judgment *precedes* the fall of Babylon (v. 19), whereas the everlasting torment of the Beast worshippers *succeeds* that great event (chap. 14. 9, 10). We gather therefore that the pouring out of the first Vial is a precursor of the doom announced as the fourth subject in that interesting chapter 14 of grave and notable events.

THE TRUMPETS AND VIALS COMPARED.

Besides a general resemblance to the plagues of Egypt, the Vials and Trumpets strikingly correspond. In the first four of each series the sphere of operation is the same, namely, the earth, the sea, the rivers, the fountains, and the sun. But in the Trumpets the area affected is restricted to a third part, *i.e.*, the Roman world. The effects produced under the Vials are different, and of a severer character, than those under the Trumpet judgments. Then the fifth, sixth, and even seventh Trumpets correspond in some general respects to the last three Vials. But in the Vials the range of the various plagues is in no wise limited to a fourth (chap. 6. 8) or third part (chap. 8) of the prophetic earth. Wherever the evil is it is searched out and none escape.

SECOND BOWL OF WRATH.

3.—"**And the second poured out his bowl on the sea; and it became blood, as of a dead man; and every living soul died in the sea.**" All the Vials are poured on the *earth*, not geographically but prophetically considered (v. 1). But the terms "earth" (v. 2) and "sea" (v. 3) both form part of the prophetic scene referred to in verse 1; that is, the term *earth* in verse 1 is of larger and wider import than the *earth* of verse 2. The latter is contrasted with the sea, and as a symbol denotes that special part of the prophetic earth then in ordered external relation to God, while the sea signifies that portion of the sphere of prophetic dealing, not organised, but revolutionary in character—the masses in general. It is important to lay hold of the force of these symbols and of their application in detail. The grand desideratum, however, is to hold in the soul and understanding the *moral* principles and teaching of the book. A detailed exposition, however interesting, and to some minds fascinating, should be subordinated to the moral element—to that which deals with the conscience and with God. The great moral principles of truth which run through all Scripture are meant to govern the heart and control the life.

The sea "became blood" is not a physical fact, as in the first Egyptian plague (Exod. 7. 17-25), when the Nile, the justly celebrated river of Egypt, with its canals, streams, and tributaries, was turned into blood literally and actually. But in the Vial plague the sea becoming blood points symbolically to a scene of *moral* death. Christianity, or at least what then represents it, is abandoned. So complete and thorough is the apostasy that the blood (*life*, moral or physical, as the case may be) is "as of a dead man." Here we have death in a double sense. First, spiritual death, as in Ephesians 2. 5, even in the case of those naturally alive; second, by apostasy, the giving up of all religious profession—the open, public renunciation of all external relationship to God, as in Jude 12—"twice dead," even when physically alive.

"Every living soul died in the sea." The masses of people within the bounds of the prophetic earth are signified by the restless *sea*, while those in special outward relation to God within that same sphere are signified by the solid *earth*. "*Every* living soul died." Each mere professor makes shipwreck of faith, of conscience, of truth, and gives up every vestige of religious profession. The apostasy and alienation from God are complete, not one left, save those who are *real* and whose names are in the Lamb's book of life.

It has been contended that a violent physical death is here signified by the term blood, but this, we judge, is a mistake. A sword symbolically sets forth death by war or violence, and that is absent here (chaps. 6. 8; 19. 15). The scene before us represents a general state of corruption and apostasy amongst the peoples and masses of mankind not in ordered relation to God, as also the open apostasy of "every" one. A *pagan* world we have read and heard of with all its disgusting and filthy practices. A *papal* Europe shrouded in moral darkness there has been, and that at no very distant date. But an *apostate* world, with its blasphemy, cruelty, and frightful misery, abandoned by God and given over to Satan, is the appalling picture in the Apocalypse, one most sure, and, moreover, not far off. The character of the times unmistakably points in that direction.

THIRD BOWL OF WRATH.

4-7.—"**And the third poured out his bowl on the rivers, and (on) the fountains of waters; and they became blood. And I heard the angel of the waters saying, Thou art righteous, Who art, and wast, the Holy One, that Thou hast judged so. For they have poured out the blood of saints and prophets, and Thou hast given them blood to drink; they are worthy. And I heard the altar saying, Yea, Lord God Almighty, true and righteous** (are) **Thy judgments.**" In the third Trumpet, to which the third Vial corresponds, the rivers and fountains come under judgment. In the former, however, they become *wormwood* (chap. 8. 11); here they are turned into *blood*. In the former all national life, character, and source of thought and action are morally poisoned; in the latter the national corruption is of a deeper kind—moral death and complete alienation from God are the results. The "rivers," the ordinary life of a nation characterised by known and accepted principles of government, social and political, its life-breath so to speak, as also "fountains of waters," the sources of prosperity and well-being, are all turned into blood, symbolically of course.* We would again remark that, allowing a certain parallelism between the Trumpets and Vials, the latter are, at the same time, of wider extent and more severe and searching than the former.

5.—"**The angel of the waters**" seems at first sight an ambiguous expression. But when it is borne in mind the large part which angels occupy in the economy of the redemption of the inheritance the expression assumes a definiteness quite in keeping with other portions of the book. Almost every subject in the Apocalypse has its angel. An angel is the intermediary between Christ and John (chap. 1. 1); the seven churches have each their angel or moral representative, not a celestial being (chaps. 2; 3); an angel challenges the universe to produce one competent to fulfil the counsels of God respecting the earth (chap. 5. 2); the numberless throng of angels worship the Lamb (vv. 11, 12); angels control the elements (chap. 7. 1); an angel seals the servants of God (vv. 2, 3); each Trumpet and each Vial has its respective angel (chaps. 8; 16); angels are the combatants in the heavenly war (chap. 12); an angel announces the Everlasting Gospel (chap. 14. 6); an angel proclaims the fall of Babylon (v. 8); an angel declares the awful doom of the worshippers of the Beast (v. 9); an angel comes out of the temple (v. 15); and another out of the altar (v. 18). If the winds, the fire, and the abyss have each an angel, the waters too have their appropriate and guardian angel. The peoples symbolised by the waters (chap. 17. 15) are controlled by an angel, all, however, under the governing hand of God.

The angel of the waters acquiesces in the divine judgment. It might be naturally supposed that he would deprecate judicial and retributive dealing in the sphere over which he presides. On the contrary, he justifies God, saying, "Thou art righteous." The plague does not overstep by a hairbreadth the just measure of strict righteousness. Then the eternity of God's Being, "Who *art*," and His past relation to men and angels, "and *wast*," are next affirmed.† "The *holy* One." This peculiar word occurs but twice in the New Testament in relation to Christ; the other instance is in chapter 15. 4.

In the Authorised Version of verse 5 the words "O Lord" and "shalt be" are unnecessary interpolations, and are rejected by most critics, while the title the "holy One" is omitted (see R.V.).

6.—"**They have poured out the blood of saints**

---

* See page 190.

† See remarks in our Exposition on chapters 1. 4, 8; 4. 8; 11. 17.

and prophets.'' This sentence conclusively proves the symbolic character of the plague. Apostate peoples and nations are referred to as ''waters.'' They had freely and wantonly poured out the blood of saints and prophets. In chapter 11. 18 the order is *prophets* and saints; here it is *saints* and prophets. In the former it is a question of public acknowledgment of service and faithfulness, hence the most responsible and distinguished company is first named; whereas in our text it is the martyrdom of all who stand for God, of all who witness for Him, negatively and positively, according to the principle in Luke 11. 50, 51. ''Saints''* is a common enough term in both Testaments, signifying true believers on God. ''Prophets''* designate those who truly witness for God in a dark and evil day.

6.—''**Thou hast given them blood to drink: they are worthy**.'' *Water* is the ordinary source of life and refreshment. *Wine* is the symbol of earth's joy. *Blood* is the witness of death. In retributive justice, in holy righteousness, God judicially gives over the persecutors of His people to drink blood, to realise in their own souls and consciences *death*. The penalty is an awful one. The drinking of blood does not mean physical death, it is infinitely worse. The punishment is as horrible as it is righteous. It is really an instalment and foretaste of the horrors of the lake of fire. ''They are worthy.'' Not only is it a righteous judgment, but these apostates have fully earned their awful doom. ''They are worthy'' to have this terrible and judicial character of death inflicted upon them, to drink it, and thus fully know its bitterness.

Then the altar speaks, not as in the Authorised Version, the angel of the altar, but the altar itself. The brazen altar is here referred to (chap. 6. 9), the altar of consuming judgment. The lives of God's saints and witnesses had been sacrificed on the altar (so He regarded it), and their souls after death are heard underneath it crying to God for vengeance on their bloodthirsty persecutors. God hears the cry. For about six thousand years it might have seemed as if God slept or was indifferent to the cruel and heartless treatment of His people in all ages. But no! The long, lingering patience of our God has now come to an end, and the slumbering vengeance of Jehovah bursts forth. The cry of the altar is a vindication of the God of wrath. It exults in the holy and righteous character of these retributive judgments. In the first book of Scripture (chap. 4. 10) we hear the cry of the blood of the first of

* See page 242.

the martyred band; now in the last book (chap. 16. 7) we listen to the cry of the altar which had borne its testimony to the slaughter of God's saints from Abel onwards. It is the appeal of the altar itself in the near approach of the final consummation of judgment under the seventh Vial. It is both an appeal to and a vindication of God in His true and righteous judgments (see chaps. 15. 3; 19. 2).

FOURTH BOWL OF WRATH.

8, 9.—"**And the fourth poured out his bowl on the sun; and it was given to it to burn men with fire. And the men were burnt with great heat, and blasphemed the Name of God, Who had authority over these plagues, and did not repent to give Him glory.**" There is a marked and striking parallelism between the first four Trumpets and the first four Vials. In both the order is the same. The great departments of nature, symbolic, of course, come under judgment, namely, the earth, the sea, the rivers, and the sun. In the Vials the whole prophetic scene is involved, whereas in the Trumpets the Roman earth is specially in view.

The previous visitation of the sun in judgment (chap. 8. 12), that is, the supreme governing authority, resulted in a scene of intense moral darkness, confined, however, to the revived Roman world. But the fourth Trumpet, both in severity and range, must pale before the greater horrors of the fourth Vial. *There* darkness, *here* intolerable agony; *there* an area of circumscribed judgment, *here* the judgment extends to the utmost bounds of Christendom; *there* the circumstances of men are in question, *here* men themselves in their own persons are the agonised sufferers.

9.—"**Burnt with great heat.**" The power of the sun is increased to such an intense degree that men are scorched or burnt with its fire. It is not, of course, a physical judgment produced by the great celestial luminary; we must therefore seek to ascertain what is the moral significance and symbolic meaning of the sign. The sun as a figure denotes *supreme government* (see on chaps. 6. 12; 8. 12; 9. 2; 12. 1). We understand, therefore, that the great governing authority on earth becomes the cause of intense and frightful anguish to men. "Burnt," or scorched, would naturally convey as much (Deut. 32. 24; Mal. 4. 1).

9.—We are next called to witness the effect of these dire plagues upon the consciences of men. Are they humbled and made repentant thereby? Are they crushed in spirit under the repeated and increasing severity of these judicial chastisements? No! They "**blasphemed the Name of**

God." What an answer on man's part to the expressed wrath of the Almighty! How incorrigibly bad and thoroughly corrupt is the will of man! Had there been godly repentance the storm of divine wrath might have been arrested, for God "had authority over these plagues." All were in His hand, and He possessed supreme control. God is the source of these apocalyptic judgments. We are not living in a world of chance, but in a world which belongs to God and which He controls, even down to the minutest circumstance of life. There was produced, not repentance, but increased hardness of heart; not glory to God, but blasphemy of His blessed Name. In this plague God and the creature stand out strongly contrasted.

FIFTH BOWL OF WRATH.

10, 11.—"**And the fifth poured out his bowl on the throne of the Beast; and his kingdom became darkened; and they gnawed their tongues with distress; and blasphemed the God of the Heaven for their distresses and their sores, and did not repent of their works.**" The seven churches (chaps. 2; 3), the seven Seals (chaps. 6; 8: 1), the seven Trumpets (chap. 8), and the seven Vials (chap. 16) are each divided into two distinct groups. In the case of the churches the division is into *three* and four, whilst in the others the grouping is reversed, *four* and three. Number seven in itself signifies *completeness*, *spiritual perfection*. When separately numbered as one, two, etc., the various parts of the whole are distinguished, and when grouped into the two unequal divisions of three and four it intimates a special and characteristic feature peculiar to each group.

We have had in the preceding Vials the four great departments of nature symbolically represented, as the earth, the sea, the rivers, and the sun. But now we pass from the realm of nature to witness a characteristic and specific subject of judgment, *i.e.*, the kingdom of the Beast, which is smitten in the centre and seat of its power. The Beast himself, or the personal head of the empire, is, with his fellow in crime, the Antichrist, reserved for an awful doom (chap. 19. 20). But till then the civil and political power of earth established by Satan (chaps. 13. 4; 17. 8) is in its strength and centre made to feel the stroke of divine judgment. The executive of the kingdom, not the subjects of it, is referred to here. The "throne," the strength and glory of the kingdom, is overwhelmed with judgment. The impious and insolent challenge, "Who is like unto the Beast? who is able to make war with him?" (chap. 13. 4) is unmistakably answered here, and subsequently too (chap. 19. 19-21).

10.—"**His kingdom became darkened.**" No doubt there is here an allusion to Exodus 10. 21-23. *There*, however, the darkness was physical, *here* it is moral. It is difficult to realise in any conceivable degree the horror of such a doom. One main characteristic of the misery endured in the eternal abode of suffering, *the lake of fire*, is darkness and blackness (Matt. 25. 30). That darkness is here foreshadowed with its accompanying consequences. "They gnawed their tongues with distress." "This is the only expression of the kind that we have in all the Word of God, and it indicates the most intense and excruciating agony."*

11.—Under the distress caused by the former Vial men blasphemed "the *Name* of God;" here there is advance in an evil sense, they blaspheme "**the God of the Heaven**," not His name merely, but God Himself. There is remorse and suffering in the morally darkened kingdom, The very knowledge that God is in Heaven and is the author and source of their misery, judicially inflicted, does not bow the heart in repentance. The will is yet unbroken. And "did not repent of their works," the very deeds which God was answering in judgment were gloried in. They loved darkness and its evil deeds. Heavier strokes must yet descend.

SIXTH BOWL OF WRATH.

12-16.—"**And the sixth poured out his bowl on the great river Euphrates; and its water was dried up, that the way of the kings from the rising of the sun might be prepared. And I saw out of the mouth of the dragon, and out of the mouth of the Beast, and out of the mouth of the false prophet. Three unclean spirits, as frogs; for they are (the) spirits of demons, doing signs; which go out to the kings of the whole habitable world to gather them together to the war of (that) great day of God the Almighty. (Behold I come as a thief. Blessed (is) he that watches and keeps his garments, that he may not walk naked, and that they (may not) see h's shame.) And He gathered them together to the place called in Hebrew Armageddon.**"

* Rev. Wm. Ramsay, "Lectures on Revelation," p. 364.

THE EUPHRATES.

"The great river Euphrates."* This justly celebrated river is the largest in western Asia, and figures largely in history and prophecy. It is first named in Genesis 2, and last mentioned in Revelation 16. 12. The two apocalyptic references to it are expressed in exactly the same terms (chaps. 9. 14; 16. 12). The Euphrates formed the limit in the east of Roman conquest, and forms the eastern boundary of enlarged Palestine† in the future. It has ever stood as a geographical barrier, a natural separating bulwark between the west and the east. The golden Bowl of the sixth angel is poured on the great river, so that its water was dried up.‡ The barrier is removed by this act of judgment, so that the eastern nations can the more readily pour their armies into Canaan.

We gather from the object in view that the Euphrates, or part, will be literally dried up, miraculously no doubt. A somewhat similar judgment will be witnessed in the west (Isa. 11. 15). Both the Nile and the Euphrates are dealt with—the western and the eastern boundaries of the land of Palestine. There need be no difficulty in accepting the statement in our text in its full and literal sense. The future is brimful of wonders and startling events, and if the

---

* See page 210.

† "In the same day the Lord made a covenant with Abram, saying, Unto thy seed have I given this land, from the river of Egypt unto the great river Euphrates" (Gen. 15. 18). Thus the Nile on the west and the Euphrates on the east are the prophetic limits of the land. David and Solomon pushed their conquests on the eastern side of the kingdom up to the borders of the great Asian river, but they were unable to hold them for any length of time. Genesis 15. 18 is of future and permanent application.

‡ An account of this remarkable and interesting river may here be given, geographically and commercially too, the largest and most important of the rivers of western Asia, and frequently referred to in Scripture.

Its entire length, from its rise in the Armenian mountains to the Persian Gulf, is about 1780 miles. Its depth and width vary according to locality and season. From the month of March to May, owing to the melting of the snow on the mountains and the heavy rains, the river rises considerably, and hence both depth and width are greatly increased. There are two sources to this river, both found in the highlands of Armenia considerably apart. These form into streams which combine at a place called *Kebben Maden*. Here the river is about 120 yards wide. About 750 miles from its mouth it flows over a large alluvial plain, where it widens to about 900 yards. After flowing through mountains for about 45 miles, it emerges at *Sumeisat*, 1195 miles from the sea, and is navigable for light vessels the whole distance, while for the last 150 miles vessels of 500 tons can safely navigate the river. Up to the time of Elizabeth it was the commercial highway to India. At *Bei* the Euphrates is distant from the nearest shore of the Mediterranean about 100 miles, and is there said to be about 630 feet above the level of that great sea. At *Kurnah*, 90 miles above the Persian Gulf, it is joined by the Tigris, and is then spoken of as *Shatt-el-Arab*. Then the river, under this new name, flows steadily on till it empties itself by several arms into the Persian Gulf, the link between the Euphrates and the Indian Ocean. From Kurnah, the meeting place of the rivers, is an area of about 108,000 square miles, and its average breadth 600 feet. There is abundance of fish in the waters. Anciently the rivers Tigris and Euphrates were connected by navigable canals, which made Nineveh and Babylon the great centres of commerce for the eastern and western worlds. There were also numerous dykes, canals, aqueducts, and other artificial means for the irrigation of the poor and unproductive soil of the country, so cleverly planned as to equal in scientific skill anything produced by our modern engineers. Alexander the Great, in fixing his seat of empire in the east, so fully appreciated the natural and artificial advantages of the river that he personally superintended the repair and enlargement of those mighty works which had so greatly helped the Babylonian empire in its commercial greatness.

river divides the east from the west, that of necessity must be removed sufficiently to allow the eastern armies under their respective kings to cross the country and assemble in Palestine. The reason of divine judgment on the river is "*that* the way of the kings FROM (not "*of*" as in the Authorised Version) the rising of the sun* might be prepared." These kings cannot be the Jews, a strange supposition. The mass of the Jewish people will enter the land from the west, while Ephraim or the ten tribes are restored chiefly from the north and south. Besides, it is not the kings *of* the east, but *from* the east, peoples on the eastern side of the Euphrates, that are in question.

We see no reason why the Turkish empire should be referred to in the naming of the Euphrates in either of the two texts where the river is named in the New Testament. Turkey is not referred to in the Scriptures at all. It needs no prophetic statement nor remarkable foresight to predict the falling to pieces of that most corrupt and the worst governed power on earth. Its dismemberment has commenced, and its complete and final overthrow is only a matter of time, and not a long one either. Palestine and adjacent countries, now part of the Ottoman empire, are rapidly coming to the front. This assemblage of opposing forces in the Holy Land is prefigured in that millennial chapter, Genesis 14. In and about Judea God will gather the nations and kingdoms to pour upon them His indignation and fierce anger (Zeph. 3. 8). Persia, Ethiopia, etc., are under the power of Russia and follow in the train of Gog, the last ruler of the Russian peoples (Ezek. 38. 2-6). Greece seems to act an independent part in the near crisis (Zech. 9. 13), but all these powers are politically hostile to restored Judah (Psa. 83; Zech. 12; 14). Egypt will be subordinate to and an ally of the Beast, and thus an object of attack by the king of the north—Israel's determined political foe (Dan. 11. 25, 29, 42-44). The Beast and Gog are opposing powers. Their policy and aims are widely different. The former is the would-be *protector* of the Jewish people; the latter their *destroyer*.

A SATANIC TRINITY.

Not only are natural hindrances and barriers removed, so that the great Asiatic powers might have the way prepared to take their allotted part in the conflict and confederacy of the last days, but Satan himself provides a "universal ministry" to effect the most

* **A beautiful Oriental and poetical expression, signifying the east, where the sun rises.**

gigantic combination of opposing forces ever witnessed. The sixth Bowl of wrath is not exhausted in the judgment on the Euphrates. There are "three unclean spirits," termed the "spirits of demons," likened to frogs—loathsome, filthy, disgusting, bred out of the mire and pestilential vapours and moral wickedness of the corrupt scene—these are sent out on their terrible mission. They are to influence by word, and sign, and miracle the peoples of the earth; to lure them on to the "war of (that) great day of God Almighty." God is about to set His King on mount Zion (Psa. 2), so the might of the whole habitable earth is gathered to thwart and defeat the divine purpose. It is a universal gathering of the powers. A trinity of evil—the concentrated malignant influence of Satan —is employed to effect the gathering together of the kings of the earth. These spirits issue out of the *mouth* of the dragon, and out of the *mouth* of the Beast, and out of the *mouth* of the False Prophet. The mouth is regarded as the *source* and *means* of destructive agency (chaps. 1. 16; 2. 16; 9. 17; 19. 15; see also Isa. 11. 4). The dragon not only works actively to effectuate his plans, but his two prime ministers share in the work—the Beast and the False Prophet. The former is the vast apostate civil and political power of Rome; the latter is the second Beast of Revelation 13, here termed for the first time the False Prophet, as by his lies and influence he can the more readily act upon the peoples. We have here a combination of direct satanic power, apostate brute force, and malignant influence, all employed in this hellish work (compare with 1 Kings 22).

ARMAGEDDON.

16.—"**And He gathered them together to the place called in Hebrew Armageddon.**" The pronoun *he* no doubt refers to God. He is behind the scenes and the actors in this judicial judgment and course of dealing. It is God Almighty, therefore, Who effects, in righteous retribution, this vast gathering of the nations, employing the dragon, His declared enemy, and the great apostate chiefs of earth to carry out *His purpose*. Why is the gathering place Armageddon? There the Canaanitish kings gave battle to Israel, but Jehovah fought with and for His people, and the signal victory granted to Israel is celebrated in glowing and triumphant strains by Deborah, the prophetess (Judges 5. 19, 20 . Now one great object which the assembled nations have before them is to crush and overthrow Israel (Psa. 83. 3-5), but God intervenes, and effectually destroys them and delivers His own, as He did in the early days of the Judges. The early victory is here alluded to as a pledge and earnest of the latter. It is not that the actual hill of Megiddo or its valley is to be the gathering centre of the nations; its circumscribed area must forbid any such notion. But the simple meaning is that God will have gathered by satanic agency many of the nations of the earth to Palestine, their object being to overthrow and crush Israel, and fling themselves in their combined might against Jehovah. But, alas for them, they do so only to their own destruction. God pours upon the assembled nations His fury (see the prophets Joel and Zephaniah). It has been remarked that the valley of Jehoshaphat is the place of *slaughter*, and Armageddon the place of *gathering* by the nations. Both places, however, are intended to present in principle certain closing scenes in the last days. Both the mountain and valley point to a future assembling of kings and peoples in the land of Palestine, and probably in the vicinity of Jerusalem. *There* the great governmental question of the sovereignty of the earth is to be decided in the complete overthrow of the nations, and in the establishment of the world kingdom of our God and of His Christ; in the settlement, too, of Israel in perpetual possession of her land, and in headship and supremacy of the nations in the millennial earth.

RETROSPECTIVE VIEW.

But now we must retrace our steps somewhat. It will be observed that verse 16 naturally follows, and indeed completes the subject of verse 14, hence the passage between (v. 15) forms a parenthesis of great moral value. "Behold I come as a thief." The kings and peoples gathered by satanic agency shall in the moment of apparent success and victory be suddenly surprised by the Advent of the Lord in glory (1 Thess. 5. 2, 3). The whole world will be asleep in midnight moral darkness, and congratulating itself on "peace and safety," when suddenly the Lord Himself bursts in upon the scene, unexpectedly, as a thief in the night. *That* aspect of the Coming neither forms our hope not causes fear (v. 4). We are not of the night, nor of darkness, and hence can never be so overtaken. To us, ere the day breaks, He appears as the bright and morning star. Then the parenthesis closes with a serious word of much-needed instruction at all times, but especially at the moment and occasion of this latter-day prophecy. The believer who in that day "watches and keeps his garments" is pronounced "blessed." It is not here a question of life or salvation, but of walk. How needful then, as at all times, to look carefully to one's ways, lest there be exposure in sight of the enemy, and they see our shame and moral nakedness.

VIAL AND TRUMPET COMPARED.

In bringing our remarks on the sixth Vial to a close we would briefly note the correspondence between it and the sixth Trumpet. In both the Euphrates is named. In both, too, the Asiatic powers take their part in conflict; various other points of resemblance may be noted by careful readers. We may further remark that the sixth Vial in itself does not present a scene of conflict by the various powers, nor does it unfold a universal slaughter; it rather points to the general gathering of the peoples from all parts of the earth, so that they are there when the Lord comes in power (Rev. 19). Other Scriptures, however, enable us to fill in details. One or two statements to emphasise points of prophetic truth are important to grasp. Judea, especially in the neighbourhood of Jerusalem, is the final gathering place of the nations and peoples of the earth. Most of the nations, particularly those in the north and east, seek to destroy the Jewish commonwealth, then politically restored and in measure upheld by the western powers. All the nations are more or less combined in undying hatred to God and to His Christ, and all are judged and punished at the Lord's Advent in power (Rev. 19; Isa. 66; Zech. 14).

SEVENTH BOWL OF WRATH.

17-21.—**"And the seventh poured out his bowl on the air; and there came out a great voice from the temple of the Heaven, from the throne, saying, It is done. And there were lightnings, and voices, and thunders; and there was a great earthquake, such as was not since men were upon the earth, such an earthquake, so great. And the great city was (divided) into three parts; and the cities of the nations fell; and great Babylon was remembered before God to give her the cup of the wine of the fury of His wrath. And every island fled, and mountains were not found. And a great hail, as of a talent weight, comes down out of Heaven upon men; and men blasphemed God because of the plague of hail, for the plague of it is exceeding great."** The events described under the previous Vial were preparatory to the final outpouring of God's wrath on the apostate civil power, and on the yet more guilty Babylon of ecclesiastical fame and history, the religious corruptress of the earth. We have just witnessed the providential judgment of God on the "great river Euphrates," and the universal gathering of the nations under the marvellous energy of Satan infused into the three frog-like* spirits of demons. The world has been warned, "Behold I come as a thief," and saints solemnly counselled to walk with undefiled garments, hence all was fully prepared under the sixth Vial. There is, therefore, no further delay. The seventh golden Bowl is now poured out, exceeding in magnitude and severity anything hitherto witnessed since man began his sorrowful history outside Eden.

17.—**"The seventh poured out his bowl on the air."** This judgment falls upon the moral life-breath of the world. The air, essential to natural life, is symbolically visited in judgment. The realm of Satan is really the sphere of this awful plague (Eph. 2. 2); only we gather that the "air," as used in this prophecy of the consummation of judgment on the organised systems of evil, denotes the ruin of all right moral influences and principles which act upon men—the destruction of the moral life of all individual, social, religious, and political society. It is a far-reaching and permeating judgment.

17.—The temple and throne unite, and He Who dwells in the one and sits on the other announces with a great voice, **"It is done."** The end has come. Details of Babylon's overthrow are unfolded in the two subsequent chapters. Here the mere fact is stated, particulars are reserved. The close of providential dealing has come, and there remains but the last and most awful stroke of judgment inflicted by the Lord in Person at His Coming. The wrath of God is closed up in the pouring out of the seventh Vial, to be followed by the more awful exhibition—open and public—the wrath of the Lamb.

18.—**"There were lightnings, and voices, and thunders."**† These symbols (in a threefold form) of almighty power in judgment occur four times. The term "voices" intimates that the execution of judgment is

* Impudence and uncleanness are characteristic of the frogs. These filthy creatures, born out of the waters and stagnant pools of Egypt, were peculiarly obnoxious to the cleanly Egyptians. The palace of the monarch and the hovel of the peasant were equally infested with the loathsome reptiles, whose croaking sounds added to the general misery (Exod. 8. 3-14). Frogs and serpents were by the ancients classed together in the expression of what was loathsome and morally disgusting. Frogs were regarded by the Greek writers and poets as the proper inhabitants of the Stygian lake, or river of hell.

† On these signs of judicial dealings, see pages 124, 246.

intelligently directed. The order in which the symbols occur differs somewhat from that in the Authorised Version. The transposition of the words in this formula of divine visitation has, no doubt, its special significance in each case; they are calculated to strike terror to the hearts of men. In addition to those signs and tokens of Jehovah's wrath upon the guilty scene "there was a great earthquake," which in magnitude and dire results exceed anything recorded in history—"such an earthquake, so great." There will be physical earthquakes in divers places (Mark 13. 8). But the vast and unparalleled upheaval under the seventh Vial is not that of the elements of nature, but symbolises a violent disruption of all government, the total collapse of authority from the highest down to the lowest. Under it thrones totter and fall, crowns are broken, sceptres are shivered; the whole framework of society is overthrown. It will be a revolution unexampled in the history of the race. The fact that this mighty convulsion is stated separately from the usual formula, "lightnings, voices, and thunders," marks its speciality and its magnitude.

19.—The disastrous effects of the mighty earthquake are next briefly and tersely stated. "**The great city* was (divided) into three parts**." That is, the vast and consolidated power of Rome, from its centre in the seven-hilled city on the Tiber on to its utmost extremities, is broken up into a tripartite division, while its utter ruin follows in due course. The break-up and dismemberment of the empire in its political and social organisation is what is signified. Satan's gigantic confederation is smashed.

19.—"**The cities of the nations fell**." The seats and centres of Gentile commerce—the political world apart from and outside the Roman earth—are involved in the general ruin, which overtakes all human combinations. From the building of Babel (Gen. 11. 1-9) till the day and hour of the seventh Vial human progress in civilisation, in religion, in social and political government, in the arts, in science, in literature, has been the aim. Here we witness judgment on all that men have built up in these and other spheres of life, from the days of Cain (Gen. 3), when the world system *without God* was inaugurated, and from Babel (Gen. 11), when human combination, secular and religious, took its rise. What a blow to the pride and ambition of man!

---

* Rome (chap. 17. 18) is thus dethroned from its sovereignty over the kings of the earth. Rome, the empire which then is the vast civil and political organisation of earth, is "the great city." Rome represents the *civil*, and Babylon the *religious* organisation of that day; both established by Satan.

DOWNFALL OF BABYLON.

19.—But the chief subject of judgment is now singled out—one more hateful to God than all others. "**Great Babylon* was remembered before God to give her the cup of the wine of the fury of His wrath.**" Babylon is a name and word of ominous signification. It is the full-blown development of all antichristian elements, of all that is opposed to God. It is the concentration of all mere human religion. The city and tower which men built on the plains of Shinar—the former the civil centre, and the latter the religious centre of gathering apart from God—have in the days of the Apocalypse attained the zenith of greatness. Popery is not Babylon, pure and simple, but is part of it. In guilt Babylon towers over all, and hence its judgment is commensurate with its sin. Undoubtedly it is the mystical Babylon that is referred to, and not the great Euphratean city which was doomed to eternal destruction (Jer. 51. 62-64). It is the false church, the corruptress of the earth, the mother or source of all that is religiously vile. The very name of Christ which she bears, and the assumption of being His body and bride, intensifies her guilt. Her title, "*great* Babylon," points to her vast assumption of religious power. The anger of God burns fiercely on this awful counterfeit and travesty of what should have stood for Him in grace, in holiness, and in testimony to the truth.

The details of Babylon's judgment, her relation to the apostate civil power, and many particulars are unfolded in the two chapters which follow; while her utter doom, celebrated in Heaven* in triumphant strains of gladness, is the subject of the first four verses of chapter 19.

20.—"**And every island fled, and mountains were not found.**"† Detached or isolated interests and governments, as islands separated from the mainland, are overwhelmed in the universal catastrophe; while seats of authority and stability, as mountains, are dissolved. Ruin is everywhere, and on everything, however seemingly firm and stable. Everything that God has not established must go in the general wreck. Such, then, are the effects of the mighty earthquake.

21.—But, in addition to this, the general horror is intensified by a hurricane of divine judgment, which

---

* The *literal* Jerusalem is grandly described in Isaiah 60; the *mystical* Jerusalem is the subject of Revelation 21. 9-22. 5. The *literal* Babylon is fully described in Jeremiah 51; the *mystical* Babylon occupies chapters 17 and 18 of the Apocalypse. In all respects Babylon is the contrast to the former, both in its historical and spiritual character.

† Under the sixth Seal "mountain and island were moved out of their places" (chap. 6. 14), here the greater severity of the judgment is intimated in their complete disappearance, "not found."

descends upon men with irresistible and crushing force, a storm of divine wrath, which even the guilty world will have to acknowledge as heaven-sent: "**A great hail as of a talent weight.**"* We have already, more than once, been told of a hailstorm, singly, and in conjunction with other destructive agencies (chaps. 11. 19; 8. 7).† But this exceeds in weight and intensity the previous hailstorms. As hail descends from Heaven, and is sharp, sudden, and disastrous in its effects, so the judgment here. The nature of it is not explained, but its severity and its source from Heaven are truths unquestionably graven on the face of the prophecy.‡

Has this crowning act of divine judgment wrought repentance? Is the will broken and the heart crushed under the mighty hand of God? No! Man is unchanged, unless the Spirit of God, in mighty sovereign grace, converts and saves. The moral effect of this awful judgment is stated in the plainest terms, "men blaspheme God"—not glorify Him, as we might naturally expect—"because of the plague of hail, for the plague of it is exceeding great." How patient is God! How perverse the creature!

---

* The Jewish talent was 125 lbs. The Egyptian and Greek talents were about 86 lbs. The former is the weight of the hail in our text, and intimates the crushing, overwhelming character of the visitation.

† See pages 182 and 246.

‡ Few persons can form a conception of the terrible character of a great hailstorm. Here is an account of one which occurred at Constantinople in the month of October, 1831, written by one who witnessed it:

"After an uncommonly sultry night, threatening clouds arose about six in the morning, and a noise between thunder and tempest, and yet not to be compared to either, increased every moment, and the inhabitants of the capital, roused from their sleep, awaited with anxious expectation the issue of this threatening phenomenon. Their uncertainty was not of long duration; lumps of ice as large as a man's foot, falling singly, and then like a thick shower of stones, which *destroyed everything with which they came in contact*. The oldest persons do not remember ever to have seen such hailstones. Some were picked up half an hour afterwards which weighed above a pound. This dreadful storm passed over Constantinople and along the Bosphorus, over Therapia, Bojukden, and Belgrade; and the fairest, nay, the only hope of this beautiful and fertile tract, the vintage, just commenced, was destroyed in a day! Animals of all kinds, and even some persons, were *killed, an innumerable number are wounded, and the damage done to the houses is incalculable*. The force of the falling masses of ice was so great that they broke to atoms all the tiles on the roofs, and, like musket balls, shattered planks."

"What would it have been if the ice masses had been fifty or one hundred times larger?"—From "Seiss on the Apocalypse," page 101.

CHAPTER XVII.

Babylon and the Beast.

BABYLON'S FALL.

We had the fall of Babylon announced as the third in the chain of events unfolded in chapter 14. Under the seventh Vial the judgment of that guilty system takes place. In other words, Revelation 14. 8 synchronises with chapter 16. 19, hence events four, five, six, and seven in chapter 14 have their place *after* the pouring out of the seventh Vial. This is important as helping to a due understanding of the various parts and visions of the book. Then the character of Babylon, her relation to the Beast, and to the kings of the earth in general, and details of her judgment are unfolded in the two following chapters (17 and 18). It must not be supposed that the subject-matter of these chapters follows on *from* the seventh Vial. The account is not consecutive. Babylon occupies a prominent place in history, and figures largely in the Scriptures as the enemy of God and enslaver of His people. She is specially singled out for judgment, and hence the need for a disclosure of her character, her relations, and her end. Why should Babylon be distinguished above all as the subject of the Lord's vengeance? By *whom* and by *what* means is her judgment executed? Chapters 17 and 18 answer these and other questions naturally suggested to inquiring minds. Thus chapters 14. 8; 16. 19; 17-19. 4 all go together, and should be read as one story.

The chapter naturally divides into two parts. The first describes the great harlot as seen by the Seer in vision (vv 1-6). The second (vv. 7-18) is more full and deeply interesting, as giving a marvellous compendium of the future history of the Beast, both in its relation to the whore and to the Lamb of God. That Rome is meant is certain from verse 18. This part of the prophecy ought to be studied carefully and with prayerfulness by all students of the prophetic Scriptures.

THE HARLOT OF SATAN AND THE BRIDE OF THE LAMB.

In every point of view these two women are set in sharp contrast. The harlot is subject to Satan. The bride is subject to Christ. It is one of the Vial angels which shows both to the wondering Seer. A wilderness* (chap. 17. 3)

* Trackless and without resources—spiritual destitution.

and a great and high mountain* (chap. 21. 10) are the respective points of observation. Great Babylon comes *out* of the earth; its historical origin is human (Gen. 11. 1-9), its latter-day development satanic, as shown in the Apocalypse. The new Jerusalem descends *out* of Heaven, its native sphere, and from God, its blessed source. Satan decks the one (chap. 17. 4); God adorns the other (chap. 19. 8). Eternal ruin is the portion of the harlot; eternal glory the happy lot of the bride.

THE GREAT HARLOT DESCRIBED (VERSES 1-6).

THE WOMAN AND THE BEAST.

1.—The Seer first beholds the great harlot sitting **"upon the† many waters"** (see Jer. 51. 13).

In the explanation of the vision (vv. 7-18) we are informed who these waters signify: "The waters which thou sawest, where the harlot sits, are peoples, and multitudes, and nations, and tongues." The introduction of "multitudes" into the usual formula expressing universality marks the heterogeneous character of those subject to her sway. "The great harlot *sits* upon the many waters." She rules and dominates the nations religiously, as the Beast does politically. Her following is an almost universal one. She herself is a vast religious system. The woman and the Beast represent distinct ideas. The former is the religious system; the latter the civil power. Corruption of the truth is characteristic of Babylon. Daring self-will and open opposition to God are marked features of the Beast. Corruption and self-will have been at work from earliest ages, and in fact were the two great evils let loose amongst the race in the period preceding the flood (Gen. 6. 11). Here we witness the full-blown development of the same crimes. Corruption is godward; violence manward. The former is embodied and concentrated in the woman, who is a licentious one, for she is termed a harlot and the mother of harlots; the Beast is openly bad and exercises brute force, trampling down ruthlessly all that opposes, and at the end daringly comes out in military force and array against Christ and His heavenly army (Rev. 19. 19).

---

* Greatness and stability—established authority.

† The insertion of the article is a questioned reading. Its place, however, in the text is supported by many competent authorities. The definite article in introducing subjects of interest is a characteristic feature of the Apocalypse. It marks the definiteness and importance of the subject so spoken of. See "*the* Heaven," "*the* rainbow," "*the* seven thunders" (chap. 10), "*the* beast" (chap. 11. 7), "*the* two wings of *the* great eagle" (chap. 12. 14), etc. The use of the article brings into prominence subjects which might otherwise be regarded as of trivial moment.

The Beast first destroys the woman, then flushed with victory and intoxicated with power madly and impiously leads on his armies against the Lamb and His militant host. The principles of Babylon have been at work from earliest times, but its highest development is yet future. It is not the papal system *alone*,* but the fusion of parties bearing the christian name into one vast system of evil. The characteristics of the papacy in the Middle Ages are evidently witnessed in the whore of the Apocalypse. "The great whore" is not only Satan's counterfeit of the true Church, but is the concentrated expression of every antichristian movement and sect then in existence, consolidated and controlled by Satan. The pretensions of the whore, or harlot, are supported by the military forces and prestige of the apostate empire, whilst her influence extends throughout the known world. This gigantic system of spiritual whoredom is, without doubt, Satan's masterpiece, and the vilest thing beneath the sun.

THE GREAT HARLOT.

2.—This, then, is Babylon the great: **"With whom the kings of the earth have committed fornication, and they that dwell on the earth have been made drunk with the wine of her fornication."** This is future, although a past resemblance may be sought for in the character and doings of the papacy in the dark times of the Middle Ages. The harlot first forms a guilty alliance with the kings of the earth, *i.e.*, the great political leaders of Christendom, and then makes drunk with the wine of her fornication "they that *dwell* on the earth," that is, the mass of christian apostates.† The wickedness of these once christian professors is then filled up. Christ, the heavenly calling, and Christianity abandoned, they give themselves up to the short-lived joys of the harlot's cup of wine. It is truly awful to contemplate the career,

* "It cannot be doubted that our most eminent divines have commonly held and taught that the apocalyptic prophecies concerning Babylon were designed by the Holy Spirit to describe the Church of Rome. Not only they who flourished at the period of the Reformation, such as Archbishop Cranmer, Bishops Ridley and Jewel, and the Authors of the Homilies, but they also who followed them in the next, the most learned age of our theology—I mean the end of the sixteenth and beginning of the seventeenth century—proclaimed openly the same doctrine. And it was maintained by those in that learned age who were most eminent for sober moderation and christian charity as well as profound erudition. It may suffice to mention the illustrious names of the two brightest luminaries of the English Church: Richard Hooker and Bishop Andrewes."—Wordsworth on the Apocalypse. Does pagan Rome or papal Rome inherit the character and features of the apocalyptic Babylon? The latter surely. In so far as popery has corrupted the truth, persecuted the saints of God, advanced arrogant and blasphemous claims, assumed universal dominion, and otherwise drunk into the spirit and adopted the principles and practices of the "Great Harlot"—she is in character the Babylon of the Apocalypse, but as we have already remarked, the Babylon of prophecy is worse—infinitely more than ever the papal system has been. We look for a fuller development of evil. Babylon is *future*.

† See pages 74, 104, 192, 235.

the character, and the doom of those *dwellers on the earth*, thus morally distinguished and singled out as the worst on the face of the globe.

SPIRITUAL FORNICATION.

Adultery, or idolatry—"with their idols have they committed adultery" (Ezek. 23. 37)—is the special sin charged upon Israel of old as being the married wife of Jehovah* (Jer. 3. 14; Isa. 54. 1). For this she was divorced.† But in the purpose and grace of Jehovah Israel will be reinstated in her former blessed relation, one never again to be forfeited so long as sun and moon endure. *Fornication*, or illicit intercourse and connection with the guilty and apostate world, is the solemn indictment against Babylon—the corrupt and licentious woman who ensnares and captivates with her short-lived pleasures all within her influence—kings and people, high and low. The seductive glitter and meretricious display of this abandoned woman affect all classes, and morally ruin those over whom she casts her golden chains and who drink of her cup. Every right and true thought of Christ perishes where the woman's blandishments are received and her smile courted.

THE BEAST ON WHICH THE WOMAN SITS.

3.—**"I saw a woman sitting upon a scarlet beast, full of names of blasphemy, having seven heads and ten horns."** The Beast, if not the most prominent figure in the vision, is yet an integral part of the prophecy. The subserviency of the Beast to the harlot is expressed by the Seer, "I saw a woman *sitting* upon a scarlet beast." The action intimates the thorough and complete subjection of the civil power. The rule and supremacy of the woman over the vast imperial and apostate power is a singular sight. The woman not only sits upon, or beside, the nations and peoples comprised within the prophetic area (v. 1), but also rules the Beast, the then dominating civil and political power on earth (v. 3).

The scene in vision where this strange sight is beheld is a *desert*, a place of loneliness and utter desolation. What a striking contrast to the display both of the woman and the Beast! The surpassing splendour of both captivates the heart and intoxicates the senses of all, save a suffering remnant to whom this pageant is as a wilderness, for God

* The royal *consort* of the King is Jerusalem (Psa. 45. 9). The *bride* and *wife* of the Lamb is the Church (Rev. 19. 7; 21. 9). The *wife* of Jehovah is Israel (Jer. 3. 14). The *mother* of the Man-Child is Israel, strictly speaking, Judah (Rev. 12. 1; Rom. 9. 5).

† A wife divorced can never again be a *virgin*; hence not Israel, but the Church is the bride of the Lamb (see 2 Cor. 11. 2; Eph. 5. 32).

is not there. It is but a grand flash, a magnificant spectacle before the final crash and overthrow.

But who is the scarlet Beast on whom the woman sits, from whom she derives her material strength, and through whom she enforces her commands? The political government of the world, its glory and greatness are indicated by the *scarlet* colour.* Without doubt it is the world power of Rome that is here referred to, revived in grandeur and greatness, and controlled by Satan. The Beast is first named in the Apocalypse in chapter 11, and is abruptly introduced into the history as a subject well known and understood.

3.—"**Full of names of blasphemy, having seven heads and ten horns.**" In chapter 13. 1 the seven heads, or complete governing authority of the empire, have upon them "*names* of blasphemy" (see margin of the Authorised Version). Here the Beast itself is said to be "*full* of names of blasphemy" (chap. 17. 3). It is not simply that the executive of the empire is given over to many and varied expressions of a blasphemous character, but the empire itself, in all its parts, is wholly corrupt; while open, blatant blasphemy characterises it throughout. "Names of blasphemy" intimate many and varied forms of rebellion and self-will against God.

3.—"**Having seven heads and ten horns.**" In the earlier notice of the "seven heads" upon the Beast there is indicated the completeness of administrative power (chap. 13. 1), but here, as is shown in the explanation (chap. 17. 10), the heads represent successive forms of government. The horns represent royal personages (v. 12). In chapter 12. 3 the dragon has seven heads and ten horns; the former being crowned,† not the latter. In chapter 13. 1 the Beast has ten horns and seven heads, the horns in this case being crowned. In our chapter, however, neither heads nor horns are crowned. The royal personages seen in the vision were not in full possession of their royal dignity; thus, in the angel's explanation of the ten-horned Beast, we read, "And the ten horns which thou sawest are ten kings, which have not yet received a kingdom, but receive authority as kings one hour with the Beast" (v. 12); that is, they reign in royal authority in conjunction with the Beast, the little horn of Daniel 7. 8, 20 being their

* The three colours in the *gate* of the Court of the Tabernacle, in the *door* of the Tabernacle, and in the *veil* dividing the holy from the most holy were blue, purple, and scarlet. The first points to Christ in His heavenly character; the second to His sufferings on earth; and the third to His assumption of the government and glory of the earth in a coming day.

† In these passages the word should read *diadems*, not "crowns." The former refers to the exercise of despotic, arbitrary power; the latter to limited monarchies—constitutional kingdoms.

master. As the actual reign of these ten kings is regarded as subsequent to the vision the horns are not crowned.

THE WOMAN IN HER GLORY.

4.—**"And the woman was clothed in purple and scarlet, and had ornaments of gold and precious stones and pearls."** Having had the state in the Beast, we again turn to witness the Church in the woman, and her ascendancy for a time over the civil power. She rides the Beast, and controls it for her own selfish ends and purposes. But she is by far the more dangerous of the two. The Beast openly blasphemes and persecutes the saints then standing for the rights of God. The woman is seductive and attractive, and having gathered to herself the weight and splendour of courts, palaces, and, in short, the tinsel glory of the world, she sits as a queen, and wins by her arts and seductive flatteries the heart of Christendom. God is displaced in the thoughts of men.

Her *vesture*, purple and scarlet, is that which particularly distinguishes pope and cardinal. Her *ornaments* of gold, precious stones, and pearls are amongst the chief symbols of papal pride and glory. Silver is not here named. In the services of the papal Church silver is being discarded for gold. But whatever resemblance there may be between Babylon and the Romish Church, the great point is that the woman is arrayed and decked out in the world's tinsel and finery. She surrounds herself with what the world regards as its highest and most valued possessions and material wealth; that, too, which it lives and labours to amass and accumulate.

4.—**"Having a golden cup in her hand full of abominations, and the unclean things of her fornication."** Babylon as a system is covered with an external grandeur and glory that attracts the natural heart and imagination of man, dazzling and bewildering him. But, worse still, she holds in her hand a golden cup. How tempting! The cup is of gold, but its contents reveal the depths of iniquity to which she has sunk. The scarlet Beast, the colour of the dragon (chap. 12. 3), was *full* of names, or expressions, of blasphemy, so here the woman's cup was "*full* of abominations, and the unclean things of her fornication." These two evils, idolatry and corruption, characterise the last phase of the professing Church on earth. "Abominations" refer to idolatry (2 Kings 23. 13; Isa. 44. 19; Ezek. 16. 36), and "fornication" to gross corruption (chaps. 2. 21; 9. 21). Idolatry and the worst forms of wickedness characterise the woman. Her cup is full of horrible evils. The climax has been reached. These things might have been looked for in the midst of the heathen, but for Christendom, *now* the scene of light, of grace, and truth, to become the very hotbed and cesspool of all that is religiously filthy and vile is indeed a marvel. Yet this chapter sketches in plain word and symbol the future of these lands. *Now* the Holy Ghost dwells in the professing Church, *then* Satan will fill it, both with his presence and awful deeds. We thank God for the sure testimony of Jesus that the Church which He builds is invulnerable (Matt. 16. 18), and its ultimate triumph secured (Eph. 5. 27).

BABYLON A MOTHER.

5.—"**Upon her forehead a name written, Mystery, Babylon the Great, the mother of the harlots, and of the abominations of the earth.**" The shameless character of Babylon is next shown. Her name is publicly borne, indelibly stamped upon her forehead, so that all may read and understand the true character of this awful system—a travesty of the true Church. Her name is a compound one. First, "Mystery."* The general usage of the word in the New Testament signifies what is now revealed, but had hitherto been a secret (Matt. 13; Eph. 5. 32, etc.). The Church is subject to Christ; the woman is subject to none. She usurps Christ's place of supremacy over the nations. She is indeed a mystery. She should have stood for God and truth, but now she is witnessed as the embodiment of error, and of all that is morally vile and wicked. Second, "Babylon the Great." It is a huge system of spiritual evil. Great and bad as Babylon was, the enslaver of God's people of old, so bad that its doom is irrevocable (Jer. 51. 64), yet it is exceeded by far in its spiritual counterpart, the great Babylon of the Apocalypse. The former was guilty, but the latter much more so. In Babylon the Great we witness the gathering up in one vast system all the evils which in past times have gone to wreck the Church. This is the culmination. The evils which have ever afflicted Christendom are here focused. The last days of the Church on earth are her worst. Christianity is the combined production of the Godhead, but Christendom is here viewed as the vilest thing on earth. Truly, the woman is entitled to the appellation "Babylon the Great." That which should be her shame and sin she publicly

* See remarks on chapters 1. 20; 10. 7.

glories in. Third, "The mother of the harlots, and of the abominations of the earth." Her offspring are numerous. She is the parent, the source of each and every religious system which courts the world. Religious idolatry of every shape and form, every ensnaring thing and object; in short, systems, things, doctrines, and objects used by Satan to turn men from God are here traced to their source—Great Babylon. The moral features of Babylon are ever the same —unchanged through all the ages. Here she is seen in her worst, because in her last and closing hours, the parent of all that is morally loathsome. This, then, is the character publicly borne by the woman, just as in ancient times it was the practice in certain places for harlots to bear their name and evil reputation on their foreheads. If the admirers of the woman fail to see her true character because intoxicated with her finery and grandeur the spiritual do not.

THE WOMAN DRUNK WITH BLOOD, AND THE WONDER OF THE SEER.

6.—"**And I saw the woman drunk with the blood of the saints, and with the blood of the witnesses of Jesus. And I wondered seeing her, with great wonder.**" One could readily understand the hatred of the pagan powers to the followers and witnesses of Jesus, but that the woman, the Church of these days and times, should herself shed the blood of God's saints is indeed a cause of wonder to the Seer. She it was who devised the hellish cruelties of the Middle Ages. The secular power is an instrument in the hands of the woman. The real instigator, the power behind the civil authority, is the whore. In her skirts is found the blood so wantonly shed in all ages. Babylon inherits the guilt of every previous persecuting religious power (Matt. 23. 35). She has never judged the past. Her history is black enough, and stained in every page with blood, the blood of those dear to God and Christ. The Seer marvels at the awful sight. The Church is here witnessed as the most wicked thing on earth. This, then, is what the professing Church is coming to. Nothing can exceed her in grandeur, in greatness, in idolatry, in filthiness, and in cruelty. "I wondered seeing her, with great wonder." The earth dwellers are drunk with her wine (v. 2), and the woman herself is drunk with blood. These two, *i.e.*, the apostates and the woman, are the worst then on the face of the earth, and on both the full fury of God's indignation bursts forth in flames of inextinguishable wrath.

THE MYSTERY OF THE WOMAN AND THE BEAST EXPLAINED (VERSES 7-18).

7.—"**And the angel said to me, Why hast thou wondered? I will tell thee the mystery of the woman, and of the Beast which carries her, which has the seven heads and the ten horns.**" We have had the mystery of Christ and the Church (Eph. 5), now the angel is going to explain to the Seer, and through him to us, the mystery of the woman and the Beast.

THE BEAST: FOUR PHASES OF ITS HISTORY.

8.—"**The Beast which thou sawest was, and is not, and is about to come up out of the abyss, and go into destruction: and they who dwell on the earth, whose names are not written in the book of life from the foundation of the world, shall wonder, seeing the Beast, that it was, and is not, and shall be present.**" Here we have the history of the greatest empire the world has ever beheld compressed into four crisp sentences, as remarkable for their brevity as for their truth. Two of them are yet future. The woman and the Beast are distinct. The former is the ecclesiastical power; the latter the civil authority. Both are viewed as wicked and apostate. The woman is viewed in the vision as in the zenith of her prosperity, proud, seductive, and murderous. She is on the highest pinnacle of pride and power just previous to her downfall. The Beast is viewed as about to enter on the third phase of its history—coming *out* of the abyss. This most awful feature is to be added to its *human* rise and history—Satan brings it out of the prison-house of demons, out of the darkness and wickedness of that domain where his authority reigns supreme.

The angel turns from the woman to the Beast when the vision is explained. John would cease to wonder at the appalling picture.

(1) The ancient empire beheld in vision **was**; that is, it existed in its imperial form in John's day, and on till its destruction in A.D. 476.

(2) "And **is not.**" It has no present political existence. The kingdoms which composed it of course remain, but the empire as such no longer exists. Modern Europe, with its many conflicting interests, jealousies, and separate kingdoms, is the result of the complete break-up of the once undivided empire of the Cæsars. The western part of the empire, which fell last, is by far the guiltiest, as being the scene of christian light and grace. These two

phases of the empire are simple matters of history, but the remaining features are prophetic, and are only written in the pages of the Sacred Volume. God lifts the veil, and we see, after the lapse of many centuries, the empire once more filling the gaze of men—an astonishment to an apostate Christendom.

(3) "Is about to come up **out of the abyss**." Satan will revive the empire, and then stamp his own character upon it. The human rise of the Beast must be carefully distinguished from its satanic revival in the midst of the seventieth prophetic week at the epoch of Satan's expulsion from Heaven (chap. 12). The Seer beholds it in vision on the eve of its revival. "Is *about* to come up." The abyss produces this monster of iniquity—the Beast. Heaven opens and gives forth the Church—the bride of the Lamb.

(4) "**Go into destruction**." This is the final phase of Gentile power. Rome came into existence 753 B.C. It passed through many trials, weathered many political storms, till it reached the zenith of its glory in the time of Christ. Its connection with Christ and Judah is the great crisis in the history of the empire. The Beast in its representative crucified the Lord after thrice declaring His innocence. Subsequently the blood of the people was shed in such multitudes that millions were involved in the most awful slaughter recorded in history, while the miserable remnants were either sold in such numbers that the slave markets were glutted with the human merchandise, and purchasers could not be found, or dispersed throughout the world. God remembers these deeds. The hour of vengeance has arrived. The Beast is consigned to the lake of fire. Final destruction overtakes the once mighty empire of the Cæsars.

SATANIC REAPPEARANCE OF THE EMPIRE

When the empire reappears in its last and satanic form it will be an object of universal wonder, save to the redeemed. What a state of things we have arrived at! Satan brings out of the darkness of the pit a power which he fashions and controls, outwardly like the empire, yet diabolically featured. Men then will wonder and worship both Satan and his human instruments (chap. 13. 4, 12). The elect had their names written in the book of life *from* the foundation of the world. Ah! these future times were all thought of and provided for in the foresight of God. This book is the same as that of chapter 13. 8, only there we are told that the book belongs to the slain Lamb. We read of another book of life in chapter 3. 5; there, however, it is the book of christian *profession*, true and false, hence some names will be erased and others stand. But in our chapter the book, or register of life, is that of *reality*, hence no name can be blotted out. All within the wide domain of Christendom shall be carried away in wonder at the reappearance of this marvellous phenomena—all save the elect. To such the true character of the Beast will be apparent.

MYSTERY OF THE BEAST.

9-13.—"**Here is the mind that has wisdom: the seven heads are seven mountains, whereon the woman sits. And there are seven kings: five have fallen, one is, the other has not yet come; and when he comes he must remain (only) a little while. And the Beast that was, and is not, he also is an eighth, and is of the seven, and goes into destruction. And the ten horns which thou sawest are ten kings, which have not yet received a kingdom, but receive authority as kings one hour with the Beast. These have one mind, and give their power and authority to the Beast.**" Of all the subjects embraced within the circle of Biblical revelation we know of none which has so occupied unintelligent minds, and produced such a wild crop of the merest conjecture as that of prophecy. Surely in all that concerns the future sobriety of thought is needful. In the domain of prophecy human learning is nigh useless. Human wisdom which would deduce facts and principles from the past or present is of no avail here. The future is alone unfolded in the Holy Scriptures. The gravest mistakes in the interpretation of the prophecies have been made, not by the ignorant multitude, but by learned men. We are absolutely dependent on the teaching of the Holy Scriptures for any knowledge we possess of coming events. God alone can unfold the future (Isa. 41. 21-23). Hence the force of the prefatory words, "Here is the mind that has wisdom." True wisdom takes its stand at the threshold of prophetic inquiry, and reverently asks, "*What is written*?"* and to that, and that only, yields implicit subjection. To the further explanation of the vision the wise are now directed. The two prominent features of the Beast which carried the woman are its seven heads and ten horns (vv. 3, 7), which occupy the chief place in the explanation. The heads are first named. There is a double application of the symbol "seven heads."

---

* "Of the dark parts of Revelation," says Warburton, "there are two sorts: one which may be cleared up by the studious application of well-employed talents; the other, which will always reside within the shadow of God's throne, where it would be impiety to intrude." *History* is open to the natural man. *Prophecy* can alone be understood by the spiritually wise.

ROME AND THE PAPACY.

(1) **"The seven heads are seven mountains, whereon the woman sits."** The seven-hilled city of Rome* is here indicated as the seat and centre of the woman's almost universal authority and influence. It is where the papacy has been located and has flourished, more or less, for 1500 years. The papacy is now slowly recovering from the wounds inflicted upon it; first in the sixteenth century, and then in our own times stripped of its temporal power. Its vitality is wonderful. Its energies are now concentrated in winning back to its fold the nations of Europe. The conversion of England is a dazzling project, and an event to be expected within a measurable time—so thinks and says the papacy. That the peoples of modern enlightened Europe will ultimately be gathered under the sway of the woman seems an evident truth from our chapter, if a sad and sorrowful one. The mighty work of the Reformation in its general and outward results is disappearing, while the acceptance of Romish principles and practices is steadily gaining ground. The persistent and insidious advance of popery in every department of life—political, social, and religious—is an alarming factor in the present situation. Protestantism as a whole is supremely indifferent. The old war cry, "No popery," cannot now rouse the nation. It is asleep. The higher critics with their infidel and destructive criticism have undermined faith in the Holy Scriptures; while the efforts of true Christians to stem the torrent of popish error are paralysed owing, in the first place, to the multiplicity of sects, in which combined action is rendered impossible, and, further, because of the growing indifference to what is of God.

POLITICAL HISTORY OF THE BEAST.

(2) **"And there are seven kings,"** *i.e.*, heads, or forms of civil and political government. The local reference to Rome in verse 9 is undoubted. But a further and additional explanation is offered. The seven heads on the Beast represent seven successive forms of government from the rise of the fourth universal empire on through its history till its end.

---

* "The seven-hilled city" is a term common enough in the history of Rome, especially in its earliest ages. It was one familiar in the social intercourse of the people, as also in its literature. Roman historians and poets seemed proud in so designating their city.

Says Wordsworth, "The unanimous voice of Roman poetry during more than five hundred years, beginning with the age of John, proclaimed Rome as *the seven-hilled city*." He also adds, "On the imperial medals of that age, which are still preserved, we see Rome figured as a woman on seven hills, precisely as she is represented in the Apocalypse."

10.—"**Five have fallen.**"* These are Kings, Consuls, Dictators, Decemvirs, and Military Tribunes.

10.—"**One is.**" This is the sixth, or imperial form of government set up by Julius Caesar, and under which John was banished to Patmos under Domitian. The previous forms of authority had ceased. The first emperor, Julius, absorbed the power covered by the old names under which Rome had been governed, and commenced the long and imperial line which became extinct in the year A.D. 476.

10.— **'The other has not yet come.**" Thus between the dissolution of the empire and its future diabolic reappearance many centuries have elapsed. "When he comes he must remain (only) a little while." This is the seventh head. It is the rise of the fallen empire under new conditions as presented in chapter 13. 1. When the Beast next comes upon the scene it will be characterised by the completeness of administrative authority of a blasphemous kind, and will be formed of ten kingdoms, each having its separate monarch, yet all in subordination to the great Gentile chief who will control the empire and hold all with a firm grasp. The brief continuance of this special form of government is plainly stated. "A little while" marks the duration of the anomalous condition of things under the revived empire, yet worse is to follow.

11.—"**And the beast that was, and is not, he also is an eighth, and is of the seven.**" The gigantic confederation of Rome is here regarded in its essential features as ever the same. He is an "eighth." We have here an advance upon the historical revival of the Beast (chap. 13. 1). For the three years and a half preceding the Advent of the Lord in power and glory the Beast is dominated and controlled by Satan. He had revived it out of the abyss. The Beast in its last and worst state comes out of the abyss, as distinct from its rise at the first (Dan. 7. 1), or its future human revival (Rev. 13. 1). It thus presents a complete picture by itself, and is thereby entitled to the appellation an "eighth." Its diabolical character as revived by Satan accounts for the use of the ordinal. We have the *human* reappearance of the empire in chapter 13, and its *hellish* revival in chapter 17.

11.—"**Is of the seven.**" There will be certain features peculiar to the Beast in the last two stages of its history. Probably the form of power under the seventh head will be

---

*** "Fallen," or "fell," intimates the ruin or destruction of a system or kingdom (chaps. 14. 8; 16. 19). The death of an individual ruler would not be so spoken of. Hence the term "kings" in our passage signifies the ruling authority for the time being. The four beasts of Daniel 7 are said to be four kings (v. 17). Thus the term *kings* must not be confined in its application to royal personages. The context in each case must determine.**

continued, and in some other respects the last holder of Gentile power will tread in the steps of his predecessor. Thus he will be of the seven, yet an eighth as a distinctive person. We may here remark that the Beast and its personal ruler are so vitally connected that the two are spoken of in interchangeable terms; thus the Beast perishes and is thrown, in the person of its last great chief, into the lake of fire. The last sovereign ruler stamps his own character upon the empire. They can be regarded separately as in Daniel 7, or identical as in our chapter.

11.—"**Goes into destruction,**" or perdition. This is accomplished at the commencement of the millennial reign, and is graphically described in chapter 19. 17-21. The fowls of Heaven are summoned to the "supper of the great God." They are called to feed and feast upon the great and mighty of the earth. The two great chiefs, heads respectively of the secular and religious powers, are consigned *alive* to the lake of fire; their subordinates and armies everlastingly perish. The first five heads fell in succession. Then the sixth came to a violent end; the seventh is merged in the eighth, which suffers a judgment more awful than history records. This head is identified with the Beast itself, and hence if it is destroyed the Beast must go into utter ruin (compare with Dan. 7. 11).

Having had the "seven heads" explained, we are now informed as to "the ten horns" (v. 12). These horns refer to royal persons. The term "horn" denotes *power* in the abstract (v. 6; Lam. 2. 3); but as used here it refers to *kings*. The ten horns therefore represent as many distinct royal personages or their kingdoms. Another has tersely said: "The ten kingdoms shall be *contemporaneous* in contradistinction to the seven heads which were *successive*." But the ten kingdoms which existed as to actual territory are here viewed as coming into power *with* the Beast. See also verse 16, not the ten horns "*upon* the beast," but the ten horns "*and* the beast" (R.V.). They do not exist as *separate* kingdoms or nationalities. There are ten, but they are coexistent with the reign of the Beast. They "received authority as kings one hour with the Beast." When the Beast reappears on the arena of history it will do so in a ten-kingdom form. It disappeared in A.D. 476, but will next come up in a form hitherto unknown in history. The revived empire will consist of ten kingdoms with their respective chiefs. The duration of the reign of these kings is measured by the reign of the Beast. But not only are these kingdoms in existence during the time that the Beast plays his terrible *rôle*, but they are subordinate to him. Willingly they place themselves in absolute subjection to the Beast. "These have one mind, and give their power and authority to the Beast." The Beast and the horns are contemporary, but the latter bow implicitly to the will of the former. When the empire was broken up, separate kingdoms were constituted—historical fact—but our prophecy demands the existence of the Beast *and* the ten kingdoms, the latter subservient to the former.

WAR WITH THE LAMB.

14.—"**These shall make war with the Lamb, and the Lamb shall overcome them; for He is Lord of lords and King of kings: and they that are with Him called, and chosen, and faithful.**" Here is recorded the final public act of the Beast and his allies. The conflict itself is fully described in chapter 19. 19-21. The angel here simply notes the fact, passing over many intervening events. The war has not been actually entered upon, but it is anticipated. Its issue is in no wise doubtful. "The Lamb shall overcome them." Victory is assured ere the conflict is entered upon, for the mighty Conqueror is King of all who reign, and Lord of all who exercise authority. He is supreme. All power in Heaven and on earth is His (Matt. 28. 18). Oh, what madness and folly for men and governments to enter the lists with God's Lamb Who will publicly wield the authority of Jehovah's throne! How touching the blessed association of the Lamb with the mighty King —tenderness and power combined (chap. 5. 5, 6).

14.—"**They that are with Him.**" The militant hosts, the heavenly armies, consist of all the redeemed then in Heaven. There will be other companies of saved persons in Heaven besides the Church (Heb. 12. 23). The whole body of heavenly saints accompany their Lord through the opened Heaven, and down to crush the confederated opposition to the rights of the Lamb. For this universal gathering of heavenly saints see Jude 14; Zechariah 14. 5; Revelation 19. 14. In the morning of the Lord's triumphal return "all the holy angels" shall swell His triumph (Matt. 25. 31; Heb. 1. 6). But "they that are with Him" must be confined to saints only. *Angels* have their part in the war in Heaven (Rev. 12. 7). *Saints* alone form the conquering army of the Lamb.

Those who take part in this conflict and who serve under such a renowned Leader are each and all spoken of as "called, and chosen, and faithful." Called in time (2 Tim. 1. 9); chosen in eternity (Eph. 1. 4); and proved faithful in all and every relation of life, and that even unto death (Matt. 25. 21-23; Rev. 2. 10). These epithets, called, chosen, and faithful can only strictly apply to saints.

INTERPRETATION OF THE WATERS.

15.—"**The waters which thou sawest, where the harlot sits, are peoples, and multitudes,* and nations, and tongues.**" The *woman* sits upon the Beast (v. 3). The *harlot* sits upon or beside many waters (v. 1). Having the explanation of these "many waters" before us we can the more readily understand the immense and universal influence which the apostate Church then exercises. The peoples and nations, organised and unformed, specially outside the limits of the existing Roman world, are ensnared and captivated by the allurements of the harlot. She sits enthroned in greatness, and richly adorned with the glories of the world, but without the affections of her deluded followers. There is display, but no reality; no heart for Christ, whose bride she impiously professes to be. Her own exaltation, and that to the spiritual ruin of the deluded millions who received her favours and court her smile, is her sole aim. Her supreme regard is for *gold* (chap. 18. 12); her least concern is for the *souls* of men (v. 13). The four divisions of the human family are employed to set forth the far-reaching influence of the woman (chaps. 7. 9; 11. 9).

DESTRUCTION OF THE HARLOT.

16, 17.—"**And the ten horns which thou sawest, and the Beast, these shall hate the harlot, and shall make her desolate and naked, and shall eat her flesh, and shall burn her with fire. For God has given to their hearts to do His mind, and to act with one mind, and to give their kingdom to the Beast, until the words of God shall be fulfilled.**" "The ten horns *and* the Beast" (see R.V. for this important emendation). The ten kingdoms combine with the Beast in hatred to the whore. What a change! It is evident that the Beast and confederate kings exist after the destruction of Babylon, as they, *i.e.*, the Beast and the horns, are the human instruments in inflicting the Lord's vengeance on that guilty and apostate system. The secular power is reserved for destruction at the hands of the Lord in Person and at His Coming in power (chap. 19). The ten horns act in conjunction with the Beast in hatred to the whore. All were united in supporting the claims and pretensions

* "Usually translated 'crowds.' "—"New Translation."

of the woman, and *now* they are equally agreed in effecting her ruin.

The world's glory and might is but a passing dream. All not founded on God withers, fades, and perishes. Babylon, when on the highest pinnacle of pride and greatness, in the zenith of her glory, is cut down. Her ruin is complete and final. In righteous retribution her partners in crime become the active instruments in her political overthrow and displacement from power over the nations.

There seems a gradation in the punishment meted out to the harlot. First, *hated*; this refers to the loathing and disgust with which her late confederates and supporters regard her. Second, made *desolate*; despoiled of her wealth, and utterly wasted (chap. 18. 19). Third, *naked*; stripped of her purple and scarlet robes, she appears before all in her true character as a shameless and abandoned woman (Ezek. 23. 29; Rev. 3. 18), her moral nakedness and shame apparent to all. Fourth, "*eat her flesh*;" there is significance in the fact that flesh is in the plural; the abundance of her wealth and all she gloried in is devoured by her late admirers, now her bitterest enemies (compare with James 5. 3; Psa. 27. 2; Micah 3. 2, 3). Fifth "*burn her with fire*;" utter social and political ruin is here indicated. The main element in the destruction of the literal Babylon was water (Jer. 51). The mystical city of that name "shall be utterly burned with fire" (chap. 18. 8). Both Babylons are doomed to everlasting desolation. The one has fallen; the other is sure to follow. There is "no healing of the bruise."

UNION OF THE POWERS IN MIND AND ACTION.

The powers who destroy Babylon glut their vengeance on the guilty system which had so long enslaved them. But here the veil is drawn aside, and we find that whatever *they* thought they were simply carrying out the divine will. God had decreed the destruction of the worst system on the face of the earth, and the Beast and his vassal kings are His instruments in doing so. "God has given to their hearts to do His mind." Note the distinction, "their *hearts*" and "His *mind*." Heartily they enter on the work of destruction, but, after all, they unknowingly accomplish the set purpose of God. The heart and mind of the destroying powers are united. They love the service to which, while they know it not, they have been divinely set apart, and they execute it with fixed determination. Such seems to be the thought conveyed in our text.

17.—Further, the ten kings "**give their kingdom to**

the Beast until the words of God shall be fulfilled." There is absolute subjection to the Beast. Unable to maintain separate and independent kingdoms the ten kings voluntarily place themselves and their kingdoms under the rule of the Beast, and from henceforth he becomes their master, allowing them but the shadow of royalty. The real power is in the hands of the Beast (chap. 13. 2-7). What is attributed to the kings in verse 13 of our chapter is traced to God as the source in verse 17. All the movements amongst the powers of Europe are in the coming crisis an accomplishment of the prophetic "words of God." We would further add that the complete subjection of the ten kings to the Beast, as indicated in verse 13, is a condition subsequent to the destruction of Babylon. They had previously given their power to the woman, now it is transferred to the Beast. The duration of the reign of the Beast in the last great crisis defines the length of time when the ten horns, or kings, exercise sovereignty* (v. 12). But that describes a state both previous and subsequent to the downfall of Babylon, whereas the abject slavery of the powers to the Beast is consequent upon and subsequent to the utter ruin of the Romish system.

God works unseen, but not the less truly, in all the political changes of the day. The astute statesman, the clever diplomatist, is simply an agent in the Lord's hands. He knows it not. Self-will and motives of policy may influence in action, but God is steadily working towards one end, *i.e.*, to exhibit the heavenly and earthly glories of His Son. Thus, instead of kings and statesmen thwarting God's purpose they unconsciously forward it. God is not indifferent, but is behind the scenes of human action. The doings of the future ten kings in relation to Babylon and the Beast—the ecclesiastical and secular powers—are not only under the direct control of God, but all is done in fulfilment of His words.

ROME, THE SEAT AND CENTRE OF THE WOMAN'S AUTHORITY.

18.—**"And the woman which thou sawest is the great city, which has kingship over the kings of the earth."** The papacy and Rome cannot be dissociated. Babylon in the future is the full-blown development of the papal system, and finds her home naturally enough in Rome, where she has ever found it. *There* the most

* "Receive power (authority) as kings *one hour* with the beast" **signifies** ***at one and the same time***; that is, the horns and Beast exist together, whether the time be limited or prolonged

blasphemous doctrines have been taught, and *there*, too, claims more than human have been advanced. There will be a fuller development of papal error in the coming apostasy. Rome, therefore, is the city here referred to. The woman is the city, not Rome actually, but the system which has its seat in Rome, the Romish Church or system, the delegate of Satan in religious corruption (chap. 16. 19), and from thence till her destruction she exercises her baneful influence over the peoples of Christendom. The last verse of this deeply interesting chapter states a truth simple, yet important withal.

An outline of the truths and subjects unfolded in the chapter may prove useful to some.

THE CHAPTER REVIEWED.

The immediate design of this and the next chapter is to supplement fully the two previous, but scant, notices of Babylon (chaps. 14. 8; 16. 19). Here a full and detailed description of her character and doom is given. But there is another subject of judgment besides that of Babylon. The Beast, the apostate secular power, occupies no unimportant place in this prophecy. The two main subjects then are Babylon, the religious system; and the Beast, the civil apostate power; the former occupying the chief place. The Beast, more prominent elsewhere (chap. 13), is here regarded as secondary in interest to Babylon, the harlot.

The chapter is divided into two parts: first, a vision beheld by the Seer (vv. 1-6); second, the interpretation of the vision by one of the Vial angels (vv. 7-18). We may here remark that the interpretation goes considerably beyond what was seen in the vision. The same principle obtains in Daniel 2 and in Matthew 13. The interpretation *adds* instruction to that found in dream, vision, or parable. The Seer first beheld the great whore ripe for judgment (v. 1). She is termed "great Babylon" because of the awful and widespread *confusion* of which she is the embodiment. She is also "the great whore" because of a frightful system of hypocrisy and lust over the souls and bodies of men. Her licentious character, moral of course, is indicated in the term "whore." She is called a woman because thereby is implied subjection (1 Cor. 11. 3). She assumes to be subject to Christ, as the Church *is* and delights to be (Eph. 5. 23-25). But in the case of the woman, her pretensions are hollow and unreal. She really cares nothing for Christ, nor will she bow to His headship or own His authority.

She sits upon or beside "many waters" (v. 1). These

waters signify vast multitudes of the human race (v. 15) over whom the woman has cast her spell, alluring them to everlasting ruin.

Then the kings and inhabitants of the earth are introduced in their respective relations to the whore (v. 2). This seems a more intimate connection than is indicated in verse 1. *There* the influence was universal; *here* is intimated direct intercourse with the whore. We gather, too, that the world at large is in view in the first verse of the chapter; in the second Christendom only. "The kings of the earth" are not the same as the "ten kings" of verse 12; these latter are kings of the Roman empire, the former signify the chiefs and leaders of Christendom generally.

Next, the woman is seen sitting upon a "scarlet Beast." This is the same Beast and the same power as that presented in chapter 13. The ancient empire of Rome, defunct for many centuries, is here witnessed on the scene of prophecy covered with the glory and government of the world, as indicated by the scarlet colour. The woman, too, is arrayed in scarlet, and the dragon bears the same colour (chap. 12. 3). How eagerly the pomp and glory of this world are sought after! The imperial power is subservient to the woman. The Beast, to whom the dragon commits universal authority, is the mere servant and tool of the woman. The secular power supports her arrogant pretensions.

But the Beast is further described as "*full* of names of blasphemy." Bad as the woman is she is never guilty of this daring and open character of impiety. Deceit, corruption, violence, pride, and shameless evils of every kind are charged home upon ecclesiastical Babylon—the whore. Blasphemy and the public denial of God and of Christ are acts of which the Beast is guilty. The names of blasphemy on the heads of the Beast (chap. 13. 1) stamp the executive, or governing authority, with this awful character of guilt, but evidently we have here the whole body politic—chiefs and people—characterised by it. Fear of God is gone. The empire in all its parts is wholly given up to this most horrible iniquity.

Then the Beast is said to have "seven heads and ten horns," several times repeated. The mention of the Beast in chapter 13. 1 is in similar terms to that of the dragon in chapter 12. 3. In the case of the *dragon* the heads, not the horns, are crowned; in the notice of the *Beast* the horns are crowned, while the heads bear the names or public expressions of blasphemy; in chapter 17 neither heads nor horns are crowned (v. 3). Such then is the general character and description of the Beast, the main supporter of the false and corrupt religious system dominating the empire, and extending her influence throughout Christendom. It does seem, at first sight, strange that the Beast—on which such a liberal grant of power is conferred by Satan (chap. 13. 4-7)—should be found a willing slave at the feet of the woman, but her dazzling splendour and seductive influence are like silken cords binding even the potent chief of the empire to the footstool of her throne.

Having had the Beast before us, we are turned again to view the woman, clothed and adorned with all that the world esteems of highest value (v. 4). She holds a golden cup in her hand; she should have been *that* in the Lord's hand. The cup is "full of abominations (idolatry) and the unclean things of her fornication."* All who drink of her cup, and millions do, are morally ruined. Then upon her forehead is stamped her name and character. She bears on her sacerdotal brow the name "Mystery," of iniquity, surely! The second part of the title, "Babylon the Great," speaks of the havoc the woman has wrought. She has filled Christendom with innumerable evils, and brought in hopeless confusion. The third part of the name, or title, of the woman is perhaps the worst of all: "The mother of the harlots, and of the abominations of the earth." Every system which copies the ways and imitates the actions of the woman, imbibing her doctrines and adopting her liturgy, and generally borrowing from or conforming to the Romish Church, now or then, must be regarded as her offspring. She is the mother, or source, of every evil religious system.

But she is a bloody system, as well as a morally licentious one. "I saw the woman drunk with the blood of the saints, and with the blood of the witnesses of Jesus" (v. 6). Papal Rome far exceeded pagan Rome in cruelty and bloodshed; and, besides, she is far more guilty as knowing better. She professed to be the spouse of Christ, and yet murdered at will those redeemed by the blood of the Lamb; no doubt the Romish Church believed that in killing the saints she was doing God service (John 16. 2), but it just shows the awful delusion which had judicially overtaken her. The wonder of the Seer was not caused by the Beast's persecution (chap. 13. 7), but by that of the woman, the professed spouse of Christ, although not she, but the Beast, actually puts the saints to death. But the woman is the power behind.

Then in the second part of the chapter the "mystery

*** Tyre, not Babylon, of old is charged with fornication; this at once shows what the character of the evil is, viewed morally.**

of the woman and of the Beast which carries her" is explained. It is a double mystery—the woman *and* the Beast; a travesty of the New Testament mystery "concerning Christ *and* the Church." In the mystery of our chapter the *woman* is first named; in that of Ephesians *Christ*, and rightly so.

The mystery of the Beast is first explained and shown under four conditions (v. 8). It "*was.*" The Beast existed as one vast consolidated empire under a long succession of imperial rulers. "*Is not.*" It has now no political existence; of course the countries and territories once within the empire remain, but the empire as such came to an inglorious end, A.D. 476. The ancient empire of world-wide fame and extent has for many centuries ceased to exist. "*Is about to come up out of the abyss.*" Its historical and yet future rise out of the *sea* (chap. 13. 1) is not the point here; comes out of the *abyss* intimates the epoch at which we have arrived and of which the chapter treats. The Apocalypse gives the history of the last prophetic half week only. "*And go into destruction,*" or perdition. This is the final and everlasting doom of the Beast (chap. 19. 20)—cast into the lake of fire *alive* with his fellow in crime the False Prophet; their master the devil will join them in the same awful place of misery a thousand years afterwards (chap. 20. 10). The resurrection of the Beast is a cause of wonder to all save the elect (v. 8). Twice the guilty and deluded world wonders, and both times in connection with the reappearance of the Beast on the platform of history (chaps. 13. 3; 17. 8).

"The seven heads are seven mountains;" these refer to the hills on which Rome reposes.* The woman sits on the Beast, and on the seven mountains, *i.e.*, the seven-hilled city of Rome. Rome is so closely interwoven with the life and growth of the papacy that to separate them would be to deal the Romish system a blow from which she could not well recover.

But, further, the seven heads also signify the various and successive forms of government beheld in the "eternal city." The heads are "seven kings," of which five are fallen. The five fallen heads have been applied to the successive kingdoms of Egypt, Assyria, Babylonia, Greece, and Persia; others consider the reference is to the first five emperors of Rome, as Augustus, Tiberius, Caligula, Claudius, and Nero. The first hypothesis cannot be right, for it is *the* Beast, *i.e.*, the Roman empire—whose condemnation of Christ and dispersion of Judah makes her pre-eminently guilty—which is before us in the pro-

* Palestine, Nierinal, Aventine, Caelian, Viminal, Esquiline, Janiculan.

phecy. Nor can the second theory be right, for the heads are *different* forms of government. There might have been some ground for terming these emperors "horns," but "heads" they cannot be. They each and all represent *one* head or form of government, viz., the imperial. After the mention of the five fallen phases of civil and political government the Seer proceeds, "one is." That is the imperial form of rule which existed in John's day—the sixth head. But another has yet "to come"—the seventh. Its continuance is but for a brief season, as the eighth, or last, phase of the empire is *the* point of interest. Satan's man and king is an eighth, having his rise out of the abyss. He is thus a distinctive object, and fully entitled to the appellation "an eighth," yet he is "of the seven" (v. 11), as the same character of rule under the seventh head will be continued. The outward forms of government will undergo but little change under the last two phases of the empire respectively arising from the *sea* and from the *abyss*. But the sure judgment of God overtakes the guilty and apostate power. It "goes into destruction," twice repeated (vv. 8, 11).

Next, the ten horns of the Beast are explained (v. 12). These horns are kings, who come within the scope of action only at the same time and along with the Beast; the duration of his existence and reign determines theirs. The whole mind and purpose of these ten sovereigns is to yield themselves entirely to the will and service of the Beast (v. 13).

Then follows the war with the Lamb. The Beast and his confederate kings and armies on the one side, as against the Lamb in His might as Lord and King* of all, and His armies on the other side (v. 14). It is the same war, the same conflict, that is grandly described in chapter 19. 11-21. In our chapter (17) the last act of the Beast and his vassal kings is *anticipated*, not actually come. Other events transpire between the account of the closing struggle (chap. 17) and its actual place in the history (chap. 19).

The waters beheld by the Seer (v. 1) signify "peoples, and multitudes, and nations, and tongues" (v. 15). An immense moral influence extending far beyond the limits of the prophetic earth. The masses of mankind, organised and unformed, are brought under the influence of the harlot. "*The* many waters" (v. 1) draws the attention to the large and multitudinous following of the whore.

The ten horns, or kings, are now seen roused into a state of unusual activity. They, with the Beast, turn round upon

* In chapter 19. 16 the order in the titles is reversed. There it is *King* of kings and Lord of lords; here it is *Lord* of lords and King of kings.

the woman, whom they had hitherto upheld, and destroy her. They reduce her to a state of desolation, and grasp at her wealth. Europe, or at least the western part of it, is carried away for a time by the dazzling and meretricious display of the woman, but ultimately snaps the fetters and makes an end of her. They act in vengeful feeling, but, after all, it is God's will which they carry out (v. 17). The ten kings are now free to give their united authority to the Beast, so that he alone occupies the scene and sphere of prophecy till destroyed by the Lord. This goes on till "the words of God shall be fulfilled." In all this the ten kings are the prominent actors.

Then the Romish system, numbering more than 200,000,000 souls in her unholy communion, is identified with Rome itself, the city (v. 18). The verse is a simple statement of a well-known and generally acknowledged fact.

In bringing this review to a close we would draw attention to the contrast between the harlot of Satan and the bride of the Lamb. The former occupies chapters 17 and 18; the latter is the main subject of the chapters which follow. The woman and a city in both portions, but set in sharp contrast.

The worldly, or purely secular side of the woman, is specially treated of in the next chapter. The system represented by Babylon is a combination of worldly pride and religious pretension. Union with the world, which is enmity with God, is the whoredom of the woman.

One in commenting on this chapter has well written: "In the chapter he (the Seer) is awed by the contemplation of her splendour and her guilt, while in chapter 18 he describes the lamentation of the world over her fate in language of almost unparalleled sublimity and pathos."

CHAPTER XVIII.

THE FALL OF BABYLON: LAMENTATION ON EARTH; TRIUMPH IN HEAVEN.

THE ANGEL AND HIS CRY.

1, 2.—"**After these things I saw another angel descending out of the Heaven, having great authority: and the earth was lightened with his glory. And he cried with a strong voice, saying, Great Babylon has fallen, has fallen.**" Although the subject of Babylon is resumed in this chapter, yet it forms a distinct and subsequent revelation contained in vision. The phrase "after these things" (cp. chaps. 4. 1; 7. 1, 9) notes a new commencement, and introduces a new set of circumstances; it also serves to direct attention to the distinctive unity of the subject or subjects so prefaced. In this point of view the chapter is an interesting one. Babylon, of course, is in the forefront of both chapters 17 and 18, and we may also add in the first three verses of the following one. Here the Beast is not once named, nor the ten kings, so active in the destruction of Babylon. In this chapter the human agents disappear, and the ruin of that awful system of corruption is traced to God as the source. Babylon, neither as a *woman* in relation to the Beast nor as a *whore* in relation to Christendom, is mentioned in the vision—one as distinctive as that in the previous chapter. The fall of Babylon (chap. 17. 16) in its civil relations does not exhaust the judgment of God upon that organised system of evil (chap. 18. 4, last clause). But of this more anon.

1.—"**Another angel,**" in contrast to the Vial angels (chaps. 17. 1; 21. 9). "Descending out of the Heaven" intimates the heavenly character of the action, and the deep interest *there* taken in the character and fate of Babylon. "Having great authority." There are orders and degrees amongst the angelic hosts.* Some are more distinguished than others in service and in position. All are characterised by might (2 Thess. 1. 7; 2 Peter 2. 11), but on some is conferred special power to act for God in certain circumstances; others, again, have a defined authority within a circumscribed area, but *universal* authority is never ascribed to an angelic being. The Lord Jesus Christ as Man and Son is the appointed Heir of *all* things (Matt. 28. 18; 11. 27; Heb. 1. 2). As Creator, His claim to universal dominion is not a conferred one, but is sovereign and independent (Col. 1. 16), founded on the rights and glory of His Person as God.

* See page 179.

The angel in our text has "great authority," and is probably the angel to whom the judgment of Babylon is committed. Here he announces its fall, but as a preliminary to further and more awful dealing. The angel has ample authority conferred upon him to deal thoroughly with the subject on hand, namely, the most iniquitous religious system on earth. "The earth was lightened with his glory." This is a testimony that God is in the scene, that it is He Who is acting in judgment. The fall of Babylon was a public event—the smoke of her burning (v. 18) as it darkened the heavens proclaimed this far and near; but the earth lightened, not by the reflection of the sun, but by the glory of the descending angel, witnessed to the fact that, whoever the actors and agents might be, yet God, as the Righteous Judge, judges Babylon. Probably the angel here referred to is none other than Christ, the same as in chapters 8. 3 and 10. 1. Christ, the Angel-Priest, on behalf of His suffering remnant (chap. 8). Christ, the Angel-Redeemer, taking possession of His inheritance (chap. 10). Christ, the Angel-Avenger of His people, taking vengeance on Babylon (chap. 18).

2.—**"He cried with a strong voice."** This is a quality in which angels excel (Psa. 103. 20).* The cry of the angel was the welcome proclamation of Babylon's downfall, not anticipative, but as having actually taken place. "Great Babylon has fallen, has fallen." The fall of that mighty system which, while guilty of falsehood and treason against Christ, yet bore His Name is here publicly announced. This in the previous chapter was executed by the western powers. There we had the Beast, to whom the power or civil authority had been entrusted,† becoming for a time the willing slave of the woman. She sits upon it in pride, an object of wonder and of admiration to all, save to those whose eyes are opened through grace to discern her true character. But the power which is with the Beast, not with the woman, gets restless under restraint, and chafes under her intolerant sway. Her wealth, too, is eagerly coveted by the civil and apostate powers. The ten kingdoms and the Beast, the whole material strength of the empire, combine to effect her ruin. In this commission of vengeance upon the worst system of evil and tyranny the sun has ever looked down upon the confederate ten kings are even more active than the Beast

---

* See page 133.

† Nebuchadnezzar received his appointment as chief of the world in civil power *directly from God* (Dan. 2. 37, 38), the succeeding powers only came upon the scene providentially, but in their case no formal grant of power or authority was directly bestowed. In the last days of the fourth empire Satan endows it with his authority and seat and power (Rev. 13. 2). What a contrast between the two empires—the *first* and the *fourth*. God established the first! Satan establishes the fourth!

himself, *i.e.*, the little horn of Daniel 7. The woman is stripped of her possessions and wealth, which go to swell the respective treasuries of the great chiefs of the empire. The woman, or the system she represents, is brought down to the lowest depths of degradation, an object of scorn and contempt even to those who before sought her favours and courted her smile. She lies before us a wreck of her former self. The apostate civil authority has triumphed over her by brute force; *then* the ten kings yield themselves and their kingdoms up to the coarse and brutal will of the Beast. Bad as things are under the woman a worse condition will ensue under the unchecked will of the Beast satanically inspired.

ANNOUNCEMENT BY THE MIGHTY ANGEL.

2, 3.—Babylon "**has become the habitation of demons, and a hold of every unclean spirit, and a hold of every unclean and hated bird. Because all the nations have drunk of the wine of the fury of her fornication; and the kings of the earth have committed fornication with her, and the merchants of the earth have been enriched through the might of her luxury.**" This is the condition of Babylon *after* and consequent upon her political downfall. She was overthrown, not destroyed. This latter is sudden. "She shall be utterly burned with fire" (v. 8) is subsequent to the burning noted in the previous chapter (v. 16).

"**Has become.**" Babylon having lost her public place of supremacy, being torn to pieces by the very powers which once formed her strength, is reduced to a state of desolation described in language of unexampled force. The description is evidently borrowed from Isaiah 13. 21, 22, in which the grandest of the Hebrew prophets foretells the ruin of Babylon, once the proud mistress of the world, now the most debased of all cities; here we have the moral counterpart. This, then, is what the professed spouse of Christ "has become." There are three parts in the description which in the aggregate constitute an awful moral horror.

(1) "**The habitation of demons.**"* Their proper home is the abyss† (Luke 8. 31, R.V.). Who demons are, whether lost angels or the souls of lost men, or a class of lost and miserable beings by themselves, to whom future torment is known and assured, we know not.‡ What an

* We may remark that the word *satyrs* (Isa. 13. 21) is rendered in the LXX. *demons*.

† The reader who desires help on the demonology of the New Testament would do well to read "Critical Studies in St. Luke's Gospel: Its Demonology and Ebionitism," by Colin Campbell, B.D. (Blackwood & Sons).

‡ See an interesting paragraph, containing probably all that is known of demons, in "From Advent to Advent; or, The Outline of the Gospel according to St. Luke," by C. E. Stuart.

amazing thought that the abyss in the underground world, and the professed spouse of Christ on earth, should both be regarded as the habitation of demons! We could readily understand the abyss as the dwelling of these emissaries of Satan, but that the professing Church should become *that* almost exceeds belief.

(2) **"A hold of every unclean spirit."** Satan establishes his spiritual forces in the ruined Church system. He makes it a hold, or stronghold, which is the force of the word, and thither the uncleanness and foulness of the pit congregate. There the doleful cry is heard and wicked deed perpetrated, "*every* (foul or) unclean spirit" gathers to ruined Babylon as to a centre.

(3) **"A hold of every unclean and hated bird."** We gather that demons and unclean spirits referred to in our text are *personal* beings. The unclean birds, birds of prey and of darkness, signify the many and varied agents of Satan (Matt. 13. 4, 32; Jer. 5. 27; especially Isa. 34. 11-15), those, of course, of a highly pernicious and destructive character. Thus is Babylon a very sink of corruption, an abomination in the sight of God.

GRAVE INDICTMENT AGAINST BABYLON.

The grounds of God's judgment on Babylon are next stated. These are:

(1) **"Because all the nations have drunk of the wine of the fury of her fornication."** The peoples of the prophetic earth have drunk, and drunk eagerly out of her golden and intoxicating cup. She has seduced the nations from their allegiance to God and Christ, and established herself in the affections of the masses of mankind. The peoples of Christendom, if not of a wider geographical area, have been captivated by the splendour of her services, her high and ornate ritual, and general display of gorgeous vestments and millinery, all so fitted to act on the ignorant mind and unbridled imagination of the populations of our cities, towns, and villages. Add to this the easy terms on which she offers salvation to her devotees, with, on the other hand, the threat of no salvation outside the pale of her communion, and need we be surprised that the nations get morally intoxicated, or mad, over a system which offers such advantages, while blind to all true judgment as to her real condition before God! At the period contemplated in our chapter the Bible will have been dethroned from its place in public, as also from the conscience of the masses of even religious people. Hence they will fall an easy prey to the seductions of Babylon.

(2) With whom **"the kings of the earth have**

committed fornication." The personal heads of the ten kingdoms which form the territorial area of the empire, when revived, must be distinguished from the kings of the earth. The former are the destroyers and burners of the woman (chap. 17. 16); they turn to hate her. Not so the kings, or chiefs, of Christendom, they lament her fate (chap. 18. 9); they, *not* the ten western kings, a specific class and number, commit fornication with Babylon. Love of display, of which the Romish Church boasts, is her argument and appeal to the senses, and before *this* god the nations will bow, but the kings of the earth, or leaders, are more guilty, more sober, as befits their position; they yield themselves up to the blandishments of the woman. The Church hugs the world for what of numbers and wealth she can get, and the world gladly welcomes her embrace, for has she not promised to open Heaven to all comers who pay well? The keys of St. Peter are dangled before kings and people, and so the chair of "The Vicar of Christ" and "Universal Bishop" will yet be exalted to a moral height far beyond that of the palmiest days of the papacy in either of the three centuries so renowned for Romish arrogance and pride, the eleventh, twelfth, and thirteenth.

(3) "**The merchants of the earth have been enriched through the might of her luxury.**" This third class has trafficked with her for gain. There has always been a numerous class of people who attach themselves to religion for what they can get, using the Church as a stepping-stone to advance their temporal interests. Babylon will offer a tempting bait to all such. The abundance of her luxuries will attract "the merchants of the earth," who will enrich themselves thereby. Soon, however, the scene will change, and these same traffickers weep and wail over the ruin of that from which they enriched themselves.

A CALL FOR SEPARATION.

4, 5.—"**And I heard another voice out of the Heaven, saying, Come out of her, my people, that ye have not fellowship in her sins, and that ye do not receive of her plagues: for her sins have been heaped on one another up to the Heaven, and God has remembered her unrighteousnesses.**" An angel descending *from* Heaven (v. 1), and a voice heard *in* Heaven (v. 4), express different actions. The latter is the expression of the mind of God, in which all in Heaven are in unison.

4.—The call, "**Come out of her, my people,**"* is,

* Compare with Jeremiah 51. 6; Isaiah 48. 20.

of course, applicable at all times, and is never out of season wherever Babylon in principle is found. But the exhortation has its special force *after* the overthrow of Babylon from its commanding greatness (chap. 17) and *before* its final doom (chap. 18). The call is imperative. Babylon as a system cannot be remodelled on scriptural lines, and hence there is ever but one course open to the faithful—one of thorough separation from that which falsely bears the Name of Christ. No doubt some real believers will be found in Babylon, even in her worst and most corrupt condition, probably to avoid persecution and death. These adherents must make a complete severance from Babylon, or if they remain in it become partakers of her plagues.*

4.—The call is based on two grounds: (1) "**that ye have not fellowship in her sins**." By remaining in it they would become partakers of her guilt. (2) "**That ye do not receive of her plagues**." The warning here is on account of consequences—judicial and governmental. Eternal security is in no wise imperilled by the divine threat. The guilt and punishment of all remaining in Babylon are here predicated. God is about to overwhelm the whole apostate ecclesiastical system with utter and irremediable ruin, and in view of this final downpour of wrath, here termed "plagues," the last call is heard, "Come out of her, my people." We would naturally conclude that the exodus of saints from Babylon is accomplished ere the last stroke falls, crushing her to powder. As another has said, "The full judgment comes after God's people are come out of her."

5.—But why such stern judgment? Why such awful dealing both from man and God? "**For her sins have been heaped on one another up to the Heaven**." Of the first Babel confederacy *without God* we read, "And they said, Go to, let us build us a city, and a tower, whose top may reach unto Heaven" (Gen. 11. 4). They would build an enduring monument of their folly, one of *stone*. But here the *sins* heaped up reach "the Heaven," the monument of her shame if she only knew it. What a striking picture is here presented, a Babel tower, not of stones but of sins; not simply sin on earth calling for judgment, but sins so aggravated, so numerous, and so bold and impious that Heaven itself is outraged.† "God has remembered her unrighteousnesses." Judgment, stern and unsparing, must take its course.

---

* These plagues are death, mourning, and famine (v. 8).

† See Ezra 9. 6; also Jeremiah 51. 9; *there* the LITERAL Babylon; *here* the MYSTICAL, the one being the counterpart of the other.

RIGHTEOUS RETRIBUTION.

6.—"**Recompense her even as she has recompensed; and double (to her) double, according to her works. In the cup which she has mixed, mix to her double.**" On textual considerations the "you" in the Authorised Version is omitted in the Revised Version, while as a matter of interpretation its introduction unduly narrows the sense of the passage. The previous verse directly addresses itself *to* the people of God, but in that before us it is *for* saints. Then, as now, the principle is asserted that God acts in retributive justice. It is a statement of the principle on which God acts towards nations, as Matthew 7. 2 shows its application to individuals. Jewish law demanded "an eye for an eye," but the vengeance here demanded goes far beyond that—the measure is doubled.

PRIDE BEFORE DESTRUCTION.

7, 8.—"**So much as she has glorified herself and lived luxuriously, so much torment and grief give to her. Because she says in her heart, I sit a queen, and I am not a widow; and I shall in no wise see grief: for this reason on one day shall her plagues come, death, and grief, and famine, and she shall be burned with fire; for strong (is the) Lord God Who has judged her.**" The principle of retributive judgment is next shown in the first part of verse 7, not in relation to what Babylon has *done* (v. 6), but because of what she *is* in herself. Having been degraded from her public place by the kings of the Roman world she yet maintains her pride. Her spirit is unbroken. Her haughtiness is asserted in spite of the fact that she sits in the dust of her former grandeur, and that her final end is at hand. The kings of the earth may *lament* over her, but *help* her they cannot. Her boasting is *within*; she says in her heart, "I sit a queen." Her public downfall had already taken place, hence the assertion of her queenly state would be out of keeping if openly expressed. "I am not a widow." Does she expect that her fortunes are to be retrieved? That she will once again mount the throne? "I shall in no wise see grief," and this while the clouds lower and the tokens on every hand presage her immediate and final judgment at the hand of God. Utter destruction is signified in the words, "she shall be burned with fire." This goes beyond the more historical scene in chapter 17. 16. The fire here makes an utter end of Babylon. The mighty God is Babylon's Judge.*

* We quote from another, "Rome means *strong*, but her strength is nothing. Strong is the Lord Who judges her."

THE DIRGE OVER BABYLON.

9, 10.—The lamentation over Babylon is taken up by all classes, for all are affected by it. The general bearing of the whole passage is so simple that detailed exposition is needless. The articles of merchandise specified in which Babylon trafficked are twenty-eight in number. The first in the list is **gold**, the last is **souls**. The ruin of Babylon will seriously affect the whole commercial and social life of the world, and it is on this account that her judgment is so deplored by those who shared in her wealth and profited by intercourse with her.

9, 10.—**"The kings of the earth"** lead in the general mourning. They were the most intimate with her, and hence more than others feel her loss. These kings, or chiefs, must not be confounded with the ten kings who hate the woman. The former mourn over her, and are unable to prevent her ruin, whereas the latter are the prime movers in her political downfall (chap. 17. 16). The kings of the earth, or, in other words, the distinguished leaders in Christendom, as apart from the ten kings of the Roman empire, are in fear. Standing afar off they witness the awful conflagration of that mighty system of evil with which they had been so closely identified, and in which they had lived and rioted in luxury. They tremble and fear at the awfulness and suddenness of the judgment, "for in one hour is thy judgment come."

11-13.—**"The merchants of the earth"** sorrow over Babylon, not because of any love they bear the system, but simply because their trade and wealth are ruined. Babylon, besides her religious character, is here viewed as the centre of vast commercial interests. The varied character of the merchandise—the product of all countries—shows the wide influence of Babylon, and how she attracts to herself as to a centre the world's riches. Think of this gigantic combination of the secular and religious trading, amongst other commodities, with the bodies and souls of men (v. 13)—named last, as of least account. In the enumeration of Babylon's merchandise she is simply the world's storehouse, or universal emporium, embracing all that is most esteemed down to that which is regarded as of least value. There are seven departments under which the various articles are classified. (1) *Valuables and ornaments*, as gold, silver, precious stones, and pearls. (2) *Costly array*, as fine linen, purple, silk, and scarlet. (3) *Sumptuous furniture*, as vessels manufactured from the most precious woods, ivory, and metals. (4) *Rich odours*, as cinnamon, frankincense, and ointments. (5) *Abundant living*, as wine, oil, flour, wheat, beasts, and sheep. (6)

Triumphal pageants, as horses and chariots. (7) *Infamous traffic* in the bodies and souls of men.

The lamentation of the merchants is interrupted by an episode narrated in verse 14, and the mournful strain is resumed in verse 15. The complete ruin of the merchandise of Babylon, that which selfishly bound to her king and peasant, leaves her a wreck. All her resources are gone; she is utterly despoiled of her former means of self indulgence; her sources of enjoyment are dried up; and, in fact, all that ministered to her pride, and everything essential to her existence, perishes in the unexpected and sudden blow from the divine hand. She is directly addressed by a voice from Heaven (v. 14).

15-17.—Then the strain is resumed, but on a wider basis. Merchants in general, which is explained to mean those "**who had been enriched through her**," take up the lamentation expressed in words similar to that of the kings (v. 10). There is one difference, however, which may be noted. The kings in their lament say "In one hour is thy *judgment* come," whereas the merchants say "In one hour so *great riches* have been made desolate." Uniting the two statements we gather that the judgment of Babylon involves the destruction of her temporal prosperity, and, further, that the stroke of vengeance from the hand of the Almighty is sudden and unlooked for.

17-19.—**Shipmasters**, **sailors**, and **all seafaring interests** suffer equally with those already named. The past greatness and riches of Babylon are remembered and mourned over in the pathetic dirge from the sea (see Ezek. 27).

The judgment of Babylon takes effect in full sight of kings, merchants, and sea traders, the various classes enriched through connection with her. *Her* torment is *their* fear.*

HEAVEN REJOICES.

20.—We have had the voice from Heaven heard *first* in verse 4, and *last* in verse 20. In this latter reference Heaven is called upon to rejoice. If there is lamentation on earth there is rejoicing in Heaven. The place and inhabitants unite in the song of triumph. There are three

* "We have the *fall* of Babylon distinguished, I think, from the *destruction* of Babylon. Her fall includes moral degradation, and being the dwelling place of unclean spirits. This is judgment on her; and she falls because of her making the nations drink of the wine of her fornication (chap. 14. 8). This we find in the ecclesiastical course, so to speak, of closing facts. Her final judgment we find in the close of the filling up the wrath of God (chap. 16. 19). The connection of the former seems to be with chapter 18. 2; of the latter with chapter 18. 21."—"Notes on the Book of Revelation," *in loco*.

This little work, by the late J. N. Darby, of 172 pages, is an invaluable aid, not in details, but in masterly unfolding of the great principles and truths contained in the Apocalypse.

classes: saints, apostles, and prophets (R.V. of v. 20). The first term is a general one, and includes believers both of Old and New Testament times; the second refers to those of Christian times (Eph. 4. 11), and "the twelve" as well; the third is, of course, the prophets of old. All the three classes mentioned are in Heaven, and there rejoice. **"God has judged your judgment upon her,"** that is, the righteous judgment passed upon Babylon by saints, apostles, and prophets—for all had suffered at her hands—is now executed by God Himself.

THE UTTER RUIN AND EVERLASTING DESOLATION OF BABYLON.

21-24.—**"And a strong angel took up a stone, as a great millstone, and cast (it) into the sea, saying, Thus with violence shall Babylon the great city be cast down, and shall be found no more at all."** The action is significant and prophetic, and sublime withal. A similar dramatic proceeding pointing to the overthrow of Babylon of old is described in Jeremiah 51. 60-64; *there*, however, Seraiah was the actor; *here* an angel of might. Both the literal and mystical cities were to be utterly and suddenly destroyed by violence. The two chapters, Jeremiah 51 and Revelation 18, should be carefully studied and compared. Then follows in verses 22 and 23 a beautifully descriptive and touching account, poetically expressed,* of her utter desolation. How complete the ruin! Joyless, dark, and silent, Babylon stands out as a monument of the utmost vengeance of God. Wickedness had sat enthroned in the midst of *that* professedly bearing the Name of Christ; but at last, when she had filled to the full her cup of iniquity, God rises in His fierce anger, His indignation burns, and Babylon falls to rise no more. Her destruction is irremediable. The chapter closes with a reiteration of the bloody character of the system† (see chaps. 17. 6; 18. 24).

---

* Compare with Jeremiah 25. 10.

† "Alas! she has erected the prisons, and prepared the rack, and lighted the fires of what she calls the holy office of the Inquisition in Italy, Spain, America, and India. She lauds one of her canonised Popes, Pius the Fifth, in her Breviary as an inflexible Inquisitor. She has engraven the massacre of St. Bartholomew's Day on her papal coins, and there represents it as a work done by an angel from Heaven. And the Roman Pontiff of that day went publicly to Church to return thanks to God for that savage and treacherous deed."—*Wordsworth*.

The term "blood" is literally *bloods*, a Hebraism, of course, but does it not point to the fact that *all* the blood so wantonly shed on earth in its numerous and varied ways is at the last found in Babylon?—a system sometimes governmentally curbed and checked, but never improved, and never repentant.

CHAPTER XIX.

THE MARRIAGE OF THE LAMB AND THE JUDGMENT OF THE REBELLIOUS NATIONS.

HEAVEN REJOICES OVER THE JUDGMENT OF BABYLON.

1-4.—**"After these things I heard as it were a loud voice of a great multitude in the Heaven, saying, Hallelujah: the salvation, and the glory, and the power of our God. For true and righteous (are) His judgments; for He has judged the great harlot which corrupted the earth with her fornication, and has avenged the blood of His bondmen at her hand. And a second time they said, Hallelujah. And her smoke goes up to the ages of ages. And the twenty-four elders and the four living creatures fell down and worshipped God Who sits upon the throne, saying, Amen, Hallelujah."** "After these things." We have had two separate visions of Babylon in which her character, guilt, and relations to the empire and Christendom, and her awful and overwhelming judgment are unfolded. Chapters 17 and 18 record a distinct vision each, which is really the filling up of the details of the historical place which Babylon occupies in chapters 14. 8; 16. 19. In a vision everything is present to the mind of the Seer. The scenes shift and change, and pass successively before the mental gaze. There is no past nor future, but all is present. Other Scriptures, however, enable us to apportion the various visions and their separate parts as well to their chronological place in the history or prophecy, as the case may be.

Now it is plain that so long as Babylon remained unjudged the true bride could not be brought out and displayed in her beauty and coronation robes. She is hid in Heaven till the usurper on earth is destroyed and removed out of sight. The whore and the bride cannot co-exist. "After these things," an apocalyptic formula (chaps. 4. 1; 18. 1), refers to the fall (chap. 17) and total destruction of Babylon (chap. 18). The *same* event is viewed very differently in Heaven and on earth. On earth the *dirge of sorrow* is heard. In Heaven the *paean of praise*. That which leads to general lamentation and mourning on earth calls forth the full rejoicing of Heaven. The cry of triumph immediately follows the destruction of Babylon. Her presence on earth had ever proved the chief hindrance to the manifestation of the glory of God, and an offence to Heaven besides. Now, however, by the total extinction of Babylon room is prepared, and the way open for the Lord God to be publicly owned on His throne, and for the Lamb to take His bride—the two great subjects of praise.

1.—The call to rejoice (chap. 18. 20) is here taken up by the heavenly hosts. **"I heard as it were a loud voice."** The words *"as it were"* inserted in the Revised Version (see also v. 6) are omitted in the Authorised Version. There is a certain purposed vagueness in the passage which is lost in the Authorised Version by the omission of the words. Who are the "great multitude" who loudly and joyously proclaim the triumph of God over the judgment of Babylon? We read of another, a Gentile company, termed a "great multitude" in chapter 7. 9, but, as we have seen, those are on earth, whereas the company before us is in Heaven. Nor can the "great multitude" of our text be identified with angels, but rather with the twenty-four elders, the mystic representatives of the redeemed translated at the Coming into the air (1 Thess. 4. 17).* The various martyred companies, that is, those of the coming crisis, are viewed as distinct from the elders. Hence, we gather that the "great multitude" is that of all saints then in Heaven.

1.—**"Hallelujah,"**† they say. This beautiful Hebrew word occurs four times in these celebrations of praise (vv. 1, 3, 4, 6), but in no other part of the New Testament. It is a word of frequent occurrence in the book of Psalms. It is the opening and closing word of each of the last five psalms—psalms which as a whole and in their united character express the millennial praise of Israel. *Hallelujah* means, "Praise ye Jehovah," or "Jah," an abbreviated form of Jehovah.

1.—**"The salvation, and the glory, and the power of our God."**‡ The article before each of the three nouns makes the subject of specific application. The first of the three terms signifies *deliverance*, the second God's *moral* glory in judgment, and the third His *might* displayed in the execution of the judgment upon the harlot. This ascription of praise is to "our God." Angels in their place and station say "our God" (chap. 7. 12). Here,

* See remarks on the term *elders* on page 122, and footnote.

† *Alleluia* in our version is from the Greek spelling of the Hebrew word *Hallelujah*. Why drop the *H*?

‡ The Rev. W. F. Wilkinson, in his useful work, "Personal Names in the Bible," considers that *Jehovah* in its etymological signification is derived from the Hebrew verb *to be*, and that its meaning to English readers is found in God's own declaration of His Name and Being to Moses, I AM THAT I AM (Exod. 3. 14), and, further, that I AM answers to *Jah*, while the larger and fuller title is the expression of *Jehovah*. Without doubt the dread and sacred name, *Jehovah*, which is never used of, nor applied to, any created being, signifies, "The necessary, continuous, eternal, personal existence of God." On this hallowed and ineffable Name of names, see pages 24, 31 of our "Exposition." See footnote on pages 142 and 170.

however, it is the language of a redeemed and heavenly company, not that of angels.

2.—The ground of their triumph is next stated. "**For true and righteous (are) His judgments.**" In chapter 15. 3 the harpers on the sea of glass sing "*Righteous* and true are Thy ways;" while in chapter 16. 7 the altar says "*True* and righteous are Thy judgments." In the former the ways of God are in view; in the latter, as also in our text, the judgment of God on His enemies is in question. It is a fundamental truth of the Scriptures, and one to be firmly maintained, that all God's dealings with His creatures, whether in grace or judgment, are characterised by truth and righteousness. Now these essential attributes of the divine Being have been conspicuously displayed in the judgment of the "great harlot," whose two great sins are once again, and for the last time, named: "which has corrupted the earth with her fornication," morally blighted and ruined the whole scene, where once the truth was known and God worshipped, "And has avenged the blood of His bondmen at her hand." The cry of the martyred band, from Abel downward, calling for judgment is heard, and God in righteous judgment pours out the indignation of His nature upon that system of harlotry and blood which had so long been a curse on the earth.

A second time, as marking the greatness of the triumph, they say "**Hallelujah**," or *Praise ye Jehovah*. "And her smoke goes up to the ages of ages" is a striking and impressive figure of the finality and perpetuity of the divinely-executed judgment. The doom of the mystical Babylon is an everlasting witness to the righteous judgment of God (compare with Isa. 34. 10).

But the volume of praise rolls on through the vault of Heaven. The elders, the representatives of the redeemed and enthroned saints, and the living creatures, the symbols of God's government in creation,* "fell down and worshipped God." How profound the worship! How fitting the action! It is God, not Christ, Who is the object of their homage. It is God Who has judged Babylon, and hence to Him the worship is rendered. Besides, Christ has not at this juncture taken up the government of the earth. *God* is the Judge of Babylon. *Christ* is the Judge of the Beast; this judgment is an event subsequent to the former, and the *first* public act of the Coming Christ (vv. 11-21). The elders and living ones say "Amen, Hallelujah." They put their seal to the truth of what has been announced, and themselves join and joy in the triumph of all in Heaven over the everlasting doom of the harlot. In chapter 5. 8

* See notes on chapter 4.

the living ones take precedence of the elders; here the elders are first named as being more directly concerned in the judgment of the harlot.

THE THRONE SPEAKS.

5.—"**And a voice came out of the throne saying, Praise our God, all ye His bondmen, (and) ye that fear Him, small and great.**" In a former vision we had the cry of the altar (chap. 16. 7, R.V.); here the throne itself speaks. In some of the past scenes, where a body of witnessing and suffering saints were in view, the altar came into prominence, but here it is *direct* judgment upon evil on the earth, for God is upon His throne, as Christ is about to sit on His. The very throne is moved to speech (symbolic, of course); thus from the centre and source of government—the *terror* of the wicked, the *joy* of the saints—goes forth a call to "praise." All who serve and all who fear Him, small and great, are invited to join in the glad song, which is a relief after the dark picture unfolded on earth. Here the terms are sufficiently wide to embrace every soul in Heaven—angels, servants, and every redeemed one. Nor is it a call addressed to an unwilling congregation. ***All*** are ready, but a new cause of joy is to be furnished, a new ground of praise. THE MARRIAGE OF THE LAMB is about to be announced.

THE MARRIAGE OF THE LAMB.

6-10.—"**And I heard as it were a voice of a great multitude, and as it were a voice of many waters, and as it were a voice of strong thunders, saying, Hallelujah, for (the) Lord our God the Almighty has taken to Himself kingly power. Let us rejoice and exult, and give Him glory; for the marriage of the Lamb is come, and His wife has made herself ready. And it was given to her that she should be clothed in fine linen, bright (and) pure; for the fine linen is the righteousnesses of the saints. And he says to me, Write, Blessed (are) they who are called to the supper of the marriage of the Lamb. And he says to me, These are the true words of God. And I fell before his feet to worship him. And he says to me, See (thou do it) not. I am thy fellow-bondman and (the fellow-bondman) of thy brethren who have the testimony of Jesus. Worship God. For the spirit of prophecy is the testimony of Jesus.**" We have transcribed in full this passage of surpassing interest.

There are two main subjects: God manifestly assuming His kingly power, and the Lamb taking to Himself His bride—the Church of the New Testament. The moment has not yet arrived for the Lord Jesus Christ, Who suffered as none ever did, to mount His throne. But all is getting ready for that grand event. O blessed moment for which creation groans and waits, for which the Church hopes and prays, and for which the wearied tribes of Israel long with eager expectation! The Nazarene is God's appointed King. But two events must necessarily take place before the throne of the world is occupied by Christ: Babylon must be judged on earth, and the marriage of the Lamb be celebrated in Heaven. We have had the one; we are now about to witness the other.

THE GRAND HALLELUJAH.

The call of the throne (v. 5) meets with a magnificent and immediate response. The praise is loud, deep, and full, and characterised by strength and grandeur. The "great multitude" (v. 6) here probably embraces all the redeemed in Heaven, save the bride. If this is so, as a careful study of the whole passage would seem to indicate, then the "great multitude" must be a larger and more comprehensive company than that mentioned in verse 1. In the former passage (v. 1) the "great multitude" is not distinguished from the elders, the representatives of the redeemed of past and present ages; while in the latter (v. 6) the "great multitude" is evidently a company apart from the bride (v. 7). The voice heard by the Seer is likened to the sound of "many waters" and "strong thunders," that is, majesty and power combined.* Having had the summons from the throne, the mighty choir takes up the strain in a voice of majesty and power—not voices, for the mind of Heaven is *one*. We now hear what fell upon the enraptured soul of the Seer; the last "Hallelujah" is sounded. It is not now Christ the object of praise, but God on the throne in holy and righteous action. The titles under which He is worshipped gather up all the various manifestations of God to His people of old. Separately they set forth distinctive relations and glories; when combined they form a tower of strength; when seen as united *in Him* the grandeur of the whole is beyond all telling. We have already remarked on the

* In various parts of the Apocalypse the symbols of *waters* and *thunders* are separately noted, but here, as also in chapter 14. 2, they are united. Waters have a double signification. First, when in *motion* is conveyed the idea of MAJESTY and GREATNESS; when *still* the symbolic reference is to NATIONS and PEOPLES; for rivers, sea, etc., see page 190.

meaning and force of these various titles in a former part of our exposition.*

We gather that *this* is the moment anticipated in chapter 11. 15. The kingdom has now come, and kingly power is assumed. This is the first great subject of praise by the heavenly host. What a relief to creation, burdened with six thousand years of sin and sorrow! But ere the second theme is announced, calling for the adoration of the redeemed, we read, "Let us rejoice and exult, and give Him glory."

In the revelation of God on His throne as Jehovah and the Almighty the whole being is bowed before Him. The soul is awed, not in fear, but in profoundest depth, and surely that is right and proper as we contemplate Him in the greatness of His Being.

But in the subject now to be introduced the affections are deeply stirred and the heart moved to its very centre. Hence the prefatory call to rejoice and give God glory, for the "marriage of the Lamb is come, and His wife has made herself ready."

THE MARRIAGE.

7.—This great and grand event is the consummation of joy to Christ as man. It is not said the marriage of the *bride*, but **the marriage of the Lamb**. It is *His* joy that is specially in view; not ours. The marriage, of which no details are given, takes place in Heaven, and on the eve of the Lord's Return in power, or the Appearing, several years at least subsequent to the Rapture (1 Thess. 4; John 14. 3). The marriage is the disclosed secret of Ephesians 5. 32. Not Israel, nor a remnant thereof, but the Church of the New Testament is the bride. Israel in her land was the wife of Jehovah (Jer. 3. 14-20; Isa. 54. 1), but the wife was divorced because of her iniquity. Israel, however, is to be reinstated in Jehovah's favour. But a divorced wife can never again be a virgin, and it is not a divorced wife but a virgin whom the Lord marries (Lev. 21. 14: compare v. 13 with 2 Cor. 11. 2). Israel, moreover, has her place and blessing *on the earth*; the marriage of the Lamb is *in Heaven*, the Church's proper home. The exclusively heavenly character of the scene forbids the application of it to Israel.†

Of whom is the bride composed? We answer unhesitat-

* See page 240. "He now reigned as the Lord God Omnipotent—that character, or those characters in which He dealt with the earth, whether as God, Creator, Promiser, and Shield of His people while strangers, or the everlasting Accomplisher of all He had promised, Jehovah, Elohim, Shaddai. All these He took now in power and reigned."—*Darby*.

† See pages 247, 248, 343, and footnotes in latter page.

ingly, *all* saints embraced between these two epochs, *i.e.*, Pentecost (Acts 2) and the Translation (1 Thess. 4. 17). These events respectively mark the commencement and the termination of the Church's sojourn on earth.

The twenty-four elders, the mystic representatives of the redeemed seen in Heaven *immediately* after the Translation (chap. 4), are named for the last time in verse four of our chapter. We gather, therefore, that the moment has now arrived when the distinct body, the Church, the bride, first comes into view. The elders divide, so to speak, and the bride and guests take their respective places in the economy of Heaven. All up till now had one place. There are *special* blessings to the saints of this Dispensation (Matt. 11. 11; Heb. 11. 40), and there are others common to all believers. Now in the course of the apocalyptic visions (chaps. 4-19. 4) no differences or distinctions of any kind appear amongst the elders. The term *elders* disappears as the various companies of saints take their allotted place in relation to the Lamb. The Church is the bride. The Church is imperishable because founded on the glory and dignity of Christ as Son of God (Matt. 16. 18). His body, too, is the *nearest* of all to Him (Eph. 1. 23), as the bride is the *dearest* object to His heart and eye. He has loved the Church with a deathless and unchangeable love, a love ever active, and knowing no cessation till He presents her in glory to Himself (Eph. 5. 25-27). The Church has weathered many a storm, has longed for her heavenly Bridegroom through cloud and sunshine, has in conjunction with the Spirit on earth ofttimes cried to Him, the Bright and Morning Star, "Come" (Rev. 22. 16, 17). We who have had our place in the Father's house, according to John 14. 3, are about to be displayed in the kingdom as the bride and wife of the Lamb. What a moment of joy! His glory and joy exceedeth.* More of the oil of gladness is poured upon His head than upon ours (Heb. 1. 9). Our place, our blessing, our gladness are wrapped up in His. "The marriage of the Lamb is come." Then shall He Who died see of the travail of His soul and be satisfied.

THE LAMB'S WIFE MAKES HERSELF READY.

7.—**"His wife has made herself ready."** In this connection the term *bride* would not be an appropriate one. Now there are two sorts of fitness, and the Church is the subject of both. First, God in the exercise of His sovereign

* The presentation of the Church in glory to Himself (Eph. 5. 27) is a *private* matter, and precedes the *public* event, the marriage of the Lamb. The one is the corollary of the other.

grace makes one fit for heavenly glory, as we read, "Giving thanks unto the Father which *hath* made us meet to be partakers of the inheritance of the saints in light" (Col. 1. 12). Second, believers have to make themselves ready ere they enter on their eternal glory. That is, the story of earth has to be gone over again in the presence of Him Who is light. Our lives have to be reviewed at the bema of Christ (2 Cor. 5. 10). The light of the throne will be cast over and upon every moment of our lives, discovering the hidden, and bringing out the true character of act, word, and service. The enigmas of life will be explained, unsolved problems cleared up, and all mistakes and misunderstandings rectified. This, and more, is the application of the judgment seat of Christ to the heavenly saints, and *precedes* the marriage. "His wife has made herself ready." The light of the throne has done its blessed work, bringing out into bold relief the whole story of her history on earth. What would it be if in glory we remembered one incident of a painful kind which had not been set right? The thought would be intolerable. But all will come out at the judgment seat as a matter between each saint and God. It will not be a public exposure before others. Nor must this be understood as signifying judicial judgment. All that has been settled on the Cross. We appear before the bema of Christ *crowned and glorified*, "raised *in* glory" (1 Cor. 15. 43), to have the light of the throne cast upon the past. What a mercy that it is so. We shall then pass from the bema with its searching light into the loved presence of the Lamb as His bride and wife for ever.

BRIDAL ROBES.

8.—**"It was given to her to be clothed in fine linen, bright (and) pure; for the fine linen is the righteousnesses of the saints."** The harlot was gorgeously arrayed, but her pomp, splendour, and ornaments were claimed as a matter of *right*. With the bride it is different; she is arrayed as a matter of *grace*. "It was given to her." Undoubtedly there are rewards for service done, as Matthew 25. 14-23 clearly show. "God is not unrighteous to forget your work and labour of love" (Heb. 6. 10). But it might be well for *us* to forget. He never will.

There is, however, another side to this question which should ever be borne in mind, namely, the sovereignty of God. His right it is to give or withhold. Many an eminent servant of God has made shipwreck of true life and service by neglect of the great balancing truth—God is sovereign.

The parable of the talents in Matthew 25 shows the *grace* of God in rewards; whilst the parable of the householder in chapter 20 of the same Gospel is a demonstration of the *sovereignty* of God in giving to all alike, irrespective of toil or length of service.

The garment of pure linen in which the Vial angels are arrayed (chap. 15. 6) expresses the righteous character of their mission, which is one of judgment.* The fine linen, pure and lustrous, of the bride is her righteousness, or "righteous acts" (R.V.), done on earth. But she claims no merit, for these righteous acts were wrought by the power of the Holy Ghost in her. Later on we have the bride covered with the glory of God (chap. 21. 11); here her own righteousness, not God's, is in question. The gaudy colours in which the harlot is arrayed present a sharp contrast to the pure, white, and bright linen of the bride. Her garments bespeak her practical character. She can now enter on the enjoyment of eternal companionship and union of the closest nature (that of wife) with her husband, the Lamb. Her deeds on *earth* have been appraised at their true value in *Heaven*. She is arrayed in them, or in the expressive words of our text, "has made herself ready." She passes from the bema to the marriage, and from thence to the kingdom.

GUESTS AT THE MARRIAGE SUPPER.

9.—"**Write, Blessed are they who are called to the supper of the marriage of the Lamb.**" The bride and guests are clearly distinguished. The former is, of course, in more immediate relation to the Lamb. The bride is wed; the guests sup.

The angel, addressing the Seer, says, "Write." This command, frequently repeated during the progress of the visions, marks the importance and speciality of the communication. "Blessed" are those called to the supper. This is not said of the bride. Her blessing, which is that of the highest order and character, is expressed in the simple words, *bride* and *wife*. What unspeakable joy is conveyed in these terms! But the guests are pronounced *blessed*. Who are they? We answer, the friends of the Bridegroom. But as the friends of the *Bridegroom* they enjoy a higher and dearer character of blessedness than they would if merely the friends of the bride. John the Baptist expressly tells us that he is a friend of the Bridegroom (John 3. 29). The Baptist was martyred before the Church was formed, hence he comes in as perhaps the most honoured

* Both in the case of the angels and of the bride the clothing is linen; but of the latter it is added "*fine* linen." See pages 173 and 318, with footnotes on both pages.

of the guests at the marriage supper. Old Testament saints constitute the large company of called guests, each one being a friend of the Bridegroom, and rejoicing in His presence and voice. The apocalyptic martyrs are not raised till *after* the marriage, hence cannot be numbered amongst the guests. Angels may be spectators of the scene, but guests they cannot be. Angels are never spoken of in the way that these are. It is called a supper, perhaps in contrast to the subsequent supper of judgment (v. 17). The former is in connection with the Lamb and His joy; the latter is in relation to God and the judgment He executes on the ungodly—administratively by the Lamb and His heavenly saints.

CERTAINTY.

9.—These divine communications, whether spoken by an angel or seen in vision by John, have attached to them all the weight and authority of God Himself. "**These are the true words of God.**"* The basis of our faith is not conjecture, but the certainty that God has spoken. The truths thus divinely authenticated are those stated within the first nine verses of the chapter. Absolute certainty is of prime importance in these days when the dogmatism of belief in a divine revelation is considered to savour of a narrow and illiberal spirit. In old times God spake *in* the prophets; in New Testament times God has spoken *in* His Son (Heb. 1. 1, 2, R.V.). How blessed, therefore, to have the confirmation of these grand and heart-gladdening truths from God Himself!

ANGELS AND SAINTS FELLOW-BONDMEN.

10.—Evidently the Seer was overwhelmed by the exalted character of the communications vouchsafed to him; probably, too, the angel who appeared to him in vision was a too glorious object for mortal gaze. "**He fell before his feet to worship him,**" not "*at* his feet" as in the Authorised Version. But angels are jealous for the glory and rights of God. *Homage* may be rendered to a creature in superior position, but *worship* is the due of the Creator alone. The movement on the part of John was instantly checked, "See (thou do it) not." To worship even the most exalted of God's creatures is idolatry. Both angels and saints worship God and Christ, as this book abundantly testifies. On a second and subsequent occasion (chap. 22. 8, 9) John was about to do so, and again prohibited by the angel.

* "Are the very truth of God, and shall veritably come to pass."—*Alford.*

10.—"**I am thy fellow-bondman.**"* The angel and the apostle were fellow-servants, rather *bondmen*. As a slave is bound for life to the service of his master, so angels and saints are bound to the everlasting service of the blessed God—His glad and willing slaves. All intelligent creatures really stand on this ground. In the case of angels the right is founded on their creation and place; in that of saints on the ground of purchase and redemption (1 Cor. 6. 19, 20). Had the passage stopped with the angel's declaration that he was a fellow-servant, or slave, with the apostle it might have been supposed that the highest in the Church† could alone be so regarded. But angels who delight to serve are also fellow-bondmen with the brethren of John, who have, or keep, "the testimony of Jesus." The testimony of Jesus in the Apocalypse is of a prophetic character, referring to His public assumption of governmental power to be displayed in the kingdom (see chap. 1. 2). If this passage, which has needlessly perplexed students, were read in connection with chapter 12. 17, where the same words occur, the difficulty would disappear. The godly remnant of Judah in the coming crisis "have the testimony of Jesus," and surely we cannot fail, with the Psalter in our hands, to understand the character of that testimony, which in their circumstances is prophetic; they long, and sigh, and pray for the open and direct intervention of God on their behalf. The presence of the Messiah, His Advent for their deliverance, is the goal of hope. The direct address of the angel to John ends with the authoritative declaration, "Worship God," a truth ever in season for Heaven and earth, for angels and men.

HEAVEN OPENED
(VERSES 11-21).

INTRODUCTORY.

11-16.—"**And I saw the Heaven opened, and behold a white horse, and One sitting on it (called) Faithful and True, and He judges, and makes war in righteousness. And His eyes are a flame of fire, and upon His head many diadems, having a Name written, which no one knows but Himself. And (He is) clothed with a garment dipped in blood; and His Name is called the Word of God. And the armies which (are) in the Heaven followed Him upon white horses, clad in white, pure, fine linen. And out of His mouth**

* Servants and slaves (bondmen) are distinguished. See Revelation 2. 20; Matthew 22. 13; for the latter see Romans 6. 20; Revelation 1. 1.

† "*First* apostles" (1 Cor. 12. 28; Eph. 4.11; Rev. 21. 14; Matt. 19. 28).

goes a sharp sword, that with it He might smite the nations; and He shall rule them with an iron rod; and He treads the winepress of the fury of the wrath of God the Almighty. And He has upon His garment and upon His thigh a Name written, King of kings, and Lord of lords." The remaining portion of the chapter to which we have given the general title, *Heaven Opened*, naturally divides into three parts: (1) the mighty Monarch and His victorious armies (vv. 11-16); (2) the call to the ravenous birds of prey to feed upon the slain, to partake of "the great supper of God" (vv. 17, 18); (3) the complete overthrow and destruction of the opposing army, the leaders consigned alive to the lake of fire, and their followers slain (vv. 19-21).

The special scene before us (vv. 11-16) is one of surpassing interest. We have had many and varied displays of Christ, for the whole book is more or less *about Him*, while all *for* us "upon whom the ends of the ages are come" (1 Cor. 10. 11, R.V.). But the present vision in its character and far-reaching results is second to none. It is unique. We have not here the Lamb enthroned as in chapter 5, but the Warrior-King great in victorious, all-conquering power. Before Christ, as here described, the hosts of earth shall quail, and the stout hearts of the mighty stand appalled; but that sight of sights is a gladdening one to saints, for they know Him. The King and Judge is their everlasting Friend.

THE HEAVEN OPENED, AND A DOOR OPENED IN HEAVEN.

11.—**"I saw the Heaven opened."** This book is full of heavenly action. The scenes in Heaven as witnessed by the Seer are numerous and diversified. Voices heard, songs sung, angels and glorified saints seen, elders and the living creatures bowed in worship, thrones, crowns, robes, harps, books, and more, tell of the happiness and ceaseless activity of Heaven's inhabitants. Glimpses *into* Heaven we have had, but Heaven itself opened is a grand and overpowering sight. In the opening of the heavenly section of the book (chap. 4) we read, "I saw, and behold, a door opened in Heaven." How much greater the astonishment of the Seer as he beholds, of course, in vision Heaven itself opened, not simply an opened door for admission. This action is in keeping with the magnificent pageant—the triumphal procession out of Heaven. A door opened in Heaven was for the Seer to pass *in*. Heaven opened was for the heavenly armies to pass *out*. Four times do we read in the New Testament of the heavens being opened

(Matt. 3. 16; John 1. 51; Acts 7. 56; Rev. 19. 11), and on each occasion in connection with Christ. Two of these instances are past, two are future. His moral glory in humiliation called for it. His manifested glory above demands it. The holy Jerusalem is seen in a subsequent vision descending out of Heaven (chap. 21. 9), but it is not said Heaven is then opened for egress; it is opened once, and that is enough.

DESCRIPTION OF THE CONQUEROR AND HIS VICTORIOUS ARMY.

11.—The first part of the description beheld by the Seer was **"a white horse,"** the symbol of victorious power.* The horseman who guides and controls bears the mystic name of "Faithful and True." Others may in measure be characterised by these qualities, but Christ alone can be so designated without qualification. He is in His Person and ways the perfect embodiment of these attributes.† Faithful in the performance of every promise and every threat, while every word and act bears the stamp of absolute truth.

11.—**"He judges and makes war in righteousness."** He comes to settle the destinies of the world for a thousand years. He is not only the mighty Warrior, but He judges the world as well as conquers it. God "hath appointed a day in which He will judge the world in righteousness by that Man Whom He hath ordained; whereof He hath given assurance unto all men in that He hath raised Him from the dead" (Acts 17. 31). The *appointed* day is about to dawn, and the *ordained* Man is before us as the Commander of the hosts of Heaven. This is no iniquitous war; it is not one undertaken for love of conquest, nor for enlargement of territory. The judging is named before the warring, because all is done intelligently. The war and its issues are wisely directed. Righteousness is characteristic of Him as Judge and as Warrior.

12.—**"His eyes are a flame of fire."** In chapters 1. 14 and 2. 18, of Christ it is said His eyes are "*as* a flame of fire," but here the "*as*" of comparison is omitted (R.V. and other authorities). "His eyes are a flame of fire;" that is the divine omniscience which observes all and searches out every hidden evil, and the piercing judgments which He executes are characteristic attributes of Him in the earlier notices, whereas in our text they are in exercise. The action is here more intense.

12.—**"Upon His head many diadems."** Crowns and

* See notes on chapter 6. 2, page 148, and footnote.

† See notes on chapter 15. 3; 21. 5.

diadems are distinguished.* The saints in Heaven have *crowns* (chap. 4. 4, 10), the expression of their royal dignity, but on the head of Christ rest *diadems*, denoting His absolute and supreme authority. The dragon has on his seven heads diadems (chap. 12. 3), and the Beast has diadems on his ten horns (chap. 13. 1). Thus both the dragon and the Beast affect supreme authority. There is but One Who can be entrusted with the exercise of absolute authority and dominion, and He is the Son of Man (Psa. 8). *Seven* diadems on the dragon, and *ten* on the Beast; but "*many*" upon the head of the conqueror Christ denote that every form and kind of government is vested in Him. The Authorised Version fails to distinguish between the symbols "crown" and "diadem;" the Revised Version, however, supplies the omission.

12.—"**Having a Name written which no one knows but Himself.**" There are certain divine names as God, Jehovah, Jesus, Christ, Lord, etc., which severally express the divine Being in a certain relation to His creatures. But here is a name *not* revealed. There is that in Christ—ever was and ever will be—which no name can express. The Son in the fulness of His divine nature can alone be known by the Father (Matt. 11. 27). Christ ever carries in Himself the knowledge of *who* and *what* He was and is.

13.—"**Clothed with a garment dipped in blood.**"† This striking and impressive figure proclaims His vengeance in judicial dealing with the opposing hosts of apostate Europe who have come out to do battle with the Lamb. In Isaiah 63. 1-4 we witness the triumphant return from the land of Edom, and from its capital city Bozrah, of the Lord with vengeance in His heart and His garments and vesture stained with the blood of His enemies, but here His garment dipped in blood is witnessed ere He enters on the conflict, a sure token that righteous vengeance shall be meted out to the full upon the gathered hosts under their two great chiefs, the Beast and the False Prophet.

13.—"**His Name is called the Word of God.**" Of the eight sacred writers of the New Testament, John is the only one who applies this title to Christ. As the Word He represents and expresses God in His Being, character, and works. He is "The Word of *Life*" (1 John 1. 1), as being in His Person and ways its living embodiment. He is termed "The Word of *God*," as perfectly expressing Him

---

* See pages 250 and 270.

† It seems absurd to apply the "garment dipped in blood" to the blood of the Cross, as many do. The Lord is here viewed on a mission of judgment, not one of grace. The blood is not His own, but that of His enemies. The context clearly determines the sense.

in judgment. As the WORD He has personal, independent, eternal existence (John 1. 1, 2); and as the WORD He is the maker of all things (v. 3). He is the Revealer of God, the ONE Who makes Him known. Our words ought to be the exact expression of what we *are*; the words of Christ were the absolute expression of what He ever is (John 8. 25). As the WORD He reveals God in His essential nature as light and love, and as the "*only* begotten Son" He declares the Father. The first without the second would have left a huge blank, for the heart craves for a known and enjoyed relationship. God is our *Father*.

The title here used of Christ has peculiar significance in this connection. It is *God* Who is here seen roused to action. His very nature demands the judgment of those who on earth madly attempt to thwart His purpose to set His Son as King on Mount Zion and put into His hands earth's government. Christ, "The Word of God," is the absolute expression of God in the scene of judgment about to take place.

THE TRIUMPHANT ARMIES.

14.—**"The armies"** in Heaven follow their renowned Leader on "white horses," for His victory is their victory, and His triumph their triumph. These armies represent the heavenly saints, those of Old Testament times and those comprising the bride. Each one is arrayed in robes which bespeak personal righteousness, which tell of personal struggle here in doing right, in maintaining the rights of God in the midst of a scene of contrariety and opposition to God and Christ. The clothing of the bride (v. 8) is the clothing of each of the militant hosts (v. 14). The armies in Heaven which triumphantly follow Christ and swell His train are not angels, but saints. What a military spectacle is here presented! These armies of saints in Heaven follow their Captain. He goes first, and heads the triumphing hosts. We have here the fulfilment of Enoch's prophecy uttered more than five thousand years ago, but alone recorded in Jude's epistle, "Behold, the Lord cometh with ten thousands of His saints" (v. 14). Zechariah (chap. 14. 5) writes of the same Coming, but to deal with the powers opposed to the Jews, whereas the apocalyptic scripture reveals as the first object of judgment the nations opposed to the Lamb. Angels, too, follow in the train and swell the triumph of the Lord (Matt. 16. 27; 25. 31; Heb. 1. 6). Triumphant power (white horses) is put forth on the day when the wrath of the Lamb is so awfully expressed. The statement of the armies in Heaven following Christ in His career of righteous war is an interruption to the general description of Christ which is now resumed. The war itself is merely mentioned (v. 19), but the personal description of the great Captain of our salvation is lengthily dwelt upon. **We delight to** hear *Him* well and much spoken of.*

CHRIST IN JUDICIAL ACTION.

15.—Next we hear of the only offensive weapon amongst the militant, heavenly hosts, **"a sharp sword."** The armies have no weapons, they need them not, for the battle is the Lord's. "Out of *His* mouth goes a sharp sword, that with it He might smite the nations."† The reference is to Isaiah 11. 4. He speaks as He did in the garden when His enemies fell to the ground (John 18. 5, 6). His Word at once smites and slays. The power is irresistible. No carnal weapon is in question, but a destructive power more terrible in its effects than any weapon forged by human skill—the spoken Word of the Lord.

15.—**"He shall rule them with an iron rod."** The second Psalm is evidently before the writer in this glorious description of almighty power. The stern and inflexible rule exercised over the rebellious nations is intimated in the firm unyielding rod of iron. "*He* shall rule," that is, govern (chap. 12. 5). Our association with Him in His government of the world (Psa. 149. 6-9), and judgment of His foes, in no wise clashes with the truth in our text, "He shall rule them with an iron rod." It is His work, and He is invested with plenitude of power to do it. The determined will of the nations must be broken and their power shivered to atoms.

15.—**"He treads the winepress of the fury of the wrath of God the Almighty."** This is not the figure of the harvest in which the good is separated from the bad, but the vintage which is unsparing vengeance on evil, on religious evil developed into apostasy (chap. 14. 17-20).‡ There are three symbols of judgment in verse 15 of our chapter. (1) A sharp sword for immediate, judicial punishment, probably death. (2) A rod of iron for righteous, inflexible government. (3) The winepress of wrath for the guiltiest of all. This latter is the expression of "extremest wrath." The Almighty God is roused. "Vengeance is Mine," saith the Lord. Again, the personal pronoun marks off the judgment as the work of the Lord

* "The description of the battle is as remarkable for its brevity as that of Christ is for its length; quite naturally, as there can properly be no sustained conflict against Him who slays with the breath of His mouth."—*Hengstenberg.*

† In chapters 1. 16 and 2. 12, the sword is said to be not only sharp, but "two-edged." Many authorities insert the word in the text of chapter 19. 15, but it is a doubtful reading.

‡ See remarks on the "winepress," page 309.

alone. "*I* have trodden the winepress *alone*; and of the peoples there was none with Me" (Isa. 63. 3).*

16.—This lengthened description closes with a grand assertion of His glory, **"He has upon His garment and upon His thigh a Name written, King of kings, and Lord of lords."**† His garment, His outward character and ways as beheld by others, bears the title expressive of universal dominion. Instead of the sword on the thigh (Psa. 45. 3), the Name here mentioned is written on it. The sword is in His mouth; the Name on the thigh. *There* one would naturally look for the sword, instead of which they read the pre-eminent dignity of Christ as Monarch of all who reign; and Lord of all lesser ruling authorities. In chapter 17. 14 the same titles are applied to the Lord; there, however, stated in inverse order, "Lord of lords" preceding "King of kings." No pen can do justice in the attempt to set forth the glorious Personage of these verses. In the interpretation of symbol and literal statement care is needed, but there is no real difficulty. Seize upon the circumstance, the occasion, and the reason of war; that actual peoples on earth are found in open, daring, armed rebellion against the authority of God, whether exercised morally or governmentally; further, that the nations on earth and the saints issuing from Heaven are literal armies, and in purpose, aims, and projects opposed. The foregoing considerations may help one out of the vague and uncertain into what is real and about to happen, and in which *we* all shall have our part.

THE GREAT SUPPER OF GOD.

17, 18.—We have had the joyous marriage supper of the Lamb; here we have the great supper of God. The epithet *great* is attached to the supper (R.V.), not to God (A.V.).

17.—**"I saw an angel standing in the sun."** He stands in the very centre, so to speak, of governmental authority. He stands where he can be seen by all, and from whence he can survey the whole scene of conflict. The supper to which he invites the ravenous birds of prey comes *after* the battle. But the birds are summoned in vision *before* the fight. The great supper is of the *dead*. Kings, captains, mighty men, horses and their

* The armies in Heaven are not said to be associated with Christ when He bathes His sword in Idumea, but they are in His victory over the Beast. In the act of taking vengeance the Lord is alone, whether in Idumea or amongst the gathered European apostate nations, but in sessional judgment His heavenly saints take part, as the promise to the overcomer in Thyatira shows (Rev. 2. 26, 27). On certain powers the *Jews* take part in the execution of judgment (Zech. 9. 13; 12. 6; 14. 14; Isa. 11. 14).

† "He is publicly, officially, and intrinsically King of kings and Lord of Lords." —"Synopsis of the Books of the Bible," vol. 5, p. 635.

riders, free and bond, small and great, lie in the silence of death, their bodies a prey to the fowls of Heaven. They have been slain by the *one* sharp sword in the heavenly army. Christ speaks, and at once judgment overtakes the gathered opposing hosts. We would again repeat this is a true and most awful literal scene. The issue of the war is anticipated, and its result disclosed. These slain rise again to meet once more their Lord, not on the horse of victorious conquering power, but on the throne where condemnation immediately follows judgment (chap. 20. 11-15). Their resurrection takes place one thousand years after their punishment on earth.

18.—Five times do we read of "**flesh**" as the food of the fowls of Heaven. Ah, what a humiliating end to the pride, pomp, strength, and chivalry of Europe! The vulture, eagle, and other birds of prey feeding upon the great and mighty whose very names may be enshrined in the pages of the history of this time (compare with Ezek. 39. 4, 17-20). "**All the birds were filled with their flesh**" (v. 21), gorged to repletion. How awful the slaughter! How immense the number of the slain!

TOTAL OVERTHROW OF THE BEAST AND CONFEDERATE KINGS AND ARMIES.

19-21.—"**And I saw the Beast, and the kings of the earth, and their armies gathered together to make war against Him that sat upon the horse, and against His army. And the Beast was taken, and the False Prophet that (was) with him, who wrought the signs before him by which he deceived them that received the mark of the Beast, and those that worshipped his image. Alive were both cast into the lake of fire which burns with brimstone. And the rest were slain with the sword of Him that sat upon the horse, which goes out of His mouth: and all the birds were filled with their flesh.**" We are now about to witness the most gigantic confederation of kings and peoples ever beheld. **The Beast** is first named as being the centre and soul of the movement. All the material strength and resources of the mighty revived empire are embraced in the term the *Beast*. Then we have mentioned "**the kings of the earth,**" the very kings who wailed over the destruction of Babylon. The political and social authorities of Christendom combine with the Beast in this insensate war.*

* The ten kings had already given themselves over to the Beast (chap. 17. 17). They are of course active in this war, for we read, "*These* shall make war with the Lamb" (chap. 17. 14), but they are not specifically mentioned in *this*, the fuller account of the war, their identity being lost, so to speak, in that of the Beast.

Next, "**their armies,**" that is, the armies of the Beast and of the kings.

All are "**gathered together.**" It may be supposed that this almost universal assemblage of powers is effected by human agency. But no Caesar or Napoleon could bring about such a vast combination, and for such a purpose as we have here. Satan is behind the movement. In chapter 16. 13, 14, 16 we have the veil lifted and the true character of it exposed. Three unclean spirits, satanic in source and character, endowed with miraculous power, "go forth unto the kings of the earth, and of the whole world to gather them to the battle (war) of that great day of God Almighty." The gathering place is also named, Armageddon (chap. 16. 16).*

After a statement of the forces in opposition by *whom* they were gathered, and *where* they were gathered to, we are next directed to the plainly-stated but startling fact that the hosts of earth are assembled "to make war against Him that sat upon the horse, and against His army." Can history furnish a parallel to this? The nations of Europe, and even of a wider area, enlightened and christianised, so deluded by Satan that they dare to enter the lists with "The King of kings and Lord of lords!" What madness! What folly! The sovereignty of the earth is really the question of that day, and is decided once and for ever by the impending battle. Their hatred is expressed against the Rider upon the white horse, the Lamb and King, the former title sarcificial, the latter regal; for whether as the Lamb slain or the King to reign, Christendom hates Him. Then comes the opposition to those who are His. They make war also "against His army." We have here the contrast between "their armies" and "His army," consisting of called, chosen, and faithful followers. *One* army as having but one mind and purpose with their renowned Leader. No details are furnished, for actual conflict there could not be. The result alone is disclosed; the awful slaughter had been already anticipated (vv. 17, 18).

20.—"**And the Beast was taken.**" The personal chief of the empire gave to it his character. The empire and its ruling head were really to all intents and purposes one. They can, of course, be distinguished as in Daniel 7, but here, and elsewhere in the Apocalypse, the Beast and its last great imperial chief are so vitally connected that the former perishes in the everlasting ruin of its head. The Beast is cast alive into the lake of fire—a man, of course, yet spoken of as "*the* Beast"—the usual designation of the empire.

---

* See page 333.

20.—"**And the False Prophet that was with him.**" This is the Antichrist, the embodiment of religious apostasy. His fellow, the Beast, is the distinguished Gentile chief on whom Satan conferred almost boundless political authority. Three times is the title "the False Prophet" used of the Antichrist as descriptive of his seductive teachings in Judea and in Christendom generally."* "Was with him," *i.e.*, the Beast, intimates that they were acting together. The Beast supplied the strength, the False Prophet the counsel. The latter is by far the more energetic of the two.

20.—"**Who wrought the signs before him**" (*i.e.*, the Beast) by which he deceived them that received the mark of the Beast, and those that worship his image. He deceived them by the miraculous signs he wrought, his grand effort being to get world-wide worship for the Beast, his superior in temporal power, although his inferior in craft and malignant satanic influence. The diabolic work of the "False Prophet," that which had been his special work as the coadjutor of the Beast, is the main subject of chapter 13. 11-17, *there* entitled "another Beast," *here* "the False Prophet," but one and the same person.

AN ETERNAL DOOM.

20.—"**Alive were both cast into the lake of fire which burns with brimstone.**" Who can paint in words the horror of such a doom? Literally, actually this is the predetermined punishment of two individuals, one a Jew and the other a Gentile, and *perhaps* both on the earth at this moment! These two men are not killed, as their deluded followers are. Physical death in their own persons they will never know, but grasped by the hand of Omnipotence, seized red-handed in their crimes, they are at once *cast* into the lake of fire—a collection of agonies unutterable. They do not proceed, nor are driven onward to their fearful doom, but are *cast* alive into it, as you would throw aside that which is worthless. A thousand years afterwards Satan joins them in the same awful place, as the next chapter unfolds. The lake of fire is never at rest. Fire and brimstone denote unspeakable torment (Isa. 30. 33). The lake, not of water, but of fire, is the eternal place of punishment for the devil and for lost men and fallen angels. It is a *place*, and not a condition. And is it not significant that the phrase, which has rightly become crystallised in our minds from earliest years as the expression of all that is dark and agonising, should

* See chapters 16. 13; 19. 20; 20. 10.

be mentioned here for the *first* time? Perhaps the first inhabitants of the lake may be those two men.

21.—"**The rest were slain with the sword of Him that sat upon the horse, which goes out of His mouth.**" The pride and armies of Europe lie in the silence of death, killed, but not by a literal sword. The angry voice of the King of kings shall strike through the serried ranks, suddenly depriving hem of their wo great chiefs; then death on the spot, the awful port on of the apostate and rebellious host. It is a terrib e story briefly told. Enoch and Elijah were taken up to Heaven without seeing death; the Beast and False Prophet (their names withheld) are cast into the lake of fire without dying. So awful is the slaughter that the fowls of Heaven are filled with the flesh of the dead. The ultimate destiny of the worshippers and adherents of the Beast is unfolded in chapters **14. 9-11**; **20. 11-15.**

CHAPTER XX.

The Millennium and the Judgment of the Dead.

INTRODUCTORY REMARKS.

From verse 6 of chapter 19 to verse 8 of chapter 21 we have traced the consecutive order of events. The *first* is the announcement of the kingly power of God and the marriage of the Lamb, and the *last* is the doom of the wicked in the lake of fire. The first is the dawn of that bright and joyous day of a thousand years, the day which is the goal of hope to the groaning creation; the second is the gloom, fixed and eternal, measured in its duration by the life time of Almighty God.

In the previous chapter we had as the prominent symbol a white *horse*; in this chapter it is a white *throne*. The former sets forth victorious power in conquest; the latter rule and sessional judgment. The horse, or rather what it represents, precedes the action of the throne, prepares the way for it, so to speak.

There are four great actions in the chapter: first, the binding of Satan in the abyss for a thousand years (vv. 1-3); second, the reign with Christ of all the heavenly saints for a thousand years (vv. 4-6); third, Satan's last and desperate attempt to regain the mastery of the world, and his utter defeat and final doom (vv. 7-10); fourth, the judgment of the wicked dead (vv. 11-15).

SATAN CONFINED IN THE ABYSS.

1-3.—**"And I saw an angel descending from the Heaven, having the key of the abyss and a great chain in his hand. And he laid hold of the dragon, the ancient serpent who is (the) devil and Satan, and bound him a thousand years. And cast him into the abyss, and shut (it) and sealed (it) over him, that he should not any more deceive the nations until the thousand years were completed; after these things he must be loosed for a little time."** The vision before us discloses an event, the natural sequence to that related at the close of the previous chapter, and yet sufficiently distinct to form a separate vision. There are three persons consigned to the lake of fire without trial—the Beast, the False Prophet, and the Assyrian (Isa. 30) at the commencement of the millennial reign; also the devil at the close of the reign. Having seen the two chief ministers of Satan, the leaders of the hosts on earth opposed to the Lamb and

His saints,* ignominiously cast alive into the lake of fire, followed by the destruction of their armies, we ask, What about the unseen spiritual being who goaded and lured on to destruction his agents and their followers? Does he escape? No! Summary judgment overtakes *him* as it did *them*. They are dealt with on earth by Christ; the devil is the subject of God's judgment from on high. The dragon, the real instigator of the rebellion so effectually crushed, is seized upon by an angel from Heaven and chained up in the abyss or bottomless pit.† He will be sent to join his followers in the lake of fire a thousand years after. He has yet other work to do on earth, but till then he is shut up and prevented from doing further mischief.

It must be borne in mind that Satan, from the time of his expulsion from the heavens (chap. 12. 9), is on the earth unseen by mortal eye, but actually on the earth, blighting, destroying, and ruining everything which has the semblance of standing for God. Thus the angel, the minister of his punishment, is witnessed by the Seer "descending from the Heaven." Satan is seized on earth. It is a reality, although no human eye may witness it.

The angel has the key of the abyss and a great chain in his hand. One need scarcely insist upon the symbolic character of the scene, for *that* seems evident on the surface. The figures, however, of the key and chain surely denote that God is supreme even over the satanic region of the abyss. Thus instrumentally, by angelic agency, He locks (the *key*) up Satan and binds him (the *chain*) secure in the abyss for a thousand years.‡ His liberty is curtailed and his sphere of operation narrowed. He is effectually curbed and restrained from doing further mischief on the earth until his prison door is unlocked (v. 7). Until the fall (Gen. 3) Satan's place was on high; consequent on the introduction of sin into the world the Heavens and earth were the enlarged sphere of his operations; then on his expulsion from the heavenly places the earth and the abyss are in a manner given over to him; now, as we have just seen, he is shut up in the abyss, confined there during the millennial reign; then for a brief season he is once more permitted to work his will on the earth, and seduce the

* The powers referred to in Zechariah 14. 2 and Psalm 83 are gathered against *Jerusalem and the Jews*, those in chapter 19 of the Apocalypse are gathered against the *Lamb and His heavenly saints*. The former have their seat in the east; the latter in the west. Thus there will be two vast hostile camps, in policy and aim opposed to each other. The north-eastern powers will be under Gog and his subordinate the king of the north. The western powers and the chiefs of Europe generally will be under the Beast and his subordinate in political authority the False Prophet or Antichrist.

† Abyss signifies *deep* (Luke 8. 31) or *bottomless*. The word occurs nine times in the New Testament, seven of these in the Apocalypse, one in Luke as we have seen, and the other in Romans 10. 7. *Out* of it the Beast ascends, and *into* it Satan is cast (Rev. 17. 8; 20. 3). The abyss is a place, but the locality is undetermined.

‡ The key of the bottomless pit in chapter 9. 2 is to *open* it; in chapter 20. 1 to *close it*.

nations from their nominal allegiance to Christ glorified and reigning; finally he is cast into the lake of fire for ever and ever.

The names of the dragon are mentioned in the order in which they occur in chapter 12. 9. There, however, he is termed "the *great* dragon." As the dragon he is the embodiment of cruelty. As the serpent he is the personification of guile. As the devil he is the arch tempter of men. As Satan he is the declared opponent of Christ and His people.* The term "dragon" represents a real historical entity, an actual living person with whom every responsible creature on earth has to do. His power and presence are, of course, controlled and limited, as he is but a creature, but his agents are so numerous and diversified, and increasingly active in their master's service, that some have gone the length of claiming for Satan the attributes of omnipotence and omniscience. These, however, are divine attributes, and necessarily belong to the Creator alone.

The dragon is seized and cast into the pit, which is then locked up and sealed "over him" (see R.V.). The seal affixed to the stone "upon the mouth of the den of lions" (Dan. 6. 17), as also upon the stone rolled to the door of the sepulchre (Matt. 27. 60, 64, 66), intimates that the judicial and governing authority pledged itself to retain in secure custody its prisoner. The door of the abyss is securely fastened.

3.—No "**more deceive the nations† until the thousand years were completed.**" The career of Satan from his first connection with the human race (Gen. 3) till his imprisonment in the abyss has been one of cruel, heartless deception. He has falsified the character of God; he has blinded the minds of men to the nature of sin and to its eternal consequences, and has so misrepresented the Gospel that millions are morally ruined by the ready acceptance of that which is "another gospel." "The whole world lieth in the evil one" is indeed a sweeping declaration (1 John 5. 19, R.V.). This solemn statement is in no wise exaggerated. The race in its then living entirety, save the elect, is at the last gathered under the banner of Satan, only to find out when too late that all have been miserably deceived (chap. 20. 7-9).

A THOUSAND YEARS.

The term a "**thousand years**" occurs in our chapter six times (vv. 2, 3, 4, 5, 6, 7). Three out of the number

* For a fuller elucidation of these names see pp. 258, 259.

† Probably there is special reference to the deception used in gathering the nations as such to Armageddon (chap. 16. 13, 14; 20. 8).

are connected with Satan; two of them assert the reign of the saints with Christ; the sixth intimates the period between the resurrection of the saints and that of the wicked. All these six occurrences of the period a *thousand years* refer to the same time, but, of course, viewed in different connections, and, in our judgment, should be regarded not in any symbolic sense, but as describing an exact and literal denomination of time. The term THE MILLENNIUM as a designation referring to the period of the Lord's reign—public and personal with His saints—over the earth is gathered from this chapter. According to Jewish reasoning the six millenniums drawing to a close answer to the six days in which the heavens and earth were made, the seventh sabbatic day of rest looking forward to that long and blessed Sabbath of a thousand years. "There remaineth therefore a Sabbath rest for the people of God" (Heb. 4. 9, R.V.).

3.—"**After these things he must be loosed for a little time.**" A group of connected events precede the loosing of Satan. "After these things" refers to more than the imprisonment in the abyss. *After* the destruction of Babylon, *after* the marriage of the Lamb, *after* the war on earth, *after* the utter rout and destruction of the Beast, the False Prophet, and their armies, and *after* the binding of the dragon and sealing of the abyss and Satan's long captivity of a thousand years he is "loosed for a little time." There are two brief periods in the coming crisis connected with the career of Satan, in both of which he displays unusual activity. First, from his expulsion from Heaven till chained in the abyss; second, from his release out of the abyss till cast into the lake of fire.

THE REIGN WITH CHRIST (VERSES 4-6).

CHRIST'S PERSONAL REIGN.

This interesting passage, round which controversy has raged for many centuries, is one which powerfully appeals to every thoughtful reader. It concerns every saint on earth. Who are they who reign with Christ in heavenly glory over this earth? Are they saints or angels? Christ's sovereignty as Man (Psa. 8) and King (Psa. 2) is the unquestionable truth of the Scriptures, a royal sovereignty to be displayed for a thousand years. Seers of old beheld it in vision. The bards of Judah sang of it. The rays of the prophetic lamp, as held in the hands of the prophets from Isaiah to Malachi, were directed on to the glories and blessings of the coming millennial kingdom. The earth, so long under the tyranny of Satan and the misrule of man, waits for its promised deliverance.

The moment has arrived for the actual realisation of the scene celebrated in Heaven, "The kingdom of the world (or world kingdom) of our Lord, and of His Christ, is come, and He shall reign to the ages of ages" (chap. 11. 15, R.V.). *There* it was announced in anticipation; *here* it is actually come. The verses in chapter 20. 4-6 are unique in this respect, that in them alone is unfolded a summary of those who share with Christ in the blessed reign of righteousness and glory. There are three classes specified.

MILLENNIAL THRONES.

4.—**"I saw thrones."** The two exiled prophets, Daniel* and John, beheld in vision the *same* thrones. The former saw them unoccupied. The heavenly sitters thereon constitute a revelation peculiar to the New Testament, and hence John supplements the vision of Daniel by adding, "they sat upon them." Both scenes refer to the commencement of the millennial reign. Nor must the thrones in our text be confounded with the twenty-four thrones of chapter 4. 4. Those seen in vision by Daniel (chap. 7. 9) and by John (chap. 20. 4) relate to the millennial government of the earth. Those beheld in the earlier vision (chap. 4) grouped around the throne of the Eternal are set in Heaven. The twelve thrones on which the apostles are to sit in sessional judgment upon Israel (Matt. 19. 28) are no doubt included in the larger and more comprehensive governing idea conveyed by the Seer (chap. 20. 4).

THE FIRST CLASS MENTIONED WHO REIGN WITH CHRIST.

4.—**"They sat upon them, and judgment was given to them."** To whom do the pronouns *they* and *them* refer? for the company mentioned is not otherwise described. Some have suggested "nations" as being the immediate antecedent (v. 3), others angels. Again, "they sat upon them" has been supposed to signify the twelve thrones of the apostles (Matt. 19. 28), and by others to mean the twenty-four heavenly thrones (Rev. 4. 4). Another class

---

* I beheld "till the thrones were *cast down*" (Dan. 7. 9). But the text in the original says exactly the opposite. It reads "till the thrones were *placed*" (R.V.), that is, set or established. We may also add that the Hebrew prophet does not conduct his readers into the millennium, but simply to its introduction. He breaks off at that point where one like the Son of Man receives from the Ancient of Days the universal and everlasting kingdom (chap. 7. 13, 14). The prophet Ezekiel takes us much further. The millennium in some of its most important features is described, such as the settlement of the tribes in parallel bands across the face of enlarged Palestine, the temple and its services, the Jewish prince, Christ's vicegerent, on the throne, the healing of the Dead Sea, etc. (Ezek. chaps. 40 to 48).

of expositors limit the application to martyrs only, supposing the pronouns to be a summary of the two classes of martyrs referred to in the text. But "*they*" are evidently a separate and independent company from the martyrs first seen in the separate state; whereas our company are witnessed enthroned—"judgment was given to them." It is never predicated of spirits that they are crowned and reign. To refer the sitters on the thrones to nations seems a far-fetched idea. Nor can the idea of enthroned angels be entertained, even if supported by the weight of such names as Ewald, P. W. Grant, and others. The reign of angels is nowhere taught in the Scriptures, but rather the contrary, "For unto the angels hath He not put in subjection the world to come whereof we speak" (Heb. 2. 5). The government of the earth is to be administered by Christ *and* His heavenly saints (see 1 Cor. 6. 2, 3). We must, too, look for a larger and broader view of the kingly reign in our text, and not narrow it down to apostles or any limited company.

The "*they*" evidently refers to a well-known class. We have already seen, more than once, the redeemed in Heaven represented by the twenty-four elders taking part in the scenes unfolded from chapters 4 to 19. They are the sum of Old Testament and New Testament believers raised or changed at the Coming into the air (1 Thess. 4. 15-17). This is a much larger body of saints than the martyrs, and hence you have nowhere to locate them in the reign, save as included in the two plural pronouns *they* and *them*. It would be strange indeed to have the reign of martyrs to the exclusion of those very saints in Heaven "made kings and priests unto God." The Old and New Testament saints in Heaven during the time of the apocalyptic judgments are the sitters on the throne beheld by the Seer.

4.—"**Judgment was given to them.**" That is, royal authority to rule is conferred on these saints. It is the fulfilment of that grand and unqualified statement, "Do ye not know that the saints shall judge the world?" (1 Cor. 6. 2).

THE SECOND CLASS WHO REIGN WITH CHRIST.

4.—"**And (I saw) the souls* of them that had been beheaded on account of the testimony of Jesus and**

* We are quite aware that the term *soul* often stands for or represents a person, as in Acts 27. 37; Genesis 12. 5, etc., but is it so in the case before us? Twice the Seer beheld the souls *of those* slain or beheaded, *i.e.*, the souls of persons. They are first beheld under the altar (chap. 6. 9), then on the eve of reunion with their bodies. But in both he sees them *out* of the body in the separate state. In our chapter John first beholds the souls of the martyrs, then he sees them as raised in life and reigning, no longer in the separate state. The soul never dies, it cannot be killed. *It* has a life which neither sword nor axe can reach (Matt. 10. 28).

for the Word of God" (R.V.). What John sees in vision is not persons but souls, the souls of martyrs in the separate state. These form an earlier class of martyrs than those who suffer under the Beast, and are evidently identical with those slain under the fifth Seal (chap. 6. 9-11). This persecution takes effect soon after the removal of the saints to the Father's house (John 14. 1-3). The grounds of this outburst of rage and cruelty are twofold: first, on account of the testimony of Jesus, which is of a prophetic character. The testimony of Jesus in the Gospels is very different from that in the Apocalypse; *there* it is the unfolding of grace, *here* it is the disclosure of judgment; *there* the Father in love, *here* God setting up the kingdom. This latter is a testimony which the apostate peoples of the earth cannot endure, hence those who receive it must suffer even to death. The second ground of this persecution is on account of the Word of God. Faithful adherence to it characterises the remnant in these times. Men will then take sides for or against the rights of God. No trimming of sails or temporising policy will be allowed. A rigid cleaving to the Word will show up the scene in its true light and character—a path so narrow and a sphere so circumscribed that death alone is the end. We gather that no saint in the coming crisis dies a natural death. He either lives through the period or is martyred.

THE THIRD CLASS WHO REIGN WITH CHRIST.

4.—**"And (I saw) those who had not worshipped the Beast, nor his image, and had not received the mark on their forehead and hand."** If the descriptive words "the testimony of Jesus" and "the Word of God" connect the previous company with those noted in chapter 6. 9-11, so here the reference to the Beast, his image, and mark on forehead or hand, unmistakably directs us to chapter 13. 15-17. How good and wise is our God to furnish us with those helps by the way. There are difficulties in every part of the divine volume, but the key to unlock the door is always *at hand*. The Apocalypse is no exception to the rule. "Was there a key sent with the book, and has this been lost? Was it thrown into the Sea of Patmos or into the Meander?" asks a distinguished theologian.

Death in one of its many forms is the only alternative to active and public support of the Beast. The Beast tramples down all rights and ruthlessly destroys all who stand in his way. The inalienable right and responsibility of the creature as such to worship God the Creator is impiously denied. It is the attempt of man on earth to take the place of God. The Antichrist, or Man of Sin, does so in the temple and amongst the Jews (2 Thess. 2. 4). The effort under the first of the Gentile monarchies (Dan. 3), as also under the *last* (Rev. 13), to banish God from the heart and conscience of man can have but one issue: death and ultimate triumph on the one hand, judgment and everlasting ruin on the other. For Nebuchadnezzar, however, there was repentance granted and mercy shown. To the Beast and his followers there will be neither.

The mystic mark on the forehead, whatever that may be, publicly proclaims the person as an adherent of the Beast; on the hand intimates active support, a willing worker in the interests of the Beast.

THE LIFE AND REIGN OF THE MARTYRS.

4.—"**And they lived and reigned with Christ a thousand years.**" The martyred saints are raised *after* the marriage and supper (chap. 19. 7-9), and just on the eve of the assumption of the kingdom, hence they are neither part of the bride nor amongst the guests at the bridal supper. The two martyred companies are specifically referred to. John has just seen their souls in the separate state, now he sees them raised—"they lived," which, of course, implies their resurrection. Death had overtaken their bodies. Hence to men they were dead, but to God they were alive, for John saw their souls. Physical death is never applied to the soul, nor is the term resurrection. The terms death and resurrection are used of the body only. We do not here refer to any figurative use of them, but to the words as literally understood. (Compare with Matt. 10. 28, which shows that the soul has life of itself which man cannot reach; also chap. 22. 32; Luke 20. 38, even *after* physical death, "all live unto Him.") The duration of the reign of these martyrs, for they have not lost but gained by laying down their lives, is now stated for the first time to be "a thousand years."

These two associated facts are clearly emphasised: the confinement of Satan and the reign of Christ for the lengthened period of one thousand years. Hallelujah! what an hour of triumph, what an answer to the life laid down under the axe of the executioner, in the dungeons of the inquisition, or under the fiend-like cruelty of a Nero!

THE REST OF THE DEAD.

5.—"**The rest of the dead did not live till the thousand years had been completed.**" That a literal resurrection and a literal reigning are meant seems unquestionable. Why depart from the simple and obvious meaning of the words, and suppose a resurrection and a reign of principles? It is *persons* and not principles which are before us in the text. It is surprising that such a far-fetched and unnatural theory should find support in certain quarters generally considered sober and orthodox.

The doctrine of a general resurrection, of good and bad alike, of just and unjust, is disproved in our text. It must be frankly conceded that the Lord's words in John 5. 28, 29 *seem* to teach a general resurrection: "Marvel not at this; for the hour is coming in which all that are in the graves shall hear His voice, and shall come forth; they that have done good unto the resurrection of life; and they that have done evil unto the resurrection of damnation" or judgment. The "hour" referred to embraces a thousand years, at the commencement of which the righteous are raised, and at its close the wicked. We are not giving an arbitrary force to the term *hour*, as in the very chapter quoted from, the *hour* of spiritual quickening, that is, of the soul, has already lasted nigh two thousand years (v. 25).

Between the resurrection of those "that have done *good*" and those "that have done *evil*" a thousand years transpire. "The rest of the dead" are the wicked raised to judgment (Rev. 20. 13). Not one saint of God will be found in this last closing scene of resurrection and consequent judgment, which is final and eternal. There is a resurrection of the just, effected at different times, commencing with Christ the firstfruit (1 Cor. 15. 23), "afterward they that are Christ's at His coming" into the air* when the living are changed and the dead in Christ of all ages raised (1 Thess. 4. 16). Then on the eve of the introduction of the millennial kingdom we have the resurrection of the apocalyptic martyrs (chap. 20. 4-6). Thus from the resurrection of Christ till those of Old and New Testament times we have a period of nigh two thousand years; again, between the raising of those latter and that of the martyrs several years, at least seven, transpire. But with the wicked dead it is far different. From Cain onwards *all* remain in their graves till after the millennial reign, when they are raised—the *last* act in time—and then judged in

* At the death of Christ "the graves were opened; and many bodies of the saints which slept arose and came out of the graves *after His resurrection*, and went into the Holy City, and appeared unto many" (Matt. 27. 52, 53). We have no reason to suppose that those saints died again and were buried. It is appointed unto men to die *once* (Heb. 9. 27). We question if the Jerusalem martyrs (Rev. 11. 11, 12) are raised simultaneously with the general body of martyrs. In our judgment the time, occasion, and circumstances are different. The Jewish witnesses perhaps take precedence.

eternity (vv. 12, 13). All such are raised at one and the same time, and find themselves after judgment in the lake of fire with the devil, the Beast, and his Jewish associate in crime, the False Prophet. Then the curtain closes only to be drawn aside once more (chap. 21. 8) for a passing glance.

INTERPRETATION OF THE VISION.

6.—**"This is the first resurrection."*** Blessed and holy he who has part in the first resurrection: over these the second death has no power; but they shall be priests of God, and of Christ, and shall reign with Him a thousand years." The vision itself occupies verse 4 (the longest verse in the apocalypse) and the first part of verse 5. Then the interpretation follows, commencing with the words, "This is the first resurrection," and continues down to the close of verse 6. The interpretation we have transcribed in full. The change which will pass over the living saints at the Coming is equivalent to the raising of the dead (1 Cor. 15. 51-54). Then every trace of mortality and corruption shall disappear, and all be glorified. The dead are raised *in* glory (v. 43). The bodies of saints, whether alive or in the grave at the Coming, are changed into the likeness of His body of glory (Phil. 3. 21). "The first resurrection" is here regarded as completed. It is a term of special blessedness and import. To have part in it was the eager desire of the apostle (Phil. 3. 11). The resurrection of the dead is equally taught in both Testaments, but resurrection *from* the dead is New Testament revelation alone, and is first taught in Mark 9. 9; then in Luke 20. 35 its application to believers is assured. The term "second resurrection" is never used of the wicked.

Every one who has part in the first resurrection is pronounced "blessed and holy." It is a matter of individual blessedness. The first term is descriptive of his happy condition; the second of his character. Happiness and holiness are inseparably associated, and must never be separated. "Over these the second death has no power." The expressions, "*first* resurrection" and "*second* death" are contrasted terms, because all who have no part in the one shall certainly share in the other. The second death *is* the lake of fire (v. 14). Into it the raised wicked dead are cast. But *this* awful death, dying yet never dead physically, has no title, no authority over those embraced in the first resurrection, for these "die no more." Their

* It may be noted here that, according to the true reading, the living and reigning is certainly resurrection. "The rest of the dead lived not until," etc.; so that it is clearly used here for resurrection, as the following words confirm: "This is the first resurrection."—"Synopsis of the Books of the Bible," vol. 5, p. 636, footnote.

bodies are immortal. They can no more die than can angels (Luke 20. 36). The "second death" has no claim over the "sons of the resurrection."

The positive blessedness of the risen and glorified saints is next declared, not simply their immunity from the eternal consequences of sin—the "second death"—"but they shall be priests of God and of Christ." Both the holy (1 Peter 2. 5) and royal character of priesthood (v. 9) shall then be in fullest exercise, unceasingly and unhinderedly. We shall have continual access into God's presence as His priests, and in association with Christ exhibit in its blessed fulness the royal virtues of Him Whom our souls delight to honour.

THE REIGN OF A THOUSAND YEARS.

6.—"**And shall reign with Him a thousand years.**"* The greatness of the statement and the grandeur of the subject leave the soul amazed. Once poor wretched sinners, then raised to such a height, only subordinate to Him Who redeemed us by His blood, and exalted us by His grace to such glory! This reign in regal power and splendour, this assumption of kingly dignity as Christ's fellow-heirs, continues for a thousand years, but the eternal state which succeeds shall disclose fresh glories and added dignities, although the mediatorial kingdom as such outlasts the longest span of life yet recorded. Methuselah lived 969 years, "*and he died*" (Gen. 5. 27). Saints in the heavens and saints on earth shall live a thousand years, and shall *not* die.

The reign of Christ and the confinement of Satan are associated facts. The tempter of men must be removed. The glory must not be dimmed nor the blessing marred by the further machinations of Satan. The reign of a thousand years is the grandest event in the history of the race. There are no details given, but simply a statement of the fact. The earthly blessings secured to Israel and the world under the sway of Christ are, in the main, the subjects of the prophets, whilst the heavenly character of the reign is unfolded from verse 9 of chapter 21 to verse 5 of chapter 22. The millennial reign is better described by the scriptural term THE KINGDOM. It consists, however, of two departments, respectively spoken of as the kingdom of the *Son* and the kingdom of the *Father* (Matt. 13. 41-43). The former relates to the earth, the latter to the heavens. Daniel 7. 27 unites the two. "Most High" is in the plural,

* We have the authority of the late Dean Alford for the statement that for the first three hundred years the whole Church understood the thousand years' reign in its plain and literal sense. He also maintained, as we do in our exposition, that verse 4 of our chapter reveals three classes of saints.

and signifies "the heavenly places," as in Ephesians 1. 3, 20. "The people (Israel) of the saints." The people and saints are distinguished. Israel on earth is the former, the changed and risen saints in the heavenlies are the latter. The people are said to belong to the saints; for, after all, the kingdom in its widest extent forms the joint dominion of Christ and His heavenly people, although Israel shall exercise sovereign rule and authority amongst the nations—their head, and not as now the tail.

SATAN'S LAST ACTION AND FINAL DOOM.

7-10.—Our chapter is apportioned into four distinct yet closely related sections. In the *first* we have the dragon bound for a thousand years and cast into the abyss, which is then sealed over him (vv. 1-3). In the *second* we have the three classes specifically brought before us who reign with Christ during the millennial era, and their blessedness (vv. 4-6). In the *third* we witness the last and universal gathering of the wicked on earth under the banner of Satan, and the final and everlasting doom of the devil in the lake of fire (vv. 7-10). In the *fourth* no denomination of time is used as in the previous sections. Here we have got to the end of time, to the close of human history, and the ushering in of the eternal state by the judgment of the dead at the great white throne (vv. 11-15).

The third section is really a continuation of the first, which had been interrupted by the calm and tranquillising sight of the various classes of heavenly saints who reign with Christ.

7.—Now the history of Satan is resumed,* connecting itself with verse 3.

8.—On the completion of the thousand years' imprisonment Satan, not now spoken of as the dragon, **"is loosed from his prison, and shall go out to deceive the nations which (are) on the four corners of the earth, Gog and Magog, to gather them together to the war, whose number is as the sand of the sea."** During the reign all Israel is saved (Jer. 31. 31-34; Rom. 11. 26), and their seed and seed's seed for ever (Isa. 59. 20, 21). But not so the Gentiles. The populations of the earth will be greatly thinned by judgments, large numbers be saved, but many will only render feigned obedience to the authority of the reigning Monarch of the earth. Not the obedience of faith, but a compelled submission under the iron rod

---

* A similar interpretation in connection with the dragon is noted in chapter 12. We have the war in Heaven (vv. 7-9). Its successful issue results in the expulsion of Satan and his angels, who are cast down to the earth. This is followed by joy and rejoicing in Heaven (vv. 10-12). Then the history of Satan is resumed which had been interrupted by the heavenly rejoicing (vv. 13-17); verse 13 connecting itself with verse 9.

(Psa. 2. 9), an obedience extorted by fear (see Psa. 18. 44; 66. 3; 81. 15; in the margin of each of those texts we read *feigned obedience*). Another consideration, which in itself fully accounts for the countless multitudes gathered by Satan from all parts of the earth, is that death even amongst the unsaved will not be the rule, rather the exception (for the principle see Isa. 65. 20); besides, the peopling of the earth shall go on as ever, but Scripture does not, so far as we know, intimate that those born during the thousand years are converted, except those amongst Israel (Isa. 59. 21). The restraint upon Satan being removed, the nations, not merely individuals, but communities and peoples who had basked under the light and blessing of Messiah's personal reign, yield themselves up to Satan. Alas! what is man? He has been tried and tested under every possible condition, in every possible way, under goodness, government, law, grace, and now under glory. The former gathering of the powers was under human leaders (chap. 19. 19). This one is on a vaster scale, and under the direct control and guidance of Satan himself. Both end in utter rout and ruin.

THE LAST HUMAN CONFEDERACY.

8.—The gathering of the nations is universal in character from the four corners of the globe, and so numerous are they that the only comparison is to the sand of the seashore. This vast assemblage is metaphorically spoken of as **Gog and Magog.*** These terms really refer to the last Czar of Russia and his land (Ezek. 38; 39). Now the last attack upon Judea is after the destruction of the western

---

* Gog, or Russia (Ezek. 38; 39). Who is Gog? The reference is to the vast and growing power of Russia, the outcome of the warlike Sclavonic tribes of ancient origin, descended from Japheth, eldest son of Noah (Gen. 10. 2). The capital cities of European and Asiatic Russia are named in the first verses of the two chapters. "Meshech" (Moscow), formerly the seat of government of European-Russia, now second city of the empire, and "Tubal" (Tobolsk), chief city of Siberia, are not only thus early designated, but Russia itself is distinctly named, and that, too, fourteen and a half centuries before she was known in history as Russia. The words in the beginning of our chapters, "The chief prince of Meshech and Tubal," should read, "Prince of Rosh, Meshech, and Tubal" (R.V.). Thus Russia—and were it still doubted, the naming of her chief cities surely establishes the fact—is clearly pointed out in the Scriptures of truth, a certain proof of the futurity of this remarkable prophecy. Russia was only known by name in history in the ninth christian century. It is derived from Ruric, a Norman pirate who really founded the empire. Her geographical position is also indicated in the prophecy: "And thou shalt come from thy place *out of the north parts*." Gog is a symbolic term for the head of all the Russias. Magog, also symbolic, is his land.

The Prophet of visions tells us of Persia, Ethiopia, and many other nations coming down under the leadership of Gog "like a cloud to cover the land." The apparently defenceless state of Judea, its numerous and thriving villages, having neither walls, bars, nor gates, seem to offer an easy prey to the nations, while the world's wealth, centralised in the Jew, will awaken the cupidity of the powers (chap. 38. 10-13). To plunder and destroy are the objects of this mighty confederation (see Isa. 33, which also refers to Gog's attack). Alas! little do they dream that Jehovah hath girded Zion with strength, and that the Keeper of Israel neither slumbers not sleeps. The Lord Jesus Christ is *there*, Israel's glory and defence, and His and their enemies only reach the Judean mountains to find a grave, and *their* wealth to swell the treasures already gathered in Immanuel's land (Ezek. 39). The chosen leader of this expedition against restored Israel is Gog, the last Czar of Russia, whose name is withheld.

powers (Rev. 19) and the eastern enemies of Israel (Zech. 14; Psa. 83). Gog (Russia) comes down upon the land to p under and destroy, not knowing that the Lord has come and made alvation the sure bulwarks of His ancient earthly people (Isa. 26. 1, 2). Hence the last attempt to destroy Israel at the *commencement* of the millennium is repeated on even a more gigantic scale at the *close*. The object is the same in both attacks, only the former comes from the north, the geographical location of Gog; whereas the latter is from *all* parts of the earth. One can thus readily understand why the terms Gog and Magog are used, so as to connect the two attempts to overthrow and destroy Israel, the one pre-millennial the other post-millennial. It will be observed that no kings or great men are named, as in the gathering under the Beast (chap. 19), but nations simply as such.

9.—"**And they went up on the breadth of the earth, and surrounded the camp of the saints and the beloved city.**" They crowd and cover the earth in its entirety. They come from north, south, east, and west. They gather under *one* leader, swayed by *one* deadly impulse of hatred, and to *one* centre. The nations have experienced for one thousand years the beneficent rule of Christ. Satan has been for one thousand years restrained, his liberty curtailed, and yet the mad attempt is entered upon to crush the camp of the saints, and to destroy the beloved city, Jerusalem. The nations converge upon Jerusalem. Christ does not intervene. It is a matter for God to take up. The camp of the saints on earth, and the "beloved city," a beautiful designation of Jerusalem in the future (Isa. 60), are surrounded by the multitudinous hosts of earth. No mention is made of how Christ and His people, heavenly or earthly, regard this last mad attempt of Satan and his deceived followers. All is silent in the camp and city. The apostate nations march into the jaws of death. Their judgment is sudden, swift, overwhelming, and final. God deals with the hosts of evil, "**Fire came down out of Heaven and devoured them**," the Authorised Version adding "*f*rom God." The words should be deleted on the authority of the critics, yet the sense is the same, for the judgment is *from God*.

SATAN CAST INTO THE LAKE OF FIRE.

10.—What of the proud boast of the perfectibility of human nature in light of the closing scene in the drama of history! For the first time in the history of the race (from Gen. 3 to Rev. 20) we have an earth without a sinner upon its surface. Satan has now to be dealt with. He is allowed to see the end of all his heartless machinations. He is foiled and defeated. His doom was fixed seven thousand years before its execution (Gen. 3. 15). His head is bruised by the woman's seed. There yet remains the one final act of everlasting judgment. "**And the devil who deceived them was cast into the lake of fire and brimstone, where (are) both the Beast and the False Prophet, and they shall be tormented day and night for the ages of ages.**"

The dragon was first cast out of Heaven, then shut up in the abyss, now cast into the lake of fire. As the *dragon* he is shut up, as *Satan* he is loosed, and as the *devil* he is cast into the lake of fire.* In this last war the dragon is not named. Satan, signifying *adversary*, is the open and declared enemy and adversary of God, of Christ, of the saints, of Israel, and in that character he stands out apart from human agents as the leader of the hosts who gather against the camp and city. But as the devil, the deceiver and tempter of men, he is cast into everlasting torment.

It is observable, too, that in the narrative the Seer changes his standpoint. In verse 7 he looks on to the end of the thousand years, whereas in verse 9 he adopts the historical tense. In the former he is the prophet; in the latter he is the historian. Need we add that the whole vision is yet future. We refer to the different points of view as John beheld them and narrates them.

10.—"**Cast into the lake of fire and brimstone.**" A lake supposes solid land on either side. "Fire and brimstone" are figures of inexpressible torment (see chap. 14. 10; Isa. 30. 33).

10.—"**The Beast and the False Prophet**" are already *there*. They were consigned to their most awful doom at the commencement of the millennial reign, and they are found in it at its close. What a pertinent and striking illustration of the Lord's words in Mark 9. 49, "Every one shall be salted with fire." Salt is preservative. Here are two men who have been salted with fire, not consumed, but preserved in torment *by* torment, and that for a thousand years. We do not contend for actual literal flames, for the devil is a spirit (see also Luke 16. 23, 24). Fire consumes natural objects. But we do most strongly insist upon that which the figures are meant to teach, "outer darkness," "wailing and gnashing of teeth," "a never dying worm and quenchless fire," "fire and brimstone," etc. The truth is that in the lake of fire mental agony and corporeal suffering are united and endured in degree proportioned to the guilt of those who have sinned. The punishment

* **For the signification of these titles see page 258.**

is in exact measure to the sin, but all is everlasting or eternal.

10.—"**They shall be tormented day and night for the ages of ages.**" The plural pronoun refers to the devil, the Beast, and the False Prophet. "Day and night" shows that the torment is without intermission, unceasing. "For the ages of ages" signifies here and in chapter 14. 11 eternity in its full and proper meaning—never-ending existence.

THE JUDGMENT OF THE DEAD (VERSES 11-15).

THE THRONE AND THE JUDGE.

11.—"**And I saw a great white throne, and Him that sat on it, from whose face the earth and the Heaven fled, and place was not found for them.**" This verse constitutes a distinct vision of itself. The words "I saw" occur again in verse 12. There are two separate visions: first, the throne and the Judge; second, the dead and their judgment. The millennium opens and closes each with an act of sessional judgment, and in both the Lord in Person is the Judge. The *living* are the subjects in the former case; the *dead* are on their trial in the latter. The throne of glory set up in Matthew 25. 31 is totally distinct from the great white throne of our chapter. The *times* of the respective judgments: the one before, and the other after the millennial reign; the *parties* judged, the living in the one case, the dead in the other; *nations*, too, in the former; *individuals* in the latter; these and other essential differences between the two thrones mark them off as fundamentally distinct. It is impossible to regard them as one and the same.

There are three great thrones: (1) in Heaven (Rev. 4. 2), from whence the universe is governed; (2) on earth (Matt. 25. 31), for the judgment of the nations in respect to their treatment of the preachers of the Gospel of the kingdom (vv. 40-45); (3) the great white throne, for the judgment of the dead (Rev. 20. 11).

11.—"**A great white throne.**"* There is but one such. We are about to view the greatest assize ever held. The august dignity of the Judge, the greatness of the occasion, the vastness of the scene, and the eternal consequences involved fitly demand the epithet *great*. The judgment is not governmental, but is one according to the nature of God Himself, Who is *light*, and that gives its own true and proper character to the throne. Greatness and purity characterise it.

* Not the throne of the Sovereign, but that of the Judge, not regal but judicial. Neither is it permanently set up, but temporally, and for a special purpose.

11.—"**Him that sat on it.**" Here the pronoun alone is used; the name of the Judge is withheld. But we learn from the Lord Himself who it is that judges. "The Father judgeth no man, but hath committed all judgment unto the Son" (John 5. 22); and, further, that the Son executes His own judgment (v. 27). It is the Lord Jesus Christ, the despised Nazarene and crucified Lord, "Who shall judge the quick and the dead" (2 Tim. 4. 1). The *quick*, or living, He has already judged (Matt. 25. 31). Now He is about to judge the *dead*. The Son of Man it is Who sits on the throne. We gather that the name is withheld because the judgment and attendant circumstances are in moral keeping with the divine nature, not so prominently with His manhood as the title Son of Man would suggest.

11.—"**From whose face the earth and the Heaven fled.**" One could readily imagine that the *present* scene, so marred and wrecked, would at once disappear before the glory and majesty of such a One, but that is not what is seen here. It is the earth and the Heaven constituted by the Lord Himself as spheres to display His glory and righteousness that cannot abide the glory of His face. The millennial scene, both in its higher and lower departments, is at the best an imperfect condition. "The earth and Heaven fled"—not passed out of existence, not annihilated. The next clause carefully guards against any such unscriptural deduction—"place was not found for them." It does not intimate the complete disappearance of the millennial earth and Heaven. Consequent upon the removal of these, new heavens and a new earth fitted, furnished, and constituted for eternity take their place—are made, not created* (Isa. 66. 22; 2 Peter 3. 13). Between the passing away of the millennial scene and the introduction of the eternal worlds, material in both cases, the great white throne is set up.† This consideration imparts profound solemnity to the scene before us. For the throne is not set on the earth, nor in relation to its dispensations and times. It is a scene outside human history entirely. We have passed *out* of time *into* eternity. The judgment therefore of the throne is final, and in its very nature eternal. We are in God's eternity. There can be no measures of

* Making supposes pre-existing material. Matter has been created once. Creation is the production of material, or matter, which never before existed. Isaiah 65. 17, 18 is millennial, and intimates a complete *moral* change.

† The removal of the present material heavens and earth, as beheld by the Seer and foretold by Peter (2 Epistle 3. 10), is in order that the "new Heaven and new earth" may take their place (Rev. 21. 1). But the question has been raised: What about the millennial saints on earth? How will they be preserved during the burning and dissolving of which Peter speaks? On this Scripture is silent. Without doubt God will care for and preserve His own during the great change. The bodies of the saints on earth will be constituted for the new conditions of life, for an earth destined never to pass away. Yet the everlasting distinction will be observed between the heavenly and earthly peoples, however close the connection may be.

time nor limitations bounded by the globe, for that by which all is measured and limited has passed away. The judgment is of persons in their individual relation to God, and is consequently final and eternal.

THE SPIRITUALLY DEAD BEFORE THE THRONE.

12.—"**And I saw the dead, the great and the small, standing before the throne**" (R.V.). A new vision. The term *dead* here has a twofold signification. First, it refers to those who had actually died, and only such are viewed in the passage. Second, all in this judgment are spiritually dead. John sees them as raised not in a separate state. Verse 13 states facts prior to verse 12, and accounts for the dead standing before the throne. There is a resurrection of the just and of the unjust (Acts 24. 15). But the resurrection of the former is special, both as to time and character. There is really no ground for the prevalent notion of a general resurrection and a general judgment. The former is negatived by the statement in verse 5 of our chapter, "The *rest* of the dead did not live till the thousand years had been completed." A general judgment is as destitute of divine authority as that of a common resurrection, for here the *dead* alone are judged, whilst in Matthew 25 and Revelation 19 the *living* only are in view a thousand years before.

12.—"**The great and the small.**" This Biblical phrase, of frequent occurrence in the Old Testament, is found five times in the Apocalypse (chaps. 11. 18; 13. 16; 19. 5, 18; 20. 12). In the first four of these references the order of the words is reversed from that in our text: "small and great." The exception is due to the greatness and majesty of the occasion. The article before the adjectives would intimate that special classes of the great and the small are there, from all ranks of men in the Church and in the world. The highest and most responsible, down to the least, are congregated and gathered round the throne.

12.—"**Standing before the throne.**" How real and present the vision was to the Seer! On what do they stand? Not on earth, for that has disappeared. The dead are maintained before the throne of omnipotent power. The throne beheld by the grandest of the prophets (Isa. 6) had an altar of sacrifice beside it; hence the righteous claim of the throne was met and answered by the altar. The throne in the innermost room of the tabernacle of old had blood—the witness of death—sprinkled upon it. But the throne before us is great and white, and there is neither altar nor blood. Oh, the horror, the despair, the agony of standing in one's sins, searched by the blaze of divine light! Caves, rocks, caverns, there are none in which the guilty soul may hide, for these have fled, and each sinner is now face to face with God, from Whom there is no escape and no shelter.

DIVINE RECORDS OF HUMAN HISTORY.

12.—"**And books were opened, and another book was opened, which is (that) of life. And the dead were judged out of the things wr tten in the books, according to their works.**" "Books were opened." Every responsible soul on earth has his life and history written above. Nothing is forgotten, nothing is too trivial, all are unerringly set down in the records of God. Infants and idiots are alone excepted. The ground of judgment is that of works, of deeds. Men are responsible for what they have done, not for what they *are* as born into the world. The existence of an evil nature in each one of the human race (Psa. 51. 5) is not the ground of judgment, and hence infants and irresponsible persons are not contemplated, and do not come in for judgment at all. We cannot help, nor are we responsible for, the *existence* of the evil nature in us, but we are responsible for its *activity*. The *root* in you you cannot help, but the *fruit* you can, and for this provision has been made in the sacrifice of Christ. Judgment is according to works, "because of *these things* cometh the wrath of God upon the children of disobedience" (Eph. 5. 6).

Literal books, or rolls, are, of course, out of question. Their awful signification is enough to appal the stoutest heart, and make the most hardened conscience quail. The ungodly dead shall be confronted with all they have thought, done, and said, from the moment of responsibility till its close. If judgment proceeds on the ground of works there can be but *one* result, *one* issue of the fair and impartial trial: condemnation, final and eternal. Twice it is said that the judgment is "according to their works." Memory, too, will be stirred in that awful moment, and add its solemn *Amen*, as the record of each one's life is read over amidst the profoundest silence and awe inspired by such a scene.

But the book of life is next opened and carefully scanned, with the result that not one name of the ungodly is found in its pages. Their names *might* have been written in that book, but mercy was despised, grace rejected, and now judgment and its execution must take their course. It is the book of life referred to in chapters 13. 8 and 17. 8, but *not* that of chapter 3. 5. This latter is the book of christian *profession*, true and false; the former is the record of all *true* believers.

COMING UP OF THE DEAD

13.—"**And the sea gave up the dead which (were) in it, and death and hades gave up the dead which were in them; and they were judged, each according to their works.**" Literally, the sea, "the sepulchre of buried nations," shall have to yield up its dead. The voice of the Son of God, for all the dead shall hear it (John 5. 28, 29), will fathom the lowest depths of the deepest sea, and the angry billows and waves shall answer to the voice of their Creator, and yield up their dead, every one. Death, too, which claimed the body, and hades the soul—the Lord has the keys of both—shall give up their dead, every one. The emperor and peasant, the high and low, the rich and poor, have been humbled to *one* dead level. Now all come forth at that voice of irresistible power and majesty, and each one is judged "according to their works."

DESTRUCTION OF DEATH AND HADES

14.—"**And death and hades were cast into the lake of fire. This is the second death (even), the lake of fire.**" All do not enter into death and hades. It is appointed unto "men once to die" (Heb. 9. 27), not unto *all* men, as the text is generally, but erroneously, read. Enoch and Elijah were caught up, and those alive at the Coming shall be changed, they will not die. When the first resurrection is completed, then death and hades are done with for saints, their work in holding respectively the body and soul is at an end. But they still continue to hold the ungodly dead in their terrible grip. Strong they are, but Christ is their Master (Rev. 1. 18). Now that their work is over they are cast into the lake of fire; they were brought into existence, so to speak, by sin, and as the lake of fire is the eternal depository of *all* contrary to God as light and love they are cast into it.

"This is the second death," that is, the lake of fire. The bodies of the wicked will be constituted to last through eternal ages; they will never die, but eternally exist in the second death. It is not extinction of existence, not annihilation, but it *is* torment during the lifetime of the Almighty and Eternal God. Nor will there be apportioned to each the same amount, measure, and degree of punishment. The place is common to all, but "*many* stripes" and "*few* stripes"

(Luke 12. 47, 48) indicate the infliction of various degrees of punishment.

CAST INTO THE LAKE OF FIRE.

15.—"**And if any one was not found written in the book of life he was cast into the lake of fire.**" Such then is the eternal doom of the wicked. The dragon, the Beast, the False Prophet, and now all the unbelieving from the days of Cain find themselves in one horror of horrors, in *one* place where memory will give point and sting to the agony of eternal separation from God, from light and happiness. May God solemnise our spirits as we ponder these realities soon to be the awful lot and portion of many.

CHAPTER XXI.

The Eternal State (verses 1-8) and the Bride in Governmental and Millennial Splendour (verses 9-27).

INTRODUCTORY.

Post-millennial, or eternal, times and events are more fully described in the first eight verses of our chapter than in any other portion of the inspired Word. The continuity of the passage with the previous chapter is self-evident. There we had the closing up of human history on earth. The unholy dead are raised, the *last* event in time, followed by the *first* recorded act of eternity—the judgment of the wicked dead. What succeeds is a new vision, in which are unfolded some of the main characteristics of the grand eternal state (vv. 1-8). The everlasting ages of God's rest (Heb. 3. 4) are the result, the force or energy of what God is in His own nature as light and love. The millennial kingdom of the Son of Man is the accomplishment of prophecy when the whole body of heavenly saints reign with Christ over the earth. The kingdom in its mediatorial character exhibits the *reign* of righteousness never before witnessed on earth, but *that* necessarily supposes contrary elements. The millennial kingdom is not a perfect condition. It is certainly an immense advance upon any previous state, and one in which immeasurable blessings are enjoyed. But perfection is only reached when righteousness *dwells*, when the work of repression is over. The eternal state is the grand consummation, the summit of holy desire, the goal of hope in its fullest sense.

The first eight verses of our chapter form the natural and fitting conclusion, not only to chapter 20, but to the section as a whole, which groups some of the most interesting events connected with man's future and final destiny (chaps. 19.-21. 8). The direct references to the eternal state are few in number, the principal passages being 1 Corinthians 15. 24-28, Ephesians 3. 21, 2 Peter 3. 13. The term "his rest" (Heb. 3 and 4) in its fullest application refers to the eternal state.

There is considerable confusion in the arrangement of the chapters.* The eighth verse of chapter 21 should have

* The division of the sacred books into chapters and verses has not proved an unqualified success. Cardinal Hugo in the thirteenth century gave us the chapters. The Jewish Rabbi, Nathan, divided Hugo's chapters into verses in the *Old* Testament in the fifteenth century. In the sixteenth century Stephens, the celebrated French printer, put the *New* Testament into verses. "Our English Bibles have Hugo's chapters throughout, the Jew's arrangement of verses in the Old Testament, and Stephens' verses in the New Testament. The first of English Bibles thus chaptered and versed is the Bishops' Bible, that immediately preceding the Authorised Version." —"Story of our English Bible," by Walter Scott.

concluded chapter 20. Then verse 9 of chapter 21 should have begun that chapter and closed with verse 5 of chapter 22. The remaining sixteen verses of the Apocalypse might have formed the concluding chapter. Had this order been adopted the subjects would have been presented in order and method. The sequence of events for more than a thousand years is narrated in that section, which in importance is second to none, namely, chapters 19.-21. 8.

May God grant reverence, sobriety of thought, and holy fear in the consideration of this sublime subject—the eternal state. Dr. Chalmers rightly observed, "While we attempt not to be wise *above* what is written, we should attempt, and that most studiously, to be wise *up* to that which is written."

A NEW HEAVEN AND A NEW EARTH.

1.—The Seer relates a new vision: "**I saw a new Heaven and a new earth.**" Both are made new, and adapted to the vast moral and physical changes which the eternal state necessitates. The "new Heaven" is for the raised and changed saints; the "new earth" is to form the habitation of those who during the millennial reign were alive on the earth—those companies described in chapters 7; 14. 1, etc. Thus, even in eternity, the everlasting distinction is preserved between the heavenly and earthly peoples of God. However close the connection they will never be united or merged in one (see Eph. 3. 15, R.V.).

The "new Heaven" in our text must not be confounded with the Heaven of Heavens, the dwelling of God. This latter subsists in moral and physical perfection, and undergoes no change.

All is new. All is according to God in His nature. All is fixed. No economic changes now. We are introduced into God's everlasting rest, into God's unchanging state, one of absolute perfection. We have not here the Lamb and the fulfilment of counsel and prophecy, nor the mediatorial kingdom and the reign of righteousness, but the kingdom given up, and God all in all (1 Cor. 15. 24-28). Time distinctions, geographical boundaries, and limitations as at present entirely disappear in the grand eternal state, which, whether in Heaven or earth, displays the energy of God Himself. The "new Heaven" and "new earth," the respective spheres of all the saved, shall be brought into blessed harmony with what God is. This is the state referred to by Isaiah 66. 22, and Peter's second Epistle 3. 13, a state in which righteousness shall *dwell*, not *reign* as in millennial times. Neither enemy nor evil shall invade either of the spheres where the redeemed will for ever dwell. Every one and everything will re-echo the glad refrain, God is light and God is love.

1.—"**For the first Heaven and the first earth had passed away.**" The undoubted reference is to the statement in the previous chapter. "From whose face the earth and the Heaven fled away" (v. 11). This dissolution, not annihilation, is effected by fire (2 Peter 3. 10). Scripture is silent as to any future act of creating material in a literal sense, and is equally silent on what some foolishly contend for, namely, annihilation or total extinction of being. Scripture knows nothing of such a baseless theory. Not an atom of matter, not a blade of grass, and surely not a sentient being in the wide universe is doomed to extinction. Our planet will be put in the crucible, altered, changed, and made new, to abide for ever. There being no sin, there can be no corruption. The new earth is eternal. The terms "*first* Heaven" and "*first* earth" are in contrast to the "*new* Heaven" and "*new* earth."

NO MORE SEA.

1.—"**And the sea is no more.**" The continuity of the earth, the same in substance after the deluge and after its destruction by fire, seems evident. It exists, but as remade.* "The sea is no more." This great, restless, destructive, and separating element of nature shall cease to exist. The sea, now essential to animal and vegetable life on earth, is not needed in God's eternity. He is not only the source of life as He ever was and is, but is then the direct sustainer of it. The sea exists in the millennial age. There we read of nations, and seas, and rivers,† but in the eternal state these no longer exist. It is *God* and *men*, and an earth without sea, all brought into ordered subjection. The conditions of life are *so* different in the everlasting state that time conditions of life and happiness are no longer needed. No sea in the new and eternal earth gives, of course, an immensely extended land surface, far exceeding that which presently exists. The countless hosts of saved Jews and Gentiles on earth during the millennial reign shall then people the new earth, but

* The earth exists *after* the passing away of Heaven and earth (chap. 20. 11-13). It cannot therefore signify cessation of existence, but means that in its *then* present condition it passes away, not that the thing itself becomes extinct, but certain time conditions cease, to give place to others of a permanent kind. A distinguished geologist has written, "I confess myself unable to find any evidence for it (extinction of our planet) in Nature, Reason, or Scripture."

† Nations as such can have no place in the eternal state, for these were the fruit of governmental judgment (Gen. 11. 1-9). The first nine verses of chapter 11 of Genesis historically precede chapter 10, and really account for the existence of the many nations mentioned in that important historical chapter. Then in the great change which Scripture refers to as "The Regeneration" (Matt. 19. 28), commonly spoken of as the millennium, we read of the dead sea, or east sea (Ezek. 47). The great sea, or the Mediterranean, is also referred to in that same interesting millennial chapter. (See Zech. 14. 8; Psa. 72. 8; Joel 3. 18, etc.).

not, we apprehend, in any distinctive or national sense, but simply as *men* in direct relation to God.

NEW JERUSALEM.

2.—"**And I saw the holy city, new Jerusalem, coming down out of the Heaven from God, prepared as a bride adorned for her husband.**" The "new Heaven" and "new earth" beheld by the Seer are not described. Of their configuration, size, and appearance we can say nothing. Their adaptation for eternal use, without change, decay, or death can surely be predicated, but not more. Without doubt they will be regions of everlasting bloom and beauty.

But now a new sight greets the eye of the Seer. He not only beholds the physical platforms on which the glories of eternity are to be displayed, but "I saw the holy city, new Jerusalem." The term "*holy* city" occurs three times in the Apocalypse (see chaps. 11. 2; 21. 2; 22. 19). The first of these references is to the literal Jerusalem in the coming crisis; the other two point to the holy character of the glorified Church. The "*beloved* city" (chap. 20. 9) is a descriptive epithet of millennial Jerusalem, the actual city of that name. The Church, the bride and wife of the Lamb, is holy in character and ways, whether during the reign (v. 10) or in the eternal state (v. 2).

But the Church is also termed "new Jerusalem" (see also chap. 3. 12). There are three Jerusalems—the heavenly (Heb. 12. 22), the earthly (Rev. 11. 2), and the mystical (chap. 21. 2, 10). The epithet "*new* Jerusalem" is in contrast to the old and literal city which has played such an important part in the world's history. The term *new* is used three times—new Heaven, new earth, new Jerusalem. If the Jewish people, as such, are in the eternal state merged in the simple appellation men, then the earthly city, Jerusalem, as a distinctive seat and centre of government will have passed away. Cities and nations are connected with time, not with eternity, and as such have no place in God's everlasting ages of unbroken rest and blessedness, in which the redeemed alone have part. The two descriptive terms "holy city" and "new Jerusalem" are both used to set forth the Church as she enters on her eternal state of blessedness, a state more deep and unchanging than even the millennial condition in which she shared in glory the rights and dignities of the Lamb. That which succeeds the public reign of the thousand years has a character peculiar to itself; in it God is all and in all.

COMING DOWN.

2.—"**Coming down out of the Heaven from God.**" This is verbally repeated in verse 10. Heaven is the proper home of the Church, and God the source of her being and happiness. It is not said the new Jerusalem "comes down *from* Heaven," but *out of* it. She has been dwelling in it. She has not had a casual acquaintance with Heaven, but knows it well and intimately, and is perfectly at home in the very dwelling place of God. The Church comes "out" of it in the love and glory of the place where God dwells. It is a marvellous statement. The "coming down" in verse 2 is a thousand years *after* the "coming down" of verse 10. The former is in eternity; the latter is at the commencement of the millennial age. In the former the Church comes down *to* the eternal earth; in the latter she rests *over* the millennial earth.

THE BRIDE PREPARED AND ADORNED.

2.—"**Prepared as a bride adorned for her husband.**" The bride is prepared in Heaven ere her public manifestation in the kingdom (v. 9), or in her descent to the earth (v. 3). The marriage was celebrated in Heaven a thousand years before the sight given us of her here. The fact is stated in chapter 19. 7, 8, to which our text clearly refers. *There* she had been adorned in robes of spotless white; *here* she is witnessed still in her bridal attire. A thousand years of love, blessedness, and companionship with her Husband and Lover are but brief. She is eternally united to Him Who died for her, and is now about to enter on a yet deeper character of blessedness in the unchanging rèst and joys of eternity. She is regarded as yet wearing her bridal robes. No soil or spot, nothing to mar their lustre, and no change in her bridal affections. The term *husband* tells of established relationship, of satisfied affection. "He that hath the bride is the bridegroom" (John 3. 29).*

---

* "Where is the chronological place of the new Jerusalem? Before, or after, or contemporary with, and to continue after the thousand years? We may confidently answer that it is the last of these; . . . there can hardly be a doubt that the *wife* mentioned (chap. 19. 7) is the same as the *bride, the wife* mentioned in chapter 21. 9. The latter is distinctly identified with the holy city, new Jerusalem (chap. 21. 2)."—"The Critical English Testament," vol. 3, p. 852.

The marriage takes place in Heaven before the warrior king and his conquering armies issue forth (chap. 19. 7); then we have the binding and confinement of Satan, and the reign of Christ for a thousand years—contemporary events—at the close of the millennial era the last satanic outburst is witnessed, followed by the resurrection and judgment of the wicked; then the eternal state is entered upon *after* the thousand years, in which the bride is still seen in her bridal robes and beauty (chap. 21. 2). Then in verse 9 the description is *retrogressive*, and shows the bride, the glorified Church during the thousand years' reign. Before the reign (chap. 19. 7), *after* the reign (chap. 21. 2), *during* the reign (chap. 21. 9).

THE NEW JERUSALEM AND THE HEAVENLY JERUSALEM.

2.—We beg the reader's careful attention to the distinction between the **new Jerusalem** of the Apocalypse, which is the glorified Church, and the *heavenly* Jerusalem spoken of by Paul (Heb. 12. 22). This latter, unlike the former, does not refer to people, but *is* the city of the living God, an actual city, the location of *all* the heavenly saints. It is the same that is referred to in the previous chapter, for which saints and patriarchs looked (Heb. 11. 10-16), a material city, built and prepared by God Himself, grand and vast beyond all telling. The city of Paul is a *material* one; the city of John is a *mystical* one.

THE TABERNACLE OF GOD WITH MEN.

3.—"**And I heard a loud voice out of the Heaven saying, Behold, the tabernacle of God (is) with men, and He shall tabernacle with them, and they shall be His people, and God Himself shall be with them, their God.**" The Revised Version reads "the *throne*," so, too, W. Kelly, but other critical editors reject it, as Tregelles, Darby, Hengstenberg, and others. The latter says: "The external testimonies for the two readings are pretty nearly equal." Were the "loud voice" heard out of the *throne* it would be the voice of God, as He, of course, sits thereon. But being heard out of the *Heaven*, as in previous announcements (chaps. 11. 15; 12. 10; 14. 2; 19. 1, 6), it may be that of saints. The loud voice heard is an exulting one, and proclaims a fact in which is wrapped up the supreme blessing of eternity—*God with men*—Emmanuel (Matt. 1. 23), not now with the Jewish people, but in a far more extended and comprehensive sense.

"Behold," attention is called to the amazing fact, "the tabernacle of God (is) with men."* God walked in Eden and talked to Adam, He appeared to the patriarchs of Israel, He dwelt in darkness in the unseen and innermost part of the tabernacle of old, God was in Christ in the days of His flesh, He dwells in the Church by His Spirit, but the actual dwelling of God with His creatures redeemed and on earth awaits the fixed and holy eternal state. This unspeakable blessing surpasses far that of the millennial reign. In chapter 7. 15 we read: "He that sitteth on the throne shall spread His tabernacle *over* them" (R.V.). But how different the preposition here, "He shall tabernacle *with* them" (R.V.). The tabernacle is the whole body of heavenly saints. The tabernacle comes down from

---

* See page 174.

"the Heaven," the natural home of the saints, but God Himself descends with them, taking His place in their midst, and tabernacles with them. Why is the word *tabernacle* and not *temple* used in this connection? We would naturally have considered that the latter term would have been the fitting one, as the tabernacle of old was set up in the wilderness, and was associated with the journeys, trials, and testings of the people. The tabernacle was the expression of a *temporary* state of things, whereas the more solid structure of stone, the temple, was a *permanent* building set up in the land. The tabernacle was a movable structure; the temple was a fixed one. We gather, therefore, that the tabernacle of God with men intimates that the saints will not settle permanently on the new earth, but move to and fro, visiting other parts of God's creation—His inheritance and ours (Eph. 1. 10, 11).

GOD WITH MEN.

3.—"**He shall tabernacle with them.**" This emphatic statement is an advance on the previous one. *There*, we read, "The tabernacle of God is with men;" *now*, "*He* shall tabernacle with them." In the one case it is the tabernacle; in the other it is Himself. What an amazing truth that God, the very God, the Maker and Sustainer of Heaven and earth, shall actually and really dwell with men on earth. This is no figure of speech, but a coming grand reality, the profound depth of which baffles human understanding.

3.—"**They shall be His people**," that is, God shall appropriate the eternal dwellers on the new earth for Himself. Israel of old was Jehovah's people. Now the appellation "His people" assumes a breadth and depth of blessing utterly unknown in Old Testament times.

3.—"**And God Himself shall be with them, their God**." In this marvellous declaration God, so to speak, comes out of His tabernacle and personally is with His people—*God Himself*. Here there is no mention of anything, tabernacle or aught else, intervening between God and His people. He is "with them," apart from any covering or external medium of communication. Then is fulfilled the Word of the Lord, "Blessed are the pure in heart, for they shall *see God*" (Matt. 5. 8). May we not, too, give an enlarged scope to the words of the apostle quoted from the Old Testament, "God hath said, I will dwell in them, and walk in them; and I will be their God, and they shall be My people?" (2 Cor. 6. 16).

3.—The topmost stone of blessing is reached in the closing words of this marvellous paragraph. "**Their God.**"

Could anything be higher? Could any character of blessing be conceived morally superior to what is here stated? God in the greatness, glory, and moral excellence of His Being! God in His own infinitude is for His people then on earth! All is wrapped up in the grand creatorial Name beyond the keenest research of a finite mind to grasp or fathom. The source, absolute and independent, of everything craved for by heart and mind is treasured up in God. What He *is* and *has* is the assured and everlasting portion of men, of all men then on the earth. The Lamb is not once named, nor any economic or other change intimated. It is God, His tabernacle, and men. God all in all, and for ever more. His lifetime measures the duration of the "new Heaven" and "new earth;" the life of God Himself the measure of the life and joy of the inhabitants of these eternal regions. We sum up: (1) God's tabernacle with men; (2) He tabernacles with them; (3) they are His people; (4) God Himself with them; (5) God, their God. In the eternal state all is fixed on a permanent basis, but measures and distinct characters of blessing there are, for even then all vessels are not of the same capacity, while all shall be filled. In these five statements we have gradation of blessing, rising up to God Himself.

EARTH'S SORROWS GONE.

4.—**"And He shall wipe away every tear from their eyes; and death shall not exist any more, nor grief, nor cry, nor distress shall exist any more, for the former things have passed away,"** It is only in the eternal state that the effects of sin, physical and moral, are completely removed. The millennial era is not, as we have seen, a perfect condition, and hence even under the beneficent sway of the Lord tears will be shed on earth. The words, "He shall wipe away every tear from their eyes," is verbally repeated in chapter 7. 17. *There*, however, it is a millennial scene; *here* it is in the everlasting state. The wiping away of tears is not an action ascribed to the Lamb either here or in the earlier scene. God does this. If He wipes away every tear, then He removes every cause and occasion of sorrow. The tear-drop will never again glisten in the eye. The eye is said to be "the fountain of sorrow," but God shall wipe it dry.

Death shall cease. The physical dead of the madly rebellious gathered under Satan covered the old earth, at least in the vicinity of Jerusalem, and the eternal inhabitants of the new earth had witnessed the awful sight (chap. 20. 7-9). But it exists no more.

"Nor grief," the same word as in chapter 18. 15,

"wailing," or mourning, the outward expression of the heart's deep sorrow.

"Nor cry," the voice of hopeless misery (Isa. 65. 19).

"Nor distress," or pain within, no internal trouble or weariness, no pain from without or from within. These things which together make up the volume of human misery exist no more, neither does that which caused them—sin. All have passed away. "The former things," of which those mentioned are part, "have passed away."

GOD ON HIS THRONE SPEAKS.

5-7.—"**And He that sat on the throne said, Behold, I make all things new. And He says (to me), Write, for these words are true and faithful. And He said to me, It is done. I am the Alpha and the Omega, the beginning and the end. I will give to him that thirsts of the fountain of the water of life freely. He that overcomes shall inherit these things, and I will be to him God, and he shall be to Me son.**" It is remarkable how often God by name or pronoun is referred to as the *source* of all blessing and action in the everlasting state. The Lamb is there as the husband and eternal companion of the Church, but as such He does not appear in the verses before us, save in one passing reference (chap. 21. 2). The kingdom has been delivered up to God, not that Christ ever ceases to reign, nor that He ever ceases to be man, but the reign of righteousness in putting down all opposing authority and rule having been accomplished we witness new triumphs of another character. God in the energy of His nature produces a scene according to what He is. It is not a question of subduing foes, but of God delighting Himself in forming a people and things according to Himself. God Himself is the actor in this scene of intense and thrilling interest.

5.—The Sitter on the throne said, "**Behold, I make all things new.**" God on the throne of omnipotence, of absolute sovereignty, declares His will—all things new. The old order of things is not improved, nor in anywise imported into the eternal state, for *that* condition demands a state of things in keeping with it; and God is the measure and source of the whole eternal state, whether of persons or things. Nothing short of what becomes God can appear in the unchanging state; hence, "*I* make *all* things new."

Then the Seer is called to write as in chapter 19. 9. Only the earlier command is given by an angel; here by God Himself. Special communications of deep import were directed to be written (Luke 10. 20; John 20. 31; Hab. 2. 2; Rev. 3. 12; 14. 13, etc.). What are the words which the Seer was commanded to write? Those just uttered by God on His throne, "Behold, I make all things new."

In this sentence is fixed the character of the eternal state. Grand words surely, and worth recording! God, too, authenticates His own magnificent declaration by adding, "for these words are true and faithful." He demands our attention, and claims our hearty and unqualified assent. "Behold, I make all things new." "Write, for these words are true and faithful." This is not promise, but the divine assertion of that which is fact when the moment comes for its realisation.

6.—**"And He said to me, It is done."** Note the change of tense. In verses 5 and 6 the word *said* occurs three times, but in the second instance it reads *saith* or *says* (R.V.). The two emphatic declarations—all things new, and it is done—are just what one would expect. The first is God's decree; the second its accomplishment.

"It is done" is verbally repeated in chapter 16. 17. The connection, however, is different. In the earlier reference the wrath of God is completed; in our text it is the permanent settlement of the eternal state that is in question; in the former, too, an angel is the speaker; here it is the voice of God that is heard.

GREATNESS OF THE SPEAKER.

6.—**"I am the Alpha and the Omega, the beginning and the end."*** The first and last letters of the Greek alphabet, followed by the explanatory phrase, "the beginning and the end," intimates that all testimony on earth had its origin in God, as its end is His glory. Creation, providence, promise, history, prediction, prophecy, testimony, love, and grace have each their source in God and in Him their end. Nothing really on the divine side ends in failure. God is seen to triumph at the end. The administration of these things on earth shows, as was the divine intention, the weakness and imperfection of the creature; but that in no wise hinders or thwarts the ultimate purpose of God. The manifestation of Himself in moral glory is the *end*.

I GIVE.

6.—We greatly love the sentence which follows: **"I will give to him that thirsts of the fountain of the water of life freely."** This is present; not future. Neither

* In chapter 1. 8 Jehovah, the Almighty, is "The Alpha and the Omega," in chapter 21. 6 it is God simply as such, no dispensational reference as in the earlier quotation, while in chapter 22. 13 it is Christ Who is "The Alpha and the Omega." In each case the divine Being uses the title of Himself. In chapter 1. 11 the words should be deleted.

hunger nor thirst shall be felt in the "new Heaven" and "new earth." The "splendid array of negatives" (v. 4) forbids the thought of thirsty ones in the eternal state, save in the lake of fire. The heart of God overflows in pity and tenderness towards the needy and unsatisfied sons and daughters of men. The "fountain," the source of life itself, is promised to the thirsty. It is God's gift, and freely given, as are all His gifts (Isa. 55. 1).

OVERCOMERS

7.—Then we have a word of wondrous cheer and strength to the tired and weary disciple, "faint yet pursuing." The promises to the overcomer in the early part of the book (chaps. 2 and 3) respect special circumstances, and are in view of special rewards. But here the encouragement to persevere to the end in the general battle of life is more ample, as the rewards are more full than those mentioned in the early portion. "**He that overcomes shall inherit these things**," those just named. But there is even yet a deeper and richer blessing in store for the overcomer, one of a personal kind, "**I will be to him God.**" He gives *Himself* to the conqueror over life's sorrows. In our judgment this truly remarkable statement even outstrips the triumphant words of Paul, "The Son of God, Who loved me, and gave Himself for me" (Gal. 2. 20). Every statement of Scripture is perfect in its place, but there are some of profounder depth than others, and that in our text is such. But the tale of grace is not exhausted, for we read, "**He shall be to Me son**." Sonship, therefore, is an eternal relationship. The overcomer has God, and God has the overcomer as son. Press on, wearied disciple, the end is near! The promises are full enough to tide you over every trial and every difficulty.

EIGHT CLASSES OF SINNERS

8.—"**But the fearful** (or cowardly), **and unbelieving, and abominable, and murderers, and fornicators, and sorcerers, and idolaters, and all liars, shall have their part in the lake which burneth with fire and brimstone: which is the second death.**" God here, as in the previous utterances, is the Speaker. As another has said, "We ought to notice how much of these eight verses is made up of direct utterances of our God." In the previous declarations God as *love* speaks, but in the final statement of eternity He speaks as *light*. God never foregoes His character as Judge of evil. The lake of fire is an actual and eternal place of punishment. In what part of the universe it is situated we know not. The current denial of eternal punishment finds no support, but absolute condemnation in the solemn passage before us. The eighth verse is as distinctly eternal as the first or second. We can introduce no measurements nor limitations within these eight verses. In them is embraced God's eternity and man's eternity, whether in Heaven, earth, or the lake of fire. There are eight classes specified:

(1) The **fearful**, or *cowardly*, refers to those who were afraid to confess Christ or identify themselves with the Gospel.

(2) **Unbelievers**, the most numerous class of any, and found amongst all classes and ranks of men.

(3) The **abominable** should be understood here in its widest sense as denoting all that is morally, religiously, and physically filthy (chaps. 17. 4, 5; 21. 27; Titus 1. 16).

(4) **Murderers** as a class are greatly on the increase. It is a solemn thing to meddle with that which peculiarly belongs to God—human life.

(5) **Fornicators** point to a sin which is awfully prevalent. The ruin of female virtue is regarded lightly, and fornicators are received into society in the knowledge of the fact, while the poor victims are outcasts from respectability. But God here reverses the judgment of man, and fornicators shall be consigned by the God of righteousness to the lake of fire.

(6) **Sorcerers** are those who profess intercourse with spirits. Death was the appointed penalty under the law for those who practised spiritualism in those days (Deut. 18. 10-12). The lake of fire is God's appointed doom for all who practise witchcraft, spiritualism, devil worship, and other forms of sorcery.

(7) **Idolaters**. All worshippers of other gods. The countless millions of heathen in the past, in the present, and notably in the future are, where God has been given up and idols turned to, given over to eternal judgment.

(8) **All liars** of every degree, kind, and character have their avenging answer in that eternal abode of misery to which everything and every one contrary to the character of God is consigned.

The "lake" *burneth*. Its fire is never exhausted. "Fire and brimstone" symbolise torment and agony of a fearful character (Isa. 30. 33). The expression "the lake of fire" occurs five times in the Apocalypse. It is remarkable that when the devil and the awful sinners mentioned in our text are in question "fire and brimstone" are added. "Which is the second death." The first death is the separation of soul and body, but not cessation of existence, nor unconsciousness, as many dream. Luke 16. 19-31, which is not said to be a parable, and Revelation 6. 9-11 shows consciousness and activity of spirit in the separate state. The lake of fire in its never-ending agony *is* the second death. There are three lists of sinners which it would be profitable to compare: 1 Corinthians 6. 9, 10, Revelation 21. 8, 22. 15. In the third list the last five named answer to the last five in the passage we have been considering.

The last notice of eternity is the never-ceasing wail of anguish in the lake of fire.

THE BRIDE IN GOVERNMENTAL AND MILLENNIAL SPLENDOUR (VERSES 9-27).

THE ETERNAL AND MILLENNIAL STATES.

The history of the race and of the ways of God with men is finally closed. The first eight verses of our chapter present some of the characteristics of the unchanging state, both in positive and negative statements, the latter more especially. The eternal blessing of the saved and the eternal doom of the wicked are set in sharp contrast. In the eternal state all is fixed. God Himself has irrevocably settled the condition of every human being. The volume of history is closed. In the scene just described the Lamb is not once named nor witnessed. God is all. God in the activity of His nature brings about an eternal calm and a deep profound sense of holy repose.

Righteousness dwells in the everlasting regions made new. But in the millennial kingdom Christ as Lamb of God and Son of Man arrests the gaze and captivates the heart. It is the shining forth of His glory. It is the sceptre in His hand. It is many diadems on His head. It is the overwhelming splendour of His reign. It is the munificent blessings He scatters in blest profusion throughout the earth. It is Christ thus and in a thousand other and varied ways and actions which makes the millennial state so magnificently grand. It is the Lord Jesus taking up the broken threads of history and weaving them all into a perfect whole. Neither Adam, Moses, Solomon, Israel, nor the Church has maintained the testimony committed to them. Every steward of grace, law, or government has proved unfaithful; every vessel of testimony has broken down. But it will be seen in the millennial kingdom that Christ, the vessel of God's glory, is the only ONE Who has ever been faithful. He receives the kingdom *from* God (Luke 19. 12), and after its administration for a thousand years He delivers it up *to* God (1 Cor. 15. 24), not only in the perfection in which it was received, but in enhanced glory.

The Church is the result of God's counsel in eternity and of His creation in time. The Church is both millennial and eternal in destiny (Eph. 3. 21), and essentially heavenly in character. The Church, next to God and to the Lamb, is the most distinguished object both in the eternal and millennial states. The Church is the bride and wife of the Lamb, and is displayed as such when Christ takes His throne and reigns. She shares His glory and throne. Her relationship as wife is an eternal one (chap. 21. 2). But in the eternal state the relation of the Church and saints to God as His tabernacle is the prominent thought in the first eight verses of the chapter. In it He dwells. The eternal state is, of course, the more profound of the two.

A MILLENNIAL SIGHT OF THE BRIDE.

9, 10.—"**And there came one of the seven angels which had the seven bowls full of the seven last plagues, and spoke with me, saying, Come here, I will show thee the bride, the Lamb's wife. And he carried me away in (the) Spirit, (and set me) on a great and high mountain, and showed me the holy city, Jerusalem, coming down out of the Heaven from God.**" After a passing allusion to the millennial reign of Christ and His heavenly saints (chap. 20. 4-6) we are brought back from the consideration of the eternal state to a lengthened description of the bride, the Lamb's wife, in her millennial relation to Israel and to the world at large. In this, the last prophetic section of the book, we see the true union of Church and state. The turning back to fill in the details of the general statement contained in chapter 20. 4-6 is by no means an arbitrary arrangement. We have several examples of a similar character in previous parts of the book. Besides, let our readers trace the sequence of events from the fall of Babylon celebrated in Heaven (chap. 19. 1-3) on till the eternal state (chap. 21. 1-8), and further carefully examine those eight verses, comparing them with what is said of the millennial state of things, and we are satisfied that they will see the suitability and scriptural arrangement thus indicated.

The place of the Church in her millennial association with Christ is not only in accordance with the purpose of God (Eph. 1. 22, 23), but is His answer to her reproach and contemptuous treatment on earth.

We have no angelic ministrations in the scene of eternity; here they are prominent. It is one of the Vial angels who shows the bride to John, as it was one of the same angels who showed him the harlot and her doom (compare chaps. 17. 1-3 with 21. 9, 10). The bride and the harlot are also respectively spoken of as a city, the former as Jerusalem, the latter as Babylon. It must be borne in mind, however, that the term *city* in this connection is but a symbol. Jerusalem (chap. 21) and Babylon (chap. 17) respectively represent a religious body of persons. The idea of city conveys the thought of an organised system of social life and activity of government, of united interests, of mutual goodwill; this and more characterise the church city of millennial and eternal days.

From verse 9 we gather that there are two indispensable conditions ere one is competent to view things or objects as God presents them. John was carried away in the *Spirit* and set on "a great and high *mountain*." His natural powers were held in abeyance while dominated and controlled by the Spirit. Then the point of view must be in keeping with the grand sight. Similarly the Spirit, and not the natural mind, was the supernatural power and capacity by which he beheld the harlot according to the thoughts of God, and most fittingly in a wilderness, for while decked out in the world's tinsel and glory it was all a desert to God, and, of course, to every spiritual mind (compare with chap. 4. 1, 2).

What the Seer beheld was "the holy city, Jerusalem,* coming down out of the Heaven from God." Twice she is said to come down. Her first descent (v. 9) is to tabernacle *over* the earth, her second *to* the new earth (vv. 2, 3), a thousand years subsequently. She comes from "the Heaven," her home, and "from God," the source of her being and happiness.

THE CITY: ITS GLORY.

11.—"**Having the glory of God**." What in Romans 5. 2 is presented as a matter of hope has here become a reality. What God can communicate of moral and external glory is beheld covering the city. She is not only the vessel of God's glory, but is the reflector of it to the world. The city bride as a glorious canopy of light and unfading beauty and brightness over the millennial scene will be the grandest sight ever beheld, and will continue to elicit for a thousand years the admiration of the world. In a lesser degree Israel will reflect the glory of Jehovah to the surrounding nations and peoples (Isa. 60). The Church will be a bright witness of God's glory and moral likeness.

* "Jerusalem" simply, the epithet *new* is added when the eternal state is in question (v. 2).

THE CITY: ITS LIGHT.

11.—"**Her light* (was) like a most precious stone, as a crystal-like jasper stone.**" In the glory of God the city shines, that glory is her light. The harlot shone in the glory of man. The bride stands out in the glory of God. In herself she is destitute of beauty. She shines only in the glory of Another. Her shining, or light, is compared to "a crystal-like jasper stone."

Amongst precious stones the jasper and sardius are remarkable for their brilliancy. These hard and indestructible gems are fit emblems of incorruption in the glorified state (1 Cor. 15. 50). The blue "wavy colours of the rainbow" in the one, and the red of the other, are flashed out in wondrous beauty. Both stones are employed to set forth the glory and majesty of God on His throne (chap. 4. 3). The jasper is solid, transparent, and brilliant as crystal, which is a native production.† There are three lists of precious stones which respectively set forth the communicable glory of God: In *creation* (Ezek. 28. 13), in which the jasper is named sixth in the list; in *grace* (Exod. 28. 17-20), the jasper is last mentioned; in *government* (Rev. 21. 19, 20), the jasper is first named. The jasper is also mentioned three times in the detailed description of the heavenly city; first, as her light (v. 11); second, as her security (v. 18); third, as the first foundation of the wall (v. 19). Thus the glory of God is the light, the security, and the foundation of the glorified Church.

THE CITY: ITS WALL.

12.—"**Having a great and high wall.**" The wall is a solid, massive, and brilliant structure. It is made of jasper (v. 18). It cannot, therefore, be broken down, nor can it be scaled, as its height forbids—144 cubits, or 216 feet (v. 17). The wall round about the city, enclosing it on all sides, denotes the most ample security (Isa. 26. 1; Zech. 2. 5). It guards and separates God's glory; guards the city and separates it from all outside. God Himself is the defence and safety of His Church. He stands between it and every hostile power, moral and physical.

The glorious wall which reflects the splendour of the city inside, telling of divine protection and absolute safety, reposes on twelve foundations (vv. 19, 20), each foundation being one stone, solid, immense, and precious. Each foundation stone is of rarest value, of priceless

* *Light* shining, or luminary, is only elsewhere employed in the New Testament and that to set forth the Church as a light-bearer in this world (Phil. 2. 15).

† See on pages 121 and 434 for further remarks on these precious stones; also on page 125 on the distinction between *glass* and *crystal* symbolically employed.

worth, of incomparable beauty, and of unfading lustre; the twelve together forming a magnificent combination of varied and brilliant hue and tint. No building on earth can be for a moment compared to this for weight, size, and splendour. "The Builder and Maker is God." The great and high wall not only bespeaks the security of those within, but guards the city from the intrusion of those without (v. 27).

THE CITY: ITS GATES.

12.—**"Having twelve gates."** The administrative number *twelve* enters largely into this description. Thus there are twelve gates, twelve angels, twelve names of Israel, twelve names of the apostles, twelve foundations, twelve pearls, while the measurements of the wall and city are multiples of twelve. The millennial Jerusalem on earth has its twelve gates (Ezek. 48. 31-34). Twelve signifies the *perfection of government* on or towards the earth. No symbolic or other numbers are spoken of in any reference to the eternal state, because earthly government, as such, is then over. Righteousness dwells, not reigns. *On* the gates are inscribed the names of the twelve tribes, and *at* the gates stand twelve angels (v. 12). The administration of Israel proceeds from the heavenly city, and this, we judge, will be in the hands of the Lord's twelve apostles—the fulfilment of Matthew 19. 28, "Ye shall sit upon twelve thrones, judging the twelve tribes of Israel." This they will do from their seat and place on high. The saints in general shall judge the world and angels (1 Cor. 6. 2, 3), but the judgment of Israel seems special and apostolic. The angels at the gates, but not inside, are servants in waiting. The perfection of angelic position is to serve. In the old economy the angels were the administrators; here it is the glorified saints (Heb. 2. 5). The angels are stationed at the gates so as to carry out the behests issued from the city. The gate was the place of public assembly. As to the location of the gates, east, north, south, and west (v. 13), the *east* is first named in the enumeration of the tribes surrounding the tabernacle; while in Ezekiel 48, in the millennial arrangement of the tribes, the *north* is first mentioned. Dan, from whom it is thought that the Antichrist will proceed, is omitted in the sealing of the tribes for millennial preservation (Rev. 7), is, however, first named of the tribes when the land is parcelled out (Ezek. 48. 1, 2); but while the idolatrous Dan is remembered in grace, yet he is farthest off from the millennial temple. The order in which the seed of Israel is restored is east, west, north, and south (Isa. 43 5, 6).

The specification in our chapter does not agree with any of the foregoing. There are no doubt divine reasons for these variations of the geographical locations in the different passages.

THE CITY: ITS PEARLS.

21.—"**The twelve gates (were) twelve pearls, every several gate was of one pearl.**" The pearl denotes unity, purity, beauty, and preciousness. Those gates of pearl remind us of the Lord's thoughts of love and beauty towards the Church. The cost of the one beautiful pearl of great value (Matt. 13. 45, 46) is beyond all telling. The Lord sold *all* that He had and bought it. But the pearl must have a setting worthy of its value, and so the gates of pearl are enclosed in the jasper wall, emblematic of the divine glory. They are also set in the four sides of the wall, so that in all parts of the earth the beauty of the Church will attract the gaze and win the admiration of the world. Its "gates shall not be shut at all by day, for night shall not be there" (v. 25). The ever-opened gates speak of perfect freedom.* It is usual to close the gates of a city at night lest an enemy steal a march unawares. But the gates of the heavenly city are never closed, for night's shadows never rest upon it.

THE CITY: FOUNDATIONS OF THE WALL.

14.—"**The wall of the city had twelve foundations.**" These are enumerated in verses 19 and 20. Each one of these stones is of vast size, of marvellous solidity, and of surpassing splendour. On the gates are the names of the tribes, while on the foundations are the names of the apostles. This latter fact recalls to mind the words of the apostle, "built upon the foundation of the apostles" (Eph. 2. 20). Both the gates and foundations have the administrative number twelve. In the structure of the city the apostles are named. Israel has no part in this. But in the power and governmental actions of the city going out through the gates Israel is prominent. "The roads leading from a city are not called after the city itself, but after the places† to which they lead, and often the gates are named in the same manner, so it is here. The city is in communication with Israel, as those who

* The gates always open and facing the four quarters of the earth would also intimate *direct intercourse* between the heavens and the earth, between the heavenly and the earthly Jerusalem. It is not said of any of the heavenly saints that they shall stand *on* the earth in millennial times, but that is not necessary; they may go to it without actually placing their feet upon its defiled surface.

† Thus in modern Jerusalem the west gate is the Jaffa gate, though Jaffa is forty miles away; the north gate the Damascus gate, though Damascus is one hundred miles away. No doubt these gates, through the attendant angels, did administrating with the tribes whose names they bear.

rule with Christ must be, but it is distinct from Israel, and built on a foundation which exclusively characterises the Church."*

The foundations were garnished, or *adorned*, with precious stones (v. 19), the same words used to describe the bride made ready for her husband (v. 2). Bengel justly remarks: "Not only did each precious stone form an ornament in the foundation, but it constituted the foundation itself." Each of the twelve foundation stones reflected some particular aspect of the divine glory. Combined they present God in the glory of His nature and Being, as constituting *one* foundation of incomparable strength and grandeur. One stands amazed at the moral truth conveyed: *God Himself in the greatness and diversified glory of His Being*, the foundation of the Church in the blessed day about to dawn. There is but *one* stone used in the building of the wall, jasper, probably the most valuable and brilliant of all. The jasper is the first foundation stone. "The colour of the sapphire, which is the second foundation, is a pure blue or deep azure; the third, chalcedony, is a grey colour, with purple, blue, and yellow; the fourth, the emerald, is green. This was the appearance of the rainbow which John saw around the throne of God. It is a fit emblem of the peace and benignity of the saving grace of God. The fifth is sardonyx, it is bluish white, or it is the onyx, with red veins, called the sardonyx, as if it were a mixture of the sardius and onyx. The sixth, sardius, is blood red; the seventh, chrysolite, blood green or golden colour; the eighth, the beryl, transparent, bluish green; the ninth, the topaz, a pale green or golden colour; the tenth, chrysoprasus, of bluish hue, a beautiful green mingled with yellow; the eleventh, a jacinth, violet or red with a mixture of yellow; twelfth, amethyst, of purple colour, or a mixture of strong blue and deep red."† These massive stones of divers colours sustain the wall. Thus are portrayed the varied glories of God throughout.

THE CITY: ITS MEASUREMENTS.

15.—"**And he that spoke with me had a golden reed (as) a measure, that he might measure the city and its gates, and its wall.**" In chapter 11. 1, 2 the temple, altar, and worshippers (all on earth) are measured, signifying that they are His, they belong to God. But here the measuring of the heavenly city is above. In the former

---

* "The Lord's Coming, Israel, and the Church," p. 289.—*T. B. Baines.*

† "The Cherubim and the Apocalypse," p. 385.—*Alexander Macleod.*

the Seer measured; in our text the angel measures. The measuring reeds, too, are different. The millennial Jerusalem on earth with its temple, courts, etc., is measured with a line of *flax* (Ezek. 40. 3). The city of gold is fittingly measured with a *golden* reed.

The city, wall, and gates were to be measured, but the result as to the latter is not stated, only that of the city and wall. The *gold* signifies divine righteousness, as the *jasper* divine glory. What the gold is amongst metals, the most valuable, so is the jasper amongst stones the most precious. The city measured by the standard of divine righteousness answers to it. It is a cube showing its perfectness on all sides, foursquare. Its length, breadth, and height are equal. In whichever way it is viewed it is perfect and complete. The unity, perfection, and divine symmetry of the Church in glory are assured. Every part is perfect, all is harmony. One has said, "It is described as being a cube, and thus presenting a square in every direction. And by this is signified that it is the *ne plus ultra* of perfection in the symmetry of its construction." The measurement of the city, "twelve thousand furlongs"—1500 miles—in length, breadth, and height, is of such vast dimensions that in size and peculiarity of structure it leaves every earthly city far, far behind. "It is alike vast and perfect, and all measured and owned of God." The wall is measured separately, but its size is quite disproportionate to that of the city (v. 17); *that* we can understand; it is "a man's measure." The wall of jasper, signifying the divine glory as the defence of the city, does not need to be of gigantic size.

THE CITY: ITS GOLD.

18.—"**The city was pure gold like unto pure glass.**" The city itself is the display of divine righteousness. We have divine righteousness now in our complete justification; it is also wrought in us so that the new nature may practically express it in a scene of contrariety, but the city itself, from its centre to its circumference and utmost bounds, is all "pure gold," transparent, too, like "pure glass." The Church, not angels, is the answer to the divine nature. All is according to Him in righteous character. In the eternal earth righteousness dwells, but the Church itself is *that*—is the living, glorified expression of divine righteousness. Oh, with what glory is the Church invested! the reflex of the nature of God. Marvellous truths are these! "The street (not streets) of the city pure gold, as transparent glass" (v. 21).

Not only will the Church itself reflect the glory of divine righteousness, but her walk and ways will agree therewith. Righteousness is now *upon* us (Rom. 3. 22), also wrought *in* us (Eph. 4. 24); we are in glory the display *of* it (Rev. 21. 18), while it is that *on* which we walk (v. 21). The street, like the city of pure gold, signifies that in all our walk holiness and righteousness characterise it, ennoble it, beautify it. "As transparent glass" means that the righteous walk and ways of the Church will reflect the glory of what she is, not only in God's sight, but actually in display and expression—the righteousness of God (2 Cor. 5. 21).

THE CITY: NO TEMPLE.

22.—"**And I saw no temple therein, for the Lord God the Almighty and the Lamb are the temple of it.**" A temple necessarily confines the presence of God and introduces the thought of near and more distant worshippers. "No temple" signifies that full and free access to God is equally granted to all. Immediate access to God without the intervention of priest or mediator is open to every one. Jehovah is the expression of moral relationship; God, *El*, the mighty One, the creatorial Name of power and sovereignty; the Almighty, omnipotent in all circumstances and over all opposing authority, and the Lamb added to these divine names and titles, form the temple. If God is in the city, and the Lamb Who has made good His glory, and in Whom the Godhead dwells (Col. 1. 19), and by Whom God is expressed (John 17. 23), a Scripture which has its application at the time contemplated in our text: What need of a temple? God in the greatness of His Being, and as the One Who has acted and ruled of old, is now revealed in glory by the Lamb. The divine presence is equally diffused. God and the Lamb make themselves known throughout every part of the vast city of gold.

THE CITY: NO CREATED LIGHT.

23.—"**And the city has no need of the sun nor of the moon to shine on it, for the glory of God did lighten it, and the lamp thereof (is) the Lamb.**" No independent yet created light as the sun, nor borrowed light as the moon, is required in the heavenly city. God is the source of her light, and the Lamb Who died for us is the lamp of the divine glory. It is He Who diffuses the light throughout every part of the city. It is concentrated in *God*, it is made known by the *Lamb*, the remembrance of whose sacrifice is eternal.

THE CITY: ITS RELATION TO NATIONS AND KINGS.

24.—"**And the nations shall walk by its light; and the kings of the earth bring their glory to it.**"* It is the Lamb Who scatters the rays of light and reveals the glory of God in the midst of and to the glorified Church, but the Church is the medium of light to the world outside. By its light the nations walk. Then kings and nations pay court and homage to the heavenly city; they bring their glory and honour to it (vv. 24-26). The rule of the heavens is acknowledged. The seat of government is in the midst of the city, and millennial kings and nations, then basking in the bright light and sunshine of the ever-glorious city, gladly bring the tribute of their grateful hearts to it. But enter it they never shall. The Church is the light and the dispenser of blessing to the world, the capital seat of all rule and government over the earth at large.

THE CITY: NO NIGHT.

25.—"**Night shall not be there.**" The city itself shall be one great body of light and glory, without and within, a light which shall never wane, and a glory which shall never fade. One perpetual high noon. No cloud shall ever cross its sky, no shadow ever rest upon it. No night with its darkness, its fears, its terrors. The long, dark night of the Church is past. She has now entered upon an eternal day which for her knows no setting sun.

THE CITY: NO DEFILEMENT.

27.—"**And nothing common, nor that maketh an abomination and a lie, shall at all enter into it; but those only who (are) written in the book of life of the Lamb.**" Sin in every phase and form is excluded from the holy city. The least spot or taint of evil could not stand the glare of the divine glory. Those who enter in and share in the heavenly blessedness are those only who are written in the book of life of the Lamb. The Church is in view in all this intensely beautiful description, that is, the complement of saints from Pentecost (Acts 2) till the Rapture (1 Thess. 4). Is there not in these closing words an intimation that *other* heavenly saints shall enter into the city? The Church is formed and complete, and, in fact, measured by God as such, so that no addition to its numbers can be thought of. Its unity and perfection as a whole are amply secured before those named in verse 27 enter into it.

* The *Authorised* reads: "The nations of *them which are saved* shall walk in the light of it." The words we have italicised should be deleted; also in verses 24, 26, "*into* it" should read "*to* it."

We judge, therefore, that Old Testament saints and the martyrs of the coming crisis shall enter into the city, that is, while not forming part of it, shall yet enter into its blessedness and glory, and share with the Church association with Christ in His universal rule and government—*all* constituting God's tabernacle (v. 3).

The Church has been viewed and described under the symbol of a city, but it is the bride, the Lamb's wife, which has been pictured in vision. That magnificent chapter, Isaiah 60, the finest literary production ever penned, is the correlative in many respects of the heavenly city, Jerusalem. The description of Israel's future in her land, in restored Jerusalem, and gathered on both sides of her millennial temple, etc., supplies much of the imagery employed in our chapter, and in the first few verses of the concluding one.

CHAPTER XXII.

Concluding Vision (verses 1-5) and Testimonies (verses 6-21).

THE RIVER AND TREE OF LIFE.

1, 2.—"**And he showed me a river of water of life, bright as crystal, proceeding out of the throne of God and of the Lamb. In the midst of its street, and of the river, on this side and on that side, (the) tree of life, producing twelve fruits, in each month yielding its fruit; and the leaves of the tree for healing of the nations.**" The throne is the prominent object in this concluding vision. It is the public millennial government of God, of which the whole passage (vv. 1-5) treats, and of which the throne is the symbol. The previous portion (chap. 21. 9-27) was introduced similarly to the one before us; there it was the bride (v. 9); *here* it is the river of life. Thus the whole section, from verse 9 of the previous chapter to verse 5 of our chapter, consists of two distinct yet closely related visions; compare the two introductory statements, "I will show thee the bride, the Lamb's wife," and "he showed me a river of water of life."

As showing how God puts His seal and stamp upon the older Revelation, and authenticates the two Testaments as *one*, it is interesting to note that the reference in the opening words of the previous chapter to the "first Heaven" and "first earth" is necessarily connected with the first chapter of Genesis; whilst the opening references in the last chapter of the Apocalypse to the river and tree of life link themselves with chapter 2 of the first book of the Bible. Thus Moses and John bridge sixteen centuries, and clasp hands in one united testimony to the truth of Holy Scripture.

1.—"**A river of water of life**" signifies fulness of life and blessing (Psa. 36. 8). "It is the beautiful symbol of life in its gladness, purity, activity, and fulness." It is no muddy nor turgid stream, but bright (as everything is in the holy city) and pellucid as the beautiful crystal. The river of gladness ever flows through the heavenly city. The joy of the bride knows no cessation, no diminution; it rather augments as the river flows and deepens in its course. The reference to Genesis 2 is undoubted. "And a river went out of Eden to water the garden" (Gen. 2. 10). There is no parting of the river in the celestial city "into four heads," as in the Edenic river; nor into east and west, as the living waters of Zechariah (chap. 14. 8). It is *one* river which flows throughout the city; *one* joy common to all, just as there is but *one* tree of life, not two trees specially named, as in the earthly garden (Gen. 2. 9). Moses first mentions the *tree* of life. John first refers to the *river* of life.

1.—"**Proceeding out of the throne of God and of the Lamb.**" Here God and the Lamb are associated in the government of the world. The might and majesty of the One, combined with the grace and meekness of the other, secure a character of government in which the Church rejoices, and under which the nations dwell in peace. It is *one* throne. God is supreme, but the Lamb administers the power and authority of the throne. This, then, is the source from whence the river of grace flows.

Jerusalem below is in many respects the counterpart of Jerusalem above. Both cities are seats of government. Both have living waters, and both have trees of fruit and healing. In the earthly millennial Jerusalem the living waters issue from under the *temple* (Ezek. 47. 1); whereas in the holy city the river flows from the *throne*.

2.—Then in the midst of the street, or broad public pathway, flows the river, on either side of which is **the tree of life.*** Neither man, innocent nor sinful, eat of the tree of life in Eden, we do not say paradise.† The cherubim and flaming sword stood in the way of access to the tree of life in the garden (Gen. 3. 24), and well that it was so, for if sinful man had eaten of its fruit he would have lived for ever a life of misery in this world. But in the city of gold and glory "the way of life is free," neither cherubim nor sword barring it. The two symbolic trees of Eden were the tree of life and the tree of the knowledge of good and evil. The former is the *first* and *last* named in the Scriptures. Life in the one and responsibility in the other are the respective principles set forth by these trees.

2.—"**Producing twelve fruits.**" This is the last instance of the employment of the governmental and administrative numeral—twelve. The saints of the heavenly city eat of its fruits—so rich and abundant that the tree yields them monthly—whilst the leaves are for the healing and blessing of the nations. *We* eat its fruit; *they* use its leaves for healing. The millennial nations are dependent on the city above for light, for government, and for healing. All this has its counterpart in that remarkable chapter, Ezekiel 47, "The fruit thereof shall be for meat, and the leaf thereof for medicine" (v. 12). Both the scene above (Rev. 22) and

* "Thus, then, as it appears, will at last be unfolded the great 'mystery of God,' and thus at last will the way be once more opened to THE TREE OF LIFE. Remarkable indeed is the mention of this TREE OF LIFE, occurring as it does in two places only of the Word of God, viz., at the *beginning* of the mystery of God, and again at its *accomplishment*."—"The Tree of Life; or, Redemption and its Fruits in Grace and Glory," p. 297.—*Rev. H. Shepherd.*

† See page 65.

the scene below (Ezek. 47) are millennial, and both exist at the *same* time, but the blessing of the former infinitely transcends that of the latter. The tree of life sustains; the river of life gladdens.

MAGNIFICENT DECLARATIONS

3-5.—"**And no curse shall be any more; and the throne of God and of the Lamb shall be in it; and His servants shall serve Him. And they shall see His face; and His Name (is) on their foreheads. And night shall not be any more, and no need of a lamp, and light of (the) sun; for (the) Lord God shall shine upon them, and they shall reign to the ages of ages.**" On the entrance of sin into the world the serpent, the source of it, was cursed (Gen. 3. 14), and the ground too (v. 17). Cain, who added to the sin of his father, completing it, so to speak, was also cursed (Gen. 4. 11). All under the works of the law are under the curse (Gal. 3. 10). But in the heavenly Jerusalem there is no more curse with its attendant train of ills and miseries. Neither the curse nor its direful effects can ever enter the holy city of God, environed by His glory.*

Once again the unity of God and the Lamb is proclaimed —a unity exercised in governmental power and action— "the throne of God *and* of the Lamb," twice repeated (vv. 1, 3). But it is set up in the midst of the Church itself, for we read the throne "shall be in *it*." Thus the throne is the strength and upholder of the city.

3.—"**His servants shall serve Him.**" God and the Lamb are so united in thought and action that the personal pronoun is here employed. God will be revealed in the Lamb; we shall serve Him. Ours will be a service without cessation, without weariness, without flagging energy. In joy and freedom our service then will be one of pure love; without a flaw, and without one legal thought. How varied the character of service! How gladly the whole being enters upon an eternal life of service to *Him!*

4.—"**They shall see His face,**" that face once so vilely covered by the spittle of man, now radiant with the glory of God. The best wine of the kingdom is being poured out. *We shall see His face.*

4.—"**His Name (is) on their foreheads.**" This signifies that we publicly, openly, belong to Him, but inasmuch as the name represents the person, so we bear His moral likeness, and give expression to all—*who* and *what* He is.†

---

* **Again we find the counterpart to "no more curse" in Zechariah 14. 11, which** refers to the removal of the curse from the earthly Jerusalem.

† His Name on the Forehead.—"Perfect reflection of Himself" (1 John 3. 2; compare chapter 13. 16).—From that useful little book, "The Symbols of the Apocalypse Briefly Defined," page 21.

5.—"**And night shall not be any more.**" This statement is verbally repeated in chapter 21. 25, but incidentally, and as a reason why the gates of the heavenly city are open perpetually; but here the statement is not contingent upon nor explanatory of any other truth, but is an absolute declaration by itself. There shall be no night and no darkness. It is one eternal day. No artificial light as a lamp nor created light as the sun is needed. The city is not dependent upon the lights of this world. She needs them not, for the "Lord God shall shine upon them." The saints in glory will bask under the direct light of God Himself.

5.—"**They shall reign to the ages of ages.**" The millennium and the eternal ages are here embraced. The saints on high shall never cease to reign. So long as Christ is on the throne, so long as He wears the crown, *that* determines the duration of the reign of the saints, for we "shall reign in life by One, Jesus Christ" (Rom. 5. 17). This character of reign is necessarily eternal, and is quite independent of economic or other change. The kingdom given up to God (1 Cor. 15. 24) is set up on the earth for a specified time, and to manifest the accomplishment of the counsels of God. The thousand years' reign comes in between the history of the world as it now exists and the eternal state. It is the kingdom of that period which the Lord delivers up, but His reign over all creatures never ceases; so long as there are angels and men—creatures of God—so long is government necessarily required. The throne is eternal, and the thrones and crowns of the saints, too, are eternal. We understand therefore the expression, "they shall reign to the ages of ages," to signify the eternal reign of the heavenly saints. Both our service and reigning are for ever and ever, or eternal.

What a glorious and triumphant close to this section of the book! How full and magnificent are the declarations, and how true! They will soon be resolved into fact in our happy experience.

May God grant grace to walk worthy of Him, and of these prophetic truths and glories so soon to be realised.

CLOSING TESTIMONIES.

THE ANGEL AUTHENTICATES THE PROPHECY.

6, 7.—"**And he said to me, These words (are) faithful and true; and (the) Lord God of the spirits of the prophets has sent His angel to show to His bondmen the things which must soon come to pass. And**

behold, I come quickly. Blessed (is) he who keeps the words of the prophecy of this book." We have several solemn affirmations as to the faithfulness and truth of God in His words and ways: by saints (chap. 15. 3; 19. 2); by the altar (chap. 16. 7); by God Himself (chap. 21.5); and here by an angel.* These prophetic visions separately and as a whole demand our closest, our most profound consideration, not because of their bearing upon *us*, but rather because the glory of our Master and the blessing of the world are involved in the faithfulness and truth of these divine unfoldings of the future (see Dan. 8. 26).

The Lord God "of the *spirits* of the prophets" (R.V.). The feelings, the hopes, the varied experiences of the prophets of old were directed by and under the control of the Lord God. *He* was with them, as He is with *us*. This unity of moral action links us up with the prophets of old in a walk and realisation of the hopes revealed then and now. Then in the words which follow we read, "hast sent His angel to show to His bondmen the things which must soon come to pass." The opening (chap. 1. 1) and close of the book are thus connected. The utmost care has been taken by the divine author of the book that these revelations of things, which *must* soon come to pass, should reach the servants, or bondmen. He counts upon their interest. The certainty of the Lord's speedy Coming, and gravity and imminence of the numerous events foretold, should surely lead to increased, prayerful, and painstaking study of this book, the only one specially addressed to servants of God as such.

COMING QUICKLY.

7.—"**And behold, I come quickly.**" The constant repetition of the conjunction *and* must not be regarded as necessarily connecting preceding statements with the immediate subject on hand. The word in the great majority of instances simply marks a new beginning without any direct reference to what has gone before.

"*Behold*, I come quickly." It is the voice of Christ we hear. It is not the announcement of a prophetic event, but the authoritative word of the Lord Himself. Three times and in different connections does He announce His Coming (vv. 7, 12, 20). In each instance the word *quickly* is found as intimating how near we are to the realisation of that blessed hope.

---

* Not the greatness and glory of the Revelations, but their faithfulness and truth are the testimony of the angel. It has been remarked that a book is valuable in proportion to its *truth*.

BLESSED.

7.—"He" (not *they*, as in chap. 1. 3) "**who keeps the words of the prophecy of this book**" is pronounced "blessed." Thus the blessing at the beginning is repeated at the close, only it seems more individual here. The completion of the book is also contemplated in the promised blessing at the close. Compare "the words of this prophecy" (chap. 1. 3) with "the words of the prophecy *of this book*"* (chap. 22. 7). To *keep* these words is to treasure them, to prize them, and act upon them.

WORSHIP OF ANGELS FORBIDDEN. GOD ALONE TO BE WORSHIPPED.

8, 9.—"**And I, John (was), he who heard and saw these things. And when I heard and saw, I fell down to worship before the feet of the angel who showed me these things. And he says to me, See (thou do it) not. I am thy fellow-bondman, and (the fellow-bondman) of thy brethren the prophets, and of those who keep the words of this book. Worship God.**" The name, John, occurs five times (chaps. 1. 1, 4, 9; 21. 2; 22. 8), three times at the commencement, and twice near the close of the book. Between these, however, personal pronouns referring to the Seer are of frequent occurrence. It seems foolish to raise any question as to the John of the Apocalypse. There is but *one* John.† Instinctively the Christian heart turns to the beloved apostle, the disciple whom Jesus loved. There was but one such, and without doubt he is the one to whom these visions and communications were vouchsafed. John is the writer of the book.

The wonderful words heard and the marvellous visions beheld, coupled with the glory and dignity of the speaker, invested the angel in the eyes of John with a right to be worshipped. But the most exalted of God's creatures themselves worship God. No angel, however exalted his standing, but would refuse divine worship. "All the angels of God worship *Him*" (Heb. 1. 6). John would have fallen at the feet of the angel to worship, but the attempted action is instantly checked, for angels are very jealous in the maintenance of the rights of God and of Christ. The angel takes, even in his more exalted

* *Book*, as applied to the completed Revelation, occurs seven times in this last and closing part (see vv. 7, 9, 10, 18 twice, 19 twice). The Revelation is complete both in its promises and threats. Nothing to be added.

† "An unknown John," remarks Hilgenfield, "whose name has disappeared from history, leaving hardly any trace behind it, can scarcely have given commands in the name of Christ and the Spirit to the seven Churches."

sphere, the place of a fellow-servant with John, with the prophets, and with "those who keep the words of this book." This is the second occasion on which one of the most distinguished of men and servants failed in the presence of these glorious scenes (chap. 19. 10). "Worship *God*" is the emphatic declaration of the angel. Creature worship is a sin against God, an affront to the Majesty of the Lord of hosts.

CONCLUSION OF THE ANGEL'S ADDRESS TO JOHN.

10, 11.—**"And he says to me, Seal not the words of the prophecy of this book. The time is near. Let him that does unrighteously do unrighteously still; and let the filthy make himself filthy still; and let him that is righteous practise righteousness still; and he that is holy, let him be sanctified still."** The command here given does not refer to any one prophecy, but to all contained in the book. There is a purposed contrast in the command to Daniel, "Shut up the words, and seal the book, to the time of the end" (chap. 12. 4). *Here* it is "seal not the words;" *there*, "seal the book." The reason given by Daniel why the words were to be shut up and the book sealed is that the time of the end was then *far off*. The reason given by John why he was not to seal the words of the prophecy is that "the time is *near*." The immediate Return of the Lord was without doubt the general expectation of Christians for the first three centuries. From the moment that the Hope was revealed the time of the end is ever regarded as at hand, as *near*. We are living in the time of the end, and hence all prophecy lies open. What was sealed is now open for our inspection, and for our profit and learning.

Then verse 11 shows the permanent condition, the immutability of the state fixed and determined at the Coming of Christ. There are two classes of bad, as opposed to two classes of good. The unrighteous as a class are contrasted with the righteous, and the filthy with the holy. Habits fix character, and character fixes destiny. Every one acts according to the truth of his nature; in this there is universal consistency. Death, or the Coming of the Lord, fixes character and destiny. The wicked remain wicked, and continue adding to their wickedness. The righteous continue righteous, and practise righteousness. In eternity sinning and suffering are united, equally so holiness and happiness. Even in the lake of fire the lost of men and angels act according to their nature; sinning and suffering goes on without cessation.

THE DIVINE SPEAKER.

12, 13.—"**Behold, I come quickly, and My reward is with Me, to render to every one as his work shall be. I (am) the Alpha and the Omega, (the) first and (the) last, the beginning and the end.**" Once again does the divine Speaker proclaim the certainty and nearness of His Return, not simply as a cheer to His waiting and expectant saints (v. 7), but with rewards, many and varied, to be bestowed according to the quality and character of service rendered. The least service shall be fittingly rewarded by the Lord when He comes, not into the air *for* us (1 Thess. 4. 17), but into the kingdom *with* us. Not the Father's house into which we are first removed (John 14. 2, 3), but the kingdom is the sphere and scene where rewards are bestowed according to service and faithfulness.

Then follows the announcement of titles essentially divine. As the book draws to a close, even as it opened, these same grand titles are asserted by Christ. None other can claim them but He (compare with chaps. 1. 8; 21. 6; 1. 17).

THE GROUND OF RIGHT TO THE CITY'S BLESSEDNESS.

14, 15.—"**Blessed (are) they that wash their robes, that they may have right to the tree of life, and that they should go in by the gates into the city. Without (are) the dogs, and the sorcerers, and the fornicators, and the murderers, and the idolaters, and every one that loves and makes a lie.**" The Authorised Version reads, "Blessed are they that do His commandments." But every critical scholar of note rejects the reading in our English Bibles. Obedience to commandments is *not* the ground on which eternal life is bestowed. It is God's gift to all who believe (John 5. 24). The reading, "that wash their robes," is in accord with chapter 7. 14, where a similar expression is employed. In both cases the mystic robes of the redeemed could alone be washed in the blood of the Lamb. In the earlier reference the application of the blood gave the saved Gentile crowd *right* to stand before the throne (chap. 7. 15); in the latter reference it is the *title* to the tree of life and entrance into the golden city (chap. 22. 14).

The classes who are debarred from entering into the city are each introduced by the definite article *the*. It is not the ungodly in general, but specific, easily defined, classes of men who are in question. Substantially the list here is the same as in chapter 21. 8. Here the fact of their exclusion from the holy city is stated, whereas the same characters are seen in the previous chapter as in the lake of fire—*from* the city of gold in chapter 22. 15; *in* the lake of fire in chapter 21. 8. In both lists special sin against *God*, and against *others*, is in the main that which distinguishes the sinners here enumerated.

JESUS IN THE DIGNITY OF HIS PERSON; JESUS IN HIS RELATION TO ISRAEL AND TO THE CHURCH.

16, 17.—"**I, Jesus, have sent Mine angel to testify these things to you in the assemblies. I am the Root and Offspring of David, the Bright (and) Morning Star. And the Spirit and the bride say, Come. And let him that hears say, Come. And let him that is athirst come; he that will, let him take (the) water of life freely.**" The calm, quiet, yet emphatic assertion of His dignity, "*I*, Jesus," is admirable, coming as it does at the close of the numerous revelations of grace, glory, and judgment in which He prominently figures. The Revelation is over now, and it simply remains to add the finishing touches to this remarkable book. Who but Jesus, Who opened it, can close it? The medium of communication between Jesus and John is an angel (compare with chap. 1. 1). "These things" were to be testified in the assemblies. What things? The whole contents of the book; nothing is to be omitted.

"*I* am the Root and Offspring of David." The "*I*" is emphatic. His connection with Israel in royalty is here asserted. As divine He is the *Root* of David's house. As man He is the *Offspring* of David. He is David's Lord and David's Son. The crown of Israel is His in virtue of Who He is, and His, too, by promise and prophecy. He was born King of the Jews (Matt. 2. 2). He died as King of the Jews (Matt. 27. 37). He shall reign as King of the Jews (Zech. 9. 9).

But He adds that which is our special portion, which connects us with Himself in a special and endearing relation, "the Bright (and) Morning Star." Before the millennial day dawns, before the judgments preceding it desolate the prophetic scene, before, too, the glories of the kingdom lift up the earth nearer Heaven, Jesus appears as the Bright and Morning Star to His bride. As the Sun of Righteousness He arises to Israel in noon-day splendour (Mal.4. 2), but that is subsequent to His Coming for us. The star is in the early morning, and precedes the shining of the sun by at least seven years.

This revelation, not of glory, but of *Himself*, the Bridegroom of the bride, at once stirs up her slumbering affections. Her heart is roused. Jesus has kindled a fire in her soul which cannot be put out. She hears Him say "I am the Bright and Morning Star." It is the voice of her Beloved, and at once the appeal is answered, "The Spirit *and* the bride say, Come," that is, to Him. The first two clauses of verse 17 are the answer to the last clause of verse 16. We have not the response of the Spirit only, but that of the bride jointly with the Spirit. It is not the Spirit *in* the bride, but both who unite in the cry to Him, *Come*. Then each individual hearer is invited to join in the glad welcome, *Come*. This is the day when the midnight cry has gone forth, "Behold the Bridegroom,"* the day of grace, of God's long-suffering mercy. So now the call goes out to every thirsty soul. Is any one wearied, disappointed? Here is a word which covers all need. "Let him that is athirst come." Again we meet with a word which is sufficiently comprehensive to embrace very willing soul on earth, for none is forgotten, "He that will, let him take (the) water of life freely."

A SOLEMN WARNING.

18, 19.—**"I testify to every one who hears the words of the prophecy of this book. If any one shall add to these things, God shall add to him the plagues which are written in this book. And if any one take from the words of the book of this prophecy, God shall take away his part from the tree of life, and out of the holy city, which are written in this book."** Wherever the words of this prophecy are read or heard this deeply solemn warning applies. It is stern denunciation by the Lord. He testifies of the awful sin, of the ruinous consequences to every soul who adds to or takes from this verbally inspired book. To tamper with the *words* of the prophecy of the book is to bring oneself under the divine lash. The plagues of the book, which are many and varied, are added in righteous retribution to those who *add to* its words. Those who *take from* the words of the prophecy shall have their part taken from the tree of life, and from the holy city. It is thus that God guards the book which above all others in the sacred canon is treated with neglect and by many with contempt.†

---

* Authorities omit the word "cometh" from Matthew 25. 6.

† "Yet the writer has transcribers of his book specially in view, and wishes to prevent them from making any arbitrary alterations, as was then often done, especially in writings of the same prophetic kind; so Grotius, Vitringa, etc."—"Bleek's Lectures on the Apocalypse," p. 355.

THE LORD'S FINAL MESSAGE TO THE CHURCH.

20.—**"He that testifies these things says, Yea, I come quickly. Amen; come, Lord Jesus."** In the preceding message, which is one of a stern character, the Lord speaks in the first person; here the change to the third person is to be noted, but in both messages Christ is the testifier. "These things" refer to all contained in the Apocalypse. Thus the whole contents of the book are vouched for by the Lord Himself.

"Yea, I come quickly." It is the final message to the Church. It is the last word from Heaven till He come. The Old Testament was closed by the announcement of His Coming. The New Testament is closed by the intimation of the same grand event. But whilst the Coming is equally applied to the descent into the air (1 Thess. 4) as to His return to Mount Olivet (Zech. 14), yet the connection is very different. Grace and judgment respectively stand related to these two comings, or rather to the two stages of the one Coming. The Old Testament closes with a threatened *curse*. The New Testament closes with a benediction of *grace*. Compare the last verse in each book.

"Yea" is the confirmation, the absolute certainty, of the truth stated, "I come quickly." This is His last spoken word. He has kept silence now for about two thousand years. But the event for which the Church prays and hopes is about to be fulfilled. The Lord is *at hand*. It has been a weary time, a waiting time, a suffering time, but His Coming, or presence, shall turn the gloom of night into gladness and everlasting joy. The shadows of time are passing away, and the first faint streaks of an eternal day, which knows neither evening nor tears, are almost discernible. Hold on, ye wearied pilgrim host! Joy cometh in the morning. We wait for *Him*, not for the fulfilment of prophecy. Is His Coming a reality in our souls? Does it influence the life, and shape the conduct, and impart vigour as we press on?

THE ANSWERING VOICE OF THE CHURCH.

20.—John, as the representative of the Church, answers the Lord's declaration. Doubtless his words formed the expression of his own desire. The aged Seer had witnessed visions and sights; had been the spectator and actor in scenes overwhelmingly grand, but on the fulfilment of this great fact they all repose: the personal return of the Lord. This was announced by the coming One Himself, and the heart of the aged apostle is thrilled. But led and controlled by the ever-present Holy Ghost he not only gives expression to his own feelings, but voices those of the whole Church, "**Amen; come, Lord Jesus.**" The *Yea* and *Amen*, Greek and Hebrew affirmatives, are united in the introduction to the book (chap. 1. 7). Here they are separated. The Lord assures us of the certainty of His Coming, "*Yea*, I come." The Church rejoices in the immutability of His word, "*Amen*; come." Can this word fail? *Impossible*. Will the Lord not keep His tryst with His people? *Surely*. "Quickly" He comes. Ah! it seems long. But according to divine reckoning the Lord has not been away quite two full days (2 Peter 3. 8). "The Lord is not slack concerning His promise." The persecutions and sorrows of Israel, the sins and griefs of a stricken earth, and the hopelessness and distractions of the professing Church call aloud for a Deliverer. All is the merest patchwork in political government and social legislation. A strong governing hand is needed, and this need will soon be met in Christ Jesus. But we have a personal interest in Him Who is Coming. For us He died, for us He lives, and for us He comes. "Amen; come, Lord Jesus," is the ardent exclamation of the Church of God.

A CLOSING BENEDICTION.

21.—"**The grace of the Lord Jesus Christ (be) with ALL THE SAINTS.**" This is the reading generally adopted by competent authorities. It is just like the heart of Christ. His unclouded favour rests upon "all the saints." The strongest and the weakest, the father and the babe, are equally objects of His grace. Irrespective, too, of the ways of His people, His grace rests upon them Through clouds and sunshine, by night and by day, in all times and circumstances, His unfailing grace is their support and strength. It is grace from beginning to end, from otherwise hopeless ruin till complete redemption.

The **Amen** closing the book is a doubtful reading.

We bring to a close these comments on this marvellous book, which have been a source of personal profit and blessing, in the earnest desire, moreover, that when *He* comes He will find a people morally prepared to greet Him.

INDEX.

"HE THAT TESTIFIES THESE THINGS SAYS,
YEA, I COME QUICKLY. AMEN,
COME, LORD JESUS."